Rick Steves'®

GREAT BRITAIN

2010

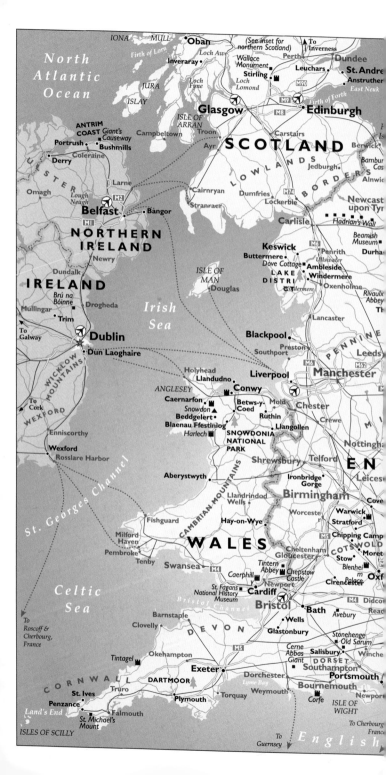

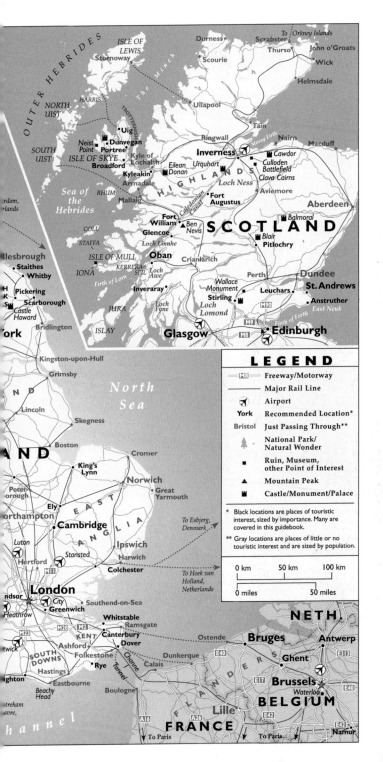

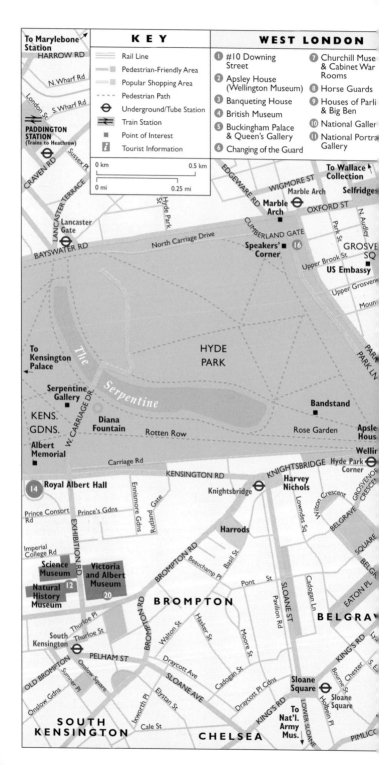

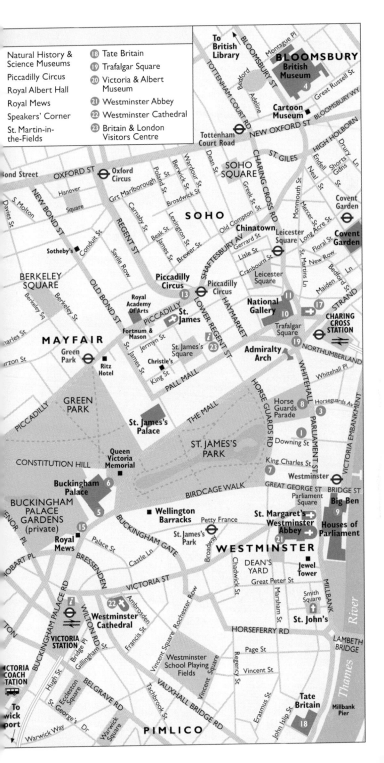

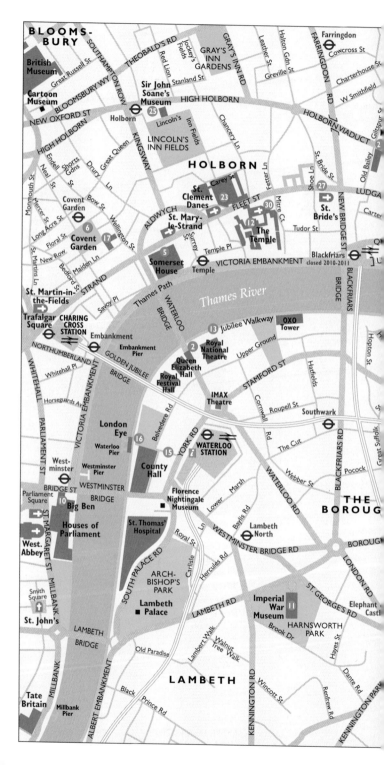

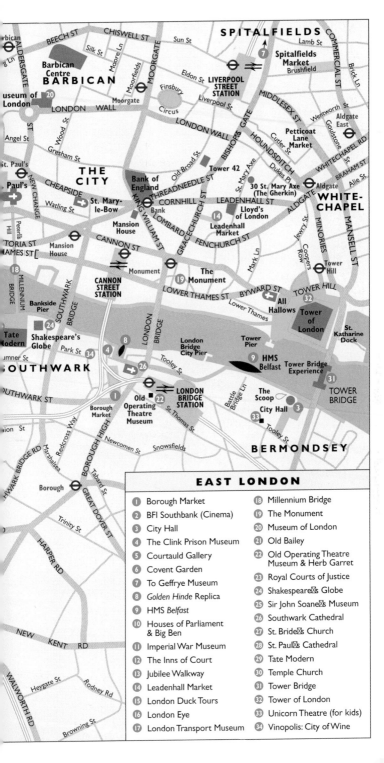

EAST LONDON

1. Borough Market
2. BFI Southbank (Cinema)
3. City Hall
4. The Clink Prison Museum
5. Courtauld Gallery
6. Covent Garden
7. To Geffrye Museum
8. *Golden Hinde* Replica
9. HMS *Belfast*
10. Houses of Parliament & Big Ben
11. Imperial War Museum
12. The Inns of Court
13. Jubilee Walkway
14. Leadenhall Market
15. London Duck Tours
16. London Eye
17. London Transport Museum
18. Millennium Bridge
19. The Monument
20. Museum of London
21. Old Bailey
22. Old Operating Theatre Museum & Herb Garret
23. Royal Courts of Justice
24. Shakespeare's Globe
25. Sir John Soane's Museum
26. Southwark Cathedral
27. St. Bride's Church
28. St. Paul's Cathedral
29. Tate Modern
30. Temple Church
31. Tower Bridge
32. Tower of London
33. Unicorn Theatre (for kids)
34. Vinopolis: City of Wine

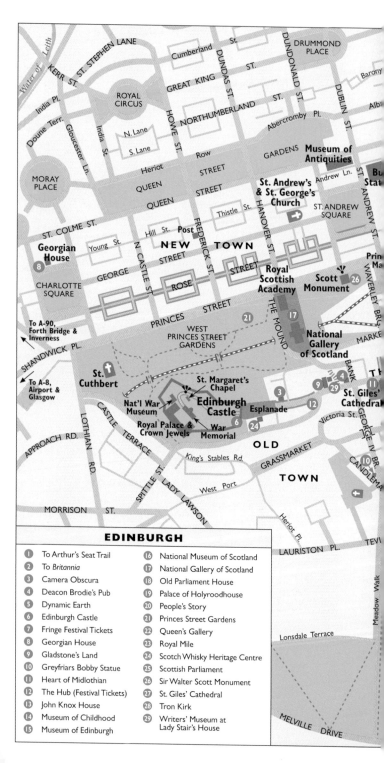

EDINBURGH

1. To Arthur's Seat Trail
2. To *Britannia*
3. Camera Obscura
4. Deacon Brodie's Pub
5. Dynamic Earth
6. Edinburgh Castle
7. Fringe Festival Tickets
8. Georgian House
9. Gladstone's Land
10. Greyfriars Bobby Statue
11. Heart of Midlothian
12. The Hub (Festival Tickets)
13. John Knox House
14. Museum of Childhood
15. Museum of Edinburgh
16. National Museum of Scotland
17. National Gallery of Scotland
18. Old Parliament House
19. Palace of Holyroodhouse
20. People's Story
21. Princes Street Gardens
22. Queen's Gallery
23. Royal Mile
24. Scotch Whisky Heritage Centre
25. Scottish Parliament
26. Sir Walter Scott Monument
27. St. Giles' Cathedral
28. Tron Kirk
29. Writers' Museum at Lady Stair's House

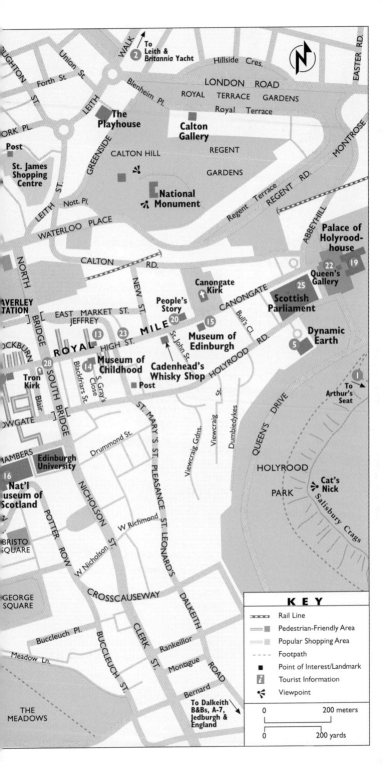

CONTENTS

Great Britain

What's so great about Britain? Plenty. You can watch a world-class Shakespeare play, do the Beatles blitz in Liverpool, and walk along a windswept hill in the footsteps of Wordsworth. Climb cobblestone streets as you wander Edinburgh's Royal Mile, or take a ferry to a windswept isle. Ponder a moody glen, wild-ponied moor, lonesome stone circle, or ruined abbey. Try getting your tongue around a few Welsh words, taste "candy floss" by the beach, and enjoy evensong at Westminster Cathedral. Stroll through a cute-as-can-be Cotswold town, try to spot an underwater monster in a loch, and sail along the Thames past Big Ben. Great Britain has it all.

Regardless of the revolution we had 230-some years ago, many American travelers feel that they "go home" to Britain. This most popular tourist destination has a strange influence and power over us. The more you know of Britain's roots, the better you'll get in touch with your own.

The Isle of Britain is small (about the size of Idaho)—600 miles long and 300 miles at its widest point. Britain's highest mountain (Scotland's Ben Nevis) is 4,400 feet, a foothill by our standards. The population is a fifth that of the United States. At its peak, in the mid-1800s, Britain owned one-fifth of the world and accounted for more than half the planet's industrial output. Today, the empire is down to the Isle of Britain itself and a few token scraps, such as Northern Ireland, Gibraltar, and the Falklands.

And yet, culturally, Britain remains a world leader. Her heritage, culture, and people cannot be measured in traditional units of power. London is a major exporter of actors, movies, and theater; of rock and classical music; and of writers, painters, and sculptors.

On the other hand, when it comes to cuisine, Britain has given the world...fish-and-chips and haggis. Bad, bland British food is almost a universal joke, headed by dishes with funny names like "bubble and squeak" and "toad in the hole." Traditionally, Britain was known for heavy, no-nonsense meals. The day started with a hearty breakfast of eggs and bacon, followed by meat pies and beer for lunch, and finished with a filling dinner of red meat and thick sauces.

But the cuisine has improved in recent years. The British have added fresh fruits and vegetables to their diet, and many regions pride themselves on using locally grown foods to make lighter, more creative variations of old favorites. Foreign influ-

ences—especially Indian and Chinese imports—are especially popular, having been adapted to local tastes.

Thankfully, one distinctive British tradition remains popular: afternoon tea served with biscuits, cookies, or little sandwiches. This four o'clock break is part pick-me-up and part social ritual.

Ethnically, the British Isles are a mix of the descendants of the early Celtic natives (in Scotland, Ireland, Wales, and Cornwall), descendants of the invading Anglo-Saxons who took southeast England in the Dark Ages, and descendants

of the conquering Normans of the 11th century...not to mention more recent immigrants from around the world. Cynics call the United Kingdom an English Empire ruled by London, whose dominant Anglo-Saxon English (50 million) far outnumber their Celtic brothers and sisters (10 million).

It's easy to think that "Britain" and "England" are one and the same. But, actually, three very different countries make up Great Britain: England, Wales, and Scotland. (Add Northern Ireland and you've got the United Kingdom—but you'll need a different guidebook.) Let's take a quick cultural tour through Great Britain's three nations.

England

Even today, England remains a cultural and linguistic touchstone for the almost one billion humans who speak English. It's the center of the United Kingdom in every way: home to four out of five UK citizens, the seat of government, the economic powerhouse, the center of higher

Britain Almanac

Official Name: The United Kingdom of Great Britain and Northern Ireland (locals say "the UK" or "Britain").

Population: Britain's 61 million people are a mix of Celtic DNA, plus about 3 percent recent immigrants, largely from India, Pakistan, and Eastern Europe. Seven in 10 British call themselves Christian (half of those are Anglican), but in any given week, more Brits visit a mosque than an Anglican church.

Latitude and Longitude: 54°N and 2°W. The latitude is similar to Alberta, Canada.

Area: From "Britannia's" 19th-century peak of power, when it dominated much of the globe, the British Empire shrunk to a quarter of its former size. Today, this nation is 95,000 square miles (about the size of Idaho). It's comprised of one large island, a chunk of another large island, and many small ones.

Geography: Most of the British Isles consist of low hills and rolling plains, with a generally moderate climate. The country's highest point is 4,408-foot Ben Nevis in western Scotland. Britain's longest river, the Severn, loops 220 miles from the mountains of Wales east into England, then south to the Bristol Channel. The Thames River runs 215 miles east–west through the heart of southern England (including London).

Biggest Cities: London is the capital, with 8 million people. Industrial Birmingham has 2.6 million, Glasgow has 2.3 million, and the port of Liverpool has 1.1 million.

Economy: The Gross Domestic Product is $2.2 trillion and the GDP per capita is $36,500. Moneymakers include banking, insurance

and business services, energy production, agriculture, shipping, and trade with the US and Germany. Heavy industry—which drove the Industrial Revolution—is now in decline. The economy and pound sterling have weakened against the euro in recent years, and most Brits oppose joining the euro monetary system. Military spending (in Iraq and Afghanistan) has pinched social services, while one in seven Brits lives in poverty.

Government: Queen Elizabeth II officially heads the country, but in practice it's the prime minister, who leads the majority party in Parliament. The British House of Commons has 659 seats. (The House of Lords is now a mere advisory body.) Britain's traditional two-party system—Labour and Conservatives ("Tories")—now has a smaller third player, the Liberal Democrats. The current prime minister, Labour leader Gordon Brown, is due to hold elections by June 2010—perhaps making way for his Conservative rival, David Cameron. Britain is a member of the European Union (but not the euro system) and is one of the five permanent members (with veto power) of the UN Security Council. In 1999, Scotland, Wales, and Northern Ireland were each granted its own Parliament.

Flag: The "Union Jack" has two red crosses on a field of blue: the English cross of St. George and the Scottish cross of St. Andrew.

The Average Brit: Eats 35 pounds of pizza and 35 pounds of chocolate a year and weighs 11.5 stone (160 pounds). He or she is 40 years old, has 1.66 children, and will live to age 79. He/she drinks 2.5 cups of tea a day, has free health care, gets 23 vacation days a year and speaks one language.

learning, and the cultural heart. And, although it lacks some of the Celtic color of other parts of Britain, you'll find plenty of variety even in "plain vanilla" England.

North England tends to be hilly with poor soil, so the traditional economy was based on livestock (grazing cows and sheep).

Today it has some of England's most beautiful landscapes, but in the 19th century it was dotted with belching smokestacks as its major cities and heartland became centers of coal and iron mining and manufacturing. Now its working-class cities and ports (such as Liverpool) are experiencing a comeback, buoyed by higher employment, tourism, and vibrant arts scenes.

South England, including London, has always had more people and more money than the north. Blessed with rolling hills, wide plains, and the River Thames, in the past this area was rich with farms and its rivers flowed with trade. High culture flourished around the epicenter in London, as it does today. London has become a thriving metropolis of eight million people.

The English people have a worldwide reputation (or stereotype) for being cheerful, courteous, and well-mannered. Cutting in line is very gauche. On the other hand, English soccer

fans can be notorious "hooligans." The English are not known for being touchy-feely or physically demonstrative (hugging and kissing), but they sure do love to talk. When times get tough, they persevere with a stiff upper lip. The understated English wit is legendary—if someone dies, it's "a bit of a drag" (but if the tea is cold, it's "ghastly"!).

England offers tourists a little of everything we associate with Britain: castles, cathedrals, and ruined abbeys; chatty locals nursing beers in village pubs; mysterious prehistoric stone circles and Roman ruins; tea, scones, and clotted cream; hikes across unspoiled, sheep-speckled hillsides; and drivers who cheerfully wave from the wrong side of the road. And then there's London, a world in itself, with monuments (Big Ben), museums (the British Museum), royalty (Buckingham Palace), theater, and nightlife, throbbing with the pulse of the global community.

You can trace England's illustrious history by roaming the countryside. Prehistoric peoples built the mysterious stone circles of Stonehenge and Avebury. Then came the Romans, who built Hadrian's Wall and baths at Bath. Viking invaders left their mark in York, and the Normans built the Tower of London. As England Christianized and unified, the grand cathedrals of Salisbury, Wells, and Durham arose. Next came

the castles and palaces of the English monarchs (Windsor and Warwick) and the Shakespeare sights from the era of Elizabeth I (Stratford-upon-Avon).

In following centuries, tiny England became a maritime empire (the *Cutty Sark* at Greenwich) and the world's first industrial power (Ironbridge Gorge). England's Romantic poets were inspired by the unspoiled nature and time-passed villages of the Lake District and the Cotswolds. In

the 20th century, the gritty urban world of 1960s Liverpool gave the world the Beatles (and the tacky tourist world of Blackpool). Finally, end your journey through English history in London—on the cutting edge of 21st-century trends.

For a thousand years, England has been a major cultural center. Parliamentary democracy, science (Isaac Newton), technology (Michael Faraday), and education (Oxford and Cambridge) were nurtured here. In literature, England has few peers in any language, producing some of the greatest legends (King Arthur, *Beowulf,* and *The Lord of the Rings*), poems (by Chaucer, Wordsworth, and Byron), novels (by Dickens, Austen, and J. K. Rowling), and plays (by William Shakespeare, England's greatest writer). London rivals

Broadway as the best scene for live theater. England is a major exporter of movies and movie actors—Laurence Olivier, Alec Guinness, Ian McKellen, Helen Mirren, Judi Dench, Kate Winslet, Keira Knightley, Ralph Fiennes, Hugh Grant, and on and on.

In popular music, England remains almost America's equal. It started in the 1960s with the "British invasion" of bands that reinfused rock and blues into America—the Beatles, the Rolling Stones, the Who. Then came successive waves in the 1970s (Elton John, Led Zeppelin, David Bowie, Pink Floyd, Queen, and the Sex Pistols), the '80s (Dire Straits, the Clash, the Cure, Elvis Costello, the Smiths, the Police, and Duran Duran), the '90s (Oasis, Spice Girls, and the rave scene), and into the 21st century (Coldplay, Amy Winehouse, Lily Allen, and Radiohead).

Wales

Humble, charming little Wales is traditional and beautiful—it sometimes feels trapped in a time warp. When you first enter Wales, it may seem like you're still in England. But soon you'll awaken to the uniqueness and crusty yet poetic vitality of this small country, and realize...you're not in Oxford anymore. And don't ask for an "English breakfast"

at your Welsh B&B—they'll smile politely and remind you that it's a "Welsh breakfast," made with Welsh ingredients.

For the tourist, Wales is a land of stout castles (the best are at Conwy and Caernarfon), salty harbors, chummy community choirs, slate-roofed villages, and a landscape of mountains, moors, and lush green fields dotted with sheep. Snowdonia National Park is a hiker's paradise, with steep but manageable mountain trails, cute-as-a-Hobbit villages (Beddgelert and Betws-y-Coed), and scenery more striking than most

anything in England. Fascinating slate-mine museums (such as at Blaenau Ffestiniog), handy home-base towns (Conwy and Ruthin), and enticing, offbeat attractions (including the "Ewe-Phoria" trained sheepdog show) round out Wales' appeal.

Perhaps Wales' best attraction is hearing the locals speak Welsh (or Cymraeg, pronounced kum-RAH-ig). The Welsh people often use this tongue-twisting and fun-to-listen-to Celtic language when speaking with each other, smoothly switching to English when a visitor asks a question. With its sometimes harsh, sometimes melodic tones, Welsh transports listeners to another time and place.

Culturally, Wales is "a land of poets and singers"—or so says the national anthem. From the myths of Merlin and King Arthur to the poetry of Dylan Thomas (1914–1953), Wales has a long literary tradition. In music, the

country nourishes its traditional Celtic folk music (especially the harp), and exports popular singers such as Tom Jones, Charlotte Church, and Jem. Popular actors born in Wales include Richard Burton and Catherine Zeta-Jones.

Scotland

Rugged, feisty, colorful Scotland is the yin to England's yang. Whether it's the looser, less-organized nature of the people, the stone and sandstone architecture, the unmanicured landscape, or simply the haggis, go-its-own-way Scotland still stands apart. The home of kilts, bagpipes, whisky, golf, lochs, and shortbread lives up to its clichéd image—and then some.

While the Scots are known for their telltale burr—and more than a few unique words (aye, just listen for a wee blether)—they're also trying to keep alive their own Celtic tongue: Gaelic (pronounced "gallic"). Though few Scots speak Gaelic in everyday life, legislation protects it, and it's beginning to be used on road signs.

That's just one small sign of the famously independent Scottish spirit. Since the days of William "Braveheart" Wallace, the Scots have chafed under English rule. Thanks to the recent trend of "devolution," Scotland is increasingly autonomous (even opening its own Parliament in 1999).

Visitors divide their time between the two Scotlands: the Lowlands (the flatter, southern area around Edinburgh and Glasgow, populated by mobile phone–toting yuppies) and the Highlands (the remote, rugged northern area, where proudly traditional Scots eke out a living).

In the Lowlands, don't miss the impressive Scottish capital of Edinburgh, with its attractions-lined Royal Mile and stirring hilltop castle. Nearby, the rival city of Glasgow offers a grittier (but quickly gentrifying) urban ambience. And golfers can't miss the seaside town of St. Andrews, with its world-famous links, vast sandy beaches, colorful university life, and an evocative ruined cathedral.

To commune with the traditional Scottish soul, head for the Highlands. Here you'll find hills, lochs (lakes), "sea lochs" (inlets), castles, and a feeling of remoteness. The "Weeping Glen" of Glencoe offers grand views and a sad tale of Scottish history. The provincial city of Inverness is a handy home base for venturing to uniquely Scottish sights (including the historic site of "Bonnie" Prince Charlie's disastrous Battle of Culloden). Ever-present whisky distilleries offer the chance to sample another uniquely

Scottish "spirit," and viewing the engineering feat of the Caledonian Canal—not to mention famous Loch Ness—inspires awe (say hi to Nessie). Hardy souls can set sail for some of Scotland's islands: Iona and Mull (from Oban), or the super-scenic Isle of Skye.

Whether going to England, Wales, Scotland, or (my choice) all three, you'll have a grand adventure—and a great experience—in Britain. Cheerio!

INTRODUCTION

This book breaks Britain into its top big-city, small-town, and rural destinations. It gives you all of the information and opinions necessary to wring the maximum value out of your limited time and money in each of these locations. If you plan a month or less for Britain and have a normal appetite for information, this book is all you need. If you're a travel-info fiend, this book sorts through all the superlatives and provides a handy rack upon which to hang your supplemental information.

Experiencing British culture, people, and natural wonders economically and hassle-free has been my goal for three decades of traveling, tour guiding, and travel writing. With this new edition, I pass on to you the lessons I've learned, updated for your trip in 2010. Note that Northern Ireland—which is part of the UK—is covered in my book *Rick Steves' Ireland*.

While including the predictable biggies (such as Big Ben, Stratford-upon-Avon, Edinburgh, and Stonehenge), this book also mixes in a healthy dose of Back Door intimacy (windswept Roman lookouts, angelic boys' choirs, and nearly edible Cotswold villages). I've been selective. For example, there are plenty of great countryside palaces, but I recommend just the best—Blenheim.

The best is, of course, only my opinion. But after spending half my adult life researching Europe, I've developed a sixth sense for what travelers enjoy. The places featured in this book will knock your spots off.

About This Book

Rick Steves' Great Britain 2010 is a personal tour guide in your pocket. I update this book every year in person, but even with annual updates, things change. For the latest, visit www.ricksteves.com/update, and for reports and experiences—good and bad—

from fellow travelers, check www.ricksteves.com/feedback.

This book is organized by destinations—each one a mini-vacation on its own, filled with exciting sights, strollable neighborhoods, homey and affordable places to stay, and memorable places to eat. In the following chapters, you'll find these sections:

Planning Your Time suggests a schedule with thoughts on how best to use your limited time.

Orientation includes specifics on public transportation, local tour options, helpful hints, easy-to-read maps, and tourist information (abbreviated **TI** in this book).

Sights, described in detail, are rated:

    ▲▲▲—Don't miss.

    ▲▲—Try hard to see.

    ▲—Worthwhile if you can make it.

    No rating—Worth knowing about.

Self-Guided Walks take you through interesting neighborhoods, with a personal tour guide in hand.

Sleeping describes my favorite hotels, from good-value deals to cushy splurges.

Eating serves up a range of options, from inexpensive pubs to fancy restaurants.

Connections outlines your options for traveling to destinations by train, bus, and plane. In car-friendly regions, I've included route tips for drivers.

British History and Culture is a quick overview of Britain, past and present.

The **appendix** is a traveler's tool kit, with telephone tips, useful phone numbers, transportation basics (on trains, buses, car rentals, driving, and flights), recommended books and films, a festival list, climate chart, handy packing checklist, hotel reservation form, and a fun British–Yankee dictionary.

Browse through this book and select your favorite sights. Then have a brilliant trip! Traveling like a temporary local, you'll get the absolute most out of every mile, minute, and dollar. I'm happy that you'll be visiting places I know and love, and meeting my favorite British people.

Planning

This section will help you get started on planning your trip—with advice on trip costs, when to go, and what you should know before you take off.

Travel Smart

Your trip to Britain is like a complex play—easier to follow and to really appreciate on a second viewing. While no one does the same

Top Destinations in Great Britain

- ISLE OF SKYE
- OBAN & SOUTHERN HIGHLANDS
- INVERNESS & NORTHERN HIGHLANDS
- BTWN. INVER. & EDIN.
- ST. ANDREWS
- GLASGOW
- EDINBURGH
- DURHAM & N.E. ENGLAND
- LAKE DISTRICT
- BLACKPOOL & LIVERPOOL
- YORK
- NORTH WALES
- IRONBRIDGE GORGE
- STRATFORD
- THE COTSWOLDS
- GREENWICH WINDSOR & CAMBRIDGE
- BATH
- LONDON
- NEAR BATH

trip twice to gain that advantage, reading this book in its entirety before your trip accomplishes much the same thing.

Design an itinerary that enables you to visit sights at the best possible times. Note holidays, festivals, colorful market days, and days when sights are closed. Sundays have the same pros and cons as they do for travelers in the US (special events, limited hours, banks and many shops closed, limited public transportation, no rush hours). Saturdays are virtually weekdays with earlier closing hours and no rush hour (though transportation connections outside of London can be less frequent than on weekdays). Sights normally closed on Monday are often open on Bank Holiday Mondays.

Great Britain at a Glance

England

▲▲▲London Thriving metropolis packed with world-class museums, monuments, churches, parks, palaces, theaters, pubs, Beefeaters, telephone boxes, double-decker buses, and all things British.

▲▲Greenwich, Windsor, and Cambridge Easy side-trips from London: Famous observatory at the maritime center of Greenwich, the Queen's palace at Windsor, and England's best university town, Cambridge.

▲▲▲Bath Genteel Georgian showcase city, built around the remains of an ancient Roman bath.

▲▲Near Bath England's mysterious heart, with the prehistoric-meets-New Age hill at Glastonbury, spine-tingling stone circles at Stonehenge and Avebury, enjoyable cathedral towns of Wells and Salisbury, delightful Dorset countryside, and rugged sights of South Wales.

▲▲The Cotswolds Remarkably quaint villages—including the cozy market town Chipping Campden, popular hamlet Stow-on-the-Wold, and handy transit hub Moreton-in-Marsh—scattered over a hilly countryside, and near one of England's top palaces at Blenheim.

▲Stratford-upon-Avon Shakespeare's hometown and top venue for seeing live performances of his plays, plus the medieval Warwick Castle and Coventry's inspiring cathedral.

▲Ironbridge Gorge Birthplace of the Industrial Revolution, with sights and museums that tell the earth-changing story.

▲Blackpool and Liverpool England's tackiest, most fun-loving beach resort at Blackpool, and the increasingly rejuvenated port city (and Beatles hometown) of Liverpool.

▲▲The Lake District Idyllic lakes-and-hills landscape, with enjoyable hikes and joyrides, time-passed valleys, William Wordsworth and Beatrix Potter sights, and the charming home-base town of Keswick.

▲▲▲**York** Walled medieval town with grand Gothic cathedral, excellent museums (Viking, Victorian, Railway), and atmospheric old center.

▲**Durham and Northeast England** Youthful working-class town with magnificent cathedral, plus nearby open-air museum, Roman remains of Hadrian's Wall, Holy Island, and Bamburgh Castle.

Wales
▲▲▲**North Wales** Scenically rugged land with the castle towns of Conwy and Caernarfon, natural beauty of Snowdonia National Park, tourable slate mines at Blaenau Ffestiniog, colorful Welsh banquet at Ruthin, and charming locals who speak a tongue-twisting old language.

Scotland
▲▲▲**Edinburgh** Proud and endlessly entertaining Scottish capital, with an imposing castle, attractions-studded Royal Mile, excellent museums, and atmospheric neighborhoods.

▲**St. Andrews** Sandy beach town that gave birth to golf and hosts Scotland's top university.

▲**Glasgow** Scotland's gritty but gentrifying "second city," a hotbed of modern architecture.

▲**Oban and the Southern Highlands** Handy home-base town of Oban—with boat trips to the isles of Mull and Iona—and the stirring "Weeping Glen" of Glencoe.

▲**Isle of Skye** Remote, dramatically scenic island with craggy mountainscapes, jagged Trotternish Peninsula, castles, distilleries, and the handy home-base towns of Portree and Kyleakin.

▲**Inverness and the Northern Highlands** Regional capital with easy access to more Highlands sights, including Culloden Battlefield (Scotland's Alamo) and monster-spotting at the famous Loch Ness.

▲**Between Inverness and Edinburgh** Whisky mecca of Pitlochry and stately castle and battlefield at Stirling.

Major Holidays and Weekends

Popular places are even busier on weekends, especially sunny weekends, which are sufficient cause for an impromptu holiday in this soggy corner of Europe. Festivals and three-day weekends can make towns, trains, buses, roads, and hotels even more crowded. Book your accommodations well in advance for these times.

A few national holidays jam things up, especially Bank Holiday Mondays. Mark these dates in red on your travel calendar: New Year's Day; Good Friday through Easter Monday (April 2–5 in 2010); the Bank Holidays that occur on the first and last Mondays in May (May 3 and 31 in 2010), the first Monday in August (Aug 2 in 2010, Scotland only), and the last Monday in August (Aug 30 in 2010, England and Wales only); and Christmas and December 26 (Boxing Day). For more information, see "Holidays and Festivals" in the appendix.

Many businesses, as well as many museums, close on Good Friday, Easter, and New Year's Day. On Christmas, virtually everything closes down, even the Tube in London (taxi rates are high). Museums are also generally closed December 24 and 26; smaller shops are usually closed December 26.

Be sure to mix intense and relaxed periods in your itinerary. To maximize rootedness, minimize one-night stands. It's worth a long drive after dinner to be settled into a town for two nights. B&Bs are also more likely to give a better price to someone staying more than one night.

Every trip (and every traveler) needs at least a few slack days (for picnics, laundry, people-watching, and so on). Pace yourself. Assume you will return.

Reread this book as you travel, and visit local TIs. Upon arrival in a new town, lay the groundwork for a smooth departure; write down (or print out from an online source) the schedule for the train or bus you'll take when you depart. Drivers can study the best route to their next destination.

While traveling, take advantage of the Internet and phones to make your trip run smoothly. By going online (at Internet cafés or your hotel) and making phone calls, you can get tourist information, learn the latest on sights (special events, tour schedules, etc.) book tickets and tours, make reservations, reconfirm hotels, research transportation connections, and keep in touch with loved ones.

Connect with the culture. Set up your own quest for the best pub, cathedral, or chocolate bar. Enjoy the friendliness of your British hosts. Slow down and be open to unexpected experiences. You speak the language—use it! Ask questions—most locals are eager to point you in their idea of the right direction. Keep a notepad in your pocket for organizing your thoughts. Wear your money belt, and learn the local cu   te prices in dollars. Those who expect to tr

Trip Costs

Five components make up your total trip costs: airfare, surface transportation, room and board, sightseeing and entertainment, and shopping and miscellany.

Airfare: A basic round-trip flight from the US to London costs $600 to $1,200, depending on where you fly from and when (cheaper in winter). If your trip extends beyond Great Britain, consider saving time and money by flying "open jaw" (into one city and out of another—for instance, into London and out of Amsterdam).

Surface Transportation: For a three-week whirlwind trip of all my recommended British destinations, allow $550 per person for public transportation (train pass, key buses, and Tube fare in London) or $750 per person for car rental (based on two people sharing a three-week rental), including parking, gas, and insurance. Leasing is worth considering for trips of two and a half weeks or more. Car rental and leases are cheapest when arranged from the US. Train passes are normally available only outside of Europe (although you can buy a bus pass in Britain). You may save money by simply buying tickets as you go (see "Transportation" in the appendix).

Room and Board: You can thrive in Britain on $115 per day per person for room and board (less in villages). A $115-per-day budget allows an average of $15 for lunch, $30 for dinner, $5 for snacks, and $65 for lodging (based on two people splitting a $160 double room that includes breakfast). Students and tightwads can do it on $60 ($35 for a bed in a hostel, $25 for meals—mostly picnics—and snacks).

Sightseeing and Entertainment: Figure on paying roughly $10–30 apiece for the major sights that charge admission (Stonehenge-$11, Shakespeare's Birthplace in Stratford-$19, Westminster Abbey-$19, Tower of London-$27), $7 for minor ones (climbing church towers), $12 for guided walks, and $20 for bus tours and splurge experiences (such as Welsh and Scottish folk evenings). For information on various sightseeing passes, see page 20.

Fortunately, many of the best sights in London are free, including the British Museum, National Gallery, National Portrait Gallery, Tate Britain, Tate Modern, Victoria & Albert Museum, and the British Library (though most request donations). An overall average of $30 a day works in most cities (allow $50 in London). Don't skimp here. After all, this category is the driving force behind your trip—you came to sightsee, enjoy, and experience Britain.

Britain's Best Three-Week Trip by Car

Day	Plan	Sleep in
1	Arrive in London, bus to Bath	Bath
2	Bath	Bath
3	Pick up car, Avebury, Wells, Glastonbury	Bath
4	South Wales, St. Fagans, Tintern	Chipping Campden
5	Explore the Cotswolds, Blenheim	Chipping Campden
6	Stratford, Warwick, Coventry	Ironbridge Gorge
7	Ironbridge Gorge, Ruthin banquet	Ruthin (if banquet) or Conwy
8	Highlights of North Wales	Ruthin or Conwy
9	Liverpool, Blackpool	Blackpool
10	South Lake District	Keswick area
11	North Lake District	Keswick area
12	Drive up west coast of Scotland	Oban
13	Highlands, Loch Ness, Scenic Highlands Drive	Edinburgh
14	Edinburgh	Edinburgh
15	Edinburgh	Edinburgh
16	Hadrian's Wall, Beamish, Durham's Cathedral and evensong	Durham
17	North York Moors, York, turn in car	York
18	York	York
19	Early train to London	London
20	London	London
21	London	London
22	Whew!	

While this three-week itinerary is designed to be done by car, it can be done by train and bus or, better yet, with a BritRail & Drive Pass (best car days: the Cotswolds, North Wales, Lake District, Scottish Highlands, Hadrian's Wall; for more on the pass, see page 710). For three weeks without a car, I'd probably cut back on the recommended sights with the most frustrating public transportation: South and North Wales, Ironbridge Gorge, and the Scottish Highlands. (Drivers can save a couple of days and a lot of miles by going directly from the Lake District to Edinburgh and skipping the long ride through the Highlands.) Lacing together the cities by train is very slick, and buses get you where the trains don't go. With more time, everything is workable without a car.

Where Do I Find Information On...?

Credit-Card Theft	See page 16.
Packing Light	See the packing list on page 735.
Phoning	See "Telephones" on page 700.
Language	See page 736.
Making Hotel Reservations	See page 28.
Tipping	See page 16.
Tourist Information Offices	See page 699.
Updates to This Book	See www.ricksteves.com/update.

Shopping and Miscellany: Figure roughly $2 per postcard, $3 for tea or an ice-cream cone, and $6 per pint of beer. Shopping can vary in cost from nearly nothing to a small fortune. Good budget travelers find that this category has little to do with assembling a trip full of lifelong and wonderful memories.

Sightseeing Priorities

Depending on the length of your trip, and taking geographic proximity into account, here are my recommended priorities:

3 days:	London
5 days, add:	Bath, Cotswolds
7 days, add:	York
9 days, add:	Edinburgh
11 days, add:	Stratford, Warwick, Blenheim
14 days, add:	North Wales, Wells/Glastonbury/Avebury
17 days, add:	Lake District, Hadrian's Wall, Durham
21 days, add:	Ironbridge Gorge, Blackpool, Scottish Highlands
24 days, add:	Choose two of the following—St. Andrews, Glasgow, Cambridge, South Wales

This list includes virtually everything on the "Britain's Best Three-Week Trip by Car" itinerary and map earlier in this chapter.

When to Go

For England and Wales, July and August are peak season—my favorite time—with very long days, the best weather, and the busiest schedule of tourist fun. For Scotland, the weather is best in May and June.

Prices and crowds don't go up during peak times as dramatically in Britain as they do in much of Europe, except for holidays and festivals. Still, travel during "shoulder season" (May, early June, Sept, and early Oct) is easier and may be a bit less expensive. Shoulder-season travelers get fewer crowds, decent weather, the full range of sights and tourist fun spots, and the ability to grab a room almost whenever and wherever they like—often at a flexible price. Winter travelers find absolutely no crowds and soft room prices, but shorter sightseeing hours and reliably bad weather. Some attractions are open only on weekends or are closed entirely in the winter (Nov–Feb). The weather can be cold and dreary, and nightfall draws the shades on sightseeing well before dinnertime. While rural charm falls with the leaves, city sightseeing is fine in the winter.

Plan for rain no matter when you go. Just keep traveling and take full advantage of bright spells. The weather can change several times in a day, but rarely is it extreme. As the locals say, "There is no bad weather—only inappropriate clothing." Bring a jacket and dress in layers. Temperatures below 32°F cause headlines, and days that break 80°F—while increasing in recent years—are still rare in Britain. July and August are not much better than shoulder months. May and June can be lovely any-where in Britain. (For more information, see the climate chart in the appendix.) And though sunshine may be rare, summer days are very long. The midsummer sun is up from 6:30 until 22:30. It's not uncommon to have a gray day, eat dinner, and enjoy hours of sunshine afterward.

Know Before You Go

Your trip is more likely to go smoothly if you plan ahead. Check this list of things to arrange while you're still at home.

You need a **passport**—but no visa or shots—to travel in Great Britain. You may be denied entry into certain European countries if your passport is due to expire within three to six months of your ticketed date of return. Get it renewed if you'll be cutting it close. It can take up to six weeks to get or renew a passport (for more on passports, see www.travel.state.gov). Pack a photocopy of your passport in your luggage in case the original is lost or stolen.

Book your rooms well in advance if you'll be traveling during any major **holidays** (see "Major Holidays and Weekends" sidebar, earlier).

Most people fly into London and remain there for a few days. Instead, consider a gentler **small-town start** in Bath (the ideal jet-lag pillow), and let London be the finale at the end of your trip. You'll be more rested and ready to tackle England's greatest city. Heathrow Airport has direct bus connections to Bath and other cities. (Bristol Airport is also near Bath.)

If you'll be in London or Stratford and want to **see a play**, check theater schedules ahead of time. For simplicity, I book plays while in Britain, but if there's something you have to see, consider buying tickets before you go. For the current schedule of London plays and musicals, visit www.officiallondontheatre.co.uk.

Even though Stratford's major Shakespeare theaters are closed for renovation for most of 2010, the town will host productions by the Bard all year (see www.rsc.org.uk for details). Note that if it's just Shakespeare you're after, with or without Stratford, you can see his plays in London, too.

To attend the **Edinburgh Festival** (Aug 13–Sept 5 in 2010), you can book tickets in advance (for details, see page 548).

If you want to **golf at St. Andrews' famous Old Course,** reserve a year ahead, or for other courses, reserve two weeks ahead. You can also try for a tee time when you arrive, but to play the Old Course, you'll need a golf handicap certificate (see page 578).

To attend the free **Ceremony of the Keys** in the Tower of London, write for tickets (see page 99).

At **Stonehenge,** anyone can see the stones from behind the rope line, but if you want to go inside the stone circle, you'll need advance reservations (see page 244).

If you're interested in **travel insurance,** do your homework before you buy. Compare the cost of the insurance to the likelihood of your using it and your potential loss if something goes wrong. For details on the many kinds of travel insurance, see www.ricksteves.com/plan/tips/insurance.htm.

Call your **debit- and credit-card companies** to let them know the countries you'll be visiting, so they won't deny your international charges. Confirm your daily withdrawal limit, and consider asking to have it raised so you can take out more cash at each ATM stop. Ask about international transaction fees.

If you'll be **renting a car** in Great Britain, bring your driver's license. Confirm pick-up hours—many car-rental offices close Saturday afternoon and all day Sunday.

If you'll be traveling to continental Europe on the **Eurostar** train, consider ordering a ticket in advance (or buy it in Britain); for details, see page 166.

Because **airline carry-on restrictions** are always changing, visit the Transportation Security Administration's website (www.tsa.gov/travelers) for an up-to-date list of what you can bring on the plane with you and what you have to check. Remember to arrive with plenty of time to get through security. Some airlines may restrict you to only one carry-on (no extras like a purse or daypack); check with your airline or at the British transportation website (www.dft.gov.uk).

Practicalities

Emergency Telephone Numbers: Dial 999 for police or medical emergencies.

Time: British schedules—and this book—use the 24-hour

clock. It's the same through 12:00 noon, then keep going: 13:00, 14:00, and so on. For anything over 12, subtract 12 and add p.m. (14:00 is 2:00 p.m.)

Britain, which is one hour earlier than most of continental Europe, is five/eight hours ahead of the East/West Coasts of the US. The exceptions are the beginning and end of Daylight Saving Time: Britain and Europe "spring forward" the last Sunday in March (two weeks after most of North America), and "fall back" the last Sunday in October (one week before North America). For a handy online time converter, try www.timeanddate.com/world clock.

Business Hours: In Britain, most stores are open Monday through Saturday from roughly 10:00 to 17:00. In London, stores stay open later on Wednesday or Thursday (until 19:00 or 20:00), depending on the neighborhood. On Sunday, when some stores are closed, street markets in London are lively with shoppers.

Watt's Up? Britain's electrical system is different from North America's in two ways: the shape of the plug (three square prongs—

not the two round prongs used in continental Europe) and the voltage of the current (220 volts instead of 110 volts). For your North American plug to work in Britain, you'll need a three-prong adapter plug, sold inexpensively at travel stores in the US, and at British airports and drugstores. As for the voltage, most newer electronics or travel appliances (such as hair dryers, laptops, and battery chargers) automatically convert the voltage—if you see a range of voltages printed on the item or its plug (such as "110–220"), it'll work in Great Britain and Europe. Otherwise, you can buy a converter separately in the US (about $20).

Discounts: While discounts (called "concessions" or "concs" in Britain) aren't listed in this book, many English sights offer discounts for seniors (loosely defined as those who are retired or willing to call themselves a senior), youths (ages 8–18), students, groups of 10 or more, and families. Always ask. To get a student or teacher ID card, visit www.isic.org or www.statravel.com.

News: British papers cover global events, and Americans can also peruse the *International Herald Tribune* (published almost daily throughout Europe and online at www.iht.com). Other newsy sites are http://news.bbc.co.uk and www.europeantimes.com. Every Tuesday, the European editions of *Time* and *Newsweek* hit the stands with articles of particular interest to travelers in Europe. Sports addicts can get their daily fix online or from *USA Today*. Many hotels have BBC (of course) and CNN television channels.

Money

This section offers advice on getting cash, using credit and debit cards, dealing with lost or stolen cards, and tipping.

Cash from ATMs

Throughout Britain, cash machines (ATMs) are the standard way for travelers to get local currency. Bring plastic—credit and/or debit cards. It's smart to bring two cards, in case one gets demagnetized or eaten by a temperamental machine.

As an emergency backup, bring several hundred US dollars in hard cash (in easy-to-exchange $20 bills). Avoid using currency exchange booths (lousy rates and/or outrageous fees); if you have currency to exchange, take it to a bank. Travelers checks are a waste of time at banks and a waste of money in fees.

You'll find ATMs all over Britain, always open and providing quick transactions. To withdraw money, you'll need a debit card (ideally with a Visa or MasterCard logo for maximum usability), plus a PIN code. Know your PIN code in numbers; there are only numbers—no letters—on European keypads.

Before you go, verify with your bank that your cards will work overseas, and alert them that you'll be making withdrawals in Europe; otherwise, the bank may not approve transactions if it perceives unusual spending patterns. (Your credit-card company may do the same thing—let them know your travel plans, too.) Also ask about international transaction fees; see "Credit and Debit Cards," below.

When using an ATM, try to take out large sums of money to reduce your per-transaction bank fees. If the machine refuses your request, try again and select a smaller amount (some ATMs limit the amount you can withdraw—don't take it personally). If that doesn't work, try a different machine.

Even in Britain, you'll need to keep your cash safe. Use a money belt—a pouch with a strap that you buckle around your waist like a belt and wear under your clothes. Thieves target tourists. A money belt provides peace of mind, allowing you to carry lots of cash safely. Don't waste time every few days tracking down an ATM—withdraw a week's worth of money, stuff it in your money belt, and travel!

Credit and Debit Cards

Visa and MasterCard are more commonly accepted than American Express. Just like at home, credit or debit cards work easily at larger hotels, restaurants, and shops, but smaller businesses prefer payment in local currency (in small bills—break large bills at a bank or larger store). If receipts show your credit-card number, don't toss these thoughtlessly.

Exchange Rate

I list prices in pounds (£) throughout this book.

1 British pound (£1) = about $1.60

While the euro (€) is now the currency of most of Europe, Britain is sticking with its pound sterling. The British pound (£), also called a "quid," is broken into 100 pence (p). Pence means "cents." You'll find coins ranging from 1p to £2 and bills from £5 to £50. Fake pound coins are easy to spot (real coins have an inscription on their outside rims; the fakes look like tree bark).

London is so expensive that some travelers try to kid themselves that pounds are dollars. But when they get home, that £1,000-pound Visa bill isn't asking for $1,000...it wants $1,600. (To get the latest rate and print a cheat sheet, see www.oanda.com.)

Scotland and Northern Ireland issue their own currency in pounds, worth the same as an English pound. English, Scottish, and Northern Ireland's Ulster pounds are technically interchangeable in each region, although Scottish and Ulster pounds are "undesirable" and sometimes not even accepted in England. Banks in any of the three regions will convert your Scottish or Ulster pounds into English pounds for no charge. Don't worry about the coins, which are accepted throughout Britain.

Fees: Credit and debit cards—whether used for purchases or ATM withdrawals—often charge additional, tacked-on "international transaction" fees of up to 3 percent plus $5 per transaction. Note that if you use a credit card for ATM transactions, it's technically a "cash advance" rather than a "withdrawal"—and subject to an additional cash-advance fee.

To avoid unpleasant surprises, call your bank or credit-card company before your trip to ask about these fees. Ask your bank if it has agreements with any British banks for lower withdrawal fees. If the fees are too high, consider getting a card just for your trip: Capital One (www.capitalone.com) and most credit unions have low-to-no international transaction fees.

If merchants offer to convert your purchase price into dollars (called dynamic currency conversion, or "DCC"), refuse this "service." You'll pay even more in fees for the expensive convenience of seeing your charge in dollars.

Dealing with "Chip and PIN": Some parts of Europe (especially Britain, Ireland, France, the Netherlands, and Scandinavia) are adopting a "chip and PIN" system for their credit and debit cards. These "smartcards" come with an embedded microchip, and cardholders enter a PIN code instead of signing a receipt. In most cases, you can still use your credit or debit card at the cashier and sign the receipt the old-fashioned way. But a few merchants might insist on the PIN code—making it helpful for you to know the PIN code for your credit card (ask your credit-card company); in a pinch, use cash or your debit card and PIN code instead. Some newer, automated pay-at-the-pump gas stations or ticket machines can no longer read the magnetic strip on American credit cards at all. Even in these situations, there's usually a cashier nearby who can take your credit or debit card and make it work.

Damage Control for Lost Cards

If you lose your credit, debit, or ATM card, you can stop people from using it by reporting the loss immediately to the respective global customer-assistance centers. Call these 24-hour US numbers collect: Visa (410/581-9994), MasterCard (636/722-7111), and American Express (623/492-8427). Diner's Club has offices in Britain (0870-190-0011) and the US (702/797-5532, call collect).

At a minimum, you'll need to know the name of the financial institution that issued you the card, along with the type of card (classic, platinum, or whatever). Providing the following information will allow for a quicker cancellation of your missing card: full card number, whether you are the primary or secondary cardholder, the cardholder's name exactly as printed on the card, billing address, home phone number, circumstances of the loss or theft, and identification verification (your birth date, your mother's maiden name, or your Social Security number—memorize this, don't carry a copy). If you are the secondary cardholder, you'll also need to provide the primary cardholder's identification-verification details. You can generally receive a temporary card within two or three business days in Europe.

If you promptly report your card lost or stolen, you typically won't be responsible for any unauthorized transactions on your account, although many banks charge a liability fee of $50.

Tipping

Tipping in Britain isn't as automatic and generous as it is in the US, but for special service, tips are appreciated, if not expected. As in the US, the proper amount depends on your resources, tipping philosophy, and the circumstances, but some general guidelines apply.

Restaurants: At a pub or restaurant with waitstaff, check the menu or your bill to see if the service is included; if not, tip about 10 percent. At pubs where you order at the counter, you don't have to tip. (Regular customers ordering a round sometimes say, "Add one for yourself" as a tip for drinks ordered at the bar—but this isn't expected.)

Taxis: To tip the cabbie, round up. For a typical ride, round up to a maximum of 10 percent (to pay a £4.50 fare, give £5; for a £28 fare, give £30). If the cabbie hauls your bags and zips you to the airport to help you catch your flight, you might want to toss in a little more. But if you feel like you're being driven in circles or otherwise ripped off, skip the tip.

Special Services: It's thoughtful to tip a pound to someone who shows you a special sight and who is paid in no other way. Tour guides at public sights often hold out their hands for tips after they give their spiel; if I've already paid for the tour, I don't tip extra unless they've really impressed me. At hotels, porters expect about 50p for each bag they carry (another reason to pack light). Leaving the maid a pound at the end of your stay is a nice touch. In general, if someone in the service industry does a super job for you, a tip of a pound or two is appropriate, but not required.

When in doubt, ask. If you're not sure whether (or how much) to tip for a service, ask your hotelier or the TI; they'll fill you in on how it's done on their turf.

Getting a VAT Refund

Wrapped into the purchase price of your British souvenirs is a Value-Added Tax (VAT) of about 17.5 percent. If you purchase more than £20 (about $32) worth of goods at a store that participates in the VAT-refund scheme, you're entitled to get most of that tax back. Getting your refund is usually straightforward and, if you buy a substantial amount of souvenirs, well worth the hassle. If you're lucky, the merchant will subtract the tax when you make your purchase. (This is more likely to occur if the store ships the goods to your home.) Otherwise, you'll need to:

Get the paperwork. Have the merchant completely fill out the necessary refund document, called a "Tax-Free Shopping Cheque." You'll have to present your passport at the store.

Get your stamp at the border or airport. Process your cheque(s) at your last stop in the EU (e.g., at the airport) with the customs agent who deals with VAT refunds. It's best to keep your purchases in your carry-on for viewing, but if they're too large or dangerous (such as knives) to carry on, track down the proper customs agent to inspect them before you check your bag. You're not supposed to use your purchased goods before you leave. If you show up at customs wearing your new Wellingtons, officials might look the other way—or deny you a refund.

Collect your refund. You'll need to return your stamped document to the retailer or its representative. Many merchants work with a service, such as Global Refund (www.globalrefund .com) or Premier Tax Free (www.premiertaxfree.com), which have offices at major airports, ports, or border crossings. These services, which extract a 4 percent fee, can refund your money immediately in your currency of choice or credit your card (within two billing cycles). If the retailer handles VAT refunds directly, it's up to you to contact the merchant for your refund. You can mail the documents from home, or quicker, from your point of departure (using a stamped, addressed envelope you've prepared or one that's been provided by the merchant). You'll then have to wait—it could take months.

Customs for American Shoppers

You are allowed to take home $800 worth of items per person duty-free, once every 30 days. The next $1,000 is taxed at a flat 3 percent. After that, you pay the individual item's duty rate. You can also bring in duty-free a liter of alcohol (slightly more than a standard-size bottle of wine; you must be at least 21), 200 cigarettes, and up to 100 non-Cuban cigars. You may take home vacuum-packed cheeses; dried herbs, spices, or mushrooms; and canned fruits or vegetables, including jams and vegetable spreads. Baked goods, candy, chocolate, oil, vinegar, mustard, and honey are OK. Fresh fruits or vegetables are not. Meats, even if canned, are generally not allowed. Remember that you'll need to carefully pack any bottles of wine and other liquid-containing items in your checked luggage, due to limits on liquids in carry-ons. To check customs rules and duty rates before you go, visit www.cbp.gov, and click on "Travel," then "Know Before You Go."

Sightseeing

Sightseeing can be hard work. Use these tips to make your visits to Britain's finest sights meaningful, fun, efficient, and painless.

Plan Ahead

Set up an itinerary that allows you to fit in all your must-see sights. For a one-stop look at opening hours in the bigger cities, see the "At a Glance" sidebars throughout this book. Most sights keep stable hours, but you can easily confirm the latest by checking their website or asking at the local TI. This is especially important on holidays, when hours can change. Don't put off visiting a must-see sight—you never know when a place will close unexpectedly for a holiday, strike, or restoration.

To get the most out of the self-guided walks and sight descriptions in this book, re-read them before you visit. When possible, visit major sights first thing (when your energy is high) and save other activities for the afternoon. Hit the museum highlights first, then go back to other things if you have the stamina and time.

Going at the right time can also help you avoid crowds. This book offers tips on specific sights. Try visiting very early, at lunch, or very late. Evening visits are usually peaceful, with fewer crowds. For specifics on London, see "London for Early Birds and Night Owls" on page 81.

At Sights

All sights have rules, and if you know about these in advance, they're no big deal.

At churches—which often offer interesting art (usually free) and a cool, welcome seat—a modest dress code (no bare shoulders or shorts) is encouraged.

Some important sights have metal detectors or conduct bag searches that will slow your entry. Major museums and sights require you to check daypacks and coats. They'll be kept safely. If you have something you can't bear to part with, stash it in a pocket or purse. To avoid checking a small backpack, carry it under your arm like a purse as you enter. From a guard's point of view, a backpack is generally a problem, whereas a purse is not.

Photography is sometimes banned at major sights. Look for signs or ask. If cameras are allowed, video cameras are as well, but flashes or tripods usually are not. Flashes damage oil paintings and distract others in the room. Even without a flash, a handheld camera will take a decent picture (or you can buy postcards or posters at the museum bookstore).

Museums have special exhibits in addition to their permanent collection. Some exhibits are included in the entry price; others come at an extra cost (which you may have to pay even if you don't want to see the exhibit).

Many sights rent audioguides, which offer excellent recorded descriptions (about £3.50). If you bring along your own pair of headphones and a Y-jack, you can sometimes share one audioguide with your travel partner and save money. Guided tours are most likely to occur during peak season (usually between £3 and £8 and widely ranging in quality).

Expect changes—artwork can be on tour, on loan, out sick, or shifted at the whim of the curator. To adapt, pick up any available free floor plans as you enter. Ask the museum staff if you can't find a particular piece.

Major sights often have an on-site café or cafeteria (usually a good place to rest and have a snack or light meal). The WCs at many sights are free and generally clean. Many places sell postcards that highlight their attractions. Before you leave, scan the postcards and thumb through the biggest guidebook (or skim its index) to be sure you haven't overlooked something that you'd like to see.

Most sights stop admitting people 30–60 minutes before closing time, and some rooms close early (often 45 minutes before the actual closing time). Guards usher people out, so don't save the best for last.

Every sight or museum offers more than what is covered in this book. Use the information in this book as an introduction—not the final word.

Sightseeing Passes and Memberships

Many sights in Britain are covered by the Great British Heritage Pass or these memberships: English Heritage or National Trust. If you're a whirlwind sightseer, seriously consider the Great British Heritage Pass, which covers the most sights.

The Great British Heritage Pass: The best deal for most travelers, this pass covers all of the major English Heritage and National Trust sights, plus many others (including several major attractions in Scotland, Wales, and Northern Ireland). Covering about 600 historic sights, this pass is good for a certain number of consecutive days (2009 prices: £32 for 4 days, £45 for 7 days, £60 for 15 days, £80 for 30 days; £72/£99/£135/£180 family pass also available for up to 2 adults and 3 kids ages 5–15, though note that kids already get discounts at sights; for more information, call 0870-242-9988 or see www.britishheritagepass.com). You can buy this pass online (£6.50 extra for shipping) or at various tourist information centers in Britain; for example, in London, this pass is sold by the Britain and London Visitors Centre on Lower Regent Street.

Memberships: Many sights in Britain are managed by either the English Heritage or the National Trust (the sights don't overlap). Both organizations sell annual memberships that allow free or discounted entry to the sights they supervise; the English Heritage also sells passes. You can join the National Trust or English Heritage online, or at just about any of their sights.

Membership in **English Heritage** includes free entry to over 400 sights in England, and half-price admission to about 100 more sights in Scotland and Wales (2009 prices: £43/1 person, £75/2 people, good for one year; discounts for students, couples, and seniors; children under 19 free, tel. 0870-333-1182, www.english -heritage.org.uk/membership). For most travelers, their Overseas Visitor Pass is a better choice than the pricier one-year membership (Visitor Pass: £20/7 days; £24/14 days; discounts for couples and families, www.english-heritage.org.uk/ovp).

Membership in the **National Trust** is best suited for garden-and-estate enthusiasts, ideally traveling by car. It covers more than

---

Get It Right

Americans tend to use "England," "Britain," and "UK" interchangeably, but they're not the same:

- **England** is in the southeast part of Britain.
- **Britain** is the name of the island.
- **Great Britain** is the political union of England, Scotland, and Wales.
- The **United Kingdom** adds Northern Ireland.
- The **British Isles** (not a political entity) also includes the independent Republic of Ireland.
- The **British Commonwealth** is a loose association of possessions and former colonies (including Canada, Australia, and India) that profess at least symbolic loyalty to the Crown.

---

300 historic houses, manors, and gardens throughout Great Britain (£48 for one year, student and couple discounts, children under 5 free, www.nationaltrust.org.uk).

CADW, the Welsh version of the National Trust, sells an **Explorer Pass** that covers many sights in Wales. If you're planning to visit at least three castles or other historic places on their list, the pass will probably save you money (3-day pass: £11/1 person, £18/2 people, £26.50/family; 7-day pass: £17.50/1 person, £29/2 people, £36/family; available at www.cadw.wales.gov.uk or individual sights).

The Bottom Line: These deals can save a busy sightseer money...but only if you choose carefully. Make a list of the sights you plan to see, check which sights are covered (visit the websites listed above), and then add up how much you'd spend if you paid individual admissions to the covered sights. Compare the total to the cost of the pass or membership. Keep in mind that an advantage to any of these deals is that you'll feel free to dip into lesser sights that normally wouldn't merit paying admission.

Fine Points: If you have children, consider the Great British Heritage family pass if you're all avid sightseers; otherwise don't get a pass or membership for them, because they get in free or cheap at most sights. Similarly, people over 60 also get "concessions" (discounted prices) at many English sights (and can get a senior discount on an English Heritage membership). If you're traveling by car and can get to the more remote sights, you're more likely to get your money's worth out of a pass or membership, especially during peak season (Easter–Oct). If you're traveling off-season (Nov–Easter) when many of the sights are closed, these deals are a lesser value.

INTRODUCTION

Sleeping

I favor accommodations (and restaurants) handy to your sightseeing activities. Rather than list hotels scattered throughout a city, I choose two or three favorite neighborhoods and recommend the best accommodations values in each, from $30 bunk beds to fancy-for-my-book $300 doubles. Outside of pricey London, you can expect to find good doubles for $80–160, including breakfast and tax. (For specifics on London, see page 127.)

I look for places that are friendly; clean; a good value; located in a central, safe, quiet neighborhood; and not mentioned in other guidebooks. I'm more impressed by a handy location and a fun-loving philosophy than hair dryers and shoeshine machines. For tips on making reservations, see page 28.

I've described my recommended accommodations using a Sleep Code (see sidebar). Prices listed are for one-night stays in peak season, include a hearty breakfast (unless otherwise noted), and assume you're booking directly and not through a TI.

You should find prices listed in this book to be good through 2010 (except during major holidays and festivals—see page 729). Prices can soften off-season, for stays of two nights or longer, or for payment in cash rather than credit card. Always mention that you found the place through this book—many of the accommodations listed offer special deals to our readers.

Official "rack rates" (the highest rates a hotel charges) can be misleading, because they often omit cheaper oddball rooms and special clearance deals. (Some fancy £120 rooms can rent for a third off if you arrive late on a slow day and ask for a deal.) With all the economic uncertainty these days, many hotels will likely be discounting deeply to snare what customers they can. Try to avoid paying rack rates. If you email several places and ask for their best prices, you'll find some eager to discount and others more passive. This can save you big bucks.

When establishing prices with a hotelier or B&B owner, confirm whether the charge is per person or per room (if a price is too good to be true, it's probably per person). Because many places in Britain charge per person, small groups often pay the same for a single and a double as they would for a triple. In this book, however, room prices are listed per room, not per person.

Many places listed have three floors of rooms and steep stairs; expect good exercise and be happy you packed light. Elevators are rare except in the larger hotels. If you're con-

Sleep Code

(£1 = about $1.60, country code: 44)

To help you easily sort through these listings, I've divided the rooms into three categories, based on the price for a double room with bath:

$$$ **Higher Priced**
$$ **Moderately Priced**
$ **Lower Priced**

To give maximum information in a minimum of space, I use the following code to describe accommodations. Prices in this book are listed per room, not per person. When a price range is given for a type of room (such as "Db-£80–120"), it means the price fluctuates with the season, size of room, or length of stay.

S = Single room, or price for one person in a double.

D = Double or twin room. (I specify double- and twin-bed rooms only if they are priced differently, or if a place has only one or the other. When reserving, you should specify.)

T = Three-person room (often a double bed with a single).

Q = Four-person room (adding an extra child's bed to a T is usually cheaper).

b = Private bathroom with toilet and shower or tub.

s = Private shower or tub only. (The toilet is down the hall.)

According to this code, a couple staying at a "Db-£80" hotel would pay a total of £80 (about $130) per night for a room with a private toilet and shower (or tub). Unless otherwise noted, credit cards are accepted and breakfast is included.

If I mention "Internet access" in a listing, there's a public terminal in the lobby for guests to use. If I say "Wi-Fi," you can generally access it in your room (usually for free), but only if you have your own laptop.

cerned about stairs, call and ask about ground-floor rooms or pay for a hotel with a "lift" (elevator).

Learn the terminology: An "en suite" room has a bathroom (toilet and shower/tub) actually inside the room; a room with a "private bathroom" can mean that the bathroom is all yours, but it's across the hall; and a "standard" room has access to a bathroom down the hall that's shared with other rooms. Figuring there's little difference between "en suite" and "private" rooms, some places charge the same for both. If you want your own bathroom inside the room, request "en suite."

If money's tight, ask for a standard room. You'll almost always have a sink in your room. And, as more rooms go "en suite," the hallway bathroom is shared with fewer standard rooms.

"Twin" means two single beds, and "double" means one double bed (in my listings, I list all two-person rooms as "doubles"). If you're willing to take either one, let them know, or you might be needlessly turned away. Most hotels offer family deals, which means that parents with young children can easily get a room with an extra child's bed or a discount for larger rooms. Call to negotiate the price. Teenage kids are generally charged as adults. Kids under five sleep almost free.

Note that to be called a "hotel," a place technically must have certain amenities, including a 24-hour reception (though this rule is loosely applied). A place called a "townhouse" or "house" (such as "London House") is like a big B&B or a small family-run hotel—with fewer amenities but more character than a "hotel."

Britain has a rating system for hotels and B&Bs. These diamonds and stars are supposed to imply quality, but I find that they mean only that the place sporting these symbols is paying dues to the tourist board. Rating systems often have little to do with value.

If you're traveling beyond my recommended destinations, you'll find accommodations where you need them. Any town with tourists has a TI that books rooms or can give you a list and point you in the right direction. In the absence of a TI, ask people on the street or in pubs or restaurants for help. Online, visit www.smoothhound.co.uk, which offers a range of accommodations for towns throughout the UK (searchable by town, airport, hotel name, or price range).

Types of Accommodations

B&Bs

Compared to hotels, bed-and-breakfast places give you double the cultural intimacy for half the price. Although you may lose some of the conveniences of a hotel—such as lounges, in-room phones, daily bed-sheet changes, and credit-card payments—I happily make the trade-off for the lower rates and personal touches. If you have a reasonable but limited budget, skip hotels and go the B&B way.

In 2010, you'll generally pay £25–50 (about $40–80) per person for a double room in a B&B in Britain. Lately the big impersonal chain hotels are offering rooms cheaper than some mom-and-pop places (but without breakfast); these are described later, under "Big, Good-Value, Modern Hotels." When considering the price of a B&B or small hotel, remember you're getting two breakfasts (up to a £25 value) for each double room.

B&Bs range from large guest houses with 15–20 rooms to small homes renting out a spare bedroom, but they typically have

---

Smoke-Free Great Britain

Great Britain's public places are now smoke-free. Hotels, B&Bs, and restaurants are required to be non-smoking (though hoteliers are permitted to designate specific rooms for smokers). In the Sleeping sections of each chapter, I've listed the rare instance in which a hotel has smoking rooms—but for the most part, the smoke truly is clearing in Britain.

---

six rooms or fewer. The philosophy of the management determines the character of a place more than its size and facilities offered. I avoid places run as businesses by absentee owners. My top listings are run by people who enjoy welcoming the world to their breakfast table.

B&Bs come with their own etiquette and quirks. Keep in mind that B&B owners are at the whim of their guests—if you're getting up early, so are they; and if you check in late, they'll wait up for you. Be considerate. It's polite to call ahead to confirm your reservation the day before, and give them a rough estimate of your arrival time. This allows them to plan their day and run errands before or after you arrive...and also allows them to give you specific directions for driving or walking to their place.

A few tips: B&B proprietors are selective as to whom they invite in for the night. At some B&Bs, children are not welcome. Risky-looking people (two or more single men are often assumed to be potential troublemakers) find many places suddenly full. If you'll be staying for more than one night, you are a "desirable." In popular weekend-getaway spots, you're unlikely to find a place to take you for Saturday night only. If my listings are full, ask for guidance. Mentioning this book can help. Owners usually work together and can call an ally to land you a bed.

B&Bs serve a hearty fried breakfast (for more about B&B breakfasts, see "Eating," later in this chapter). You'll figure out quickly which parts of the "fry" you like and don't like. Your hosts prefer to know this up front, rather than serve you the whole shebang and have to throw out uneaten food. Because your B&B owner is also the cook, there's usually a quite limited time span when breakfast is served (typically about an hour—make sure you know when it is). It's an unwritten rule that guests shouldn't show up at the very end of the breakfast period and expect a full cooked breakfast—instead, aim to arrive at least 10 minutes before breakfast ends. If you do arrive late (or if you need to leave before breakfast is served), most B&B hosts are happy to let you help yourself to cereal, fruit, and coffee; ask politely whether it might be possible.

B&Bs are not hotels: If you want to ruin your relationship with your hostess, treat her like a hotel clerk. Americans often assume they'll get new towels each day. The British don't, and neither will you. Hang them up to dry and reuse.

Be aware of luggage etiquette. A large bag in a compact older building can easily turn even the most graceful of us into a bull in a British china shop. If you've got a backpack, don't wear it indoors. If your host offers to carry your bag upstairs, accept—they're adept at maneuvering luggage up tiny staircases without damaging their walls and banisters. Finally, use your room's luggage racks—putting bags on empty beds can dirty and scuff nice comforters. Treat these lovingly maintained homes as you would a friend's house.

In almost every B&B, you'll encounter unusual bathroom fixtures. The "pump toilet" has a flushing handle that doesn't kick in unless you push it just right: too hard or too soft, and it won't go. Be decisive but not ruthless. There's also the "dial-a-shower," an electronic box under the shower head where you'll turn a dial to select the heat of the water, and (sometimes with a separate dial or button) turn on or shut off the flow of water. If you can't find the switch to turn on the shower, it may be just outside the bathroom.

Rooms in most B&Bs come with a hot-water pot, cups, tea bags, and coffee packets (if you prefer decaf, buy a jar at a grocery before leaving home, and dump into a baggie for easy packing). Electrical outlets have switches that turn the current on or off; if your electrical appliance isn't working, flip the switch.

Most B&Bs come with thin walls and doors. This can make for a noisy night, especially with people walking down the hall to use the bathroom. If you're a light sleeper, bring earplugs. And please be quiet in the halls and in your rooms (talk softly, and keep the TV volume low). Those of us getting up early will thank you for it.

Your B&B bedroom probably won't include a phone, and in the mobile-phone age, street phone booths can be few and far between. Some B&B owners will allow you to use their phone (with an international phone card), but many are disinclined to let you ring up charges. That's because the British are generally charged for each local call (whether from a fixed line or a mobile phone), and rates are expensive. Therefore, to be polite, ask to use their phone only in an emergency—and offer to use an international calling card (with a toll-free access number) or to pay them for the call. If you plan to stay in B&Bs and make frequent calls, consider buying a British mobile phone (see page 704). And if you're bringing your laptop, look for places with Wi-Fi (noted in my hotel listings).

Many B&B owners are also pet owners. And, while pets are rarely allowed into guest rooms, and B&B proprietors are typically very tidy, those with pet allergies might be bothered. I've tried to list which B&Bs have pets, but if you're allergic, ask about pets when you reserve.

Big, Good-Value, Modern Hotels

Hotel chains—popular with budget tour groups—offer predictably comfortable, no-frills accommodations at reasonable prices. These hotels are popping up in big cities across Britain. Some are located near the train station, on major roads, or outside the city center. What you lose in charm, you gain in savings.

These hotels are ideal for families, offering simple, clean, and modern rooms for up to four people (two adults/two children) for £60–90, depending on the location. Note that couples or families (up to four) pay the same price for a room. Most rooms have a double bed, single bed, five-foot trundle bed, private shower, WC, and TV. Hotels usually have an attached restaurant, good security, an elevator, and a 24-hour staffed reception desk. Breakfast is always extra. Of course, they're as cozy as a Motel 6, but many travelers love them. You can book over the phone or online with a credit card, then pay when you check in. When you check out, just drop off the key, Lee.

Although you can reserve by phone, booking online will generally net you a discount. The biggies are Travelodge (reservations tel. 0870-085-0950, www.travelodge.co.uk) and Premier Inn (reservations tel. 0870-242-8000, www.premierinn.co.uk). The Irish chain Jurys Inn also has some hotels in Britain (book online at www.jurysinns.com).

Couples could also consider Holiday Inn Express, which are spreading throughout Britain. These are like a Holiday Inn Lite, with cheaper prices and no restaurant. Many of their hotels allow only two per room, but some take up to four (doubles cost about £60–100; make sure "Express" is part of the name, or you'll pay more for a regular Holiday Inn; reservations tel. 0871-423-4896, www.hiexpress.co.uk).

More Hotel Deals Online: For recommendations for online hotel deals in London, as well as using auction-type sites, see page 127.

Hostels

If you're traveling alone, hosteling is the best way to conquer hotel loneliness. Hostels are also a tremendous source of local and budget travel information. You'll pay an average of £20 for a bed and £3 for breakfast. Anyone of any age can hostel in Britain. While there are no membership concerns for private hostels, International Youth Hostel Federation (IYHF) hostels require membership. Those without cards simply buy one-night guest memberships for £3.

Britain has hundreds of hostels of all shapes and sizes. Choose your hostel selectively. Hostels can be historic castles or depressing tenements, serene and comfy or overrun by noisy school groups. Unfortunately, many of the IYHF hostels have become overpriced and, in general, I no longer recommend them. The only time I do is if you're on a very tight budget, want to cook your own meals, or are traveling with a group that likes to sleep on bunk beds in big rooms. But many of the informal private hostels are more fun, easygoing, and cheaper. These alternatives to the IYHF hostels are more common than ever, and allow you to enjoy the benefits of hosteling. Good listings are plentiful at Hostels of Europe (www.hostelseurope.com) and Hostels.com. You can also book online for many hostels (for London: www.hostellondon.com, for England and Wales: www.yha.org.uk, and for Scotland: www.hostel-scotland.co.uk).

Phoning

To make international calls to Britain to line up hotel reservations, you'll need to know its country code: 44. To call from the US or Canada, dial 011-44-local number (drop the initial 0 from the local number). If calling Britain from another European country, dial 00-44-local number (without the initial zero). For more information on telephoning, see "Communicating" in the appendix.

Making Reservations

Given the quality of the places I've found for this book, I'd recommend that you reserve your rooms in advance, particularly if you'll be traveling during peak season. Book several weeks ahead, or as soon as you've pinned down your travel dates. Note that some national holidays merit your making reservations far in advance (see "Major Holidays and Weekends" sidebar on page 6). Just like at home, holidays that fall on a Monday, Thursday, or Friday can turn the weekend into a long holiday, so book the entire weekend well in advance.

Requesting a Reservation: To make a reservation, contact hotels directly by email, phone, or fax. Email is the clearest, most economical way to make a reservation. Or you can go straight to the hotel website; many have secure online reservation forms and can instantly inform you of availability and any special deals. But be sure you use the hotel's official site and not a booking agency's site—otherwise you may pay higher rates than you should. If phoning from the US, be mindful of time zones (see page 12).

The hotelier wants to know these key pieces of information (also included in the sample request form on page 734):

- number and type of rooms
- number of nights

- date of arrival
- date of departure
- any special needs (e.g., bathroom in the room or down the hall, twin beds vs. double bed, air-conditioning, quiet, view, ground floor, etc.)

When you request a room for a certain time period, use the European style for writing dates: day/month/year. For example, a two-night stay in July would be "2 nights, 16/07/10 to 18/07/10." Consider in advance how long you'll stay; don't just assume you can tack on extra days once you arrive.

If you don't get a reply to your email or fax, it usually means the hotel is already fully booked (but you can try sending the message again, or call to follow up).

Confirming a Reservation: If the hotel's response tells you its room availability and rates, it's not a confirmation. You must tell them that you want that room at the given rate. Many hoteliers will request your credit-card number for a one-night deposit to hold the room. While you can email your credit-card information (I do), it's safer to share that personal info by phone call, fax, two successive emails, or secure online reservation form (if the hotel has one on its website).

Canceling a Reservation: If you must cancel your reservation, it's courteous to do so with as much advance notice as possible—at least three days. Simply make a quick phone call or send an email. Family-run hotels and B&Bs lose money if they turn away customers while holding a room for someone who doesn't show up. Understandably, most hotels bill no-shows for one night.

Hotels in larger cities such as London sometimes have strict cancellation policies. For example, you might lose a deposit if you cancel within two weeks of your reserved stay, or you might be billed for the entire visit if you leave early. Ask about cancellation policies before you book.

If canceling by email, request confirmation that your cancellation was received to avoid being accidentally billed.

Reconfirming Your Reservation: Always call to reconfirm your room reservation a few days in advance from the road. Smaller hotels and B&Bs appreciate knowing your time of arrival. If you'll be arriving after 17:00, be sure to let your hotelier know. On the small chance that a hotel loses track of your reservation, bring along a hard copy of their emailed or faxed confirmation. Don't have the TI reconfirm rooms for you; they'll take a commission.

Reserving Rooms While You Travel: If you enjoy having a flexible itinerary, you can make reservations while you travel, calling hotels or B&Bs a few days to a week before your visit. If you prefer the flexibility of traveling without any reservations at all, you'll have greater success snaring rooms if you arrive at your destination early in the day. When you anticipate crowds (week-ends are worst), call hotels around 9:00 on the day you plan to arrive, when the hotel clerk knows who'll be checking out and just which rooms will be available.

Most TIs in Britain can book you a room in their town, and also often in nearby towns. They generally charge a £4 fee, and you'll pay a 10 percent "deposit" at the TI and the rest at the B&B (meaning that you pay extra and the B&B loses money, as the TI keeps the "deposit"). This can be useful in a pinch, but it's a better deal for everyone (except the TIs) to book direct, using the listings in this book.

Eating

Britain's reputation for miserable food is now dated, and the British cuisine scene is lively, trendy, and pleasantly surprising. (Unfortunately, it's also very expensive.) Even the basic, traditional pub grub has gone "upmarket," with "gastropubs" serving fresh vegetables rather than soggy fries and mushy peas.

All British eateries are now smoke-free. Restaurants and pubs that sell food are non-smoking indoors; establishments keep their smokers contented by allowing them to light up in doorways and on outdoor patios.

The Great British Breakfast

The traditional "fry," often included in the cost of your room, is famous as a hearty way to start the day. Also known as a "heart attack on a plate," the breakfast is especially feast-like if you've just come from the land of the skimpy continental breakfast across the Channel.

The standard fry gets off to a healthy start with juice and cereal or porridge. (Try Weetabix, a soggy British cousin of shredded wheat and perhaps the most absorbent material known to human-kind.) Next, with tea or coffee, you get a heated plate with a fried egg, Canadian-style bacon or sausage, a grilled tomato, sautéed mushrooms, and baked beans. Toast comes on edge on a rack (to cool quickly and crisply) with butter and marmalade or jam. Try kippers (herring fillets smoked in an oak fire). This protein-stuffed meal is great for stamina, and tides many travelers over until dinner. To avoid wasting food, remember to order only what you'll eat. There's nothing wrong with skipping the fry—few Brits actually start their day with this heavy breakfast. Many progressive B&B owners offer vegetarian, organic, or other creative variations on the traditional breakfast.

These days, the best coffee is served in a *cafetière* (also called a "French press"). When your coffee has steeped as long as you like, plunge down the filter and pour. To revitalize your brew, pump the plunger again.

Tips on Budget Eating

You have plenty of inexpensive choices: pub grub, daily specials, ethnic restaurants, cafeterias, fast food, picnics, fish-and-chips, greasy-spoon cafés, pizza, and more.

Portions are huge and, with locals feeling the pinch of their recession, **sharing plates** is generally just fine. Ordering two drinks, a soup or side salad, and splitting a £10 meat pie can make a delicious, filling meal. On a limited budget, I'd share a main course in a more expensive place for a nicer eating experience. Plus, if you split a meal, the price is cut in half—and you might lose a little weight.

Pub grub is the most atmospheric budget option. You'll usually get fresh, tasty buffets under ancient timbers, with hearty lunches and dinners priced at £6–10 (explained later, under "Pub Grub and Beer").

Classier restaurants have some affordable deals. Lunch is usually cheaper than dinner; a top-end, £25-for-dinner-type restaurant often serves the same quality two-course lunch deals for £10. Look for early-bird dinner specials, allowing you to eat well and affordably (generally two courses-£17, three courses-£20), but early (about 17:30–19:00, last order by 19:00).

Ethnic restaurants from all over the world add spice to Britain's cuisine scene. Eating Indian or Chinese is cheap (even cheaper if you take it out). Middle Eastern stands sell gyro sandwiches, falafel, and *shwarmas* (lamb in pita bread). An Indian samosa (greasy, flaky meat-and-vegetable pie) costs £2, can be microwaved, and makes a very cheap, if small, meal. (For more options, see "Indian Food," later.) You'll find all-you-can-eat Chinese and Thai places serving £6 meals and offering £3.50 take-away boxes. While you can't "split" a buffet, you can split a take-away box. Stuff one full and you and your partner can eat in a park for under £2 each—making the Chinese take-away box Britain's cheapest hot meal.

Most large **museums** (and some historic **churches**) have handy, moderately priced cafeterias.

Fast-food places, both American and British, are everywhere.

Cheap chain restaurants, such as steak houses and pizza places, serve no-nonsense food in a family-friendly setting (steak-house meals about £10; all-you-can-stomach pizza around £5). For specific chains to keep an eye out for, see "Good Chain Restaurants," later.

Picnicking saves time and money. Clean park benches and

polite pigeons abound in most neighborhoods. You can easily get prepared food to go (e.g., see "Ethnic restaurants," earlier). Munch a relaxed "meal on wheels" picnic during your open-top bus tour or river cruise to save 30 precious minutes for sightseeing.

Bakeries sell yogurt, cartons of "semi-skimmed" milk, pastries, and pasties (PASS-teez). Pasties are "savory" (not sweet) meat pies that originated in the Cornish mining country; they had big crust handles so miners with filthy hands could eat them and toss the crust.

Good **sandwich shops** and corner **grocery stores** are a hit with local workers eating on the run. Try boxes of orange juice (pure, by the liter), fresh bread, tasty English cheese, meat, a tube of Colman's English mustard, local eatin' apples, bananas, small tomatoes, a small tub of yogurt (drinkable), trail mix, nuts, plain or chocolate-covered digestive biscuits, and any local specialties.

At **open-air markets** and **supermarkets,** you can get produce in small quantities (three tomatoes and two bananas cost me £1). Supermarkets often have good deli sections, even offering Indian dishes, and sometimes salad bars. Decent packaged sandwiches (£3) are sold everywhere.

Good Chain Restaurants

I know, I know—you're going to Britain to enjoy characteristic little hole-in-the-wall pubs, so mass-produced food is the furthest thing from your mind. But several excellent chains with branches across the UK can be a nice break from pub grub. I've recommended these restaurants throughout this book, but if you see a location that I haven't listed...go for it.

Wagamama is a mod noodle bar serving up reliably delicious pan-Asian dishes, usually with long shared tables and busy servers toting high-tech handheld ordering computers (typically £6–12 main dishes).

At **Yo! Sushi,** freshly prepared sushi dishes trundle past on a conveyor belt. Color-coded plates tell you how much each dish costs (£1.75–5), and a picture-filled menu explains what you're eating. Just help yourself.

Marks & Spencer Simply Food, an offshoot of the department store chain, is a picnicker's and budget traveler's dream-come-true. They have a wide range of tasty, high-quality prepared salads, sandwiches, and more, all ready to take away (no seating, but plasticware is provided). Most Marks & Spencer (M&S) department stores have a grocery store in the basement—with the

---

Sounds Bad, Tastes Good

The British have a knack for making food sound disgusting.
Here are a few examples:

Toad in the Hole: Sausage dipped in batter and fried
Bubble and Squeak: Leftovers, usually potatoes, veggies, and
meat, all fried up together
Bap: Small roll
Treacle: Golden syrup, similar to light molasses

---

same delicious packaged items as in the Simply Food outlets—and
sometimes an inexpensive Café Revive on the top floor. Sainsbury's
supermarkets also feature surprisingly good prepared food; Tesco
is a distant third.

Ask and **Pizza Express** restaurants serve quality pasta and
pizza in a pleasant, sit-down atmosphere that's family-friendly.

On the High Street of most British cities you'll find an array
of healthier-than-expected fast food. **Pret A Manger** and **Eat** offer
inexpensive and generally good sandwiches and salads to go.

Afternoon Tea

People of leisure punctuate their day with an "afternoon tea" at a
tearoom. You'll get a pot of tea, small finger foods (like cucumber sandwiches and tarts), homemade scones, jam, and thick
clotted cream. A lighter "cream" tea gets you tea and a scone or
two. Tearooms, which often serve appealing light meals, are usually open for lunch and close at about 17:00, just before dinner.
For more on this most English of traditions, see "Taking Tea in
London" on page 154.

Pub Grub and Beer

Pubs are a basic part of the British social scene, and, whether you're
a teetotaler or a beer-guzzler, they should be a part of your travel
here. "Pub" is short for "public house." It's an extended living room
where, if you don't mind the stickiness, you can feel the pulse of
Britain.

Smart travelers use the pubs to eat, drink, get out of the
rain, watch the latest sporting event, and make new friends.
Unfortunately, many city pubs have been afflicted with an excess
of brass, ferns, and video games. Most traditional atmospheric
pubs are in the countryside and smaller towns.

Pub grub gets better each year. In London, it offers the
best indoor eating value. For £6–10, you'll get a basic, budget hot
lunch or dinner in friendly surroundings. The *Good Pub Guide*,
published annually by the British Consumers Union, is excellent

(www.thegoodpubguide.co.uk). Pubs that are attached to restaurants, advertise their food, and are crowded with locals are more likely to have fresh food and a chef than to be the kind of pub that sells only lousy microwaved snacks.

Pubs generally serve traditional dishes, such as fish-and-chips, vegetables, "bangers and mash" (sausages and mashed potatoes), roast beef with Yorkshire pudding (batter-baked in the oven), and assorted meat pies, such as steak-and-kidney pie or shepherd's pie (stewed lamb topped with mashed potatoes). Side dishes include salads (sometimes even a nice self-serve salad bar), vegetables, and—invariably—"chips" (French fries). "Crisps" are potato chips. A "jacket potato" (baked potato stuffed with fillings of your choice) is almost a meal in itself. A "ploughman's lunch" is a modern "traditional English meal" of bread, cheese, and sweet pickles that nearly every tourist tries...once. These days, you'll likely find more Italian pasta, curried dishes, and quiche on the menu than traditional fare.

Meals are usually served from 12:00 to 14:00 and from 18:00 to 20:00, not throughout the day. There's usually no table service. Order at the bar, then take a seat and they'll bring the food when it's ready (or sometimes you pick it up at the bar). Pay at the bar (sometimes when you order, sometimes after you eat). Don't tip unless it's a place with full table service. Servings are hearty, service is quick, and you'll rarely spend more than £10. (If you're on a tight budget, consider sharing a meal—note the size of portions around you before ordering.) A beer or cider adds another couple of pounds. (Free tap water is always available.) Because pubs make more money selling drinks than food, many stop cooking fairly early.

The British take great pride in their **beer.** They think that drinking beer cold and carbonated, as Americans do, ruins the taste. Most pubs will have lagers (cold, refreshing, American-style beer), ales (amber-colored, cellar-temperature beer), bitters (hop-flavored ale, perhaps the most typical British beer), and stouts (dark and somewhat bitter, like Guinness). At pubs, long-handled pulls are used to pull the traditional, rich-flavored "real ales" up from the cellar. These are the  connoisseur's favorites: fermented naturally, varying from sweet to bitter, often with a hoppy or nutty flavor. Notice the fun names. Short-hand pulls at the bar mean colder, fizzier, mass-produced, and less interesting keg beers. Mild beers are sweeter, with a creamy malt flavoring. Irish cream ale is a smooth, sweet experience. Try the draft cider (sweet or dry)...carefully.

Order your beer at the bar and pay as you go, with no need to tip. An average beer costs £3. Part of the experience is standing before a line of "hand pulls," or taps, and wondering which beer to choose.

Drinks are served by the pint (20-ounce imperial size) or the half-pint. (It's almost feminine for a man to order just a half; I order mine with quiche.) Proper British ladies like a shandy—half beer and half 7-Up.

Besides beer, many pubs actually have a good selection of wines by the glass, a fully stocked bar for the gentleman's "G and T" (gin and tonic), and the increasingly popular bottles of alcohol-plus-sugar (such as Bacardi Breezers) for the younger, working-class set. Pimm's is a refreshing fruity summer cocktail, traditionally popular during Wimbledon. It's an upper-class drink—a rough bloke might insult a pub by claiming it sells more Pimm's than beer. Teetotalers can order from a wide variety of soft drinks. Children are served food and soft drinks in pubs, but you must be 18 to order a beer.

Pub hours vary. Pubs generally serve beer Monday–Saturday 11:00–23:00 and Sunday 12:00–22:30, though many are open later, particularly on Friday and Saturday. As it nears closing time, you'll hear shouts of "Last orders." Then comes the 10-minute warning bell. Finally, they'll call "Time!" to pick up your glass, finished or not, when the pub closes.

A cup of darts is free for the asking. People go to a public house to be social. They want to talk. Get vocal with a local. This is easiest at the bar, where people assume you're in the mood to talk (rather than at a table, where you're allowed a bit of privacy). The pub is the next best thing to having relatives in town. Cheers!

Indian Food

Eating Indian food is "going local" in cosmopolitan, multi-ethnic Britain. You'll find recommended Indian restaurants in most British cities, and even small towns. Take the opportunity to sample food from Britain's former colony. Indian cuisine is as varied as the country itself, featuring more exotic spices than British or American cuisine—some hot, some sweet. Indian food is very vegetarian-friendly, offering many dishes to choose from on any given menu.

For a simple meal that costs about £10–12, order one dish with rice and naan (Indian flatbread that can be ordered plain, with garlic, or other ways). Many restaurants offer a fixed-price combination meal that offers more variety, and is simpler and cheaper than ordering à la carte. For about £20, you can make a mix-and-match platter out of several sharable dishes, including *dal* (lentil soup) as a starter; one or two meat or vegetable dishes with sauce (for example, chicken curry, chicken tikka masala in a creamy tomato sauce, grilled fish tandoori, chickpea *chana* masala, or the spicy

British Chocolate

My chocoholic readers are enthusiastic about British chocolates. Like other dairy products, chocolate seems richer and creamier here than it does in the US, so even the basics like Kit Kat and Twix have a different taste. Some favorites include Cadbury Gold bars (filled with liquid caramel), Cadbury Crunchie bars, Nestlé's Lion bars (layered wafers covered in caramel and chocolate), Cadbury's Boost bars (a shortcake biscuit with caramel in milk chocolate), Cadbury Flake bars (crumbly folds of melt-in-your-mouth chocolate), and Galaxy chocolate bars (especially the ones with hazelnuts). Thornton shops (in larger train stations) sell a box of sweets called the Continental Assortment, which comes with a tasting guide. The highlight is the mocha white-chocolate truffle. British M&Ms, called Smarties, are better than American ones. At ice-cream vans, look for the beloved traditional "99p"—a vanilla soft-serve cone with a small Flake bar stuck right into the middle.

vindaloo dish); *raita* (a cooling yogurt that's added to spicy dishes); rice; naan; and an Indian beer (wine and Indian food don't really mix) or chai (a cardamom- and cinnamon-spiced tea).

Desserts (Sweets)

To the British, the traditional word for dessert is "pudding," although it's also referred to as "sweets" these days. Sponge cake, cream, fruitcake, and meringue are key players.

Trifle is the best-known British concoction, consisting of sponge cake soaked in brandy or sherry (or orange juice for children), then covered with jam and/or fruit and custard cream. Whipped cream can sometimes put the final touch on this "light" treat.

Castle puddings are sponge puddings cooked in small molds and topped with Golden Syrup (a popular brand and a cross between honey and maple syrup). Bread-and-butter pudding consists of slices of French bread baked with milk, cream, eggs, and raisins (similar to the American preparation), served warm with cold cream. Hasty pudding, supposedly the invention of people in a hurry to avoid the bailiff, is made from stale bread with dried fruit and milk. Queen of puddings is a breadcrumb pudding topped with warm jam, meringue, and cream. Treacle pudding is a popular steamed pudding whose "sponge" mixture combines flour, suet (animal fat), butter, sugar, and milk. Christmas pudding (also called plum pudding) is a dense mixture with dried, candied fruit served with brandy butter or hard sauce. Sticky toffee pudding is a moist cake made with dates, heated and drizzled with toffee sauce,

How Was Your Trip?

Were your travels fun, smooth, and meaningful? If you'd like to share your tips, concerns, and discoveries, please fill out the survey at www.ricksteves.com/feedback. I value your feedback. Thanks in advance—it helps a lot.

and served with ice cream or cream. Banoffee pie is the delicious British answer to banana cream pie.

The British version of custard is a smooth, yellow liquid. Cream tops most everything custard does not. There's single cream for coffee. Double cream is really thick. Whipped cream is familiar, and clotted cream is the consistency of whipped butter.

Fool is a dessert with sweetened pureed fruit (such as rhubarb, gooseberries, or black currants) mixed with cream or custard and chilled. Elderflower is a popular flavoring for sorbet.

Scones are tops, and many inns and restaurants have their secret recipes. Whether made with fruit or topped with clotted cream, scones take the cake.

Traveling as a Temporary Local

We travel all the way to Europe to enjoy differences—to become temporary locals. You'll experience frustrations. Certain truths that we find "God-given" or "self-evident," such as cold beer, ice in drinks, bottomless cups of coffee, hot showers, and bigger being better, are suddenly not so true. One of the benefits of travel is the eye-opening realization that there are logical, civil, and even better alternatives.

Americans are enjoying a surge in popularity in Europe these days. But if there is a negative aspect to the image the British have of Americans, it's that we are big, loud, aggressive, impolite, rich, superficially friendly, and a bit naive.

The British (and Europeans in general) place a high value on speaking quietly in restaurants and on trains. Listen while on the bus or in a restaurant—the place can be packed, but the decibel level is low. Try to adjust your volume accordingly to show respect for their culture.

While the British look bemusedly at some of our Yankee excesses—and worriedly at others—they nearly always afford us individual travelers all the warmth we deserve. Judging from all the happy feedback I receive from travelers who have used this book, it's safe to assume you'll enjoy a great, affordable vacation— with the finesse of an independent, experienced traveler.

Thanks, and have a brilliant holiday!

Back Door Travel Philosophy
From *Rick Steves' Europe Through the Back Door*

Travel is intensified living—maximum thrills per minute and one of the last great sources of legal adventure. Travel is freedom. It's recess, and we need it.

Experiencing the real Europe requires catching it by surprise, going casual..."Through the Back Door."

Affording travel is a matter of priorities. (Make do with the old car.) You can travel—simply, safely, and comfortably—anywhere in Europe for $120 a day plus transportation costs (allow more for bigger cities). In many ways, spending more money only builds a thicker wall between you and what you came to see. Europe is a cultural carnival, and, time after time, you'll find that its best acts are free and the best seats are the cheap ones.

A tight budget forces you to travel close to the ground, meeting and communicating with the people, not relying on service with a purchased smile. Never sacrifice sleep, nutrition, safety, or cleanliness in the name of budget. Simply enjoy the local-style alternatives to expensive hotels and restaurants.

Connecting with people carbonates your experience. Extroverts have more fun. If your trip is low on magic moments, kick yourself and make things happen. If you don't enjoy a place, maybe you don't know enough about it. Seek the truth. Recognize tourist traps. Give a culture the benefit of your open mind. See things as different but not better or worse. Any culture has much to share.

Of course, travel, like the world, is a series of hills and valleys. Be fanatically positive and militantly optimistic. If something's not to your liking, change your liking. Travel is addictive.

Travel can make you a happier American as well as a citizen of the world. Our Earth is home to six and a half billion equally important people. It's humbling to travel and find that people don't have the "American Dream"—they have their own dreams. Europeans like us, but, with all due respect, they wouldn't trade passports.

Thoughtful travel engages us with the world. In tough economic times, it reminds us what is truly important. By broadening perspectives, travel teaches new ways to measure quality of life.

Globe-trotting destroys ethnocentricity, helping you understand and appreciate different cultures. Rather than fear the diversity on this planet, celebrate it. Among your prized souvenirs will be the strands of different cultures you choose to knit into their own character. The world is a cultural yarn shop, and Back Door travelers are weaving the ultimate tapestry. Join in!

ENGLAND

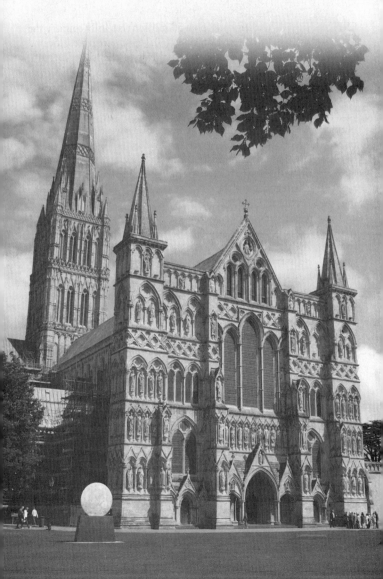

ENGLAND

England (pop. 50 million) is a hilly country the size of Louisiana (50,346 square miles) located in the lower two-thirds of the isle of Britain. Scotland is to the north and the English Channel is to the south, with the North Sea to the east and Wales (and the Irish Sea) to the west. Fed by ocean air from the southwest, the climate is mild, with a chance of cloudy, rainy weather almost any day of the year.

England has an economy that can stand alongside many much larger nations. It boasts high-tech industries (software, chemical, aviation), international banking, and textile manufacturing, and is a major exporter of beef. Though farms and villages remain, England is now an urban, industrial, and post-industrial colossus.

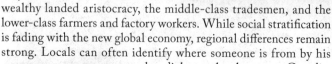

England was traditionally very class-conscious, with the wealthy landed aristocracy, the middle-class tradesmen, and the lower-class farmers and factory workers. While social stratification is fading with the new global economy, regional differences remain strong. Locals can often identify where someone is from by his or her dialect or local accent—Geordie, Cockney, or Queen's English.

One thing that sets England apart from its fellow UK countries (Scotland, Wales, and Northern Ireland) is its ethnic makeup. Traditionally, those countries had Celtic roots, whereas the English mixed in Saxon and Norman blood. In the 20th century, England welcomed many Scots, Welsh, and Irish as low-wage workers. More recently, it's become home to immigrants from former colonies of its worldwide empire—

England

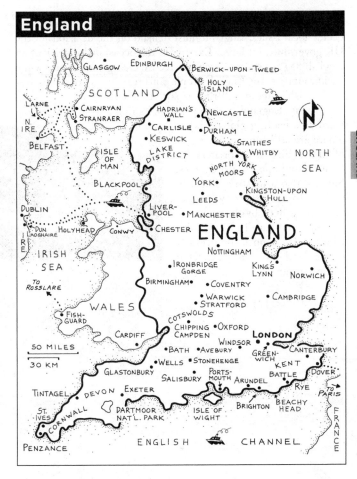

particularly from India/Pakistan/Bangladesh, the Caribbean, and Africa—and to many workers from poorer EU countries in Eastern Europe. These days it's not a given that every "English" person speaks English. Nearly one in three citizens does not profess the Christian faith. As the world becomes increasingly interconnected by communications technology, it's possible for many immigrants to physically inhabit the country while remaining closely linked to their home culture—rather than truly assimilating into England.

This is the current English paradox. England—the birthplace and center of the extended worldwide family of English-speakers—is losing its traditional Englishness. Where Scotland, Wales, and Northern Ireland have cultural movements to preserve their local languages and customs, England does not. Politically, there is no "English" party in the UK Parliament. In fact, Scotland,

Wales, and Northern Ireland now have their own parliaments to decide local issues; England must depend on the decisions of the UK government at large. Except for the occasional display of an English flag at a soccer match (the red St. George's cross on a white background), many English people don't really think of themselves as "English"—more as "Brits," a part of the wider UK.

Today, England tries to preserve its rich past as it races forward as a leading global player.  There are still hints of its legacy of farms, villages, Victorian lamplighters, and upper-crust dandies, but it's also a jostling world of unemployed factory workers, investment bankers, soccer matches, and faux-Tudor suburbs. Modern England is a culturally diverse land in transition. Catch it while you can.

LONDON

London is more than 600 square miles of urban jungle. With eight million people—who don't all speak English—it's a world in itself and a barrage on all the senses. On my first visit I felt extremely small.

London is more than its museums and landmarks. It's a living, breathing, thriving organism...a coral reef of humanity. The city has changed dramatically in recent years, and many visitors are surprised to find how "un-English" it is. White people are now a minority in major parts of the city that once symbolized white imperialism. Arabs have nearly bought out the area north of Hyde Park. Chinese take-outs outnumber fish-and-chips shops. Eastern Europeans pull pints in British pubs. Many hotels are run by people with foreign accents (who hire English chambermaids), while outlying suburbs are home to huge communities of Indians and Pakistanis. London is a city of eight million separate dreams, inhabiting a place that tolerates and encourages them. With the English Channel Tunnel making travel between Britain and the Continent easier than ever, many locals see even more holes in their bastion of Britishness. London is learning—sometimes fitfully—to live as a microcosm of its formerly vast empire. In anticipation of the 2012 Olympic Games, London is busy spiffing up the place, especially its rapidly developing Olympic Park in East London.

With just a few days here, you'll get no more than a quick splash in this teeming human tidal pool, but with a good orientation, you'll find London manageable and fun. You'll get a sampling of the city's top sights, history, and cultural entertainment, and a good look at its ever-changing human face.

Blow through the city on the open deck of a double-decker orientation tour bus, and take a pinch-me-I'm-in-London walk through the West End. Ogle the crown jewels at the Tower of London, hear the chimes of Big Ben, and see the Houses of Parliament in action. Cruise the Thames River, and take a spin on the London Eye. Hobnob with the tombstones in Westminster Abbey, and visit with Leonardo, Botticelli, and Rembrandt in the National Gallery. Enjoy Shakespeare in a replica of the Globe Theatre, then marvel at a glitzy, fun musical at a modern-day theater. Whisper across the dome of St. Paul's Cathedral, then rummage through our civilization's attic at the British Museum. And sip your tea with pinky raised and clotted cream dribbling down your scone.

Planning Your Time

The sights of London alone could easily fill a trip to Britain. It's a great one-week getaway. On a three-week tour of Britain I'd give it three busy days. You won't be able to see everything, so don't try. You'll keep coming back to London. After dozens of visits, I still enjoy a healthy list of excuses to return. If you're flying in, consider starting your trip in Bath and making London your British finale—if you plan to enjoy a play or concert, a night or two of jet lag is bad news.

Here's a suggested schedule:

Day 1: 9:00–Tower of London (crown jewels first, then Beefeater tour, then White Tower); 12:30–Munch a sandwich on the Thames while cruising from the Tower to Westminster Bridge; 14:00–Tour Westminster Abbey; 15:30–Follow the self-guided Westminster Walk (see page 68). When you're finished, you could return to the Houses of Parliament and pop in to see the House of Commons in action.

Day 2: 8:30–If traveling around Britain, spend 30 minutes on the phone getting all essential elements of your trip nailed down. If you know where you'll be and when, call those B&Bs now. 9:00–Take a double-decker hop-on, hop-off London sightseeing bus tour (start at Victoria Street and hop off for the Changing of the Guard); 11:30–Buckingham Palace (guards change most days, but worth confirming); 13:00–Covent Garden for lunch, shopping, and people-watching; 14:30–Tour the British Museum. Have a pub dinner before a play, concert, or evening walking tour.

Day 3: Choose among these remaining London highlights: Tour British Library, Imperial War Museum, the two Tates (Tate Modern on the south bank for modern art, Tate Britain on the North Bank for British art), St. Paul's Cathedral, or the Museum of London; take a spin on the London Eye or a cruise to Kew or

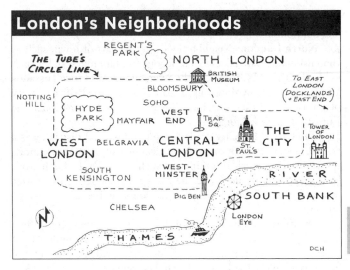

London's Neighborhoods

Greenwich; enjoy a Shakespearean play at Shakespeare's Globe; do some serious shopping at one of London's elegant department stores or open-air markets; or take another historic walking tour.

Orientation to London

(area code: 020)

To grasp London more comfortably, see it as the old town in the city center without the modern, congested sprawl. The Thames River runs roughly west to east through the city, with most of the visitor's sights on the North Bank. Mentally—maybe even physically with scissors—trim down your map to include only the area between the Tower of London (to the east), Hyde Park (west), Regent's Park (north), and the South Bank (south). This is roughly the area bordered by the Tube's Circle Line. This four-mile stretch between the Tower and Hyde Park (about a 90-min walk) looks like a milk bottle on its side (see map above) and holds 80 percent of the sights mentioned in this chapter.

Sprawling London becomes much more manageable if you think of it as a collection of neighborhoods:

Central London: This area contains Westminster and what Londoners call the West End. The **Westminster** district includes Big Ben, Parliament, Westminster Abbey, and Buckingham Palace—the grand government buildings from which Britain is ruled. Trafalgar Square, London's gathering place, has major museums. The **West End** is the center of London's cultural life, with bustling squares: Piccadilly Circus and Leicester Square host cinemas, tourist traps, and nighttime glitz. Soho and Covent

Garden are thriving people-zones with theaters, restaurants, pubs, and boutiques.

North London: Neighborhoods in this part of town, such as Bloomsbury, Fitzrovia, and Marylebone, contain major sights such as the British Museum and the over-hyped Madame Tussauds Waxworks. Nearby, along busy Euston Road, is the British Library plus a trio of train stations, including St. Pancras International, the Eurostar launchpad for Paris.

The City: "The City," today's modern financial district, was a walled town in Roman times. Now gleaming skyscrapers are interspersed with historical landmarks such as St. Paul's Cathedral, legal sights (Old Bailey), and the Museum of London. The Tower of London and Tower Bridge lie just outside The City's eastern border.

The South Bank: The South Bank of the Thames River offers major sights (Tate Modern, Shakespeare's Globe, London Eye) linked by a riverside walkway. Pedestrian bridges connect the South Bank with The City and Trafalgar Square.

West London: This huge area contains neighborhoods such as Mayfair, Belgravia, Chelsea, South Kensington, and Notting Hill. It's home to London's wealthy, and has many trendy shops and enticing restaurants. Here you'll find a range of museums (Victoria and Albert Museum, Kensington Palace, Tate Britain, and more), recommended hotels, lively Victoria Station, and the vast green expanses of Hyde Park and Kensington Gardens.

East London: London's version of Manhattan—the Docklands—has sprung up far to the east around Canary Wharf. Energized by big businesses and gearing up to host parts of the 2012 Olympics, the Docklands shows you London at its most modern. Historic Greenwich lies just south of the Docklands/Canary Wharf area, across the Thames.

Tourist Information

The **Britain and London Visitors Centre,** a block off Piccadilly Circus, is the best tourist information service in town (June–Sept Mon–Fri 9:30–18:30, Sat 9:00–17:00, Sun 10:00–16:00; Oct–May Mon–Fri 9:30–18:00, Sat–Sun 10:00–16:00; 1 Lower Regent Street, tel. 020/8846-9000, toll tel. 0870-156-6366, www.visitbritain .com, www.visitlondon.com).

This TI has many different departments. It's a great one-stop-shopping place to get tourist information, buy advance tickets to big sights, buy sightseeing passes, arrange coach tours, buy theater tickets, plan travel beyond London, and even book trains to the Continent. Bring your itinerary and a checklist of questions.

Entering the lobby, check out the various departments and get in the right line for what you need. At the Tourist Information

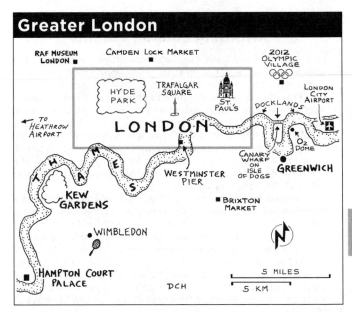

Greater London

RAF MUSEUM LONDON ■

CAMDEN LOCK MARKET ■

2012 OLYMPIC VILLAGE

HYDE PARK

TRAFALGAR SQUARE

ST. PAUL'S

DOCKLANDS

LONDON CITY AIRPORT

← TO HEATHROW AIRPORT

L O N D O N

O₂ DOME

CANARY WHARF ON ISLE OF DOGS

GREENWICH

WESTMINSTER PIER

KEW GARDENS

■ BRIXTON MARKET

● WIMBLEDON

■ HAMPTON COURT PALACE

DCH

5 MILES

5 KM

T H A M E S

LONDON

desk handling both London and Britain inquiries, pick up various free publications: the *London Planner* (a great free monthly that lists all the sights, events, and hours), walking tours info, a theater guide, the London bus map, and the Thames River Services brochure. The staff sells a good £1 map and all the various sightseeing deals, including the London Pass (described on page 50) and the Great British Heritage Pass and English Heritage membership (both described on page 20).

The Entertainment and Tickets desk sells tickets to plays (20 percent booking fee). The Hotels and Travel desk sells long-distance bus tickets and passes, train tickets (convenient for reservations), and Fast Track tickets to some of London's attractions. The Fast Track tickets, which allow you to skip the queue at the sights at no extra cost, are worthwhile for places that sometimes have long ticket lines, such as the Tower of London, the London Eye, and Madame Tussauds Waxworks. (If you'll be going to the Waxworks, buy tickets here, since—at £20—they're cheaper than at the sight itself.)

The Visitors Centre reserves hotel rooms, but you can avoid their £5 booking fee by contacting hotels on your own. A Rail Europe section books the Eurostar and train travel or train passes on the Continent.

Upstairs, there are even more brochures, Internet access (£1/20 min), and comfy chairs where you can read or get organized. If you visit only one TI, make it this one, the Britain and

Affording London's Sights

London is, in many ways, Europe's most expensive city, with the dubious distinction of having some of the world's most expensive admission prices. Fortunately, many of its best sights are free.

Free Museums: Many of the city's biggest and best museums won't cost you a dime. Free sights include the British Museum, British Library, National Gallery, National Portrait Gallery, Tate Britain, Tate Modern, Wallace Collection, Imperial War Museum, Victoria and Albert Museum, Natural History Museum, Science Museum, National Army Museum, Sir John Soane's Museum, the Museum of London, the Geffrye, and, on the outskirts of town, the Royal Air Force Museum London.

Several museums, such as the British Museum, request a donation of a few pounds, but whether you contribute or not is up to you. If I spend money for an audioguide, I feel fine about not otherwise donating. If that makes you uncomfortable, donate.

Free Churches: Smaller churches let worshippers (and tourists) in free, although they may ask for a donation. The big sightseeing churches—Westminster Abbey and St. Paul's—charge steep admission fees, but offer free evensong services daily. Westminster Abbey offers free organ recitals most Sundays at 17:45.

Other Freebies: There are plenty of free performances, such as lunch concerts at St. Martin-in-the-Fields (see page 125) and summertime movies at The Scoop amphitheater, near City Hall (Tube: London Bridge, schedule at www.morelondon.com—click "The Scoop"). For other freebies, check out www.freelondon listings.co.uk. There's no charge to enjoy the pageantry of the Changing of the Guard, rants at Speaker's Corner in Hyde Park, displays at Harrods, and the people-watching scene at Covent Garden. It's free to view the legal action at Old Bailey and the legislature at work in the Houses of Parliament. And you can get into a bit of the Tower of London by attending Sunday services in the Tower's chapel (chapel access only).

Sightseeing Deals: If you buy a paper Travelcard or rail ticket at a National Rail station (such as Paddington or Victoria), you may be eligible for two-for-one discounts at many popular sights, such as the Tower of London, Westminster Abbey, and Madame Tussauds Waxworks. Get details and print out vouchers at www.daysoutguide.co.uk, or look for brochures with coupons at major train stations.

Good-Value Tours: The £7–9 city walking tours with professional guides are one of the best deals going. And with the free Royal London walking tour (see page 64), you always get at least your money's worth. Hop-on, hop-off big-bus tours (£15–25), while expensive, provide a great overview, and include free boat tours as well as city walks. A one-hour Thames ride to Greenwich costs £8.40 one-way, but generally comes with an entertaining commentary. A three-hour bicycle tour is about £16–19.

Pricey...But Worth It?: Big-ticket sights worth their admission fees are Kew Gardens (£13), Shakespeare's Globe (£10.50), and the Cabinet War Rooms, with its fine Churchill Museum (£13). The London Eye has become a London must-see (£17).

Although Kensington Palace (£12.50) and Hampton Court Palace (£14) are expensive, they are well-presented and a reasonable value if you have a real interest in royal history. The Queen charges big time to open her palace to the public: Buckingham Palace (£16.50, Aug–Sept only) and her art gallery and carriage museum (adjacent to the palace, about £8 each, £14.50 for both) are expensive but interesting. Madame Tussauds Waxworks is pricey but still fun and popular (£25, £20 if purchased at TI, drops to £16 after 17:00 if booked on the Waxworks' website). The Vinopolis wine museum provides a way to get a buzz and call it museum-going (from £25, includes five small glasses of wine).

Many smaller museums cost only around £5. My favorites include the Courtauld Gallery (free on Mon until 14:00) and the Wellington Museum at Apsley House (£5.70).

Not Worth It: Gimmicky, overpriced, bad-value enterprises include the London Dungeon (£20) and the Dalí Universe (great location next to the popular London Eye, but for £14.50, skip it).

Theater: Compared with Broadway's prices, London theater is a bargain. Seek out the freestanding "tkts" booth at Leicester Square to get discounts from 25 to 50 percent (though not necessarily for the hottest shows; see page 121). A £5 "groundling" ticket for a play at Shakespeare's Globe is the best theater deal in town (see page 123). Tickets to the Open Air Theatre at north London's Regent's Park start at £10 (see page 124).

London doesn't come cheap. But with its many free museums and affordable plays, this cosmopolitan, cultured city offers days of sightseeing thrills without requiring you to pinch your pennies (or your pounds).

London Visitors Centre. Unfortunately, London's many Tourist Information Centres (which represent themselves as TIs at major train and bus stations and airports) are now simply businesses selling advertising space to companies with fliers to distribute.

The **London Pass** is worth considering only if you're a whirlwind sightseer (£39/1 day, £52/2 days, £63/3 days, £87/6 days, includes 160-page guidebook, toll tel. 0870-242-9988, www.londonpass.com). It covers plenty of sights that cost £11–17, including the Tower of London, St. Paul's Cathedral, Shakespeare's Globe, Cabinet War Rooms, Kensington Palace, Windsor Palace, and Kew Gardens. But if you saw just these sights without the pass, you'd pay about £90, roughly the cost of a six-day London Pass. Note that busy sightseers can make a short pass work for a longer trip by seeing only covered sights while the pass is valid, and touring London's many free sights before or after the pass' validity period. Think through your sightseeing plans carefully before you buy.

Arrival in London

By Train: London has nine major train stations, all connected by the Tube (subway). All have ATMs, and many of the larger stations also have shops, fast food, exchange offices, and luggage storage. From any station, you can ride the Tube or taxi to your hotel. For more info on train travel, see page 163 and www.nationalrail.co.uk.

By Bus: The bus ("coach") station is one block southwest of Victoria Station, where you can also take the Tube. For more info on bus travel, see www.nationalexpress.com.

By Plane: London has five airports. Most tourists arrive at Heathrow or Gatwick airports, although flights from elsewhere in Europe may land at Stansted, Luton, or London City airports. For specifics on getting from London's airports to downtown London, see "London Connections" on page 158.

Helpful Hints

Theft Alert: The Artful Dodger is alive and well in London. Be on guard, particularly on public transportation and in places crowded with tourists. Tourists, considered naive and rich, are targeted. More than 7,500 purses are stolen annually at Covent Garden alone. Wear your money belt.

Pedestrian Safety: Cars drive on the left side of the road, so before crossing a street, I always look right, look left, then look right again just to be sure. Many crosswalks are even painted with instructions, reminding foreign guests to "Look right" or "Look left."

Medical Problems: Local hospitals have good-quality 24-hour-a-day emergency care centers where any tourist who needs help can drop in and, after a wait, be seen by a doctor. Your hotel has details. St. Thomas' Hospital, immediately across the river from Big Ben, has a good reputation.

Festivals: For one week in February and another in September, fashionistas descend on the city for **London Fashion Week.** The famous **Chelsea Flower Show** blossoms May 25–29 in 2010 (book tickets ahead for this popular event at www.rhs .org.uk/chelsea). During the annual **Trooping the Colour** on June 13, there are military bands and pageantry, and the Queen's birthday parade. Tennis fans pack the stands at the **Wimbledon Tennis Championship** June 21–July 4 in 2010 (www.wimbledon.org), and partygoers head for the **Notting Hill Carnival** August 29–30 in 2010.

Winter: London dazzles year-round, so consider visiting in winter, when airfares and hotel rates are generally cheaper and there are fewer tourists. For ideas on what to do, see the "Winter Activites in London" article at www.ricksteves.com/winteracts.

Internet Access: The **easyInternetcafé** chain offers dozens of computers per store (generally daily 8:00–22:00, £3/30 min). You'll find branches at Trafalgar Square (456 Strand), Bayswater (Queensway, second floor of Whiteley's Shopping Centre), Oxford Street (#358, opposite Bond Street Tube station), and Kensington High Street (#160–166). Your hotelier can direct you to the nearest Internet café.

Travel Bookstores: Located in Covent Garden, **Stanfords Travel Bookstore** is good and stocks current editions of my books (Mon, Wed, and Fri 9:00–19:30, Tue 9:30–19:30, Thu 9:00–20:00, Sat 10:00–20:00, Sun 12:00–18:00, 12–14 Long Acre, Tube: Covent Garden, tel. 020/7836-1321, www.stanfords .co.uk).

Two impressive **Waterstone's** bookstores have the biggest collection of travel guides in town: on Piccadilly (Mon–Sat 9:00–22:00, Sun 11:30–18:00, 203 Piccadilly, tel. 020/7851-2400) and on Trafalgar Square (Mon–Sat 9:30–21:00, Sun 12:00–18:00, Costa Café on second floor, tel. 020/7839-4411).

Baggage Storage: Train stations have replaced their lockers with more secure baggage-storage counters, known as "left luggage." Each bag must go through a scanner (just like at the airport), so lines can be slow. Expect long waits in the morning to check in (up to 45 min) and in the afternoon to pick up (each item-£8/24 hours, most stations daily 7:00–22:00). You can also store bags at the airports (similar rates and hours, www.excess-baggage.com). If leaving London and returning later, you may be able to leave a box or bag at your hotel for free—assuming you'll be staying there again.

Getting Around London

To travel smart in a city this size, you must get comfortable with public transportation. London's excellent taxis, buses, and subway (Tube) system make a private car unnecessary. An £8 congestion charge levied on any private car entering the city center has been effective in cutting down traffic jam delays and bolstering London's public transit. The revenue raised subsidizes the buses, which are now cheaper, more frequent, and even more user-friendly than before. Today, the vast majority of vehicles in the city center are buses, taxis, and service trucks. (Drivers can find out more information on the congestion charge at www.cclondon.com.)

Public-Transit Passes: Oyster Cards and Travelcards

London has the most expensive public transit in the world—you will definitely save money on your Tube and bus rides using a multi-ride pass. There are two options: plastic Oyster cards and paper Travelcards (details online at www.tfl.gov.uk, click "Tickets").

Oyster Cards

An Oyster card (a plastic card embedded with a computer chip) is the standard, smart way to economically ride the Tube, buses, and Docklands Light Railway (DLR).

You prepay an amount, and fares are automatically deducted each time you use your card. On each type of transport, you simply touch the card to the yellow card reader at the turnstile/entrance, it flashes green, and you've paid your fare. (You'll need the card to exit the Tube and DLR turnstiles, but not to exit buses.)

With an Oyster card, you'll pay only £1.80–2.40 per ride on the Tube (in Zones 1–6 off-peak) instead of £4.50 per ride with a full-fare ticket. For the bus, it's £1.20 versus £2. A price cap guarantees you'll never pay more than the One-Day Travelcard price within a 24-hour period (see "One-Day Travelcard," described later). An Oyster card is worth considering if you'll be in London for even a few days, and it is especially handy if you're not sure you'll ride enough each day to justify a Travelcard.

You can buy Oyster cards at any Tube station ticket window. With the standard **pay-as-you-go Oyster card,** you load up your Oyster with as much credit you want (there's no minimum, but start with at least £10). When your balance gets low, you simply pay more money (at a ticket window or machine) to keep riding. To see how much credit remains on your card, swipe it at any automatic ticket machine. You can also see a record of all your travels (and what you paid). Try it. Pay-as-you-go Oyster balances never expire (though they need reactivating at a ticket window every two years); you can use the card whenever you're in London, or lend it to someone else. The only downside, and it's minor, is that you pay a £3 one-time refundable deposit for the card itself (you can turn in your card for the £3 refund at any ticket window, but allow 20 minutes for the process).

The **Seven-Day Oyster card** is another good possibility to consider, even for a visit as short as four days. Technically a seven-day Travelcard (see below), this odd hybrid is generally issued on a plastic Oyster card. The least expensive version is £25.80 and covers unlimited peak-time travel through Zones 1 and 2 (no deposit required, cards covering more zones are also available).

Travelcards

A paper Travelcard works like a traditional ticket: You buy it at any Tube station ticket window or machine, then feed it into a turnstile (and retrieve it) to enter and exit the Tube. On a bus, just show it to the driver when you get on. If you take at least two rides a day, a Travelcard is a better deal than buying individual tickets. Like the Oyster card, Travelcards are valid on the Tube, buses, and Docklands Light Railway. Before you buy a card, estimate where you'll be going; there's a card for Zones 1 and 2, and another for Zones 1–6 (which includes Heathrow Airport).

The **One-Day Travelcard** gives you unlimited travel for a day; cheaper off-peak versions are good for travel after 9:30 on weekdays and anytime on weekends (**Zones 1–2:** £7.20, off-peak version £5.60; **Zones 1–6:** £14.80, off-peak version £7.50).

Which Pass to Buy?

Trying to decide between an Oyster and a Travelcard? Here's what I recommend:
- For one to two days, get a One-Day Travelcard each day.
- For three consecutive days, buy a pay-as-you-go Oyster card.
- For four consecutive days, choose a Seven-Day Oyster card (£25.80), or a pay-as-you-go Oyster card. Or you could buy a One-Day Travelcard each day (total £22.40–28.80 in Zones 1-2).

- For five or more days in a row, a Seven-Day Oyster card is usually your best bet. But if you aren't sure if you'll ride enough each day to justify the expense, get the pay-as-you-go Oyster card instead.
- If your trip involves travel to Heathrow Airport, depending on the time of day you travel, you may be better off just paying £4.50 for a full-fare ticket to or from Heathrow, and buying a Zones 1–2 Travelcard for the rest of your time in London.

Other Discounts

Groups of 10 or more adults can travel all day on the Tube for £3.70 each (but not on buses). Kids 11–17 pay £1 when part of a group of 10.

Families: A paying adult can take up to four kids (age 10 and under) for free on the Tube and Docklands Light Railway all day, every day. In the Tube, use the manual gate, rather than the turnstiles, to be waved in. Families with older kids can consider the "Zip" card: Kids ages 11–15 travel for £1 on the Tube and for free on buses. Apply online, and pick up the card in London (takes 3 weeks; requires £5 deposit and digital photo, see www.tfl.gov.uk).

River Cruises: A Travelcard or a Seven-Day Oyster card gives you a 33 percent discount on most Thames cruises (see "Cruises" on page 66).

Sightseeing Deal: Buy a paper Travelcard or rail ticket at a National Rail station and you may qualify for two-for-one discounts at many popular sights (look for brochures with coupons at major train stations or print out vouchers at www.daysoutguide .co.uk).

By Tube

London's subway system (called the Tube or Underground, but never "subway," which refers to a pedestrian underpass) is one of this planet's great people-movers and often the fastest long-distance transport in town (runs Mon–Sat about 5:00–24:00, Sun about 7:00–23:00).

Start by studying a Tube map (free at any station). Each line has a name (such as Circle, Northern, or Bakerloo) and two directions (indicated by the end-of-the-line stops). Find the line that will take you to your destination, and figure out roughly what direction (north, south, east, or west) you'll need to go to get there.

You can use paper tickets, Travelcards, or an Oyster card to pay for your journey. At the Tube station, feed your paper ticket or Travelcard into the turnstile, reclaim it, and hang on to it—you'll need it to get through the turnstile at the end of your journey. If using a plastic Oyster card, touch the card to the yellow card reader when you enter and exit the station.

Find your train by following signs to your line and the (general) direction it's headed (such as Central Line: east). Some tracks are shared by several lines, so double-check before boarding a train. First, make sure your destination is one of the stops listed on the sign at the platform. Also, check the electronic signboards that announce which train is next, and make sure the destination (the end-of-the-line stop) is the one you want. Some trains, particularly on the Circle and District lines, split off for other directions, but each train has its final destination marked above its windshield.

Trains run roughly every 3–10 minutes. If one train is absolutely packed and you notice another to the same destination is coming in three minutes, wait to avoid the sardine experience. The system can be fraught with construction delays and breakdowns, so pay attention to signs and announcements explaining necessary detours (the Circle Line is notorious for problems). Rush hours (8:00–10:00 and 16:00–19:00) can be packed and sweaty. Bring something to do to make your waiting time productive. If you get confused, ask for advice from a local, a blue-vested staff person, or at the information window located before the turnstile entry.

Remember that you can't leave the system without feeding your ticket or Travelcard to the turnstile or touching your Oyster card to an electronic reader. If you have a single-trip paper ticket, the turnstile will eat your now-expired ticket; if it's a Travelcard, it will spit out your still-valid card. Save walking time by choosing the best street exit—check the maps on the walls or ask any station personnel. For Tube and bus information, visit www.tfl.gov.uk (and check out the journey planner).

Any ride in Zones 1–6 (the center of town all the way out to Heathrow Airport) costs a steep £4.50 for adults paying cash. If you plan to ride the Tube and buses more than twice in one day, you'll save money by getting a Travelcard (or for visits of four days or more, an Oyster card is a good choice).

If you do buy a single Tube ticket, you can avoid ticket-window lines in stations by using the coin-op machines; practice on the punchboard to see how the system works (hit "Adult Single" and your destination). These tickets are valid only on the day of purchase.

London

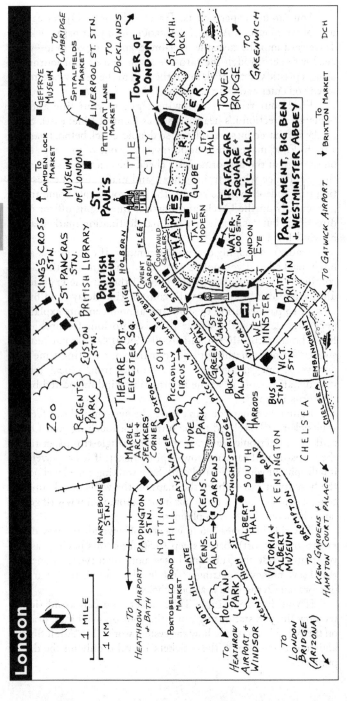

Tube Etiquette

- When waiting at the platform, get out of the way of those exiting the train. Board only after everyone is off.
- Avoid using the hinged seats near the doors of some trains when the car is jammed; they take up valuable standing space.
- In a crowded train, try not to block the exit. If you're blocking the door when the train stops, step out of the car and to the side, let others off, then get back on.
- Talk softly in the cars. Listen to how quietly Londoners communicate and follow their lead.
- On escalators, stand on the right and pass on the left (even though Brits do the opposite behind the wheel). But note that in some passageways or stairways, you might be directed to walk on the left (same as car direction).
- When leaving a station, it's polite to hold the door for the person behind you.
- Flash photos are not allowed on the Tube or in any of the stations because they can affect the drivers' vision.
- Discreet eating and drinking are fine (nothing smelly); drinking alcohol and smoking are not.

By Bus

If you figure out the bus system, you'll swing like Tarzan through the urban jungle of London. Pick up a free bus map at a TI, transport office, or some major museums; it will list the bus routes best for sightseeing (also see "Handy Bus Routes" sidebar, next page).

The first step in mastering the bus system is learning how to decipher the bus-stop signs. Find a bus stop and study the signs mounted on the pole next to the stop. You'll see a chart listing (alphabetically) the destinations served by buses that pick up at this spot or nearby; the names of the buses; and alphabet letters that identify exactly where the buses pick up. After locating your destination, remember or write down the bus name and bus stop letter. Next, refer to the neighborhood map (also on the pole) to find your bus stop. Just match your letter with a stop on the map. Make your way to that stop—you'll know it's yours because it will have the same letter on its pole—and wait for the bus with the right name to arrive. Some fancy stops have electric boards indicating the minutes until the next bus arrives; but remember to check the name on the bus before you hop on. Crack the code and you're good to go.

On almost all buses, you'll pay at a machine at the bus stop (no change given), then show your ticket or pass as you board. You can also use Travelcards and Oyster cards (see page 52). If you're using an Oyster card, touch it to the electronic card reader as you

Handy Bus Routes

Since London instituted a congestion charge for cars, the public bus system has gotten faster, easier, and cheaper than ever. Tube-oriented travelers need to get over their tunnel vision, learn the bus system, and get around fast and easy. The best views are upstairs on a double-decker.

Here are some of the most useful routes:

Route #9: Knightsbridge (Harrods) to Hyde Park Corner to Piccadilly Circus to Trafalgar Square. This is one of two "Heritage Routes," using old-style double-decker buses.

Routes #11 and #24: Victoria Station to Westminster Abbey to

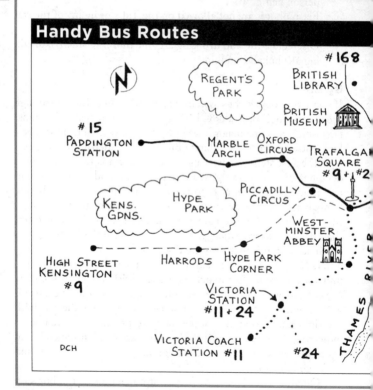

Handy Bus Routes

N

REGENT'S PARK

#168
BRITISH LIBRARY

BRITISH MUSEUM

#15
PADDINGTON STATION

MARBLE ARCH   OXFORD CIRCUS

TRAFALGAR SQUARE
#9 + #2

KENS. GDNS.

HYDE PARK

PICCADILLY CIRCUS

WEST-MINSTER ABBEY

HIGH STREET KENSINGTON
#9

HARRODS

HYDE PARK CORNER

THAMES RIVER

VICTORIA STATION
#11 + 24

DCH

VICTORIA COACH STATION #11

#24

Trafalgar Square (#11 continues to St. Paul's and Liverpool Street Station).

Route #RV1: Tower of London to Tower Bridge to Tate Modern/Shakespeare's Globe to London Eye/Waterloo Station/County Hall Travel Inn accommodations to Aldwych to Covent Garden (a scenic South Bank joyride).

Route #15: Paddington Station to Oxford Circus to Regent Street/TI to Piccadilly Circus to Trafalgar Square to Fleet Street to St. Paul's to Tower of London. This is the other "Heritage Route" that uses old-style double-decker buses.

Route #168: Waterloo Station/London Eye to Covent Garden and then near British Museum and British Library.

In addition, several buses (including #6, #13, #15, #23, #139, and #159) make the corridor run from Trafalgar, Piccadilly Circus, and Oxford Circus to Marble Arch. Check the bus stop closest to your hotel—it might be convenient to your sightseeing plans.

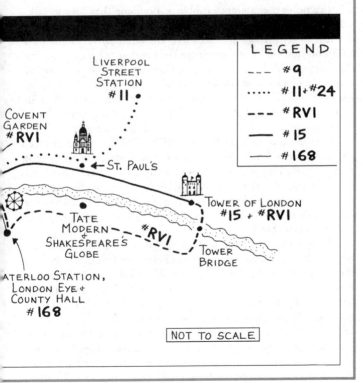

board; no need to do so when you hop off. On "Heritage Routes" #9 and #15 (which use older double-decker buses), you still pay a conductor; take a seat, and he or she will come around to collect your fare or verify your pass.

Any bus ride in downtown London costs £2 for those paying cash, £1.20 if using an Oyster card. If you're staying longer, consider the £16.60 Seven-Day bus pass. If you have a Travelcard or Oyster card, save your feet and get in the habit of hopping buses for quick little straight shots, even just to get to a Tube stop. During bump-and-grind rush hours (8:00–10:00 and 16:00–19:00), you'll usually go faster by Tube.

By Taxi

London is the best taxi town in Europe. Big, black, carefully regulated cabs are everywhere. (Though historically known as "black cabs," some of London's official taxis are now covered with wildly colored ads.)

I've never met a crabby cabbie in London. They love to talk, and they know every nook and cranny in town. I ride in one each day just to get my London questions answered (drivers must pass a rigorous test on "The Knowledge" of London geography to earn their license). Rides start at £2.20. Connecting downtown sights is quick and easy, and will cost you about £6–8 (for example, St. Paul's to the Tower of London). For a short ride, three adults in a cab generally travel at close to Tube prices, and groups of four or five adults should taxi everywhere. Telephoning a cab will get you one in a few minutes (toll tel. 0871-871-8710; £2 surcharge, plus extra fee to book ahead by credit card), but it's generally not necessary—hailing a cab is easy and costs less. If a cab's top light is on, just wave it down. Drivers flash lights when they see you wave. They have a tight turning radius, so you can hail cabs going in either direction. If waving doesn't work, ask someone where you can find a taxi stand.

Don't worry about meter cheating. Licensed British cab meters come with a sealed computer chip and clock that ensures you'll get the regular tariff #1 most of the time (Mon–Fri 6:00–20:00), tariff #2 during "unsociable hours" (Mon–Fri 20:00–22:00 and Sat–Sun 6:00–22:00), and tariff #3 at night (nightly 22:00–6:00) and on holidays. (Rates go up about 15–20 percent with each higher tariff.) All extra charges are explained in writing on the cab wall. The only way a cabbie can cheat you is by taking a needlessly long route. Another pitfall is taking a cab when traffic is bad to a destination efficiently served by the Tube. On a recent trip to London, I hopped in a taxi at South Kensington for Waterloo Station and hit bad traffic. Rather than spending 20 minutes and £2–4 on the Tube, I spent 40 minutes and £16 in a taxi.

Tip a cabbie by rounding up (maximum 10 percent). If you over-drink and ride in a taxi, be warned: Taxis charge £40 for "soiling" (a.k.a., pub puke). If you forget this book in a taxi, call the Lost Property office and hope for the best (toll tel. 0845-330-9882).

Tours in London

▲▲▲Hop-on, Hop-off Double-Decker Bus Tours

Two competitive companies (Original and Big Bus) offer essentially the same two tours of the city's sightseeing highlights, with

nearly 30 stops on each route. Big Bus tours are a little more expensive (£25), while Original tours are cheaper (£21 with this book) and nearly as good.

LONDON

These two-hour, once-over-lightly bus tours drive by all the famous sights, providing a stress-free way to get your bearings and see the biggies. They stop at a core group of sights regardless of which overview tour you're on: Piccadilly Circus, Trafalgar Square, Big Ben, St. Paul's, the Tower of London, Marble Arch, Victoria Station, and elsewhere. With a good guide and nice weather, sit back and enjoy the entire two hours. Narration is important—so hop on and hop off to see the sights or to change guides (if yours is more boring than entertaining).

Each company offers at least one route with live (English-only) guides, and a second (sometimes slightly different route) comes with tape-recorded, dial-a-language narration. In addition to the overview tours, both Original and Big Bus include river cruises and three walking tours.

Pick up a map from any flier rack or from one of the countless salespeople, and study the complex system. Note: If you start at Victoria Station at 9:00, you'll finish near Buckingham Palace in time to see the Changing of the Guard at 11:30; ask your driver for the best place to hop off. Sunday morning—when the traffic is light and many museums are closed—is a fine time for a tour. Unless you're using the bus tour mainly for hop-on, hop-off transportation, consider saving money by taking a night tour (described later).

Buses run about every 10–15 minutes in summer, every 20 minutes in winter, and operate daily. They start at about 8:00 and run until early evening in summer, until late afternoon in winter. The last full loop usually leaves Victoria Station about 17:00 (confirm by checking the schedule or asking the driver).

Daily Reminder

Sunday: The Tower of London and British Museum are both especially crowded today. The Speakers' Corner in Hyde Park rants from early afternoon until early evening. These places are closed: Banqueting House, Sir John Soane's Museum, and legal sights (Houses of Parliament, City Hall, and Old Bailey; the neighborhood called The City is dead). Westminster Abbey and St. Paul's are open during the day for worship but closed to sightseers. Many stores are closed, and some minor sights don't open until noon. The Camden Lock, Spitalfields, Greenwich, and Petticoat Lane street markets flourish, but Portobello Road and Brixton are closed. Except for the Globe, theaters are quiet, as most actors take today off.

Monday: Virtually all sights are open except for Apsley House, Sir John Soane's Museum, Vinopolis, and a few others. The Courtauld Gallery is free until 14:00. The Houses of Parliament are usually open until 22:30. The Portobello Road market is sparse.

Tuesday: Virtually all sights are open, except for Vinopolis and Apsley House. The British Library is open until 20:00. On the first Tuesday of the month, Sir John Soane's Museum is also open 18:00–21:00. The Houses of Parliament are usually open until 22:30.

Wednesday: Virtually all sights are open, except for Vinopolis. Westminster Abbey is open until 19:00.

Thursday: All sights are open, plus evening hours at the British Museum (selected galleries until 20:30), National Portrait

You can buy tickets from drivers or from staff at street kiosks (credit cards accepted at kiosks at major stops such as Victoria, ticket good for 24 hours).

Original London Sightseeing Bus Tour: For a live guide on the city highlights tour, look for a yellow triangle on the front of the bus. A red triangle means a longer, tape-recorded multilingual tour that includes Madame Tussauds—avoid it, unless you have kids who'd enjoy the entertaining recorded kids' tour. A blue triangle connects far-flung museums, while green, black, and purple triangle routes link major train stations to the central routes. All routes are covered by the same ticket. Keep it simple and just take the city highlights tour (£24, £21 after £3 discount with this book, limit two discounts per book, they'll rip off the corner of this page—raise bloody hell if the staff or driver won't honor this discount, also online deals, info center at 17 Cockspur Street, tel. 020/8877-1722, www.theoriginaltour.com). Your ticket includes a City Cruises "River Red Rover" all-day river cruise ticket (normally £11.50; for details see "Cruises: To Greenwich" on page 67), as well as three free 90-minute walking tours.

Gallery (until 21:00), and Vinopolis (until 22:00).

Friday: All sights are open, plus evening hours at the British Museum (selected galleries until 20:30), National Gallery (until 21:00), National Portrait Gallery (until 21:00), Vinopolis (until 22:00), Victoria and Albert Museum (until 22:00), and Tate Modern (until 22:00). The Houses of Parliament close early today (15:00). Best street market today: Spitalfields.

Saturday: Most sights are open except legal ones (Old Bailey, City Hall, Houses of Parliament; skip The City). Vinopolis is open until 22:00, and the Tate Modern until 22:00. Best street markets: Portobello, Camden Lock, Greenwich.

Notes: The St. Martin-in-the-Fields church offers **concerts** at lunchtime (free, Mon, Tue, and Fri at 13:00) and in the evening (jazz: £5-8, Wed at 20:00; classical: £6-25, at 19:30 Thu-Sat, sometimes Tue). **Evensong** occurs daily at St. Paul's (Mon-Sat at 17:00 and Sun at 15:15), Westminster Abbey (Mon-Fri at 17:00—may be spoken on Wed, Sat-Sun at 15:00), and Southwark Cathedral (weekdays at 17:30, Sat at 16:00, Sun at 15:00, no service on Wed or alternate Mon). **London by Night Sightseeing Tour** buses leave from Victoria Station every evening (19:30-21:30, only at 19:30 in winter). The **London Eye** spins nightly (until 20:00-21:30, depending on the season). See also the "London for Early Birds and Night Owls" sidebar on page 81.

Big Bus London Tours: For £25 (£20 online if you pick a specific date; requires printer), you get the same basic overview tours: Red buses come with a live guide, while the blue route has a recorded narration and a longer path around Hyde Park. Your ticket includes three silly one-hour London walks, as well as river cruises on the Thames (similar to "Rover" ticket mentioned above; cruises operated by City Cruises). These pricier tours tend to have better, more dynamic guides than Original, and more departures as well—meaning shorter waits for those hopping on and off (daily 8:30–18:00, winter until 16:30, info center at 48 Buckingham Palace Road, tel. 020/7233-9533, www.bigbustours.com).

At Night: The **London by Night Sightseeing Tour** offers a two-hour circuit, but after hours, with no extras (e.g., walks, river cruises), and at a lower price. Although the narration can be pretty lame, the views at twilight are grand—though note that it stays light until late on summer nights (£15, £11 online, drivers take cash only; May–late Sept departs 19:30, 20:30, and 21:30 from Victoria Station, Jan–April and late Sept–late Dec departs 19:30 only, no tours between Christmas and New Year; Taxi Road, at front of station near end of Wilton Road; or board at any stop, such as Paddington Station, Marble Arch, Trafalgar Square, London Eye, or Tower of London; tel. 020/8545-6109, www.london-by-night .net). For a memorable and economical evening, munch a scenic picnic dinner on the top deck. There are plenty of take-away options in the train stations and near the various stops.

▲▲Walking Tours

Several times a day, top-notch local guides lead (sometimes big) groups through specific slices of London's past. Look for brochures at TIs or ask at hotels, although the latter usually push higher-priced bus tours. *Time Out,* the weekly entertainment guide (£3 at newsstands) lists some, but not all, scheduled walks. Check with the various tour companies by phone or online to get their full picture.

To take a walking tour, simply show up at the announced location and pay the guide. Then enjoy two chatty hours of Dickens, Harry Potter, the Plague, Shakespeare, Legal London, the Beatles, or whatever is on the agenda.

London Walks: This leading company lists its extensive daily schedule in a beefy, plain *London Walks* brochure. Pick it up at St. Martin-in-the-Fields on Trafalgar Square, or access it on their website. Their two-hour walks cost £7 (cash only, walks offered year-round—even Christmas, private tours for groups-£100, tel. 020/7624-3978, for a recorded listing of today's walks call 020/7624-9255, www.walks.com). They also run Explorer day trips, a good option for those with limited time and transportation (£12 plus £10–40 for transportation and any admission costs, cash only, trips change most days: Stonehenge/Salisbury, Oxford/Cotswolds, Cambridge, Bath, and so on; fewer trips offered in winter).

Sandemans New London Tours: This company employs English-speaking students to give three-hour London tours. The fast-moving, youthful tours are light, irreverent, entertaining, and fun. Best of all, one of their tours—Royal London—is free (daily at 11:00, meet at Wellington Arch, Tube: Hyde Park Corner, Exit 2; they push for tips at the end and cross-promote their evening pub crawl). Their other tours include Old City (£9, daily at 10:00, meet at sundial opposite the Tower Hill Tube station exit); Grim Reapers (£9, daily at 14:00, also meets at Tower Hill Tube sundial); and a Pub Crawl (£12, Tue–Sat at 19:30, meet at Belushi's at 9 Russell Street, Tube: Covent Garden). Look for the guides in their red T-shirts (www.newlondon-tours.com).

The Beatles: Fans of the Fab Four can take one of three Beatles walks (London Walks, above, has two that run 5/week; Big Bus, previous page, includes a daily walk with their bus tour). For a photo op, go to Abbey Road and walk the famous crosswalk (at intersection with Grove End Road, Tube: St. John's Wood). The Beatles Store is at 231 Baker Street (daily 10:00–18:30, next to Sherlock Holmes Museum, Tube: Baker Street, tel. 020/7935-4464, www.beatlesstorelondon.co.uk).

Jack the Ripper: Each walking tour company seems to make most of its money with "haunted" and Jack the Ripper tours. Many guides are historians and would rather not lead these lightweight tours—but tourists pay more for gore (the ridiculously juvenile London Dungeon is one of the city's top sights). You'll find plenty of Ripper tours, but for a little twist, you might consider the scary walk given by Ripping Yarns, guided by Yeoman Warders of the Tower of London (£7, pay at end, 2.5 hours, nightly at 18:45 at Tower Hill Tube station, no tours between Christmas and New Year, mobile 07813-559-301, www.jack-the-ripper-tours.com).

Local Guides—Standard rates for London's registered "Blue Badge" guides usually run about £120 for four hours and £190 or more for nine hours (tel. 020/7780-4060, www.touristguides.org .uk, www.blue-badge.org.uk).

Consider Sean Kelleher (£120/half-day, £200/day, also conducts tours about the history of transportation in London, tel. 020/8673-1624, mobile 07764-612-770, seankelleher@bt internet.com) or Britt Lonsdale (£150/half-day, £220/day, great with families, tel. 020/7386-9907, mobile 07813-278-077, brittl @btinternet.com).

Drivers: Robina Brown leads small group tours in her Toyota Previa minivan (with car £270/half-day, £410–600/day; without car £120/half-day, £200/day; prices vary by destination, tel. 020/7228-2238, www.driverguidetours.com, robina@driverguide tours.com). Janine Barton provides a similar driver-and-guide tour and similar prices (tel. 020/7402-4600, http://seeitinstyle .synthasite.com, jbsiis@aol.com). Robina's and Janine's services are particularly helpful for travelers with disabilities who want to see more of London.

London Duck Tours

A bright-yellow amphibious WWII-vintage vehicle (the model that landed troops on Normandy's beaches on D-Day) takes a gang of 30 tourists past some famous sights on land—Big Ben, Trafalgar Square, Piccadilly Circus—then splashes into the Thames for a cruise. All in all, it's good fun at a rather steep price. The live guide works hard, and it's kid-friendly to the point of goofiness (£20, 2/ hr, daily 10:00–17:00, 75 min—45 min on land and 30 min in the river, £2.50 online booking fee, these book up in advance, departs from Chicheley Street—you'll see the big ugly vehicle parked 100 yards behind the London Eye, Tube: Waterloo or Westminster, tel. 020/7928-3132, www.londonducktours.co.uk).

Bike Tours

London, like Paris, is committed to making more bike paths, and many of its best sights can be laced together with a pleasant pedal through its parks.

London Bicycle Tour Company: Three tours covering London are offered daily from their base at Gabriel's Wharf on the south bank of the Thames. Sunday is the best, as there is less car traffic (Central Tour—£16, April–Oct daily at 10:30, 6 miles, 2.5 hours, includes Westminster, Covent Garden, and St. Paul's; West Tour—£19, April–Oct Sat–Sun at 12:00, Nov–March only on Sun, 9 miles, 3.5 hours, includes Westminster, Hyde Park, Buckingham Palace, and Covent Garden; East Tour—£19, April–Oct Sat–Sun at 14:00, Nov–March only on Sat, 9 miles, 3.5 hours, includes south side of the river to Tower Bridge, then The City to the East End). They also rent bikes (office open daily 10:00–18:00, west of Blackfriars Bridge on the South Bank, 1a Gabriel's Wharf, tel. 020/7928-6838, www.londonbicycle.com).

Fat Tire Bike Tours: Daily bike tours cover the highlights of downtown London. The spiel is light and irreverent rather than scholarly, but the price is right. This is a fun way to see the sights and enjoy the city on two wheels (£16, daily June–Aug at 11:00 and 15:30, March–May and Sept–Nov at 11:00, Dec–Feb by reservation only, covers 7 miles in 4 hours, pay when you show up—no reservations needed except for kids' bikes or in winter, Queensway Tube station, mobile 078-8233-8779, www.fattirebiketourslondon.com).

▲▲Cruises

Boat tours with entertaining commentaries sail regularly from many points along the Thames. It's a bit confusing, because several companies offer essentially the same trip. Your basic options are to use the boats to go downstream to the Tower and Greenwich, upstream to Kew Gardens and Hampton Court, or just enjoy a round-trip scenic tour cruise. Most people depart from the Westminster Pier (at the base of Westminster Bridge across the street from Big Ben). You can catch many of the same boats (with less waiting) from Waterloo Pier at the London Eye across the river. For pleasure and efficiency, consider combining a one-way cruise (to Kew Gardens, Greenwich, or wherever) with a Tube or train ride back.

Buy boat tickets at the small ticket offices on the docks. While individual Tube and bus tickets don't work on the boats, a Travelcard or Seven-Day Oyster card can snare you a 33 percent discount on most cruises (just show the card when you pay for the cruise, not valid with pay-as-you-go Oyster cards). Children and seniors get discounts. You can purchase drinks and scant, pricey snacks on board. Clever budget travelers pack a picnic and munch while they cruise.

Thames Boat Piers

Although Westminster Pier is the most popular, it's not the only dock in town. Consider all the options:

Westminster Pier, at the base of Big Ben, offers round-trip sightseeing cruises and lots of departures in both directions.

Waterloo Pier, at the base of the London Eye, is a good, less-crowded alternative to Westminster, with many of the same cruise options.

Embankment Pier is near Covent Garden, Trafalgar Square, and Cleopatra's Needle (the obelisk on the Thames). You can take a round-trip cruise from here, or catch a boat to the Tower of London and Greenwich.

Tower Pier is at the Tower of London. Boats sail west to Westminster Pier or east to Greenwich.

Bankside Pier (near Tate Modern and Shakespeare's Globe) and **Millbank Pier** (near Tate Britain) are connected to each other by the Tate Boat ferry service.

LONDON

Here are some of the most popular cruise options:

To the Tower of London: City Cruises boats sail 30 minutes to the Tower from Westminster Pier (£6.90 one-way, £8.70 round-trip, one-way included with Big Bus London tour; covered by £11.50 "River Red Rover" ticket that includes Greenwich; daily April–Oct roughly 10:00–21:00, until 18:00 in winter, every 20 min).

To Greenwich: Two companies—City Cruises and the Thames River Services—head to Greenwich from Westminster Pier. The cruises are usually narrated by the captain, with most commentary given on the way to Greenwich. The companies' prices are the same, though **City Cruises** offers a few more alternatives (£8.40 one-way, £11 round-trip; or get their £11.50 all-day, hop-on, hop-off "River Red Rover" ticket to have option of getting off at the London Eye and Tower of London—included with Original London bus tour; daily April–Oct generally 10:00–17:00, less off-season, about every 40 min, 75 min to Greenwich; also departs for Greenwich from the pier at the Tower of London for less: £6.90 one-way, £8.70 round-trip, 30 min; tel. 020/7740-0400, www.citycruises.com). The **Thames River Services** goes to Greenwich from Westminster Pier a bit more frequently and a little quicker (£8.40 one-way, £11 round-trip, April–Oct 10:00–16:00, July–Aug until 17:00, daily 2/hr; Nov–March shorter hours and runs every 40 min; 1 hour to Greenwich, tel. 020/7930-4097, www.thamesriverservices .co.uk).

To Kew Gardens: Boats run by the Westminster Passenger Services Association leave for Kew Gardens from Westminster Pier (£11 one-way, £17 round-trip, cash only, 4/day, April–Oct daily 10:30–14:00, 90 min, narrated for 45 min, tel. 020/7930-2062, www.wpsa.co.uk). Some boats continue on to **Hampton Court Palace** for an additional £3 (and 90 min). Because of the river current, you'll sometimes save 30 minutes cruising from Hampton Court back into town (depends on the tide).

Round-Trip Cruises: The London Eye operates its own "River Cruise," offering a 40-minute live-guided circular tour from Waterloo Pier (£12, reservations recommended, departures daily generally at :45 past the hour, April–Oct 10:45–18:45, Nov–March 11:45–16:45, closed mid-Jan–mid-Feb, toll tel. 0870-500-0600, www.londoneye.com).

From Tate to Tate: The Tate Boat service for art-lovers connects the Tate Modern and Tate Britain with a sleek, 220-seat catamaran (£5 one-way or £12 for a day ticket, discounted with Travelcard, buy ticket at gallery desk or on board, runs daily every 40 min, from Tate Modern 10:10–16:50, from Tate Britain 10:30–17:10, 18-min trip, tel. 020/7887-8888, www.tate.org.uk).

On Regent's Canal: Consider exploring London's canals by taking a cruise on historic Regent's Canal in north London. The good ship *Jenny Wren* offers 90-minute guided canal boat cruises from Walker's Quay in Camden Town through scenic Regent's Park to Little Venice (£8.50, Aug daily at 10:30, 12:30, 14:30 and 16:30, April–July and Sept–Oct daily at 12:30 and 14:30, Sat–Sun also at 16:30; Walker's Quay, 250 Camden High Street, 3-min walk from Tube: Camden Town; tel. 020/7485-4433, www.walkersquay.com). While in Camden Town, stop by the popular, punky Camden Lock Market to browse through trendy arts and crafts (daily 10:00–18:00, busiest on weekends, a block from Walker's Quay, www.camdenlock.net).

Self-Guided Walk

Westminster Walk

Just about every visitor to London strolls along historic Whitehall from Big Ben to Trafalgar Square. This quick nine-stop walk gives meaning to that touristy ramble. Under London's modern traffic and big-city bustle lie 2,000 fascinating years of history. You'll get a whirlwind tour as well as a practical orientation to London.

Start halfway across **Westminster Bridge** (❶) for that "Wow, I'm really in London!" feeling. Get a close-up view of the **Houses of Parliament** and **Big Ben** (floodlit at night). Downstream you'll see the **London Eye.** Down the stairs to Westminster Pier are boats to the Tower of London and Greenwich (downstream) or

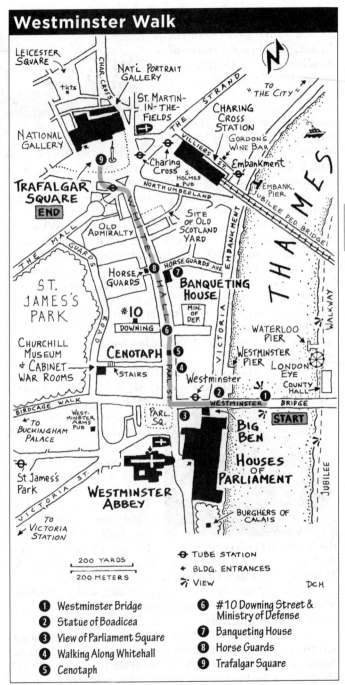

Westminster Walk

LONDON

1. Westminster Bridge
2. Statue of Boadicea
3. View of Parliament Square
4. Walking Along Whitehall
5. Cenotaph
6. #10 Downing Street & Ministry of Defense
7. Banqueting House
8. Horse Guards
9. Trafalgar Square

Kew Gardens (upstream).

En route to Parliament Square, you'll pass a **statue of Boadicea** (❷), the Celtic queen defeated by Roman invaders in A.D. 60.

For fun, call home from a pay phone near Big Ben at about three minutes before the hour, to let your loved one hear the bell ring. You'll find four red phone booths lining the north side of **Parliament Square** (❸) along Great George Street.

Wave hello to Churchill in Parliament Square. To his right is **Westminster Abbey** with its two stubby, elegant towers.

Head north up Parliament Street, which turns into **Whitehall** (❹), and walk toward Trafalgar Square. You'll see the thought-provoking **Cenotaph** (❺) in the middle of the street, reminding passersby of Britain's many war dead. To visit the Churchill Museum and Cabinet War Rooms (see page 75), take a left before the Cenotaph, on King Charles Street.

Continuing on Whitehall, stop at the barricaded and guarded **#10 Downing Street** (❻) to see the British "White House," home of the prime minister. Break the bobby's boredom and ask him a question.

Nearing Trafalgar Square, look for the 17th-century **Banqueting House** across the street (❼) and the **Horse Guards** (❽) behind the gated fence (Changing of the Horse Guards Mon–Sat at 11:00, Sun at 10:00, dismounting ceremony daily at 16:00).

The column topped by Lord Nelson marks **Trafalgar Square** (❾). The stately domed building on the far side of the square is the **National Gallery** (free), which has a classy café upstairs in the Sainsbury wing. To the right of the National Gallery is **St. Martin-in-the-Fields Church** and its Café in the Crypt.

To get to Piccadilly from Trafalgar Square, walk up Cockspur Street to Haymarket, then take a short left on Coventry Street to colorful **Piccadilly Circus.**

Near Piccadilly you'll find the **Britain and London Visitors Centre** (on Lower Regent Street) and piles of theaters. **Leicester Square** (with its half-price "tkts" booth for plays, see page 121) thrives just a few blocks away. Walk through seedy **Soho** (north of

Shaftesbury Avenue) for its fun pubs (consider my recommended Soho "Food Is Fun" Three-Course Dinner Crawl on page 150). From Piccadilly or Oxford Circus, you can take a taxi, bus, or the Tube home.

Sights in London

Central London
Westminster

▲▲▲**Westminster Abbey**—The greatest church in the English-speaking world, Westminster Abbey is the place where England's kings and queens have been crowned and buried since 1066. A thousand years of English history—3,000 tombs, the remains of 29 kings and queens, and hundreds of memorials to poets, politicians, and warriors—lie within its stained-glass splendor and under its stone slabs. Like a stony refugee camp huddled outside St. Peter's Pearly Gates, this place has many stories to tell. The steep admission includes an excellent audioguide, worthwhile if you have the time and interest. To experience the church more vividly, take a live tour, or attend evensong or an organ concert (see below). You can even have a sandwich or bowl of soup in the cloister...but you can't take photos.

Two tiny **museums** ring the cloisters: the Chapter House (where the monks held daily meetings, notable for its fine architecture, stained glass, and faded but well-described medieval art), and the Abbey Museum (which tells of the abbey's history, royal coronations, and burials). Look into the impressively realistic eyes of Henry VII's funeral effigy (one of a fascinating series of wax-and-wood statues that, for three centuries, graced royal coffins during funeral processions).

Cost: £15, £30 family ticket for three, includes cloisters, audioguide, and Abbey Museum.

Hours and Information: Abbey open Mon–Fri 9:30–16:30, Wed until 19:00, Sat 9:30–14:30, last entry one hour before closing, closed Sun to sightseers but open for services; Abbey Museum open daily 10:30–16:00; cloisters open daily 8:00–18:00; £3 90-min guided tours, 5/day in summer; Tube: Westminster or St. James's Park. Info desk tel. 020/7222-5152 or 020/7654-4834, www .westminster-abbey.org.

Avoiding Crowds: The main entrance, on the Parliament Square side, often has a sizable line; visit early, during lunch, or late

London at a Glance

▲▲▲**Westminster Abbey** Britain's finest church and the site of royal coronations and burials since 1066. **Hours:** Mon–Fri 9:30–16:30, Wed until 19:00, Sat 9:30–14:30, closed Sun to sightseers except for worship. See page 71.

▲▲▲**Churchill Museum and Cabinet War Rooms** Underground WWII headquarters of Churchill's war effort. **Hours:** Daily 9:30–18:00. See page 75.

▲▲▲**National Gallery** Remarkable collection of European paintings (1250–1900), including Leonardo, Botticelli, Velázquez, Rembrandt, Turner, Van Gogh, and the Impressionists. **Hours:** Daily 10:00–18:00, Fri until 21:00. See page 77.

▲▲▲**British Museum** The world's greatest collection of artifacts of Western civilization, including the Rosetta Stone and the Parthenon's Elgin Marbles. **Hours:** Daily 10:00–17:30, Thu–Fri until 20:30 but only a few galleries open after 17:30. See page 88.

▲▲▲**British Library** Impressive collection of the most important literary treasures of the Western world. **Hours:** Mon–Fri 9:30–18:00, Tue until 20:00, Sat 9:30–17:00, Sun 11:00–17:00. See page 90.

▲▲▲**St. Paul's Cathedral** The main cathedral of the Anglican Church, designed by Christopher Wren, with a climbable dome and daily evensong services. **Hours:** Mon–Sat 8:30–16:30, closed Sun except for worship. See page 94.

▲▲▲**Tower of London** Historic castle, palace, and prison, today housing the crown jewels and a witty band of Beefeaters. **Hours:** March–Oct Tue–Sat 9:00–17:30, Sun–Mon 10:00–17:30; Nov–Feb Tue–Sat 9:00–16:30, Sun–Mon 10:00–16:30. See page 97.

▲▲**London Eye** Enormous observation wheel, dominating—and offering commanding views over—London's skyline. **Hours:** Daily June–Sept 10:00–21:00, July–Aug until 21:30, Oct–May until 20:00. See page 101.

▲▲**Tate Modern** Works by Monet, Matisse, Dalí, Picasso, and Warhol displayed in a converted powerhouse. **Hours:** Daily 10:00–18:00, Fri–Sat until 22:00. See page 104.

▲▲**Houses of Parliament** London's famous Neo-Gothic landmark, topped by Big Ben and occupied by the Houses of Lords and Commons. **Hours** (both Houses): Generally Mon–Tue 14:30–22:30, Wed–Thu 11:30–17:50, Fri 9:30–15:00, closed Sat–Sun. See page 74.

▲▲**National Portrait Gallery** A *Who's Who* of British history, featuring portraits of this nation's most important historical figures. **Hours:** Daily 10:00–18:00, Thu–Fri until 21:00. See page 80.

▲▲**Victoria and Albert Museum** The best collection of decorative arts anywhere. **Hours:** Daily 10:00–17:45, Fri until 22:00. See page 111.

▲▲**Imperial War Museum** Examines the military history of the bloody 20th century. **Hours:** Daily 10:00–18:00. See page 103.

▲▲**Shakespeare's Globe** Timbered, thatched-roofed reconstruction of the Bard's original wooden "O." **Hours:** Theater complex, museum, and actor-led tours generally daily May–Sept 9:00–17:00, Oct–April 10:00–17:00; in summer, morning theater tours only. Plays are also held here. See page 104.

▲▲**Tate Britain** Collection of British painting from the 16th century through modern times, including works by William Blake, the Pre-Raphaelites, and J. M. W. Turner. **Hours:** Daily 10:00–17:50, first Fri of the month until 21:40. See page 108.

▲**Courtauld Gallery** Fine collection of paintings filling one wing of the Somerset House, a grand 18th-century palace. **Hours:** Daily 10:00–18:00. See page 84.

▲**Buckingham Palace** Britain's royal residence with the famous Changing of the Guard. **Hours:** Palace—Aug–Sept only, daily 9:45–18:00; Guard—May–July daily at 11:30, Aug–April every other day. See page 85.

▲**Old Operating Theatre Museum** 19th-century hall where surgeons performed amputations for an audience of aspiring med students. **Hours:** Daily 10:30–17:00. See page 107.

to avoid tourist hordes. Midmornings are most crowded, whereas weekdays after 14:30 are less congested; come then and stay for the 17:00 evensong.

Music: The church hosts **evensong** performances daily, sung every night but Wednesday, when it is spoken (Mon–Fri at 17:00; Sat–Sun at 15:00). A free 30-minute **organ recital** is usually held on Sunday at 17:45.

▲▲**Houses of Parliament (Palace of Westminster)**—This Neo-Gothic icon of London, the royal residence from 1042 to 1547, is now the meeting place of the legislative branch of government. The Houses of Parliament are located in what was once the Palace of Westminster—long the palace of England's medieval kings—until it was largely destroyed by fire in 1834. The palace was rebuilt in the Victorian Gothic style (a move away from Neoclassicism back to England's Christian and medieval heritage, true to the Romantic Age) and completed in 1860.

Tourists are welcome to view debates in either the bickering House of Commons or the genteel House of Lords. You're only allowed inside when Parliament is in session, indicated by a flag flying atop the Victoria Tower at the south end of the building (generally Mondays through Thursdays, plus some Fridays). While the actual debates are generally quite dull, it is a thrill to be inside and see the British government inaction.

Cost and Hours: Free, both Houses usually open Mon–Tue 14:30–22:30, Wed–Thu 11:30–17:50, Fri 9:30–15:00, closed Sat–Sun, generally less action and no lines after 18:00, Tube: Westminster. Tel. 020/7219-4272; see www.parliament.uk for schedule. The House of Lords has more pageantry, shorter lines, and less interesting debates (tel. 020/7219-3107 for schedule, and visit www.parliamentlive.tv for a preview).

Visiting the Houses of Parliament (HOP): Enter the venerable HOP midway along the west side of the building (across the street from Westminster Abbey) through the Visitor Entrance (with the tourist ramp, next to the St. Stephen's Entrance—if lost, ask a guard). As you enter, you'll be asked if you want to visit the House of Commons or the House of Lords. Inquire about the wait—an hour or two is not unusual. If there's a long line for the House of Commons and you just want a quick look inside the grand halls of this grand building, start with the House of Lords. Once inside you can switch if you like.

Just past security, you enter the vast and historic **Westminster Hall,** which survived the 1834 fire. The hall was built in the 11th century, and its famous self-supporting hammer-beam roof was added in 1397. Racks of brochures here explain how the British government works, and plaques describe the hall. The Jubilee Café, open to the public, has live video feeds showing exactly what's going on in each house. Just seeing the café video is a fun experience (and can help you decide which house—if either—you'd actually like to see). Walking through the hall and up the stairs, you'll enter the busy world of government with all its high-powered goings-on.

Houses of Parliament Summer Recess Tours: Though Parliament is in recess during much of August and September, you can get a behind-the-scenes peek at the royal chambers of both houses with a tour (£13, 75 min, tours generally Tue–Thu, times vary so confirm in advance; book ahead through Keith Prowse ticket agency—toll tel. 0870-906-3773, www.keithprowse.com, no booking fee).

The **Jewel Tower,** across the street from the Parliament building's St. Stephen's Gate, is a rare remnant of the old Palace of Westminster used by kings until Henry VIII. The crude stone tower (1365–66) was a guard tower in the palace wall, overlooking a moat. It contains a fine little exhibit on Parliament and the tower. Next to the tower (and free) is a quiet courtyard with picnic-friendly benches (£3, daily March–Oct 10:00–17:00, Nov–Feb 10:00–16:00, tel. 020/7222-2219).

Big Ben, the clock tower (315 feet high), is named for its 13-ton bell, Ben. The light above the clock is lit when the House of Commons is sitting. The face of the clock is huge—you can actually see the minute hand moving. For a good view of it, walk halfway over Westminster Bridge.

▲▲▲**Churchill Museum and Cabinet War Rooms**—This is a fascinating walk through the underground headquarters of

the British government's fight against the Nazis in the darkest days of the Battle for Britain. The 27-room nerve center of the British war effort was used from 1939 to 1945. Churchill's room, the map room, and other rooms are just as they were in 1945. For all the blood, sweat, toil, and tears details, pick up the excellent, essential, and included audioguide at the entry and follow the 60-minute tour; be patient—it's well worth it.

Don't bypass the Churchill Museum (entrance is a half-dozen rooms into the exhibit), which shows the man behind the famous cigar, bowler hat, and V-for-victory sign—allow an hour for that museum alone. It shows his wit, irascibility, work ethic, American ties, writing talents, and drinking habits. A long touch-the-screen timeline lets you zero in on events in his life from birth (November 30, 1874) to his appointment as prime minister in 1940. It's all the more amazing considering that, in the 1930s, the man who would become my vote for greatest statesman of the 20th century was considered a washed-up loony ranting about the growing threat of fascism.

Cost, Hours, Location: £13, daily 9:30–18:00, last entry one hour before closing; on King Charles Street, 200 yards off Whitehall, follow the signs, Tube: Westminster. Tel. 020/7930-6961, www.iwm.org.uk. The museum's gift shop is great for anyone nostalgic for the 1940s.

Nearby: If you're hungry, get your rations at the Switch Room café (in the museum) or, for a nearby pub lunch, try the Westminster Arms (food served downstairs, on Storey's Gate, a couple of blocks south of Cabinet War Rooms).

Horse Guards—The Horse Guards change daily at 11:00 (10:00 on Sun), and there's a colorful dismounting ceremony daily at 16:00. The rest of the day, they just stand there—terrible for video cameras (on Whitehall, between Trafalgar Square and #10 Downing Street, Tube: Westminster, www.changing-the-guard.com). Buckingham Palace pageantry is canceled when it rains, but the Horse Guards change regardless of the weather.

▲Banqueting House—England's first Renaissance building was designed by Inigo Jones around 1620. It's one of the few London

landmarks spared by the 1698 fire and the only surviving part of the original Palace of Whitehall. Don't miss its Rubens ceiling, which, at Charles I's request, drove home the doctrine of the legitimacy of the divine right of kings. In 1649—divine right ignored—Charles I was beheaded on the balcony of this building by order of a Cromwellian Parliament. Admission includes a restful 20-minute audiovisual history, which shows the place in banqueting action; a 30-minute audioguide—interesting only to history buffs; and a look at the exquisite banqueting hall.

Cost, Hours, Location: £4.80, includes audioguide, Mon–Sat 10:00–17:00, closed Sun, last entry at 16:30, subject to closure for government functions, aristocratic WC, immediately across Whitehall from the Horse Guards, Tube: Westminster. Tel. 020/3166-6154 or 020/3166-6155, www.hrp.org.uk. Just up the street is Trafalgar Square.

On Trafalgar Square

▲▲Trafalgar Square—London's recently renovated central square, the climax of most marches and demonstrations, is a thrilling place to simply hang out. Lord Nelson stands atop his

Trafalgar Square

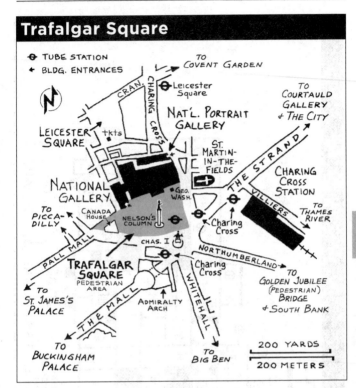

⊖ TUBE STATION
◆ BLDG. ENTRANCES

TO COVENT GARDEN

Leicester Square

LEICESTER SQUARE

CRAN.

CHARING CROSS

tkts

NAT'L. PORTRAIT GALLERY

ST. MARTIN-IN-THE-FIELDS

TO COURTAULD GALLERY & THE CITY

THE STRAND

CHARING CROSS STATION

VILLIERS

TO THAMES RIVER

NATIONAL GALLERY

GEO. WASH.

TO PICCA-DILLY

Canada House

NELSON'S COLUMN

Charing Cross

CHAS. I

NORTHUMBERLAND

PALL MALL

TRAFALGAR SQUARE
PEDESTRIAN AREA

Charing Cross

TO GOLDEN JUBILEE (PEDESTRIAN) BRIDGE & SOUTH BANK

TO ST. JAMES'S PALACE

THE MALL

ADMIRALTY ARCH

WHITEHALL

TO BUCKINGHAM PALACE

TO BIG BEN

200 YARDS
200 METERS

LONDON

185-foot-tall fluted granite column, gazing out toward Trafalgar, where he lost his life but defeated the French fleet. Part of this 1842 memorial is made from his victims' melted-down cannons. He's surrounded by spraying fountains,

giant lions, hordes of people, and—until recently—even more pigeons. A former London mayor decided that London's "flying rats" were a public nuisance and evicted Trafalgar Square's venerable seed salesmen (Tube: Charing Cross).

▲▲▲**National Gallery**—Displaying Britain's top collection of European paintings from 1250 to 1900—including works by Leonardo, Botticelli, Velázquez, Rembrandt, Turner, Van Gogh, and the Impressionists—this is one of Europe's great galleries.

While the collection is huge, following the route suggested on the highlights map (see pages 78–79) will give you my best

National Gallery Highlights

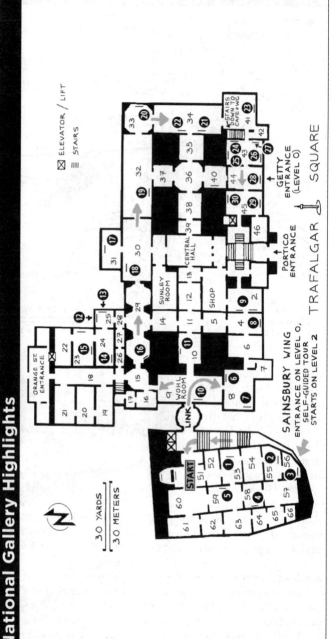

LONDON

MEDIEVAL & EARLY RENAISSANCE
1. ANONYMOUS – The Wilton Diptych
2. UCCELLO – Battle of San Romano
3. VAN EYCK – The Arnolfini Marriage

ITALIAN RENAISSANCE
4. BOTTICELLI – Venus and Mars
5. CRIVELLI – The Annunciation, with Saint Emidius

HIGH RENAISSANCE
6. MICHELANGELO – Entombment
7. RAPHAEL – Pope Julius II
8. HOLBEIN – The Ambassadors
9. DA VINCI – The Virgin of the Rocks; Virgin and Child with St. Anne and St. John the Baptist

VENETIAN RENAISSANCE
10. TINTORETO – The Origin of the Milky Way
11. TITIAN – Bacchus and Ariadne

NORTHERN PROTESTANT ART
12. VERMEER – A Young Woman
13. "A Peepshow"
14. REMBRANDT – Belshazzar's Feast
15. REMBRANDT – Self-Portrait

BAROQUE & ROCOCO
16. RUBENS – The Judgment of Paris
17. VAN DYCK – Equestrian Portrait of Charles I
18. VELÁZQUEZ – The Rokeby Venus
19. CARAVAGGIO – The Supper at Emmaus
20. BOUCHER – Pan and Syrinx

BRITISH
21. CONSTABLE – The Hay Wain
22. TURNER – The Fighting Téméraire
23. DELAROCHE – The Execution of Lady Jane Grey

IMPRESSIONISM & BEYOND
24. MONET – Gare St. Lazare
25. MONET – The Water-Lily Pond
26. MANET – Corner of a Café-Concert (a.k.a. The Waitress)
27. RENOIR – Boating on the Seine
28. SEURAT – Bathers at Asnières
29. VAN GOGH – Sunflowers
30. CÉZANNE – Bathers

quick visit. The audioguide tour (suggested £3.50 donation) is one of the finest I've used in Europe.

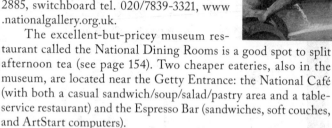

Cost, Hours, Location: Free, but suggested donation of £1–2; daily 10:00–18:00, Fri until 21:00; last entry to special exhibits 45 min before closing, free one-hour overview tours daily at 11:30 and 14:30; no photography, on Trafalgar Square, Tube: Charing Cross or Leicester Square. Recorded info tel. 020/7747-2885, switchboard tel. 020/7839-3321, www.nationalgallery.org.uk.

The excellent-but-pricey museum restaurant called the National Dining Rooms is a good spot to split afternoon tea (see page 154). Two cheaper eateries, also in the museum, are located near the Getty Entrance: the National Café (with both a casual sandwich/soup/salad/pastry area and a table-service restaurant) and the Espresso Bar (sandwiches, soft couches, and ArtStart computers).

▲▲**National Portrait Gallery**—Put off by halls of 19th-century characters who meant nothing to me, I used to call this "as interesting as someone else's yearbook." But a selective walk through this 500-year-long *Who's Who* of British history is quick and free, and puts faces on the story of England. The collection is well-described, not huge, and in historical sequence, from the 16th century on the second floor to today's royal family on the ground floor.

Some highlights: Henry VIII and wives; portraits of the "Virgin Queen" Elizabeth I, Sir Francis Drake, and Sir Walter Raleigh; the only real-life portrait of William Shakespeare; Oliver Cromwell and Charles I with his head on; portraits by Gainsborough and Reynolds; the Romantics (William Blake, Lord Byron, William Wordsworth, and company); Queen Victoria and her era; and the present royal family, including the late Princess Diana.

Cost, Hours, Location: Free, but suggested donation of £3; daily 10:00–18:00, Thu–Fri until 21:00, last entry to special exhibits 45 min before closing, excellent themed audioguides—£2 suggested donation; entry 100 yards off Trafalgar Square, around corner from National Gallery, opposite Church of St. Martin-in-the-Fields; Tube: Charing Cross or Leicester Square. Tel. 020/7306-0055, recorded info tel. 020/7312-2463, www.npg.org.uk.

The elegant Portrait Restaurant on the top floor is pricey but has a fine view of Trafalgar Square (£15–20 entrées, reservations smart, tel. 020/7312-2490). The Portrait Café in the basement (take the lift down) is cheaper and offers sandwiches, salads, and pastries.

London for Early Birds and Night Owls

Most sightseeing in London is restricted to the hours between 10:00 and 18:00. Here are a few exceptions:

Sights Open Early
Every day several sights open at 9:30 or earlier.
Shakespeare's Globe: May–Sept daily at 9:00.
Churchill Museum and Cabinet War Rooms: Daily at 9:30.
Kew Gardens: Daily at 9:30.
Madame Tussauds Waxworks: Mon–Fri at 9:30, Sat–Sun at 9:00 (opens daily at 9:00 mid-July–Aug).
Westminster Cathedral: Daily at 7:00.
Buckingham Palace: Aug–Sept daily at 9:45.
St. Paul's Cathedral: Mon–Sat at 8:30.
Westminster Abbey: Mon–Sat at 9:30.
British Library: Mon–Sat at 9:30.
Tower of London: Tue–Sat at 9:00.
Houses of Parliament: Fri at 9:30.

Sights Open Late
Every night in London at least one sight is open late, in addition to the London Eye. Here's the scoop from Monday through Sunday:
London Eye: July–Aug daily until 21:30, June and Sept until 21:00, otherwise until 20:00.
Houses of Parliament (when in session): Mon–Tue until 22:30.
British Library: Tue until 20:00.
Sir John Soane's Museum: First Tue of month until 21:00.
National Gallery: Fri until 21:00.
Vinopolis: Thu–Sat until 22:00, Sun until 18:00.
British Museum (some galleries): Thu–Fri until 20:30.
National Portrait Gallery: Thu–Fri until 21:00.
London Transport Museum: Some Fri until 21:00.
Victoria and Albert Museum: Fri until 22:00.
Tate Modern: Fri–Sat until 22:00.
Clink Prison Museum: Sat–Sun until 21:00 in summer.

▲**St. Martin-in-the-Fields**—The church, built in the 1720s with a Gothic spire atop a Greek-type temple, is an oasis of peace on the wild and noisy Trafalgar Square. St. Martin cared for the poor. "In the fields" was where the first church stood on this spot (in the 13th century), between Westminster and The City. Stepping inside, you still feel a compassion for the needs of the people in this neighborhood—the church serves the homeless and houses a Chinese community center. The modern east window—with grill-work bent into the shape of a warped cross—was installed in 2008 to replace one damaged in World War II.

A new freestanding glass pavilion to the left of the church serves as the entrance to the church's underground areas. There you'll find the concert ticket office, a gift shop, brass-rubbing center, and the fine support-the-church Café in the Crypt (listed on page 143).

Cost, Hours, Location: Church entry free, donations welcome, audioguide available, open daily, Tube: Charing Cross. Tel. 020/7766-1100, www2.stmartin-in-the-fields.org.

Music: The church is famous for its concerts. Consider a free lunchtime concert (Mon, Tue, and Fri at 13:00), an evening concert (£6–25, at 19:30 Thu–Sat and on some Tue), or live jazz in the church's café (£5–8, Wed at 20:00). See the church's website for the concert schedule.

West End and Nearby

To explore this area during dinner, take my recommended Soho "Food Is Fun" Three-Course Dinner Crawl, and munch your way from Covent Garden to Soho (see page 150).

▲▲**Piccadilly Circus**—London's most touristy square got its name from the fancy ruffled shirts—*picadils*—made in the neighborhood long ago. Today, the square (Tube: Piccadilly), while pretty grotty, is surrounded by fascinating streets swimming with youth on the rampage. Look no further than the gargantuan **Ripley's Believe-It-Or-Not Museum** to capture the gimmicky flavor of today's Piccadilly. For over-stimulation in a grimy mall that smells like teen spirit, drop by the extremely trashy **Trocadero Center** for its Funland arcade games, nine-screen cinema, and 10-lane bowling alley (admission to Trocadero is free; individual attractions cost £2–10; located between Piccadilly and Leicester Squares on Coventry Street, Tube: Piccadilly Circus). Chinatown, to the east, swelled when the former British colony of Hong Kong was returned to China in 1997, but is now threatened by developers. Nearby Shaftesbury Avenue and Leicester Square teem with fun-seekers, theaters, Chinese restaurants, and street singers.

Soho—North of Piccadilly, seedy Soho has become seriously trendy and is well worth a gawk. But Soho is also London's red light district (especially near Brewer and Berwick Streets), where "friendly models" wait in tiny rooms up dreary stairways, and voluptuous con artists sell strip shows. Though venturing up a stairway to check out a model is interesting, anyone who goes into any one of the shows will be ripped off. Every time. Even a £5 show in a "licensed bar" comes with a £100 cover or minimum (as it's printed on the drink menu) and a "security man." You may accidentally buy a £200 bottle of bubbly. And suddenly, the door has no handle.

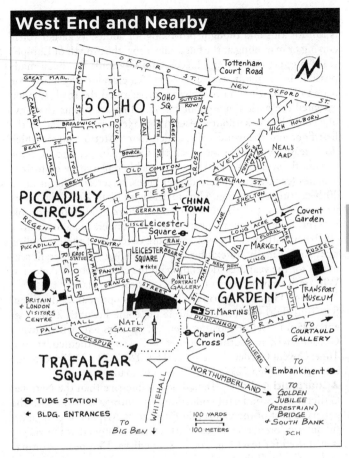

West End and Nearby

Telephone sex ads are hard to avoid these days in London. Phone booths are littered with racy fliers of busty ladies "new in town." Some travelers gather six or eight phone booths' worth of fliers and take them home for kinky wallpaper.

▲▲**Covent Garden**—The centerpiece of this boutique-ish shopping district is an iron-and-glass arcade. The opera house borders the square, and venerable theatres are nearby. The area is a people-watcher's delight, with cigarette eaters, Punch-and-Judy acts, food that's good for you (but not your wallet), trendy crafts, sweet whiffs of marijuana, two-tone hair (neither natural), and faces that could set off a metal detector (Tube: Covent Garden). For better Covent Garden lunch deals, walk a block or two away from the eye of this touristic hurricane (check out the places north of the Tube station along Endell and Neal Streets).

▲**London Transport Museum**—This newly renovated museum is fun for kids and thought-provoking for adults. Whether you're cursing or marveling at the buses and Tube, the growth of Europe's third-biggest city (after Moscow and Istanbul) has been made possible by its public transit system. An elevator transports you back to 1800, when horse-drawn vehicles ruled the road. London invented the notion of a public bus traveling a set route that anyone could board without a reservation. Next, you descend to the first floor and the world's first underground Metro system, which used steam-powered locomotives (the Circle Line, c. 1865). On the ground floor, horses and trains are quickly replaced by motorized vehicles (cars, taxis, double-decker buses, streetcars), resulting in 20th-century congestion. How to deal with it? In 2003, car drivers were slapped with a congestion charge. Today, a half-billion people ride the Tube every year. Learn how city planners hope to improve efficiency with better tracks and more coverage of the expanding East End. Finally, an exhibit lets you imagine four different scenarios for the year 2055 depending on the choices you make today. Will fresh strawberries in December destroy the planet?

Cost, Hours, Location: £10, includes optional £2 donation, Sat–Thu 10:00–18:00, Fri 11:00–18:00, some Fri until 21:00, last entry 45 min before closing, pleasant upstairs café with Covent Garden view, in southeast corner of Covent Garden courtyard, Tube: Covent Garden. Switchboard tel. 020/7379-6344 or recorded info tel. 020/7565-7299, www.ltmuseum.co.uk.

▲**Courtauld Gallery**—Though less impressive than the National Gallery, this wonderful collection of paintings is still a joy. The gallery is part of the Courtauld Institute of Art, and the thoughtful description of each piece of art reminds visitors that the gallery is still used for teaching. You'll see medieval European paintings and works by Rubens, the Impressionists (Manet, Monet, and Degas), Post-Impressionists (such as Cézanne), and more. Besides the permanent collection, a quality selection of loaners and temporary exhibits are often included in the entry fee.

Cost, Hours, Location: £5, free Mon until 14:00, open daily 10:00–18:00, last entry at 17:30; downstairs cafeteria, lockers, and WC; bus #6, #9, #11, #13, #15, or #23 from Trafalgar Square; Tube: Temple or Covent Garden. Tel. 020/7848-1194 or 020/7848-2777, recorded info tel. 020/7848-2526, www.courtauld.ac.uk.

Somerset House: The Courtauld Gallery is located at Somerset House, a grand 18th-century civic palace that offers a marvelous public space (housing temporary exhibits) and a riverside terrace with several eateries (between the Strand and the Thames). The palace once held the national registry that recorded Britain's births, marriages, and deaths: "...where they hatch 'em, match 'em, and dispatch 'em." Step into the courtyard to enjoy the fountain. Go ahead...walk through it. The 55 jets get playful twice an hour. In the winter, this becomes a popular ice-skating rink with a toasty café for viewing (www.somerset-house.org.uk).

Buckingham Palace

There are three palace sights that require admission: the State Rooms, Queen's Gallery, and Royal Mews. You can pay for each separately, or buy a combo-ticket. The combo-ticket for £29.50 admits you to all three sights; a cheaper version for £14.50 covers the Queen's Gallery and Royal Mews. Many tourists are more interested in the Changing of the Guard, which costs nothing at all to view.

▲**State Rooms at Buckingham Palace**—This lavish home has been Britain's royal residence since 1837. When the Queen's at home, the royal standard flies (a red, yellow, and blue flag); otherwise, the Union Jack flaps in the wind. The Queen now opens her palace to the public—but only in August and September, when she's out of town.

Cost, Hours, Location: £16.50 for lavish State Rooms and throne room, includes audioguide, Aug–Sept only, daily 9:45–18:00, last admission 15:45; only 8,000 visitors a day by timed entry; come early to the Palace's Visitor Entrance (opens 9:15) or book ahead in person or by phone or online (£1.25 extra); Tube: Victoria. Tel. 020/7766-7300, www.royalcollection.org.uk.

▲**Queen's Gallery at Buckingham Palace**—Queen Elizabeth's personal collection of art is on display in a wing adjoining the Palace. Her 7,000 paintings make up the finest private art collection in the world, rivaling Europe's biggest national art galleries. It's actually a collection of collections, built on by each successive monarch since the 16th century. She rotates her paintings, enjoying some privately in her many palatial residences while sharing others with her subjects in public galleries in Edinburgh and London. Small, thoughtfully presented, and always exquisite displays fill the handful of rooms open to the public. You're in "the most important building in London," so security is tight. In addition to the permanent collection, you'll see temporary exhibits and a room full of the Queen's personal jewelry. Compared to the crown jewels at the Tower, it may be Her Majesty's bottom drawer—but it's still a dazzling pile of diamonds. Temporary exhibits change about twice a year and are lovingly described by the included audioguide. Though admission tickets come with an entry time, this is only enforced during rare days when crowds are a problem.

Cost, Hours, Location: £8.50, daily 10:00–17:30, last entry one hour before closing, Tube: Victoria. Tel. 020/7766-7301 but Her Majesty rarely answers. Men shouldn't miss the mahogany-trimmed urinals.

Royal Mews—Located to the left of Buckingham Palace, the Queen's working stables, or "mews," are open to visitors. The visit is likely to be disappointing unless you follow the included guided tour, in which case it's thoroughly entertaining—especially if you're interested in horses and/or royalty. The 40-minute tours show off a few of the Queen's 30 horses, a fancy car, and a bunch of old carriages, finishing with the Gold State Coach (c. 1760, 4 tons, 4 mph). Queen Victoria said absolutely no cars. When she died, in 1901, the mews got its first Daimler. Today, along with the hay-eating transport, the stable is home to five Rolls-Royce Phantoms, with one on display.

Cost, Hours, Location: £7.50, April–July and Oct Sat–Thu 11:00–16:00, Aug–Sept 10:00–17:00, last entry 45 min before closing, closed Fri and Nov–March, 2 tours/hr, Buckingham Palace Road, Tube: Victoria. Tel. 020/7766-7302.

▲▲Changing of the Guard at Buckingham Palace—The stone-faced, red-coated, bearskin-hatted guards change posts with much fanfare, in a 40-minute ceremony accompanied by a brass band. It happens at 11:30 daily from May through July, and every other day the rest of the year (no ceremony in very wet weather). The exact schedule is subject to change, so call 020/7766-7300 for the day's plan, or check www.changing-the-guard.com or www.royalcollection.org.uk (click "Visit," then "Changing the Guard"). Then hop into a big black taxi and say, "Buck House, please" (a.k.a. Buckingham Palace).

Most tourists just show up and get lost in the crowds, but those who know the drill will enjoy the event more. The best place to see it is from on the circular Victoria Memorial in front of the Palace. More on that later, but here's the lowdown on what goes down.

It's just after 11:00, and the on-duty guards—actually working at nearby St. James's Palace—are ready to finish their shift. At 11:15, these tired guards, along with the band, head out to the Mall and then take a right turn for Buckingham Palace. Meanwhile, their replacement guards—fresh for the day—gather at 11:00 at their Wellington Barracks, 500 yards east of the palace (on Birdcage Walk), for a review and inspection. At 11:30, they also head for Buckingham Palace. As both the tired and fresh guards converge on the palace, the Horse Guard enters the fray, marching

Buckingham Palace Area

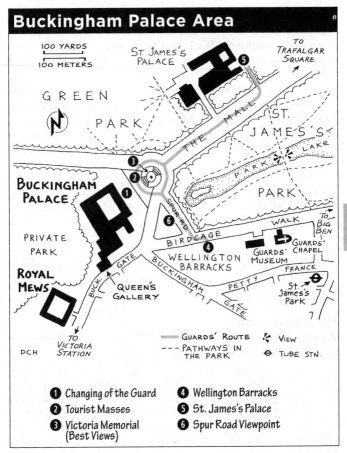

100 YARDS
100 METERS

ST JAMES'S PALACE

TO TRAFALGAR SQUARE

GREEN PARK

THE MALL

ST. JAMES'S PARK

LAKE

BUCKINGHAM PALACE

PRIVATE PARK

ROYAL MEWS

QUEEN'S GALLERY

SPUR RD

BIRDCAGE WALK

WELLINGTON BARRACKS

GUARDS' MUSEUM

GUARDS' CHAPEL

TO BIG BEN

FRANCE

BUCK. GATE

BUCKINGHAM GATE

PETTY

St. James's Park

TO VICTORIA STATION

DCH

━━━ GUARDS' ROUTE
--- PATHWAYS IN THE PARK

↙ VIEW
⊖ TUBE STN.

1 Changing of the Guard
2 Tourist Masses
3 Victoria Memorial (Best Views)
4 Wellington Barracks
5 St. James's Palace
6 Spur Road Viewpoint

LONDON

down the Mall from the Horse Guard Barracks on Whitehall. At 11:45, it's a perfect storm of Red Coat pageantry, as all three groups converge. Everyone parades around, the guard changes (passing the regimental flag, or "color") with much shouting, the band plays a happy little concert, and then they march out. A few minutes later, fresh guards set up at St. James's Palace, the tired ones dress down at the barracks, and the tourists disperse.

So to recap, the event actually takes place in stages over the course of an hour, at several different locations. The main event is in the forecourt right in front of the Palace (between the Palace and the fence) from 11:30 to 12:00. To see it close up, you'll need to get here by no later than 10:30 to get a place right next to the fence.

But there's equal pageantry elsewhere. Get out your map and strategize. You could see the guards mobilizing at Wellington

Barracks or St. James's Palace (11:00–11:30). Or watch them parade with bands down The Mall and Spur Road (11:30). After the ceremony at Buckingham Palace is over (and many tourists have gotten bored and gone home), the parades march back along those same streets (12:10).

Pick one event and find a good, unobstructed place from which to view it. The key is to either get right up front along the road or fence, or find some raised elevation to stand or sit on—a balustrade or a curb—so you can see over people's heads. Don't come without a plan and end up milling around in the mobs and seeing nothing.

For the best overall view, stake out the high ground on the circular Victoria Memorial (come before 11:00 to get a place). From the Memorial, you have good views of the palace as well as the arriving and departing parades along The Mall and Spur Road. The actual changing of the guard in front of the palace is a nonevent. It is interesting, however, to see nearly every tourist in London gathered in one place at the same time. Afterward, stroll through nearby St. James's Park (Tube: Victoria, St. James's Park, or Green Park).

North London

▲▲▲**British Museum**—Simply put, this is the greatest chronicle of civilization...anywhere. A visit here is like taking a long hike

through *Encyclopedia Britannica* National Park. While the vast British Museum wraps around its Great Court (the huge entrance hall), the most popular sections of the museum fill the ground floor: Egyptian, Assyrian, and ancient Greek, with the famous Elgin Marbles from the Athenian Parthenon. The museum's stately Reading Room—famous as the place where Karl Marx hung out while formulating his ideas on communism and writing *Das Kapital*—sometimes hosts special exhibits. From the Great Court,

doorways lead to all wings. Huge winged lions (which guarded an Assyrian palace 800 years before Christ) guard these great galleries. For a brief tour, connect these ancient dots:

Start with the **Egyptian** section. Wander from the Rosetta Stone past the many statues. At the end of the hall, climb the stairs to mummy land.

Back at the winged lions, explore the dark, violent, and mysterious **Assyrian** rooms. The Nimrud Gallery is lined with royal propaganda reliefs and wounded lions (from the ninth century B.C.).

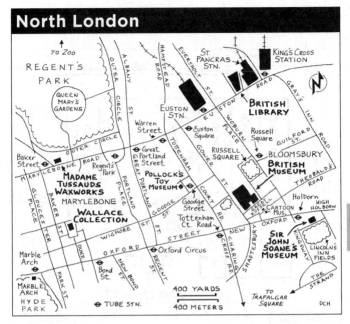

North London

To Zoo

REGENT'S PARK

QUEEN MARY'S GARDENS

OUTER CIRCLE

ALBANY ST.

HAMPSTEAD ROAD

EVERSHOLT ST.

St. PANCRAS STN.

KING'S CROSS STATION

GRAY'S INN ROAD

BRITISH LIBRARY

EUSTON ROAD

EUSTON STN.

Euston Square

WOBURN PLACE

GOWER ST.

Russell Square

RUSSELL SQUARE

GUILFORD ST.

BLOOMSBURY

BRITISH MUSEUM

THEOBALD'S ROAD

Warren Street

MARYLEBONE ROAD

Baker Street

Regent's Park

Great Portland Street

TOTTENHAM COURT ROAD

GREAT PORTLAND ST.

PORTLAND PLACE

MADAME TUSSAUDS WAXWORKS

MARYLEBONE

POLLOCK'S TOY MUSEUM

GOODGE ST.

Goodge Street

COURT RD.

GREAT RUSSELL ST.

Holborn

HIGH HOLBORN

CARTOON MUS.

WALLACE COLLECTION

Tottenham Ct. Road

NEW OXFORD ST.

SIR JOHN SOANE'S MUSEUM

KINGSWAY

LINCOLN'S INN FIELDS

WIGMORE ST.

OXFORD STREET

NEW CHARING CROSS RD.

SHAFTESBURY

GLOUCESTER PLACE

BAKER ST.

DUKE ST.

Marble Arch

OXFORD ST.

Oxford Circus

REGENT ST.

NEW BOND ST.

Bond St.

THE STRAND

PARK ST.

MARBLE ARCH

HYDE PARK

⊖ **TUBE STN.**

400 YARDS

400 METERS

TO TRAFALGAR SQUARE

DCH

N

The most modern of the ancient art fills the **Greek** section. Find Room 11, behind the winged lions, and start your walk through Greek art history with the simple and primitive Cycladic fertility figures. Later, painted vases show a culture really into partying. The finale is the Elgin Marbles. The much-wrangled-over bits of the Athenian Parthenon (from about 450 B.C.) are even more impressive than they look. To best appreciate these ancient carvings, take the audioguide tour (see "Tours," below).

Be sure to venture upstairs to see artifacts from **Roman Britain** (Room 50) that surpass anything you'll see at Hadrian's Wall or elsewhere in Britain. Nearby, the Dark Age Britain exhibits offer a worthwhile peek at that bleak era; look for the Sutton Hoo Burial Ship artifacts from a seventh-century royal burial on the east coast of England (Room 41). A rare Michelangelo cartoon (preliminary sketch) is in Room 90.

Cost, Hours, Location: Museum free but a £3, $5, or €5 donation requested; temporary exhibits extra, daily 10:00–17:30, Thu–Fri until 20:30—but not all galleries open after 17:30, least crowded weekday late afternoons, Great Russell Street, Tube: Tottenham Court Road. Switchboard tel. 020/7323-8000, general info tel. 020/7323-8299, collection questions tel. 020/7323-8838, www.britishmuseum.org.

Tours: The 90-minute Highlights tours, led by licensed guides, are expensive but meaty, giving an introduction to the

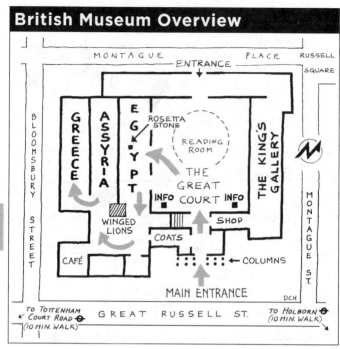

British Museum Overview

(map: MONTAGUE PLACE, RUSSELL SQUARE, ENTRANCE; BLOOMSBURY STREET; GREECE, ASSYRIA, EGYPT; ROSETTA STONE, READING ROOM, THE GREAT COURT, THE KING'S GALLERY; WINGED LIONS, INFO, INFO, SHOP, COATS, CAFÉ, COLUMNS; MONTAGUE ST.; MAIN ENTRANCE; TO TOTTENHAM COURT ROAD (10 MIN. WALK); GREAT RUSSELL ST.; TO HOLBORN (10 MIN. WALK))

LONDON

museum's masterpieces (£8, 90 min, daily at 10:30, 13:00, and 15:00). The free 30-minute eyeOpener tours focus on select rooms (daily 11:00–15:30, generally running every half-hour). There are three audioguide tours: Museum Highlights (90 min) and Parthenon Sculptures (60 min) are both substantial and cerebral, plus there's a fun Family Tour. The cost is £3.50 each or £5.50 for two tours (must leave photo ID).

▲▲▲**British Library**—Here, in just two rooms called "The Treasures of the British Library," are the literary gems of Western civilization, from early Bibles to the Magna Carta to Shakespeare's *Hamlet* to Lewis Carroll's *Alice's Adventures in Wonderland.* You'll see the Lindisfarne Gospels transcribed on an illuminated manuscript, as well as Beatles lyrics scrawled on the back of a greeting card. The British Empire built its greatest monuments out of paper,  and it's with literature that England made her lasting contribution to civilization and the arts.

Cost, Hours, Location: Free but donations appreciated,

British Library Highlights

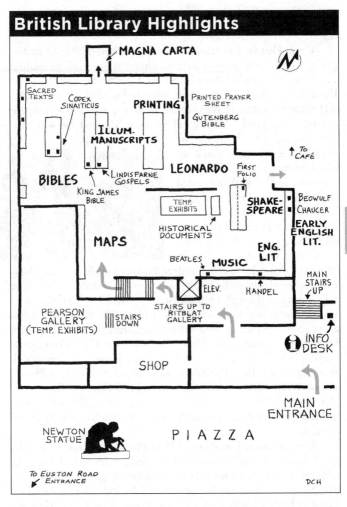

MAGNA CARTA

SACRED TEXTS

CODEX SINAITICUS

PRINTING

PRINTED PRAYER SHEET

GUTENBERG BIBLE

ILLUM. MANUSCRIPTS

To CAFÉ

LEONARDO

FIRST FOLIO

BEOWULF

BIBLES

LINDISFARNE GOSPELS

KING JAMES BIBLE

SHAKE-SPEARE

CHAUCER

EARLY ENGLISH LIT.

TEMP. EXHIBITS

HISTORICAL DOCUMENTS

MAPS

BEATLES

MUSIC

ENG. LIT.

MAIN STAIRS UP

HANDEL

ELEV.

PEARSON GALLERY (TEMP. EXHIBITS)

STAIRS DOWN

STAIRS UP TO RITBLAT GALLERY

INFO DESK

SHOP

MAIN ENTRANCE

NEWTON STATUE

PIAZZA

To EUSTON ROAD ENTRANCE

DCH

temporary exhibits extra, Mon–Fri 9:30–18:00, Tue until 20:00, Sat 9:30–17:00, Sun 11:00–17:00; helpful free computers give you extra info; ground-floor café, self-service cafeteria upstairs; Tube: King's Cross St. Pancras, walk a block west to 96 Euston Road; Euston Tube station is also close; bus #10, #30, #73, #91, #205, or #390. Library tel. 020-7412-7332, www.bl.uk.

▲**Wallace Collection**—Sir Richard Wallace's fine collection of 17th-century Dutch Masters, 18th-century French Rococo, medieval armor, and assorted aristocratic fancies fills the sumptuously furnished Hertford House on Manchester Square. From the rough and intimate Dutch life-scapes of Jan Steen to the pink-cheeked Rococo fantasies of François Boucher, a wander through this little-visited mansion makes you nostalgic for the days of empire.

Cost, Hours, Location: Free, daily 10:00–17:00, £3 audio-guide, free guided tours or lectures almost daily—call to confirm times, just north of Oxford Street on Manchester Square, Tube: Bond Street. Tel. 020/7563-9500, www.wallacecollection.org.

▲**Madame Tussauds Waxworks**—This is gimmicky and expensive but dang good. The original Madame Tussaud did wax casts

of heads lopped off during the French Revolution (such as Marie-Antoinette's). She took her show on the road and ended up in London in 1835. And now it's much easier to be featured. The gallery is one big photo-op—a huge hit with the kind of travelers who skip the British Museum. After looking a hundred famous people in their glassy eyes and surviving a silly hall of horror, you'll board a Disney-type ride and cruise through a kid-pleasing "Spirit of London" time trip. Your last stop is the auditorium for a 12-minute stage show (runs every 15 min). They've dumped anything really historical (except for what they claim is the blade that beheaded Marie-Antoinette) because "there's no money in it and we're a business." Now, it's all about squeezing Brad Pitt's bum, gambling with George Clooney, and partying with Beyoncé, Britney, and Bill Clinton. The unpopular Gordon Brown is the first prime minister in 150 years not to be immortalized in wax—but President Obama has already joined the club.

Cost, Hours, Location: £25 (£20 if purchased from TI), £37 combo-ticket with London Eye, cheaper for kids. Check the website for discounts on this pricey waxtravaganza. From 17:00 to closing, it's £16 if you buy online, £11 for kids (does not include London Eye). Children under 5 are always free. Open Mon–Fri 9:30–17:30, Sat–Sun 9:00–18:00, mid-July–Aug and school holidays daily 9:00–18:00; Marylebone Road, Tube: Baker Street. Toll tel. 08709-990-046, www.madametussauds.com.

Sir John Soane's Museum—Architects, along with fans of interior decor, eclectic knickknacks, and Back Door sights, love this quirky place. Tour this furnished home on a bird-chirping square and see 19th-century chairs, lamps, and carpets, wood-paneled nooks and crannies, and stained-glass skylights. The townhouse is cluttered with Soane's (and his wife's) collection of ancient relics, curios, and famous paintings, including Hogarth's series on *The Rake's Progress* (read the fun plot) and several excellent Canalettos. In 1833, just before his death, Soane established his house as a museum, stipulating that it be kept as nearly as possible in the state he left it. If he visited today, he'd be entirely satisfied. You'll leave wishing you'd known the man.

Cost, Hours, Location: Free but donations much appreciated, Tue–Sat 10:00–17:00, last entry 30 min before closing, first Tue of the month also 18:00–21:00, closed Sun–Mon, long entry lines on Sat and first Tue, good £1 brochure, £5 guided tours Sat at 11:00, 13 Lincoln's Inn Fields, quarter-mile southeast of British Museum, Tube: Holborn. Tel. 020/7405-2107.

LONDON

Cartoon Museum—This humble but interesting museum is located in the shadow of the British Museum. While its three rooms are filled with British cartoons unknown to most Americans, the satire of famous bigwigs and politicians—from Napoleon to Margaret Thatcher, the Queen, and Tony Blair—shows the power of parody to deliver social commentary. Upstairs, you'll see pages spanning from *Tarzan* to *Tank Girl*, *Andy Capp* to the British *Dennis the Menace*—interesting only to comic-book diehards.

Cost, Hours, Location: £5; Tue–Sat 10:30–17:30, Sun 12:00–17:30, closed Mon; 35 Little Russell Street—go one block south of the British Museum on Museum Street and make a right, Tube: Tottenham Court Road. Tel. 020/7580-8155, www.cartoon museum.org.

Pollock's Toy Museum—This rickety old house, with glass cases filled with toys and games lining its walls and halls, is a time-warp experience that brings back childhood memories to people who grew up without batteries or computer chips. Though the museum is small, you could spend a lot of time here, squinting at the fascinating toys and dolls that entertained the children of 19th- and early 20th-century England. The included information is great. The story of Theodore Roosevelt refusing to shoot a bear cub while on a hunting trip was celebrated in 1902 cartoons, resulting in a new, huggable toy: the Teddy Bear. It was popular for good reason—it could be manufactured during World War I without rationed products, it coincided with the new belief that soft toys were good for a child's development, it was an acceptable "doll for boys," and it's *the* toy children keep long after they've grown up.

Cost, Hours, Location: £5, kids-£2, Mon–Sat 10:00–17:00, closed Sun, last entry 30 min before closing, 1 Scala Street, Tube: Goodge Street. Tel. 020/7636-3452, www.pollockstoymuseum .com. Call before you go to make sure it's open.

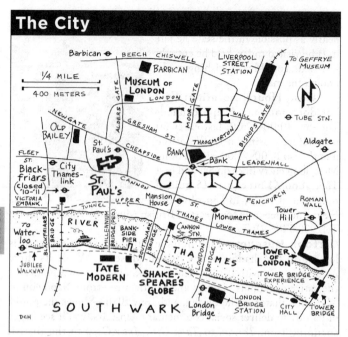

The City

When Londoners say "The City," they mean the one-square-mile business center in East London that 2,000 years ago was Roman Londinium. The outline of the Roman city walls can still be seen in the arc of roads from Blackfriars Bridge to Tower Bridge. Within The City are 23 churches designed by Sir Christopher Wren, mostly just ornamentation around St. Paul's Cathedral. Today, while home to only 5,000 residents, The City thrives with nearly 500,000 office workers coming and going daily. It's a fascinating district to wander on weekdays, but because almost nobody actually lives here, it's dull in the evenings and on Saturday and Sunday.

St. Paul's Cathedral and Nearby

▲▲▲St. Paul's Cathedral—Wren's most famous church is the great St. Paul's, its elaborate interior capped by a 365-foot dome. Since World War II, St. Paul's has been Britain's symbol of resistance. Despite 57 nights of bombing, the Nazis failed to destroy the cathedral, thanks to the St. Paul's volunteer fire watchmen, who stayed on the dome.

St. Paul's is England's national church. There's been a church on this spot since 604. After the Great Fire of 1666 destroyed

St. Paul's Cathedral

TO
St. Paul's ⊖

HIGH
ALTAR

ENTER

NAVE

DOME

CHOIR

BISHOP'S
THRONE

DCH

① Nave
② Wellington Monument
③ Dome
④ Choir & High Altar
⑤ HUNT – The Light of the World
⑥ MOORE – Mother and Child

⑦ American Memorial Chapel
⑧ John Donne Statue
⑨ Nelson & Cornwallis Monuments
⑩ Climb the Dome
   (2 Possible Entrances)
⑪ Crypt Entrance

the old cathedral, Wren created a Baroque masterpiece. Even now, as skyscrapers encroach, the dome of St. Paul's rises majestically above the rooftops of the neighborhood.

Inside, this big church *feels* big. At 515 feet long and 250 feet wide, it's Europe's fourth-largest, after Rome (St. Peter's), Sevilla, and Milan. The spaciousness is accentuated by the relative lack of decoration. The simple, cream-colored ceiling and the clear glass in the windows light everything evenly.

There are many legends buried here: Horatio Nelson, who wore down Napoleon; the Duke of Wellington, who finished Napoleon off; and even Charles Cornwallis, who was finished off by George Washington at Yorktown. Often the site of historic funerals (Queen Victoria and Winston Churchill), St. Paul's most famous ceremony was a wedding—when Prince Charles married Lady Diana Spencer in 1981.

During your visit, you can climb the dome for a great city view and have some fun in the Whispering Gallery. Whisper sweet nothings into the wall, and your partner (and anyone else) standing far away can hear you. For best effects, try whispering (not talking) with your mouth close to the wall, while your partner stands a few dozen yards away with his or her ear to the wall. The crypt (included with admission) is a world of historic bones and interesting cathedral models.

Cost, Hours, Location: £11, includes church entry and dome climb; Mon–Sat 8:30–16:30, last church entry 16:00, last dome entry 16:15, closed Sun except for worship, £3 tours and £4 audioguides, no photography allowed, cheery café and pricier restaurant in crypt, Tube: St. Paul's; bus #4, #11, #15, #23, #26, or #100. Don't head for St. Paul's Church near Covent Garden; your destination is St. Paul's Cathedral, in The City. Recorded info tel. 020/7246-8348, office tel. 020/7236-8350, www.stpauls.co.uk.

Music: The evensong services are free, but nonpaying visitors are not allowed to linger afterward (Mon–Sat at 17:00, Sun at 15:15, 40 min).

▲**Old Bailey**—To view the British legal system inaction—lawyers in little blond wigs speaking legalese with a British accent—spend a few minutes in the visitors' gallery at the Old Bailey, called the "Central Criminal Court." Don't enter under the dome; signs point you to the two visitors' entrances.

Cost, Hours, Location: Free, generally Mon–Fri 10:00–13:00 & 14:00–17:00 depending on caseload, closed Sat–Sun, reduced hours in Aug; no kids under 14; no bags, mobile phones, cameras, or food, but small purses OK; Eddie at Bailey's Café across the street at #30 stores bags for £2; 2 blocks northwest of St. Paul's on Old Bailey Street, follow signs to public entrance, Tube: St. Paul's. Tel. 020/7248-3277.

▲**Museum of London**—London, a 2,000-year-old city, is so littered with ruins that when a London builder finds Roman antiquities, he simply documents the finds, moves the artifacts to a museum, and builds on. If you're asking, "Why did the Romans build their cities underground?" a trip to the creative and entertaining Museum of London is a must.

The museum features London's distinguished citizens through history—from Neanderthals to Romans to Elizabethans to Victorians to Mods to today. The museum's displays are chronological, spacious, and informative without being overwhelming. Scale models and costumes help you visualize everyday life in the city at different periods. There are enough whiz-bang multimedia displays (including the Plague and the Great Fire) to spice up otherwise humdrum artifacts. This regular stop for the local school kids gives the best overview of London history in town.

London's Story at the Museum of London: Here you can walk through London's history from prehistory to the present. First, zip quickly through a half-million years, when Britain morphed from peninsula to island, Neanderthals speared mammoths, and Stone Age humans huddled in crude huts on the South Bank of the Thames.

In 54 B.C., Julius Caesar invaded, and the Romans built "Londinium" on the North Bank. The settlement quickly became the hub of Britain and a river-trade town, complete with arenas, forums, baths, a bridge across the Thames, and a city wall. That wall—arcing from the present Tower of London to St. Paul's—defined the city's boundaries for the next 1,500 years. The Museum of London sits on the northwest perimeter of the city wall, and you can look out the windows to see a crumbling remnant along the street, now called "London Wall."

When Rome could no longer defend the city (A.D. 410), it fell to the Saxons (becoming "Lundenburg") and later, the Normans (in 1066), who built the Tower of London. Medieval London was devastated by the Black Death plague of 1348. As the city recovered and grew even bigger, it became clear to wannabe kings that whoever controlled London controlled Britain.

When Queen Elizabeth I brought peace to the land, London thrived as a capital of theaters (the Globe and Rose), arts, and ideas. Then, just when things were going so well, the city was disintegrated by the Great Fire of 1666, which left London a blank slate.

The exhibits covering 1666 to the present have been closed for years, but they're scheduled to reopen in spring 2010 with great fanfare. You'll see the opulence of rebuilt Georgian London in the Museum's prized possession—the Lord Mayor's Coach, a golden carriage pulled by six white horses that looks right out of Cinderella. Next, stroll through a multimedia "pleasure garden" and take a "Victorian Walk," experiencing what it was like to live in the world's greatest city.

Two world wars and the car changed 20th-century London into a concrete jungle. But it remained a cultural capital of elegance (see an Art Deco elevator from Selfridges) and a global trendsetter (Beatles-era memorabilia).

Finally, displays on the 21st century—including the terrorist bombings of July 7, 2005—weave contemporary London into the tapestry of history.

Cost, Hours, Location: Free, daily 10:00–18:00, until 21:00 first Thu of month, last entry 30 min before closing, Tube: Barbican or St. Paul's plus a five-minute walk, tel. 020/7814-5530, recorded info tel. 020/7001-9844, www.museumoflondon.org.uk.

Tower of London and Nearby

▲▲▲**Tower of London**—The Tower has served as a castle in wartime, a king's residence in peace time, and, most notoriously, as the prison and execution site of rebels. You can see the crown jewels, take a witty Beefeater tour, and ponder the executioner's block that dispensed with Anne Boleyn, Sir Thomas More, and troublesome heirs to the throne.

William I, still getting used to his new title of "the Conqueror," built the stone "White Tower" (1077–1097) to keep the Londoners in line. The Tower also served as an effective lookout for seeing invaders coming up the Thames. His successors enlarged it to its present 18-acre size. Because of the security it provided, it has served over the centuries as the Royal Mint, the Royal Jewel House, and as a prison and execution site.

The Tower's hard stone and glittering jewels represent the ultimate power of the monarch. The crown jewels include the world's largest cut diamond—the 530-carat Star of Africa—placed in the royal scepter. When Queen Elizabeth II opens Parliament, she checks out the Imperial State Crown with its 3,733 jewels, including Elizabeth I's pearl earrings.

You'll find more bloody history per square inch in this original tower of power than anywhere else in Britain, though the actual execution site (in the courtyard) looks just like a lawn. Not all prisoners died at the block—Richard III supposedly ordered two teenage princes strangled in their prison cells because they were a threat to his throne.

Today, while the Tower's military purpose is history, it's still home to the Beefeaters (the 25 Yeoman Warders and their families), who host three million visitors a year. Although these men (and one woman) are no longer expected to protect the monarch, the Beefeaters have evolved into great entertainers, leading groups of tourists through the Tower.

For a refreshingly different Tower experience, come on Sunday mornings, when visitors are welcome on the grounds for free to worship in the Royal Chapel. You get in without the lines, but you can only see the chapel—no sightseeing (9:15 Communion or 11:00 service with fine choral music, meet at west gate 30 minutes early, dress for church).

Cost, Hours, Location: £17, family-£47; audioguide-£4; March–Oct Tue–Sat 9:00–17:30, Sun–Mon 10:00–17:30; Nov–Feb Tue–Sat 9:00–16:30, Sun–Mon 10:00–16:30; last entry 30 min before closing, the long but fast-moving ticket lines are worst on Sun, no photography allowed of jewels, in chapels, or in the White Tower; Tube: Tower Hill. Switchboard toll tel. 0844-482-7777,

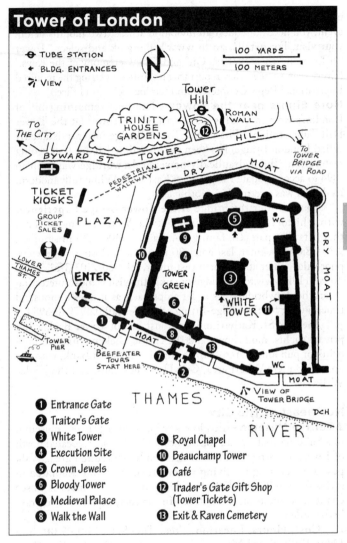

Tower of London

- ☉ TUBE STATION
- ← BLDG. ENTRANCES
- ⭷ VIEW

100 YARDS
100 METERS

1 Entrance Gate
2 Traitor's Gate
3 White Tower
4 Execution Site
5 Crown Jewels
6 Bloody Tower
7 Medieval Palace
8 Walk the Wall
9 Royal Chapel
10 Beauchamp Tower
11 Café
12 Trader's Gate Gift Shop (Tower Tickets)
13 Exit & Raven Cemetery

booking toll tel. 0844-482-7799.

Avoid long lines by buying your ticket online (www.hrp.org .uk), at any London TI, at the Trader's Gate gift shop down the steps from the Tower Hill Tube stop, or at the Welcome Centre to the left of the normal ticket line (credit card only). After your visit, consider taking the boat to Greenwich from here (see cruise info on page 67).

Ceremony of the Keys: This pageantry-filled ceremony is held every night at precisely 21:30, when the Tower of London is locked up (as it has been for the last 700 years). To attend this free 30-minute event, you need to request an invitation at least two months before your visit. For details, go to www.hrp.org.uk and select "Tower Of London," then "What's On" and "The Ceremony of the Keys." (Every year, some readers report that it's difficult getting the required International Reply Coupons from their local US post office.)

More Sights near the Tower—The best remaining bit of London's Roman Wall is just north of the Tower (at the Tower Hill Tube station). The iconic Tower Bridge (often mistakenly called London Bridge) has been freshly painted and is undergoing restoration. The hydraulically powered drawbridge was built in 1894 to accommodate the growing East End. While fully modern, its design was a retro Neo-Gothic look.

You can tour the bridge at the **Tower Bridge Experience,** with a history exhibit and a peek at the Victorian engine room that lifts the span (£6, family £14, daily 10:00–18:30 in summer, 9:30–18:00 in winter, last entry 30 min before closing, good view, poor value, enter at the northwest tower, tel. 020/7403-3761, Tube: Tower Hill, www.towerbridge.org.uk). The visit is most interesting when the drawbridge lifts to let ships pass, as it does a thousand times a year; for the bridge-lifting schedule, call 020/7940-3984.

The chic **St. Katharine Dock,** just east of Tower Bridge, has private yachts, mod shops, and the classic Dickens Inn, fun for a drink or pub lunch. Across the bridge is the South Bank, with the upscale Butlers Wharf area, City Hall, museums, and the Jubilee Walkway.

Northeast of The City

▲**Geffrye Museum**—This low-key but well organized museum, in a building that was an 18th-century almshouse, is located north of Liverpool Street Station in the trendy Shoreditch area. Walk past a dozen English living rooms, furnished and decorated in styles from 1600 to 2000, then descend the circular stairs to see changing exhibits on home decor. In summer, explore the fragrant herb garden.

Cost, Hours, Location: Free, Tue–Sat 10:00–17:00, Sun 12:00–17:00, closed Mon, garden open April–Oct, 136 Kingsland Road, Shoreditch, Tube: Liverpool Street, then 10-min ride north on bus #149 or #242. If you're here after the new Hoxton Tube Station opens in mid-2010, you can take the East London line directly to the museum. Tel. 020/7739-9893, www.geffrye -museum.org.uk.

South Bank

▲**Jubilee Walkway**—The South Bank is a thriving arts and cultural center tied together by this riverside path, a popular, pub-

crawling pedestrian promenade called the Jubilee Walkway. Stretching from Tower Bridge past Westminster Bridge, it offers grand views of the Houses of Parliament and St. Paul's. On a sunny day, this is the place to see London out strolling. The Walkway hugs the river except just east of London Bridge, where it cuts inland for a couple of blocks. Plans are underway to expand the path into a 60-mile "Greenway" encircling the city, scheduled to open in 2012 for the Olympic Games and Elizabeth's 60th year as queen (www.jubileewalkway.org.uk).

▲▲**London Eye**—This giant Ferris wheel, towering above London opposite Big Ben, is the world's highest observational wheel and London's answer to the Eiffel Tower. While the experience is memorable, London doesn't have much of a skyline and the price is borderline outrageous. But whether you ride or not, the wheel is a sight to behold. Designed like a giant bicycle wheel, it's a pan-European under-

taking: British steel and Dutch engineering, with Czech, German, French, and Italian mechanical parts. It's also very "green," running extremely efficiently and virtually silently. You start with a short "pre-flight" exhibit in the ticket hall, then step aboard. Twenty-five people ride in each of its 32 air-conditioned capsules for the 30-minute rotation. Each capsule has a bench, but most people stand. From the top of this 443-foot-high wheel—the highest public viewpoint in the city—even Big Ben looks small. You go around only once. Built to celebrate the new millennium, the Eye's original five-year lease has been extended, and it's becoming a permanent fixture on the London skyline. Thames boats come and go from here using the Waterloo Pier at the foot of the wheel.

Cost, Hours, Location: £17, or £37 combo-ticket with Madame Tussauds Waxworks, £10 extra buys a Fast Track ticket that lets you jump the queue, other packages available. Buy tickets there, in advance by calling 0870-500-0600, or save 10 percent by booking online at www.londoneye.com. Open daily July–Aug 10:00–21:30, June and Sept 10:00–21:00, Oct–May 10:00–20:00, closed Dec 25 and a few days in Jan for annual maintenance, Tube: Waterloo or Westminster.

LONDON

The South Bank

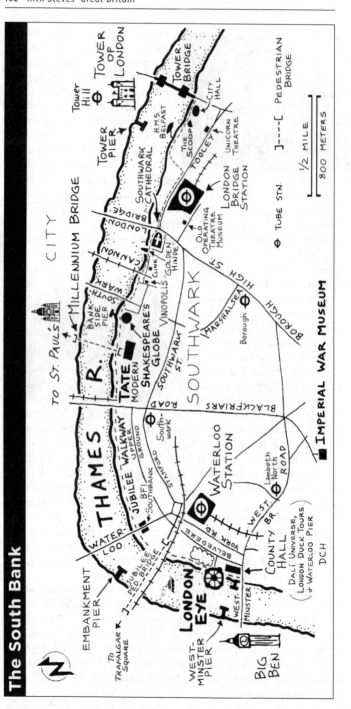

By the Eye: The area next to the London Eye has developed a cotton-candy ambience of kitschy, kid-friendly attractions. There's an aquarium, a game arcade, and a new "Movieum" dedicated to movies filmed in London, from Harry Potter to *Star Wars*. I'd skip the overpriced Dalí Universe (£14.50) of mind-bending art by Salvador Dalí and Picasso.

▲▲**Imperial War Museum**—This impressive museum covers the wars of the last century—from WWI biplanes to the rise of fascism to Monty's Africa campaign tank to the Cold War, the Cuban Missile Crisis, the troubles in Northern Ireland, the wars in Iraq, and terrorism.

The core of the permanent collection, located downstairs, takes you step by step through World Wars I and II. Then you move on to conflicts since 1945. Most of the displays are low-tech—glass cases hold dummies in uniforms, weapons, newspaper clippings, ordinary objects from daily life—but have excellent explanations. Two multimedia experiences hammer home the horrors of war. The Trench Experience lets you walk through a dark, chaotic, smelly WWI trench. The Blitz Experience film assaults the senses with the noise and intensity of a WWII air raid on London. Also, the cinema shows a rotating selection of films.

In the entry hall are the large exhibits—including Montgomery's tank, several field guns, and, dangling overhead, vintage planes. Imagine the awesome power of the 50-foot V-2 rocket, the kind the Nazis rained down on London, which could arrive silently and destroy a city block. Its direct descendant is the Polaris missile, capable of traveling nearly 3,000 miles in 20 minutes and obliterating an entire city.

Besides exhibits on the world wars, the museum has several other permanent sections. The "Secret War" peeks into the intrigues of espionage in World Wars I and II. The section on the Holocaust is one of the best on the subject anywhere, and there are always several temporary exhibitions that are top-notch.

War wonks will love the place, as will general history buffs who enjoy patiently reading displays. For the rest, there are enough multimedia exhibits and submarines for the kids to climb in to keep it interesting.

Rather than glorify war, the museum does its best to shine a light on the 100 million deaths of the 20th century. It shows everyday life for people back home and never neglects the powerful human side of one of humankind's most persistent traits.

Cost, Hours, Location: Free, daily 10:00–18:00, temporary exhibits extra, often guided tours on weekends—ask at info desk, £4 audioguide, Tube: Lambeth North or bus #12 or bus #159. Tel. 020/7416-5000, www.iwm.org.uk.

LONDON

The museum is housed in what was the Royal Bethlam Hospital. Also known as "the Bedlam asylum," the place was so wild it gave the world a new word for chaos. Back in Victorian times, locals—without reality shows and YouTube—paid admission to visit the asylum on weekends for entertainment.

▲▲**Tate Modern**—Dedicated in the spring of 2000, the striking museum across the river from St. Paul's opened the new century with art from the old one. Its powerhouse collection of Monet, Matisse, Dalí, Picasso, Warhol, and much more is displayed in a converted powerhouse. Of equal interest are the many temporary exhibits featuring cutting-edge art. Each year, the main hall features a different monumental installation by a prominent artist.

Cost, Hours, Location: Free but £3 donations appreciated, fee for special exhibitions, daily 10:00–18:00, Fri–Sat until 22:00—a good time to visit, last entry 45 min before closing, audioguide-£2, children's audioguide-£1; free guided tours at 11:00, 12:00, 14:00, and 15:00—confirm at info desk; view restaurant on top floor; cross the Millennium Bridge from St. Paul's; Tube: Southwark, London Bridge or Mansion House plus a 10–15-min walk; or connect by Tate Boat ferry from Tate Britain for £5 one-way, discounted with Travelcard. Switchboard tel. 020/7887-8888, recorded info tel. 020/7887-8008, www.tate.org.uk.

▲**Millennium Bridge**—The pedestrian bridge links St. Paul's Cathedral and the Tate Modern across the Thames. This is London's first new bridge in a century. When

it first opened, the $25 million bridge wiggled when people walked on it, so it promptly closed for an $8 million, 20-month stabilization; now it's stable and open again (free). Nicknamed the "blade of light" for its sleek minimalist design (370 yards long, four yards wide, stainless steel with teak planks), its clever aerodynamic handrails deflect wind over the heads of pedestrians.

▲▲**Shakespeare's Globe**—This replica of the original Globe Theatre was built, half-timbered and thatched, as it was in

Shakespeare's time. (This is the first thatched roof in London since they were outlawed after the Great Fire of 1666.) The Globe originally accommodated 2,200 seated and another 1,000 standing. Today, slightly smaller and leaving space for reasonable aisles, the theater holds 800 seated and 600

Crossing the Thames on Foot

You can cross the Thames on any of the bridges that carry car traffic over the river, but London's two pedestrian bridges are more fun. The Millennium Bridge connects the sedate St. Paul's Cathedral with the great Tate Modern. The Golden Jubilee Bridge, well-lit with a sleek, futuristic look, links bustling Trafalgar Square on the North Bank with the London Eye and Waterloo Station on the South Bank.

groundlings. Its promoters brag that the theater melds "the three A's"—actors, audience, and architecture—with each contributing to the play. The working theater hosts authentic performances of Shakespeare's plays with actors in period costumes, modern interpretations of his works, and some works by other playwrights (generally all summer at 14:00 and 19:30—but confirm). For details on seeing a play, see page 123.

The complex has three parts: the theater itself, the box office, and the "Globe Exhibition" museum. The **Globe Exhibition** ticket (£10.50) includes both a tour of the theater and the museum. First, you browse on your own through displays of Elizabethan-era costumes, music, script-printing, and special effects. There are early folios and objects that were dug up on the site. A video and scale models help put Shakespearean theater within the context of the times. (The Globe opened one year after England mastered the seas by defeating the Spanish Armada. The debut play was Shakespeare's Julius Caesar.)

Next comes the tour of the theater—you must take the tour at the time stamped on your ticket, but you can come back to the museum afterward; tickets are good all day. The guide (usually an actor) leads you into the theater to see the stage and the different seating areas for the different classes of people. You take a seat and learn how the new Globe is similar to the old Globe (open-air performances, standing-room by the stage, no curtain) and how it's different (female actors today, lights for night performances, concrete floor). It's not a backstage tour—you don't see dressing rooms or costume shops or sit in on rehearsals, though you may see workers building sets for a new production. You mostly sit and listen. The guides are energetic, theatrical, and knowledgeable, bringing the Elizabethan period to life. You can't tour the theater during a live performance, but you can see the museum, then tour the nearby (and less interesting) Rose Theatre instead.

Cost, Hours, Location: £10.50 includes museum and one-hour tour, £7.50 on Rose Theater days; tickets good all day; complex open daily 9:00–17:00; Exhibition and tours May–Sept 9:00–17:00—Globe tours offered mornings only in summer with Rose tours in afternoon, Oct–April daily 10:00–17:00—Globe tours run all day in winter; tours go every 15–30 min; on the South Bank directly across Thames over Southwark Bridge from St. Paul's, Tube: Mansion House or London Bridge plus a 10-min walk. Tel. 020/7902-1400 or 020/7902-1500, www.shakespeares -globe.org.

The Swan at the Globe café is open daily (11:00–1:00 in the morning, tel. 020/7928-9444).

Southwark

The next several sights are in Southwark, on the South Bank. The area stretching from the Tate Modern to London Bridge, known as Southwark (SUTH-uck), was for centuries the place Londoners would go to escape the rules and decency of the city and let their hair down. Bearbaiting, brothels, rollicking pubs, and theater—you name the dream, and it could be fulfilled just across the Thames. A run-down warehouse district through the 20th century, it's been gentrified with classy restaurants, office parks, pedestrian promenades, major sights (such as the Tate Modern and Shakespeare's Globe—described earlier), and this colorful collection of lesser sights. The area is easy on foot and a scenic—though circuitous— way to connect the Tower of London with St. Paul's.

Vinopolis: City of Wine—While it seems illogical to have a huge wine museum in beer-loving London, Vinopolis makes a good case. Built over a Roman wine store and filling the massive vaults of an old wine warehouse, the museum offers an excellent audioguide with a light yet earnest history of wine to accompany your sips of various mediocre reds and whites, ports, and champagnes. Allow some time, as the audioguide takes 90 minutes—and the sipping can slow things down pleasantly. This place is popular. Booking ahead for Friday and Saturday nights is a must.

Cost, Hours, Location: Various tour options range from £25 to £75 (save 20 percent by booking online at www.vinopolis.co.uk). Each includes about five wine tastes and an audioguide. Some packages also include whiskey (the new wine), other spirits, or a meal (Thu–Fri 12:00–22:00, Sat 11:00–22:00, Sun 12:00–18:00, closed Mon–Wed, last entry 2.5 hours before closing, between the Globe and Southwark Cathedral at 1 Bank End, Tube: London Bridge. Tel. 020/7940-8300 or toll tel. 0870-241-4040.

The Clink Prison Museum—Proudly the "original clink," this was, until 1780, where law-abiding citizens threw Southwark troublemakers. Today, it's a low-tech torture museum filling grotty old rooms with papier-mâché gore. Unfortunately, there's little that seriously deals with the fascinating problem of law and order in Southwark, where 18th-century Londoners went for a good time.

Cost, Hours, Location: Overpriced at £5, Mon–Fri 10:00–18:00, Sat–Sun until 21:00, 1 Clink Street, Tube: London Bridge. Tel. 020/7403-0900, www.clink.co.uk. Call before you come to make sure they're open.

Golden Hinde Replica—This is a full-size replica of the 16th-century warship in which Sir Francis Drake circumnavigated the globe from 1577 to 1580. Commanding this ship, Drake earned the reputation as history's most successful pirate. The original is long gone, but this boat has logged more than 100,000 miles, including a voyage around the world. The ship is fun to see, but its interior is not worth touring.

Cost, Hours, Location: £7, Mon–Sat 10:00–17:30, Sun 10:30–17:00, may be closed if rented out for pirate birthday parties, school groups, or weddings, Tube: London Bridge. Tel. 020/7403-0123, www.goldenhinde.org.

Southwark Cathedral—While made a cathedral only in 1905, it's been the neighborhood church since the 13th century, and comes with some interesting history. The enthusiastic docents give impromptu tours if you ask.

Cost, Hours, Location: Free but £4 suggested donation, daily 10:00–18:00, last entry 30 min before closing, £2.50 audio-guide, £2.50 guidebook, no photos without permission, Tube: London Bridge. Tel. 020/7367-6700, http://cathedral.southwark.anglican.org.

Music: The cathedral hosts evensong services (weekdays at 17:30, Sat at 16:00, Sun at 15:00, no service on Wed or alternate Mon).

▲**Old Operating Theatre Museum and Herb Garret**—Climb a tight and creaky wooden spiral staircase to a church attic, where you'll find a garret used to dry medicinal herbs, a fascinating exhibit on Victorian surgery, cases of well-described 19th-century medical paraphernalia, and a special look at "anesthesia, the defeat of pain." Then you stumble upon Britain's oldest operating theater, where limbs were sawed off way back in 1821.

Cost, Hours, Location: £5.60, daily 10:30–17:00, closed Dec 15–Jan 5, 9a St. Thomas Street, Tube: London Bridge. Tel. 020/7188-2679, www.thegarret.org.uk.

Near the Tower Bridge

HMS Belfast—"The last big-gun armored warship of World War II" clogs the Thames just upstream from the Tower Bridge. This huge vessel—now manned with wax sailors—thrills kids who always dreamed of sitting in a turret shooting off their imaginary guns. If you're into WWII warships, this is the ultimate. Otherwise, it's just lots of exercise with a nice view of Tower Bridge.

Cost, Hours, Location: £10.70, daily March–Oct 10:00–18:00, Nov–Feb 10:00–17:00, last entry one hour before closing, Tube: London Bridge. Tel. 020/7940-6300, www.hmsbelfast.iwm.org.uk.

City Hall—The glassy, egg-shaped building near the south end of Tower Bridge is London's City Hall, designed by Sir Norman Foster, the architect who worked on London's Millennium Bridge and Berlin's Reichstag. City Hall is where London's mayor works, the blonde, flamboyant, conservative, former journalist and author Boris Johnson. He consults here with the Assembly representatives of the city's 25 districts. An interior spiral ramp allows visitors to watch and hear the action below in the Assembly Chamber—ride the lift to the second floor (the highest visitors can go) and spiral down. On the lower ground floor is a large aerial photograph of London, an information desk, and a handy cafeteria. Next to City Hall is the outdoor amphitheatre called The Scoop.

Cost, Hours, Location: City Hall is open to visitors Mon–Fri 8:00–17:30, Tube: London Bridge station plus 10-min walk, or Tower Hill station plus 15-min walk. Tel. 020/7983-4000, www.london.gov.uk/gla/city_hall.

West London

▲▲Tate Britain—The world's best collection of British art, Tate Britain specializes in works from the 16th century through modern times. This is everyday art, with realistic paintings rooted in the people, landscape, and stories of the British Isles. You'll see Hogarth's stage sets, Gainsborough's ladies, Blake's angels, Constable's clouds, Turner's tempests, the swooning realism of the Pre-Raphaelites, and the camera-eye portraits of Hockney and Freud. What you won't see here are the fleshy goddesses, naked cherubs, and Madonna-and-child altarpieces so popular elsewhere in Europe. The largely Protestant English abhorred the "graven images" of the wealthy Catholic world.

The collection is constantly in motion, but the basic layout stays the same: a roughly chronological walk through British paintings from 1500 to 1901 in the west half of the building, the 20th century in the east, and the swirling works of J. M. W. Turner in the adjoining Clore Gallery.

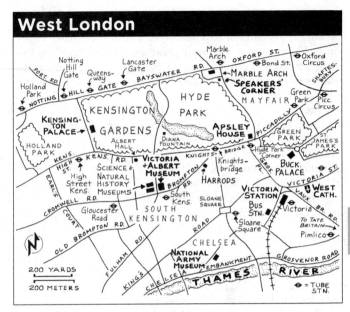

West London

Cost, Hours, Location: Free, £2 donation requested, temporary exhibits extra, daily 10:00–17:50, first Fri of the month until 21:40, last entry 50 min before closing, fine and necessary £3.50 audioguide; free tours: Mon–Fri at 11:00 on art from 1500 to 1800, 12:00 on art from 1800 to 1900, 14:00 on Turner, and 15:00 on art from the 20th century; Sat–Sun tours at 12:00 and 15:00 on collection highlights; call to confirm schedule, kids' activities on weekends; no photography allowed without advance permission, café and restaurant; Tube: Pimlico, then 7-min walk; or arrive directly at museum by taking the Tate Boat ferry from Tate Modern; or take bus #87 from National Gallery or bus #88 from Oxford Circus. Recorded info tel. 020/7887-8008, switchboard tel. 020/7887-8888, www.tate.org.uk.

▲**Apsley House (Wellington Museum)**—Having beaten Napoleon at Waterloo, Arthur Wellesley, the First Duke of Wellington, was once the most famous man in Europe. He was given London's ultimate address, #1 London. His newly refurbished mansion offers a nice interior, a handful of world-class paintings, and a glimpse at the life of the great soldier and two-time prime minister. Those who know something about Wellington ahead of time will appreciate the place much more than those who don't, as there's scarce biographical background.

An 11-foot-tall marble statue of Napoleon, clad only in a fig leaf, greets you. Napoleon commissioned the sculptor Canova to make it for him but didn't like it, and after Napoleon's defeat, it was eventually sold to Wellington as a war trophy. It's one of several images Wellington acquired of his former foe to have in his home. The two great men were polar opposites—Napoleon the daring general and champion of revolution, Wellington the play-it-safe strategist and conservative politician—but they're forever linked in history.

The core of the collection is a dozen first-floor rooms decorated with fancy wallpaper, chandeliers, a few pieces of furniture, and wall-to-wall paintings from Wellington's collection. You'll see fancy dinnerware and precious objects given to the Irish-born general by the crowned heads of Europe, who were eternally grateful to him for saving their necks from the guillotine. The highlight is the large ballroom, the Waterloo Gallery, decorated with Van Dyck's *Charles I on Horseback* (over the main fireplace), Velazquez's earthy *The Water-Seller of Seville* (to the left of Van Dyck), Jan Steen's playful *The Dissolute Household* (to the right), and a large portrait of Wellington by Goya (farther right).

Downstairs is a small gallery of Wellington memorabilia, including a pair of Wellington boots, which the duke popularized—Brits today still call rubber boots "wellies."

Cost, Hours, Location: £5.70, free on June 18—Waterloo Day, Wed–Sun 11:00–17:00 April–Oct, until 16:00 Nov–March, closed Mon–Tue, well-described by included audioguide which has sound bites from the current Duke of Wellington who still lives at Apsley, 20 yards from Hyde Park Corner Tube station. Tel. 020/7499-5676, www.english-heritage.org.uk. Hyde Park's pleasant and picnic-wonderful rose garden is nearby.

▲**Hyde Park and Speakers' Corner**—London's "Central Park," originally Henry VIII's hunting grounds, has more than 600 acres of lush greenery, the huge man-made Serpentine Lake, the royal Kensington Palace and Orangery, and the ornate neo-Gothic Albert Memorial across from the Royal Albert Hall. The western half of the park is known as Kensington Gardens. On Sundays from just after noon until early evening, Speakers'

Corner offers soapbox oratory at its best (northeast corner of the park, Tube: Marble Arch). Characters climb their stepladders, wave their flags, pound emphatically on their sandwich boards, and share what they are convinced is their wisdom. Regulars have resident hecklers—who know their lines and are always ready with a verbal jab or barb. "The grass roots of democracy" is actually a holdover from when the gallows stood here and the criminal was allowed to say just about anything he wanted to before he swung. I dare you to raise your voice and gather a crowd—it's easy to do.

The **Princess Diana Memorial Fountain** honors the "People's Princess" who once lived in nearby Kensington Palace. The low-key circular stream, great for cooling off your feet on a hot day, is in the south central part of the park, near the Albert Memorial and Serpentine Gallery. (Don't be confused

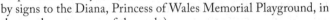

by signs to the Diana, Princess of Wales Memorial Playground, in the northwest corner of the park.)

▲▲**Victoria and Albert Museum**—The world's top collection of decorative arts (vases, stained glass, fine furniture, clothing, jewelry, carpets, and more) is a surprisingly interesting assortment of crafts from the West, as well as Asian and Islamic cultures. The V&A grew out of the Great Exhibition of 1851, that ultimate celebration of the Industrial Revolution. Now "art" could be brought to the masses through modern technology and mass production. The museum was founded on the idealistic Victorian notion that anyone can be continually improved by education and example. After much support from Queen Victoria and Prince Albert, the museum was renamed for the royal couple, and its present building was opened in 1909.

In 2004, the V&A received several grants for refurbishment projects to take place over the next 10 years. Changes so far include a new café, renovated sculpture gallery, and reopened Islamic room. The refurbished Medieval and Renaissance galleries reopen in late 2009. During this chaotic time, exhibits will likely be rearranged, so check with the information desk for current room closures, carry a copy of the museum's detailed map, and ask a nearby guard if you can't find one of the objects.

Many visitors start with the **British Galleries** (upstairs)—a one-way tour stretching through 400 years of high-class British lifestyles, almost a museum in itself.

In Room 46A are the plaster casts of **Trajan's Column,** a copy

of Rome's 140-foot spiral relief telling the story of the conquest of Romania. (The V&A's casts are copies made for the benefit of 19th-century art students who couldn't afford a railpass.)

Room 46B, which has plaster casts of **Renaissance sculptures,** may be closed until 2010 (if so, you can peek down into it from the upper mezzanine). Compare Michelangelo's monumental David with Donatello's girlish David, and see Ghiberti's bronze Baptistery doors.

In Room 48A are **Raphael's "cartoons,"** seven of the full-size designs by Raphael that were used to produce tapestries for the Sistine Chapel (approximately 13' x 17', done in tempera on paper, now mounted on canvas). The cartoons were sent to factories in Brussels, cut into strips (see the lines), and placed on the looms. The scenes are the reverse of the final product—lots of left-handed saints.

The museum is large and gangly, with 150 rooms and more than 12 miles of corridors. Just wandering works well here, but also consider catching one of the free one-hour orientation tours or buying the fine £5 *V&A Guide Book*.

Cost, Hours, Location: Free, £3 donation requested, possible pricey fee for special exhibits, daily 10:00–17:45, Fri until 22:00; free 60-min tours daily on the half-hour from 10:30–15:30; Tube: South Kensington, a long tunnel leads directly from the Tube station to museum. Tel. 020/7942-2000, www.vam.ac.uk.

▲**Natural History Museum**—Across the street from Victoria and Albert, this mammoth museum is housed in a giant, wonderful Victorian, Neo-Romanesque building. Built in the 1870s specifically for the huge collection (50 million specimens), it has two halves: the Life Galleries (creepy-crawlies, human biology, "our place in evolution," and awesome dinosaurs) and the Earth Galleries (meteors, volcanoes, earthquakes, and so on). Exhibits are wonderfully explained, with lots of creative, interactive displays. Pop in, if only for the wild collection of dinosaurs and the roaring *Tyrannosaurus rex*.

Cost, Hours, Location: Free, fees for special exhibits, daily 10:00–17:50, last entry at 17:30, occasional tours, a long tunnel leads directly from South Kensington Tube station to museum. Tel. 020/7942-5000, www.nhm.ac.uk.

▲**Science Museum**—Next door to the Natural History Museum, this sprawling wonderland for curious minds is kid-perfect. It offers hands-on fun, from moonwalks to deep-sea exploration, with trendy technology exhibits, an IMAX theater (£8, kids-£6.25), and cool rotating themed exhibits, including "Cosmos and Culture: How Astronomy Has Shaped Our World," on display through 2010.

Cost, Hours, Location: Free entry, daily 10:00–18:00, Exhibition Road, Tube: South Kensington. Toll tel. 0870-870-4868, www.sciencemuseum.org.uk.

▲▲**Kensington Palace**—In 1689, King William and Queen Mary moved from Whitehall in central London to the more pristine and peaceful village of Kensington (now engulfed by London).

Sir Christopher Wren renovated an existing house into Kensington Palace, which became the center of English court life until 1760, when the royal family moved into Buckingham Palace. Since then, lesser royals have bedded down in Kensington Palace. Princess Diana lived here from her 1981 marriage to Prince Charles until her death in 1997. Today it's home to three of Charles' cousins and to employees of the royal family. The palace, while still functioning as a royal residence, also welcomes visitors with an impressive string of royal apartments and a few rooms of royal dresses. Enjoy a re-created royal tailor and dressmaker's workshop, the 17th-century splendor of the apartments of William and Mary, and the bed where Queen Victoria was born—fully clothed, it is said.

Cost, Hours, Location: £12.50, includes excellent audio-guide, daily 10:00–18:00, until 17:00 in winter, last entry one hour before closing, a 10-min hike through Kensington Gardens from either Queensway or High Street Kensington Tube station. Toll tel. 0870-751-5170 or 0844-482-7777, www.hrp.org.uk.

Nearby: Garden enthusiasts enjoy popping into the secluded Sunken Garden, 50 yards from the exit. Consider afternoon tea at the nearby Orangery (see page 154), built as a greenhouse for Queen Anne in 1704.

Victoria Station—From underneath this station's iron-and-glass canopy, trains depart for the south of England and Gatwick Airport. And though Victoria Station is famous and a major Tube stop, few tourists actually take trains from here—most just come to take in the exciting bustle. It's a fun place to just be a "rock in a river" teeming with commuters and services. The station is surrounded by big red buses and taxis, travel agencies, and lousy eateries. It's next to the main bus station (National Express) and the best inexpensive lodgings in town.

Westminster Cathedral—This, the largest Catholic church in England, just a block from Victoria Station, is striking, but not very historic or important to visit. Opened in 1903, it has a brick neo-Byzantine flavor (surrounded by glassy office blocks). While it's definitely not Westminster Abbey, half the tourists wandering around inside seem to think it is. The highlight is the lift to the viewing gallery atop its 273-foot bell tower (£3 for the lift, tower open daily 9:30–12:30 & 13:00–17:00 in summer, Thu–Sat 9:00–17:00 in winter).

Cost, Hours, Location: Free entry, daily 7:00–19:00; 5-min walk from Victoria Station or take bus #11, #24, #148, #211, or #507 to museum's door; just off Victoria Street, Tube: Victoria, www.westminstercathedral.org.uk.

National Army Museum—This museum is not as awe-inspiring as the Imperial War Museum, but it's still fun, especially for kids into soldiers, armor, and guns. And while the Imperial War

Museum is limited to wars of the 20th century, this tells the story of the British Army from 1415 through the Bosnian conflict and Iraq, with lots of Redcoat lore and a good look at Waterloo. Kids enjoy trying on a Cromwellian helmet, seeing the skeleton of Napoleon's horse, and peering out from a WWI trench through a working periscope.

Cost, Hours, Location: Free, daily 10:00–17:30, Royal Hospital Road, Chelsea, Tube: Sloane Square. Tel. 020/7730-0717 or 020/7881-2455, www.national-army-museum.ac.uk.

East London

The Docklands are easy to combine with an excursion to Greenwich; you can catch a boat (or the Tube) to Greenwich, then stop by the Docklands on the way back in the afternoon, when it's especially lively at the end of the workday.

▲▲**The Docklands**—Survey the skyline or notice the emergence of an entire new Tube network, and it becomes clear that London is shifting east. This vibrant city center will become even more important in the near future, as it will host several events during the 2012 Olympics. The heart of this new London is the Docklands, filling the Isle of Dogs—a peninsula created by a hairpin bend in the Thames—with gleaming skyscrapers springing out of a futuristic, modern art–filled people zone below.

By the late 1700s, 13,000 ships a year were loaded and unloaded in London, congesting the Thames. In 1802 the world's largest-of-its-kind harbor was built here in the Docklands, organizing shipping for the capital of the empire upon which the sun never set. When Britannia ruled the waves, the Isle of Dogs hosted the world's leading harbor. But with the advent of container shipping in the 1960s, London's shipping industry moved to deep-water ports. The Docklands became a derelict and dangerous wasteland—the perfect place to host a new, vibrant economic center. Over the past few decades, Britain's new Information Age industries—banking, finance, publishing, and media—have vacated downtown London and set up shop here.

Those 1802 West India warehouses survive, but rather than trading sugar and rum, today they house the Museum of London Docklands (described later) and a row of happening restaurants. And where sailors once drank grog while stevedores unloaded cargo, today thousands of office workers populate a forest of skyscrapers, towering high above the remnants of the Industrial Age. If you simply stroll around, you'll find this one of the most exciting hours of free entertainment London has to offer. This is today's London—and there's not a tourist in sight.

The Tube and Docklands Light Railway stations are awe-inspiring. Explore sprawling underground malls and delightfully peaceful, green parks with pedestrian bridges looping over the now-tranquil canals. Though you can't get up the skyscrapers, the ground-floor levels are welcoming with fun art. Photographers can't help but catch jumbo jets gliding past gleaming towers, goofy pose-with-me statues, and trendy pubs filled with trendier young professionals. Jubilee Park is an oasis of green in this Manhattan of Britain.

The Canary Wharf Tower (with its pyramid cap), once the tallest in Europe, remains the tallest in the UK—for now. Like its little sister skyscrapers, owned by HSBC (Hong Kong Shanghai Banking Corporation) and Citigroup, it's filled with big banks, finance, and media companies. The stubby building just to one side, occupied by an American bank, is a painfully truthful metaphor.

This pedestrian-friendly district is well-served by signs. Follow them over the pedestrian bridge to the **Museum of London Docklands,** which tells the story of the world's leading 19th-century port (£5, daily 10:00–18:00, last entry 30 min before closing, West India Quay, Canary Wharf, tel. 020/7001-9844, www.museumindocklands.org.uk). Between the bridge and the museum is a line of fun, mod eateries (£10 main courses, huge variety of cuisines).

Getting There: Ride the Tube's Jubilee Line (just 15 min from Westminster, frequent departures) to its Canary Wharf stop, or take the Docklands Light Railway from Bank to Canary Wharf (this makes a good stop en route to or from Greenwich). At Canary Wharf, the Jubilee Line station and DLR station are a short walk apart.

Greater London

To locate the following sights, see the map on page 47.

▲▲**Kew Gardens**—For a fine riverside park and a palatial greenhouse jungle to swing through, take the Tube or the boat to every

botanist's favorite escape, Kew Gardens. While to most visitors the Royal Botanic Gardens of Kew are simply a delightful opportunity to wander among 33,000 different types of plants, to the hardworking organization that runs the gardens, it's a way to promote understanding and preservation of the botanical diversity of our planet. The Kew Tube station drops you in an herbal little business community, a two-block walk from Victoria Gate (the main garden entrance). Pick up a map brochure and check at the gate for a monthly listing of best blooms.

Garden-lovers could spend days exploring Kew's 300 acres. For a quick visit, spend a fragrant hour wandering through three buildings: the **Palm House,** a humid Victorian world of iron, glass, and tropical plants built in 1844; a **Waterlily House** that Monet would swim for; and the **Princess of Wales Conservatory,** a modern greenhouse with many different climate zones growing countless cacti, bug-munching carnivorous plants, and more. The latest addition to the gardens is the **Rhizotron and Xstrata Treetop Walkway,** a 200-yard-long scenic steel walkway that puts you high in the canopy 60 feet above the ground.

Cost, Hours, Location: £13, discounted to £11 45 min before closing, kids under 17 free, £5 for Kew Palace only; April–Aug Mon–Fri 9:30–18:30, Sat–Sun 9:30–19:30; closes earlier Sept–March, last entry to gardens 30 min before closing, galleries and conservatories close at 17:30 in high season—earlier off-season, free 60-min walking tours daily at 11:00 and 14:00, £4 narrated floral 40-min hop-on, hop-off joyride on little tram departs on the hour from 11:00 from near Victoria Gate, Tube: Kew Gardens, boats run April–Oct between Kew Gardens and Westminster Pier—see page 68. Switchboard tel. 020/8332-5000, recorded info tel. 020/8332-5655, www.kew.org.

Nearby: For a sun-dappled lunch, walk 10 minutes from the Palm House to the Orangery (£6 hot meals, daily 10:00–17:30).

▲**Hampton Court Palace**—Fifteen miles up the Thames from downtown (£15 taxi ride from Kew Gardens) is the 500-year-old palace of Henry VIII. Actually, it was the palace of his minister, Cardinal Wolsey. When Wolsey, a clever man, realized Henry VIII was experiencing a little palace envy, he gave the mansion to his king. The Tudor palace was also home to Elizabeth I and Charles I. Sections were updated by Christopher Wren for William and Mary. The stately palace stands overlooking the Thames and includes some impressive Tudor rooms, including a Great Hall with a magnificent hammer-beam ceiling. The industrial-strength Tudor kitchen was capable of keeping 600 schmoozing courtiers thoroughly—if not well—fed. The sculpted garden features a rare Tudor tennis court and a popular maze.

The palace, fully restored after a 1986 fire, tries hard to please, but it doesn't quite sparkle. From the information center in the main courtyard pick up audioguides for self-guided tours of various wings of the palace (free). The Tudor kitchens, Henry VIII's apartments, and the King's apartments are most interesting. The

Georgian rooms are pretty dull. The maze in the nearby garden is a curiosity some find fun (maze free with palace ticket, otherwise £3.50).

Cost and Hours: The palace costs £14, or £38 for families; daily April–Oct 10:00–18:00, Nov–March 10:00–16:30, last entry one hour before closing. Toll tel. 0870-751-5175, recorded info toll tel. 0870-752-7777, www.hrp.org.uk.

Getting There: The train (2/hr, 30 min) from London's Waterloo station drops you across the river from the palace (just walk across the bridge). Note that there are often discounts available for people riding the train from London to the palace. Check online or at the ticket office at Waterloo station for the latest offers.

Consider arriving at or departing from the palace by boat (connections with London's Westminster Pier, see page 68); it's a relaxing and scenic three-hour cruise past two locks and a fun mix of old and new riverside.

Royal Air Force Museum London—A hit with aviation enthusiasts, this huge aerodrome and airfield contain planes from World War II's Battle of Britain up through the Gulf War. You can climb inside some of the planes, try your luck in a cockpit, and fly with the Red Arrows in a flight simulator.

Cost, Hours, Location: Free, daily 10:00–18:00, last entry 30 min earlier, café, shop, parking, Grahame Park Way, Tube: Colindale—top of Northern Line Edgware branch. Tel. 020/8205-2266, www.rafmuseum.org.uk.

Shopping in London

Harrods—Harrods is London's most famous and touristy department store. With more than four acres of retail space covering seven floors, it's a place where some shoppers could spend all day. (To me, it's still just a department store.) Big yet classy, Harrods has everything from elephants to toothbrushes (Mon–Sat 10:00–20:00, Sun 12:00–18:00, mandatory storage for big backpacks-£3, no shorts or flip-flops, on Brompton Road, Tube: Knightsbridge, tel. 020/7730-1234, www.harrods.com).

Sightseers should pick up the free *Store Guide* at any info post. Here's what I enjoy: On the ground floor, find the Food Halls, with their Edwardian tiled walls, creative and exuberant displays, and staff in period costumes—not quite like your local supermarket back home.

Descend to the lower ground floor and follow signs to the Egyptian Escalator (in the center of the store), where you'll find a memorial to Dodi Fayed and Princess Diana. Photos and flowers honor the late princess and her lover, who both died in a car crash in Paris in 1997. Inside a small, clear pyramid, you can see a wine glass still dirty from their last dinner and the engagement ring that Dodi purchased the day before they died. True Di-hards can go back up one level to the ground floor and follow signs to Door #3 in Menswear. A huge (and more than a little creepy) bronze statue shows Di and Dodi releasing a symbolic albatross. It was commissioned by Dodi Fayed's father, Mohamed Al Fayed, who owns Harrods.

Back in the center of the store, ride the Egyptian Escalator—lined with pharaoh-headed sconces, papyrus-plant lamps, and hieroglyphic balconies (Al Fayed is from Egypt)—to the fourth floor. From the escalator, make a U-turn left and head to the far corner of the store (toys) to find child-size luxury cars that actually work. A junior Jaguar or Mercedes will set you back about $13,000. The Mini Hummer H3 ($23,000) is as big as my car.

Also on the fourth floor is **The Georgian Restaurant,** where you can enjoy a fancy afternoon tea (see page 155). For non–tea drinkers, 27 other eateries are scattered throughout the store, including a sushi bar, kosher deli, pizzeria, classic pub, and—for the truly homesick—a Krispy Kreme.

Many of my readers report that Harrods is overpriced, snooty, and teeming with American and Japanese tourists. Still, it's the palace of department stores. The nearby Beauchamp Place is lined with classy and fascinating shops.

Harvey Nichols—Once Princess Diana's favorite, "Harvey Nick's" remains the department store du jour (Mon–Sat 10:00–20:00, Sun 12:00–18:00, near Harrods, 109–125 Knightsbridge, Tube: Knightsbridge, tel. 020/7235-5000, www.harveynichols.com). Want to pick up a little £20 scarf for the wife? You won't do it here—they're more like £200. The store's fifth floor is a veritable food fest, with a gourmet grocery store, a fancy restaurant, a Yo! Sushi bar, and a lively café. Consider a take-away tray of sushi to eat on a bench in the Hyde Park rose garden two blocks away.

Toys—The biggest toy store in Britain is **Hamleys,** which in 2010 marks its 250th anniversary of delighting children. Seven floors buzz with 28,000 toys, managed by a staff of 200. Employees, some dressed in playful costumes, give demos of the latest gadgets. At the "Build-a-Bear Factory," kids can pick out a made-to-order teddy bear and watch while it's stuffed and sewn (Mon–Fri 10:00–20:00, Sat 9:00–20:00, Sun 12:00–18:00, 188–196 Regent Street, toll tel. 0870-333-2455, www.hamleys.com).

Street Markets—Antique buffs, people-watchers, and folks who brake for garage sales love London's street markets. There's good early-morning market activity somewhere any day of the week. The best are Portobello Road and Camden Market. Any London TI has a complete, up-to-date list. If you like to haggle, there are no holds barred in London's street markets. Warning: Markets attract two kinds of people—tourists and pickpockets.

The best are **Portobello Road** (Mon–Wed and Fri–Sat 8:00–18:30, Thu 8:00–13:00, sparse on Mon, closed Sun, Tube: Notting Hill Gate, near recommended B&Bs, tel. 020/7229-8354, www.portobelloroad.co.uk) and **Camden Lock Market** (daily 10:00–18:00, Tube: Camden Town, tel. 020/7284-2084, www.camdenlockmarket).

Famous Auctions—London's famous auctioneers welcome the curious public for viewing and bidding. You can preview estate catalogs or browse auction calendars online. To ask questions or set up an appointment, contact **Sotheby's** (Mon–Fri 9:00–16:30, closed Sat–Sun, café, 34–35 New Bond Street, Tube: Oxford Circus, tel. 020/7293-5000, www.sothebys.com) or **Christie's** (Mon–Fri 9:00–17:00, Sat–Sun usually 12:00–17:00 but weekend hours vary—call ahead, 8 King Street, Tube: Green Park, tel. 020/7839-9060, www.christies.com).

Entertainment in London

Theater (a.k.a. "Theatre")

London's theater rivals Broadway's in quality and usually beats it in price. Choose from 200 offerings—Shakespeare, musicals, comedy, thrillers, sex farces, cutting-edge fringe, revivals starring movie stars, and more. London does it all well. I prefer big, glitzy—even bombastic—musicals over serious chamber dramas, simply because London can deliver the lights, sound, dancers, and multimedia spectacle I rarely get back home.

Most theaters, marked on tourist maps (also see map on next page), are found in the West End between Piccadilly and Covent Garden. Box offices, hotels, and TIs offer a handy, free *London Theatre Guide* and *Entertainment Guide*. From home it's easy to check www.officiallondontheatre.co.uk for the latest on what's currently playing in London.

Performances are nightly except Sunday, usually with one or two matinees a week (Shakespeare's Globe is the rare theater that offers performances on Sun, May–Sept). Tickets range from about £11 to £55. Matinees are generally cheaper and rarely sell out.

To book a seat, simply call the theater box office direct, ask about seats and available dates, and buy a ticket with your credit card. You can call from the US as easily as from London. Arrive

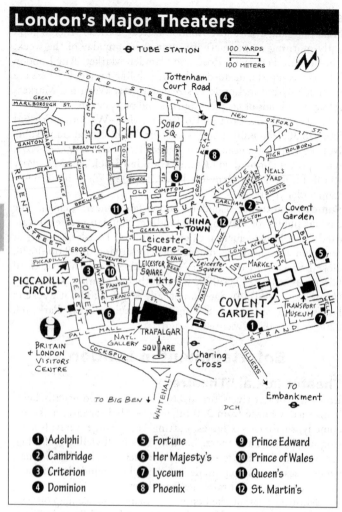

London's Major Theaters

⊕ TUBE STATION

100 YARDS
100 METERS

- ❶ Adelphi
- ❷ Cambridge
- ❸ Criterion
- ❹ Dominion
- ❺ Fortune
- ❻ Her Majesty's
- ❼ Lyceum
- ❽ Phoenix
- ❾ Prince Edward
- ❿ Prince of Wales
- ⓫ Queen's
- ⓬ St. Martin's

about 30 minutes before the show starts to pick up your ticket and to avoid lines.

For a booking fee, you can reserve online. Most theater websites link you to a preferred ticket vendor, usually www.ticket master.co.uk or www.seetickets.com. Keith Prowse Ticketing is also handy by phone or online (US tel. 800-669-8687, toll tel. 0844-209-0382, www.keithprowse.com).

Although booking through an agency is quick and easy, prices are inflated by a standard 25 percent fee. Ticket agencies (whether in the US, at London's TIs, or scattered throughout the city) are scalpers with an address. If you're buying from an agency, look at the ticket carefully (your price should be no more than 30 percent over the printed face value; the 17.5 percent VAT is already included in the face value), and understand where you're sitting according to the floor plan (if your view is restricted, it will state this on the ticket; for floor plans of the various theaters, see www.theatre monkey.com). Agencies are worthwhile only if a show you've just got to see is sold out at the box office. They scarf up hot tickets, planning to make a killing after the show is sold out. US booking agencies get their tickets from another agency, adding even more to your expense by involving yet another middleman. Many tickets sold on the street are forgeries. Although some theaters have booking agencies handle their advance sales, you'll stand a good chance of saving money and avoiding the middleman by simply calling the box office direct to book your tickets (international phone calls are cheap, and credit cards make booking a snap).

Theater Lingo: Stalls (ground floor), dress circle (first balcony), upper circle (second balcony), balcony (sky-high third balcony), slips (cheap seats on the fringes). Many cheap seats have a restricted view (behind a pillar).

Cheap Theater Tricks: Most theaters offer cheap returned tickets, standing-room, matinee, and senior or student standby deals. These "concessions" (discounted tickets) are indicated with a "conc" or "s" in the listings. Picking up a late return can get you a great seat at a cheap-seat price. If a show is "sold out," there's usually a way to get a seat. Call the theater box office and ask how.

If you don't care where you sit, you can often buy the absolutely cheapest seats (those with an obstructed view or in the nosebleed section) at the box office; tickets generally cost less than £20. Many theaters are so small that there's hardly a bad seat. After the lights go down, scooting up is less than a capital offense. Shakespeare did it.

Half-Price "tkts" Booth: This famous ticket booth at **Leicester** (LESS-ter) **Square** sells discounted tickets for top-price seats to shows on the push list—but only on the day of the performance (generally £2.50 service charge per ticket, Mon–Sat 10:00–19:00, Sun 12:00–15:00, matinee tickets from noon, lines often form early, list of shows available online at www.tkts.co.uk). Most tickets are half-price; other shows are discounted 25 percent. Note that the real half-price booth (with its "tkts" name) is a freestanding kiosk at the edge of the garden in Leicester Square. Several dishonest outfits nearby advertise "official half-price tickets"; avoid these.

Here are some sample prices: A top-notch seat to *Chicago* costs £59 if you buy it directly from the theater; the same seat costs £32.50 at Leicester Square. The cheapest balcony seat is £20 through the theater. Half-price tickets can be a good deal, unless you want the cheapest seats or the hottest shows. But check the board; occasionally they sell cheap tickets to good shows. For example, a first-class

What's On in the West End

Here are some of the perennial favorites that you're likely to find among the West End's evening offerings. If spending the time and money for a London play, I like a full-fledged high-energy musical.

Generally, you can book tickets for free at the box office or for a £2–3 fee by telephone or online. See the theater map on page 120 for locations.

Musicals

Billy Elliot—This adaptation of the popular British film is part family drama, part story of a boy who just has to dance, set to a score by Elton John (£17.50–50, Mon–Sat 19:30, matinees Thu and Sat 14:30, Victoria Palace Theatre, Victoria Street, Tube: Victoria, tel. 0870-895-5577, www.billyelliotthemusical.com).

Chicago—A chorus-girl-gone-bad forms a nightclub act with another murderess to bring in the bucks (£20–59, Mon–Thu 20:00, Fri 17:30 and 20:30, Sat 15:00 and 20:00, Cambridge Theatre, Earlham Street, Tube: Covent Garden, booking toll tel. 0844-412-4652, www.chicagothemusical.com).

Jersey Boys—This fast-moving, easy-to-follow show tracks the rough start and rise to stardom of Frankie Valli and The Four Seasons. It's light, but the music is so catchy that everyone leaves whistling the group's classics (£20–60, Mon–Sat 19:30, matinees Tue and Sat 14:30, Prince Edward Theatre, Old Compton Street, Tube: Leicester Square, tel. 0844-482-5151, www.jerseyboys london.com).

Les Misérables—Claude-Michel Schönberg's musical adaptation of Victor Hugo's epic follows the life of Jean Valjean as he struggles with the social and political realities of 19th-century France. This inspiring mega-hit takes you back to the days of France's struggle for a just and modern society (£12.50–52.50, Mon–Sat 19:30, matinees Wed and Sat 14:30, Queen's Theatre, Shaftesbury Avenue, Tube: Piccadilly Circus, box office toll tel. 0844-482-5160, www.lesmis.com).

The Lion King—In this Disney extravaganza, Simba the lion learns about the delicately balanced circle of life on the savanna (£30–59.50, Tue–Sat 19:30, matinees Wed and Sat 14:00, Sun

seat to the long-running *Les Misérables* (which rarely sells out) costs £52.50 when you go through the theater ticket office, but you'll pay £30.50 at the tkts booth.

West End Theaters: The commercial (nonsubsidized) theaters cluster around Soho (especially along Shaftesbury Avenue) and Covent Garden. With a centuries-old tradition of pleasing the masses, these present London theater at its glitziest. See the "What's On in the West End" sidebar.

Royal Shakespeare Company: If you'll ever enjoy Shakes-

15:00, Lyceum Theatre, Wellington Street, Tube: Charing Cross or Covent Garden, booking toll tel. 0844-844-0005, theater info tel. 020/7420-8100, www.thelionking.co.uk).

Mamma Mia!—This energetic, spandex-and-platform-boots musical weaves together a slew of ABBA hits to tell the story of a bride in search of her real dad as her promiscuous mom plans her Greek Isle wedding. The production has the audience dancing by the time it reaches its happy ending (£19.50–58, Mon–Thu and Sat 19:30, Fri 20:30, matinees Fri 17:00 and Sat 15:00, Prince of Wales Theatre, Coventry Street, Tube: Piccadilly Circus, box office toll tel. 0844-482-5138, www.mamma-mia.com).

Phantom of the Opera—A mysterious masked man falls in love with a singer in this haunting Andrew Lloyd Webber musical about life beneath the stage of the Paris Opera (£20–55, Mon–Sat 19:30, matinees Tue and Sat 14:30, Her Majesty's Theatre, Haymarket, Tube: Piccadilly Circus or Leicester Square, US toll-free tel. 800-334-8457, London booking toll tel. 0844-412-2707, www.thephantomoftheopera.com).

We Will Rock You—Whether or not you're a Queen fan, this musical tribute (more to the band than to Freddie Mercury) is an understandably popular celebration of their work (£27.50–60, Mon–Sat at 19:30, matinee Sat 14:30, Dominion Theatre, Tottenham Court Road, Tube: Tottenham Court Road, Ticketmaster toll tel. 0844-847-1775, www.queenonline.com/wewillrockyou).

Thrillers

The Mousetrap—Agatha Christie's whodunit about a murder in a country house has been stumping audiences for over 50 years (£13.50–36, Mon–Sat 19:30, matinees Tue 15:00 and Sat 16:00, St. Martin's Theatre, West Street, Tube: Leicester Square, box office toll tel. 0844-499-1515, www.the-mousetrap.co.uk).

The Woman in Black—The chilling tale of a solicitor who is haunted by what he learns when he closes a reclusive woman's affairs (£13.50–39, Mon–Sat 20:00, matinees Tue 15:00 and Sat 16:00, Fortune Theatre, Russell Street, Tube: Covent Garden, box office toll tel. 0870-060-6626, www.thewomaninblack.com).

peare, it'll be in Britain. The RSC performs at various theaters around London and in Stratford year-round. To get a schedule, contact the RSC (Royal Shakespeare Theatre, Stratford-upon-Avon, tel. 01789/403-444, www.rsc.org.uk).

Shakespeare's Globe: To see Shakespeare in a replica of the theater for which he wrote his plays, attend a play at the Globe. In this round, thatch-roofed, open-air theater the plays are performed much as Shakespeare intended—under the sky with no amplification.

The play's the thing from late April through October (usually Mon 19:30, Tue–Sat 14:00 and 19:30, Sun either 13:00 and/or 18:30, tickets can be sold out months in advance). You'll pay £5 to stand and £15–33 to sit, usually on a backless bench. Because only a few rows and the pricier Gentlemen's Rooms have seats with backs, many consider £1 cushions and £3 add-on back rests a good investment. Dress for the weather. The £5 "groundling" tickets—while open to rain—are most fun. Scurry in early to stake out a spot on the stage's edge, where the most interaction with the actors occurs. You're a crude peasant. You can lean your elbows on the stage, munch a picnic dinner (yes, you can bring in food), or walk around. I've never enjoyed Shakespeare as much as here, performed as it was meant to be in the "wooden O." If you can't get a ticket, consider waiting around. Plays can be long, and many groundlings leave before the end. Hang around outside and beg or buy a ticket from someone leaving early (groundlings are allowed to come and go).

For information on plays or £10.50 tours of the theater and museum (see page 104), contact the theater at tel. 020/7902-1400 or 020/7902-1500 (or see www.shakespeares-globe.org). To reserve tickets for plays, call or drop by the box office (Mon–Sat 10:00–18:00, Sun 10:00–17:00, stays open one hour later on performance days, New Globe Walk entrance, tel. 020/7401-9919). You can also reserve online (£2 booking fee per transaction). A few non-Shakespeare plays are also presented each year.

The theater is on the South Bank, directly across the Thames over the Millennium Bridge from St. Paul's Cathedral (Tube: Mansion House or London Bridge). The Globe is inconvenient for public transport, but the courtesy phone in the lobby gets a mini-cab in minutes. (These minicabs have set fees—e.g., £8 to South Kensington—but generally cost less than a metered cab and provide good, honest service.) During theater season, there's a regular supply of black cabs outside the main foyer on New Globe Walk.

Outdoor Theater in Summer: Enjoy Shakespearean drama and other plays under the stars at the **Open Air Theatre,** in leafy Regent's Park in north London. Food is allowed: You can bring your own picnic; order à la carte from the theater menu; or pre-order a £22.50 picnic supper from the theater at least one week in advance (tickets £10–50; season runs late May–mid-Sept, box office open April–late May Mon–Sat 10:00–18:00, closed Sun; late May–mid-Sept Mon–Sat 10:00–20:00, Sun 10:00–until start of play on performance days only; order tickets online after mid-Jan or by phone Mon–Sun 9:00–21:00; £1 booking fee by phone, no fee if ordering online or in person; toll tel. 0844-826-4242, www.openairtheatre.org; grounds open 1.5 hours prior to evening performances, one hour prior to 2:30 matinee, and 30 min prior to earlier matinees; 10-min walk north of Baker Street Tube, near Queen Mary's Gardens within Regent's Park; detailed directions and more info at www.openairtheatre.org).

Fringe Theatre: London's rougher evening-entertainment scene is thriving, filling pages in *Time Out*. Choose from a wide range of fringe theater and comedy acts (generally £5).

Classical Music
Concerts at Churches
For easy, cheap, or free concerts in historic churches, check the TIs' listings for **lunch concerts,** especially:
- St. Bride's Church, with free lunch concerts twice a week at 13:15 (generally Tue, Wed, or Fri—confirm by phone or online, church tel. 020/7427-0133, www.stbrides.com).
- St. James's at Piccadilly, with 50-minute concerts on Monday, Wednesday, and Friday at 13:10 (suggested donation £3, info tel. 020/7381-0441, www.st-james-piccadilly.org).
- St. Martin-in-the-Fields, offering free concerts on Monday, Tuesday, and Friday at 13:00 (suggested £3.50 donation, church tel. 020/7766-1100, www.smitf.org).

St. Martin-in-the-Fields also hosts fine candlelight **evening concerts** (£6–25, at 19:30 Thu–Sat, sometimes Tue) and live jazz in its underground Café in the Crypt (£5–8, Wed at 20:00).

Evensong and Organ Recitals at Churches
Evensong services are held at several churches, including:
- St. Paul's Cathedral (Mon–Sat at 17:00, Sun at 15:15).
- Westminster Abbey (Mon–Tue and Thu–Fri at 17:00, Sat–Sun at 15:00; there's a service on Wed, but it's spoken, not sung).
- Southwark Cathedral (Mon–Tue and Thu–Fri at 17:30; Sat at 16:00, Sun at 15:00, no service on Wed or alternate Mon, tel. 020/7367-6700, www.southwark.anglican.org/cathedral).
- St. Bride's Church (Sun at 18:30, tel. 020/7427-0133, www.stbrides.com).

Free **organ recitals** are often held on Sunday at 17:45 in Westminster Abbey (30 min, tel. 020/7222-5152). Many other churches have free concerts; ask for the *London Organ Concerts Guide* at the TI.

Prom Concerts and Opera
For a fun classical event (mid-July–mid Sept), attend a **Prom Concert** (shortened from "Promenade Concert") during the annual festival at the Royal Albert Hall. Nightly concerts are offered at give-a-peasant-some-culture prices to "Promenaders"—those willing to stand throughout the performance (£5 standing-room spots sold at the door, £7 restricted-view seats, most £22–30 but depends

on performance, Tube: South Kensington, tel. 020/7589-8212, www.bbc.co.uk/proms).

Some of the world's best **opera** is belted out at the prestigious Royal Opera House, near Covent Garden (box office tel. 020/7304-4000, www.roh.org.uk), and at the less-formal Sadler's Wells Theatre (Rosebery Avenue, Islington, Tube: Angel, info tel. 020/7863-8198, box office toll tel. 0844-412-4300, www.sadlerswells.com).

Evening Museum Visits

Many museums are open an evening or two during the week, offering fewer crowds. See a list on page 81.

Tours

Guided **walks** are offered several times a day. **London Walks** is the most established company. Daytime walks vary by theme: ancient London, museums, legal London, Dickens, Beatles, Jewish quarter, Christopher Wren, and so on. In the evening, expect a more limited choice: ghosts, Jack the Ripper, pubs, or literary themed. Get the latest from their brochure or website, or call for a recorded listing of that day's walks. Show up at the listed time and place, pay the guide, and enjoy the two-hour tour (£7, cash only, tel. 020/7624-3978, recorded info 020/7624-9255, www.walks.com).

To see the city illuminated at night, consider a **bus** tour. A one-hour **London by Night Sightseeing Tour** leaves every evening from Victoria Station and other points (see page 63).

Summer Evenings Along the South Bank

If you're visiting London in summer, consider the South Bank.

Take a trip around the **London Eye** while the sun sets over the city (Ferris wheel spins until 21:00). Then cap your night with an evening walk along the pedestrian-only **Jubilee Walkway,** which runs east–west along the river. It's where Londoners go to escape the heat. This pleasant stretch of the walkway—lined with pubs and casual eateries—goes from the London Eye past Shakespeare's Globe to Tower Bridge (you can walk in either direction; see www.jubileewalkway.com for maps and Tube stops).

If you're in the mood for a movie, take in a flick at the **BFI Southbank,** located just across the river, alongside Waterloo Bridge. Run by the British Film Institute, the state-of-the-art theater shows mostly classic films, as well as art cinema (£8.60, £5 on Tue, Tube: Waterloo or Embankment, box office tel. 020/7928-3232, check www.bfi.org.uk for schedules).

Farther east along the South Bank is **The Scoop**—an outdoor amphitheater next to City Hall. It's a good spot for outdoor movies, concerts, dance, and theater productions throughout the summer— with Tower Bridge as a scenic backdrop. These events are free, nearly nightly, and family-friendly. For the latest event schedule, see www.morelondon.com and click on "The Scoop" (next to City Hall, Riverside, The Queen's Walkway, Tube: London Bridge).

Cruises

During the summer, boats sail as late as 21:00 between Westminster Pier (near Big Ben) and the Tower of London. (For details, see page 66.)

A handful of outfits run Thames River evening cruises with four-course meals and dancing. **London Showboat** offers the best value (£75, April–Oct Wed–Sun, Nov–March Thu–Sat, 3.5 hours, departs at 19:00 from Westminster Pier and returns by 22:30, reservations necessary, tel. 020/7740-0400, www.citycruises.com). Dinner cruises are also offered by **Bateaux London** (£65–120, tel. 020/7695-1800, www.bateauxlondon.com). For more on cruising, get the *River Thames Boat Services* brochure from a London TI.

Sleeping in London

London is perhaps Europe's most expensive city for rooms. Cheaper rooms are relatively dumpy. Don't expect £130 cheeriness in a £80 room. For £70, you'll get a double with breakfast in a safe, cramped, and dreary place with minimal service and the bathroom down the hall. For £90, you'll get a basic, clean, reasonably cheery double in a usually cramped, cracked-plaster building with a private bath, or a soulless but comfortable room without breakfast in a huge Motel 6–type place. My London splurges, at £150–260, are spacious, thoughtfully appointed places good for entertaining or romancing. Off-season, it's possible to save money by arriving late without a reservation and looking around. Competition softens prices, especially for multinight stays. Check hotel websites for special deals. All of Britain's accommodations are now nonsmoking.

Hearty English or generous buffet breakfasts are included unless otherwise noted, and TVs are standard in rooms, but may come with only the traditional five British channels (no cable).

Looking for Hotel Deals Online

Given the high hotel prices and relatively weak dollar, consider using the Internet to help score a hotel deal. Various websites list rooms in high-rise, three- and four-star business hotels. You'll give up the charm and warmth of a family-run establishment, and breakfast will probably not be included, but you might find the price is right.

Start by checking the websites of several chains to get an idea of typical rates and to check for online-only deals. Big London

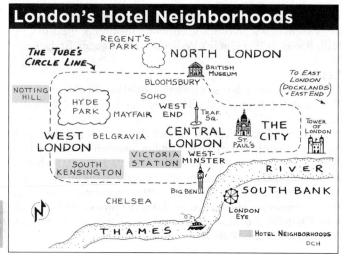

London's Hotel Neighborhoods

hotel chains include the following: Millennium/Copthorne (www.millenniumhotels.com), Thistle Hotels (www.thistle.com), Intercontinental/Holiday Inn (www.ichotelsgroup.com), Radisson (www.radisson.com), Hilton (www.hilton.com), and Red Carnation (www.redcarnationhotels.com). For information on no-frills, Motel 6–type chains, see "Big, Good-Value, Modern Hotels," below.

Auction-type sites (such as www.priceline.com or www.hotwire.com) can be great for matching flexible travelers with empty hotel rooms, often at prices well below the hotel's normal rates.

Other favorite accommodation discount sites mentioned by my readers include www.londontown.com (an informative site with a discount booking service), http://athomeinlondon.co.uk and www.londonbb.com (both list central B&Bs), www.lastminute.com, www.visitlondon.com, http://roomsnet.com, and www.eurocheapo.com. Read candid reviews of London hotels at www.tripadvisor.com. And check the "Graffiti Wall" at www.ricksteves.com for the latest tips and discoveries.

For a good overview on finding London hotel deals, go to www.smartertravel.com and click "Travel Guides," then "London."

Big, Good-Value, Modern Hotels

These places—popular with budget tour groups—are well-run and offer elevators, 24-hour reception, and all the modern comforts in a no-nonsense, practical package. With the notable exception of my second listing, they are often located on busy streets in dreary train-station neighborhoods, so use common sense after dark and wear your money belt. The doubles for £90–100 are a great value for

Sleep Code

(£1 = about $1.60, country code: 44, area code: 020)
S = Single, **D** = Double/Twin, **T** = Triple, **Q** = Quad, **b** = bathroom,
s = shower only. Unless otherwise noted, credit cards are accepted and prices include breakfast.

To help you easily sort through these listings, I've divided the rooms into three categories, based on the price for a double room with bath:

$$$ **Higher Priced**—Most rooms £115 or more.
$$ **Moderately Priced**—Most rooms between £70–115.
$ **Lower Priced**—Most rooms £70 or less.

London. Midweek prices are generally higher than weekend rates. Breakfast is always extra. Online bookings are often the easiest way to make reservations, and will generally net you a discount.

$$ Jurys Inn Islington rents 200-plus compact, comfy rooms near King's Cross station (Db/Tb-£89–139, some discounted rooms available online, 2 adults and 2 kids under age 12 can share one room, 60 Pentonville Road, Tube: Angel, tel. 020/7282-5500, fax 020/7282-5511, www.jurysinns.com).

$$ Premier Inn London County Hall, literally down the hall from a $400-a-night Marriott Hotel, fills one end of London's massive former County Hall building. This family-friendly place is wonderfully located near the base of the London Eye and across the Thames from Big Ben. Its 313 efficient rooms come with all the necessary comforts (Db-£109–119 for 2 adults and up to 2 kids under age 16, book in advance, no-show rooms released at 15:00, some easy-access rooms, 500 yards from Westminster Tube stop and Waterloo Station, Belvedere Road, central reservations toll tel. 0870-242-8000, reception desk toll tel. 0870-238-3300, easiest to book online at www.premierinn.com).

$$ Premier Inn London Southwark, with 59 rooms, is near Shakespeare's Globe on the South Bank (Db for up to 2 adults and 2 kids-£99–110, Bankside, 34 Park Street, toll tel. 0870-990-6402, www.premierinn.com).

$$ Premier Inn King's Cross St. Pancras, with 276 rooms, is just east of King's Cross and St. Pancras stations (Db-£90–114, 26–30 York Way, toll tel. 0870-990-6414, www.premierinn.com).

Other **$$ Premier Inns** charging £87–114 per room include **London Euston** (big, blue, Lego-type building packed with vacationing families, on handy but noisy street at corner of Euston Road and Dukes Road, Tube: Euston, toll tel. 0870-238-3301), **London Kensington Earl's Court** (11 Knaresborough Place,

Tube: Earl's Court or Gloucester Road, toll tel. 0870-238-3304), and **London Putney Bridge** (£79–89, farther out, 3 Putney Bridge Approach, Tube: Putney Bridge, toll tel. 0870-238-3302). Avoid the **Tower Bridge** location, which is an inconvenient, 15-minute walk from the nearest Tube stop. For any of these, call 0870-242-8000 or—the best option—book online at www.premierinn.com.

$$ Hotel Ibis London Euston St. Pancras, which feels a bit classier than a Premier Inn, rents 380 rooms on a quiet street a block behind and west of Euston Station (Db-£90–115, up to £150 during special events, no family rooms, 3 Cardington Street, tel. 020/7388-7777 or 020/7304-7712, fax 020/7388-0001, www .ibishotel.com, h0921@accor.com).

$$ Travelodge London Kings Cross is another typical chain hotel with lots of cookie-cutter rooms, just 200 yards south of King's Cross Station (Db-£52–98, family rooms, can be noisy, Grays Inn Road, toll tel. 0871-984-6256). Other convenient Travelodge London locations are the nearby **Kings Cross Royal Scot, Euston, Marylebone, Covent Garden, Liverpool Street,** and **Farringdon.** For details on all Travelodge hotels, see www .travelodge.co.uk.

Victoria Station Neighborhood (Belgravia)

The streets behind Victoria Station teem with little, moderately-priced-for-London B&Bs. It's a safe, surprisingly tidy, and decent area without a hint of the trashy, tour-

isty glitz of the streets in front of the station. West of the tracks is Belgravia, where the prices are a bit higher and your neighbors include Andrew Lloyd Webber and Margaret Thatcher (her policeman stands outside 73 Chester Square). Decent eateries abound (see page 151).

All the recommended hotels are within a five-minute walk of the Victoria Tube, bus, and train stations. On hot summer nights, request a quiet back room. Nearby is the 400-space Semley Place NCP **parking garage** (£32/day, possible discounts with hotel voucher, just west of the Victoria Coach Station at Buckingham Palace Road and Semley Place, toll tel. 0845-050-7080, www.ncp.co.uk). The handy **Pimlico Launderette** is about five blocks southwest of Warwick Square (daily 8:00–19:00, self-service or full service, south of Sutherland Street at 3 Westmoreland Terrace, tel. 020/7821-8692). **Launderette Centre** is a block northeast of Warwick Square (Mon–Fri 8:00–22:00, Sat–Sun until 19:00, about £7 wash and dry, £11 full-service, 31 Churton Street, tel. 020/7828-6039).

Victoria Station Neighborhood

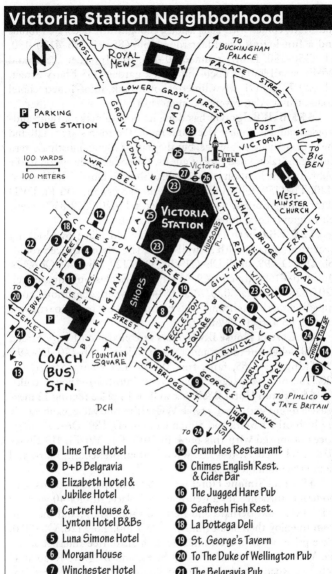

1 Lime Tree Hotel
2 B+B Belgravia
3 Elizabeth Hotel & Jubilee Hotel
4 Cartref House & Lynton Hotel B&Bs
5 Luna Simone Hotel
6 Morgan House
7 Winchester Hotel
8 Cherry Court Hotel
9 Bakers Hotel
10 easyHotel Victoria
11 Ebury Wine Bar
12 Jenny Lo's Tea House
13 To La Poule au Pot Rest.
14 Grumbles Restaurant
15 Chimes English Rest. & Cider Bar
16 The Jugged Hare Pub
17 Seafresh Fish Rest.
18 La Bottega Deli
19 St. George's Tavern
20 To The Duke of Wellington Pub
21 The Belgravia Pub
22 The Thomas Cubitt Pub
23 Grocery Stores (4)
24 Launderettes (2)
25 Bus Tours – Day (2)
26 Bus Tours – Night
27 Tube, Taxis & City Buses

$$$ Lime Tree Hotel, enthusiastically run by Charlotte and Matt, comes with 28 spacious, thoughtfully decorated rooms and a fun-loving breakfast room (Sb-£85–95, Db-£120–150, Tb-£150–180, family room-£170–195, free Internet access and Wi-Fi, small lounge opens into quiet garden, 135 Ebury Street, tel. 020/7730-8191, www.limetreehotel.co.uk, info@limetreehotel.co.uk, trusty Alan covers the night shift).

$$$ B+B Belgravia has done its best to make a tight-and-tangled old guesthouse sleek and mod. The rooms are small and the management is absentee, but the staff of young, mostly Eastern Europeans takes good care of guests, the coffee is always on in the lobby, and the location is unbeatable (Sb-£99, Db-£120, Db twin-£130, Tb-£150, Qb-£160, free Internet access and Wi-Fi, DVD library, loaner bikes, 64 Ebury Street, tel. 020/7259-8570, www.bb-belgravia.com, info@bb-belgravia.com).

$$$ Elizabeth Hotel is a stately old place overlooking Eccleston Square, with 37 well-worn, slightly overpriced rooms (Sb-£99, D-£99, small Db-£119, big Db-£129, Tb-£149, Qb-£159, Quint/b-£169, air-con-£9, Wi-Fi, 37 Eccleston Square, tel. 020/7828-6812, fax 020/7828-6814, www.elizabethhotel.com, info@elizabethhotel.com). The Elizabeth also rents apartments sleeping up to six (£259/night).

$$ Cartref House B&B offers rare charm on Ebury Street, with 10 delightful rooms and a warm welcome (Sb-£70, Db-£95, Tb-£126, Qb-£155, fans, free Wi-Fi, 129 Ebury Street, tel. 020/7730-6176, www.cartrefhouse.co.uk, info@cartrefhouse.co.uk).

$$ Lynton Hotel B&B is a well-worn place renting 12 inexpensive rooms with small prefab WCs. It's a fine value, exuberantly run by brothers Mark and Simon Connor (D-£80, Db-£90, these prices promised with this book in 2010, free Wi-Fi, 113 Ebury Street, tel. 020/7730-4032, www.lyntonhotel.co.uk, mark-and-simon@lyntonhotel.co.uk).

$$ Luna Simone Hotel rents 36 fresh, spacious rooms with modern bathrooms. It's a well-managed place, run for 40 years by twins Peter and Bernard and Bernard's son, Mark, and they still seem to enjoy their work (Sb-£70, Db-£100, Tb-£120, Qb-£150, these prices with cash and this book in 2010, free Internet access and Wi-Fi, corner of Charlwood Street and Belgrave Road at 47 Belgrave Road, handy bus #24 to Victoria Station and Trafalgar Square stops out front, tel. 020/7834-5897, www.lunasimonehotel.com, lunasimone@talk21.com).

$$ Morgan House rents 11 good rooms and is entertainingly run, with lots of travel tips and friendly chat from owner Rachel Joplin and her staff, Danilo and Fernanda (S-£52, D-£72, Db-£92, T-£92, family suites-£112–132 for 3–4 people, Wi-Fi, 120 Ebury Street, tel. 020/7730-2384, www.morganhouse.co.uk, morganhouse@btclick.com).

$$ Winchester Hotel has 19 small rooms and is an adequate value for the price (Db-£89–99, Tb-£115, Qb-£140, Internet access, 17 Belgrave Road, tel. 020/7828-2972, www.londonwinchester hotel.co.uk, info@londonwinchesterhotel.co.uk). If you need a cab, call your own to avoid excessive fares. They also rent a few apartments around the corner (£125–230, see website for details).

$ Cherry Court Hotel, run by the friendly and industrious Patel family, rents 12 very small, basic, incense-scented rooms in a central location (Sb-£48, Db-£55, Tb-£80, Qb-£95, Quint/b-£110, these prices promised with this book through 2010, 5 percent fee to pay with credit card, fruit-basket breakfast in room, air-con, laundry, free Internet access and Wi-Fi, peaceful garden patio, 23 Hugh Street, tel. 020/7828-2840, fax 020/7828-0393, www.cherry courthotel.co.uk, info@cherrycourthotel.co.uk).

$ Jubilee Hotel is a well-run slumber mill with 24 tiny rooms and many tiny beds. It's a bit musty and its windows only open a few inches, but the price is right (S-£39, Sb-£59, tiny D-£59, tiny Db-£65, Db-£69, Tb-£89, Qb-£105, ask for the 5 percent Rick Steves discount when booking, pay Internet access and Wi-Fi, 31 Eccleston Square, tel. 020/7834-0845, www.jubileehotel.co.uk, stay@jubileehotel.co.uk, Bob Patel).

$ Bakers Hotel is a well-worn cheapie, with 10 tight rooms, but it's well-located and offers youth hostel prices and a small breakfast (S-£30–35, D-£50–55, Db-£60–65, T-£60–65, Tb-£70–75, family room-£70–75, 126 Warwick Way, tel. 020/7834-0729, www.bakershotel.co.uk, reservations@bakershotel.co.uk, Amin Jamani).

$ easyHotel Victoria is a radical concept—offering what you need to sleep well and safe—and no more. Their 77 rooms fit the old floor plan, so some rooms are tiny windowless closets, while others are quite spacious. All rooms are well-ventilated and come with an efficient "bathroom pod"—just big enough to take care of business. Prices are the same for one person or two. You get two towels, soap and shampoo, and a clean bed—no breakfast, no fresh towels, and no daily cleaning. Rooms range from £25 to £65, depending on their size and when you book: "The earlier you book, the less you pay" (reserve only through website, 36 Belgrave Road, tel. 020/7834-1379, www.easyHotel.com, enquiries@victoria.easyHotel.com). They also have branches at South Kensington, Earl's Court, Paddington, and Heathrow and Luton airports (see their website for details).

"South Kensington," She Said, Loosening His Cummerbund

To stay on a quiet street so classy it doesn't allow hotel signs, surrounded by trendy shops and colorful restaurants, call "South Ken"

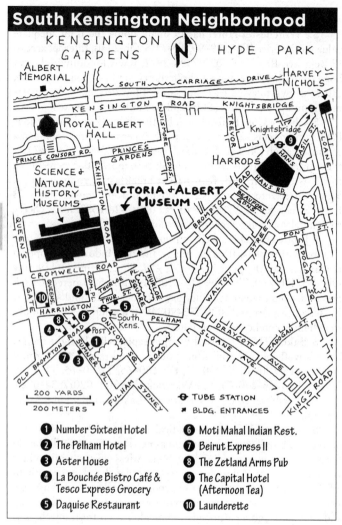

South Kensington Neighborhood

KENSINGTON GARDENS

HYDE PARK

ALBERT MEMORIAL

SOUTH CARRIAGE DRIVE

HARVEY NICHOLS

KENSINGTON ROAD

KNIGHTSBRIDGE

ROYAL ALBERT HALL

Knightsbridge

PRINCE CONSORT RD.

PRINCES GARDENS

HARRODS

SCIENCE & NATURAL HISTORY MUSEUMS

VICTORIA & ALBERT MUSEUM

BEAUFORT GDNS.

CROMWELL ROAD

THURLOE SQUARE

WALTON STREET

PONT ST.

HARRINGTON

South Kens.

PELHAM

DRAYCOTT AVE.

SLOANE AVE.

CADOGAN ST.

OLD BROMPTON ROAD

SUMNER PL.

Post

ONSLOW SQ.

SLOANE

KINGS ROAD

FULHAM   SYDNEY

200 YARDS
200 METERS

⊖ TUBE STATION
◼ BLDG. ENTRANCES

1 Number Sixteen Hotel
2 The Pelham Hotel
3 Aster House
4 La Bouchée Bistro Café & Tesco Express Grocery
5 Daquise Restaurant

6 Moti Mahal Indian Rest.
7 Beirut Express II
8 The Zetland Arms Pub
9 The Capital Hotel (Afternoon Tea)
10 Launderette

your London home. Shoppers like being a short walk from Harrods and the designer shops of King's Road and Chelsea. When I splurge, I splurge here. Sumner Place is just off Old Brompton Road, 200 yards from the handy South Kensington Tube station (on Circle Line, two stops from Victoria Station, direct Heathrow connection). The handy **launderette** is on the corner of Queensberry Place and Harrington Road (Mon–Fri 7:30–21:00, Sat 9:00–20:00, Sun 10:00–19:00, bring 50p and £1 coins).

$$$ Number Sixteen, for well-heeled travelers, packs over-the-top formality and class into its 42 rooms, plush lounges, and tranquil garden. It's in a labyrinthine building, with modern decor throughout—perfect for an urban honeymoon (Db-£200—but soft, ask for discounted "seasonal rates" especially in July–Aug—subject to availability, breakfast buffet in the garden-£17, elevator, 16 Sumner Place, tel. 020/7589-5232, fax 020/7584-8615, US tel. 800-553-6674, www.firmdalehotels.com, sixteen@firmdale.com).

$$$ The Pelham Hotel, a 52-room business-class hotel with a pricey mix of pretense and style, is not quite sure which investment company owns it. It's genteel, with low lighting and a pleasant drawing room among the many perks (Db-£180–260, breakfast extra, lower prices Aug and weekends, Web specials can include free breakfast, air-con, pay Internet access and Wi-Fi, elevator, gym, 15 Cromwell Place, tel. 020/7589-8288, fax 020/7584-8444, US tel. 1-888-757-5587, www.pelhamhotel.co.uk, reservations @pelhamhotel.co.uk).

$$$ Aster House, run by friendly and accommodating Simon and Leonie Tan, has a cheerful lobby, lounge, and breakfast room. Its rooms are comfy and quiet, with TV, phone, and air-conditioning. Enjoy breakfast or just lounging in the whisper-elegant Orangery, a Victorian greenhouse (Sb-£120, Db-£180, bigger Db-£225, 20 percent discount with this book through 2010 if you book three or more nights, additional 5 percent off for five or more nights with cash, check website for specials, VAT not included, pay Internet access and Wi-Fi, 3 Sumner Place, tel. 020/7581-5888, fax 020/7584-4925, www.asterhouse.com, asterhouse@btinternet.com). Simon and Leonie offer free loaner mobile phones to their guests.

Notting Hill and Bayswater Neighborhoods

Residential Notting Hill has quick bus and Tube access to downtown, and, for London, is very "homely" (Brit-speak for cozy). It's also peppered with trendy bars and restaurants, and is home to the famous Portobello Road Market (see "Street Markets," on page 119).

Popular with young international travelers, Bayswater's Queensway street is a multicultural festival of commerce and eateries. The neighborhood does its dirty clothes at Galaxy Launderette (£6 self-service, £8–10 full-service, daily 8:00–20:00, staff on hand with soap and coins, 65 Moscow Road, at corner of St. Petersburgh Place and Moscow Road, tel. 020/7229-7771). For Internet access, you'll find several stops along busy Queensway, and a self-serve bank of easyInternetcafé computer terminals on the food circus level of the Whiteleys Shopping Centre (daily 8:30–24:00, corner of Queensway and Porchester Gardens).

Near Kensington Gardens Square

Several big old hotels line the quiet Kensington Gardens Square (not to be confused with the much bigger Kensington Gardens

Notting Hill and Bayswater Neighborhoods

⊖ TUBE STN.

1/4 MILE

400 METERS

1. Phoenix Hotel
2. Vancouver Studios & Princes Square Guest Accommodation
3. Kensington Gardens Hotel
4. Westland Hotel
5. London Vicarage Hotel
6. To Norwegian YWCA
7. Maggie Jones Restaurant
8. The Churchill Arms Pub & Thai Kitchens
9. The Prince Edward Pub
10. Café Diana
11. Royal China Restaurant
12. Whiteleys Mall (Food Court, Grocery, Internet)
13. Tesco Grocery
14. Spar Market
15. The Orangery (Afternoon Tea)
16. Launderette

adjacent to Hyde Park), a block west of bustling Queensway, north of Bayswater Tube station. These hotels are quiet for central London.

$$$ Phoenix Hotel, a Best Western modernization of a 130-room hotel, offers American business-class comforts; spacious, plush public spaces; and big, fresh, modern-feeling rooms. Its prices—which range from value to rip-off—are determined by a greedy computer program, with huge variations according to expected demand. See their website and book online to save money (Db-£90–165, elevator, impersonal staff, 1–8 Kensington Gardens Square, tel. 020/7229-2494, fax 020/7727-1419, US tel. 800-528-1234, www.phoenixhotel.co.uk, info@phoenixhotel.co.uk).

$$$ Vancouver Studios offers 45 modern rooms with fully equipped kitchenettes (utensils, stove, microwave, and fridge) rather than breakfast (small Sb-£79, Db-£125, Tb-£170, extra bed-£15, 10 percent discount for week-long stay or more, welcoming lounge and garden, near Kensington Gardens Square at 30 Prince's Square, tel. 020/7243-1270, fax 020/7221-8678, www .vancouverstudios.co.uk, info@vancouverstudios.co.uk).

$$ Kensington Gardens Hotel laces 17 pleasant rooms together in a tall, skinny building with lots of stairs and no elevator (Ss-£57, Sb-£64, Db-£86, Tb-£105; book by phone or email for these special Rick Steves prices, rather than through the pricier website; continental breakfast served at sister hotel next door, Wi-Fi, 9 Kensington Gardens Square, tel. 020/7221-7790, fax 020/7792-8612, www.kensingtongardenshotel.co.uk, info @kensingtongardenshotel.co.uk, Rowshanak).

$$ Princes Square Guest Accommodation is a big, impersonal 50-room place that's well-located, practical, and a good value, especially with its online discounts (Sb-£65–115, Db-£85–150, Tb-£110–175, elevator, 23–25 Princes Square, tel. 020/7229-9876, www.princessquarehotel.co.uk, info@princessquarehotel.co.uk).

Near Kensington Gardens

$$$ Westland Hotel is comfortable, convenient (5-min walk from Notting Hill neighborhood), and feels like a wood-paneled hunting lodge with a fine lounge. The rooms are spacious, recently refurbished, and quite plush. Their £130 doubles (less your 10 percent discount—see below) are the best value, but check their website for specials (Sb-£110, Db-£130, deluxe Db-£152, cavernous deluxe Db-£172, sprawling Tb-£165–193, gargantuan Qb-£186–220, Quint/b-£234, 10 percent discount with this book in 2010—claim upon booking or arrival; elevator, garage-£12/day, pay Wi-Fi, between Notting Hill Gate and Queensway Tube stations at 154 Bayswater Road, tel. 020/7229-9191, fax 020/7727-1054, www .westlandhotel.co.uk, reservations@westlandhotel.co.uk, Jim and

Nora ably staff the front desk).

$$$ London Vicarage Hotel is family-run, understandably popular, and elegantly British in a quiet, classy neighborhood. It has 17 rooms furnished with taste and quality, a TV lounge, and facilities on each floor. Mandy and Monika maintain a homey and caring atmosphere (S-£55, Sb-£93, D-£93, Db-£122, T-£117, Tb-£156, Q-£128, Qb-£172, 20 percent less in winter—check website, free Wi-Fi; 8-min walk from Notting Hill Gate and High Street Kensington Tube stations, near Kensington Palace at 10 Vicarage Gate; tel. 020/7229-4030, fax 020/7792-5989, www .londonvicaragehotel.com, vicaragehotel@btconnect.com).

Near Holland Park

$ Norwegian YWCA (Norsk K.F.U.K.)—where English is definitely a second language—is for women 30 and under only (and men 30 and under with Norwegian passports). Located on a quiet, stately street, it offers a study, TV room, piano lounge, and an open-face Norwegian ambience (goat cheese on Sundays!). They have mostly quads, so those willing to share with strangers are most likely to get a bed (July–Aug: Ss-£36, shared double-£35/bed, shared triple-£30/bed, shared quad-£26/bed, includes breakfast year-round plus sack lunch and dinner Sept–June, £20 key deposit required, pay Wi-Fi, 52 Holland Park, tel. 020/7727-9346 or 020/7727-9897, www.kfukhjemmet.org.uk, kontor@kfukh jemmet.org.uk). With each visit, I wonder which is easier to get—a sex change or a Norwegian passport?

Other Neighborhoods

North of Marble Arch: **$$$ The 22 York Street B&B** offers a casual alternative in the city center, renting 10 stark, hardwood, comfortable rooms (Sb-£89, Db-£120, two-night minimum, Internet access and Wi-Fi, inviting lounge; from Baker Street Tube station, walk 2 blocks down Baker Street and take a right to 22 York Street; tel. 020/7224-2990, www.22yorkstreet.co.uk, mc@22yorkstreet .co.uk, energetically run by Liz and Michael Callis).

$$$ The Sumner Hotel, in a 19th-century Georgian townhouse, is located a few blocks north of Hyde Park and Oxford Street, a busy shopping destination. Decorated with fancy modern Italian furniture, this swanky place packs in all the extras (Db-£160–190, 20 percent discount with this book in 2010, extra bed-£30, free Wi-Fi, 54 Upper Berkeley Street just off Edgware Road, Tube: Marble Arch, tel. 020/7723-2244, fax 0870-705-8767, www .thesumner.com, hotel@thesumner.com, manager Peter).

Near Covent Garden: **$$$ Fielding Hotel,** located on a charming, quiet pedestrian street just two blocks east of Covent Garden, offers 24 no-frills rooms and a good location (Db-£115–

140, Db with sitting room-£160, pricier rooms are bigger with better bathrooms, no breakfast, no kids under 6, free Wi-Fi, 4 Broad Court, Bow Street, tel. 020/7836-8305, fax 020/7497-0064, www .thefieldinghotel.co.uk, reservations@the-fielding-hotel.co.uk, manager Graham Chapman).

Near Buckingham Palace: **$$ Vandon House Hotel,** run by Central College in Iowa, is packed with students most of the year, but rents its 32 rooms to travelers from late May through August at great prices. The rooms, while institutional, are comfy, and the location is excellent (S-£46, D-£70, Db-£90, Tb-£99, Qb-£119, only twin beds, elevator, Internet access and Wi-Fi; on a tiny road 3-min walk west of St. James's Park Tube station or 7-min walk from Victoria Station, near east end of Petty France Street at 1 Vandon Street; tel. 020/7799-6780, www.vandonhouse.com, info @vandonhouse.com).

Near Euston Station and the British Library: The **$$$ Methodist International Centre (MIC),** a modern, youthful, Christian hotel and conference center, fills its lower floors with international students and its top floor with travelers. The 28 rooms are modern and simple yet comfortable, with fine bathrooms, phones, and desks. The atmosphere is friendly, safe, clean, and controlled; it also has a spacious lounge and game room (annex S-£85, Sb-£140, deluxe Sb-£150, annex D-£95, Db-£155, deluxe Db-£175, Tb-£195; Sb-£95 and Db-£108 with £115 membership; 3-bedroom annex is great for families, check website for specials, elevator, Wi-Fi; on a quiet street a block west of Euston Station, 81–103 Euston Street—not Euston Road, Tube: Euston Station; tel. 020/7380-0001, www .micentre.com, reservations@micentre.com). From June through August, when the students are gone, they also rent simpler twin rooms (S or D-£50, includes one breakfast, extra breakfast-£12.50).

Hostels

$ London Central Youth Hostel is the flagship of London's hostels, with 300 beds and all the latest in security and comfortable efficiency. Families and travelers of any age will feel welcome in this wonderful facility. You'll pay the same price for any bed in a 4- to 8-bed single-sex dorm—with or without private bathroom—so try to grab one with a bathroom (£20–30 per bunk bed—fluctuates with demand, £3/night extra for non-members, breakfast-£4; includes sheets, towel and locker; families or groups welcome to book an entire room, free Wi-Fi, members' kitchen, laundry, book long in advance, between Oxford Street and Great Portland Street Tube stations at 104 Bolsover Street, toll tel. 0870-770-6144 or 0845-371-9154, www.yha.org.uk, londoncentral@yha.org.uk).

$ St. Paul's Youth Hostel, near St. Paul's, is clean, modern, friendly, and well-run. Most of the 190 beds are in shared, single-sex bunk rooms (bed-£22–26 depending on number of beds in room and demand, twin D-£54–61, bunk-bed Q-£96, non-members pay £3 extra, cheap meals, open 24 hours, 36 Carter Lane, Tube: St. Paul's, tel. 020/7236-4965 or toll tel. 0845-371-9012, www.yha.org .uk, stpauls@yha.org.uk).

$ A cluster of three **St. Christopher's Inn** hostels, south of the Thames near London Bridge, have cheap dorm beds (£20–25, 161–165 Borough High Street, Tube: Borough or London Bridge, tel. 020/7407-1856, www.st-christophers.co.uk).

Dorms

$ The **University of Westminster** opens its dorm rooms to travelers during summer break, from mid-June until late September. Located in several high-rise buildings scattered around central London, the rooms—some with private bathrooms, others with shared bathrooms nearby—come with access to well-equipped kitchens and big lounges (S-£26–35, Sb-£35–55, D-£47–60, Db-£52–95, apartment Sb-£48–80, apartment Db-£58–90, weekly rates, tel. 020/7911-5181, www.wmin.ac.uk/comserv, unilet vacations@westminster.ac.uk).

$ **University College London** also has rooms for travelers, from mid-June until mid-September (S-£27–30, D-£55, breakfast extra, minimum 3-night stay, www.ucl.ac.uk/residences).

$ **Ace Hotel,** a budget hotel within four townhouses set in a residential neighborhood, has contemporary decor (£18–29 per bed in 3- to 8-bed dorms, bunk-bed D-£53–57, bunk-bed Db-£57–61, Db with patio-£99, pay Internet access, lounge and garden, 16–22 Gunterstone Road, West Kensington, tel. 020/7602-6600, www .ace-hotel.co.uk, reception@ace-hotel.co.uk).

Heathrow and Gatwick Airports
At or near Heathrow Airport

It's so easy to get to Heathrow from central London, I see no reason to sleep there. But if you do, here are some options.

$$ **Yotel,** at the airport, has small sleep dens that offer a place to catch a quick nap (four hours-£37–64), or to stay overnight (tiny "standard cabin"—£59/8 hours, "premium cabin"—£82/8 hours; cabins sleep 1–2 people; price is per cabin not person, reserve online for free or by phone for small fee). Prices vary by day, week, and time of year, so check their website. All rooms are only slightly larger than a double bed, and have private bathrooms and free Internet access and Wi-Fi. Windowless rooms have oddly purplish lighting (Heathrow Terminal 4, tel. 020/7100-1100, www.yotel .com, customer@yotel.com).

$ **easyHotel** is your cheapest bet, with 53 pod-like rooms on two floors (£25–45, no elevator, no breakfast, pay Internet access and Wi-Fi; Brick Field Lane, take local bus #140 from airport's Central Bus Station or the £4 "Hotel Hoppa" shuttle bus #H8 or #H3 from Terminals 1, 2, or 3—runs 2–3/hr; on-demand shuttle available, tel. 020/8897-9237, www.easyhotel.com, enquiries @heathrow.easyhotel.com).

$$ Hotel Ibis London Heathrow is a chain hotel offering predictable value (Db-£77, Db-£52 on Fri–Sun, check website for specials as low as £45, breakfast-£7, pay Internet access and Wi-Fi; 112–114 Bath Road, take local bus #105, #111, #140, #285, #423, or #555 from airport's Central Bus Station or #555 direct from Terminal 4, or the £4 "Hotel Hoppa" shuttle bus #H6 from Terminals 1, 2, or 3; tel. 020/8759-4888, fax 020/8564-7894, www .ibishotel.com, h0794@accor.com).

$$ Jurys Inn, another hotel chain, tempts tired travelers with 300-plus cookie-cutter rooms (Db-£85–105, check website for deals, breakfast extra; on Eastern Perimeter Road, Tube: Hatton Cross plus 5-min walk; take the £3.20 Tube one stop from Terminals 1, 2, or 3; or two stops from Terminals 4 or 5; or the £4 "Hotel Hoppa" shuttle bus #H9 from Terminals 1, 2, or 3; or buses #285, #482, #490, or #555; tel. 020/8266-4664, fax 020/8266-4665, www.jurysinns.com).

At or near Gatwick Airport

$$ Yotel, with small rooms, has a branch right at the airport (Gatwick South Terminal, see prices and contact info in Heathrow listing, earlier).

$$ Gatwick Airport Central Premier Inn rents cheap rooms 350 yards from the airport (Db-£75, £67 Fri–Sun, breakfast-£8, £2 shuttle bus from airport—must reserve in advance, Longbridge Way, North Terminal, toll tel. 0870-238-3305, frustrating phone tree, www.premierinn.com). Four more Premier Inns are within a five-mile radius from the airport.

$$ Barn Cottage, a converted 16th-century barn flanked by a tennis court and swimming pool, sits in the peaceful countryside, with a good pub just two blocks away. Its two wood-beamed rooms, antique furniture, and large garden make you forget Gatwick is 10 minutes away (S-£55, D-£75, cash only, Church Road, Leigh, Reigate, Surrey, tel. 01306/611-347, warmly run by Pat and Mike Comer). Don't confuse this place with others of the same name; this Barn Cottage has no website. A taxi from Gatwick to here runs about £15; the Comers can take you back to the airport or train station for about £10.

$ Gatwick Airport Travelodge has budget rooms about a mile from the airport (Db-£39–57, breakfast extra, Wi-Fi, Church Road, Lowfield Heath, Crawley, £4 "Hotel Hoppa" shuttle bus from airport, toll tel. 0871-984-6031, www.travelodge.co.uk).

For Longer Stays

Staying a week or longer? Consider the advantages that come with renting a furnished apartment, or "flat," as the British say. Complete with a small, equipped kitchen and living room, this option can also sometimes work for families or groups on shorter visits. Among the many organizations ready to help, the following have been recommended by local guides and readers: www .perfectplaceslondon.co.uk, www.homefromhome.co.uk, www .london33.com, www.london-house.com, www.gowithit.co.uk, www.aplacelikehome.co.uk, and www.regentsuites.com.

Sometimes you can save money by renting directly from the apartment owner (check www.vrbo.com). Readers also report success using Craig's List (http://london.craigslist.co.uk; search within "holiday rentals").

Read the conditions of rental carefully and ask lots of questions. If a certain amenity is important to you (such as Wi-Fi or a washing machine in the unit), ask specifically about it and what to do if it stops working. Plot the location carefully (plug the address into http://maps.google.com), and remember to factor in travel time and costs from outlying neighborhoods to central London. Finally, it's a good idea to buy trip cancellation/interruption insurance, as many weekly rentals are nonrefundable.

Eating in London

In London, the sheer variety of foods—from every corner of its former empire and beyond—is astonishing. You'll be amazed at the number of hopping, happening new restaurants of all kinds.

If you want to dine (as opposed to eat), drop by a London newsstand to get a weekly entertainment guide or an annual restaurant guide (both have extensive restaurant listings). Visit www.london-eating.co.uk or www.squaremeal.co.uk for more options.

The thought of a £40 meal in Britain generally ruins my appetite, so my London dining is limited mostly to easygoing, fun, inexpensive alternatives. I've listed places by neighborhood—handy to your sightseeing or hotel. Considering how expensive London can be, if there's any good place to cut corners to stretch your budget, it's by eating cheap.

Pub grub is the most atmospheric budget option. Many of London's 7,000 pubs serve fresh, tasty buffets under ancient timbers, with hearty lunches and dinners priced £7–9.

Ethnic restaurants—especially Indian and Chinese—are popular, plentiful, and cheap. Most large museums (and many churches) have inexpensive, cheery cafeterias. Of course, picnicking is the fastest and cheapest way to go. Good grocery stores and sandwich shops, fine park benches, and polite pigeons abound in Britain's most expensive city.

London (and all of Britain) is now smoke-free, thanks to a recent smoking ban. Expect restaurants and pubs that sell food to be non-smoking indoors, with smokers occupying patios and doorways outside.

Central London
Near Trafalgar Square

These eateries are within about 100 yards of Trafalgar Square. To locate the following restaurants, see the map on the next page.

St. Martin-in-the-Fields Café in the Crypt is just right for a tasty meal on a monk's budget—maybe even on a monk's tomb. You'll dine sitting on somebody's gravestone in an ancient crypt. Their enticing buffet line is kept stocked all day, serving breakfast, lunch, and dinner (£6–8 cafeteria plates, Mon–Wed 8:00–20:00, Thu–Sat 8:00–21:00, Sun 11:00–18:00, profits go to the church, underneath Church of St. Martin-in-the-Fields on Trafalgar Square, Tube: Charing Cross, tel. 020/7766-1158 or 020/7766-1100). Wednesday evenings at 20:00 come with a live jazz band (£5–8 tickets). While here, check out the concert schedule for the busy church upstairs (or visit www.smitf.org).

The Chandos Pub's Opera Room floats amazingly apart from the tacky crush of tourism around Trafalgar Square. Look for it opposite the National Portrait Gallery (corner of William IV Street and St. Martin's Lane) and climb the stairs to the Opera Room. This is a fine Trafalgar rendezvous point and wonderfully local pub. They serve traditional, plain-tasting £6–7 pub meals— meat pies are their specialty. The ground-floor pub is stuffed with regulars and offers snugs (private booths), the same menu, and more serious beer drinking (kitchen open daily 11:00–18:00, order and pay at the bar, 29 St. Martin's Lane, Tube: Leicester Square, tel. 020/7836-1401).

Gordon's Wine Bar, with a simple, steep staircase leading into a candlelit 15th-century wine cellar, is filled with dusty old bottles, faded British memorabilia, and local nine-to-fivers. At the "English rustic" buffet, choose a hot meal or cold meat dish with a salad, or a hearty (and splittable) plate of cheeses, bread, and pickles (£7.50). Then step up to the wine bar and consider the many varieties of wine and port available by the glass. This place is passionate about port. The low, carbon-crusted vaulting deeper in the back seems to intensify the Hogarth-painting atmosphere. Although it's crowded, you can normally corral two chairs and grab the corner of a table. On hot days, the crowd spills out into a leafy back patio (arrive before 17:30 to get a seat, Mon–Sat 11:00–23:00, Sun 12:00–22:00, 2 blocks from Trafalgar Square, bottom

Central London Eateries

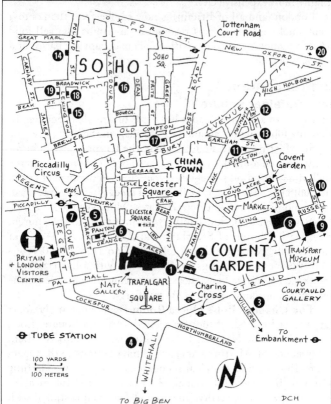

1 St. Martin-in-the-Fields
   Café in the Crypt

2 The Chandos Pub's Opera Room

3 Gordon's Wine Bar

4 The Lord Moon of the Mall Pub

5 Stockpot & Woodlands South
   Indian Vegetarian Restaurant

6 West End Kitchen

7 Criterion Restaurant

8 Just Falafs

9 To The Food Balcony, Joe Allen,
   Livebait & PJ's Bar and Grill

10 Ristorante Zizzi

11 Belgo Centraal

12 Neal's Yard Eateries

13 Food for Thought Café

14 Yo! Sushi

15 Wagamama Noodle Bar

16 Busaba Eathai Thai Rest.
   & Côte Restaurant

17 Y Ming Chinese Rest.

18 Andrew Edmunds Rest.

19 Mildred's Vegetarian Rest.
   & Fernandez & Wells

20 To The Princess Louise Pub

of Villiers Street at #47, Tube: Embankment, tel. 020/7930-1408, manager Gerard Menan).

The Lord Moon of the Mall pub has real ales on tap and good, cheap pub grub, including a two-meals-for-the-price-of-one deal (£8, Mon–Fri 14:00–22:00). The pub fills a great old former Barclays Bank building a block down Whitehall from Trafalgar Square (daily 9:00–22:00, no kids after 18:00, 16–18 Whitehall, Tube: Charing Cross or Embankment, tel. 020/7839-7701). Nearby are several cheap cafeterias and pizza joints.

Near Piccadilly

Hungry and broke in the theater district? Head for Panton Street (off Haymarket, 2 blocks southeast of Piccadilly Circus) where several hardworking little places compete, all seeming to offer a three-course meal for about £8.50. Peruse the entire block (vegetarian, Pizza Express, Moroccan, Thai, Chinese, and two famous eateries) before making your choice. **Stockpot** is a meat, potatoes, gravy, and mushy-peas kind of place, famous and rightly popular for its edible, cheap English meals (Mon–Sat 7:00–23:30, Sun 7:00–22:00, 38–40 Panton Street, cash only). The **West End Kitchen** (across the street at #5, same hours and menu) is a direct competitor that's also well-known and just as good. Vegetarians prefer the **Woodlands South Indian Vegetarian Restaurant** at #37 Panton Street.

The palatial **Criterion** offers grand-piano ambience beneath gilded tiles and chandeliers in a dreamy Byzantine church setting from 1880. It's right on Piccadilly Circus but a world away from the punk junk. The house wine is great, as is the food. After 19:00, the menu becomes really expensive. Anyone can drop in for coffee or a drink (£17–19 fixed-price meals, Mon–Sat 12:00–14:30 & 17:30–23:30, Sun 12:00–15:30 & 17:30–22:30, 224 Piccadilly, tel. 020/7930-0488).

The Wolseley is the grand 1920s showroom of a long-defunct British car. The last Wolseley drove out with the Great Depression, but today this old-time bistro bustles with formal waiters serving traditional Austrian and French dishes in an elegant black-marble-and-chandeliers setting fit for its location next to the Ritz. While the food can be unexceptional, prices are reasonable, and the presentation and setting are grand. Reservations are a must (£16.50 plates; cheaper soup, salad, and sandwich menu available; Mon–Fri 7:00–24:00, Sat 8:00–24:00, Sun 8:00–23:00, 160 Piccadilly, tel. 020/7499-6996). They're popular for their fancy cream or afternoon tea (£9.75–19.75, served Sun–Fri 15:30–18:30, Sat 15:30–17:30).

Pub Appreciation

The pub is the heart of the people's England, where all manner of folks have, for generations, found their respite from work and a home-away-from-home. England's classic pubs are national treasures, with great cultural value and rich history, not to mention good beer and grub.

The Golden Age for pub-building was in the late Victorian era (c. 1880–1905), when pubs were independently owned and land prices were high enough to make it worthwhile to invest in fixing up pubs. The politics were pro-pub as well: Conservatives, backed by Big Beer, were in, and temperance-minded Liberals were out.

Especially in class-conscious Victorian times, traditional pubs were divided into sections by elaborate screens (now mostly gone), allowing the wealthy to drink in a more refined setting, while commoners congregated on the pub's rougher side. These were really "public houses," featuring nooks (snugs) for groups and clubs to meet, friends and lovers to rendezvous, and families to get out of the house at night. Since many pub-goers were illiterate, pubs were simply named for the picture hung outside (e.g., The Crooked Stick, The Queen's Arms—meaning her coat of arms).

Historic pubs still dot the London cityscape. The only place to see the very oldest-style tavern in the "domestic tradition" is at **Ye Olde Cheshire Cheese,** which was rebuilt in 1667 from a 16th-century tavern (open daily, 145 Fleet Street, Tube: Temple or St. Paul's, Blackfriars station is nearest but is closed until 2011; tel. 020/7353-6170). Imagine this place in the pre-Victorian era: With no bar, drinkers gathered around the fireplaces, while tap boys shuttled tankards up from the cellar. (This was long before barroom taps were connected to casks in the cellar. Oh, and don't say "keg"—that's a gassy modern thing.)

Late Victorian pubs, such as the lovingly restored 1897 **Princess Louise** (open daily 12:00–23:00, 208 High Holborn, Tube: Holborn, tel. 020/7405-8816) are more common. These places are fancy, often coming with heavy embossed wallpaper ceilings, decorative tile work, fine-etched glass, ornate carved stillions (the big central hutch for storing bottles and glass), and even urinals equipped with a place to set your glass. London's best Art Nouveau pub is **The Black Friar** (c. 1900–1915), with fine carved capitals, lamp holders, and quirky phrases worked into the decor (open daily, Tube: Temple or St. Paul's, across from the Blackfriars Tube station—station closed until 2011—at 174 Queen Victoria Street, tel. 020/7236-5474).

The "former-bank pubs" represent a more modern trend in pub building. As banks increasingly go electronic, they're moving

Historic Pubs

ST. PAUL'S

BANK OF ENGLAND

ROYAL COURTS

St. Paul's

TO TRAFALGAR SQUARE

Black-friars (closed 10–11)

THE TEMPLE

Temple

THAMES RIVER

TATE MODERN

GLOBE

TO TOWER OF LONDON →

Bank

Mansion House

Monu-ment

Mayfair

STREET WIDTH EXAGGERATED FOR CLARITY

400 YARDS
400 METERS

DCH

⊖ TUBE STATION
⋏ VIEW

Historic Pubs
① Ye Olde Cheshire Cheese
② The Black Friar
③ The Old Bank of England
④ The Counting House

Other Eatery
⑤ De Gustibus Sandwiches

LONDON

out of lavish, high-rent old buildings. Many of these former banks are being refitted as pubs with elegant bars and free-standing stillions, providing a fine centerpiece. Three such pubs are **The Old Bank of England** (closed Sat–Sun, 194 Fleet Street, Tube: Temple, tel. 020/7430-2255), **The Jugged Hare** (open daily, 172 Vauxhall Bridge Road, see map on page 131, Tube: Victoria, tel. 020/7828-1543, also see listing on page 152), and **The Counting House** (closed Sat–Sun, 50 Cornhill, Tube: Bank, tel. 020/7283-7123, also see listing on page 157).

Go pubbing in the evening for a lively time, or drop by during the quiet late morning (from 11:00), when the pub is empty and filled with memories. For more information, see Bob Steel's website, www.aletrails.com. Bob also offers London Heritage pub tours (about £50 per group for a leisurely half-day private walk).

Near Covent Garden

Covent Garden bustles with people and touristy eateries. Although the area feels overrun, there are some good options.

Just Falafs is a healthy fast-food option in the chaos of Covent Garden. Located in the southeast corner, where rows of outdoor café tables line the tiny shop, they offer falafel sandwiches with yummy vegetarian-friendly extras (£4–6 sandwiches, daily until about 21:00, 27b Covent Gardens Square, tel. 020/7240-3838).

The Food Balcony, with great people-watching overlooking the Jubilee Market Piazza, is a sticky food circus of ethnic places serving £6 meals on disposable plates and wobbly plastic tables (closes at 18:30). A handy Wagamama Noodle Bar is around the corner on Tavistock Street (see description in next section).

Joe Allen, tucked in a basement a block away, serves modern international cuisine with both style and hubbub. Downstairs off a quiet street with candles and white tablecloths, it's comfortably spacious and popular with the theater crowd (meals for about £30, £15 two-course specials and £17 three-course specials 17:00–18:45, open Mon–Fri 8:00–24:45, Sat 11:30–24:45, Sun 11:30–23:45, piano music after 21:00, 13 Exeter Street, tel. 020/7836-0651).

Livebait Restaurant is an upscale fish-and-chips place with an elegant yet simple tiled interior. Their forte is fresh and well-prepared fish (£14–20 main courses, specials before 19:00, Mon–Sat 12:00–23:00, Sun 12:00–21:00, 21 Wellington Street, tel. 020/7836-7161).

Ristorante Zizzi is a fun, top-end Italian chain with a crisp contemporary atmosphere, an open pizza oven adding warmth and action, and a sharp local clientele (£7–10 pizzas, pastas, and salads; great chicken Caesar, daily 12:00–23:00, 20 Bow Street, tel. 020/7836-6101).

PJ's Bar and Grill, a tired diner that seems to be a hit with locals, serves decent "modern European" food. It's family-friendly, with more intimate seating in the back (£10–15 meals, Mon–Sat 12:00–24:00, Sun 11:30–16:00, 30 Wellington Street, 020/7240-7529).

Belgo Centraal serves hearty Belgian specialties in a vast 400-seat underground lair. It's a seafood, chips, and beer emporium dressed up as a mod-monastic refectory—with noisy acoustics and waiters garbed as Trappist monks. The classy restaurant section is more comfortable and less rowdy, but usually requires reservations. It's often more fun just to grab a spot in the boisterous beer hall, with its tight, communal benches (no reservations accepted). The same menu and specials work on both sides. Belgians claim they eat as well as the French and as heartily as the Germans. Specialties include mussels, great-tasting fries, and a stunning array of dark, blond, and fruity Belgian beers. Belgo actually makes Belgian things trendy—a formidable feat (£10–14 meals; Mon–Sat 12:00–23:00, Sun 12:00–22:30, Mon–Fri £5–6.30 "beat the clock" meal specials 17:00–18:30—the time you order is the price you pay—including main dishes, fries, and beer; no meal-splitting after 18:30, and you must buy food with beer; daily £7.50 lunch special 12:00–17:00; 1 kid eats free for each parent ordering a regular entree; 1 block north of Covent Garden Tube station at intersection of Neal and Shelton streets, 50 Earlham Street, tel. 020/7813-2233).

Neal's Yard is *the* place for cheap, hip, and healthy eateries near Covent Garden. The neighborhood is a tabouli of fun, hippie-type cafés. One of the best is the vegetarian **Food for Thought,** packed with local health nuts (good £5 vegetarian meals, £7.50 dinner plates, Mon–Sat 12:00–20:30, Sun 12:00–17:00, 2 blocks north of Covent Garden Tube station, 31 Neal Street, near Neal's Yard, tel. 020/7836-0239).

Near Soho and Chinatown

London has a trendy scene that most Beefeater-seekers miss entirely. These restaurants are scattered throughout the hipster, gay, and strip-club district, teeming each evening with fun-seekers and theater-goers. Even if you plan to have dinner elsewhere, it's a treat just to wander around this lively area.

Beware of the extremely welcoming women standing outside the strip clubs (especially on Great Windmill Street). Enjoy the sales pitch—but only fools fall for the "£5 drink and show" lure. They don't get back out without emptying their wallet...literally.

Yo! Sushi is a futuristic Japanese-food-extravaganza experience. It's pricey—those plates add up fast—but it's a memorable experience, complete with thumping rock, Japanese cable TV, and a 195-foot-long conveyor belt—the world's longest sushi bar. For £1 you get unlimited green tea or water (from spigot at bar, with or without gas). Snag a bar stool and grab dishes as they rattle by (priced by color of dish; check the chart: £1.75–5 per dish, £1.75 for miso soup, daily 12:00–23:00, 2 blocks south of Oxford Street, where Lexington Street becomes Poland Street, 52 Poland Street, tel. 020/7287-0443). If you like Yo!, there are several locations around town, including a handy branch a block from the London Eye on Belvedere Road, as well as outlets within Selfridges, Harvey Nichols department stores, and Whiteleys Mall on Queensway.

Wagamama Noodle Bar is a noisy pan-Asian, organic slur-pathon. As you enter, check out the kitchen and listen to the roar of the basement, where benches rock with happy eaters. Everybody sucks. Stand against the wall to feel the energy of all this "positive eating." Portions are huge and splitting is allowed (£7–11 meals,

The Soho "Food Is Fun" Three-Course Dinner Crawl

For a multicultural, movable feast, consider enjoying a drink and eating (or splitting) one course at each of these places. Start around 17:30 to avoid lines, get in on early-bird specials, and find waiters willing to let you split a meal. Prices, though reasonable by London standards, add up. Servings are large enough to share. All are open nightly. Arrive at 17:30 at **Belgo Centraal** and split the early-bird dinner special—a kilo of mussels, fries, and dark Belgian beer. At **Yo! Sushi,** have beer or sake and a few dishes, then slurp your last course at **Wagamama Noodle Bar.** For a low-calorie dessert, people-watch at Leicester Square.

Mon–Sat 11:30–23:00, Sun 12:00–22:00, crowded after 19:00, 10A Lexington Street, tel. 020/7292-0990 but no reservations taken). If you like this place, handy branches are all over town, including one near the British Museum (4 Streatham Street), Kensington (26 High Street), in Harvey Nichols (109 Knightsbridge), Covent Garden (1 Tavistock Street), Leicester Square (14 Irving Street), Piccadilly Circus (8 Norris Street), Fleet Street (#109), and next to the Tower of London (Tower Place).

Busaba Eathai Thai Restaurant is a hit with locals for its snappy service, casual-yet-high-energy ambience, and good, inexpensive Thai cuisine. You'll sit communally around big, square 16-person hardwood tables or in two-person tables by the window—with everyone in the queue staring at your noodles. They don't take reservations, so arrive by 19:00 or line up (£7–10 meals, Mon–Thu 12:00–23:00, Fri–Sat 12:00–23:30, Sun 12:00–22:00, 106 Wardour Street, tel. 020/7255-8686). They have two other handy locations: at 22 Store Street, near the British Museum and Goodge Street Tube; and 8–13 Bird Street, just off Oxford Street and across from the Bond Street Tube.

Côte Restaurant is a contemporary French bistro chain, serving good-value French cuisine at the right prices (£9–13 mains, early dinner specials, Mon–Wed 8:00–23:00, Thu–Fri 8:00–24:00, Sat 10:00–24:00, Sun 10:00–22:30, 124–126 Wardour Street, tel. 020/7287-9280).

Y Ming Chinese Restaurant—across Shaftesbury Avenue from the ornate gates, clatter, and dim sum of Chinatown—has dressy European decor, serious but helpful service, and authentic Northern Chinese cooking (good £10 meal deal offered 12:00–18:00, £7–10 plates, open Mon–Sat 12:00–23:45, closed Sun, 35–36 Greek Street, tel. 020/7734-2721).

Andrew Edmunds Restaurant is a tiny, candlelit place where you'll want to hide your camera and guidebook and act as local as possible. This little place—with a jealous and loyal clientele— is the closest I've found to Parisian quality in a cozy restaurant in London. The modern European cooking and creative seasonal menu are worth the splurge (£25 meals, Mon–Sat 12:30–15:00 & 18:00–22:45, Sun 13:00–15:30 & 18:00–22:30, come early or call ahead, request ground floor rather than basement, 46 Lexington Street in Soho, tel. 020/7437-5708).

Mildred's Vegetarian Restaurant, across from Andrew Edmunds, has cheap prices, an enjoyable menu, and a plain-yet-pleasant interior filled with happy eaters (£7–9 meals, Mon–Sat 12:00–23:00, closed Sun, vegan options, 45 Lexington Street, tel. 020/7494-1634).

Fernandez & Wells is a delightfully simple little wine, cheese, and ham bar. Drop in and grab a stool as you belly up to the big wooden bar. Share a plate of top-quality cheeses and/or Spanish or French hams with fine bread and oil, while sipping a nice glass of wine and talking with Juan or Toby (Mon–Sat 11:00–22:00, Sun 12:00–19:00, quality sandwiches at lunch, wine/cheese/ham bar after 16:00, 43 Lexington Street, tel. 020/7734-1546).

West London

Near Victoria Station Accommodations

I've enjoyed eating at these places, a few blocks southwest of Victoria Station (see the map on page 131).

Ebury Wine Bar, filled with young professionals, provides a cut-above atmosphere, delicious £13–18 entrées, and a £15.50 two-course special at lunch and from 18:00 to 20:00. In the delightful back room, the fancy menu features modern European cuisine with a French accent; at the wine bar, find a cheaper bar menu that's better than your average pub grub. This is emphatically a "traditional wine bar," with no beers on tap (Mon–Sat 11:00–23:00, Sun 18:00–22:30, reserve after 20:00, at intersection of Ebury and Elizabeth Streets, near bus station, 139 Ebury Street, tel. 020/7730-5447).

Jenny Lo's Tea House is a simple budget place serving up reliably tasty £7–8 eclectic Chinese-style meals to locals in the know. While the menu is small, everything is high quality. Jenny clearly learned from her father, Ken Lo, one of the most famous Cantonese chefs in Britain, whose fancy place is just around the corner (Mon–Sat 11:30–15:00 & 18:00–22:00, closed Sun, cash only, 14 Eccleston Street, tel. 020/7259-0399).

La Poule au Pot, ideal for a romantic splurge, offers a classy, candlelit ambience with well-dressed patrons and expensive but good country-style French cuisine (£18.75 two-course lunch specials, £25 dinner plates, daily 12:30–14:30 & 18:45–23:00, Sun until

22:00, £50 for dinner with wine, leafy patio dining, reservations smart, end of Ebury Street at intersection with Pimlico Road, 231 Ebury Street, tel. 020/7730-7763).

Grumbles brags it's been serving "good food and wine at non-scary prices since 1964." Offering a delicious mix of "modern eclectic French and traditional English," this unpretentious little place with cozy booths inside and four nice sidewalk tables is *the* spot to eat well in this otherwise workaday neighborhood (£8–16 plates, £11 early-bird specials 18:00–19:00, open Mon–Sat 12:00–14:30 & 18:00–22:45, Sun 12:00–22:30, reservations wise, half a block north of Belgrave Road at 35 Churton Street, tel. 020/7834-0149). Multitaskers take note: The self-service launderette down the street is open evenings.

Chimes English Restaurant and Cider Bar comes with a fresh country farm ambience, serious ciders (rare in London), and very good, traditional English food. Experiment with the cider—it's legal here...just barely (£8–12 meals, £13 two-course specials, hearty salads, Mon–Sat 12:00–15:00 & 17:30–22:15, Sun 12:00–23:15, 26 Churton Street, tel. 020/7821-7456).

The Jugged Hare, a 10-minute walk from Victoria Station, is a pub in a lavish old bank building, its vaults replaced by tankards of beer and a fine kitchen. They have a fun, traditional menu with more fresh veggies than fries, and a plush and vivid pub scene good for a meal or just a drink (£8–10 meals, daily 12:00–21:30, 172 Vauxhall Bridge Road, tel. 020/7828-1543).

Seafresh Fish Restaurant is the neighborhood place for plaice—either take-out on the cheap or eat-in, enjoying a chrome-and-wood mod ambience with classic and creative fish-and-chips cuisine. Though Mario's father started this place in 1965, it feels like the chippie of the 21st century (meals-£5 to go, £6–13 to sit, Mon–Fri 12:00–15:00 & 17:00–22:30, Sat 12:00–22:30, closed Sun, 80–81 Wilton Road, tel. 020/7828-0747).

La Bottega is an Italian delicatessen that fits its upscale Belgravia neighborhood. It offers tasty, freshly cooked pastas (£5.50), lasagnas, and salads at its counter (lasagna and salad meal-£8), along with great sandwiches (£3) and a good coffee bar with pastries. It's not cheap, but it's fast (order at the counter), and the ingredients would please an Italian chef (Mon–Fri 8:00–18:30, Sat 9:00–18:00, closed Sun, on corner of Ebury and Eccleston Streets, tel. 020/7730-2730). Grab your meal to go, or enjoy the good Belgravia life with locals, either sitting inside or on the sidewalk.

St. George's Tavern is *the* pub for a meal in this neighborhood. They serve dinner from the same fun menu in three zones: on the sidewalk to catch the sun and enjoy some people-watching, in the sloppy pub, and in a classier back dining room (£7–10 meals, proud of their sausages, Mon–Sat 10:00–22:00, Sun until 21:00, corner of Hugh Street and Belgrave Road, tel. 020/7630-1116).

Drinking Pubs that Serve Food: If you want to have a pub meal or just enjoy a drink surrounded by interesting local crowds, consider three pubs in the neighborhood, each with a distinct character: **The Duke of Wellington** is a classic neighborhood pub with forgettable grub, woodsy sidewalk seating, and an inviting interior (food served Mon–Sat 12:00–15:00 & 18:00–21:00, Sun 12:00–15:00 only, 63 Eaton Terrace, tel. 020/7730-1782). **The Belgravia Pub** is a sports bar with burgers, a stark interior, and a little outdoor garden (daily 12:00–21:30, corner of Ebury Street and South Eaton Place at 152 Ebury Street, tel. 020/7730-6040). **The Thomas Cubitt Pub,** packed with young professionals, is the neighborhood's trendy new "gastropub," great for a drink or pricey meals (44 Elizabeth Street, tel. 020/7730-6060).

Cheap Eats: For groceries, a handy **Marks & Spencer Simply Food** is inside Victoria Station (Mon–Sat 7:00–24:00, Sun 8:00–22:00), along with a **Sainsbury's Market** (daily 6:00–23:00, at rear entrance, on Eccleston Street; a second Sainsbury's is just north of the station on Victoria Street). A larger Sainsbury's is on Wilton Road near Warwick Way, a couple of blocks southeast of the station (daily 6:00–24:00). A string of good ethnic restaurants line Wilton Road (near the Seafresh Fish Restaurant, recommended earlier). For affordable, if forgettable, meals, try the row of cheap little eateries on Elizabeth Street.

Near Notting Hill and Bayswater Accommodations

The road called Queensway is a multi-ethnic food circus, lined with lively and inexpensive eateries. See the map on page 136.

Maggie Jones, a £40 splurge, is where Charles Dickens meets Ella Fitzgerald—exuberantly rustic and very English with a 1940s-jazz sound track. You'll get solid English cuisine, including huge plates of crunchy vegetables, served by a young and casual staff. It's pricey, but the portions are huge (especially the meat and fish pies—their specialty). You're welcome to save lots by splitting your main course. The candlelit upstairs is the most romantic, while the basement is kept lively with the kitchen, tight seating, and lots of action. If you eat well once in London, eat here—and do it quick, before it burns down (daily 12:30–14:30 & 18:30–23:00, reservations recommended, 6 Old Court Place, just east of Kensington Church Street, near High Street Kensington Tube stop, tel. 020/7937-6462).

The Churchill Arms pub and **Thai Kitchens** (same location) are local hangouts, with good beer and a thriving old-English ambience in front, and hearty £6 Thai plates in an enclosed patio in the back. You can eat the Thai food in the tropical hideaway or in the atmospheric pub section. The place is festooned with

Taking Tea in London

Once the sole province of genteel ladies in fancy hats, afternoon tea has become more democratic in the 21st century. While some tearooms—such as the £37-a-head tea service at the Ritz and the finicky Fortnum & Mason—still require a jacket and tie (and a big bank account), most welcome tourists in jeans and sneakers.

The cheapest "tea" on the menu is generally a "cream tea"; the most expensive is the "champagne tea." **Cream tea** is simply a pot of tea and a homemade scone or two with jam and thick clotted cream. **Afternoon tea** generally is a cream tea, plus a tier of three plates holding small finger foods (such as cucumber sandwiches) and an assortment of small pastries. **Champagne tea** includes all of the goodies, plus a glass of champagne. For maximum pinkie-waving taste per calorie, slice your scone thin like a miniature loaf of bread. **High tea** generally means a more substantial late afternoon or early evening meal, often served with meat or eggs and eaten at a "higher" (i.e., kitchen) table.

Tearooms, which often also serve appealing light meals, are usually open for lunch and close at about 17:00, just before dinner. At all the places listed below, it's perfectly acceptable to order one afternoon tea and one cream tea (at about £5) and split the afternoon-tea goodies. The fancier places, such as Harrods and The Capital Hotel, are happy to bring you seconds and thirds of your favorites, turning tea into an early dinner.

The Orangery at Kensington Palace serves four different varieties of tea meals, from the £12.50 "Orangery tea" to the £25 "Tregothnan tea" in its bright white hall near Princess Di's former residence. You can also order treats à la carte. The portions aren't huge, but who can argue with eating at a princess' house? (Tea served 15:00–18:00, no reservations taken; located on map on page 136, a 10-min walk through Kensington Gardens from either Queensway or High Street Kensington Tube stations to the orange brick building, about 20 yards from Kensington Palace; tel. 020/7938-1406, www.hrp.org.uk.)

The National Dining Rooms, a restaurant/café within the National Gallery on Trafalgar Square, is both classy and convenient. The restaurant can book up in advance, but you can generally waltz in for afternoon tea at the café. To play it safe, arrive in the early afternoon to reserve a tea time, then visit the National Gallery (page 77) before or after your appointed time (£4 cakes and tarts, £5.50 cream tea, £14.50 afternoon tea, tea served 15:00–17:00, located in Sainsbury Wing of National Gallery, Tube: Charing Cross or Leicester Square, tel. 020/7747-2525, www.thenationaldiningrooms.co.uk).

The Café at Sotheby's, located on the ground floor of the auction giant's headquarters, is manna for shoppers taking a break from fashionable New Bond Street. There are no windows—just a long leather bench, plenty of mirrors, and a dark-wood room where waiters serve sweet treats and the £5.50 mix-and-match Neal's Yard cheese plate to locals in the know

(£3 cakes and creams, £6.50 "small tea," £13.75 afternoon tea must be ordered 24 hours in advance—call 020/7293-5077, café open Mon–Fri only 9:30–11:30 & 12:00–16:45, afternoon tea served 15:00–16:45, 34-35 New Bond Street, Tube: Bond Street or Oxford Circus, www.sothebys.com/cafe/restaurant.html).

For a classier experience with an attentive waitstaff, try **The Capital Hotel,** a luxury hotel a half-block from Harrods. The Capital caters to weary shoppers with its intimate, linen-table-cloth tearoom. It's where the ladies-who-lunch meet to decide whether to buy that Versace gown they've had their eye on. Even so, casual clothes, kids, and sharing plates—with a £2.50 split-tea service charge—are all OK (£18.50 afternoon tea, daily 15:00–17:30, call to book ahead, especially on weekends, see map on page 134, 22 Basil Street, Tube: Knightsbridge, tel. 020/7589-5171).

Two famous department stores—Fortnum & Mason and Harrods—serve afternoon tea for sky-high prices. **Fortnum & Mason's St. James's Restaurant,** on the fourth floor, offers plush seats under the elegant tearoom's chandeliers. You'll get the standard three-tiered silver tea tray: finger sandwiches on the bottom, fresh scones with jam and clotted cream on the first floor, and decadent pastries and "tartlets" on the top floor, with unlimited tea. Consider it dinner (about £30–38, Mon–Sat 14:00–18:30, Sun 12:00–16:30, dress up a bit for this—no shorts, "children must be behaved," 181 Piccadilly, reserve in advance online or at toll tel. 0845-602-5694, www.fortnumandmason.com).

At **Harrods' Georgian Restaurant** you (along with 200 of your closest friends) can enjoy a fancy tea under a skylight as a pianist tickles the keys of a Bösendorfer, the world's most expensive piano (£21 afternoon tea, includes finger sandwiches and pastries with free refills, served daily from 15:45, last order at 17:15, on Brompton Road, Tube: Knightsbridge, reservations tel. 020/7225-6800, store tel. 020/7730-1234, www.harrods.com).

If you want the teatime experience but are put off by the price, try the department stores on Oxford Street. **John Lewis** has a mod third-floor brasserie that serves a nice £10 afternoon-tea platter (on Oxford Street one block west of the Bond Street Tube station). **Selfridges'** afternoon tea, served after 15:00 in the Gallery Restaurant, is pricier at £16.50. Near the Ritz, consider the £9.75 cream tea or the £19.75 afternoon tea at **The Wolseley** (see listing on page 145).

Many museums and bookstores have cafés serving afternoon tea goodies à la carte, where you can put together a spread for less than £10; **Waterstone's** fifth-floor café and the **Victoria and Albert Museum** café are two of the best.

The modern **teapod,** on the South Bank, serves cream tea for £5 and afternoon tea for £10, along with sandwiches, soups, salads, and pastries (Mon–Fri 8:30–18:00, Sat 9:00–19:00, Sun 10:00–19:00, 31 Shad Thames, 200 yards from the Tower Bridge, tel. 020/7407-0000).

Churchill memorabilia and chamber pots (including one with Hitler's mug on it—hanging from the ceiling farthest from Thai Kitchen—sure to cure the constipation of any Brit during World War II). Arrive by 18:00 or after 21:00 to avoid a line. During busy times, diners are limited to an hour at the table (daily 12:00–22:00, 119 Kensington Church Street, tel. 020/7792-1246).

The Prince Edward serves good grub in a quintessential pub setting (£7–10 meals, Mon–Sat 11:00–15:00 & 18:00–23:00, Sun 11:00–22:30, plush-pubby indoor seating or sidewalk tables, family-friendly, free Wi-Fi, 2 blocks north of Bayswater Road at the corner of Dawson Place and Hereford Road, 73 Prince's Square, tel. 020/7727-2221).

Café Diana is a healthy little eatery serving sandwiches, salads, and Middle Eastern food. It's decorated—almost shrine-like—with photos of Princess Diana, who used to drop by for pita sandwiches (daily 8:00–23:00, 5 Wellington Terrace, on Bayswater Road, opposite Kensington Palace Garden Gates—where Di once lived, tel. 020/7792-9606).

Royal China Restaurant is filled with London's Chinese, who consider this one of the city's best eateries. It's dressed up in black, white, and gold, with candles, brisk waiters, and fine food (£7–11 dishes, daily 12:00–23:00, dim sum until 16:45, 13 Queensway, tel. 020/7221-2535).

Whiteleys Mall Food Court offers a fun selection of ethnic and fast-food chain eateries among Corinthian columns, and a multiscreen theater in a delightful mall (daily 9:00–23:00; options include Yo! Sushi, good salads at Café Rouge, pizza, Starbucks, and a coin-op Internet place; second floor, corner of Porchester Gardens and Queensway).

Supermarket: **Tesco** is a half-block from the Notting Hill Gate Tube stop (Mon–Sat 8:00–23:00, Sun 11:00–17:00, near intersection with Pembridge Road, 114–120 Notting Hill Gate). The smaller **Spar Market** is at 18 Queensway (Mon–Sat 7:00–24:00, Sun 9:00–24:00), and **Marks & Spencer** can be found in Whiteleys Mall (Mon–Sat 10:00–20:00, Sun 12:00–18:00).

Near South Kensington Accommodations

Popular eateries line Old Brompton Road and Thurloe Street (Tube: South Kensington), and a huge variety of cheap eateries are clumped around the Tube station. See the map on page 134.

The **Tesco Express** grocery store is handy for picnics (daily 7:00–24:00, 50–52 Old Brompton Road).

La Bouchée Bistro Café is a classy, hole-in-the-wall touch of France. This candlelit, woody bistro serves a two-course, £11.50 special weekdays at lunch and from 17:30–18:30, and £17 *plats du* *jour* all *jour* (daily 12:00–15:00 & 17:30–23:30, 56 Old Brompton Road, tel. 020/7589-1929).

Daquise, an authentic-feeling 1930s Polish time warp, is ideal if you're in the mood for kielbasa and kraut. It's likeably dreary—fast, cheap, family-run—and a much-appreciated part of the neighborhood (£10 meals, weekday lunch special, daily 12:00–23:00, 20 Thurloe Street, tel. 020/7589-6117).

Moti Mahal Indian Restaurant, with minimalist-yet-classy mod ambience and attentive service, offers delicious Indian and Bangladeshi cuisine. Chicken *jalfrezi* and butter chicken are the favorites (£10 dinners, Mon–Sat 11:30–14:30 & 17:30–23:00, Sun 12:00–23:30, 3 Glendower Place, tel. 020/7584-8428).

Beirut Express II has fresh, well-prepared Lebanese cuisine, with quick-serve barstools and take-away service in the front, and a sit-down restaurant in the back (65 Old Brompton Road, tel. 020/7591-0123).

The Zetland Arms serves good pub meals in a classic pub atmosphere on its noisy and congested ground floor, and in a more spacious and comfy upstairs—used only in the evenings. Large groups may find it too crowded after 18:00 (same menu throughout, £6–10 meals, food served daily 12:00–21:30, 2 Bute Street, tel. 020/7589-3813).

Elsewhere in London

Between St. Paul's and the Tower: **The Counting House,** formerly an elegant old bank, offers great £8–10 meals, nice homemade meat pies, fish, and fresh vegetables. The fun "nibbles menu" is available from 15:00 to 22:00 (Mon–Fri 11:00–23:00, closed Sat–Sun, gets really busy with the buttoned-down 9-to-5 crowd after 12:15, near Mansion House in The City, 50 Cornhill, tel. 020/7283-7123).

Near St. Paul's: **De Gustibus Sandwiches** is where a top-notch artisan bakery meets the public, offering fresh, you-design-it sandwiches, salads, and soups with simple seating or take-out picnic sacks (great parks nearby), just a block below St. Paul's (Mon–Fri 7:00–17:00, closed Sat–Sun, from church steps follow signs to youth hostel a block downhill, 53–55 Carter Lane, tel. 020/7236-0056; another outlet is inside the Borough Market in Southwark).

Near the British Library: Drummond Street (running just west of Euston Station) is famous in London for very cheap and good Indian vegetarian food. Consider **Chutneys** (124 Drummond, tel. 020/7388-0604) and **Ravi Shankar** (133–135 Drummond, tel. 020/7388-6458) for a good *thali* (both generally open daily until 21:30, later Fri–Sat).

London Connections

Airports

Phone numbers and websites for London's airports and major airlines are listed in the appendix. For accommodations at and near the major airports, see page 140.

Heathrow Airport

Heathrow Airport is one of the world's busiest airports. Think about it: 68 million passengers a year on 470,000 flights from 180 destinations riding 90 airlines, like some kind of global maypole dance. Read signs and ask questions. For Heathrow's airport, flight, and transfer information, call the switchboard at 0870-000-0123 (www.heathrowairport.com).

Heathrow has five terminals: T-1 (mostly domestic and Irish flights, with some European); T-2 (mainly European flights; may close in 2010 for renovation); T-3 (flights from North and South America and Asia); T-4 (European and US flights; ongoing renovation may shuffle airlines); and T-5 (British Airways flights only). To travel between terminals, you can take the Heathrow Express and Connect trains (free), buses (free), or the Tube (requires a ticket).

It's critical to confirm which terminal your flight will use (check your plane ticket or call your airline in advance), because if it's T-4 or T-5, you'll need to allow extra time. Taxi drivers generally know which terminal you'll need, but bus drivers may not. If you're taking the Tube to the airport, note that some Piccadilly Line subway cars post which airlines are served by which terminals.

Each terminal has an airport information desk (generally daily 6:00–22:00), car-rental agencies, exchange bureaus, ATMs, a pharmacy, a **VAT refund desk** (tel. 020/8910-3682; you must present the VAT claim form from the retailer here to get your tax rebate on items purchased in Britain—see page 17 for details), and **baggage storage** (£8/item for 24 hours, hours vary by terminal but generally daily 5:30–23:00, www.left-baggage.co.uk). Get online 24 hours a day at Heathrow's **Internet access points** (at each terminal—T-4's is up on the mezzanine level) and with a laptop at pay-as-you-go wireless "hotspots"—including many hosted by T-Mobile—in its departure lounges. There's a **post office** on the first floor of T-2. Each terminal has cheap **eateries**.

Heathrow's small **"TI"** (tourist info shop), even though it's a for-profit business, is worth a visit to pick up free information: a simple map, the *London Planner,* and brochures (daily 6:30–22:00, 5-min walk from T-3 in Tube station, follow signs to Underground; bypass queue for transit info to reach window for London questions).

Getting to London from Heathrow Airport

You have several options for traveling the 14 miles between Heathrow Airport and downtown London. For one person on a budget, the Tube or bus is cheap but slow. To speed things up, though you'll spend a little more, combining the Heathrow Connect train with either a Tube or taxi ride (between Paddington Station and your hotel) is nearly as fast and less than half the cost of taking a cab the whole way. For groups of four or more, a taxi is faster and easier, as well as cheaper. Some options are better than others for a specific terminal.

By Tube (Subway): For £4.50, the Tube takes you from any terminal to downtown London in 50–60 minutes on the Piccadilly Line (6/hr; depending on your destination, may require a transfer, buy ticket at the Tube station ticket window). Note that if you arrive at Terminal 4, you need to take the free Heathrow Connect train to the Heathrow Central terminal (from Terminal 5, take the free Heathrow Express train), which can add 20 minutes to your

trip (especially critical if your return plans involve getting back to these terminals). If you plan to use the Tube for transport in London, it may make sense to buy a Travelcard (Zones 1–6) or Oyster card at the Tube station ticket window at the airport. For information on these passes, see page 52.

If you're taking the Tube from downtown London to the airport, note that the Piccadilly Line trains don't stop at every terminal on every run. Trains either go to T-4, T-1, T-2, and T-3 (in that order); or T-1, T-2, T-3, and T-5 (so allow extra time if going to T-4 or T-5). Check before you board.

By Bus: Most buses depart from the outside common area called the Central Bus Station. It serves T-1, T-2, and T-3, and is a 5-minute walk from any of these terminals. To get to T-4 or T-5 from the Central Bus Station, go inside, go downstairs, and follow signs to take the Tube to your terminal (free, but runs only every 15–20 min to those terminals).

National Express has regular service from Heathrow's Central Bus Station to Victoria Coach Station in downtown London, near several of my recommended hotels. While slow, the bus is affordable and convenient for those staying near Victoria Station (£4, 1–3/hr, 45–75 min, toll tel. 0871-781-8181, calls 10p/min, www .nationalexpress.com).

By Train: Two different trains run between Heathrow Airport and London's Paddington Station. At Paddington Station, you're

LONDON

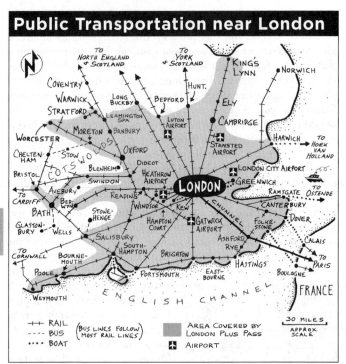

Public Transportation near London

in the thick of the Tube system, with easy access to any of my recommended neighborhoods—Notting Hill Gate is just two Tube stops away. The **Heathrow Connect** train is the slightly slower, much cheaper option serving T-1, T-2, T-3, and T-4; you can get to T-5 if you transfer at T-1, T-2, or T-3 (£6.90 one-way, 2/hr, 25–28 min, toll tel. 0845-678-6975, www.heathrowconnect.com). The **Heathrow Express** train is fast (15 min to downtown from T-1, T-2, and T-3; 21 min from T-5; not good for T-4) and runs more frequently (4/hr), but it's pricey (£16.50 "express class" one-way, £32 round-trip, ask about discount promos at ticket desk, kids under 16 ride half-price, under 5 ride free, buy ticket before you board or pay a £3 surcharge to buy it on the train, covered by BritRail pass, daily 5:10–23:25, toll tel. 0845-600-1515, www.heathrowexpress .co.uk). At the airport, you can use either the Heathrow Express or Heathrow Connect as a free transfer between terminals.

By Taxi: Taxis from the airport cost about £45–70 to west and central London (one hour). For four people traveling together, this can be a deal. Hotels can often line up a cab back to the airport for about £30–40. For the cheapest taxi to the airport, don't order one from your hotel. Simply flag down a few and ask them for their best "off-meter" rate.

Getting to Bath from Heathrow Airport

By Bus: Direct buses run daily from Heathrow to Bath (£19, 10/day direct, 2–3 hrs, more frequent but slower with transfer in London, toll tel. 0871-781-8181, calls 10p/min, www.nationalexpress.com). BritRail passholders may prefer the 2.5-hour Heathrow–Bath bus/train connection via Reading (BritRail passholders just pay £15 for bus; otherwise £50–65 depending on time of day, about £10 cheaper when bought in advance; tel. 0118-957-9425, buy bus ticket from www.railair.com, train ticket from www.firstgreatwestern .co.uk). First catch the RailAir Link shuttle bus (2/hr, 45 min) to Reading (RED-ding), then hop on the express train (2/hr, 60 min) to Bath. Factoring in the connection in Reading—which can add at least an hour to the trip—the train is a less convenient option than the direct bus to Bath. For more bus information, see "By Bus," page 57.

Gatwick Airport

More and more flights land at Gatwick Airport, halfway between London and the South Coast (recorded airport info toll tel. 0870-000-2468).

Getting to London: Gatwick Express trains—clearly the best way into London from here—shuttle conveniently between Gatwick and London's Victoria Station (£16.90, £28.80 round-trip, 4/hr, 30 min, runs 5:00–24:00 daily, purchase tickets on train at no extra charge, toll tel. 0845-850-1530, www.gatwickexpress .com). If you're traveling with two or three other adults, buy your tickets at the station before boarding, and you'll travel for the price of two. The only restriction on this impressive deal is that you have to travel together. So if you see another couple in line, get organized and save 50 percent.

You can save a few pounds by taking Southern Railway's slower and less frequent shuttle between Gatwick's South Terminal and Victoria Station (£10.90, up to 4/hr, 45 min, toll tel. 0845-127-2920, www.southernrailway.com). A train also runs from Gatwick to St. Pancras International Station (£8.90, 8/hr, 60 min, www .firstcapitalconnect.co.uk), useful for travelers taking the Eurostar train (to Paris or Brussels) or staying in the St. Pancras/King's Cross neighborhood.

Getting to Bath: To get to Bath from Gatwick, you can catch a bus to Heathrow and take the bus to Bath from there (10/day, 4–5 hrs, £25 one-way, transfer at Heathrow Airport, www.national express.com—see above). By train, the best Gatwick–Bath connection involves a transfer in Reading (£45–60 one-way depending on time of day, £23 in advance, hourly, 2.5 hrs, www.firstgreat western.co.uk; avoid transfer in London, where you'll have to change stations).

London's Other Airports

Stansted Airport: If you're using Stansted (airport toll tel. 0870-0000-303, www.stanstedairport.com), you have several options for getting into or out of London. The National Express bus runs between the airport and downtown London's Victoria Coach Station (£8, £17 round-trip, 2–3/hr, 1.5 hrs, runs 24 hours a day, picks up and stops throughout London, toll tel. 0871-781-8181—calls 10p/min, www.nationalexpress.com). Or you can take the faster, pricier Stansted Express train (£18 one-way, £26.80 round-trip, connects to London's Tube system at Tottenham Hale and Liverpool Street, 4/hr, 45 min, 5:00–23:00, toll tel. 0845-850-0150, www.stanstedexpress.com). Stansted is expensive by cab; figure £99 one-way from central London.

Luton Airport: For Luton (airport tel. 01582/405-100, www.london-luton.co.uk), there are two choices into or out of London. The fastest way is to go by rail to London's St. Pancras International Station (£11.50 one-way, 1–5/hr, 25–45 min, check schedule to avoid the slower trains, toll tel. 0845-712-5678, www.eastmidlandstrains.co.uk); catch the 10-minute shuttle bus (£1) from outside the terminal to the Luton Airport Parkway train station. The Green Line express bus #757 runs to London's Victoria Station (£13 one-way, £14.50 round-trip, small discount for easyJet passengers who buy online, 2–4/hr, 1.25–1.5 hrs, 24 hours a day, toll tel. 0844-801-7261, www.greenline.co.uk). If you're sleeping at Luton, consider easyHotel (see listing on page 140).

London City Airport: There's a slim chance you might use London City Airport (tel. 020/7646-0088, www.londoncityairport.com). To get into London, take the Docklands Light Railway (DLR) to the Bank Tube station, which is one stop east of St. Paul's on the Central Line (£4 one-way, covered by Travelcard, £2.20–2.70 on Oyster card, 22 min, tel. 020/7222-1234, www.tfl.gov.uk/dlr).

Connecting London's Airports by Bus

More and more travelers are taking advantage of cheap flights out of London's smaller airports. The handy **National Express bus** runs between Heathrow, Gatwick, Stansted, and Luton airports—easier than having to cut through the center of London—although traffic can be bad and increase travel times (toll tel. 0871-781-8181, calls 10p/min, www.nationalexpress.com).

From Heathrow Airport to: Gatwick Airport (1–4/hr, 1.25–1.5 hrs, £19.50 one-way, £36.50 round-trip, allow at least three hours between flights), **Stansted Airport** (1–2/hr, 1.5–1.75 hrs, £22.50 one-way, £29.30 round-trip), **Luton Airport** (hourly, 1–1.5 hrs, £19.90 one-way, £24.50 round-trip).

Discounted Flights from London

London is one of Europe's cheapest places to fly into and out of. For information, see "Cheap Flights" on page 720.

Trains and Buses

Britain is covered by a myriad of rail systems (owned by different companies), which together are called National Rail. London, the country's major transportation hub, has a different train station for each region. There are nine main stations:

Euston—Serves northwest England, North Wales, and Scotland.

King's Cross—Serves northeast England and Scotland, including York and Edinburgh.

Liverpool Street—Serves east England, including Essex and Harwich.

London Bridge—Serves south England, including Brighton.

Marylebone—Serves southwest and central England, including Stratford-upon-Avon.

Paddington—Serves south and southwest England, including Heathrow Airport, Windsor, Bath, South Wales, and the Cotswolds.

St. Pancras International—Serves north and south England, plus Eurostar to Paris or Brussels.

Victoria—Serves Gatwick Airport, Canterbury, Dover, and Brighton.

Waterloo—Serves southeast England, including Dover and Salisbury.

Any train station has schedule information, can make reservations, and can sell tickets for any destination. Most stations offer a baggage-storage service (£8/bag for 24 hours, look for *left luggage* signs); because of long security lines, it can take a while to check or pick up your bag (www.excess-baggage.com). For more details on the services available at each station, see www.nationalrail.co.uk/stations.

Buying Tickets: For general information, call 0845-748-4950 (or visit www.nationalrail.co.uk or www.eurostar.com; £5 booking fee for telephone reservations).

Railpasses: For train travel outside London, consider getting a BritRail pass. Options include passes that cover England as well as Scotland and Wales, England-only passes, England/Ireland passes, "London Plus" passes (good for travel in most of southeast England but not in London itself—see pass coverage on map on page 160), and BritRail & Drive passes (which offer you some rail days and some car-rental days). For specifics, contact your travel agent or see www.ricksteves.com/rail.

London's Train Stations

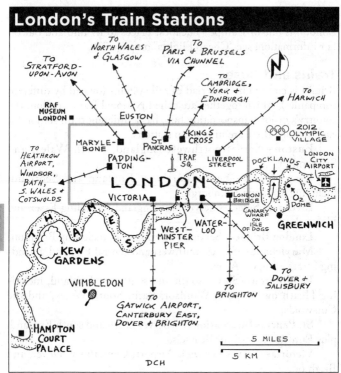

LONDON

By Train
To Points West
From Paddington Station to: Bath (2/hr, 1.5 hrs; also consider a guided Evan Evans tour by bus—see the next page), **Oxford** (2–5/hr, 1 hr, possible transfer in Reading), **Penzance** (every 1–2 hours, 5–5.75 hrs, possible change in Plymouth), and **Cardiff** (2/hr, 2 hrs).

To Points North
From King's Cross Station: Trains run at least hourly, stopping in **York** (2 hrs), **Durham** (3 hrs), and **Edinburgh** (4.5 hrs). Trains to **Cambridge** also leave from here (2/hr, 1 hr).

  From Euston Station to: Conwy (nearly hourly, 3.25–4 hrs, transfer in Chester or Crewe), **Liverpool** (hourly, 2 hrs, more with transfer), **Blackpool** (hourly, 3 hrs, transfer at Preston), **Keswick** (9/day, 3–3.5 hrs, transfer to bus at Penrith), **Glasgow** (1–2/hr, 4.5–5 hrs direct, some may leave from King's Cross Station).

From London's Other Stations
Trains run between London and **Canterbury,** leaving from

Charing Cross Station and arriving in Canterbury West, as well as from London's Victoria Station and arriving in Canterbury East (2/hr, 1.5 hrs).

Direct trains leave for **Stratford-upon-Avon** from Marylebone Station, located near the southwest corner of Regents Park (every 2 hrs, 2.25 hrs).

Other Destinations: Dover (1–2/hr, 1.75–2.25 hrs; from Waterloo, Charing Cross, or Victoria Station), **Brighton** (4–5/hr, 1 hr, from Victoria Station and London Bridge Station), **Portsmouth** (3/hr, 1.5–2 hrs, most from Waterloo Station, a few from Victoria Station), and **Salisbury** (1–2/hr, 1.5 hrs, direct from Waterloo Station).

By Bus

National Express' excellent bus service is considerably cheaper than the train, and a fine option for destinations within England (call toll tel. 0871-781-8181—calls 10p/min, or visit www.national express.com or the bus station a block southwest of Victoria Station).

To Bath: The National Express bus leaves from Victoria Station nearly hourly (3.25–3.75 hrs, avoid those with layover in Bristol, sample fares one-way-£19, round-trip-£29).

To get to Bath via Stonehenge, consider taking a guided bus tour from London to Stonehenge and Bath, and abandoning the tour in Bath (be sure to confirm that Bath is the last stop). **Evan Evans'** tour is £69 and includes admissions (£44 without admissions). The tour leaves from the Victoria Coach station every morning at 8:45 (you can stow your bag under the bus), stops in Stonehenge (45 min), and then stops in Bath for lunch and a city tour before returning to London (offered year-round). You can book the tour at the Victoria Coach station or the Evan Evans office (258 Vauxhall Bridge Road, near Victoria Coach station, tel. 020/7950-1777, US tel. 866-382-6868, www.evanevans.co.uk, reservations@evanevanstours.co.uk). Golden Tours also runs a Stonehenge–Bath tour (£59, £39 without admissions, check website for seasonal tour days; departs from Fountain Square, located across from Victoria Coach Station, US tel. 800-548-7083, toll tel. 0844-880-6981, www.goldentours.co.uk, reservations@golden tours.co.uk).

To Other Destinations: Oxford (2–4/hr, 1.75–2.25 hrs), **Cambridge** (about hourly, 2–2.5 hrs), **Canterbury** (about hourly, 2–2.5 hrs), **Dover** (about hourly, 2.5–3.25 hrs), **Penzance** (6/day, 8.5–9 hrs, overnight available), **Cardiff** (every 1–2 hrs, 3.25 hrs), **Liverpool** (8/day direct, 5.25–6 hrs, overnight available), **Blackpool** (4/day direct, 6.25–7 hrs, overnight available), **York** (4/day direct, 4.75–5.25 hrs), **Durham** (4/day direct, 6–7.5 hrs),

Glasgow (2/day direct, 8–9 hrs, train is a much better option), **Edinburgh** (2/day direct, 8.75–9.75 hrs, go by train instead).

To **Dublin, Ireland:** The bus/boat journey takes 9–10 hours (£35–43, 3/day, toll tel. 0871-781-8181, calls 10p/min, www.national express.com). Consider a 75-minute Ryanair flight instead (www .ryanair.com).

Crossing the Channel
By Eurostar Train

The fastest, most convenient way to get from Big Ben to the Eiffel Tower is by rail. Eurostar, a joint service of the Belgian, British, and French railways, is the speedy passenger train that zips you (and up to 800 others in 18 sleek cars) from downtown London to downtown Paris or Brussels (15/day, 2.5 hrs) faster and more easily than flying. The actual tunnel crossing is a 20-minute, silent, 100-mile-per-hour nonevent. Your ears won't even pop. Eurostar's monopoly expires at the beginning of 2010, and Air France has already announced plans to start a competing high-speed rail service between London and Paris in late autumn of 2010.

Eurostar Fares

Channel fares are reasonable but complicated. Prices vary depending on how far ahead you reserve, whether you can live with restrictions, and whether you're eligible for any discounts (children, youths, seniors, round-trip travelers, and railpass holders all qualify).

Fares can change without notice, but typically a **one-way, full-fare ticket** (with no restrictions on refundability) runs about $425 first-class and $300 second-class. **Cheaper seats** come with more restrictions and can sell out quickly (figure $80–160 for second class, one-way). Those traveling with a railpass that covers France or Britain

Eurostar Routes

should look first at the **passholder** fare ($85–130 for second-class, one-way Eurostar trips). For more details, visit www.ricksteves .com/rail/eurostar.htm.

Buying Eurostar Tickets

Because only the most expensive (full-fare) ticket is fully refundable, don't reserve until you're sure of your plans. But if you wait too long, the cheapest tickets will get bought up.

Once you're confident about the time and date of your crossing, you can check and book fares by phone or online in the US and pay to have your ticket delivered to you in the US. (Order online at www.ricksteves.com/rail/eurostar.htm, prices listed in dollars; order by phone at US tel. 800-EUROSTAR.) Or you can order in Britain (toll tel. 08705-186-186, £5 booking fee by phone, www.eurostar.com, prices listed in pounds).

If you buy from a US company, you'll pay for ticket delivery in the US; if you book with the British company, you'll pick up your ticket at the train station. In continental Europe, you can buy your Eurostar ticket at any major train station in any country or at any travel agency that handles train tickets (expect a booking fee). In Britain, tickets can be issued only at the Eurostar office in St. Pancras International Station.

Remember that Britain's time zone is one hour earlier than France or Belgium (and the rest of Europe). Times listed on tickets are local times (departure from London is British time, arrival in Paris is French time).

Eurostar by Tour

A tour company called Britain Shrinkers sells one- and two-day tours via the Eurostar to Paris, Brussels, or Bruges, enabling you to side-trip to these cities from London for less than most train tickets alone. For example, you'll pay £99 for a one-day Paris "tour" (unescorted Mon–Sat day trip with Métro pass; tel. 207-713-1311 or www.britainshrinkers.com). This can be a particularly good option if you need to get to Paris from London on short notice, when only the costliest fares are available.

Taking the Eurostar

Eurostar trains depart from and arrive at London's St. Pancras International Station. Check in at least 30 minutes in advance for your Eurostar trip. It's very similar to an airport check-in: You pass through airport-like security, show your passport to customs officials, and find a TV monitor to locate your departure gate. There are a few airport-like shops, newsstands, horrible snack bars, and cafés (bring food for the trip from elsewhere), pay-Internet terminals, and a currency-exchange booth with rates about the same as you'll find on the other end.

Crossing the Channel Without Eurostar

The old-fashioned ways of crossing the Channel are usually cheaper than Eurostar (taking the bus is cheapest). They're generally also twice as romantic, complicated, and time-consuming.

By Train and Boat

To Paris: You'll take a train from London to the port of Dover, then catch a ferry to Calais, France, before boarding another train for Paris. Trains go from London's Charing Cross, Waterloo, or Victoria stations to **Dover's** Priory station (1–2/hr, 1.75–2.25 hrs; bus or taxi from station to ferry dock). P&O Ferries sail from Dover to Calais; TGV trains run from Calais to Paris. You'll need to book your own train tickets to Dover and from Calais to Paris. The prices listed here are for the ferry only (from £25 one-way or £50 round-trip online, more at dock or by phone, book early for best fares; 22/day, 1.5 hrs, toll tel. 0871-664-5645, www.poferries.com).

To Amsterdam: Stena Line's Dutchflyer service combines train and ferry tickets between London and Amsterdam via the ports of **Harwich** and Hoek van Holland. Trains go from London's Liverpool Street station to Harwich (hourly, 1.5 hrs). Stena Line ferries sail from Harwich to Hoek van Holland (7.5 hrs), where you can transfer to a train to Amsterdam or other Dutch cities (ferry—from £32, from £60 with cabin, book at least 2 weeks in advance for best price, 13 hrs total travel time, Dutchflyer toll tel. 0870-545-5455, www.stenaline.co.uk, Dutch train info at www.ns.nl).

For additional European ferry info, visit www.aferry.to. For UK train and bus info, go to www.traveline.org.uk.

By Bus

You can take the bus from London direct to **Paris** (4/day, 8.25–9.75 hrs), **Brussels** (3–4/day, 7.75–9.25 hrs), or **Amsterdam** (4/day, 11.75–12.75 hrs) from Victoria Coach Station (by ferry or Chunnel, day or overnight). Sample prices to Paris for economy fares booked at least two days in advance: £25 one-way, £52 round-trip, book online early for best fares (toll tel. 0871-781-8181, calls 10p/min; visit www.eurolines.co.uk and look for "funfares").

By Plane

Check with budget airlines for inexpensive round-trip fares to Paris or Brussels (see "Cheap Flights" on page 720).

GREENWICH, WINDSOR, AND CAMBRIDGE

Three of the best day-trip possibilities near London are Greenwich, Windsor, and Cambridge (listed from nearest to farthest). Greenwich is England's maritime capital; Windsor has a very famous castle; and Cambridge is easily England's best university town.

Getting Around

By Train: The British rail system uses London as a hub and normally offers same-day, round-trip fares that cost virtually the same as one-way fares. For day trips, these "cheap day return" tickets, available if you depart London after 9:30 on weekdays or anytime Sat–Sun, are best. You can save a little money (both one-way and round-trip) if you purchase advance tickets before 18:00 on the day before your trip.

By Train Tour: London Walks offers a variety of Explorer day trips year-round by train for about £12 plus transportation costs (pick up their walking-tour brochures at the TI or hotels, tel. 020/7624-3978, www.londonwalks.com; see listing on page 64).

London Day Trips

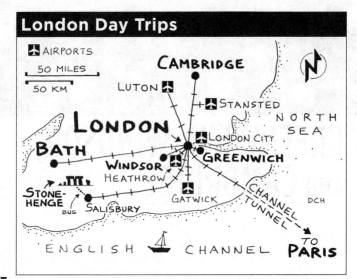

GREENWICH

Greenwich

Tudor kings favored the palace at Greenwich (GREN-ich). Henry VIII was born here. Later kings commissioned Inigo Jones and Christopher Wren to beautify the town and palace. Yet in spite of Greenwich's architectural and royal treats, this is England's maritime capital, and visitors go for all things salty. Although Greenwich's main attraction—the *Cutty Sark* clipper—is closed for restoration through 2010, the town is still worth a visit. It has the world's most famous observatory, stunning Baroque architecture, appealing markets, a fleet of nautical shops, and hordes of tourists. And where else can you set your watch with such accuracy?

Planning Your Time

Upon arrival, stroll past the *Cutty Sark* dry dock and walk the shore-line promenade. Enjoy lunch or a drink in the venerable Trafalgar Tavern before heading up to the National Maritime Museum and then through the park to the Royal Observatory Greenwich.

Getting to Greenwich

It's a joy by boat, or a snap by Tube.

By Boat: From central London, cruise down the Thames from the piers at Westminster or the Tower of London (2/hr, about 1 hour; see page 67).

By Tube: Take the Tube to Bank and change to the Docklands Light Railway (DLR), which takes you right to Cutty

Sark Station in central Greenwich (one stop before the main—but less central—Greenwich Station, 20 min, all in Zone 2, covered by any Tube pass). Some DLR trains terminate at Island Gardens (from which you can generally catch another train to Greenwich's Cutty Sark Station within a few minutes, though it may be more memorable to get out and walk under the river through the long Thames pedestrian tunnel). Many DLR trains terminate at Canary Wharf, so make sure you get on one that continues to Lewisham or Greenwich.

A fun way to return to London is to ride the DLR back to Canary Wharf and get off there to explore the Docklands area (London's Manhattan, most interesting at the end of the work-day, see page 114). When you're done exploring, hop on the speedy Jubilee line and zip back to Westminster in 15 minutes.

By Train: Mainline trains also go from London (Charing Cross, Cannon Street, Waterloo East, and London Bridge stations) several times an hour to Greenwich Station (10-min walk from the sights). Though the train is fast and cheap, I prefer the Tube.

Orientation to Greenwich

(area code: 020)
Covered markets and outdoor stalls make weekends lively. Save time to browse the town. Wander beyond the touristy Church Street and Greenwich High Road to where flower stands spill onto the side streets, and antique shops sell brass nautical knick-knacks. King William Walk, College Approach, Nelson Road, and Turnpin Lane are all worth a look. If you need pub grub, Greenwich has almost 100 pubs, some boasting that they're mere milliseconds from the prime meridian.

Tourist Information

Until March 2010, the Greenwich TI is located across from Cutty Sark Station at 46 Greenwich Church Street. After that you'll find it back within the Old Royal Naval College, inside the new Discover Greenwich Centre (just east of the closed-for-restoration *Cutty Sark* at 2 Cutty Sark Gardens, Pepys House). Regardless of the location, the hours and phone number remain the same (daily 10:00–17:00, toll tel. 0870-608-2000, www.greenwichwhs.org.uk). Guided walks depart from the TI and cover the big sights (£6, daily at 12:15 and 14:15).

Helpful Hints

Markets: Thanks to its markets, Greenwich throbs with day-trippers on weekends. The **Greenwich Market** is an entertaining mini-Covent Garden, located between College Approach

Greenwich

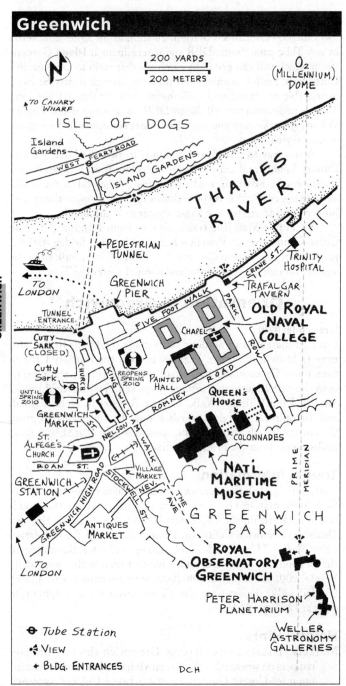

GREENWICH

TO CANARY WHARF

200 YARDS
200 METERS

O₂ (MILLENNIUM) DOME

ISLE OF DOGS

Island Gardens

WEST FERRY ROAD

ISLAND GARDENS

THAMES RIVER

PEDESTRIAN TUNNEL

CRANE ST.

TRINITY HOSPITAL

GREENWICH PIER

FIVE FOOT WALK

TRAFALGAR TAVERN

PARK ROW

OLD ROYAL NAVAL COLLEGE

TO LONDON

TUNNEL ENTRANCE

CHAPEL

CUTTY SARK (CLOSED)

Cutty Sark

CHURCH ST.

REOPENS SPRING 2010

PAINTED HALL

ROMNEY ROAD

UNTIL SPRING 2010

KING WILLIAM WALK

QUEEN'S HOUSE

GREENWICH MARKET

NELSON ST.

COLONNADES

St. ALFEGE'S CHURCH

ROAN ST.

VILLAGE MARKET

NAT'L. MARITIME MUSEUM

PRIME MERIDIAN

GREENWICH STATION

STOCKWELL ST.

NEV.

THE AVE.

GREENWICH PARK

GREENWICH HIGH ROAD

Antiques Market

ROYAL OBSERVATORY GREENWICH

TO LONDON

PETER HARRISON PLANETARIUM

WELLER ASTRONOMY GALLERIES

⊖ Tube Station
⋅ View
+ Bldg. Entrances

DCH

and Nelson Road (Wed 11:00–18:00, Thu–Fri 10:00–17:00, Sat–Sun 10:00–17:30, Wed–Fri best for antiques, lots of crafts and food on weekends, tel. 020/7515-7153, www.greenwich market.net). The **Antiques Market** sells old odds and ends at high prices on Greenwich High Road, near the post office (Sat–Sun only 9:30–17:30). The **Village Market** has a little bit of everything—antiques, books, food, and flowers (Sat–Sun only 9:30–17:30, across Nelson Road from the Greenwich Market, enter from Stockwell Street or King William Walk).

Supermarket: If you're picnicking, visit the handy **Marks & Spencer Simply Food** across from the *Cutty Sark* dry dock (Mon–Sat 8:00–21:00, Sun 10:00–21:00, 55 Greenwich Church Street, tel. 020/7228-2545).

Sights in Greenwich

▲▲*Cutty Sark*—The Scottish-built *Cutty Sark* is closed for restoration until late 2010—call 020/8858-2698 or check www.cutty sark.org.uk for updates. She was the last of the great China tea clippers and was the queen of the seas when first launched in 1869. With 32,000 square feet of sail, she could blow with the wind 300 miles in a day. You may be able to view some of the renovation from an observation window in the *Cutty Sark* gift shop adjacent to the dry dock (hours vary—call ahead).

Old Royal Naval College—Now that the Royal Navy has moved out, the public is invited in to see the college's elaborate Painted Hall and Chapel, grandly designed by Christopher Wren and completed by other architects in the 1700s. You'll also find fine descriptions and an altar painting by American Benjamin West (free, Mon–Sat 10:00–17:00, Sun 12:30–17:00, sometimes closed for private events, choral service Sun at 11:00 in chapel—all are welcome, in the two college buildings farthest from river). Guides give 90-minute tours covering the hall and chapel, along with three other places not open to the general public (£5, daily at 11:30 and 14:00, call ahead to check availability, tel. 020/8269-4799, www.oldroyalnavalcollege.org).

Stroll the Thames to Trafalgar Tavern—From the *Cutty Sark*

dry dock, pass the pier and wander east along the Thames on Five Foot Walk (named for the width of the path) for grand views in front of the Old Royal Naval College (see above). Founded by William III as a naval hospital and designed by Wren, the college was split in two because Queen Mary didn't want the view from Queen's House blocked. The riverside view is good,

GREENWICH

too, with the twin-domed towers of the college (one giving the time, the other the direction of the wind) framing Queen's House, and the Royal Observatory Greenwich crowning the hill beyond.

Continuing downstream, just past the college, you'll see the **Trafalgar Tavern.** Dickens knew the pub well, and he used it as the setting for the wedding breakfast in *Our Mutual Friend.* Built in 1837 in the Regency style to attract Londoners downriver, the tavern is popular with Londoners (and tourists) for its fine lunches. The upstairs Nelson Room is still used for weddings. Its formal moldings and elegant windows with balconies over the Thames are a step back in time (food served Mon–Sat 12:00–22:00, Sun 12:00–16:00, elegant ground-floor dining room as well as the more casual pub, Park Row, tel. 020/8858-2909).

From the pub, enjoy views of the former Millennium Dome a mile downstream. The Dome languished for nearly a decade after its controversial construction and brief life as a millennial "world's fair" site. Plans for a casino and hotel project fell through, although it has come in handy as an emergency homeless shelter. It was finally bought by a developer a few years ago and rechristened "The O_2" in honor of the telecommunications company that paid for the naming rights. Currently, it hosts concerts and sporting events, and will see action during the 2012 Summer Olympics. Whatever it's called, locals will no doubt continue to grumble about its original cost.

From the Trafalgar Tavern, you can walk the two long blocks up Park Row, and turn right into the park leading up to the Royal Observatory Greenwich.

Queen's House—This building, the first Palladian-style villa in Britain, was designed in 1616 by Inigo Jones for James I's wife, Anne of Denmark. All traces of the queen are long gone, and the Great Hall and Royal Apartments now serve as an art gallery for rotating exhibits from the National Maritime Museum. The Orangery is now home to the great J. M. W. Turner painting *Battle of Trafalgar.* His largest (so big that a wall had to be opened to get it in here) and only royal commission, it is surrounded by Christ-like paintings of Admiral Nelson's death (free, daily 10:00–17:00, last entry 30 min before closing, tel. 020/8858-4422, recorded info tel. 020/8312-6565, www.nmm.ac.uk).

▲▲National Maritime Museum—Great for anyone remotely interested in the sea, this museum holds everything from a *Titanic* passenger's pocket watch and Captain Scott's sun goggles (from his 1910 Antarctic expedition) to the uniform Admiral Nelson wore when he was killed at Trafalgar. Under a big glass roof—accompanied by the sound of creaking wooden ships and crashing waves—slick, modern displays depict lighthouse technology, a whaling cannon, and a Greenpeace "survival pod." Kids love the

All Hands and Bridge galleries, where they can send secret messages by Morse code and operate a miniature dockside crane.

Note that some parts of the museum, such as the Nelson's Navy gallery, are closed for renovation until 2012 (free, daily 10:00–17:00, last entry 30 min before closing; look for family-oriented events posted at entrance—singing, treasure hunts, storytelling—particularly on weekends; toll tel. 0870-781-5168, www .nmm.ac.uk).

▲▲**Royal Observatory Greenwich**—Located on the prime meridian (0° longitude), the observatory is the point from which all time is measured. However, the observatory's early work had nothing to do with coordinating the world's clocks to Greenwich Mean Time (GMT). The observatory was founded in 1675 by Charles II to find a way to determine longitude at sea. Today, the Greenwich time signal is linked with the BBC (which broadcasts the famous "pips" worldwide at the top of the hour).

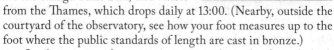

GREENWICH

Look above the observatory to see the orange Time Ball, also visible from the Thames, which drops daily at 13:00. (Nearby, outside the courtyard of the observatory, see how your foot measures up to the foot where the public standards of length are cast in bronze.)

In the courtyard, set your wristwatch to the digital clock showing GMT to a tenth of a second, and straddle the prime meridian.

Inside, check out the historic astronomical instruments and camera obscura. In the Time Galleries, see timepieces through the ages, including John Harrison's prizewinning marine chronometers that helped 18th-century sailors calculate longitude (the highlight for fans of Dava Sobel's *Longitude*). The observatory is also home to the state-of-the-art, 120-seat Peter Harrison Planetarium, an education center, and the Weller Astronomy Galleries, where interactive displays allow you to guide a space mission and touch a 4.5-billion-year-old meteorite.

Cost and Hours: Free entry to observatory, planetarium shows-£6; observatory open daily 10:00–17:00, last entry 30 min before closing; courtyard open until 20:00; planetarium shows hourly Mon–Fri 13:00–16:00, Sat–Sun 11:00–16:00, fewer in winter, 30 min; tel. 020/8858-4422, www.nmm.ac.uk.

Observatory Grounds and Viewpoint: Before you leave the observatory grounds, enjoy the view from the overlook—the symmetrical royal buildings, the Thames, the Docklands and its busy cranes (including the tallest building in the UK, Canary Wharf Tower, a.k.a. One Canada Square), the huge O_2 (Millennium) Dome, and the square-mile City of London, with its skyscrapers and the dome of St. Paul's Cathedral. At night (17:00–24:00), look for the green laser beam that the observatory projects into the sky (best viewed in winter), extending along the prime meridian for 15 miles.

Windsor

WINDSOR

Windsor, an easy, compact walking town of about 30,000 people, originally grew up around the royal residence. In 1070, William the Conqueror continued his habit of kicking Saxons out of their various settlements, taking over what the locals called "Windlesora" (meaning "riverbank with a hoisting crane")—which later became "Windsor." William built the first fortified castle on a chalk hill above the Thames; later kings added on to his early designs, rebuilding and expanding the castle and surrounding gardens.

By setting up primary residence here, modern monarchs increased Windsor's popularity and prosperity—most notably Queen Victoria, whose stern statue glares at you as you approach the castle. After her death, Victoria rejoined her beloved husband, Albert, in the Royal Mausoleum at Frogmore House, a mile south of the castle, in a private section of the Home Park (house and mausoleum rarely open; check www.royalcollection.org.uk). The current Queen considers Windsor her primary residence, and the one where she feels most at home. You can tell if Her Majesty is in residence by checking to see which flag is flying above the round tower: If it's the royal standard (a red, yellow, and blue flag) instead of the Union Jack, the queen is at home.

Though 99 percent of visitors just come to see the castle and go, some enjoy spending the night. Windsor's charm is most evident when the tourists are gone. Consider overnighting here, since parking and access to Heathrow Airport are easy, day-tripping into London is feasible, and an evening at the horse races (on Mondays) is hoof-pounding, heart-thumping fun.

Getting to Windsor

By Train: Windsor has two train stations—Windsor & Eton Central (5-min walk to palace, TI inside) and Windsor & Eton Riverside (5-min walk to palace and TI). First Great Western trains run between London's Paddington Station and Windsor & Eton Central (2/hr, 35 min, change at Slough, £8 one-way standard class, £9–11 same-day return). South West Trains run between London's Waterloo Station and Windsor & Eton Riverside (2/hr, 1 hr, possible change at Staines, £8.50 one-way standard class, £9–15 same-day return; info toll tel. 0845-748-4950, www.national rail.co.uk).

If you're day-tripping into London from Windsor, ask at the train station about combining a same-day return train ticket with a One-Day Travelcard as one ticket (£12–21, lower price for travel after 9:30, covers rail transportation to and from London and doubles as an all-day Tube and bus pass in town, rail ticket may also qualify you for half-price London sightseeing discounts—ask or look for brochure at station, or go to www.daysoutguide .co.uk).

By Bus: Green Line buses #701 and #702 run from London's Victoria Colonnades (between the Victoria train and coach stations) to the Parish Church stop on Windsor's High Street, before continuing on to Legoland (£1–8.50 one-way, £9–12.50 round-trip, prices vary depending on time of day, 1–2/hr, 1.25 hours to Windsor, tel. 01344/782-222, www.rainbowfares.com).

By Car: Windsor is 20 miles from London and just off Heathrow Airport's landing path. The town (and then the castle and Legoland) is well-signposted from the M4 motorway. It's a convenient first stop if you're arriving at and renting a car from Heathrow, and saving London until the end of your trip.

From Heathrow Airport: Buses #71 and #77 make the 45-minute trip between Terminal 5 and Windsor, dropping you in the center of town on Peascod Street (about £7, 1–2/hr, toll tel. 0871-200-2233, www.firstgroup.com). London black cabs can charge whatever they like from Heathrow to Windsor (and do); avoid them by calling a local cab company, such as Windsor Radio Cars (£20, tel. 01753/677-677).

Orientation to Windsor

(area code: 01753)

Windsor's pleasant pedestrian shopping zone litters the approach to its famous palace with fun temptations. You'll find most shops and restaurants around the castle on High and Thames Streets, and down the pedestrian Peascod Street (PESS-cot), which runs perpendicular to High Street.

Windsor

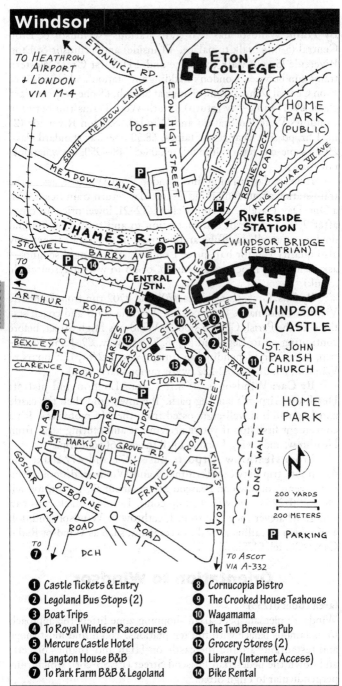

WINDSOR

1 Castle Tickets & Entry
2 Legoland Bus Stops (2)
3 Boat Trips
4 To Royal Windsor Racecourse
5 Mercure Castle Hotel
6 Langton House B&B
7 To Park Farm B&B & Legoland
8 Cornucopia Bistro
9 The Crooked House Teahouse
10 Wagamama
11 The Two Brewers Pub
12 Grocery Stores (2)
13 Library (Internet Access)
14 Bike Rental

Tourist Information
The TI is adjacent to Windsor & Eton Central Station, in the Windsor Royal Shopping Centre's Old Booking Hall (April–Sept Mon–Sat 9:30–17:30, Sun 10:00–16:00; Oct–March Mon–Sat 10:00–17:00, Sun 10:00–16:00; tel. 01753/743-900, www.windsor .gov.uk). The TI sells discount tickets to Legoland for £34.

Arrival in Windsor
By Train: The train to Windsor & Eton Central Station from Paddington (via Slough) will spit you out in a shady shopping pavilion (which houses the TI), only a few minutes' walk from the castle. If you instead arrive at Windsor & Eton Riverside train station (from Waterloo, via Staines), you'll see the castle as you exit—just follow the wall to the castle entrance.

By Car: Follow signs from the M4 motorway for pay-and-display parking in the center. River Street Car Park is closest to the castle, but pricey and often full. The cheaper, bigger Alexandra Car Park (near the riverside Alexandra Gardens) is farther west. To walk to the town center from the Alexandra Car Park, head east through the tour-bus parking lot toward the castle. At the souvenir shop, walk up the stairs (or take the elevator) and cross the overpass to the Windsor & Eton Central Station. Just beyond the station, you'll find the TI in the Windsor Royal Shopping Centre.

Helpful Hints
Internet Access: Get online for free at the **library,** located on Bachelors' Acre, between Peascod and Victoria Streets (Mon and Thu 9:30–17:00, Tue 9:30–20:00, Wed 14:00–17:00, Fri 9:30–19:00, Sat 9:30–15:00, closed Sun, tel. 01753/743-940, www.rbwm.gov.uk).

Supermarkets: Pick up picnic supplies at **Marks & Spencer** (Mon–Sat 9:00–18:00, Sun 11:00–17:00, 130 Peascod Street, tel. 01753/852-266) or at **Waitrose** (Mon–Tue and Sat 8:30–19:00, Wed–Fri 8:30–20:00, Sun 11:00–17:00, King Edward Court Shopping Centre, just south of the Windsor & Eton Central Station, tel. 01753/860-565). Just outside the castle, you'll find long benches near the statue of Queen Victoria—great for people-watching while you munch.

Bike Rental: Extreme Motion, near the river in Alexandra Gardens, rents 21-speed mountain bikes as well as helmets (£12/4 hrs, £17/day, helmets-£1–1.50, £100 credit-card deposit required, bring passport as ID, summer daily 10:00–22:00, tel. 01753/830-220, www.extrememotion.com).

WINDSOR

Sights in Windsor

▲▲Windsor Castle

Windsor Castle, the official home of England's royal family for 900 years, claims to be the largest and oldest occupied castle in the world. Thankfully, touring it is simple. You'll see immense grounds, lavish staterooms, a crowd-pleasing dollhouse, an art gallery, and the chapel.

Cost, Hours, Information: £15.50, family pass–£41, daily March–Oct 9:45–17:15, Nov–Feb 9:45–16:15, last entry 1.25 hours before closing, tel. 020/7766-7304, www.royalcollection.org.uk.

Tours: As you enter, ask about the warden's free 30-minute guided walks around the grounds (2/hr). They cover the grounds but not the castle, which is well-described by the included audioguide (skip the official guidebook).

Other Activities: The **Changing of the Guard** takes place on alternate days at 11:00 (ceremonies begin a little earlier—get there by 10:45), except in very wet weather (and never on Sun). There's an **evensong** in the chapel nightly at 17:15—free for worshippers.

❷ Self-Guided Tour: Immediately upon entering, you pass through a simple modern building housing a **historical overview** of the castle. This excellent intro is worth a close look, since you're basically on your own after this. Inside, you'll find the motte (artificial mound) and bailey (fortified stockade around it) of William the Conqueror's castle. Dating from 1080, this was his first castle in England.

Follow the signs to the staterooms/gallery/dollhouse. **Queen Mary's Dollhouse**—a palace in miniature (1:12 scale, from 1924) and "the most famous dollhouse in the world"—often comes with the longest wait. If dollhouses aren't your cup of tea, you can skip that line and go immediately into the lavish **staterooms.** Strewn with history and the art of a long line of kings and queens, they're the best I've seen in Britain—and well-restored after the devastating 1992 fire. Take advantage of the talkative docents in each room, who are happy to answer your questions.

The adjacent gallery is a changing exhibit featuring the **royal art collection** (and some big names, such as Michelangelo and Leonardo). Signs direct you (downhill) to **St. George's Chapel.** Housing numerous royal tombs, it's a fine example of Perpendicular Gothic, with classic fan vaulting spreading out from each pillar (dating from about 1500). The simple chapel containing the tombs of the current Queen's parents, King George VI and "Queen Mother" Elizabeth, and younger sister, Princess Margaret, is along the church's north aisle. Next door is the sumptuous 13th-century **Albert Memorial Chapel,** redecorated after the death of Prince Albert in 1861 and dedicated to his memory.

More Sights in Windsor

Legoland Windsor—Paradise for Legomaniacs under 12, this huge, kid-pleasing park has dozens of tame but fun rides (often with very long lines) scat-tered throughout its 150 acres. The impressive Mini-land has 40 million Lego pieces glued together to cre-ate 800 tiny buildings and a mini-tour of Europe, and the Creation Centre boasts an 80 percent-scale Boeing 747 cockpit, made of two

million bricks. Several of the more exciting rides involve getting wet, so dress accordingly or buy a cheap disposable poncho in the gift shop. Though you may be tempted to hop on the Hill Train at the entrance, it's faster and more convenient to walk down into the park. Food is available in the park, but you can save money by bringing a picnic.

Cost: Adults-£36, £32.40 in advance online, £34 at Windsor TI; children-£27, £24 online or from TI; free for ages 2 and under; optional £10/person "Q-Bot" ride-reservation gadget allows you to bypass lines; coin lockers-£1.

Hours: Mid-July–Aug daily 10:00–19:00, Sept–Oct and April–mid-July Thu–Mon only and closes 1–2 hours earlier, closed Nov–mid-March except around Christmas, call or check website for exact schedule.

Information: Toll tel. 0871-222-2001, www.legoland.co.uk.

Getting There: A £4.50 round-trip shuttle bus runs from opposite Windsor's Theatre Royal on Thames Street, and from the Parish Church stop on High Street (2/hr). If day-tripping from London, ask about rail/shuttle/park admission deals from Paddington or Waterloo train stations. For drivers, the park is on B3022 Windsor/Ascot road, two miles southwest of Windsor and 25 miles west of London. Legoland is clearly signposted from the M3, M4, and M25 motorways. Parking is easy and free.

Eton College—Across the bridge from Windsor Castle, you'll find many post-castle tourists filing toward the most famous "public" (the equivalent of our "private") high school in Britain. Eton was founded in 1440 by King Henry VI; today it educates about 1,300 boys (ages 13–18), who live on campus. Eton has molded the characters of 18 prime ministers, as well as members of the royal family, most recently princes William and Harry. The college is sparse on sights, but the public is allowed into the schoolyard, chapel, cloisters, and the Museum of Eton Life (£6, access only by one-hour guided tour at 14:00 and 15:15; tours available mid-April–Sept Wed and Fri–Sun, daily June–July; Oct–Nov Wed and Fri only; closed late Nov–mid-April and about once a month for special events, so call ahead, no photos in chapel, no food or drink allowed, tel. 01753/671-177, www.etoncollege.com).

Boat Trips—Cruise up and down the Thames River for relaxing views of the castle, the village of Eton, Eton College, and the Royal Windsor Racecourse. Relax onboard and nibble a picnic (£5, family pass-£12.50, 40 min; mid-Feb–Oct roughly 2/hr daily 10:00–17:00; Nov Sat–Sun hourly 10:00–16:00, closed Mon–Fri; closed Dec–mid-Feb; tel. 01753/851-900, www.frenchbrothers.co.uk). The same company also offers a longer two-hour circular trip (£8, 1–2/day).

Horse Racing—The horses race near Windsor every Monday evening at the Royal Windsor Racecourse (£8–18 entry, off A308 between Windsor and Maidenhead, tel. 01753/498-400, www.windsor-racecourse.co.uk). The romantic way to get there is by a 10-minute shuttle boat (£5.50 round-trip, see "Boat Trips," above). The famous Ascot Racecourse (described next) is also nearby.

Near Windsor

Ascot Racecourse—Located seven miles southwest of Windsor and just north of the town of Ascot, this royally owned racecourse is one of the most famous horse-racing venues in the world. Originally opened in 1711, it is best known for June's five-day Royal Ascot race meeting, attended by the Queen and 299,999 of her loyal subjects. For many, the outlandish hats worn on Ladies Day (Thursday) are more interesting than the horses. Royal Ascot is usually the third week in June (June 15–19 in 2010), and the pricey tickets go on sale the preceding November (see website for details). In addition to Royal Ascot, the racecourse runs the ponies year-round—funny hats strictly optional (regular tickets generally £10–20, online discounts, children 16 and under free; parking-£5–7, more for special races; dress code enforced in some areas and on certain days, toll tel. 0870-727-1234, www.ascot.co.uk).

Sleeping in Windsor

(area code: 01753)
Most visitors stay in London and do Windsor as a day trip. But here are a few suggestions for those staying the night.

Sleep Code

(£1 = about $1.60, country code: 44)
S = Single, **D** = Double/Twin, **T** = Triple, **Q** = Quad, **b** = bathroom,
s = shower only. Unless otherwise noted, credit cards are
accepted.

To help you sort easily through these listings, I've divided
the rooms into three categories based on the price for a
standard double room with bath:

$$$ Higher Priced—Most rooms £100 or more.
$$ Moderately Priced—Most rooms between £60-100.
$ Lower Priced—Most rooms £60 or less.

$$$ Mercure Castle Hotel, with 108 business-class rooms,
is as central as can be, just down the street from Her Majesty's
weekend retreat (Db-£120–165, nonrefundable online deals,
breakfast-£16, air-con, free Wi-Fi, 18 High Street, tel. 01753/851-
577, www.mercure.com, h6618@accor.com).

$$ Langton House B&B is a stately Victorian home with
three well-appointed rooms lovingly maintained by Paul and Sonja
Fogg (Sb-£70, Db-£90, Tb-£110, Qb-£130, 5 percent extra if paying by credit card, family-friendly, guest kitchen, free Internet
access and Wi-Fi, 46 Alma Road, tel. & fax 01753/858-299, www
.langtonhouse.co.uk, paul@langtonhouse.co.uk).

$$ Park Farm B&B, bright and cheery, is convenient for
drivers visiting Legoland (Sb-£65, Db-£85, Tb-£95, Qb-£105, ask
about family room with bunk beds, cash only—credit card solely for
reservations, free Wi-Fi, pay phone in entry, access to shared fridge
and microwave, free off-street parking, 1 mile from Legoland on
St. Leonards Road near Imperial Road, 5-min bus ride or 1.25-mile
walk to castle, £4 taxi ride from station, tel. 01753/866-823, www
.parkfarm.com, stay@parkfarm.com, Caroline and Drew Youds).

Eating in Windsor

Cornucopia Bistro, a favorite with locals, is a welcoming little
place two minutes from the TI and castle, just beyond the tourist
crush. They serve tasty international dishes with everything made
proudly from scratch. The hardwood floors add a rustic elegance (£11
two-course lunches, £10–14 dinner entrées, Tue–Sat 12:00–14:30
& 18:00–21:30, Sun 12:00–14:30, closed Mon, 6 High Street, tel.
01753/833-009).

The Crooked House is a touristy 17th-century timber-
framed teahouse, serving fresh, hearty £8–10 lunches and cream

teas in a tipsy interior or outdoors on its cobbled lane (Mon–Fri 10:30–18:00, Sat–Sun 10:00–19:00, 51 High Street, tel. 01753/857-534). The important-looking building next door is the Guildhall, which hosted the weddings of both Prince Charles (to Camilla) and Elton John. It's also the home of the town's public WC.

Wagamama offers modern Asian food, mostly in the form of noodle soups. The setting is informal and communal, much like its London siblings (£7–10 main dishes, Mon–Sat 12:00–23:00, Sun 12:00–22:00, just off High Street, on the left as you face the entrance to Windsor Royal Shopping Centre, tel. 01753/833-105).

The Two Brewers Pub, tucked away near the top of Windsor Great Park's Long Walk, serves meals in a cozy Old World atmosphere. Befriend the barman and he may point out a minor royal (open for drinks Mon–Sat 11:30–23:00, Sun 12:00–22:30; lunch served Mon–Sat 12:00–14:00, Sun 12:00–16:00; dinner served Mon–Thu 18:00–22:00, appetizers only Fri–Sat 18:30–21:30, no evening meal on Sun, reservations smart for meals, kids under 18 must sit outside, 34 Park Street, tel. 01753/855-426).

CAMBRIDGE

Cambridge

Cambridge, 60 miles north of London, is world-famous for its prestigious university. Wordsworth, Isaac Newton, Tennyson, Darwin, and Prince Charles are a few of its illustrious alumni. The university dominates—and owns— most of Cambridge, a historic town of 100,000 people that's more pleasant than its rival, Oxford. Cambridge is the epitome of a university town, with  busy bikers, stately residence halls, plenty of bookshops, and proud locals who can point out where DNA was originally modeled, the atom was first split, and electrons were initially discovered.

In medieval Europe, higher education was the domain of the Church, and was limited to ecclesiastical schools. Scholars lived in "halls" on campus. This academic community of residential halls, chapels, and lecture halls connected by peaceful garden courtyards survives today in the colleges that make up the universities of Cambridge and Oxford. By 1350 (Oxford is roughly 100 years older), Cambridge had eight colleges, each with a monastic-type courtyard and lodgings. Today, Cambridge has 31 colleges. While students' lives revolve around their independent college, the university organizes lectures, presents degrees, and promotes research.

Planning Your Time

Cambridge is worth most of a day but not an overnight. Arrive in time for the 11:30 walking tour—an essential part of any visit—and spend the afternoon touring King's College Chapel and Fitzwilliam Museum (closed Mon except Bank Holidays), or simply enjoying the ambience of this stately old college town.

The university schedule has three terms: the Lent term from mid-January to mid-March, the Easter term from mid-April to mid-June, and the Michaelmas term from early October to early December. The colleges are closed to visitors during exams—in mid-April and late June—but King's College Chapel and the Trinity Library stay open, and the town is never sleepy.

Getting to Cambridge

By Train: It's an easy trip from London, about an hour away. Catch the train from London's King's Cross Station (2/hr, fast trains leave at :15 and :45 past the hour and run in each direction, 45 min, £19 one-way standard class, £20 same-day return after 9:30, operated by First Capital Connect, toll tel. 0845-748-4950, www.firstcapitalconnect.co.uk or www.nationalrail.co.uk).

By Bus: National Express coaches run from London's Victoria Coach Station to the Parkside stop in Cambridge (hourly, 2–3 hrs, £11.50, toll tel. 0871-781-8181).

Orientation to Cambridge

(area code: 01223)

Cambridge is congested but small. Everything is within a pleasant walk. There are two main streets, separated from the river by the most interesting colleges. The town center, brimming with tearooms, has a TI and a colorful open-air market (clothes and food Mon–Sat 9:30–16:00; arts, crafts, and food Sun 9:30–16:30; on Market Square).

Tourist Information

An info kiosk on the train station platform dispenses free city maps and sells fancier ones. If it's closed, you can buy a map from a machine with a £1 coin, or get a free one from the nearby bike-rental shop (see "Helpful Hints," below). The official TI is well-signposted, just off Market Square. They book rooms for £5, and sell bus tickets and a £0.30 mini-guide/map (Mon–Fri 10:00–17:30, Sat 10:00–17:00, Easter–Sept also Sun 11:00–15:00—otherwise closed Sun, phones answered from 9:00, Wheeler Street, tel. 01223/464-732 or toll 0871-226-8006, room-booking tel. 01223/457-581, www .visitcambridge.org).

Cambridge

MAGDALENE COLLEGE

JESUS GREEN

NORTHAMPTON

MAG. BR. BRIDGE

QUAYSIDE

THE

St. JOHN'S COLLEGE

200 YARDS
200 METERS

WESLEY HOUSE

WREN LIBRARY

JESUS LANE

SIDNEY SUSSEX COLLEGE

TRINITY COLLEGE

ST. JOHN'S

SIDNEY

HOBSON

KING

N

HOSTEL

TRINITY

GREEN

CHRIST'S COLLEGE

BUS STN.

GARRET

St. MARY'S

MKT.

DRUMMER

CLARE COLLEGE

MARKET SQUARE

PETTY

CURRY

B

EMMANUEL

ST. ANDREW'S

REGENT ST.

To NATIONAL EXPRESS COACH STOP

CHAPEL

KING'S COLLEGE

KING'S PARADE

BENET

St. EDWARD'S

WHEELER

CORN EXCH.

POST

St. TIBB'S

DOWNING

P

B

THE BACKS

QUEEN'S COLLEGE

PEMBROKE

PEMBROKE COLLEGE

DOWNING COLLEGE

SILVER ST.

MILL LANE

TRUMPINGTON ST.

SIDGWICK

PETER-HOUSE

To TRAIN STATION ½ MILE

LAUNDRESS GREEN

To MUSEUM OF CLASSICAL ARCHAEOLOGY (REOPENS SPRING 2010)

RIVER CAM

FITZWILLIAM MUSEUM

DCH

NOTE: MANY ROADS ARE PEDESTRIAN OR RESTRICTED

☐ OTHER COLLEGES (NOT ALL SHOWN)
P PARKING

- - - PATHS
Ⓑ BUS STOPS

❶ Michaelhouse Café
❷ Café Carradines
❸ The Eagle Pub
❹ Marks & Spencer
❺ Sainsbury's
❻ Trinity Punt
❼ Scudamore's Punts (2)

CAMBRIDGE

Arrival in Cambridge

By Train: To get to downtown Cambridge from the train station, take a 25-minute walk (any free map can help); a £5 taxi ride; or bus marked *Citi1, Citi3,* or *Citi7* (£1.30, every 5–10 min).

By Car: Drivers can follow signs from the M11 motorway to any of the handy central short-stay parking lots. Or you can leave the car at one of five park-and-ride lots outside the city, then take the shuttle into town (free parking, £2.50 shuttle, buy ticket from machine or driver).

Helpful Hints

Festival: The **Cambridge Folk Festival** gets things humming and strumming (likely July 29–Aug 1 in 2010, www.cambridge folkfestival.co.uk).

Bike Rental: Station Cycles, located about a half-block to your right as you exit the station, rents bikes (£8/half-day, helmets-50p, £50–75 deposit, cash or credit card) and stores luggage (£3–4/bag depending on size; Mon–Fri 8:00–18:00, Wed until 19:00, Sat 9:00–17:00, Sun 10:00–16:00, tel. 01223/307-125, www.stationcycles.co.uk). They have a second location near the center of town (inside the Grand Arcade, on Corn Exchange Street near Wheeler, Mon–Fri 8:00–19:00, Wed until 20:00, Sat 9:00–19:00, Sun 10:00–18:00, tel. 01223/307-655).

Tours in Cambridge

▲▲**Walking Tour of the Colleges**—A walking tour is the best way to understand Cambridge's mix of "town and gown." The walks provide a good rundown of the historic and scenic highlights of the university, as well as some fun local gossip.

The TI offers **daily walking tours** (£10, 2 hrs, includes admission to King's College Chapel if it's open; July–Aug daily at 10:30, 11:30, 13:30, and 14:30, no 10:30 tour Sun; April–June and Sept daily at 11:30 and 13:30; Oct–March Mon–Sat at 11:30 and 13:30, Sun at 13:30; tel. 01223/457-574, www.visitcambridge.org). Drop by the TI (the departure point) one hour early to snare a spot. If you're visiting on a Sunday, call the day before to reserve a spot with your credit card and confirm departure time.

Private guides are also available through the TI (basic 1-hour tour-£3.50/person, £50 minimum; 1.5-hour tour-£4/person, £58 minimum; 2-hour tour-£4.50/person, £65 minimum; does not include individual college entrance fees, tel. 01223/457-574, www.visitcambridge.org).

Walking and Punting Ghost Tour—If you're in Cambridge on the weekend, consider a £5 ghost walk Friday evenings at 18:00, or a spooky £16 trip on the River Cam followed by a walk most Saturdays at 20:00 (book ahead for both, tel. 01223/457-574, www .visitcambridge.org).

Bus Tours—City Sightseeing hop-on, hop-off bus tours are informative and cover the outskirts, including the American WWII Cemetery (£12, 80 min for full 21-stop circuit, departs every 20 min in summer, every 40 min in winter, first bus leaves train station at 10:06, last bus at 17:46, recorded commentary with some live English-language guides, can use credit card to buy tickets in their office in train station, tel. 01223/423-578, www.city -sightseeing.com). Walking tours go where the buses can't—right into the center.

Sights in Cambridge

In Cambridge

▲▲**King's College Chapel**—Built from 1446 to 1515 by Henrys VI–VIII, England's best example of Perpendicular Gothic is the single most impressive building in town. Stand inside, look up, and marvel, as Christopher Wren did, at what was the largest single span of vaulted roof anywhere—2,000 tons of incredible fan vaulting. Wander through the Old Testament, with 26 stained-glass windows from the 16th century, the most Renaissance stained glass anywhere in one spot. The windows were removed to keep them safe during World War II, and then painstakingly replaced. Walk to the altar and admire Rubens' masterful *Adoration of the Magi* (£5, erratic hours depending on school schedule and events; during academic term usually Mon–Fri 9:30–15:30, Sat 9:30–15:15, Sun 13:15–14:15; during breaks—see "Planning Your Time," earlier—it's open Mon–Sat 9:30–16:30, Sun 10:00–17:00). When school's in session, you're welcome to enjoy an evensong service (Mon–Sat at 17:30, Sun at 15:30, tel. 01223/331-212, recorded info tel. 01223/331-155, www.kings.cam.ac.uk/chapel).

▲▲**Trinity College and Wren Library**—Nearly half of Cambridge's 83 Nobel Prize winners have come from this richest and biggest of the town's colleges, founded in 1546 by Henry VIII. Don't miss the 1695 Wren-designed library, with its wonderful carving and fascinating original manuscripts. There's a small fee to visit the campus (£2.50), but if you just want to see Wren Library (free), enter from the riverside entrance, located by the Garret Hostel Bridge. The Wren Library should remain open during planned renovation that may close the grounds through July 2010 (otherwise campus open daily 10:00–17:00; library open Mon–Fri 12:00–14:00, Nov–mid-June also Sat 10:30–12:30, always closed Sun and during exams; only 15 people allowed in at a time, tel. 01223/338-400, www.trin.cam.ac.uk). Just outside the library entrance, Sir Isaac Newton, who spent 30 years at Trinity, clapped his hands and timed the echo to measure the speed of sound as it raced down the side of the cloister and back. In the library's 12 display cases (covered with cloth that you flip back), you'll see handwritten works by Sir Isaac Newton and John Milton, alongside A. A. Milne's original *Winnie the Pooh* (the real Christopher Robin attended Trinity College).

▲▲**Fitzwilliam Museum**—Britain's best museum of antiquities and art outside London is the Fitzwilliam. Enjoy its wonderful paintings (Old Masters and a fine English section featuring Gainsborough, Reynolds, Hogarth, and others, plus works by all the famous Impressionists); old manuscripts; and Greek, Egyptian, and Mesopotamian collections. Watch your step—a visitor tripped a few years ago and accidentally smashed three 17th-century Chinese vases. Amazingly, the vases were restored and are now on display in Gallery 17...in a protective case (free, audio/videoguide-£3, Tue–Sat 10:00–17:00, Sun 12:00–17:00, closed Mon except Bank Holidays, no photos, Trumpington Street, tel. 01223/332-900, www.fitzmuseum.cam.ac.uk).

Museum of Classical Archaeology—Though this museum—reopening after renovation in spring 2010—contains no originals, it offers a unique chance to see accurate copies (19th-century casts) of virtually every famous ancient Greek and Roman statue. More than 450 statues are on display (free, likely Mon–Fri 10:00–17:00, sometimes also Sat 10:00–13:00 during term, closed Sun, Sidgwick Avenue, tel. 01223/330-402, www.classics.cam.ac.uk/museum). The museum is a five-minute walk west of Silver Street Bridge; after crossing the bridge, continue straight until you reach a sign reading *Sidgwick Site*. The museum is in the long building on the corner to your right; the entrance is on the opposite side.

▲**Punting on the Cam**—For a little levity and probably more exercise than you really want, try hiring one of the traditional flat-bottom punts at the river and

pole yourself up and down (or around and around, more likely) the lazy Cam. Once you get the hang of it, it's a fine way to enjoy the scenic side of Cambridge. It's less crowded in late afternoon (and less embarrassing).

Two companies rent punts and offer tours. **Trinity Punt,** just north of Garrett Hostel Bridge, is run by Trinity College students (£12/hr, £40 deposit, 45-min tours-£30/boat, can share ride and cost with up to 2 others, cash only, ask for quick and free lesson, Easter–mid-Oct

Mon–Fri 11:00–17:30, Sat–Sun 10:00–17:30, return punts by 18:30, no rentals mid-Oct–Easter, tel. 01223/338-483). **Scudamore's** has two locations: Mill Lane, just south of the central Silver Street Bridge, and the less-convenient Quayside at Magdalene Bridge, at the north end of town (£16–18/hr, £80 deposit required—can use credit card, 45-min tours-£14/person, save £2 by buying at TI, open daily June–Aug 9:00–22:00, Sept–May at least 10:00–17:00, weather permitting, tel. 01223/359-750, www.scudamores.com).

Near Cambridge

Imperial War Museum Duxford—This former airfield, nine miles south of Cambridge, is nirvana for aviation fans and WWII buffs. Wander through seven exhibition halls housing 200 vintage aircraft (including Spitfires, B-17 Flying Fortresses, a Concorde, and a Blackbird), as well as military land vehicles and special displays on Normandy and the Battle of Britain. On many weekends, the museum holds special events, such as air shows (extra fee)—check the website for details (£16, show local bus ticket for discount, daily mid-March–late Oct 10:00–18:00, late Oct–mid-March 10:00–16:00, last entry one hour before closing, tel. 01223/835-000, http://duxford.iwm.org.uk).

Getting There: The museum is located off A505 in Duxford. From Cambridge you can take the bus marked *Citi7* from the train station (45 min) or from Emmanuel Street's Stop A (55 min; bus runs 2/hr Mon–Sat, www.stagecoachbus.com/cambridge). On Sundays and Bank Holidays, catch the #132 bus, run by private bus operator Myalls, from the train station or the Drummer Street bus station (40 min, first bus around 10:00, then every 2 hours until 18:00, tel. 01763/243-225).

Eating in Cambridge

While picnicking is scenic and saves money, the weather may not always cooperate. Here are a few ideas for fortifying yourself in central Cambridge.

The **Michaelhouse Café** is a heavenly respite from the crowds, tucked into the repurposed St. Michael's Church, just north of Great St. Mary's Church. At lunch, choose from salads, soups, and sandwiches, as well as a few hot dishes and a variety of tasty baked goods (£5–10 light meals, £4 "fill your plate" special available 14:30–15:00, open Mon–Sat 8:00–17:00, breakfast served 8:00–11:30, lunch served 11:30–15:00, hot drinks and baked goods available all the time, closed Sun, Trinity Street, tel. 01223/309-147).

Café Carradines is a cozy cafeteria that serves traditional British food at reasonable prices, including a Sunday roast lunch for £7 (Mon–Sat 8:00–17:00, Sun 10:00–16:00, down the stairs at 23 Market Street, tel. 01223/361-792).

The Eagle Pub, near the TI, is a good spot for a quick drink or a pub lunch. Look at the carefully preserved ceiling in its "Air Force Bar," signed by local airmen during World War II. Science fans can also celebrate the discovery of DNA—Francis Crick and James Watson first announced their findings here in 1953 (Mon–Sat 11:00–23:00, Sun 12:00–22:30, food served 12:00–14:30 & 17:00–21:30, pleasant patio, 8 Benet Street, tel. 01223/505-020).

Supermarkets: There's a **Marks & Spencer Simply Food** grocery at the train station and a larger store at 6 Sidney Street (Mon–Sat 9:00–18:00, Sun 11:00–17:00, tel. 01223/355-219). **Sainsbury's** supermarket, with slightly longer hours, is at 44 Sidney Street, on the corner of Green Street. A good picnic spot is Laundress Green, a grassy park on the river, at the end of Mill Lane near the Silver Street Bridge punts. There are no benches, so bring something to sit on. Remember, the college lawns are private property, so walking or picnicking on the grass is generally not allowed. When in doubt, ask at the college's entrance.

Cambridge Connections

From Cambridge by Train to: York (hourly, 2.5 hrs, transfer in Peterborough), **Stratford-upon-Avon** (hourly, 4 hrs, inconvenient change in London or Birmingham), **London** (3/hr, 1 hr). Train info: Toll tel. 0845-748-4950, www.nationalrail.co.uk.

By Bus to: London (hourly, 2–3 hrs), **Heathrow Airport** (1–2/hr, 2–3 hrs). Bus info: Toll tel. 08717-818-181, www.national express.com.

BATH

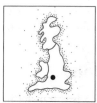

The best city to visit within easy striking distance of London is Bath—just a 90-minute train ride away. Two hundred years ago, this city of 85,000 was the trendsetting Hollywood of Britain. If ever a city enjoyed looking in the mirror, Bath's the one. It has more "government-listed" or protected historic buildings per capita than any other town in England. The entire city, built of the creamy warm-tone limestone called "Bath stone," beams in its cover-girl complexion. An architectural chorus line, it's a triumph of the Georgian style. Proud locals remind visitors that the town is routinely banned from the "Britain in Bloom" contest to give other towns a chance to win. Bath's narcissism is justified. Even with its mobs of tourists (2 million per year) and greedy prices, Bath is a joy to visit.

Bath's fame began with the allure of its (supposedly) healing hot springs. Long before the Romans arrived in the first century, Bath was known for its warm waters. Romans named the popular spa town Aquae Sulis, after a local Celtic goddess. The town's importance carried through Saxon times, when it had a huge church on the site of the present-day abbey and was considered the religious capital of Britain. Its influence peaked in 973 with King Edgar's sumptuous coronation in the abbey. Later, Bath prospered as a wool town.

Bath then declined until the mid-1600s, languishing to just a huddle of huts around the abbey, with hot, smelly mud and 3,000 residents, oblivious to the Roman ruins 18 feet below their dirt floors. In fact, with its own walls built upon ancient ones, Bath was no bigger than that Roman town. Then, in 1687, Queen Mary, fighting infertility, bathed here. Within 10 months she gave birth to a son...and a new age of popularity for Bath.

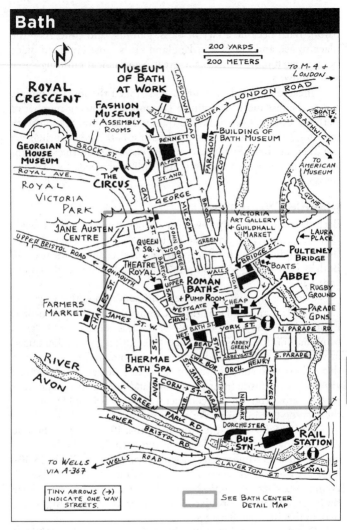

The revitalized town boomed as a spa resort. Ninety percent of the buildings you'll see today are from the 18th century. Local architect John Wood the Elder was inspired by the Italian architect Andrea Palladio to build a "new Rome." The town bloomed in the Neoclassical style, and streets were lined not with scrawny sidewalks but with wide "parades," upon which the women in their stylishly wide dresses could spread their fashionable tails.

Beau Nash (1673–1762) was Bath's "master of ceremonies." He organized both the daily regimen of aristocratic visitors and the city, lighting the streets, improving security, banning swords, and opening the Pump Room. Under Nash's fashionable baton, Bath became a city of balls, gaming, and concerts—the place to see and be seen in England. This most civilized place became even more so with the great Neoclassical building spree that followed.

These days, modern tourism has stoked the local economy, as has the fast morning train to London. (A growing number of Bath professionals catch the 7:13 train to Paddington Station every morning.) With renewed access to Bath's soothing hot springs via the Thermae Bath Spa, the venerable waters are in the spotlight again, attracting a new generation of visitors in need of a cure or a soak.

Planning Your Time

Bath deserves two nights even on a quick trip. On a three-week Britain getaway, spend three nights in Bath, with one day for the city and one day for side-trips (see next chapter). Ideally, use Bath as your jet-lag recovery pillow, and do London at the end of your trip.

Consider starting a three-week British vacation this way:

Day 1: Land at Heathrow. Connect to Bath by National Express bus—the better option—or the less convenient bus/train combination (for details, see page 161). Although you don't need or want a car in Bath, and some rental companies have an office there, those who land early and pick up their cars at the airport can visit Windsor Castle (near Heathrow) and/or Stonehenge on their way to Bath. (You can also consider flying into Bristol.) If you have the evening free in Bath, take a walking tour.

Day 2: 9:00–Tour the Roman Baths; 10:30–Catch the free city walking tour; 12:30–Picnic on the open deck of a Bath tour bus; 14:00–Free time in the shopping center of old Bath; 15:30–Tour the Fashion Museum or Museum of Bath at Work. Take the evening walking tour (unless you did last night), enjoy the Bizarre Bath comedy walk, consider seeing a play, or go for a nighttime soak in the Thermae Bath Spa.

Day 3 (and possibly 4): By car, explore nearby sights. Without a car, consider a one-day Avebury/Stonehenge/cute towns minibus tour from Bath (Mad Max tours are best; see "Tours in Bath" later in this chapter).

Orientation to Bath

(area code: 01225)

Bath's town square, three blocks in front of the bus and train station, is a cluster of tourist landmarks, including the abbey, Roman and medieval baths, and the Pump Room.

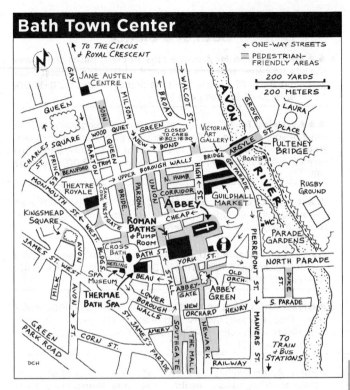

Bath Town Center

Tourist Information

The TI is in the abbey churchyard (Mon–Sat 9:30–18:00, Sun 10:00–16:00, closes one hour early Mon–Sat Oct–May, toll tel. 0870-420-1278, www.visitbath.co.uk, note that their 0906 info number costs 50p/min). The TI sells a chintzy £1 city map. The £1.25 map, available in their shop, is much better—or just use the one included in the free *Bath Visitors' Guide and Map*. While you're at the TI, browse through scads of fliers, books, and maps, or ask them to book you a room (booking tel. 0844-847-5256). They don't print an events flier, so look at the local paper or their daily events board. You can also buy the Great British Heritage Pass here (see page 20).

Arrival in Bath

The Bath Spa **train station** has a national and international tickets desk and a privately run travel agency masquerading as a TI.

Immediately surrounding the train station is a sea of construction, as Bath gets a new mall and underground parking garage (due to be completed in 2011). To get to the TI from the train station, walk two blocks up Manvers Street and turn left at the triangular "square," following the small TI arrow on a signpost.

Bath at a Glance

▲▲▲**Roman and Medieval Baths** Ancient baths that gave the city its name, tourable with good audioguide. **Hours:** Daily July–Aug 9:00–22:00, March–June and Sept–Oct 9:00–18:00, Nov–Feb 9:30–17:30. See page 200.

▲▲▲**Walking Tours** Free top-notch tours, helping you make the most of your visit, led by The Mayor's Corps of Honorary Guides. **Hours:** Sun–Fri at 10:30 and 14:00, Sat at 10:30 only; additional evening walks offered May–Sept Tue and Fri at 19:00. See page 198.

▲▲**Royal Crescent and the Circus** Stately Georgian (Neoclassical) buildings from Bath's late 18th-century glory days. **Hours:** Always viewable. See page 204.

▲▲**Fashion Museum** 400 years of clothing under one roof, plus opulent Assembly Rooms. **Hours:** Daily March–Oct 10:30–18:00, Nov–Feb 10:30–17:00. See page 205.

▲▲**Museum of Bath at Work** Gadget-ridden circa-1900 engineer's shop, foundry, factory, and office, best enjoyed with a live tour. **Hours:** April–Oct daily 10:30–17:00, Nov–March weekends only. See page 206.

▲**Pump Room** Swanky Georgian hall, ideal for a spot of tea or a taste of unforgettably "healthy" spa water. **Hours:** Daily 9:30–12:00 for coffee and breakfast, 12:00–14:30 for lunch, 14:30–16:30 for afternoon tea (open for dinner during Bath International Music Festival, July–Aug and Christmas holidays only). See page 201.

The **bus station** is west of the train station, just south of Dorchester Street.

My recommended B&Bs are all within a 10- to 15-minute walk or a £4–5 taxi ride from the train station.

Helpful Hints

Festivals: The **Bath Literature Festival** is an open book February 27–March 7 in 2010 (www.bathlitfest.org.uk). The **Bath International Music Festival** bursts into song every spring (classical, folk, jazz, contemporary; May 28–June 12 in 2010, see www.bathmusicfest.org.uk), overlapped by the eclectic **Bath Fringe Festival** (theater, walks, talks, bus trips; May 28–June 13 in 2010, www.bathfringe.co.uk). The **Jane Austen Festival** unfolds genteelly in late September (www.janeausten.co.uk/festival). Bath's festival box office sells tickets for most

▲**Thermae Bath Spa** Relaxation center that put the bath back in Bath. **Hours:** Daily 9:00–22:00. See page 201.

▲ **Abbey** 500-year-old Perpendicular Gothic church, graced with beautiful fan vaulting and stained glass. **Hours:** April–Oct Mon–Sat 9:00–18:00, Sun 13:00–14:30 & 16:30–17:30; Nov–March Mon–Sat 9:00–16:30, Sun 13:00–14:30 & 16:30–17:30. See page 203.

▲**Pulteney Bridge and Parade Gardens** Shop-strewn bridge and relaxing riverside gardens. **Hours:** Bridge—always open; gardens—April–Sept daily 10:00–dusk, shorter hours off-season. See page 203.

▲**Georgian House at No. 1 Royal Crescent** Best opportunity to explore the interior of one of Bath's high-rent Georgian beauties. **Hours:** Mid-Feb–Oct Tue–Sun 10:30–17:00, Nov Tue–Sun 10:30–16:00, closed Mon and Dec–mid-Feb. See page 205.

▲ **American Museum** An insightful look primarily at colonial/early-American lifestyles, with 18 furnished rooms and eager-to-talk guides. **Hours:** Mid-March–Oct Tue–Sun 12:00–17:00, closed Mon and Nov–mid-March. See page 207.

Jane Austen Centre Exhibit on 19th-century Bath-based novelist, best for her fans. **Hours:** Mid-March–mid-Nov daily 9:45–17:30, July–Aug Thu–Sat until 19:00; mid-Nov–mid-March Sun–Fri 11:00–16:30, Sat 9:45–17:30. See page 206.

BATH

events, and can tell you exactly what's on tonight (2 Church Street, tel. 01225/463-362, www.bathfestivals.org.uk). The city's local paper, the *Bath Chronicle,* publishes a "What's On" event listing on Fridays (www.thisisbath.com).

Internet Access: You can get online at the Bath library (£1/20 min with free library membership, Mon–Thu 9:30–19:00, Fri–Sat 9:30–17:00, Sun 13:00–16:00, in The Podium shopping centre on Northgate Street near Pulteney Bridge, tel. 01225/394-041, www.bathnes.gov.uk), or ask your hotel or the TI for recommended Internet cafés.

Laundry: Bring lots of £0.20 and £1 coins, as there are no change machines at these launderettes. **Spruce Goose Launderette** is around the corner from the recommended Brocks Guest House, on the pedestrian lane called Margaret's Buildings (self-service daily 8:00–20:00; full-service Mon, Wed, and

Fri 9:00–13:00—but book ahead; tel. 01225/483-309). **Speedy Wash** can pick up your laundry before 11:00 anywhere in town for same-day service (£12/bag, Mon–Fri 7:30–17:30, Sat 8:30–13:00 but no pickup, closed Sun, no self-service, most hotels work with them, 4 Mile End, London Road, tel. 01225/427-616).

Car Rental: Enterprise provides a pickup service for customers to and from their hotels (extra fee for one-way rentals, at Lower Bristol Road outside Bath, tel. 01225/443-311, www.enterprise.com). Others include **Thrifty** (pickup service and one-way rentals available, in the Burnett Business Park in Keynsham—between Bath and Bristol, tel. 01179/867-997, www.thrifty.co.uk) and **National Europcar** (one-way rentals available, £7 by taxi from the train station, at Brassmill Lane—go west on Upper Bristol Road, tel. 01225/481-982 or 01761/479-205). Skip **Avis**—it's a mile from the Bristol train station, and you'd need to rent a car to get there. Most offices close Saturday afternoon and all day Sunday, which complicates weekend pickups. I recommend that you take the train or bus from downtown London to Bath, and rent a car as you leave Bath.

Parking: Parking in the city center is difficult—short-term street parking is available but pricey (about £2.50/hr, 2-hour maximum, buy pay-and-display tickets from machine), with cheaper parking in parking lots. For more information, visit www.bathnes.gov.uk/bathnes.

Tours in Bath

▲▲▲**Walking Tours**—The **Mayor's Corps of Honorary Guides** offers free two-hour tours led by volunteers who want to share their love of Bath with its many visitors (as the city's mayor first did when he took a group on a guided walk back in the 1930s). Their chatty, historical, and gossip-filled walks are essential for your understanding of this town's amazing Georgian social scene. How else would you learn that the old "chair ho" call for your sedan chair evolved into today's "cheerio" farewell? Tours leave from outside the Pump Room in the abbey churchyard (free, no tips, year-round Sun–Fri at 10:30 and 14:00, Sat at 10:30 only; additional evening walks May–Sept Tue and Fri at 19:00; tel. 01225/477-411, www.thecityofbath.co.uk). Tip for theatergoers: When your guide stops to talk outside the Theatre Royal, skip out for a moment, pop into the box office, and see about snaring a great deal on a play for tonight.

For a **private tour,** call the local guides' bureau (£60/2 hrs, tel. 01225/337-111). For **Ghost Walks** and **Bizarre Bath** tours, see "Nightlife in Bath," later.

BATH

▲▲**City Bus Tours**—City Sightseeing's hop-on, hop-off bus tours zip through Bath. Jump on a bus anytime at one of 17 sign-posted pickup points, pay the driver, climb upstairs, and hear recorded commentary about Bath. City Sightseeing has two 45-minute routes: a city tour (unintelligible audio recording on half the buses, live guides on the other half—choose the latter), and a "Skyline" route outside town (all live guides, stops near the American Museum—15-min walk). On a sunny day, this is a multitasking tourist's dream come true: You can munch a sandwich, work on a tan, snap great photos, and learn a lot, all at the same time. Save money by doing the bus tour first—ticket stubs get you minor discounts at many sights (£11, ticket valid for 2 days and both tour routes, generally 4/hr daily in summer 9:30–18:30, in winter 10:00–15:00, tel. 01225/330-444, www .city-sightseeing.com).

Taxi Tours—Local taxis, driven by good talkers, go where big buses can't. A group of up to four can rent a cab for an hour (about £20) and enjoy a fine, informative, and—with the right cabbie—entertaining private joyride. It's probably cheaper to let the meter run than to pay for an hourly rate, but ask the cabbie for advice.

To Stonehenge, Avebury, and the Cotswolds

Bath is a good launch pad for visiting Wells, Avebury, Stonehenge, and more.

Mad Max Minibus Tours—Operating daily from Bath, Maddy and Paul offer thoughtfully organized, informative tours that run with entertaining guides and a maximum group size of 16 people. Their **Stone Circles** full-day tour covers 110 miles and visits Stonehenge, the Avebury Stone Circles, and two cute villages, Lacock and Castle Combe. Photogenic Lacock is featured in parts of the BBC's *Pride and Prejudice* and the *Harry Potter* movies, and Castle Combe, the southernmost Cotswold village, is as sweet as they come (£30 plus £6.50 Stonehenge entry, tours run daily 8:45–16:30, arrive 10 min early, leaves early to beat the Stonehenge hordes). Their shorter tour of **Stonehenge and Lacock** leaves daily at 13:15 and returns at 17:15, and on some days leaves at 8:45 and returns at 12:45 (£15 plus £6.50 Stonehenge entry).

Mad Max also offers a **Cotswold Discovery** full-day tour, a picturesque romp through the countryside with stops and a cream tea opportunity in the Cotswolds' quainter villages, including Stow-on-the-Wold, Bibury, Tetbury, the Coln Valley, The Slaughters (optional walk between the two villages), and others (£32.50; runs Sun, Tue, and Thu 8:45–17:15; arrive 10 min early). If you request it in advance, you can bring your luggage along and use the tour as transportation to Stow or, for £2.50 extra, Moreton-in-Marsh, with easy train connections to Oxford.

BATH

All tours depart from Bath at the Glass House shop on the corner of Orange Grove, a one-minute walk from the abbey. Arrive 10 minutes before your departure time and bring cash—credit cards are not accepted. It's better to book ahead—as far ahead as possible in summer—for these popular tours. Online or email reservations are preferable to calling (phone answered daily 8:00–18:00, tel. 07990/505-970, www.madmax.abel.co.uk, maddy@madmax.abel.co.uk). Please honor or cancel your seat reservation.

More Bus Tours—If Mad Max is booked, don't fret. Plenty of companies in Bath offer tours of varying lengths, prices, and destinations. Note that the cost of admission to sights is usually not included with any tour.

Scarper Tours runs a minibus tour to Stonehenge (£14, 10 percent Rick Steves discount if you book direct, does not include £6.50 Stonehenge entry fee, departs from behind the abbey, daily Easter–Sept at 10:00 and 14:00, Oct–Easter at 13:00 only, tel. 07739/644-155, www.scarpertours.com). The three-hour tour (two hours there and back, an hour at the site) includes driver narration en route.

Celtic Horizons, run by retired teacher Alan Price, offers tours from Bath to a variety of destinations, such as Stonehenge, Avebury, and Wells. He can provide a convenient transfer service (to or from London, Heathrow, Bristol Airport, the Cotswolds, and so on), with or without a tour itinerary en route. Allow about £25/hour for a group (his comfortable minivan seats up to 8 people) and £125 for Heathrow–Bath transfers. It's best to make arrangements and get pricing information by email at alan@celtichorizons.com (cash only, tel. 01373/461-784, http://celtichorizons.com).

Sights in Bath

In the Town Center

▲▲▲Roman and Medieval Baths—In ancient Roman times, high society enjoyed the mineral springs at Bath. From Londinium, Romans traveled so often to Aquae Sulis, as the city was called, to "take a bath" that finally it became known simply as Bath. Today, a fine museum surrounds the ancient bath. It's a one-way system leading you past well-documented displays, Roman artifacts, mosaics, a temple pediment, and the actual mouth of the spring, piled high with Roman pennies. Enjoy some

quality time looking into the eyes of Minerva, goddess of the hot springs. The included audioguide makes the visit easy and plenty informative. For those with a big appetite for Roman history, in-depth 40-minute guided tours leave from the end of the museum at the edge of the actual bath (included with ticket, on the hour, a poolside clock is set for the next departure time). The water is greenish because of algae—don't drink it. You can revisit the museum after the tour (£11, £14.50 combo-ticket includes Fashion Museum—a £3.50 savings, family ticket available, daily July–Aug 9:00–22:00, March–June and Sept–Oct 9:00–18:00, Nov–Feb 9:30–17:30, last entry one hour before closing, tel. 01225/477-785, www.romanbaths.co.uk). The museum and baths are fun to visit in the evening in summer—romantic, gas-lit, and all yours.

After touring the Roman Baths, stop by the attached Pump Room for a spot of tea, or to gag on the water.

▲**Pump Room**—For centuries, Bath was forgotten as a spa. Then, in 1687, the previously barren Queen Mary bathed here, became pregnant, and bore a male heir to the throne. A few years later, Queen Anne found the water eased her painful gout. Word of its wonder waters spread, and Bath earned its way back on the aristocratic map. High society soon turned the place into one big pleasure palace. The Pump Room, an elegant Georgian hall just above the Roman Baths, offers visitors their best chance to raise a pinky in this Chippendale grandeur. Above the newspaper table and sedan chairs, a statue of Beau Nash himself sniffles down at you. Drop by to sip coffee or tea or to enjoy a light meal (daily 9:30–12:00 for coffee and £6–9 breakfast, 12:00–14:30 for £6–10 lunches, 14:30–16:30 for £17.50 traditional afternoon tea, tea/coffee and pastries also available in the afternoons; open for dinner July–Aug, during Bath International Music Festival, and Christmas holidays only; live music daily—string trio or piano, times vary; tel. 01225/444-477). For just the price of a coffee (£3), you're welcome to drop in anytime—except during lunch—to enjoy the music and atmosphere.

The Spa Water: This is your chance to eat a famous (but forgettable) "Bath bun" and split a drink of the awful curative water (£0.50). The water comes from the King's Spring and is brought to you by an appropriately attired server, who explains that the water is 10,000 years old, pumped from nearly 100 yards deep, and marinated in 43 wonderful minerals. Convenient public WCs (which use plain old tap water) are in the entry hallway that connects the Pump Room with the baths.

▲**Thermae Bath Spa**—After simmering unused for a quarter-century, Bath's natural thermal springs once again offer R&R for the masses. The state-of-the-art spa is housed in a complex of three buildings that combine historic structures with controversial (and expensive) new glass-and-steel architecture.

Is the Thermae Bath Spa worth the time and money? The experience is pretty pricey and humble compared to similar German and Hungarian spas. Because you're in a tall, modern building in the city center, it lacks a certain old-time elegance. Jets are very limited, and the only water toys you'll see are big foam noodles. There's no cold plunge—the only way to cool off between steam rooms is to step onto a small, unglamorous balcony. The Royal Bath's two pools are essentially the same, and the water isn't particularly hot in either—in fact, the main attraction is the rooftop view from the top one (best with a partner or as a social experience).

That said, this is the only natural thermal spa in the UK, and a chance to bathe in Bath. If you visit, bring your own swimsuit and come for a couple of hours (Fri night and Sat afternoon are most crowded). Or consider an evening visit, when—on a chilly day—Bath's twilight glows through the steam from the rooftop pool.

Cost: The cheapest spa pass is £22 for two hours, which gains you access to the Royal Bath's large, ground-floor "Minerva Bath"; the four steam rooms and the waterfall shower; and the view-filled, open-air, rooftop thermal pool. If you want to stay longer, it's £32/4 hrs and £52/day (towel, robe, and slippers-£9). The much-hyped £37.50 Twilight Package includes three hours and a meal (one plate, drink, robe, towel, and slippers). This package's appeal is not the mediocre meal, but to be on top of the building at a magical hour (which you can do for less money at the regular rate). Thermae also has all the "pamper thyself" extras: massages, mud wraps, and various healing-type treatments, including "watsu"—water shiatsu (£40–70 extra).

Hours: Daily 9:00–22:00, last entry at 19:30.

Location and Information: It's 100 yards from the Roman and Medieval Baths, on Beau Street. Tel. 01225/331-234, book treatments at www.thermaebathspa.com. There's a salad-and-smoothies café for guests. No kids under 16 allowed.

Cross Bath: This renovated, circular Georgian structure across the street from the main spa provides a simpler and less-expensive bathing option. It has a hot-water fountain that taps directly into the spring, making its water temperature higher than the spa's (£13/90 min, daily 10:00–20:00, last entry at 18:30, changing rooms, no access to Royal Bath, no kids under 12).

Spa Visitor Center: Also across the street, in the Hetling Pump Room, this free, one-room exhibit explains the story of the spa (Mon–Sat 10:00–17:00, Sun 10:00–16:00, £2 audioguide).

▲**Abbey**—The town of Bath wasn't much in the Middle Ages, but an important church has stood on this spot since Anglo-Saxon times. King Edgar I was crowned here in 973, when the church was much bigger (before the bishop packed up and moved to Wells). Dominating the town center, today's abbey—the last great medieval church of England—is 500 years old and a fine example of Late Perpendicular Gothic, with breezy fan vaulting and enough stained glass to earn it the nickname "Lantern of the West." The glass, red-iron gas-powered lamps, and heating grates on the floor are

all remnants of the 19th century. The window behind the altar shows 52 scenes from the life of Christ. A window to the left of the altar shows Edgar's coronation (worth the £2.50 donation; April–Oct Mon–Sat 9:00–18:00, Sun 13:00–14:30 & 16:30–17:30; Nov–March Mon–Sat 9:00–16:30, Sun 13:00–14:30 & 16:30–17:30; handy flier narrates a self-guided 19-stop tour, tel. 0122/422-462, www.bathabbey.org). Posted on the door is the schedule for concerts, services, and **evensong** (at 16:00 or 17:15, check schedule on website). The facade (c. 1500, but mostly restored) is interesting for some of its carvings. Look for the angels going down the ladder. The statue of Peter (to the left of the door) lost his head to mean iconoclasts; it was re-carved out of his once super-sized beard. Take a moment to appreciate the abbey's architecture from the Abbey Green square.

A small but worthwhile exhibit, the abbey's **Heritage Vaults** tells the story of Christianity in Bath since Roman times (free, Mon–Sat 10:00–15:30, closed Sun, entrance just outside church, south side).

▲**Pulteney Bridge, Parade Gardens, and Cruises**—Bath is inclined to compare its shop-lined Pulteney Bridge to Florence's Ponte Vecchio. That's pushing it. But to best enjoy a sunny day, pay about £1 to enter the Parade Gardens below the bridge (April–Sept daily 10:00–dusk, shorter hours off-season, includes deck chairs, ask about concerts held some Sun at 15:00 in summer, www.bathnes.gov.uk). Taking a siesta to relax peacefully at the riverside provides a wonderful break (and memory).

Across the bridge, at Pulteney Weir, tour boat companies run **cruises** (£8, £4 one-way, up to 7/day if the weather's good, 60 min to Bathampton and back, WCs on board, tel. 01225/312-900). Just take whatever boat is running—all stop in Bathampton (allowing

you to hop off and walk back). Boats come with picnic-friendly sundecks.

Guildhall Market—The little shopping mall, located across from Pulteney Bridge, is a frumpy time warp in this affluent town—fun for browsing and picnic shopping. Its cheap Market Café is recommended in "Eating in Bath."

Victoria Art Gallery—This two-story gallery, next to Pulteney Bridge, is filled with paintings from the late 17th century to the present (free, includes audioguide, Tue–Sat 10:00–17:00, Sun 13:30–17:00, closed Mon, WC, tel. 01225/477-233, www.victoriagal.org.uk).

▲▲Royal Crescent and the Circus—If Bath is an architectural cancan, these are its knickers. These first Georgian "condos" by John Wood (the Elder and the Younger) are well-explained by the city walking tours. "Georgian" is British for "Neoclassical," or

dating from the 1770s. As you cruise the Crescent, pretend you're rich. Then pretend you're poor. Notice the "ha ha fence," a drop-off in the front yard that acted as a barrier, invisible from the windows,

for keeping out sheep and peasants. The refined and stylish **Royal Crescent Hotel** sits unmarked in the center of the crescent. You're welcome to (politely) drop in to explore its fine ground-floor public spaces and back garden. A gracious and traditional tea is served in the garden out back (£12.50 cream tea, £22.50 afternoon tea, daily 15:00–17:00, sharing is OK, reserve a day in advance in summer, tel. 01225/823-333).

Picture the round Circus as a coliseum turned inside out. Its Doric, Ionic, and Corinthian capital decorations pay homage to its Greco-Roman origin, and are a reminder that Bath (with its seven hills) aspired to be "the Rome of England." The frieze above the first row of columns has hundreds of different panels, each representing the arts, sciences, and crafts. The first floor was high off the ground, to accommodate aristocrats on sedan chairs and women with sky-high hairdos. The tiny round windows on the top floors were the servants' quarters. And though the building fronts are uniform, the backs are higgledy-piggledy, infamous for their

BATH

"hanging loos." Stand in the middle of the Crescent among the grand plane trees, on the capped old well. Imagine the days when there was no indoor plumbing, and the servant girls gathered here to fetch water—this was gossip central. If you stand on the well, your clap echoes three times around the circle (try it).

▲**Georgian House at No. 1 Royal Crescent**—This museum (corner of Brock Street and Royal Crescent) offers your best look into a period house. Your visit is limited to four roped-off rooms, but if you take your time and talk to the docents stationed in each room, it's worth the £5 admission to get behind one of those classy Georgian facades. The docents are determined to fill you in on all the fascinating details of Georgian life...like how high-class women shaved their eyebrows and pasted on carefully trimmed strips of furry mouse skin in their place. On the bedroom dresser sits a bowl of black beauty marks and a head-scratcher from those pre-shampoo days. Fido spent his days in the kitchen treadmill powering the rotisserie (mid-Feb–Oct Tue–Sun 10:30–17:00, Nov Tue–Sun 10:30–16:00, last entry 30 min before closing, closed Mon and Dec–mid-Feb, £2 guidebook available, no photos, "no stiletto heels, please," tel. 01225/428-126, www.bath-preservation-trust .org.uk). Its WC is accessible from the street (under the entry steps, across from the exit and shop).

▲▲**Fashion Museum**—Housed underneath Bath's Assembly Rooms, this museum displays four centuries of fashion, organized by theme (bags, shoes, underwear, wedding dresses, and so on). Follow the included audioguide tour, and allow about an hour— unless you pause to lace up a corset and try on a hoop underdress (£7, £14.50 combo-ticket covers Roman Baths—saving you £3.50, family ticket available, daily March–Oct 10:30–18:00, Nov–Feb 10:30–17:00, last entry one hour before closing, on-site self-service café, tel. 01225/477-173, www.fashionmuseum.co.uk).

The **Assembly Rooms,** which you can see for free en route to the museum, are big, grand, empty rooms. Card games, concerts, tea, and dances were held here in the 18th century, before the advent of fancy hotels with grand public spaces made them obsolete. Note the extreme symmetry (pleasing to the aristocratic eye) and the high windows (assuring privacy). After the Allies bombed the historic and well-preserved German city of Lübeck, the Germans picked up a Baedeker guide and chose a similarly lovely city to bomb: Bath. The Assembly Rooms—gutted in this wartime tit-for-tat by WWII bombs—have since been restored to their original splendor. (Only the chandeliers are original.)

Below the Fashion Museum (to the left as you leave, 20 yards away) is one of the few surviving sets of **iron house hardware.** "Link boys" carried torches through the dark streets, lighting the way for big shots in their sedan chairs as they traveled from one affair to the next. The link boys extinguished their torches in the black conical "snuffers." The lamp above was once gas-lit. The crank on the left was used to hoist bulky things to various windows (see the hooks). Few of these sets survived the dark days of the WWII Blitz, when most were collected and melted down, purportedly to make weapons to feed the British war machine. (Not long ago, these well-meaning Brits finally found out that all of their patriotic extra commitment to the national struggle had been for naught, since the metal ended up in junk heaps.)

▲▲**Museum of Bath at Work**—This is the official title for Mr. Bowler's Business, a 1900s engineer's shop, brass foundry, and fizzy-drink factory with a Dickensian office. It's just a pile of meaningless old gadgets—until the included audioguide resurrects Mr. Bowler's creative genius. Featuring other Bath creations through the years, including a 1914 car and the versatile plasticine (proto-Play-Doh), the museum serves as a vivid reminder that there was an industrial side to this spa town. Don't miss the fine "Story of Bath Stone" in the basement (£5, April–Oct daily 10:30–17:00, Nov–March weekends only except closed in Dec, last entry at 16:00, Julian Road, 2 steep blocks up Russell Street from Assembly Rooms, tel. 01225/318-348, www.bath-at-work.org.uk).

Jane Austen Centre—This exhibition focuses on Jane Austen's tumultuous, sometimes troubled five years in Bath (circa 1800, during which time her father died), and the influence the city had on her writing. There's little of historic substance here; you'll walk through a Georgian townhouse that she didn't live in (one of her real addresses in Bath was a few houses up the road, at 25 Gay Street), and see mostly enlarged reproductions of artifacts associated with her writing. The museum describes various places from two novels set in Bath (*Persuasion* and *Northanger Abbey*). After a live intro (15 min, 2/hr) explaining how this romantic but down-to-earth woman dealt with the silly, shallow, and arrogant aristocrats' world, where "the doing of nothings all day prevents one from doing anything," you see a 15-minute video and wander through the rest of the exhibit (£7; mid-March–mid-Nov daily 9:45–17:30, July–Aug Thu–Sat until 19:00; mid-Nov–mid-March Sun–Fri 11:00–16:30, Sat 9:45–17:30; between Queen's Square and the Circus at 40 Gay Street, tel. 01225/443-000, www.janeausten.co.uk). Jane Austen–themed walking tours of the city begin at the TI and end at the Centre (£5, 90 min, Sat–Sun at 11:00, July–Aug also Fri–Sat at 16:00, no reservation necessary).

Outer Bath
Building of Bath Collection—This offers an intriguing behind-the-scenes look at how the Georgian city was actually built (£4, mid-April–Oct Sat–Mon 10:30–17:00, last entry 30 min before

closing, closed Tue–Fri and Nov–mid-April, north of the city center on a street called "The Paragon," tel. 01225/333-895, www .bath-preservation-trust.org.uk).

▲**American Museum**—I know, you need this in Bath like you need a Big Mac. The UK's only museum dedicated to American history, this may be the only place that combines Geronimo and Groucho Marx. It has thoughtful exhibits on the history of Native Americans and the Civil War, but the museum's heart is with the decorative arts and cultural artifacts that reveal how Americans lived from colonial times to the mid-19th century. Each of the 18 completely furnished rooms (from a plain 1600s Massachusetts dining/living room to a Rococo Revival explosion in a New Orleans bedroom) is hosted by eager guides, waiting to fill you in on the everyday items that make domestic Yankee history surprisingly interesting. (In the Lee Room, look for the original mouse holes, lovingly backlit, in the floor boards.) One room is a quilter's nirvana. You can easily spend an afternoon here, enjoying the surrounding gardens, arboretum, and trails (£8, mid-March–Oct Tue–Sun 12:00–17:00, last entry one hour before closing, closed Mon and Nov–mid-March, at Claverton Manor, tel. 01225/460-503, www.americanmuseum.org). The museum is outside of town and a headache to reach if you don't have a car (10–15-min walk from bus #18 or the hop-on, hop-off bus stop).

Activities in Bath

Walking—The Bath Skyline Walk is a six-mile wander around the hills surrounding Bath (leaflet at TI). Plenty of other scenic paths are described in the TI's literature. For additional options, get *Country Walks around Bath*, by Tim Mowl (£4.50 at TI or bookstores).

Hiking the Canal to Bathampton—An idyllic towpath leads from the Bath Spa train station, along an old canal to the sleepy village of Bathampton. Immediately behind the station, cross the footbridge and find where the canal hits the river. Turn left, noticing the series of Industrial-Age locks, and walk along the towpath, giving thanks that you're not a horse pulling a barge. You'll be in Bathampton in less than an hour, where a classic pub awaits with a nice lunch and cellar-temp beer.

Boating—The Bath Boating Station, in an old Victorian boathouse, rents rowboats, canoes, and punts (£7 per person/first hour, then £3/additional hour, Easter–Sept daily 10:00–18:00, closed off-season, Forester Road, one mile northeast of center, tel. 01225/312-900, www.bathboating.co.uk).

Swimming and Kids' Activities—The Bath Sports and Leisure Centre has a fine pool for laps as well as lots of water slides. Kids have entertaining options in the mini-gym "Active Zone" area, which includes a rock wall and a "Zany Zone" indoor playground (£3.70, Mon–Fri 8:00–22:00, closes earlier Sat–Sun, kids' hours limited, call for open swim times, just across North Parade Bridge, tel. 01225/486-905, www.aquaterra.org).

Shopping—There's great browsing between the abbey and the Assembly Rooms (Fashion Museum). Shops close around 17:30, and many are open on Sunday (11:00–16:00). Explore the antique shops lining Bartlett Street, just below the Assembly Rooms.

Nightlife in Bath

For an up-to-date list of events, pick up the local newspaper, the *Bath Chronicle*, on Fridays, when the "What's On" schedule appears (www.thisisbath.com). Younger travelers may enjoy the party-ready bar, club, and nightlife recommendations at www .itchybath.co.uk.

▲▲▲**Bizarre Bath Street Theater**—For an immensely entertaining walking tour comedy act "with absolutely no history or culture," follow Dom, J. J., or Noel Britten on their creative and entertaining Bizarre Bath walk. This 90-minute "tour," which plays off local passersby as well as tour members, is a belly laugh a minute (£8, or £7 for Rick Steves readers, includes some minor discounts in town, April–Oct nightly at 20:00, smaller groups Mon–Thu, heavy on magic, careful to insult all minorities and sensitivities, just racy enough but still good family fun, leaves from The Huntsman pub near the abbey, confirm at TI or call 01225/335-124, www.bizarrebath.co.uk).

▲**Theatre Royal Performance**—The 18th-century, 800-seat Theatre Royal, newly restored and one of England's loveliest, offers a busy schedule of London West End–type plays, including many "pre-London" dress-rehearsal runs (£15–39, shows generally start at 19:30 or 20:00, matinees at 14:30, box office open Mon–Sat 10:00–20:00, Sun 12:00–20:00, tel. 01225/448-844, www.theatreroyal.org.uk). Forty nosebleed spots on a bench (misnamed "standbys") go on sale at noon Monday through Saturday for that day's evening performance (£5, pay cash at box office or—for £3 more—call and book with credit card, 2 tickets maximum). Same-day "standing places" go on sale at 18:00 (12:00 for matinees) for £3 (pay cash at box office, 2 tickets maximum). Or you can snatch up any last-minute seats for £10–15 a half-hour before "curtain up."

A handy cheap sightseers' tip: During the free Bath walking tour, your guide stops here. Pop into the box office, ask what's playing tonight, and see if there are many seats left. If the play sounds good and plenty of seats remain unsold, you're fairly safe to come back 30 minutes before curtain time to buy a ticket at that cheaper price. Oh...and if you smell jasmine, it's the ghost of Lady Grey, a mistress of Beau Nash.

Evening Walks—Take your choice: comedy (Bizarre Bath, described above), history, or ghost tour. The free city history walks (a daily standard described on page 198) are offered on some summer evenings (2 hours, May–Sept Tue and Fri at 19:00, leave from Pump Room). **Ghost Walks** are a popular way to pass the after-dark hours (£7, cash only, 90 min, year-round Thu–Sat at 20:00, leave from The Garrick's Head pub to the left and behind Theatre Royal as you face it, tel. 01225/350-512, www .ghostwalksofbath.co.uk). The cities of York and Edinburgh—which have houses thought to be actually haunted—are better for these walks.

Pubs—Most pubs in the center are very noisy, catering to a rowdy twentysomething crowd. But on the top end of town you can still find some classic old places with inviting ambience and live music. These are listed in order from closest to farthest away (from the center of town):

The Old Green Tree, the most convenient of all these pubs, is a rare traditional pub right in the town center (locally brewed real ales, no children, 12 Green Street, tel. 01225/448-259; also recommended under "Eating in Bath" for lunch).

The Star Inn is much appreciated by local beer-lovers for its fine ale and "no machines or music to distract from the chat." It's a "spit 'n' sawdust" place, and its long bench, nicknamed "death row," still comes with a complimentary pinch of snuff from tins on the ledge. Try the Bellringer Ale, made just up the road (Mon–Fri 12:00–14:30 & 17:30–23:00, Sat–Sun 12:00–23:00, no food served, 23 The Vineyards, top of The Paragon/A4 Roman Road, tel. 01225/425-072, generous and friendly welcome from Paul, who runs the place).

The Bell has a jazzy, pierced-and-tattooed, bohemian feel, but with a mellow, older crowd. They serve pizza on the large concrete terrace out back in summer, and there's some kind of activity nearly every night, usually involving live music (Mon–Sat 11:00–23:00, Sun 12:00–10:30, sandwiches served all day, 103 Walcot Street, tel. 01225/460-426).

Summer Nights at the Baths—In July and August, you can stretch your sightseeing day at the Roman Baths, open nightly until 22:00 (last entry 21:00), when the gas lamps flame and the baths are far less crowded and more atmospheric. To take a dip yourself, consider popping in to the Thermae Bath Spa (last entry at 19:30).

BATH

Sleeping in Bath

Bath is a busy tourist town. Accommodations are expensive, and low-cost alternatives are rare. By far the best budget option is the YMCA—it's central, safe, simple, very well-run, and has plenty of twin rooms available. To get a good B&B, make a telephone reservation in advance. Competition is stiff, and it's worth asking any of these places for a weekday, three-nights-in-a-row, or off-season deal. Friday and Saturday nights are tightest (with many rates going up by about 25 percent)—especially if you're staying only one night, since B&Bs favor those lingering longer. If staying only Saturday night, you're very bad news to a B&B hostess. If you're driving to Bath, stowing your car near the center will cost you (though some less-central B&Bs have parking)—see "Parking" on page 198, or ask your hotelier. Almost every place provides Wi-Fi at no charge to its guests.

B&Bs near the Royal Crescent

These listings are all a 15-minute uphill walk or an easy £4–5 taxi ride from the train station. Or take any hop-on, hop-off bus tour from the station, get off at the stop nearest your B&B (likely Royal Avenue—confirm with driver), check in, then finish the tour later in the day. The Marlborough Lane places have easier parking but are less centrally located.

$$$ The Town House, overlooking the Assembly Rooms, is genteel, deluxe, and homey, with three fresh, mod rooms that have a hardwood stylishness. In true B&B style, you'll enjoy a gourmet breakfast at a big family table with the other guests (Db-£95–100 or £115–130 Fri–Sat, 2-night minimum, Wi-Fi, 7 Bennett Street, tel. & fax 01225/422-505, www.thetownhousebath.co.uk, stay @thetownhousebath.co.uk, Alan and Brenda Willey).

$$ Brocks Guest House has six rooms in a Georgian townhouse built by John Wood the Younger in 1765. Located between the prestigious Royal Crescent and the courtly Circus, it was redone in a way that would make the great architect proud (Db-£79–87, Tb-£99, Qb-£115, prices go up about 10 percent Fri–Sat, Wi-Fi, little top-floor library, 32 Brock Street, tel. 01225/338-374, fax 01225/334-245, www.brocksguesthouse.co.uk, brocks@brocksguesthouse .co.uk, run by Sammy and her husband Richard).

$$ Parkside Guest House has five thoughtfully appointed Edwardian rooms—tidy, clean, and homey, with nary a doily in sight—and a spacious back garden (Db-£77, this price is for Rick Steves readers, 11 Marlborough Lane, tel. & fax 01225/429-444, www.parksidebandb.co.uk, post@parksidebandb.co.uk, Erica and Inge Lynall).

Sleep Code

(£1 = about $1.60, country code: 44, area code: 01225)
S = Single, **D** = Double/Twin, **T** = Triple, **Q** = Quad, **b** = bathroom,
s = shower only. Unless otherwise noted, credit cards are accepted.

   To help you sort easily through these listings, I've divided the rooms into three categories based on the price for a standard double room with bath:

  $$$ Higher Priced—Most rooms £100 or more.
   $$ Moderately Priced—Most rooms between £60-100.
    $ Lower Priced—Most rooms £60 or less.

$$ Elgin Villa rents five comfy, nicely maintained rooms (Ss-£40, Sb-£55, Ds-£68, Db-£85, Tb-£99, Qb-£120, more expensive for Sat-only stay, discount for 3 nights, includes substantial un-fried breakfast, Wi-Fi, parking, 6 Marlborough Lane, tel. 01225/424-557, www.elginvilla.co.uk, stay@elginvilla.co.uk, Anna).

$$ Cornerways B&B, located on a noisy street, is simple and well-worn, with four rooms and old-fashioned homey touches (Sb-£45-55, Db-£65-75, 15 percent discount with this book and 3-night stay in 2010, Wi-Fi, DVD library, free parking, 47 Crescent Gardens, tel. 01225/422-382, www.cornerwaysbath.co.uk, info@cornerwaysbath.co.uk, Sue Black).

B&Bs East of the River

These listings are a 10-minute walk from the city center. Although generally a better value, they are less conveniently located.

$$$ Villa Magdala rents 18 stately, hotelesque rooms in a freestanding Victorian townhouse opposite a park. In a city that's so insistently Georgian, it's fun to stay in a mansion that's decorated so enthusiastically Victorian (Db-£95-130, less off-season, fancier rooms and family options described on website, inviting lounge, Wi-Fi, free parking, in quiet residential area on Henrietta Street, tel. 01225/466-329, fax 01225/483-207, www.villamagdala.co.uk, enquiries@villamagdala.co.uk; Roy and Lois).

$$$ The Ayrlington, next door to a lawn-bowling green, has 14 attractive rooms with Asian decor and hints of a more genteel time. Though this well-maintained hotel fronts a busy street, it's quiet and tranquil. Rooms in the back have pleasant views of sports greens and Bath beyond. For the best value, request a standard double with a view of Bath (twin Db-£80-105, standard Db-£100-130, fancy Db-£120-170, big deluxe Db-£130-195, prices spike 30 percent on weekends, see website for specifics, Wi-Fi, fine garden, easy parking, 24–25 Pulteney Road, tel. 01225/425-495, fax 01225/469-029, www.ayrlington.com, mail@ayrlington.com). If you stay here three weeknights, you get a free pass to the Thermae Bath Spa (worth £22/person).

$$ Holly Villa Guest House, with a cheery garden, six bright rooms, and a cozy TV lounge, is enthusiastically and thoughtfully run by chatty, friendly Jill and Keith McGarrigle (Ds-£60–65, Db-£65–75, Tb-£80–95, cash only, Wi-Fi, free parking; 8-min walk from station and city center—walk over North Parade Bridge, take the first right, and then take the second left to 14 Pulteney Gardens; tel. 01225/310-331, www.hollyvilla.com, jill @hollyvilla.com).

$$ 14 Raby Place is another good value, mixing Georgian glamour with homey warmth and modern, artistic taste within its

five rooms. Luddite Muriel Guy keeps things simple and endearingly friendly. She's a fun-loving live wire who serves organic food for breakfast (S-£35, Db-£70, Tb-£80, cash only; 14 Raby Place—go over bridge on North Parade Road, left on Pulteney Road, cross to church, Raby Place is first row of houses on hill; tel. 01225/465-120).

In the Town Center

$$$ Three Abbey Green Guest House, with seven rooms, is newly renovated, bright, fresh, and located in a quiet, traffic-free courtyard only 50 yards from the abbey and the Roman Baths. Its spacious rooms are a fine value (Db-£85–135, four-poster Db-£145–175, family rooms-£135–195, 2-night minimum on weekends, Internet access and Wi-Fi, tel. 01225/428-558, www.three abbeygreen.com, stay@threeabbeygreen.com, Sue and Derek). They also rent self-catering apartments (Db-£135–155, Qb-£160–195, higher prices are for Fri–Sat, 2-night minimum).

$$$ Harington's Hotel rents 13 fresh, modern, and newly refurbished rooms on a quiet street in the town center. This stylish place feels like a boutique hotel, but with a friendlier, more laid-back vibe (Sb-£79–130, standard Db-£88–130, superior Db-£98–140, large superior Db-£108–150, Tb-£138–180, prices vary substantially depending on demand, Wi-Fi, attached restaurant-bar open all day, 10 Queen Street, tel. 01225/461-728, fax

Bath Accommodations

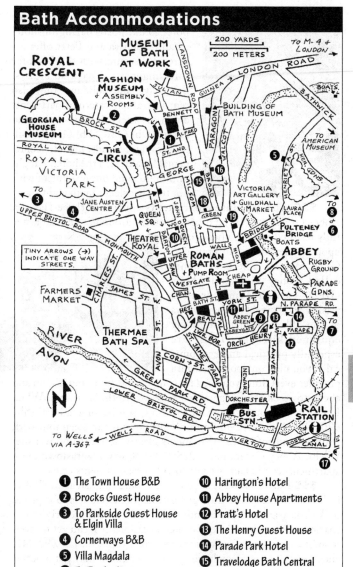

200 YARDS
200 METERS

TO M-4 & LONDON →

ROYAL CRESCENT

MUSEUM OF BATH AT WORK

FASHION MUSEUM & ASSEMBLY ROOMS

GEORGIAN HOUSE MUSEUM

THE CIRCUS

LONDON ROAD

BUILDING OF BATH MUSEUM

BOATS

ROYAL AVE.

ROYAL VICTORIA PARK

TO AMERICAN MUSEUM

JANE AUSTEN CENTRE

UPPER BRISTOL ROAD

VICTORIA ART GALLERY & GUILDHALL MARKET

LAURA PLACE

QUEEN SQ.

THEATRE ROYAL

PULTENEY BRIDGE
BOATS
ABBEY

TINY ARROWS (→) INDICATE ONE WAY STREETS.

ROMAN BATHS & PUMP ROOM

RUGBY GROUND

PARADE GDNS.

FARMERS' MARKET

JAMES ST. W.

WESTGATE

CHEAP

N. PARADE RD.

TO

RIVER AVON

THERMAE BATH SPA

S. PARADE

ABBEY GREEN
ABBEYGATE

YORK ST.
BEAU

LWR. BOR.

ORCH.

HENRY

DORCHESTER

LOWER BRISTOL RD.

BUS STN.

RAIL STATION

TO WELLS VIA A-367

WELLS ROAD

CLAVERTON ST.

CANAL

1 The Town House B&B
2 Brocks Guest House
3 To Parkside Guest House & Elgin Villa
4 Cornerways B&B
5 Villa Magdala
6 To The Ayrlington
7 To Holly Villa Guest House
8 To 14 Raby Place
9 Three Abbey Green Guest House
10 Harington's Hotel
11 Abbey House Apartments
12 Pratt's Hotel
13 The Henry Guest House
14 Parade Park Hotel
15 Travelodge Bath Central
16 YMCA
17 White Hart Hostel
18 St. Christopher's Inn
19 Library (Internet Access)

BATH

01225/444-804, www.haringtons hotel.co.uk, post@haringtonshotel .co.uk). Melissa and Peter offer a 5 percent discount with this book for three-night stays except on Fridays, Saturdays, and holidays. They also rent several self-catering apartments down the street that can sleep up to three (Db-£130, Tb-£150, much pricier on weekends, includes continental breakfast in the hotel, 2-night minimum), and one apartment with hot tub that sleeps up to eight.

$$$ Abbey House Apartments consist of three flats on Abbey Green and several others scattered around town—all taste-

fully restored by Laura (who, once upon a time, was a San Francisco Goth rocker). The apartments called Abbey View and Abbey Green (which comes with a washer and dryer) both have views of the abbey from their nicely equipped kitchens. These are especially practical and economical if you plan on cooking. Laura

provides everything you need for simple breakfasts, and it's fun and cheap to stock the fridge or get take-away ethnic cuisine. When Laura meets you to give you the keys, you become a local (Sb-£90, Db-£100–175, 2-night minimum, rooms can sleep four with Murphy and sofa beds, apartments clearly described on website, Wi-Fi, Abbey Green, tel. 01225/464-238, www.laurastownhouse apartments.co.uk, laura@laurastownhouseapartments.co.uk).

$$$ Pratt's Hotel is as proper and olde English as you'll find in Bath. Its creaks and frays are aristocratic. Even its public places make you want to sip a brandy, and its 46 rooms are bright and spacious. Since it's in the city center, occasionally it can get noisy—request a quiet room, away from the street (Sb-£90, Db-£90–140, check website for specials, drop-ins after 16:00 may get a better rate if room available, dogs-£7.50 but children under 15 free with 2 adults, attached restaurant-bar, elevator, 4 blocks from station on South Parade, tel. 01225/460-441, fax 01225/448-807, www .forestdale.com, pratts@forestdale.com).

$$ The Henry Guest House is a simple, vertical place, renting eight clean rooms. It's friendly, well-run, and just two blocks in front of the train station (S-£40–45, Sb-£55–65, Db-£85–105, extra bed-£15, family room-£135, 2-night minimum on weekends,

Wi-Fi, 6 Henry Street, tel. 01225/424-052, www.thehenry.com, stay@thehenry.com). Steve and Liz also rent two self-catering apartments nearby that sleep up to eight with cots and a sleeper couch—email for group prices.

$$ Parade Park Hotel rents 35 modern, basic rooms in a very central location (S-£49, Sb-£69, D-£69, small Db-£85, large Db-£95–105, Tb-£115, Qb-£110–160, no Wi-Fi, lots of stairs, lively bar downstairs and noisy seagulls, 8–10 North Parade, tel. 01225/463-384, www.paradepark.co.uk, info@paradepark.co.uk).

$$ Travelodge Bath Central, which offers 66 American-style, characterless-yet-comfortable rooms, worries B&Bs with its reasonable prices. As it's located over a nightclub, request a room on the third floor—especially on weekends (Db/Tb/Qb-£70 on weeknights, £85–95 Fri–Sat, prices vary widely—as low as £39 on weeknights if you book online in advance, up to 2 kids sleep free, breakfast extra, Wi-Fi, 1 York Building at George Street, toll tel. 08719-846-219, www.travelodge.co.uk). This is especially economical for families of four (who enjoy the Db price). Another Travelodge is located about a mile from the train station (similar prices, free parking, Rossiter Road, toll tel. 08719-846-407).

Bargain Accommodations

Bath's Best Budget Beds: **$** The **YMCA,** centrally located on a leafy square, has 200 beds in industrial-strength rooms—all with sinks and prison-style furnishings. The place is a godsend for budget travelers—safe, secure, quiet, and efficiently run. With lots of twin rooms and no double beds, this is the only easily accessible budget option in downtown Bath (S-£28, twin D-£44, T-£60, Q-£72, dorm beds-£16, £1/person more Fri–Sat, WCs and showers down the hall, includes continental breakfast, cooked breakfast-£2.20, cheap lunches, linens, lockers, Internet access and Wi-Fi, laundry facilities, down a tiny alley off Broad Street on Broad Street Place, tel. 01225/325-900, fax 01225/462-065, www.bathymca.co.uk, stay@bathymca.co.uk).

Sloppy Backpacker Dorms: **$–$$ White Hart Hostel** is a simple nine-room place offering adults and families good, cheap beds in two- to six-bed dorms (£15/bed, S-£25, D-£40, Db-£50–70, family rooms, kitchen, fine garden out back, 5-min walk behind train station at Widcombe—where Widcombe Hill hits Claverton Street, tel. 01225/313-985, www.whitehartbath.co.uk). The White Hart also has a pub with a reputation for decent food. **$ St. Christopher's Inn,** in a prime, central location, is part of a chain of low-priced, high-energy hubs for backpackers looking for beds and brews. Their beds are so cheap because they know you'll spend money on their beer (46 beds in 4- to 12-bed rooms-£15–21.50, D-£52–58, higher prices on weekends or if you don't book online, check website for specials, Internet access, laundry, lounge with video, lively "Belushi's" pub and bar downstairs, 9 Green Street, tel. 01225/481-444, www.st-christophers.co.uk).

Eating in Bath

Bath is bursting with eateries. There's something for every appetite and budget—just stroll around the center of town. A picnic dinner of deli food or take-out fish-and-chips in the Royal Crescent Park or down by the river is ideal for aristocratic hoboes. The restaurants I recommend are small and popular—reserve a table on Friday and Saturday evenings. Most pricey little bistros offer big savings with their two- and three-course lunches and "pre-theater" specials. In general, you can get two courses for £10 at lunch or £12 in the early evening (compared to £15 for a main course after 18:30 or 19:00). Restaurants advertise their early-bird specials, and as long as you order within the time window, you're in for a cheap meal.

Romantic French and English

Tilleys Bistro, popular with locals, serves healthy French, English, and vegetarian meals with candlelit ambience. Owners Dawn and Dave make you feel as if you are guests at a special dinner party in their elegant living room. Their fun menu lets you build your own meal, and there's an interesting array of £7 starters. If you cap things off with the cheese plate and a glass of the house port, you'll realize you're enjoying one of Dave's passions (Mon–Sat 12:00–14:30 & 18:30–22:30, Sun 18:30–22:30 only, reservations smart, 3 North Parade Passage, tel. 01225/484-200).

The Garrick's Head is an elegantly simple gastropub right around the corner from the Theatre Royal, with a pricey restaurant on one side and a bar serving affordable snacks on the other. You're welcome to eat from the bar menu, even if you're in the fancy dining room or outside enjoying some great people-watching (Mon–Sat 11:00–21:00, Sun 12:00–21:00, 8 St. John's Place, tel. 01225/318-368).

The Circus Café and Restaurant is a relaxing little eatery serving rustic European cuisine. They have a romantic interior, with a minimalist modern atmosphere, and four tables on the peaceful street (£7 lunches, £12 dinner plates, open Mon–Sat 12:00–24:00, closed Sun, reservations smart, 34 Brock Street, tel. 01225/466-020).

Casanis French Bistro-Restaurant is a local hit. Chef Laurent, who hails from Nice, cooks "authentic Provençal cuisine" from the south of France, while his wife Jill serves. The decor matches the cuisine—informal, relaxed, simple, and top-quality. The intimate Georgian dining room upstairs is a bit nicer and more

Bath Restaurants

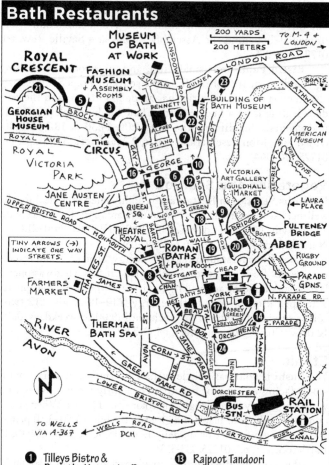

1. Tilleys Bistro & Demuths Vegetarian Rest.
2. The Garrick's Head
3. The Circus Café & Rest.
4. Casanis French Bistro-Rest.
5. Bistro Papillon
6. Loch Fyne Restaurant
7. Yen Sushi
8. Thai Balcony Restaurant
9. Ocean Pearl Oriental Buffet & Waitrose Supermarket
10. Wagamama
11. Martini Restaurant
12. Ask Restaurant
13. Rajpoot Tandoori
14. Yak Yeti Yak
15. Boston Tea Party & Seafoods Fish & Chips
16. Chandos Deli
17. Crystal Palace Pub
18. The Old Green Tree
19. The Cornish Bakehouse
20. Guildhall Market
21. Royal Crescent Hotel (Afternoon Tea)
22. The Star Inn
23. The Bell
24. Marks & Spencer & Café Revive

spacious than the ground floor (£11.50 two-course lunch specials, £20 three-course early dinner from 18:00–19:00, closed Sun–Mon, immediately behind the Assembly Rooms at 4 Saville Row, tel. 01225/780-055).

Bistro Papillon is small, fun, and unpretentious, dishing up "modern-rustic cuisine from the south of France." The cozy, checkered-tablecloth interior has an open kitchen, and the outdoor seating is on a fine pedestrian lane (£8 lunch plates, £13–15 main courses for dinner, Tue–Sat 12:00–14:30 & 18:30–22:00, closed Sun–Mon, reservations smart, 2 Margaret's Buildings, tel. 01225/310-064).

Vegetarian and Seafood

Demuths Vegetarian Restaurant is highly rated and ideal for the well-heeled vegetarian. Its stark, understated interior comes with a vegan vibe (£15 main dishes, daily 10:00–15:30 & 18:00–21:00, 2 North Parade Passage, tel. 01225/446-059).

Loch Fyne Restaurant, a high-energy, Scottish chain restaurant, serves fresh fish at reasonable prices. It fills what was once a lavish bank building with a bright, airy, and youthful atmosphere. The open kitchen adds to the energy (£10–18 meals, £12 two-course special plus wine from lunch until 19:00 on weekdays, daily 12:00–21:30, 24 Milsom Street, tel. 01225/750-120).

Ethnic

Yen Sushi is your basic little sushi bar—stark and sterile, with stools facing a conveyor belt that constantly tempts you with a variety of freshly made delights on color-coded plates. When you're done, they tally your plates and give you the bill (£1.50–3.50 plates, you can fill up for £12 or so, daily 12:00–15:00 & 17:30–22:30, 11 Bartlett Street, tel. 01225/333-313).

Thai Balcony Restaurant's open, spacious interior is so plush, it'll have you wondering, "Where's the Thai wedding?" While locals debate which of Bath's handful of Thai restaurants serves the best food or offers the lowest prices, there's no doubt that Thai Balcony's fun and elegant atmosphere makes for a memorable and enjoyable dinner (£8 two-course lunch special, £8–9 plates, daily 12:00–14:00 & 18:00–22:00, reservations smart on weekends, Saw Close, tel. 01225/444-450).

Ocean Pearl Oriental Buffet is famous for being the restaurant Asian tourists eat at repeatedly. It offers a practical, 40-dish, all-you-can-eat buffet in the modern Podium Shopping Centre and spacious seating in a high, bright dining hall overlooking the river. You'll pay £6.50 for lunch, £13 for dinner, or you can fill up a take-away box for just £4 (daily 12:00–15:00 & 18:00–22:30, in the Podium Shopping Centre on Northgate Street, tel. 01225/331-238).

Wagamama, a stylish, youthful, and modern chain of noodle shops, continues its quest for world domination. There's one in almost every mid-sized city in the UK, and after you've sampled their udon noodles, fried rice, or curry dishes, you'll know why. Diners enjoy huge portions in a sprawling, loud, and modern hall. Bowls are huge enough for light eaters on a tight budget to share (£7–9 meals, Mon–Sat 12:00–23:00, Sun 12:00–22:00, good vegetarian options, 1 York Buildings, George Street, tel. 01225/337-314).

Martini Restaurant, a hopping, purely Italian place, has class and jovial waiters. It offers a very good eating value (£12–16 entrées, £7–9 pizzas, daily 12:00–14:30 & 18:00–22:30, plenty of veggie options, daily fish specials, extensive wine list, reservations smart on weekends, 9 George Street, tel. 01225/460-818; Mauro, Nunzio, Franco, and chef Luigi).

Ask Restaurant is part of a chain of Italian eateries, serving standard-quality pizza and pasta in a big, 200-seat place with a loud and happy local crowd (£7 pizza and pasta, good salads, daily 12:00–23:00, George Street but entrance on Broad Street, tel. 01225/789-997).

Rajpoot Tandoori serves—by all assessments—the best Indian food in Bath. You'll hike down deep into a cellar, where the plush Indian atmosphere and award-winning cooking make paying the extra pounds palatable. The seating is tight and the ceilings low, but it's air-conditioned (£8 three-course lunch special, £10 plates, £20 dinners, daily 12:00–14:30 & 18:00–23:00, 4 Argyle Street, tel. 01225/466-833, Ali).

Yak Yeti Yak is a fun Nepalese restaurant, with both Western and sit-on-the-floor seating. Sera and his wife, Sarah, along with their cheerful, hardworking Nepali team, cook up great traditional food (and plenty of vegetarian plates) at prices a sherpa could handle (£6–7 lunches, £4 veggie plates, £7 meat plates, daily 12:00–14:30 & 17:00–22:30, 5 Pierrepont Street, tel. 01225/442-299).

Simple Options

Light Meals: **Boston Tea Party** feels like a Starbucks—if there were only one. It's fresh and healthy, serving extensive breakfasts, light lunches, and salads. The outdoor seating overlooks a busy square (daily 7:30–19:00, 19 Kingsmead Square, tel. 01225/313-901). **Chandos Deli** has good coffee and tasty £6–7 sandwiches made on artisan breads. This upscale but casual eight-table place serves breakfast and lunch to dedicated foodies who don't want to pay too much (Mon–Sat 9:00–17:00, Sun 11:00–17:00, 12 George Street, tel. 01225/314-418).

Pubs: **Crystal Palace Pub** is an inviting place just a block away from the abbey, facing the delightful little Abbey Green.

With a focus on food rather than drink, they serve "pub grub with a Continental flair" in three different spaces, including a picnic-table back patio (£8–10 meals, daily 12:00–20:30, last order by 20:00, no kids after 16:30, Abbey Green, tel. 01225/482-666). **The Old Green Tree,** in the old town center, serves satisfying lunches to locals in a characteristic pub setting. As Bath is not a good pub-grub town, this is likely the best you'll do in the center (real ales on tap, lunch Mon–Sat 12:00–15:00 only, no children, can be crowded on weekend nights, 12 Green Street, tel. 01225/448-259).

Fast Food: **Seafoods Fish & Chips** is respected by lovers of greasy fried fish in Bath. There's diner-style and outdoor seating, or you can get your food to go (£4–5 meals, Mon–Sat 11:30–23:00, takeout until 22:00, Sun 12:00–20:00, 38 Kingsmead Square, tel. 01225/465-190). **The Cornish Bakehouse,** near the Guildhall Market, has freshly baked £2 take-away pasties (open until 17:30, off High Street at 11A The Corridor, tel. 01225/426-635). Munch your picnic enjoying buskers from a bench on the Abbey Square.

Produce Market and Café: **Guildhall Market,** across from Pulteney Bridge, has produce stalls with food for picnickers. At its inexpensive **Market Café,** you can slurp a curry or sip a tea while surrounded by stacks of used books, bananas on the push list, and honest-to-goodness old-time locals (£4 meals including fried breakfasts all day, Mon–Sat 8:00–17:00, closed Sun, tel. 01225/461-593 a block north of the abbey, on High Street).

Supermarkets: **Waitrose,** at the Podium Shopping Centre, is great for picnics, with a good salad bar (Mon–Fri 8:30–20:00, Sat 8:30–19:00, Sun 11:00–17:00, just west of Pulteney Bridge and across from post office on High Street). **Marks & Spencer,** near the train station, has a grocery at the back of its department store and the pleasant, inexpensive **Café Revive** on the top floor (Mon–Wed and Sat 8:30–18:00, Thu–Fri 8:30–19:00, Sun 11:00–17:00, 16–18 Stall Street).

Bath Connections

Bath's train station is called Bath Spa (toll tel. 0845-748-4950). The National Express bus station is just west of the train station (bus info toll tel. 0871-781-8181, www.nationalexpress.com). For all public bus services in southwestern England, see www.travelinesw.com.

From London to Bath: To get from London to Bath and see Stonehenge to boot, consider an all-day organized **bus tour** from London (and skip the return trip; see page 165).

From Bath to London: You can catch a **train** to London's Paddington Station (2/hr, 1.5 hrs, £48 one-way after 9:30, cheaper in advance, www.firstgreatwestern.co.uk) or save money—but not time—by taking the National Express **bus** to Victoria Station (direct buses nearly hourly, a little over 3 hours, one-way-£18, round-trip-£27.50).

From Heathrow to Bath: See page 161. Also consider taking a minibus with Alan Price (see "Celtic Horizons" on page 200).

From Bath to London's Airports: You can reach **Heathrow** directly and easily by National Express bus (10/day, 2–3 hrs, £19 one-way, toll tel. 0871-781-8181, calls 10p/min, www.national express.com) or by a train-and-bus combination (take twice-hourly train to Reading, catch twice-hourly airport shuttle bus from there, allow 2.5 hours total, £50–65 depending on time of day, about £10 cheaper when bought in advance, BritRail passholders just pay £15 for bus). Or take the Celtic Horizons minibus to Heathrow.

You can get to **Gatwick** by train (about hourly, 2.5 hrs, £45–60 one-way depending on time of day, £23 in advance, transfer in Reading) or by bus (10/day, 4–5 hrs, £25 one-way, transfer at Heathrow Airport).

Between Bristol Airport and Bath: Located about 20 miles west of Bath, this airport is closer than Heathrow, but they haven't worked out good connections to Bath yet. From Bristol Airport, your most convenient options are to take a taxi (£35) or call Alan Price (see "Celtic Horizons" on page 200). Otherwise, at the airport you can hop aboard the Bristol International Flyer (city bus #330 or #331), which takes you to the Temple Meads train station in Bristol (£9, 2–4/hr, 30 min, buy bus ticket at airport info counter or from driver, tell driver you want the Temple Meads train station). At the Temple Meads Station, check the departure boards for trains going to the Bath Spa train station (4/hr, 15 min, £6). To get from Bath to Bristol Airport, just reverse these directions: Take the train to Temple Meads, then catch the International Flyer bus.

From Bath by Train to: Salisbury (1–2/hr, 1 hr), **Portsmouth** (hourly, 2.25 hrs), **Exeter** (1–2/hr, 1.5–2 hrs, transfer in Bristol or Westbury), **Penzance** (1–2/hr, 4.5–5 hrs, one direct, most 1–2 transfers), **Moreton-in-Marsh** (hourly, 2.5–3 hrs, 2–3 transfers), **York** (2/hr, 4–4.5 hrs, 1–2 transfers in Birmingham, Bristol, and/or London), **Oxford** (hourly, 1–1.5 hrs, transfer in Didcot), **Cardiff** (hourly, 1–1.5 hrs), **Birmingham** (2/hr, 2 hrs, transfer in Bristol), and **points north** (from Birmingham, a major transportation hub, trains depart for Blackpool, Scotland, and North Wales; use a train/bus combination to reach Ironbridge Gorge and the Lake District).

From Bath by Bus to: Salisbury (hourly, 2.75 hrs, transfer in Warminster; or 1/day direct at 10:35, 1.5 hrs on National Express #300), **Portsmouth** (1/day direct, 3 hrs), **Exeter** (4/day, 3.5–4 hrs, transfer in Bristol), **Penzance** (2/day, 7–8 hrs, transfer in Bristol),

Cheltenham or **Gloucester** (4/day, 2.5 hrs, transfer in Bristol), **Stratford-upon-Avon** (1/day, 4 hrs, transfer in Bristol), and **Oxford** (1/day direct, 2 hrs, more with transfer). Buses to **Wells** depart nearly hourly, but the last direct bus back leaves before the evensong service is finished (1.25 hrs, last return 17:43, or take 18:15 bus to Bristol, then train to Bath—see page 239). For bus connections to **Avebury** and **Glastonbury,** see the next chapter.

NEAR BATH

Glastonbury • Wells • Avebury • Stonehenge •
Salisbury • South Wales

Ooooh, mystery, history. Glastonbury is the ancient home of Avalon, King Arthur, and the Holy Grail. Nearby, medieval Wells gathers around its grand cathedral, where you can enjoy an evensong service. Then get Neolithic at every Druid's favorite stone circles, Avebury and Stonehenge. Salisbury is known for its colorful markets and soaring cathedral.

An hour west of Bath, at St. Fagans National History Museum, you'll find South Wales' story vividly told in a park full of restored houses. Relish the romantic ruins and poetic wax of Tintern Abbey, the lush Wye River Valley, and the quirky Forest of Dean.

Planning Your Time

In England: Avebury, Glastonbury, and Wells make a wonderful day out from Bath. Splicing in Stonehenge is possible but stretching it. Everybody needs to see Stonehenge, but I'll tell you now, it looks just like you think it will look. You'll know what I mean when you pay to get in and rub up against the rope fence that keeps tourists at a distance. Avebury is the connoisseur's circle: more subtle and welcoming.

Wells is simply a cute town, much smaller and more medieval than Bath, with a uniquely beautiful cathedral that's best experienced at the 17:15 evensong service (Sunday at 15:15). Glastonbury is normally done surgically, in two hours: See the abbey, climb the tor, ponder your hippie past (and where you are now), then scram. Just an hour from Bath, Salisbury makes a pleasant stop, particularly on a market day (Tue, Sat, and every other Wed), though its cathedral looks striking anytime.

Sights near Bath

In Wales: Think of the South Wales sights as a different grouping. Ideally, they fill the day you leave Bath for the Cotswolds. Anyone interested in Welsh culture can spend four hours in St. Fagans National History Museum. Castle-lovers and romantics will want to consider seeing Tintern Abbey, the Forest of Dean, and the castles of Cardiff, Caerphilly, and Chepstow.

For a great day in South Wales, consider this schedule: 9:00–Leave Bath for South Wales; 10:30–Tour St. Fagans; 15:00–Stop at Tintern Abbey and/or a castle of your choice, then drive to the Cotswolds; 18:00–Set up in your Cotswolds home base.

Getting Around the Region

By Car: Drivers can do a 133-mile loop, from Bath to Avebury (25 miles) to Stonehenge (30 miles) to Glastonbury (50 miles) to Wells

(6 miles) and back to Bath (22 miles). A loop from Bath to South Wales is 100 miles, mostly on the 70-mph motorway. Each Welsh sight is just off the motorway.

By Bus and Train: Wells and Glastonbury are both easily accessible by bus from Bath. Bus #173 goes direct from Bath to **Wells** (hourly, 1.25 hrs), where you can catch bus #375, #376, or #377 to continue on to **Glastonbury** (4/hr, 20 min). Wells and Glastonbury are also connected to each other by a 9.5-mile foot and bike path.

Many different buses run between Bath and **Avebury,** all requiring one or two transfers (hourly, 1.5 hrs). There is no bus between Avebury and Stonehenge.

A one-hour train trip connects Bath to **Salisbury** (2/hr). With the best public transportation of all these towns, Salisbury is a good jumping-off point for Stonehenge or Avebury by bus or car. The Stonehenge Tour runs buses between Salisbury, Old Sarum, and Stonehenge (see page 249). Buses also run regularly from Salisbury to Avebury (1–2/hr, 1.5–2.5 hrs; Wilts & Dorset bus #2 leaves from St. Paul's Church on Fisherton Street, near the train station, then transfer in Devizes to Stagecoach's bus #49 to Avebury; other combinations possible, some with 2 transfers).

Various bus companies run these routes, including Stagecoach, Bodmans Coaches, the First Bus Company, and Wilts & Dorset. To find fare information, check with Traveline South West, which combines all the information from these companies into an easy-to-use website that covers all the southwest routes (tel. 0871-200-2233, www.travelinesw.com). Buses run much less frequently on Sundays.

To get to **South Wales** from Bath, take a train to Cardiff (transfer in Bristol), then connect by bus (or train) to the sights.

By Tour: From Bath, the most convenient and quickest way to see Avebury and Stonehenge if you don't have a car is to take an all-day bus tour, or a half-day tour just to Stonehenge. Of those tours leaving from Bath, Mad Max is the liveliest (see page 199).

Glastonbury

Marked by its hill, or "tor," and located on England's most powerful line of prehistoric sites (called a "ley line"), the town of Glastonbury gurgles with history and mystery.

In A.D. 37, Joseph of Arimathea—Jesus' wealthy uncle—brought vessels containing the blood of Jesus to Glastonbury, and, with them, Christianity came to England. (Joseph's visit is plausible—long before Christ, locals traded lead to merchants from the Levant.) Although this story is "proven" by fourth-century writings and accepted by the Church, the King-Arthur-and-the-Holy-Grail legends it inspired are not.

Those medieval tales came when England needed a morale-boosting folk hero for inspiration during a war with France. They pointed to the ancient Celtic sanctuary at Glastonbury as proof enough of the greatness of the fifth-century warlord Arthur. In 1191, his supposed remains (along with those of Queen Guinevere) were dug up from the abbey garden, and Glastonbury became woven into the Arthurian legends. Reburied in the abbey choir, their gravesite is a shrine today. Many think the Grail trail ends at the bottom of the Chalice Well, a natural spring at the base of the Glastonbury Tor.

The Glastonbury Abbey was England's most powerful abbey by the 10th century, and was part of a nationwide network of monasteries that by 1500 owned one-sixth of all English land and had four times the income of the Crown. Then Henry VIII dissolved the abbeys in 1536. He was particularly harsh on Glastonbury—he not only destroyed the abbey but also hung and quartered the abbot, sending the parts of his body on four different national tours...at the same time.

But Glastonbury rebounded. In an 18th-century tourism campaign, thousands signed affidavits stating that they'd been healed by water from the Chalice Well, and once again Glastonbury was on the tourist map. Today, Glastonbury and its tor are a center for searchers, too creepy for the mainstream church but just right for those looking for a place to recharge their crystals.

Orientation to Glastonbury

(area code: 01458)

Tourist Information

The TI is on High Street—as are many of the dreadlocked folks who walk it (Mon–Thu 10:00–16:00, Fri–Sat 10:00–16:30, closed Sun, tel. 01458/832-954, www.glastonburytic.co.uk). The TI has several booklets about cycling and walking in the area. The 50p *Glastonbury Town Trail* brochure outlines a good tor-to-town walk (a brisk 10 min). The TI's *Glastonbury Millennium Trail* pamphlet (60p) sends visitors on a historical scavenger hunt, following 20 numbered marble plaques embedded in the pavement throughout the town.

The TI, which occupies a fine 15th-century townhouse, is also home to the **Lake Village Museum**—two humble rooms featuring tools made of stones, bones, and antlers. Preserved in and excavated from the local peat bogs, these tools offer an interesting look at the lives of marshland people in pre-Roman times (£2.50, same hours as TI).

Getting to the Tor

The **Tor Bus** shuttles visitors from the town center and abbey to the base of the tor. If you ask, the bus will stop at the Somerset Rural Life Museum and the Chalice Well (£2.50 round-trip, 2/hr, on the half-hour, daily Easter–Sept 9:30–19:30, Oct–Easter 10:00–15:30, bus does not run during lunchtime, catch bus at St. Dunstan's parking lot in the town center, pick up schedule at TI).

A **taxi** to the tor costs £4 one-way—an easier, more economical choice for couples or groups.

Helpful Hints

Market Day: Tuesday is market day for crafts, knickknacks, and produce on the main street. There's also a country market Tuesday mornings in the Town Hall.

Glastonbury Festival: Every summer (June 23–27 in 2010), the gigantic Glastonbury Festival—billing itself as the "largest music and performing arts festival in the world"—brings all manner of postmodern flower children to its notoriously muddy "Healing Fields." Music fans and London's beautiful people make the trek to see the hottest new English and American bands. If you're near Glastonbury during the festival, anticipate increased traffic and crowds (especially on public transportation; over 135,000 tickets generally sell out), even though the actual music venue is six miles east of town (www.glastonburyfestivals.co.uk).

Sights in Glastonbury

▲▲**Glastonbury Abbey**—The evocative ruins of the first Christian sanctuary in the British Isles stand mysteriously alive in

a lush 36-acre park. Start your visit in the good little museum, where a model shows the abbey in its pre–Henry VIII splendor, and exhibits tell the story of a place "grandly constructed to entice even the dullest of minds to prayer." Then head out to explore the green park, dotted with bits of the ruined abbey.

In the 12th century, because of its legendary connection with Joseph of Arimathea, Glastonbury was the leading Christian pilgrimage site in all of Britain. The popular abbey grew very wealthy, and employed a thousand people to serve the needs of the pilgrims. Then, in 1171, Thomas Becket was martyred at Canterbury and immediately canonized by the pope (who thanked God for the opportunity to rile up the Christian public in England against King Henry II). This was a classic church-state power struggle. The king was excommunicated, and had to crawl through the streets of London on his knees and submit to a whipping from each bishop in England. Religious pilgrims abandoned Glastonbury for Canterbury, leaving Glastonbury suddenly a backwater.

NEAR BATH

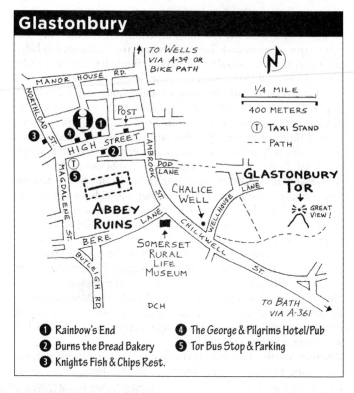

Glastonbury

TO WELLS VIA A-39 OR BIKE PATH

N

¼ MILE

400 METERS

Ⓣ TAXI STAND

--- PATH

MANOR HOUSE RD.

NORTHLOAD ST.

POST

HIGH STREET

LAMBROOK ST.

MAGDALENE ST.

Ⓣ

POP LANE

CHALICE WELL

WELLHOUSE LANE

GLASTONBURY TOR

←

☀ GREAT VIEW!

ABBEY RUINS

BERE LANE

BUTLEIGH RD.

CHILKWELL ST.

SOMERSET RURAL LIFE MUSEUM

DCH

TO BATH VIA A-361

❶ Rainbow's End
❷ Burns the Bread Bakery
❸ Knights Fish & Chips Rest.

❹ The George & Pilgrims Hotel/Pub
❺ Tor Bus Stop & Parking

In 1184 there was a devastating fire in the monastery, and in 1191 the abbot here "discovered"—with the help of a divine dream—the tomb and bodies of King Arthur and Queen Guinevere. Of course, this discovery rekindled the pilgrim trade in Glastonbury.

Then, in 1539, King Henry VIII ordered the abbey's destruction. When Glastonbury Abbot Richard Whiting questioned the king's decision, he was branded a traitor, hung at the top of Glastonbury Tor (after carrying up the plank that would support his noose), and his body cut into four pieces. His head was stuck over the gateway to the former abbey precinct. After this harsh example, the other abbots accepted the king's dissolution of England's abbeys. Many returned to monastic centers in France.

Today, the abbey attracts people who find God within. Tie-dyed, starry-eyed pilgrims seem to float through the grounds naturally high. Others lie on the grave of King Arthur, whose burial site is marked in the center of the abbey ruins.

The only surviving intact building on the grounds is the abbot's conical kitchen. Here you'll often find Matilda the pilgrim and her monk friend demonstrating life in the abbey kitchen in a kind

NEAR BATH

of medieval cooking show. If you'd like to see the demo, it's best to phone ahead for the schedule, especially off-season. They also offer earnest, costumed "Living History" reenactments (included with your ticket), generally daily March through October at 10:30, 12:00, 14:00, and 16:00—confirm times when you enter.

Cost, Hours, Information: £5, daily June–Aug 9:00–18:00, Sept–May 9:30 or 10:00 to dusk, closing times vary in the winter, last entry 30 min before closing, nearby pay parking, several guided walks offered daily, informative but long-winded 40-min audioguide-£2, as you enter ask about various tour and "show" times, tel. 01458/832-267, www.glastonburyabbey.com.

Somerset Rural Life Museum—Exhibits in this free, extremely kid-friendly museum include peat digging, cider-making, and cheesemaking. The Abbey Farmhouse is now a collection of domestic and work mementos that illustrate the life of Victorian farm laborer John Hodges "from the cradle to the grave." The fine 14th-century tithe barn (one of 30 such structures that funneled tithes to the local abbey), with its beautifully preserved wooden ceiling, is filled with Victorian farm tools and enthusiastic school-children (free, Tue–Sat 10:00–17:00, closed Sun–Mon, last entry 30 min before closing, free parking, 15-min walk from abbey, at intersection of Bere Lane and Chilkwell Street, tel. 01458/831-197, www.somerset.gov.uk/museums).

Chalice Well—The well is surrounded by a peaceful garden. According to tradition, Joseph of Arimathea brought the chalice from the Last Supper to Glastonbury in A.D. 37. Even if the chalice is not in the bottom of the well and the water is red from iron ore and not Jesus' blood, the tranquil setting is one where nature's harmony is a joy to ponder. The stones of the well shaft date from the 12th century and are believed to have come from the church in  Glastonbury Abbey (which was destroyed by fire). During the 18th century, pilgrims flocked to Glastonbury for the well's healing powers. Even today, there's a moment of silence at noon for world peace and healing. Have a drink or take some of the precious water home (£3.50, daily April–Oct 10:00–17:30, Nov–March 10:00–16:00, last entry 30 min before closing, water bottles available for purchase, on Chilkwell Street/A361, drivers can park at Rural Life Museum and walk 5 min, tel. 01458/831-154, www.chalicewell.org.uk).

▲Glastonbury Tor—Seen by many as a Mother Goddess symbol, the tor—a natural plug of sandstone on clay—has an undeniable geological charisma.

Climbing the tor is the essential activity on a visit to Glastonbury. A fine Somerset view rewards those who hike to its 520-foot summit. From its top you can survey a former bogland that is still below sea level at high tide. The ribbon-like manmade drainage canals that glisten as they slice through the farmland are the work of Dutch engineers, imported centuries ago to turn the marshy wasteland into something usable.

Looking out, find Glastonbury (at the base of the hill) and Wells (marked by its cathedral) to the right. Above Wells, a TV tower marks the 996-foot high point of the Mendip Hills. It was lead from these hills that attracted the Romans (and, perhaps, Jesus' uncle Joe) so long ago. Stretching to the left, the hills define what was the coastline before those Dutch engineers arrived.

The tor-top tower is the remnant of a chapel dedicated to St. Michael. Early Christians often summoned St. Michael, the warrior angel, to combat pagan gods. When a church was built upon a pagan holy ground like this, it was frequently dedicated to Michael. But apparently those pagan gods fought back: St. Michael's Church was destroyed by an earthquake in 1275.

Getting There: The tor is a short bus ride or walk from the town center. Drivers can park at the nearby Rural Life Museum. For details, see "Getting to the Tor" on page 227.

New Age Shopping—Part of the fun of a visit to Glastonbury is just being in a town where every other shop and eatery is a New Age place. If you need spiritual guidance or just a rune reading, wander through the **Glastonbury Experience,** a New Age mall at the bottom of High Street. Locals who are not into this complain that on High Street you can buy any kind of magic crystal or incense, but not a roll of TP. But, as this counterculture is their town's bread and butter, they do their best to sit in their pubs and go "Ommmmm."

Eating in Glastonbury

Glastonbury has no shortage of healthy eateries. The vegetarian **Rainbow's End** is one of several fine lunch cafés for beans, salads, herbal teas, yummy homemade sweets, and New Age people-watching (£8 meals, daily 10:00–16:00, a few doors up from the TI, 17 High Street, tel. 01458/833-896). If you're looking for a midwife or a male-bonding tribal meeting, check their notice board.

Burns the Bread makes hearty pasties (savory meat pies) as well as fresh pies, sandwiches, delicious cookies, and pastries. Ask about the Torsy Moorsy Cake, or try a gingerbread man made with real ginger. Grab a pasty and picnic with the ghosts of Arthur and Guinevere in the abbey ruins (Mon–Sat 6:00–17:00, Sun 11:00–17:00, 14 High Street, tel. 01458/831-532).

Knights Fish and Chips Restaurant has been in business since 1909 because it serves good food (Mon 17:00–21:30, Tue–Sat 12:00–14:15 & 17:00–21:30, closed Sun, eat in or take away, 5 Northload Street, tel. 01458/831-882).

For visitors suffering a New Age overdose, the wonderfully Old World pub in **The George and Pilgrims Hotel** might be exactly what the doctor ordered (1 High Street, also rents rooms for £85–95, tel. 01458/831-146).

Glastonbury Connections

The nearest train station is in Bath. Local buses are run by First Bus Company (toll tel. 0845-606-4446, www.firstgroup.com).

From Glastonbury by Bus to: Wells (4/hr, 20 min, bus #375/#376/#377 runs frequently, bus #29 only 6/day), **Bath** (hourly, allow 2 hours, take bus #375/#376/#377 or #29 to Wells, transfer to bus #173 to Bath, 1.25 hours between Wells and Bath). Buses are sparse on Sundays (generally one bus every hour).

Wells

Because this wonderfully preserved little town has a cathedral, it can be called a city. While it's the biggest town in Somerset, it's England's smallest cathedral city (pop. 9,400), with one of its most interesting cathedrals and a wonderful evensong service. Wells has more medieval buildings still doing what they were originally built to do than any town you'll visit. Market day fills the town square on Wednesday and Saturday.

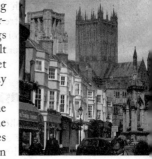

Tourist Information: The TI, on the main square, has information about the town's sights and nearby cheese factories (April–Oct Mon–Sat 10:00–17:00, Sun 10:00–16:00; Nov–March Mon–Sat 11:00–16:00, closed Sun; tel. 01749/672-552, www.wellstourism.com).

Local Guide: Edie Westmoreland offers town walks in the summer by appointment (£15/group of 2–5 people, £4/person for 8 or more, 1.5-hour tours usually start at Penniless Porch on town square, book three days in advance, tel. 01934/832-350, mobile 07899-836-706, ebwestmoreland@btinternet.com).

Sights in Wells

▲▲Wells Cathedral

England's first completely Gothic cathedral (dating from about 1200) is the highlight of the city. Locals claim this church has the largest collection of medieval statuary north of the Alps.

Cost, Hours, Information: Requested £5.50 donation—not intended to keep you out, daily Easter–Sept 7:00–19:00 or dusk, Oct–Easter 7:00–18:00; 45-min tours Mon–Sat April–Oct at 10:00, 12:00, 13:00, 14:00, and 15:00; pay £3 photography fee at info desk, no flash in choir, good shop, handy Cathedral Cloister Restaurant, tel. 01749/674-483, www.wellscathedral.org.uk.

❂ **Self-Guided Tour:** Begin in front of the cathedral. The newly restored west front displays almost 300 original 13th-century carvings of kings and the **Last Judgment.** The bottom row of niches is empty, too easily reached by Cromwell's men, who were hell-bent on destroying "graven images." Stand back and imagine it as a grand Palm Sunday welcome with a cast of hundreds—all gaily painted back then, choristers singing boldly from holes above the doors and trumpets tooting through the holes up by the 12 apostles.

Inside, you're immediately struck by the general lightness and the unique "scissors" or hourglass-shaped **double arch** (added in 1338 to transfer weight from the west—where the foundations were sinking under the tower's weight—to the east, where they were firm). You'll be greeted warmly, reminded how expensive it is to maintain the cathedral, and given a map of its highlights.

The warm tones of the stone interior give the place a modern feel. Until Henry VIII and the Reformation, the interior was painted a gloomy red and green; later it was whitewashed. Then, in the 1840s, the church experienced the Victorian "great scrape," as locals peeled moldy whitewash off and revealed the bare stone we see today. The floral ceiling painting is based on the original medieval design. A single pattern was discovered under the 17th-century whitewash and repeated throughout.

Small, ornate 15th-century pavilion-like chapels flank the altar, carved in lacy Gothic for wealthy townsmen. The **pulpit** features a post-Reformation, circa-1540 English script—rather than the standard Latin. Since this was not a monastery church, the Reformation didn't destroy it as it did the Glastonbury Abbey church.

Don't miss the fine 14th-century stained glass (the "Golden Window" on the east wall). The medieval **clock,** which depicts the earth at the center of the universe, does a silly but much-loved joust on the quarter-hour (north transept, its face dates from 1390, notice how—like clockwork—every other rider gets clobbered). The outer ring shows hours, the second ring shows minutes, and the inner ring shows the dates of the month and phases of the moon. The **crucifix** was carved out of a yew tree by a German prisoner of war during World War II. After the war ended, many of Britain's German prisoners figured there was little in Germany to go home to, so they stayed, assimilating into British culture.

In the **choir** (the central zone where the daily services are sung), the embroidery work on the cushions is worth a close look. It celebrates the hometowns of important local church leaders.

Head over to the south transept. Notice the **carvings** on the pillars. The figures depict medieval life—a man with a toothache, another man with a thorn in his foot, and, around the top, a ticked-off farmer chasing fruit stealers. Look at the tombstones set in the floor. Notice there is no brass. After the Reformation, in the 1530s, the church was short on cash, so they sold the brass to pay for roof repairs. The **old font** survives from the previous church (A.D. 705) and has been the site of Wells baptisms for nearly a thousand years. In the far end of this transept, a little of the muddy green and red that wasn't whitewashed survives.

In the apse, or east end, find the **Lady Chapel** with its beautiful medieval glass windows. In the 17th century, Puritan troops trashed the precious original glass. Much was repaired, but many of the broken panes were like a puzzle that was never figured out. That's why today many of the windows are simply kaleidoscopes of colored glass.

Well-worn steps lead to the grand fan-vaulted **Chapter House**—an intimate place for the theological equivalent of a huddle among church officials. The cathedral **Reading Room** (£1, Fri–Sat 14:30–16:30 only), with a few old manuscripts, offers a peek into a real 15th-century library.

More Cathedral Sights
▲▲**Cathedral Evensong Service**—The cathedral choir takes full advantage of heavenly acoustics with a nightly 45-minute evensong service. You will sit right in the old "quire" as you listen to a great pipe organ and boys', girls', and men's voices (Mon–Sat at 17:15, Sun at 15:00, generally no service when school is out July–Aug unless a visiting choir performs, to check call 01749/674-483

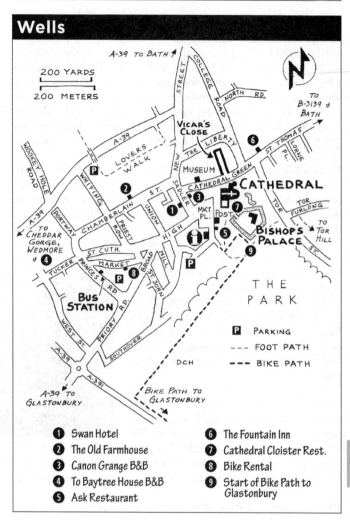

Wells

1 Swan Hotel
2 The Old Farmhouse
3 Canon Grange B&B
4 To Baytree House B&B
5 Ask Restaurant
6 The Fountain Inn
7 Cathedral Cloister Rest.
8 Bike Rental
9 Start of Bike Path to Glastonbury

or visit www.wellscathedral.org.uk). At 17:05 (Sun at 15:05) the verger ushers visitors to their seats. There's usually plenty of room.

On weekdays and Saturdays, if you need to catch the 17:43 bus to Bath, request a seat on the north side of the presbytery, so you can slip out the side door without disturbing the service (10-min walk to station from cathedral; or go at 18:15 via Bristol—explained under "Wells Connections," later).

The cathedral also hosts several evening **concerts** each month (£10–25, most around £18, generally Thu–Sat at 19:00 or 19:30, box office open Mon–Sat 14:00–16:30, closed Sun, tel. 01749/832-201). Concert tickets are also available at the TI.

Cathedral Green—In the Middle Ages the cathedral was enclosed within the "Liberty," an area free from civil jurisdiction until the 1800s. The Liberty included the green on the west side of the cathedral, which, from the 13th to the 17th centuries, was a burial place for common folk, including 17th-century plague victims. During the Edwardian period, a local character known as Boney Foster used to dig up the human bones and sell them to tourists. The green later became a cricket pitch, then a field for grazing animals. Today it's the perfect setting for an impressive cathedral.

Vicar's Close—Lined with perfectly pickled 14th-century houses, this is the oldest continuously occupied complete street in Europe (since 1348, just a block north of the cathedral). It was built to house the vicar's choir, and it still houses church officials.

Bishop's Palace—Next to the cathedral stands the moated Bishop's Palace, built in the 13th century and still in use today

as the residence of the Bishop of Bath and Wells. The interior offers a look at elegant furniture and clothing (not worth the £5.50, April–Oct Sun–Fri 10:30–18:00, Sat 10:30–14:00, closed Nov–March some Sat–Sun for events—call to confirm, last entry one hour before closing, £2 guidebook, tel. 01749/678-691, www.bishops palace.org.uk).

The palace's spring-fed moat, built in the 14th century to protect the bishop during squabbles with the borough, now serves primarily as a pool for swans. The bridge was last drawn in 1831. On the grounds (past the old-timers playing a proper game of croquet—daily after 13:30) is a fine garden, home to the idyllic springs and wells that gave the city its name.

More Sights and Best Views—The mediocre **city museum** is next door to the cathedral (£3; Easter–Oct Mon–Sat 11:00–17:00, Sun 11:00–16:00; Nov–Easter daily 11:00–16:00; 8 Cathedral Green, tel. 01749/673-477, www.wellsmuseum.org.uk). For a fine **cathedral-and-town view** from your own leafy hilltop bench, hike 10 minutes from here up Tor Hill.

Near Wells

Bike Ride from Wells to Glastonbury Tor—This 9.5-mile cycling and foot path is part of the West Country Way Cycle Route (although much of the Wells–Glastonbury segment is on rural highways). Look for the signs that lead you to Glastonbury (small blue metal signs say *byway*, with a red number 3).

You can rent a bike in Wells at **Bike City** (£7.50/half-day, £15/ day, Mon–Thu 9:00–17:30, Fri–Sat 9:00–17:00, closed Sun, helmets available, near the bus station on Market Street, tel. 01749/671-711, www.bikecity.biz). They give route advice and handy maps. There is no bike rental in Glastonbury.

Cheddar Cheese—If you're in the mood for a picnic, drop by any local aromatic cheese shop for a great selection of tasty Somerset cheeses. Real farmhouse cheddar puts American cheddar to Velveeta shame. The **Cheddar Gorge Cheese Company,** eight miles west of Wells, is a dairy farm with a guide and a viewing area, giving guests a chance to see the cheesemaking process and enjoy a sample (£2, daily 10:00–16:00; take A39, then A371 to Cheddar Gorge; tel. 01934/742-810, www.cheddargorgecheeseco .co.uk).

Scrumpy Farms—Scrumpy is the wonderfully dangerous hard cider brewed in this part of England. You don't find it served in many pubs because of the unruly crowd it attracts. Scrumpy, at 8 percent alcohol, will rot your socks. "Scrumpy Jack," carbonated mass-produced cider, is not real scrumpy. The real stuff is "rough farmhouse cider." This is potent stuff. It's said some farmers throw a side of beef into the vat, and when fermentation is done only the teeth remain.

TIs list local cider farms open to the public, such as **Mr. Wilkins' Land's End Cider Farm,** a great Back Door travel experience (free, Mon–Sat 10:00–20:00, Sun 10:00–13:00; west of Wells in Mudgley, take B3139 from Wells to Wedmore, then B3151 south for 2 miles, farm is a quarter-mile off B3151—tough to find, get close and ask locals; tel. 01934/712-385). Glastonbury's **Somerset Rural Life Museum** also has a cider exhibit.

Apples are pressed from August through December. Hard cider, while not quite scrumpy, is also typical of the West Country, but more fashionable, "decent," and accessible. You can get a pint of hard cider at nearly any pub, drawn straight from the barrel— dry, medium, or sweet.

Castle of Nunney—The centerpiece of the charming village of Nunney (between Bath and Glastonbury, off A361) is a striking 14th-century castle surrounded by a fairy-tale moat. Its rare, French-style design brings to mind the Paris Bastille. The year 1644 was a tumultuous one for Nunney. Its noble family was royalist (and likely closet Catholics). They defied Parliament, so Parliament ordered their castle "slighted" (deliberately destroyed) to ensure that it would threaten the order of the land no more. Looking at this castle, so daunting in the age of bows and arrows, you can see how it was no match for modern cannon. The pretty Mendip village of Nunney, with its little brook, is worth a wander too.

Sleeping in Wells

Wells is a pleasant overnight stop with a handful of agreeable B&Bs. The first three places listed below are within a short walk of the cathedral.

$$ Swan Hotel, a Best Western facing the cathedral, is a big, comfortable 50-room hotel. Prices for their Tudor-style rooms vary based on whether you want extras such as a four-poster bed or a view of the cathedral (Sb-£100, Db-£134, often cheaper if you just show up, ask about weekend deals, Sadler Street, tel. 01749/836-300, fax 01749/836-301, www.swanhotelwells.co.uk, info@swan hotelwells.co.uk).

$ The Old Farmhouse, a five-minute walk from the town center, welcomes you with a secluded front garden and two tastefully decorated rooms (Db-£75–80, 2-night minimum, secure parking, 62 Chamberlain Street, tel. 01749/675-058, www.wellsholiday.com, theoldfarmhousewells@hotmail.com, charming owners Felicity and Christopher Wilkes).

$ Canon Grange B&B is a 15th-century watch-your-head beamed house directly in front of the cathedral. It has five homey rooms and a cozy charm (Sb-£50, Db-£68, Db with cathedral view-£74, ask for 10 percent Rick Steves discount with stay of 2 or more nights, family room, on the cathedral green, tel. 01749/671-800, www.canongrange.co.uk, canongrange@email.com, Annette and Ken).

$ Baytree House B&B is a modern, practical home at the edge of town (on a big road, a 10-minute walk to the center), renting five modern, fresh, and comfy rooms (Db-£64, family rooms, Wi-Fi, plush lounge, free parking, near where Strawberry Way hits the A39 road to Cheddar at 85 Portway, tel. 01749/677-933, mobile 07745-287-194, www.baytree-house.co.uk, stay@baytree -house.co.uk, Amanda Bellini).

Sleep Code

(£1 = about $1.60, country code: 44, area code: 01749)

S = Single, **D** = Double/Twin, **T** = Triple, **Q** = Quad, **b** = bathroom, **s** = shower only. Unless otherwise indicated, you can assume credit cards are accepted and breakfast is included.

To help you sort easily through these listings, I've divided the rooms into two categories based on the price for a standard double room with bath:

$$ Higher Priced—Most rooms £80 or more.

$ Lower Priced—Most rooms less than £80.

Eating in Wells

Downtown Wells is tiny. A good variety of eating options are within a block or two of its market square, including classic pubs, **Ask Restaurant** (a popular Italian chain, £8 pizza and pastas, right on the square in the Market Hall, tel. 01749/677-681), a good pasties-to-go **bakery** (on Sadler Street), and little delis and bakeries serving light meals. **The Fountain Inn** serves good pub grub (50 yards behind the cathedral on St. Thomas Street, tel. 01749/672-317).

For a handy if not heavenly lunch, consider the **Cathedral Cloister Restaurant** in the cathedral, along a lovely stone corridor with leaded windows overlooking cloister tombstones (£4–6 lunches, Mon–Sat 10:00–17:00, Sun 13:00–17:00; closes at 16:30 and occasionally on Sun in winter).

Wells Connections

The nearest train station is in Bath. The bus station in Wells is actually a bus lot, at the intersection of Priory and Princes Roads. Local buses are run by First Bus Company (for Wells, toll tel. 0845-606-4446, www.firstgroup.com), and buses to and from London are run by National Express (toll tel. 0871-781-8181, www.nationalexpress.com).

From Wells by Bus to: Bath (hourly, 1.25 hrs, last bus #173 leaves at 17:43), **Glastonbury** (4/hr, 20 min, bus #375/#376/#377 runs frequently, bus #29 only 6/day), **London's Victoria Coach Station** (£28–30, hourly, 4 hrs, change in Bristol, buses run daily 6:10–18:15).

If you miss the 17:43 bus to Bath, you can catch the 18:15 bus to Bristol, then take a 15-minute train ride to Bath, arriving at 19:35.

NEAR BATH

Avebury

Avebury is a prehistoric open-air museum, with a complex of fascinating Neolithic sites all gathered around the great stone henge

(circle). Because the area sports only a thin skin of topsoil over chalk, it is naturally treeless (similar to the area around Stonehenge). Perhaps this unique landscape—where the land connects with the big sky—made it the choice of prehistoric societies for their religious monuments. Whatever the case, Avebury dates to 2800 B.C.— six centuries older than Stonehenge.

This complex, the St. Peter's Basilica of Neolithic civilization, makes for a fascinating visit. Many enjoy it more than Stonehenge.

Orientation to Avebury

Avebury, just a little village with a big stone circle, is easy to reach by car, but may not be worth the hassle by public transportation (see "Getting Around the Region" on page 224).

Tourist Information

The TI is located within the town chapel. Notice the stone work: It's a mix of bricks and broken stones from the ancient circle (June–Oct Tue–Sun 9:30–17:00, closed Mon, shorter hours Nov–May, Green Street, tel. 01672/539-179, www.visitwiltshire.co.uk). For good information on the Avebury sights, see the websites of the English Heritage (www.english-heritage.org.uk) and the National Trust (www.nationaltrust.org.uk).

Arrival by Car

You must pay to park in Avebury, and your only real option is the flat-fee National Trust parking lot, which is a three-minute walk from the village (£5, £3 after 15:00, summer 9:00–18:00, off-season 9:00–16:00). No other public parking is available in the village.

Sights in Avebury

▲▲Avebury Stone Circle—The stone circle at Avebury is bigger (16 times the size), less touristy, and, for many, more interesting than Stonehenge. You're free to wander among 100 stones, ditches, mounds, and curious patterns from the past, as well as the village of Avebury, which grew up in the middle of this fascinating 1,400-foot-wide Neolithic circle.

In the 14th century, in a kind of frenzy of religious paranoia, Avebury villagers buried many of these mysterious pagan stones. Their 18th-century descendants hosted social events in which they broke up the remaining pagan stones (topple, heat, douse with cold water, and scavenge broken stones as building blocks). In modern times, the buried stones were dug up and re-erected. Concrete markers show you where the missing broken-up stones once stood.

To make the roughly half-mile walk around the circle, you'll hike along an impressive earthwork henge—a 30-foot-high outer bank surrounding a ditch 30 feet deep, making a 60-foot-high rampart. This earthen rampart once had stones standing around the perimeter, placed about every 30 feet, and four grand causeway entries. Originally, two smaller circles made of about 200 stones stood within the henge (free, always open).

Avebury

Legend:
— ROAD
--- FOOTPATH
P PARKING
•••• STANDING STONES

TO SWINDON

Direction of Summer Sunrise

ALEXANDER KEILLER MUSEUM
2
1
HIGH ST.
TO CALNE
EARTHEN RAMPARTS
GREEN ST.
i AVEBURY STONE CIRCLE

RITUAL PROCESSION WAY

TO CHERHILL HORSE & BATH
P
3
BECKHAMPTON RD.
B-4003

SILBURY HILL
A-4361
A-4
TO DEVIZES
A-361

ROMAN ROAD
A-4

½ MILE
800 METERS

1 Circle Restaurant
2 The Red Lion Pub
3 Mrs. Dixon's B&B

WEST KENNET LONG BARROW
RIVER KENNET
B-4003
A-4
TO MARLBOROUGH

THE SANCTUARY "WOOD HENGE"
Direction of Winter Sunrise

DCH

▲**Ritual Procession Way**—Also known as West Kennet Avenue, this double line of stones provided a ritual procession way leading from Avebury to a long-gone wooden circle dubbed "The Sanctuary." This "wood henge," thought to have been 1,000 years older than everything else in the area, is considered the genesis of Avebury and its big stone circle. Most of the stones standing along the procession way today were reconstructed in modern times.

▲**Silbury Hill**—This pyramid-shaped hill is a 130-foot-high, yet-to-be-explained mound of chalk just outside of Avebury.

Over 4,000 years old, this mound is considered the largest man-made object in prehistoric Europe (with the surface area of London's Trafalgar Square and the height of the Nelson Column). It's a reminder that we've only just scratched the surface of England's mysterious, ancient, and religious landscape.

Inspired by a legend that the hill hid a gold statue in its center, locals tunneled through Silbury Hill in 1830, undermining the

structure. Work is currently underway to restore the hill, which remains closed to the public. Archaeologists (who date things like this by carbon-dating snails and other little critters killed in its construction) figure Silbury Hill took only 60 years to build in about 2200 B.C. This makes Silbury Hill the last element built at Avebury and contemporaneous with Stonehenge. Some think it may have been an observation point for all the other bits of the Avebury site. You can still see evidence of a spiral path leading up the hill and a moat at its base.

The Roman road detoured around Silbury Hill. (Roman engineers often used features of the landscape as visual reference points when building roads. Their roads would commonly kink at the crest of hills or other landmarks, where they realigned with a new visual point.) Later the hill sported a wooden Saxon fort, which likely acted as a look-out for marauding Vikings. And in World War II, the Royal Observer Corps stationed men up here to count and report Nazi bombers on raids.

West Kennet Long Barrow—A pull-out on the road just past Silbury Hill marks the West Kennet Long Barrow (a 15-min walk from Silbury Hill). This burial chamber, the best-preserved Stone Age chamber tomb in the UK, stands intact on the ridge. It lines up with the rising sun on summer solstice. You can walk inside the barrow.

Cherhill Horse—Heading west from Avebury on A4 (toward Bath), you'll see an obelisk (a monument to some important earl) above you on the downs, or chalk hills, near the village of Cherhill. You'll also see a white horse carved into the chalk hillside. Above it are the remains of an Iron Age hill fort known as Oldbury Castle—described on an information board at the roadside pull-out. There is one genuinely prehistoric white horse in England (the Uffington White Horse); the Cherhill Horse, like all the others, is just an 18th-century creation. Prehistoric discoveries were all the rage in the 1700s, and it was a fad to make your own fake ones. Throughout southern England, you can cut into the thin layer of topsoil and find chalk. Now, so they don't have to weed, horses like this are cemented and painted white.

Alexander Keiller Museum—This archaeology museum has an interactive exhibit in a 17th-century barn (£5, daily April–Oct 10:00–18:00, Nov–March 10:00–16:00 or dusk, last entry 30 min before closing, tel. 01672/539-250).

Eating and Sleeping in Avebury

The pleasant **Circle Restaurant** serves healthy, hearty à la carte lunches, including vegan and gluten-free dishes, and cream teas on most days (daily April–Oct 10:00–17:30, Nov–March 11:00–15:30, next to National Trust store and the Alexander Keiller museum, tel. 01672/539-514).

The Red Lion has inexpensive, greasy pub grub; a creaky, well-worn, dart-throwing ambience; and a medieval well in its dining room (£6–12 meals, daily 12:00–22:00, tel. 01672/539-266).

Sleeping in Avebury makes lots of sense—the stones get lonely and are wide open all night. **$ Mrs. Dixon's B&B,** up the road from the public parking lot, rents three cramped and homey rooms. Look for the green-and-white *Bed & Breakfast* sign from the main road (S-£40, D-£60, these prices promised with this book in 2010, cash only, parking available in back, 6 Beckhampton Road, tel. 01672/539-588, run by earthy Mrs. Dixon and crew).

Stonehenge

As old as the pyramids, and older than the Acropolis and the Colosseum, this iconic stone circle amazed medieval Europeans,

who figured it was built by a race of giants. And it still impresses visitors today. As one of Europe's most famous sights, Stonehenge does a valiant job of retaining an air of mystery and majesty (partly because cordons, which keep hordes of tourists from trampling all over it, create the illusion that it stands alone in a field). Although some people are underwhelmed by Stonehenge, most of its nearly one million annual visitors find that it's worth the trip.

NEAR BATH

Getting to Stonehenge

By Public Transportation: Catch a train to Salisbury, then go by bus or taxi to Stonehenge (for details, see page 249). Note that there is no public transportation between Avebury and Stonehenge.

By Car: Stonehenge is well-signed just off A303. It's about 15 minutes north of Salisbury, an hour east of Glastonbury, and an hour south of Avebury. From Salisbury, head north on A345 (Castle Road) through Amesbury, go west on A303 for 1.5 miles, veer right onto A344, and it's just ahead on the left, with the parking lot on the right.

By Bus Tour: For tours of Stonehenge from Bath, see page 199 (Mad Max is best); for tours from Salisbury, see page 249.

Orientation to Stonehenge

Cost: £6.50, covered by English Heritage Pass and Great British Heritage Pass (see page 20).

Hours: Daily June–Aug 9:00–19:00, mid-March–May and Sept–mid-Oct 9:30–18:00, mid-Oct–mid-March 9:30–16:00, last entry 30 min before closing.

When to Go: Shorter hours and possible closures June 20–22 due to huge, raucous solstice crowds; £3 parking fee likely in summer—refundable with paid admission.

Information: Entry includes a worthwhile hour-long audio-guide—though they sometimes run out (tel. 01980/623-108 or toll tel. 0870-333-1181, www.english-heritage.org.uk/stonehenge).

Reaching the Inner Stones: Special one-hour access to the stones' inner circle—before or after regular visiting hours—costs an extra £14 and must be reserved well in advance. Details can be found on the English Heritage website (look for a link to "Stone Circle Access") or by calling 01722/343-830.

Planned Changes: Future plans for Stonehenge call for the creation of a new visitors center and museum, designed to blend in with the landscape and make the stone circle feel more pristine. Visitors will park farther away and ride a shuttle bus to the site.

Self-Guided Tour

The entrance fee includes a good audioguide, but this commentary will help make your visit even more meaningful.

Walk in from the parking lot, buy your ticket, pick up your included audioguide, and head through the ugly underpass beneath the road. On the way up the ramp, notice the artist's rendering of what Stonehenge once looked like. As you approach the massive structure, walk right up to the knee-high cordon and let your fellow 21st-century tourists melt away. It's just you and the druids...

England has hundreds of stone circles, but Stonehenge—which literally means "hanging stones"—is unique. It's the only one that has horizontal cross-pieces (called lintels) spanning the vertical monoliths, and the only one with stones that have been made smooth and uniform. What you see here is a bit more than half the original structure—the rest was quarried centuries ago for other buildings.

Now do a slow counterclockwise spin around the monument, and ponder the following points. As you walk, mentally flesh out the missing pieces and re-erect the rubble. Knowledgeable guides posted around the site are happy to answer your questions.

This was a hugely significant location to prehistoric peoples. There are some 500 burial mounds within a three-mile radius of Stonehenge—most likely belonging to kings and chieftains. Built in phases between 3000 and 1000 B.C., Stonehenge's original function may have been simply as a monumental gravestone for a ritual burial site. (So goes one recently popular theory.) But that's not the end of the story, as the monument was expanded over the millennia.

Stonehenge still functions as a remarkably accurate celestial calendar. As the sun rises on the summer solstice (June 21), the "heel stone"—the one set apart from the rest, near the road—lines up with the sun and the altar at the center of the stone circle. A study of more than 300 similar circles in Britain found that each was designed to calculate the movement of the sun, moon, and stars, and to predict eclipses in order to help early societies know when to plant, harvest, and party. Even in modern times, as the summer solstice sun sets in just the right slot at Stonehenge, pagans boogie.

In addition to being a calendar, Stonehenge is built at the precise point where six ley lines intersect. Ley lines are theoretical lines of magnetic or spiritual power that crisscross the globe. Belief in the power of these lines has gone in and out of fashion over time: They are believed to have been very important to prehistoric peoples, but then were largely ignored until the New Age movement of the 20th century. Without realizing it, you follow these ley lines all the time: Many of England's modern highways are built on top of prehistoric paths, and many churches are built on the site of prehistoric monuments where ley lines intersect. If you're a skeptic, ask one of the guides at Stonehenge to demonstrate the ley lines with a pair of L-shaped divining rods...it's creepy and convincing.

Notice that two of the stones (facing the entry passageway) are blemished. At the base of one monolith, it looks like someone has pulled back the stone to reveal a concrete skeleton. This is a clumsy repair job to fix damage done by souvenir-seekers long ago, who actually rented hammers and chisels to take home a piece of Stonehenge. On the stone to the right of the repaired one, notice that the back isn't covered with the same thin layer of protective lichen as the others. The lichen—and some of the stone itself—was sandblasted off to remove graffiti. (No wonder they've got Stonehenge roped off now.)

Stonehenge's builders used two different types of stones. The tall, stout monoliths and lintels are made of sandstone blocks called sarsen stones. Most of the monoliths weigh about 25 tons (the largest is 45 tons), and the lintels are about seven tons apiece. These sarsen stones were brought from "only" 20 miles away. The shorter stones in the middle, called "bluestones," came from the south coast of Wales—240 miles away. (Close if you're taking a train, but far if you're packing a megalith.) Imagine the logistical puzzle of floating six-ton stones up the River Avon, then rolling them on logs about 20 miles to this position...an impressive feat, even in our era of skyscrapers.

Why didn't the builders of Stonehenge use what seem like perfectly adequate stones nearby? This, like many other questions about Stonehenge, remains shrouded in mystery. Think again about the ley lines. Ponder the fact that many experts accept none of the explanations of how these giant stones were transported. Then imagine congregations gathering here 4,000 years ago, raising thought levels, creating a powerful life force transmitted along the ley lines. Maybe a particular kind of stone was essential for maximum energy transmission. Maybe the stones were levitated here. Maybe psychics really do create powerful vibes. Maybe not. But it's as unbelievable as electricity used to be.

Salisbury

Salisbury, set in the middle of the expansive Salisbury Plain, is a favorite stop for its striking cathedral and intriguing history.

Salisbury was originally settled during the Bronze Age, possibly as early as 600 B.C., and later became a Roman town called Sarum. The modern city of Salisbury developed when the old settlement outgrew its boundaries, prompting the townspeople to move the city from a hill to the river valley below. Most of today's visitors come to marvel at the famous Salisbury Cathedral, featuring England's tallest spire and largest cathedral green. Collectors, bargain hunters, and foodies savor Salisbury's colorful market days. And archaeologists dig the region around Salisbury, with England's highest concentration of ancient sites. The town itself is pleasant and walkable, and is a convenient base camp for visiting the ancient sites of Stonehenge and Avebury, or for exploring the countryside.

Salisbury

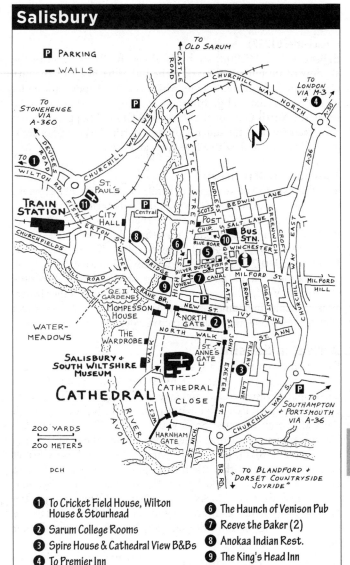

P PARKING
— WALLS

TO OLD SARUM

TO STONEHENGE VIA A-360

TO LONDON VIA M-3 ❹

CHURCHILL WAY NORTH

CASTLE ROAD

WEST

CHURCHILL WAY

CASTLE STREET

❶

WILTON RD.

DEVIZES ROAD

FISH

ST. PAUL'S

❶❶

TRAIN STATION

CITY HALL

Central

CHURCHFIELDS

MERTON ST.

ENDLESS ST.

BEDWIN LANE

SCOTS LANE

POST

CHIP.

Blue Boar

SALT LANE

BUS STN.

❿

WINCHESTER

GREENWICH

CROFT

EAST

TO LONDON VIA M-3

A-36

A-30

MILL ROAD

WATER

BRIDGE ST.

❽

❻

❺

SILVER

BUTCH

FISH

❼

NEW CANAL

MILFORD ST.

MILFORD HILL

GIGANT ST.

CRANE BR.

Q.E. II GARDENS

MOMPESSON HOUSE

NEW ST.

❷

NORTH GATE

IVY ST.

BROWN ST.

CATH. ST.

QUEEN

TRIN.

ST. ANN

WATER-MEADOWS

THE WARDROBE

SALISBURY & SOUTH WILTSHIRE MUSEUM

NORTH WALK

ST. ANNE'S GATE

ST. JOHN

EXETER ST.

❸

FRIARY LANE

WEST WALK

CATHEDRAL

CATHEDRAL CLOSE

RIVER AVON

200 YARDS
200 METERS

HARNHAM GATE

ST. NICH.

NEW BR. RD.

CHURCHILL WAY S.

❷

TO SOUTHAMPTON & PORTSMOUTH VIA A-36

TO BLANDFORD & "DORSET COUNTRYSIDE JOYRIDE"

DCH

❶ To Cricket Field House, Wilton House & Stourhead

❷ Sarum College Rooms

❸ Spire House & Cathedral View B&Bs

❹ To Premier Inn

❺ Charter 1227 Rest. & Market Square

❻ The Haunch of Venison Pub

❼ Reeve the Baker (2)

❽ Anokaa Indian Rest.

❾ The King's Head Inn

❿ Launderette

❶❶ Bus to Avebury

NEAR BATH

Orientation to Salisbury

(area code: 01722)

Salisbury (pop. 45,000) stretches along the River Avon in the shadow of its huge landmark cathedral. The heart of the city clusters around Market Square, which is also a handy parking lot on nonmarket days. High Street, a block to the west, leads to the medieval North Gate of the Cathedral Close. Shoppers explore the streets south of the square. The area north of Market Square is generally residential, with a few shops and pubs.

Tourist Information

The TI, just off Market Square, hands out free city maps, books rooms for no fee, sells a £1 city guide, sells train tickets with a £1.10 surcharge, and offers free Internet access (May Mon–Sat 9:30–17:00, Sun 10:00–16:00; June–Sept Mon–Sat 9:30–18:00, Sun 10:00–16:00; Oct–April Mon–Sat 9:30–17:00, closed Sun; Fish Row, tel. 01722/334-956, www.visitwiltshire.co.uk).

Ask the TI about 1.5-hour walking tours (£4, April–Oct daily at 11:00, Nov–March Sat–Sun only, depart from TI; other itineraries available, including £4 Ghost Walk May–Sept Fri at 20:00; tel. 01722/320-349, www.salisburycityguides.co.uk).

Arrival in Salisbury

By Train: From the train station, it's a 10-minute walk into the town center. Leave the station to the left, walk about 50 yards down South Western Road, and take the first right (at The Railway Tavern) onto Mill Road, following it around the bend and through the traffic roundabouts. Soon you'll see the Queen Elizabeth Gardens and the cathedral spire on your right. The road becomes Crane Bridge Road, then Crane Street, and finally New Street before intersecting with Catherine/St. John Street. Market Square and the TI are one long block north (left) on Catherine Street, and it's another two short blocks beyond that to the bus station. The Salisbury Cathedral and recommended Exeter Street B&Bs are to the south (right), down St. John Street (which becomes Exeter Street).

By Car: Drivers will find several pay parking lots in Salisbury—simply follow the blue *P* signs. The "Central" lot, behind the giant red-brick Sainsbury's store, is within a 10-minute walk of the TI or cathedral and is best for overnight stays (enter from Churchill Way West or Castle Street, lot open 24 hrs). The "Old George Mall" parking garage is closer to the cathedral and has comparable daytime rates (1 block north of cathedral, enter from New Street; garage open Mon–Sat 7:00–20:00, Sun 10:00–17:00).

Helpful Hints

Market Days: For centuries Salisbury has been known for its lively markets. On Tuesdays and Saturdays, Market Square hosts the charter market, with general goods. Every other Wednesday is the farmers market. There are also special markets, such as one with French products. Ask the TI for a current schedule.

Festivals: The Salisbury International Arts Festival runs for just over two weeks at the end of May and beginning of June (likely May 21–June 6 in 2010, www.salisburyfestival.co.uk).

Internet Access: The TI offers a single stand-up Internet terminal at no charge for a quick email check.

Laundry: Washing Well has full-service (£7–13 per load depending on size, 2-hour service, Mon–Sat 8:00–17:30) as well as self-service (Mon–Sat 16:00–21:00, Sun 7:00–20:00, last self-service wash one hour before closing; 28 Chipper Lane, tel. 01722/421-874).

Getting to the Stone Circles: You can get to Stonehenge from Salisbury on **The Stonehenge Tour** bus. Their distinctive red-and-black double-decker buses leave from the Salisbury train station and make a circuit to Stonehenge and Old Sarum (£11, £17.50 with Stonehenge admission, tickets good all day, buy ticket from driver, June–mid-Oct daily 9:30–17:00, 1–2/hr, none on June 21 due to solstice crowds, shorter hours off-season, 30 min from station to Stonehenge, tel. 01722/336-855, check www.thestonehengetour.info for timetable).

A **taxi** from Salisbury to Stonehenge costs about £40 (corral a few fellow tourists and share the cost, call for exact price, includes round-trip from Salisbury to Stonehenge plus an hour at the site, entry fee not included, tel. 01722/339-781 or mobile 07971-255-690, brian@salisburytaxis.co.uk, Brian MacNeillie).

For buses to Avebury's stone circle, see "Salisbury Connections," later.

Sights in Salisbury

▲▲Salisbury Cathedral—This magnificent cathedral, visible for miles around because of its huge spire (the tallest in England at 404 feet), is a wonder to behold. The surrounding enormous grassy field (called a "close") makes the Gothic masterpiece look even larger. What's more impressive is that all this was built in a mere 38 years—astonishingly fast for the Middle Ages. When the old hill town

NEAR BATH

of Sarum was moved down to the valley, its cathedral had to be replaced in a hurry. So, in 1220, the townspeople began building, and in 1258 their sparkling-new cathedral was ready for ribbon-cutting. Because the structure was built in just a few decades, its style is uniform, rather than the patchwork of styles common in cathedrals of the time (which often took centuries to construct).

Cost and Hours: £5 suggested donation; mid-June–Aug Mon–Sat 7:15–19:15, Sun 7:15–18:15; Sept–mid-June daily 7:15–18:15; Chapter House usually opens Mon–Sat at 9:30, Sun at 12:45, closes 30–45 min before the rest of the cathedral, and closes entirely for special events; choral evensong Mon–Sat at 17:30, Sun at 15:00; excellent cafeteria, tel. 01722/555-120, recorded info tel. 01722/555-113, www.salisburycathedral.org.uk. This working cathedral opens early for services—be respectful if you arrive when one is in session.

Tower Tours: Imagine building a cathedral on this scale before the invention of cranes, bulldozers, or modern scaffolding. An excellent tower tour (1.5–2 hours) helps visitors understand how it was done. You'll climb in between the stone arches and the roof to inspect the vaulting and trussing; see a medieval winch that was used in the construction; and finish with the 330-step climb up the narrow tower for a sweeping view of the Wiltshire countryside (£8; early June–Aug Mon–Sat at 11:15, 14:15, 15:15, and 17:00, Sun at 14:15 and 16:15; May–early June and Sept Mon–Sat at 11:15, 14:15, and 15:15, Sun at 14:15 and 16:15; fewer off-season but usually one at 14:15, no tours in Dec except Christmas week; maximum 12 people, can reserve by calling 01722/555-156).

◑ **Self-Guided Tour:** You'll feel the architectural harmony the moment you enter the church. Volunteer guides posted at the entry are ready to answer your questions. (Free guided tours of the cathedral nave are offered—about twice hourly—when enough people assemble.)

As you look down the nave, notice how the stone columns march identically down the aisle, like a thick gray forest of tree trunks. The arches overhead soar to grand heights, helping church-goers appreciate the vast and amazing heavens.

From the entrance, head to the far wall (the back-left corner). You'll find a model showing how this cathedral was built so quickly in the 13th century. Next to that is the "oldest working clock in existence," dating from the 14th century (the hourly bell has been removed, so as not to interrupt worship services). On the wall by the clock is a bell from the decommissioned ship HMS *Salisbury*. Look closely inside the bell to see the engraved names of crew members' children who were baptized on the ship.

Wander down the aisle past monuments and knights' tombs. When you get to the transept, examine the columns where the arms of the church cross. These posts were supposed to support a more modest bell tower, but when a heavy tower was added 100 years later, the columns bent under the enormous weight, causing the tower to lean sideways. Although the posts were later reinforced, the tower still tilts about 2.5 feet.

Continue down the left side of the choir, and dip into the Morning Chapel. At the back of this chapel, find the spectacular glass prism engraved with images of Salisbury—donated to the church in memory of a soldier who died at the D-Day landing at Normandy.

The oldest part of the church is at the apse (far end), where construction began in 1220: the Trinity Chapel. The giant, modern stained-glass window ponders the theme "prisoners of conscience."

After you leave the nave, pace the cloister and follow signs to the medieval **Chapter House.** All English cathedrals have a chapter house, so called because it's where the daily Bible verse, or chapter, is read. These spaces often served as gathering places for conducting church or town business. Here you can see a modest display of cathedral items plus one must-see display: one of the four original copies of the Magna Carta, a document as important to the British as the Constitution is to Americans. This "Great Charter," dating from 1215, settled a dispute between the slimy King John and some powerful barons. Revolutionary for limiting the monarch's power, the Magna Carta constitutionally guaranteed that the monarch was not above the law. This was one of the first major victories in the long battle between monarchs and nobles.

▲**Cathedral Close**—The enormous green surrounding the cathedral is the largest in England, and one of the loveliest. It's cradled in

the elbow of the River Avon and ringed by row houses, cottages, and grand mansions. The church owns the houses on the green and rents them to lucky people with holy connections. A former prime minister, Edward Heath, lived on the green, not because of his political influence, but because he was once the church organist.

The benches scattered around the green are an excellent place for having a romantic moonlit picnic or for gazing thoughtfully at the leaning spire. Although you may be tempted to linger until it's late, don't—this is still private church property, and the heavy medieval gates of the close shut at about 23:00.

A few houses are open to the public, such as the overpriced Mompesson House and the medieval Wardrobe. The most interesting attraction is the...

▲**Salisbury and South Wiltshire Museum**—Occupying the building just opposite the cathedral entry, this eclectic, sprawling collection was heralded by travel writer Bill Bryson as one of England's best. While that's a stretch, the museum does offer a little something for everyone, including exhibits on local archaeology and history, a costume gallery, the true-to-its-name "Salisbury Giant" puppet once used by the tailors' guilds during parades, some J. M. W. Turner paintings of the cathedral interior, and a collection of exquisite Wedgwood china and other ceramics. The highlight is the "Stonehenge Gallery," with informative and interactive exhibits explaining the ancient structure. Since there's not yet a good visitors center at the site itself, this makes for a good pre- or post-Stonehenge activity (£6, Mon–Sat 10:00–17:00, July–Aug Sun 12:00–17:00, Sept–June closed Sun, 65 The Close, tel. 01722/332-151, www.salisburymuseum.org.uk).

Sleeping in Salisbury

Salisbury's town center has very few affordable accommodations, and I've listed them below—plus a couple of good choices a little farther out. The town gets particularly crowded during the arts festival (late May–early June).

$$ Cricket Field House, outside of town on A36 toward Wilton, overlooks a cricket pitch and golf course. It has 17 clean, comfortable rooms, a gorgeous garden, and plenty of parking (Sb-£60–68, Db-£70–95, Tb-£105–120, Qb-£100–130, price depends on season, Wilton Road, tel. & fax 01722/322-595, www.cricket fieldhouse.co.uk, cricketfieldcottage@btinternet.com, Brian and Margaret James). Though this place works best for drivers, it's just a 15-minute walk from the train station or a five-minute bus ride from the city center.

$$ Sarum College is a theological college renting 48 rooms in its building right on the peaceful Cathedral Close. Much of the year, it houses visitors to the college, but it usually has rooms for tourists as well—except the week after Christmas, when they close. The slightly institutional but clean rooms share hallways with libraries, bookstores, and offices, and the five attic rooms come with grand cathedral views (S-£45, Sb-£60, D-£70, Db-£95–105 depending on size, meals available at additional cost, elevator, 19 The Close, tel. 01722/424-800, fax 01722/338-508, www.sarum .ac.uk, hospitality@sarum.ac.uk).

$ Spire House B&B, just off the Cathedral Close, is classy and cozy. The four bright, surprisingly quiet rooms come with busy wallpaper, and three have canopied beds (Db-£75, Tb-£85, cash only, no kids under age 8, free Wi-Fi, 84 Exeter Street,

tel. 01722/339-213, www.salisbury-bedandbreakfast.com, spire
.enquiries@btinternet.com, friendly Lois).

$ Cathedral View B&B, with four rooms next door at #83,
is simpler, but still offers a good value in an outstanding location
(Db-£75, Tb-£90, cash only, 2-night minimum on weekends, no
kids under age 10, free Wi-Fi, 83 Exeter Street, tel. 01722/502-
254, www.cathedral-viewbandb.co.uk, enquiries@cathedral-view
bandb.co.uk, Wenda and Steve).

$ Premier Inn, just two miles from the city center, offers
dozens of prefab and predictable rooms ideal for drivers and families (Db-£65, more during special events, 2 kids ages 15 and under
sleep free, breakfast-£5–8, pay Wi-Fi, possible noise from nearby
trains, off roundabout at A30 and Pearce Way, toll tel. 08701-977-
225, fax 01722/337-889, www.premierinn.com).

Eating in Salisbury

There are plenty of atmospheric pubs all over town. For the best
variety of restaurants, head to the Market Square area. Many
places offer great "early bird" specials before 20:00.

Charter 1227, an upstairs eatery overlooking Market Square,
is a handy place for a nice meal (£10 two-course lunch, £12.27
three-course early-bird dinner before 19:00, open Tue–Sat 12:00–
14:30 & 18:00–21:30, closed Sun–Mon, dinner reservations smart,
6 Ox Row, tel. 01722/333-118).

The Haunch of Venison, possibly dating back to 1320, is a
Salisbury institution with creaky, crooked floors and the mummi-
fied hand of a cheating card player on display (actually a replica; to
the left of the fireplace in the House of Lords room). Downstairs,
the "occasionally haunted" half-timbered pub serves nouvelle pub
grub (£5–8 meals). The restaurant upstairs, while a little preten-
tious, has a good reputation for its traditional fare (£8–13 main
dishes; pub open Mon–Sat 11:00–23:00, Sun 12:00–22:00, food
served 12:00–14:30 & 18:00–21:00, reservations smart for dinner, 1
Minster Street, tel. 01722/411-313).

Reeve the Baker, with a branch just up the street from the
TI, crafts an array of high-calorie delights and handy pick-me-
ups for a fast and affordable lunch. The long cases of pastries and
savory treats will make you drool (Mon–Fri 8:00–17:30, Sat 8:00–
17:00, Sun 10:00–16:00, cash only; one location is next to the TI
at 2 Butcher Row, another is at the corner of Market and Bridge
Streets at 61 Silver Street, tel. 01722/320-367).

Anokaa is a splurge that's highly acclaimed for its updated
Indian cuisine. You won't find the same old chicken *tikka* here,
but clever newfangled variations on Indian themes, dished up in

a dressy contemporary setting (£9–15 main dishes, £8 lunch buffet, daily 12:00–14:00 & 17:30–22:30, 60 Fisherton Street, tel. 01722/414-142).

The King's Head Inn is a youthful chain pub with a big, open, modern interior and fine outdoor seating overlooking the pretty little River Avon. Its extensive menu has something for everyone (£3–4 sandwiches, £5–8 main dishes, Mon–Fri 7:00–24:00, Sat–Sun 8:00–24:00, kids welcome during the day but they must order meals by 20:30, free Wi-Fi, 1 Bridge Street, tel. 01722/342-050).

Salisbury Connections

From Salisbury by Train to: London's Waterloo Station (1–2/hr, 1.5 hrs), **Bath** (1–2/hr, 1 hr), **Oxford** (2/hr, 2 hrs, 1–2 transfers), **Portsmouth** (hourly, 1.25–1.75 hrs, possible transfers in Southampton and Havant), **Exeter** (1–2/hr, 1.5–3.5 hrs, some require transfers), **Penzance** (roughly hourly, 5–6 hrs, 1–3 transfers). Train info: toll tel. 0845-748-4950, www.nationalrail.co.uk.

By Bus to: Bath (hourly, 2.75 hrs, transfer in Warminster, www.travelinesw.com; or one direct bus/day at 10:35, 1.5 hrs on National Express #300, toll tel. 0871-781-8181, www.national express.com), **Avebury** (1–2/hr, 1.5–2.5 hrs, transfer in Devizes, Pewsey, or Marlborough, www.travelinesw.com). Many of Salisbury's long-distance buses are run by Wilts & Dorset (tel. 01722/336-855, www.wdbus.co.uk). National Express buses go once a day to **Bath** (morning only at 10:35, 1.5 hrs) and **Portsmouth** (at 15:00 or 18:25, 1.5 hrs, possible change at Southampton).

Near Salisbury

Old Sarum

Right here, on a hill overlooking the plain below, is where the original town of Salisbury was founded many centuries ago. Though little remains of the old town, the view of the valley is amazing...and a little imagination can transport you back to *very* olde England.

Human settlement in this area stretches back to the Bronze Age, and the Romans, Saxons, and Normans all called this hilltop home. From about 500 B.C. through A.D. 1220, Old Sarum flourished, giving rise to a motte-and-bailey castle, a cathedral, and scores of wooden homes along the town's outer ring. The town grew so quickly that by the Middle Ages it had outgrown its spot on the hill. In 1220, the local bishop successfully petitioned to move the entire city to the valley below, where space and water was plentiful. So, stone by stone, Old Sarum was packed up and shipped to New Sarum, where builders used nearly all the rubble from the old city to create a brand-new town with a magnificent cathedral.

Old Sarum was eventually abandoned altogether, leaving only a few stone foundations. The grand views of Salisbury from here have "in-spired" painters for ages and provided countless picnickers with a scenic backdrop: Grab a sandwich or snacks from one of the grocery stores in Salisbury or at the excellent Waitrose supermarket on the road between Salisbury and Sarum (Old Sarum entry-£3.50, daily July–Aug 9:00–18:00, April–June and Sept 10:00–17:00, Feb–March and Oct 10:00–16:00, Nov–Jan 11:00–15:00, last entry 30 min before closing, 2 miles north of Salisbury off A345, accessible by Wilts & Dorset bus #5 or #6 or via the Stonehenge Tour Bus—see page 249, tel. 01722/335-398, www.english-heritage.org.uk).

Wilton House

This sprawling estate, with a grand mansion and lush gardens, has been owned by the Earls of Pembroke since King Henry VIII's time. Inside the mansion you'll find a collection of paintings by Rubens, Rembrandt, Van Dyck, and Brueghel, along with quirky odds and ends, such as a lock of Queen Elizabeth I's hair. The perfectly proportioned Double Cube Room has served as everything from a 17th-century state dining room to a secret D-Day planning room during World War II...if only the portraits could talk. The Old Riding School houses a skippable 20-minute film that dramatizes the history of the Pembroke family. Outside, classic English gardens feature a river lazily winding its way through grasses and under Greek-inspired temples. Jane Austen fans particularly enjoy this stately home, where parts of 2005's Oscar-nominated *Pride & Prejudice* were filmed. But, alas, Mr. Darcy has checked out (house and gardens-£12, gardens only-£5; house open Easter weekend and May–Aug Sun–Thu 12:00–17:00, last entry 45 min before closing, closed Sat except holiday weekends; gardens open 2 weeks in mid-April and May–Aug daily 11:00–17:30, Sept Sat–Sun 11:00–17:30, last entry one hour before closing; house and gardens closed Oct–April, except house open Easter weekend and gardens open mid-April; 5 miles west of Salisbury via A36 to Wilton's Minster Street; or bus #60, #60A, or #61 from Salisbury to Wilton; tel. 01722/746-729 or 01722/746-714, www.wiltonhouse.com).

Stourhead

For a serious taste of traditional English landscape, don't miss this 2,650-acre delight. Stourhead, designed by owner Henry Hoare II in the mid-18th century, is a wonderland of rolling hills, meandering paths, placid lakes, and colorful trees, punctuated by classically inspired bridges and monuments. It's what every other English estate aspires to be—like nature, but better (house and garden-£11.60, or £7 to see just one; house open mid-March–Oct Fri–Tue 11:00–17:00, closed Wed–Thu; garden open year-round daily 9:00–18:00, 28 miles west of Salisbury off B3092 in town of Stourton, 3 miles northwest of Mere, tel. 01747/841-152, www.nationaltrust.org.uk).

Drivers or ambitious walkers can visit nearby **King Alfred's Tower,** and climb its 205 steps for glorious views of the estate and surrounding countryside (£2.50 to climb tower; April–Aug Fri–Tue 11:00–17:00, closed Wed–Thu; Sept–Oct Sat–Sun only 11:00–17:00; closed Nov–March; 2.5 miles northwest of Stourhead, off Tower Road).

Dorset Countryside Joyride

The region of Dorset, just southwest of Salisbury, is full of rolling fields, winding country lanes, quaint cottages, and villages stuffed with tea shops. Anywhere you go in the area will take you someplace charming, so consider this tour only a suggestion and feel free to get pleasantly lost in the English countryside. You'll be taking some less-traveled roads, so bring along a good map.

Starting in Salisbury, take A354 through Blandford Forum to Winterborne Whitechurch. From here, follow signs and small back roads to the village of Bere Regis, where you'll find some lovely 15th-century buildings, including one with angels carved on the roof. Follow A35 and B3075 to Wareham, where T. E. Lawrence (a.k.a. Lawrence of Arabia) lived; he's buried in nearby Moreton. Continue south on A351 to the dramatic and romantic **Corfe Castle.** This was a favorite residence for medieval kings until it was destroyed by a massive gunpowder blast during a 17th-century siege (£5.50, daily April–Sept 10:00–18:00, March and Oct 10:00–17:00, Nov–Feb 10:00–16:00, tel. 01929/481-294, www.nationaltrust.org.uk). Retrace A351 to Wareham, and then take A352 to Dorchester.

Just northeast of Dorchester on A35, near the village of Stinsford, novelist Thomas Hardy was born in 1840; you'll find his family's cottage nearby in Higher Bockhampton (£3.50, mid-March–Oct Sun–Thu 11:00–17:00, closed Fri–Sat and Nov–mid-March, tel. 01305/262-366, www.nationaltrust.org.uk). Although Hardy's heart is buried in Stinsford with his first wife, Emma, the rest of him is in Westminster Abbey's Poets' Corner. Take A35 back to Dorchester. Just west of Dorchester, stay on A35 until it connects to A37; then follow A352 north toward Sherborne.

About eight miles north of Dorchester, on the way to Sherborne, you'll find the little town of **Cerne Abbas,** named for an abbey in the center of town. There are only two streets to wander, so take this opportunity to recharge with a cup of tea and a scone. Abbots Tea Room has a nice cream tea (pot of tea,

Dorset Joyride

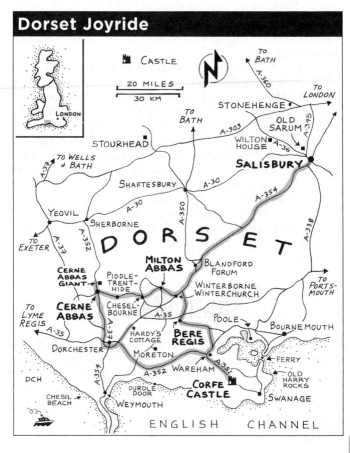

scone, jam, and clotted cream). They also run a B&B (Db-£70–80, less for 2-night stays, cash only, 7 Long St., tel. 01300/341-349, abbots@3Lambs.com). Up the street, you can visit the abbey and its well, reputed to have healing powers.

Just outside of town, a large chalk figure, the **Cerne Abbas Giant,** is carved into the green hillside. Chalk figures such as this one can be found in many parts of the region. Because the soil is only a few inches deep, the overlying grass and dirt can easily be removed to expose the bright white chalk bedrock beneath, creating the outlines. While nobody is sure exactly how old the figures are, or what their original purpose was, they are faithfully maintained by the locals, who mow and clear the fields at least once a year. This particular figure, possibly a fertility god, looks friendly...maybe a little too friendly. Locals claim that if a woman who's having trouble getting pregnant sleeps on the giant for one night, she will soon be able to conceive a child. (A couple of years ago, controversy surrounded this giant, as a 180-foot-tall, donut-hoisting Homer Simpson was painted onto the adjacent hillside. No kidding.)

Leaving Cerne Abbas on country roads toward Piddletrenthide (on the aptly named River Piddle), continue through Cheselbourne to **Milton Abbas.** (This area, by the way, has some of the best town names in the country, such as Droop, Plush, Pleck, and Folly.) The village of Milton Abbas looks overly perfect. In the 18th century, a wealthy man bought up the town's large abbey and estate. His new place was great...except for the neighbors, a bunch of vulgar villagers with houses that cluttered his view from the garden. So he had the town demolished and rebuilt a mile away. What you see now is probably the first planned community, with identical houses, a pub, and a church. The estate is now a "public school," which is what the British call an expensive private school. From Milton Abbas, signs lead you back to Winterborne Whitechurch, and the A354 to Salisbury.

South Wales

Although the best bits of Wales lie to the north (see North Wales chapter), there are a few worthwhile sights in the southern part of the country, not far from Bath (see map on page 224). Note that many of the sights mentioned here—including Caerphilly Castle, Chepstow Castle, and Tintern Abbey—are included in Wales' Explorer Pass (described on page 21). For more on Wales, see the Wales country introduction on page 454.

▲Cardiff and Nearby

The Welsh capital of Cardiff (pop. 320,000) has a newly renovated waterfront area, with shops and entertainment. It's also home to the 74,000-seat Millennium Stadium, which will see football (soccer) action during the 2012 London Summer Olympics.

Cardiff's helpful **TI** is located in the Old Library, a five-minute walk from Cardiff Castle and a 10-minute walk from the train station (Mon–Sat 9:30–18:00, Sun 10:00–16:00, The Hayes, toll tel. 08701-211-258, www.visitcardiff.com). They have Internet access (£1/30 min) and storage lockers (small-£3, large-£5, both require refundable £3 deposit, lockers open Mon–Sat 9:30–17:30, Sun 10:00–15:30).

Cardiff Castle (Castell Caerdydd)

A visit to Cardiff's castle is interesting only if you catch one of the entertaining tours of the interior. With its ornate clock tower, the castle is the latest in a series of fortresses erected on the site by Romans, Normans, and assorted British lords. The interior is a Victorian fantasy, and there's a visitors center, with a film and exhibits.

Cost and Hours: £12 with 50-min tour, £9 without tour, tours at least every 20 min, free audioguide with either ticket, daily March–Oct 9:00–18:00, Nov–Feb 9:00–17:00, last tour and entry one hour before closing, tel. 02920/878-100, www.cardiffcastle.com.

▲▲St. Fagans National History Museum/ Amgueddfa Werin Cymru (Museum of Welsh Life)

This best look at traditional Welsh folk life has three sections: open-air folk museum, main museum (which you walk through as you enter), and castle/garden. Outside, in a 100-acre park that surrounds a castle, you'll find displays of more than 40 carefully reconstructed old houses from all corners of this little country. Each house is fully furnished and comes equipped with a local expert warming up beside a toasty fire, happy to tell you anything you want to know about life in this old cottage. Ask questions!

Cost and Hours: Free, parking-£2.50, daily 10:00–17:00, tel. 02920/573-500, www.museumwales.ac.uk/en/stfagans. While

everything is well-explained, the £2 museum guidebook (or 30p map)—available at the information desk as you enter—is a good investment. If you see construction in process, it's to build more storage for the museum's sizable collection of artifacts.

Getting There: To get from the Cardiff train station to the museum in the village of St. Fagans, catch bus #32 (9/day, 6/day Sun, 20 min, toll tel. 0871-200-2233, www.traveline-cymru.info). Drivers leave M4 at Junction 33 and follow the signs. Leaving the museum, jog left on the freeway, take the first exit, and circle back, following signs to M4.

◐ Self-Guided Tour: If the sky's dry, see the scattering of houses first. Otherwise, in the main museum building, head to Gallery One, a recently renovated multimedia gallery with artifacts from Welsh life—including elaborately carved "love spoons" as well as new memorabilia near and dear to local hearts (such as mementos from triumphant rugby teams). Don't miss the costume exhibit, hidden behind a gallery of farming equipment. Spend an hour in the large building's fascinating museum.

Head outside, where a small train trundles among the exhibits from Easter to October (five stops, 50p/stop, whole circuit takes

45 min). The castle interior is royal enough and surrounded by a fine garden.

The highlight of the open-air museum is the Rhyd-y-Car 1805 row house, which displays ironworker cottages as they might have looked in 1805, 1855, 1895, 1925, 1955, and 1985, offering a fascinating zip through Welsh domestic life from hearths to microwaves.

Step into an old schoolhouse, a chapel, or a blacksmith's shop to see traditional craft makers in action. Head over to the farm and wander among the livestock and funky old outbuildings. Then beam a few centuries forward to the House for the Future, an optimistic projection of domestic life in Wales 50 years from now. The timber house blends traditional building techniques with new technologies aimed at sustainability. The roof collects water and soaks up solar energy. The earth that was removed to make way for the foundation was made into bricks that were then used in the structure.

Eating at St. Fagans: The coffee shop near the entrance and the restaurant upstairs are both handy, but you'll eat light lunches better, cheaper, and with more atmosphere in the park at the Gwalia Tea Room. The Plymouth Arms pub just outside the museum serves the best food.

▲Caerphilly Castle

The impressive but gutted old castle, spread over 30 acres, is the second largest in Europe after Windsor. English Earl Gilbert de Clare erected this squat behemoth to try to establish a stronghold in Wales. With two concentric walls, it was considered to be a brilliant arrangement of defensive walls and moats. Attackers had to negotiate three drawbridges and four sets of doors and portcullises just to reach the main entrance. For the record, there were no known successful enemy forays beyond the current castle's inner walls.

The castle has its own leaning tower—the split and listing tower reportedly out-leans Pisa's—and, some say, a resident ghost. Legend has it that de Clare, after learning of his wife Alice's infidelity, exiled her back to France and had her lover killed. Upon learning of her paramour's fate, Alice died of a broken heart. Since then, the "Green Lady," named for her husband's jealousy, has reportedly roamed the ramparts.

Exhibits at the castle display clever catapults, castle-dwellers' tricks for harassing intruders, and a good dose of Welsh history.

Cost and Hours: £3.70; April–Oct daily 9:00–17:00; Nov–

March Mon–Sat 9:30–16:00, Sun 11:00–16:00; last entry 30 min before closing, tel. 02920/883-143, www.cadw.wales.gov.uk.

Getting There: The town of Caerphilly—the castle is located right in the center—is nine miles north of Cardiff. To get there, take the train from Cardiff to Caerphilly (2–4/hr, 20 min) and walk five minutes. It's 20 minutes by car from St. Fagans (exit #32, following signs from M4).

Chepstow, Tintern, and Nearby

If you're seduced into spending the night in this charming area, you'll find plenty of B&Bs near the Tintern Abbey, or in the castle-crowned town of Chepstow, located just down the road (a one-hour drive from Bath).

The **Chepstow TI** is helpful (daily Easter–early Oct 9:30–17:00, off-season 10:00–15:30, Bridge Street, tel. 01291/623-772, www .visitwyevalley.com). Pick

up the £1.50 *Chepstow Town Trail* guide for a 21-stop, 1.5-hour stroll around the village. The walk begins at the town gate, where, in medieval times, folks arriving to sell goods or livestock were hit up for tolls.

The **Tintern TI,** north of the abbey and the village of Tintern, is housed within a former railway station (April–Oct daily 10:30–17:30, closed Nov–March, café, railway exhibit, The Old Station, tel. 01291/689-566, www .visitwyevalley.com).

Chepstow Castle

Perched on a hill overlooking the pleasant village of Chepstow on one side and the Wye River on the other, this castle is worth a short stop for drivers heading for Tintern Abbey, or a 10-minute walk from the Chepstow train station (uphill going back).

The stone-built bastion dating to 1066 was among the first castles the Normans plunked down to secure their turf in Wales,

and it remained in use through 1690. While many castles of the time were built first in wood, Chepstow, then a key foothold on the England–Wales border, was built from stone from the start for durability. As you clamber along the battlements, you'll find architectural evidence of military

NEAR BATH

renovations through the centuries, from Norman to Tudor right up through Cromwellian additions. You can tell which parts date from Norman days—they're the ones made of yellow sandstone instead of the grayish limestone that makes up the rest of the castle.

Cost and Hours: £3.70; April–Oct daily 9:00–17:00; Nov–March Mon–Sat 9:30–16:00, Sun 11:00–16:00; last entry 30 min before closing, guidebook-£3.50, in Chepstow village a half-mile from train station, tel. 01291/624-065, www.cadw.wales.gov.uk.

▲▲Tintern Abbey

Inspiring monks to prayer, William Wordsworth to poetry, J. M. W. Turner to a famous painting, and rushed tourists to a thoughtful moment, this verse-worthy ruined-castle-of-an-abbey merits a five-mile detour off the motorway. Founded in 1131 on a site chosen by Norman monks for its tranquility, it functioned as an austere Cistercian abbey until its dissolution in 1536. The monks followed a strict schedule. They rose several hours after midnight for the first of eight daily prayer sessions, and spent the rest of their time studying, working the surrounding farmlands, and meditating. Dissolved under Henry VIII's Act of Suppression in 1536, the magnificent church moldered in relative obscurity until tourists in the Romantic era (mid-18th century) discovered the wooded Wye valley and abbey ruins. J. M. W. Turner made his first sketches in 1792, and William Wordsworth penned "Lines Composed a Few Miles Above Tintern Abbey..." in 1798.

Most of the external walls of the 250-foot-long, 150-foot-wide church still stand, along with the exquisite window tracery and outlines of the sacristy, chapter house, and dining hall. The daylight that floods through the roofless ruins highlights the Gothic decorated arches—in those days a bold departure from Cistercian simplicity.

It's flooded with tourists in the summer, so visit early or late to miss the biggest crowds. The abbey's shop sells Celtic jewelry and other gifts. Take an easy 15-minute walk up to St. Mary's Church for a view of England just over the River Wye.

Cost and Hours: £3.70; April–Oct daily 9:00–17:00; Nov–March Mon–Sat 9:30–16:00, Sun 11:00–16:00; last entry 30 min before closing, occasional summertime events in the cloisters (check website for schedule), tel. 01291/689-251, www.cadw.wales.gov.uk.

Getting There: From Cardiff, catch a 40-minute train to Chepstow; from there, take a 20-minute ride on bus #69 (runs every 2 hrs) or a taxi to the abbey.

▲Wye River Valley and Forest of Dean

This land is lush, mellow, and historic. Local tourist brochures explain the Forest of Dean's special dialect, its strange political autonomy, and its oaken ties to Trafalgar and Admiral Nelson.

Sleeping: **$$ Florence Country House Hotel,** snuggled in the lower Wye Valley north of Tintern on the way to Monmouth,

 is located just off the 177-mile-long Offa's Dyke Path. On a nice day, hotel guests can eat on the garden terrace of this 17th-century hotel and share the scenery with the cows lazing along the riverbanks (Sb-£35–38, Db-£70–76, request river view, includes breakfast, no kids under 10, tel. 01594/530-830, www.florencehotel.co.uk, enquiries@florencehotel.co.uk, kind owners Dennis and Kathy).

For a medieval night, check into the **$ St. Briavels Castle B&B/Youth Hostel** (70 beds, £16–19 beds in 4- to 16-bed dorms, non-members-£3 extra, includes breakfast, private 4- to 8-bed rooms available, reception daily 8:00–10:00 & 17:00–23:00, hostel closed to guests daily 10:00–17:00, curfew at 23:30, kitchen and lounge, brown-bag lunches and evening meals available, toll tel. 0845-371-9042 or 0870-770-6040, www.yha.org.uk, stbriavels @yha.org.uk).

Eating: The **hostel** hosts medieval banquets on most Wednesday and Saturday nights in summer (£15, for hostel guests only, ask staff for schedule). An 800-year-old Norman castle used by King John in 1215 (the year he signed the Magna Carta), the hostel is comfortable (as castles go), friendly, and in the center of the quiet village of St. Briavels just north of Tintern Abbey. For dinner, eat at the hostel or walk "just down the path and up the snyket" to **The Crown Inn** (decent food and local pub atmosphere).

Cardiff Connections

From Cardiff by Train to: Caerphilly (2–4/hr, 20 min), **Bath** (hourly, 1–1.5 hrs), **Birmingham** (2–3/hr, 2 hrs, some change in Bristol, once an hour direct), **London** (2/hr, 2 hrs, to London Paddington), **Chepstow** (about hourly, 40 min; then bus #69 to Tintern—runs every 2 hrs, 20 min). Train info: toll tel. 0871-200-2233, www.traveline-cymru.info.

Route Tips for Drivers

Bath to South Wales: Leave Bath following signs for A4, then M4. It's 10 miles north (on A46 past a village called Pennsylvania) to the M4 freeway. Zip westward, crossing a huge suspension bridge into Wales (£5.10 toll westbound only). Stay on M4 (not

NEAR BATH

THE COTSWOLDS

The Cotswold Hills, a 25-by-90-mile chunk of Gloucestershire, are dotted with enchanting villages and graced with England's greatest countryside palace, Blenheim. As with many fairy-tale regions of Europe, the present-day beauty of the Cotswolds was the result of an economic disaster. Wool was a huge industry in medieval England, and Cotswold sheep grew the best wool. A 12th-century saying bragged, "In Europe the best wool is English. In England the best wool is Cotswold." The region prospered. Wool money built fine towns and houses. Local "wool" churches are called "cathedrals" for their scale and wealth. Stained-glass slogans say things like "I thank my God and ever shall, it is the sheep hath paid for all."

With the rise of cotton and the Industrial Revolution, the woolen industry collapsed. Ba-a-a-ad news. The wealthy Cotswold towns fell into a depressed time warp; the homes of impoverished nobility became gracefully dilapidated. Today, visitors enjoy a harmonious blend of man and nature—the most pristine of English countrysides decorated with time-passed villages, rich wool churches, tell-me-a-story stone fences, and "kissing gates" you wouldn't want to experience alone. Appreciated by throngs of 21st-century Romantics, the Cotswolds are enjoying new prosperity.

The north Cotswolds are best. Two of the region's coziest towns, Chipping Campden and Stow-on-the-Wold, are eight and four miles, respectively, from Moreton-in-Marsh, which has the best public transportation connections. Any of these three towns makes a fine home base for your exploration of the thatch-happiest of Cotswold villages and walks.

Planning Your Time

The Cotswolds are an absolute delight by car and, with patience, enjoyable even without a car. On a three-week British trip, I'd spend two nights and a day in the Cotswolds. The Cotswolds' charm has a softening effect on many uptight itineraries. You could enjoy days of walking from a home base here.

Chipping Campden and Stow-on-the-Wold are quaint without being overrun, and both have good accommodations. Stow has a bit more character for an overnight stay, and offers the widest range of choices. The plain town of Moreton is the only one of the three with a train station. With a car, consider really getting away from it all by staying in one of the smaller villages.

If you want to take in some Shakespeare, note that Stow, Chipping Campden, and Moreton are only a 30-minute drive from Stratford, which offers a great evening of world-class entertainment (see Stratford-upon-Avon chapter).

One-Day Driver's 100-Mile Cotswold Blitz, Including Blenheim: Use a good map and reshuffle to fit your home base: 9:00–Browse through Chipping Campden, following the self-guided walk; 10:00–Joyride through Snowshill, Stanway, Stanton, the Slaughters, and Bourton-on-the-Water; 13:00–Have lunch at Stow-on-the-Wold, then follow the self-guided walk; 15:00–Drive 30 miles to Blenheim Palace and take the hour-long tour (last tour departs at 16:45); 18:00–Drive home for just the right pub dinner. (If planning on a gourmet countryside pub dinner, reserve in advance by phone.)

Two-Day Plan by Public Transportation: This plan is best for weekdays, when buses run more frequently than on weekends. Make your home base in Moreton-in-Marsh.

Day 1: Take the early bus to Chipping Campden, then bus to Stow (via Moreton). Rent a bike in Stow and explore the countryside, or take a bus to Bourton-on-the-Water and walk to the Slaughters. Have an early dinner in Stow, then return to Moreton at 18:45.

Day 2: Take a day trip to Blenheim Palace via Oxford (train to Oxford, bus to palace); or rent a bike and ride to Chastleton House; or take a day-long countryside walk.

Getting Around the Cotswolds
By Bus

The Cotswolds are so well preserved, in part, because public transportation to and within this area has long been miserable.

To explore the towns, use the bus routes that hop through the region nearly hourly, lacing together main stops and ending at rail stations. In each case, there are about eight buses per day; the entire trip takes about an hour; and on some routes you can get an all-day, unlimited Rover Ticket (£6, individual fares about £2, buy

The Cotswolds

1 Stanway House
2 Snowshill Lavender
3 Sheepscombe House B&B
4 Hidcote Manor Garden
5 Cotswold Farm Park
6 Chastleton House

— MAJOR ROAD
— MINOR ROAD
···· COTSWOLD WAY FOOTPATH

DCH

Rover Ticket from driver on participating routes, including #855, #860, and #865). With the help of the TI or the Traveline info line (toll tel. 0871-200-2233), you can put together a one-way or return trip by public transportation, making for a fine Cotswolds day. Ask the TI for the *Explore the Cotswolds by Public Transport* timetables, which summarize all of the bus routes in the area in separate central, north, and south editions (or download them at www.cotswoldsaonb.org.uk). If you're traveling one-way between two train stations, remember that the Cotswold villages—generally pretty clueless when it comes to the needs of travelers without a car—have no baggage-check services. You'll need to improvise; ask sweetly at the nearest TI or business. Note that bus service is poor on Saturdays and essentially nonexistent on Sundays. For specifics, consult any TI, visit www.traveline.org.uk, or call 0871-200-2233.

While I've based this information on Moreton, you can derive Stow and Chipping Campden bus connections from this same write-up. Here are the bus lines that leave from Moreton:

From Moreton-in-Marsh to Chipping Campden: Buses #21 and #22 run from Moreton-in-Marsh to Chipping Campden to Stratford-upon-Avon. These are the only buses that go all the way through to Chipping Campden. (Bus #H3, which you may see on timetables, connects Stratford and Chipping Campden, but doesn't go all the way to Moreton.)

From Moreton-in-Marsh to Stow-on-the-Wold: Bus #855 goes from Moreton-in-Marsh to Stow-on-the-Wold to Bourton-on-the-Water to Northleach to Cirencester to the Kemble train station. Bus #801 goes from Moreton-in-Marsh to Stow-on-the-Wold to the Slaughters to Bourton-on-the-Water, and ends at Cheltenham.

By Bike

Despite narrow roads and high hedgerows (blocking some views), bikers enjoy the Cotswolds free from the constraints of bus schedules. For each area, TIs have fine route planners that indicate which peaceful, paved lanes are particularly scenic for biking. In summer, it's smart to book your bike rental a couple days ahead.

In **Moreton-in-Marsh,** the nice folks at the Toy Shop rent mountain bikes. You can stop in the shop to rent a bike, or call ahead to pick up or drop off at other times—they're flexible (£15/day with route maps, bike locks, and helmets; shop open Mon and Wed–Fri 9:00–13:00 & 14:00–17:00, Sat 9:00–17:00, closed Sun and Tue, High Street, tel. 01608/650-756).

In **Chipping Campden,** try Cotswold Country Cycles (£15/day, tandem-£30/day, includes helmets and route maps, delivery for a fee, daily 9:30–dusk, 2 miles north of town at Longlands Farm Cottage, tel. 01386/438-706, mobile 07746-107-728, www.cotswoldcountrycycles.com).

By Foot

Walking guidebooks abound, giving you a world of choices for each of my recommended stops (choose a book with clear maps). Villages are generally no more than three miles apart, and most have pubs

that would love to feed and water you. For a list of guided walks, ask at any TI for the free *Cotswold Lion* newspaper. The walks range from 2 to 12 miles, and often involve a stop at a pub or tearoom (April–Sept; Lion newspaper also online at www.cotswoldsaonb .org.uk—click on "Publications").

By Car

Distances here are wonderfully short (but only if you invest in the Ordnance Survey map of the Cotswolds, sold locally at TIs and newsstands). Here are distances from Moreton: **Broadway** (10 miles), **Chipping Campden** (8 miles), **Stratford-upon-Avon** (17 miles), **Warwick** (23 miles), **Stow** (4 miles), **Blenheim Palace** (20 miles).

Robinson Goss Self Drive, six miles north of Moreton-in-Marsh, offers £28–47 one-day rentals, including everything but gas. They're in the middle of nowhere, but may pick you up for a charge of about £1/mile (Mon–Fri 8:30–17:00, Sat 8:30–12:00, closed Sun, tel. 01608/663-322, www.robgos.co.uk).

Car hiking is great. In this chapter, I cover the postcard-perfect (but discovered) villages. With a car and the local Ordnance Survey map (Tour Map #8, £5), you can easily ramble about and find your own gems. The problem with having a car is that you are less likely to walk. Consider taking a taxi or bus somewhere, so that you can walk back to your car and enjoy the scenery.

By Taxi

Two or three town-to-town taxi trips can make more sense than renting a car. Though taking a cab cross-country seems extravagant (about £2.50/mile), the distances are short (Stow to Moreton is 4 miles, Stow to Chipping Campden is 10), and one-way walks are lovely. If you call a cab, confirm that the meter will start only when you are actually picked up. Consider hiring a cab at the hourly "touring rate" (£28–30), rather than the meter rate (e.g., £20 Stow to Chipping Campden). For a few more bucks, you can have a joyride peppered with commentary.

Note that the drivers listed below are not typical city taxi services (with many drivers on call), but are mostly individuals—it's smart to book ahead if you're arriving in high season, since they can book up in advance on weekends.

To scare up a driver in Moreton, call Richard at **Four Shires** (mobile 07747-802-555) or **Iain's Taxis** (mobile 07789-897-966, £30/hr); in Stow, call Iain (above) or **Tony Knight** (mobile 07887-714-047, £28/hr); and in Chipping Campden, call Iain (above) or **Cotswold**

Cotswold Appreciation 101

Much history can be read into the names of the area. *Cotswold* could come from the Saxon phrase meaning "hills of sheep's coats." Or it could mean shelter ("cot" like cottage) on the open upland ("wold").

In the Cotswolds, a town's main street (called High Street) needed to be wide to accommodate the sheep and cattle being marched to market (and, today, to park tour buses). Some of the most picturesque cottages were once humble row houses of weavers' cottages, usually located along a stream for their waterwheels (good examples in Bibury and Castle Combe). The towns run on slow clocks and yellowed calendars. An entire village might not have a phone booth.

Fields of yellow (rapeseed) and pale blue (linseed) separate pastures dotted with black and white sheep. In just about any B&B, when you open your window in the morning you'll hear sheep baaing. The decorative "toadstool" stones dotting front yards throughout the region are medieval staddle stones, which buildings were set upon to keep the rodents out.

Cotswold walls and roofs are made of the local limestone. The limestone roof tiles hang by pegs. To make the weight more bearable, the smaller, lighter tiles are higher up. An extremely strict building code keeps towns looking what many locals call "overly quaint."

Towns are small, and everyone seems to know everyone. The area is provincial yet ever-so-polite, and people commonly rescue themselves from a gossipy tangent by saying, "It's all very...mmm...yyya."

This is walking country. The English love their walks and vigorously defend their age-old right to free passage. Once a year the Rambling Society organizes a "Mass Trespass," when each of the country's 50,000 miles of public footpaths is walked. By assuring each path is used at least once a year, they stop landlords from putting up fences. Any paths found blocked are unceremoniously unblocked.

Questions to ask locals: Do you think foxhunting should have been banned? Who are the Morris men? What's a kissing gate?

Private Hire (mobile 07980-857-833, £28/hr). Tim Harrison at **Tour the Cotswolds** specializes in tours of the Cotswolds and its gardens (mobile 07779-030-820, www.tourthecotswolds.co.uk; Tim co-runs a recommended B&B in Snowshill—see page 281).

By Tour

Departing from Bath, **Mad Max Minibus Tours** offers a "Cotswold Discovery" full-day tour, and can drop you off in Stow with your luggage if you arrange it in advance (see page 199 of the Bath chapter).

While none of the Cotswold towns offers regularly scheduled walks, many have voluntary warden groups who love to meet visitors and give walks for just a small donation (about £2/person; specific contact information appears below for Chipping Campden).

Chipping Campden

Just touristy enough to be convenient, the north Cotswolds town of Chipping Campden (CAM-den) is a ▲▲ sight. This market town, once the home of the richest Cotswold wool merchants, has some incredibly beautiful thatched roofs. Both the great British historian G. M. Trevelyan and I call Chipping Campden's High Street the finest in England.

Orientation to Chipping Campden

(area code: 01386)
Walk the full length of High Street; its width is characteristic of market towns. Go around the block on both ends. On one end, you'll find impressively thatched homes (out Sheep Street, past the public WC and ugly gas station, and right on Westington Street). Walking north on High Street, you'll pass the Market Hall, the wavy roof of the first great wool mansion, a fine and free memorial garden, and, finally, the town's famous 15th-century Perpendicular Gothic "wool" church. (This route is the same as the self-guided town walk described below.)

Tourist Information

Chipping Campden's TI is tucked away in the old police station on High Street. Get the £1 town guide, which includes a map

(April–Oct daily 9:30–17:00; Nov–March Mon–Thu 10:00–13:00, Fri–Sun 10:00–16:00; tel. 01386/841-206, www.chippingcampden online.org).

Helpful Hints:

Internet Access: Try the occasionally open **library** (High Street, tel. 01386/840-692, www.gloucestershire.gov.uk/libraries) or **Butty's at The Old Bakehouse,** a casual eatery and Internet café (reasonably priced sandwiches and snacks, free Wi-Fi, pay Internet access-£1.50/15 min, £2.50/30 min, £4/hour, Mon–Sat 7:30–14:30, closed Sun, adjacent to the recommended The Old Bakehouse B&B on Lower High Street, tel. 01386/840-401).

Bike Rental: Call **Cotswold Country Cycles** (see "Getting Around the Cotswolds—By Bike," page 268).

Taxi: Try **Cotswold Private Hire** or **Tour the Cotswolds** (see "Getting Around the Cotswolds—By Taxi," page 269).

Parking: Find a spot anywhere along High Street and park for free with no time limit. There's also a pay-and-display lot (90-min maximum) on High Street (across from TI).

Tours: The local members of the **Cotswold Voluntary Wardens** would be happy to show you around town for a small donation to their conservation society (£2/person, 1-hour walk, walks July–Sept Wed at 14:30, meet at Market Hall). Tour guide and coordinator Ann Colcomb can help arrange for a walk on other days as well (tel. 01386/832-131, www.cotswoldsaonb.com).

Self-Guided Walk

Welcome to Chipping Campden

This 500-yard walk through "Campden" (as locals call their town) takes you from the TI to the church in about 30 minutes.

If it's open, begin at the **Magistrate's Court** (can be closed for meetings, events, and even weddings). This meeting room is in the old police station, located above the TI (free, same hours as TI, ask at TI to go up). Under the open-beamed courtroom, you'll find a humble little exhibit on the town's history.

Campden's most famous monument, the **Market Hall,** stands in front of the TI, marking the town center. It was built in 1627 by the 17th-century Lord of the Manor, Sir Baptist Hicks.

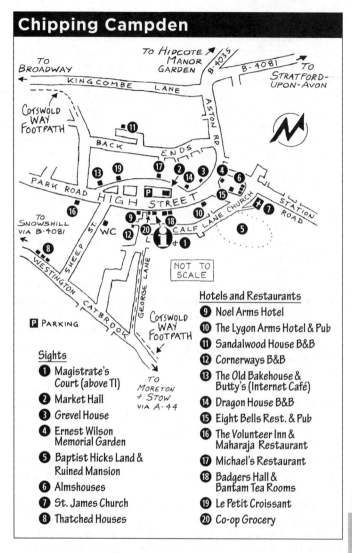

Chipping Campden

Sights

❶ Magistrate's Court (above TI)
❷ Market Hall
❸ Grevel House
❹ Ernest Wilson Memorial Garden
❺ Baptist Hicks Land & Ruined Mansion
❻ Almshouses
❼ St. James Church
❽ Thatched Houses

Hotels and Restaurants

❾ Noel Arms Hotel
❿ The Lygon Arms Hotel & Pub
⓫ Sandalwood House B&B
⓬ Cornerways B&B
⓭ The Old Bakehouse & Butty's (Internet Café)
⓮ Dragon House B&B
⓯ Eight Bells Rest. & Pub
⓰ The Volunteer Inn & Maharaja Restaurant
⓱ Michael's Restaurant
⓲ Badgers Hall & Bantam Tea Rooms
⓳ Le Petit Croissant
⓴ Co-op Grocery

P PARKING

THE COTSWOLDS

(Look for the Hicks family coat of arms on the building's facade.) Back then, it was an elegant—even over-the-top—shopping hall for the townsfolk who'd come here to buy their produce. In the 1940s, it was almost sold to an American, but the townspeople heroically raised money to buy it first, then gave it to the National Trust for its preservation.

The timbers inside are true to the original. Study the classic Cotswold stone roof, still held together with wooden pegs nailed in from underneath. (Tiles were cut and sold with peg holes, and stacked like waterproof scales.) Buildings all over the region still use these stone shingles. Today, the hall hosts local fairs.

Chipping Campden's **High Street** has changed little architecturally since 1840. (The town's street plan survives from the 12th century.) Notice the harmony of the long rows of buildings. While the street comprises different styles through the centuries, everything you see was made of the same Cotswold stone—the only stone allowed today.

To be level, High Street arcs with the contour of the hillside. Because the street is so wide, you know this was a market town. In past centuries, livestock and packhorses laden with piles of freshly shorn fleece would fill the streets. Campden was a sales and distribution center for the wool industry, and merchants from as far as Italy would come here for the prized raw wool.

High Street has no house numbers—people know the houses by their names. In the distance, you can see the town church (where this walk ends).

• *Hike up High Street to just before the first intersection.*

In 1367, William Grevel built what's considered Campden's first stone house: **Grevel House** (on the left). Sheep tycoons had big homes. Imagine back then, when this fine building was surrounded by humble wattle-and-daub huts. It had newfangled chimneys, rather than a crude hole in the roof. (No more rain inside!) Originally a "hall house" with just one big, tall room, it got its upper floor in the 16th century. The finely carved central bay window is a good early example of the Perpendicular Gothic style. The gargoyles scared away bad spirits—and served as rain spouts. The boot scrapers outside each door were fixtures in that muddy age—especially in market towns, where the streets were filled with animal dung.

• *Continue up High Street for about 100 yards. Go past Church Street (which we'll walk up later). Across the street, you'll find a small Gothic arch leading into a garden.*

The small and secluded **Ernest Wilson Memorial Garden,** once the church's vegetable patch, is now a botanist's delight. It's filled with well-labeled plants that the Victorian botanist Ernest Wilson brought back to England from his extensive travels in Asia. There's a complete history of the garden on the board to the left of the entry (free, open daily until dusk).

• *Backtrack to Church Street. Turn left, walk past the Eight Bells Inn, and head across the street.*

Sprawling adjacent to the town church, the area known as **Baptist Hicks Land** holds Hicks' huge estate and manor house. This influential Lord of the Manor was from "a family of substance," merchants of silk and fine clothing as well as moneylenders. Beyond the ornate gate, only a few outbuildings and the

THE COTSWOLDS

charred corner of his mansion survive. The mansion was burned by Royalists in 1645 during the Civil War—notice how Cotswold stone turns red when burned. Hicks housed the poor, making a show of his generosity, adding a long row of almshouses (with his family coat of arms) for neighbors to see as they walked to church. These almshouses (lining Church Street on the left) house pensioners today, as they have since the 17th century.

• *Walk along the wall that lines the Hicks estate to the church, where a scenic, tree-lined lane leads to the front door. On the way, notice the 12 lime trees, one for each of the apostles, that were planted in about 1760 (sorry, no limes).*

One of the finest churches in the Cotswolds, **St. James Church** graces one of its leading towns. Both the town and the church were built by wool wealth. The church is Perpendicular Gothic, with lots of light and strong verticality. Before you leave, notice the fine vestments and altar hangings behind protective blue curtains (near the back of the church). Tombstones pave the floor—memorializing great wool merchants through the ages.

At the altar is a brass relief of William Grevel, the first owner of the Grevel House (see above), and his wife. But it is Sir Baptist Hicks who dominates the church. His huge, canopied tomb is the ornate final resting place for Hicks and his wife, Elizabeth. Study their faces, framed by fancy lace ruffs (trendy in the 1620s).

Adjacent—as if in a closet—is a statue of their daughter, Lady Juliana, and her husband, Lutheran Yokels. Juliana commissioned the statue in 1642, when her husband died, but had it closed until *she* died in 1680. Then the doors were opened, revealing these two people living happily ever after—at least in marble. The hinges have likely been used only once.

Sleeping in Chipping Campden

(area code: 01386)

In Chipping Campden—as in any town in the Cotswolds—B&Bs offer a better value than hotels. Rooms are generally tight on Saturdays (when many charge a bit more and are reluctant to rent to one-nighters) and in September, which is considered a peak month. Parking is never a problem. Always ask for a discount if staying longer than one or two nights.

$$$ Noel Arms Hotel, the characteristic old hotel on the main square, has welcomed guests for 600 years. Its lobby is

Sleep Code

(£1 = about $1.60, country code: 44)
S = Single, **D** = Double/Twin, **T** = Triple, **Q** = Quad, **b** = bathroom,
s = shower only. Unless noted otherwise, you can assume credit cards are accepted.

To help you sort easily through these listings, I've divided the rooms into three categories based on the price for a standard double room with bath:

$$$ Higher Priced—Most rooms £90 or more.
$$ Moderately Priced—Most rooms between £65-90.
$ Lower Priced—Most rooms £65 or less.

decorated with ancient weaponry, and comes with a whiff of the medieval ages. Its 26 rooms are well-furnished with antiques (Sb-£95–115, standard Db-£130, bigger Db-£160, fancier four-poster Db-£180–200, midweek deals, some ground-floor doubles, includes breakfast, attached restaurant/bar, High Street, tel. 01386/840-317, fax 01386/841-136, www.noelarmshotel.com, reception@noel armshotel.com).

$$ The Lygon Arms Hotel, attached to the popular pub of the same name, has small public areas and 10 cheery, open-beamed rooms (one small older Db-£70–80, huge "superior" Db-£95–120, lovely courtyard Db-£130–160, lower prices are for midweek or multinight stays, family deals, free Wi-Fi, High Street, go through archway and look for hotel reception on the left, tel. 01386/840-318, www.lygonarms.co.uk, sandra@lygonarms.co.uk, Sandra Davenport).

$$ Sandalwood House B&B is a big, comfy home with a pink flowery lounge and a sprawling back garden. Just a five-minute walk from the center of town, it's in a quiet, woodsy, pastoral setting. Its two cheery, pastel rooms are bright and spacious (D/Db-£70–75, T-£90, cheaper if you order a light breakfast instead of full, self-catering apartment sleeps four-£400–500/week, cash only, no kids under age 10, free Wi-Fi, off-street parking, friendly Bobby the cat, tel. & fax 01386/840-091—preferred method of booking, Diana Bendall). To get to Sandalwood House, go west on High Street; at the church and the Volunteer Inn, turn right and then right again; look for a sign in the hedge on the left, and head up the long driveway.

$$ Cornerways B&B is a fresh, bright, and comfy modern home (not "oldie worldie") a block off High Street. It's run by the delightful Carole Proctor, who can "look out the window and see the church where we were married." The huge, light, airy loft rooms are great for families (Db-£70, Tb-£90, Qb-£110, 2-night minimum, £5 off for 3 or more nights, children's discount, cash only, free Wi-Fi, off-street parking, George Lane, just walk through the arch beside Noel Arms Hotel, tel. 01386/841-307, www.corner ways.info, carole@cornerways.info).

$$ The Old Bakehouse rents five small but pleasant rooms in a 600-year-old home with a plush fireplace lounge. Hardworking Sarah lives just up the road—phone ahead with an arrival time, or call her mobile phone if she's not there when you arrive (Sb-£45, Db-£70, family deals, £5 off for 2 or more nights, cash only, free Wi-Fi, fun attic room that sleeps up to 5 has beams running through it, Lower High Street, tel. & fax 01386/840-979, mobile 07702-359-530, www.chippingcampden-cotswolds.co.uk, oldbake house@chippingcampden-cotswolds.co.uk). In addition to the B&B, Sarah runs **Butty's at the Old Bakehouse,** a casual eatery and Internet café (see "Helpful Hints," earlier).

$ Dragon House B&B rents two tidy rooms—with medieval beams and a shared lounge—right on the center of High Street. They have laundry machines and a sumptuous, stay-awhile garden (Db-£65, £5 off for 3 or more nights, cash only, off-street parking available, near Market Hall, tel. & fax 01386/840-734, www.dragonhouse-chipping-campden.com, info@dragonhouse -chipping-campden.co.uk, Valerie and Graeme the potter). They also have a cottage that sleeps up to six (Sat to Sat only, £250–750/ week depending on month).

Eating in Chipping Campden

This town—so filled with wealthy residents and tourists—comes with lots of choices. Here are some local favorites:

Eight Bells is a charming 14th-century inn on Leysbourne with a classy and woody restaurant and a more colorful pub (£15–20 dinners, daily 12:00–14:00 & 18:30–21:00, reservations recommended, tel. 01386/840-371).

The Volunteer Inn serves Indian dishes in their **Maharaja** restaurant (£6–17 meals, daily 17:00–23:00, grassy courtyard out back, Lower High Street, tel. 01386/849-281). **The Lygon Arms** pub also has good food (£8–15 meals, daily).

Michael's, a fun Mediterranean restaurant on High Street, serves hearty portions and breaks plates at closing every Saturday night (Tue–Sun 10:30–14:30 & 19:00–22:00, closed Sun nights and Mon, tel. 01386/840-826).

Picnic: The **Co-op** grocery store is the town's small "supermarket" (Mon–Sat 7:00–22:00, Sun 7:00–20:00, across from the market and next to TI on High Street). Munch lunch across the street, on the benches on the little green.

Tearooms

To visit a cute tearoom, try one of these places, located in the town center.

Badgers Hall Tea Room is great for a wide selection of homemade cakes, crumbles, and scones. Along with light lunches, they serve an afternoon tea—a tall tray of dainty sandwiches, pastries, and scones with tea—for half the London price (£25 for 2 people, daily 10:00–16:30; also rents three rooms—Db-£98–110, 2-night minimum, no kids under age 10, Wi-Fi, High Street, tel. 01386/840-839, www.badgershall.com, Karen).

Bantam Tea Rooms, near the Market Hall, is also a good value (Mon–Sat 10:00–17:00, Sun 10:30–17:00, High Street, tel. 01386/840-386).

Le Petit Croissant, a cheery little French deli with a tearoom in the back, serves pastries, quiche, cheese, and wine (Mon–Fri 9:00–17:00, Sat 8:30–17:00, closed Sun, Lower High Street, tel. 01386/841-861).

Near Chipping Campden

Located to the west of Chipping Campden, these are my nominations for the cutest Cotswold villages. Like marshmallows in hot chocolate, Stanway, Stanton, and Snowshill nestle side by side, awaiting your arrival. (Note the Stanway House's limited hours when planning your visit.) Other easy-to-access sights to the west and north of Chipping Campden are also included below.

▲▲Stanway House

The Earl of Wemyss (pronounced "Weemz"), whose family tree charts relatives back to 1202, opens his melancholy home and grounds to visitors just two days a week in the summer. Walking through his house offers a unique glimpse into the lifestyles of England's eccentric and fading nobility.

Cost and Hours: £6, June–Aug Tue and Thu only 14:00–17:00, tel. 01386/584-469, www.stanwayfountain .co.uk. His lordship himself narrated the audioguide to his home (£2).

Getting There: By car, leave B4077 at a statue of (the Christian) George slaying the dragon (of pagan superstition); you'll round the corner and see the manor's fine 17th-century Jacobean gatehouse. There's no real public transportation to Stanway.

➋ **Self-Guided Tour:** Start with the grounds, then head into the house itself.

The Earl recently restored "the tallest fountain in Britain" on the grounds—300 feet tall, gravity-powered, and quite impressive (fountain spurts for 30 min at 14:45 and 16:00 on opening days).

The bitchin' Tithe Barn (near where you enter the grounds) dates to the 14th century, and predates the manor. It was originally where monks—in the days before money—would accept one-tenth of whatever the peasants produced. Peek inside: This is a great hall for village hoedowns. While the Tithe Barn is no longer used to greet motley peasants and collect their feudal "rents," the lord still gets rent from his vast landholdings, and hosts community fêtes in his barn.

Stepping into the obviously very lived-in palace, you're free to wander around pretty much as you like, but keep in mind that a family does live here. His lordship is often roaming about as well. The place feels like a time warp. Ask a staff member to demonstrate the spinning rent-collection table. In the great hall, marvel at the one-piece oak shuffleboard table and the 1780 Chippendale exercise chair (half an hour of bouncing on this was considered good for the liver).

The manor dogs have their own cutely painted "family tree," but the Earl admits that his last dog, C. J., was "all character and no breeding." Poke into the office. You can psychoanalyze the lord by the books that fill his library, the videos stacked in front of his bed (with the mink bedspread), and whatever's next to his toilet.

The place has a story to tell. And so do the docents stationed in each room—modern-day peasants who, even without family trees, probably have relatives going back just as far in this village. Really. Talk to these people. Probe. Learn what you can about this side of England.

From Stanway to Stanton: These towns are separated by a row of oak trees and grazing land, with parallel waves echoing the furrows plowed by medieval farmers. Centuries ago, farmers were allotted long strips of land called "furlongs." The idea was to dole out good and bad land equitably. (One square furlong equals an acre.) Over centuries of plowing these, furrows were formed. Let someone else drive, so you can hang out the window under a canopy of oaks, passing stone walls and sheep. Leaving Stanway on the road to Stanton, the first building you'll see (on the left, just outside Stanway) is a thatched cricket pavilion overlooking the village cricket green. Dating only from 1930, it's raised up (as medieval buildings were) on rodent-resistant staddle stones. Stanton's just ahead; follow the signs.

▲Stanton

Pristine Cotswold charm cheers you as you head up the main street of the village of Stanton. Stanton's **Church of St. Michael** betrays a pagan past. It's safe to assume any church dedicated to St. Michael (the archangel who fought the devil) sits upon a sacred pagan site. Stanton is actually at the intersection of two ley lines (geographic lines along which many prehistoric sights are found). You'll see St. Michael's well-worn figure (with a sundial) above the door as you enter. Inside, above the capitals in the nave, find the pagan symbols for the sun and the moon. Although the church probably dates back to the ninth century, today's building is mostly from the 15th century, with 13th-century transepts. On the north transept, medieval frescoes show faintly through the 17th-century whitewash. (Once upon a time, medieval frescoes were considered too "papist.") Imagine the church interior colorfully decorated throughout. Original medieval glass is behind the altar. The list of rectors (left side wall) goes back to 1269. Finger the grooves in the back pews, worn away by sheepdog leashes. (A man's sheepdog accompanied him everywhere.)

Horse Rides and Sleeping near Stanton: Anyone can enjoy the Cotswolds from the saddle. Jill Carenza's **Cotswolds Riding Centre,** set just outside Stanton village, is in the most scenic corner of the region. The facility has 50 horses, and takes rank beginners on an hour-long scenic "hack" through the village and into the high country (£27/person for a group hack, £37/person for a semi-private hack, £47 for a private one-person hack; lessons, longer rides, rides for experts, and pub tours available; well signposted in Stanton, tel. 01386/584-250, www.cotswoldsriding.co.uk).

Jill rents five rooms at her **$$ Vine B&B,** but it takes a backseat to the horses. There's no greeting or check-in, and guests wander around wondering which room is theirs. Still, it's convenient if you want to ride all day (Ds/Db-£69, most rooms with four-poster beds, some stairs, tel. 01386/584-250, fax 01386/584-888, info @cotswoldsriding.co.uk).

Snowshill

Another nearly edible little bundle of cuteness, Snowshill (SNOWS-hill) has a photogenic triangular square with a characteristic pub at its base.

▲**Snowshill Manor**—Dark and mysterious, this old palace is filled with the lifetime collection of Charles Paget Wade. It's one big, musty celebration of craftsmanship, from finely carved spinning wheels to frightening samurai armor to tiny elaborate figurines carved by prisoners from the bones of meat served at dinner. Taking seriously his family motto, "Let Nothing Perish," Wade dedicated his life and fortune to preserving things finely crafted. The house (whose management made me promise not to promote it as an eccentric collector's pile of curiosities) really shows off Mr. Wade's ability to recognize and acquire fine examples of craftsmanship. It's all very...mmm...yyya.

This popular sight allows in only 22 people every 10 minutes, and entry times are doled out at the ticket desk (no reservations taken). It can be up to an hour's wait—even more on busy days, especially weekends. A good strategy is to arrive close to the opening time (12:00), and if there's a wait, enjoy the surrounding gardens (it's a 15-min walk up to the manor itself).

Cost and Hours: £8.50, manor house open mid-March–Oct Wed–Sun 12:00–17:00, last entry 50 min before closing, closed Mon–Tue and Nov–March, restaurant, tel. 01386/852-410, www.nationaltrust.org.uk/snowshillmanor.

Getting There: The manor overlooks the town square, but there's no direct access from the square. Park at the shop and follow the walkway through the garden to get to the house. A golf-cart-type shuttle to the house is available for those who need assistance.

Snowshill Lavender—In 2000, farmer Charlie Byrd realized that tourists love lavender. He planted his farm with 250,000

plants, and now visitors come to wander among his 53 acres, which burst with gorgeous lavender blossoms from mid-June through late August. His fragrant fantasy peaks late each July. Farmer Byrd produces lavender oil (an herbal product valued since ancient times for its healing, calming, and fragrant qualities) and sells it in a delightful shop, along with many other lavender-themed items. Lavender—so famous in France's Provence—is not indigenous to this region, but it fits the climate and soil just fine. A free flier in the shop explains the variations of flowers blooming.

Cost, Hours, Location: £2.50, daily late May–late Aug 10:00–17:00, tel. 01386/854-821, www.snowshill-lavender.co.uk, info@snowshill-lavender.co.uk. It's a half-mile out of Snowshill on Chipping Campden Road (easy parking).

Sleeping near Snowshill: The pretty, one-pub village of Snowshill holds a gem of a B&B. **$$$ Sheepscombe House**

B&B is a clean and pristine home on a working sheep farm. It's immersed in the best of Cotswold scenery, with plenty of sheep in the nearby fields. Jacki and Tim Harrison rent three modern, spacious, and thoughtfully appointed rooms (Db-£90–100, Tb-£130–150, folding cots available, free Wi-Fi, just a third of a mile south of Snowshill—look for signs, tel. 01386/853-769, www.broadway-cotswolds.co.uk/sheepscombe.html, reservations @snowshill-broadway.co.uk). Tim, who's happy to give you a local's perspective on this area, also runs Tour the Cotswolds car service (see page 271).

More Sights near Chipping Campden

▲**Hidcote Manor Garden**—If you like gardens, the grounds around this manor house (which has only a few rooms open to the public) are worth a look. Located northeast of Chipping Campden, Hidcote is where garden designers pioneered the notion of creating a series of outdoor "rooms," each with a unique theme (e.g., maple room, red room, and so on) and separated by a yew-tree hedge. Follow your nose through a clever series of small gardens that lead delightfully from one to the next. Among the best in England, Hidcote Gardens are at their fragrant peak from May through July (£9; July–Aug daily 10:00–18:00; mid-March–June and Sept Sat–Wed 10:00–18:00, closed Thu–Fri; Oct Sat–Wed 10:00–17:00, closed Thu–Fri; last entry one hour before closing; closed Nov–mid-March; tearoom, 4 miles northeast of Chipping Campden on B4035, tel. 01386/438-333, www.nationaltrust.org.uk/hidcote).

▲**Cotswold Farm Park**—Here's a delight for young and old alike. This park is the private venture of the Henson family, who are passionate about preserving rare and endangered breeds of local animals. While it feels like a kids' zone (with all the family-friendly facilities you can imagine), it's actually a fascinating chance for anyone to get up close and (very) personal with piles of mostly cute animals, including the sheep that made this region famous—the big, woolly  Cotswold Lion. A busy schedule of demonstrations gives you a look at local farm life. Take full advantage of the excellent (and included) audioguide, narrated by founder Joe Henson and filled with his passion for the farm's mission. Buy a bag of seed (50p) upon arrival, or have your map eaten by munchy goats as I did. Check the events board as you enter for times for the milking, shearing, or well-done "sheep show." Tykes love the little tractor rides, maze, and zip line, but the "touch barn" is where it's at for little kids (£6.75, kids-£5.50, daily mid-March–early Sept 10:30–17:00, last entry 30 min before closing, closed off-season, good £2 guidebook, decent cafeteria, tel. 01451/850-307, www.cotswold farmpark.co.uk, well signposted 15 minutes from Stow just off the Tewkesbury road—B4077).

Broadway—This postcard-pretty town, a couple of miles west of Chipping Campden, is filled with inviting shops and fancy tea-houses. Because most big bus tours stop here, I give Broadway a miss. But with a new road that allows traffic to skirt the town, Broadway has gotten cuter than ever. Broadway has good bus connections with Chipping Campden (bus #21, tel. 0871-200-2233—calls are 10p/min, www.traveline.org.uk).

Stow-on-the-Wold

Located 10 miles south of Chipping Campden, Stow-on-the-Wold—with a name that means "meeting place on the uplands"—is the highest point of the Cotswolds. Despite its crowds, it retains its charm, and it merits ▲▲. Most of the tourists are day-trippers, so even summer nights are peaceful. Stow has no real sights other than the town itself, some good pubs, antiques stores, and

cute shops draped seductively around a big town square. Visit the church, with its evocative old door guarded by ancient yew trees and the tombs of wool tycoons. A visit to Stow is not complete until you've locked your partner in the stocks on the green.

Orientation to Stow-on-the-Wold

(area code: 01451)

Tourist Information

At the TI on the main square, get the handy little 50p walking-tour brochure called *Town Trail* and the free *Cotswold Events* guide (TI may move in late 2009 and hours may change; likely open March–Oct Mon and Wed 9:00–16:30, Tue and Thu–Sat 10:00–16:00, closed Sun, Nov–Feb may have shorter hours, tel. 01451/831-082).

THE COTSWOLDS

Helpful Hints

Internet Access: Try the erratically open **library** in St. Edwards Hall on the main square (tel. 01451/830-352) or the **youth hostel** (17:00–23:00 nightly).

Taxi: See "Getting Around the Cotswolds—By Taxi" (page 269).

Parking: Park anywhere on Market Square free for two hours, or overnight between 16:00 and 11:00 (free 18:00–9:00 plus any 2 hours—they note your license so you can't just move to another spot, £50 tickets for offenders). One "Long Stay" lot is 400 yards north of the town square at the Tesco supermarket (free, follow the signs).

Self-Guided Walk

Welcome to Stow-on-the-Wold

This little four-stop walk covers about 500 yards and takes about 45 minutes.

Start at the **Stocks on the Market Square.** Imagine this village during the time when people were publicly ridiculed here as a punishment. Stow was born in pre-Roman times; it's where three trade routes crossed at a high point in the region (altitude: 800 feet). This main square hosted an international fair starting in 1107, and people came from as far away as Italy for the wool fleeces. This grand square was a vast, grassy expanse. Picture it in the Middle Ages (before the buildings in the center were added): a public commons and grazing ground, paths worn through the grass, and no well. Until 1867, Stow had no running water; women fetched water from the "Roman Well" a quarter-mile away.

A thin skin of topsoil covers the Cotswold limestone, from which these buildings were made. The **Stow Lodge** (next to the church) lies a little lower than the church, and sits on the spot where locals quarried stones for the church. That building, originally the rectory, is now a hotel. The church (where we'll end this little walk) is made of Cotswold stone, and marks the summit of the hill upon which the town was built. The stocks are a great photo op (my kids locked me in for a photo our family used for a Christmas card).

• *Walk past the youth hostel to the market, and cross to the other side of the square. Notice how locals seem to be a part of a tight little community.*

For 500 years, the **Market Cross** stood in the market,

Stow-on-the-Wold

TO BROADWAY & CHIPPING CAMPDEN

TO MORETON-IN-MARSH, STRATFORD-UPON-AVON, WARWICK

NOT TO SCALE

TESCO SUPERMKT

P "Long Stay"

PATH TO BROADWELL

TO UPPER SWELL, FORD & STANWAY

A 424

B 4077

A 429

FOSSEWAY

HIGH ST.

BUS STOP

PARSON'S CORNER

WC

Stocks

THE SQUARE

11

8

1

CHURCH

15

i

2

14

13

POST

SHEEP ST.

DIGBETH

12

4

PARK ST.

5

8

WC

P

TO

10

TO LOWER SWELL

B. 4068

7

6

TO UPPER & LOWER ODDINGTON

DCH

A 429

BACK WALLS

TO BOURTON-ON-THE-WATER & THE SLAUGHTERS

P PARKING

1 Stow Lodge Hotel & Rest.
2 The Kings Arms Hotel & Pub
3 The Old Stocks Hotel & Rest.
4 Number Nine B&B; Greedy's Fish & Chips; The Prince of India
5 Chipping House B&B; Cross Keys Cottage
6 The Pound B&B
7 West Deyne B&B

8 Tall Trees B&B
9 Youth Hostel
10 To Little Broom B&B
11 The Queen's Head
12 The Eagle & Child
13 The Coffee House
14 Market Cross
15 Library (Internet)

reminding all Christian merchants to "trade fairly under the sight of God." Notice the stubs of the iron fence in the concrete base—a reminder of how countless wrought-iron fences were cut down and given to the government to be melted down during World War II. (Recently, it's been disclosed that all that iron ended up in junk heaps—frantic patriotism just wasted.) The plaque on the cross honors the Lord of the Manor, who donated money back to his tenants, allowing the town to finally finance running water in 1878. Scan the square for a tipsy shop locals call the "wonky house." Because it lists (tilts) so severely, it's a listed building—the facade is protected (but the interior is modern and level). The Kings Arms, with its great gables and scary chimney, was once where travelers parked their horses before spending the night. In the 1600s, this was considered the premium "posting house" between London and Birmingham. Today, the Kings Arms cooks up some of the best food in town, and rents rooms upstairs (see "Sleeping in and near Stow," later).

During the English Civil War, which pitted Parliamentarians against Royalists, Stow-on-the-Wold remained staunchly loyal to the king. (Charles I is said to have eaten at the Kings Arms before a great battle.) Because of its allegiance, the town has an abundance of pubs with royal names (King's This and Queen's That).

• *Walk past the Kings Arms down Digbeth Street to the little triangular park located in front of the Methodist Church and across from the Royalist Hotel. This hotel—along with about 20 others—claims to be the oldest in England, dating from 947.*

Just beyond the small grassy triangle with benches is the place where—twice a year, in May and October—the Gypsy Horse Fair attracts Roma (Gypsies) and Travelers (Irish Tinkers) from far and wide. They congregate down the street on the Maugersbury Road. Locals paint a colorful picture of the Roma, Travelers, and horses inundating the town. The young women dress up because the fair also functions as a marriage market.

• *Hike up Sheep Street. You'll pass a boutique-filled former brewery yard, Fleece Alley (just wide enough for a single file of sheep to walk on, which made them easier to count on market days), and a fine antique bookstore. Turn right on Church Street, which leads past the best coffee shop in town (the Coffee House), and find the church.*

Before entering the **church,** circle it. On the back side, a door is flanked by two ancient yew trees. While to many it looks like the Christian "Behold, I stand at the door and knock" door, J. R. R. Tolkien fans see something quite different. Tolkien hiked the Cotswolds, and had a passion for sketching evocative trees such as this. *Lord of the Rings* enthusiasts are convinced this must be the inspiration for the door into Moria.

Although the church (open daily—apart from services—9:00–18:00) dates from Saxon times, today's structure is from the 15th century. Its history is played up in leaflets and plaques just inside the door. The floor is paved with the tombs of big shots who made their money from wool and are still boastful in death. (Find the tombs crowned with the bales of wool.)

During the English Civil War (1615), more than 1,000 soldiers were imprisoned here. The tombstone in front of the altar remembers the Royalist Captain Keyt. His long hair, lace, and sash indicate he was a "cavalier," and true blue to the king (Cromwellians were called "round heads"—named for their short hair). Study the crude provincial art—childlike skulls and (in the upper corners) symbols of his service to the king (armor, weapons).

On the right wall, a monument remembers the many boys from this small town who were lost in World War I (50 out of a population of 2,000). There were far fewer in World War II. The biscuit-shaped plaque (to the left) remembers an admiral from Stow who lost four sons defending the realm. It's sliced from an ancient fluted column (which locals believe is from Ephesus, Turkey). While most of the windows are Victorian (19th-century), the two sets high up in the clerestory are from the dreamier Pre-Raphaelite school (c. 1920).

Finally, don't miss the kneelers, made by a committed band of women known as "the Kneeler Group." They meet most Tuesday mornings (except sometimes in summer) at 10:30 in the Church Room to needlepoint, sip coffee, and enjoy a good chat. (The vicar assured me that any tourist wanting to join them would be more than welcome. The help would be appreciated and the company would be excellent.)

Sleeping in and near Stow

(£1 = about $1.60, country code: 44, area code: 01451)

In Stow

$$$ **Stow Lodge Hotel** fills the historic church rectory with lots of old English charm. Facing the town square, with its own sprawling and peaceful garden, this lavish old place offers 21 large, thoughtfully appointed rooms with soft beds, stately public spaces, and a cushy-chair lounge (Db-£85–145 depending on season, closed Jan, pay Internet access and free Wi-Fi, off-street parking, The Square, tel. 01451/830-485, fax 01451/831-671, www.stowlodge.com, enquiries@stowlodge.com, helpful Hartley family).

$$$ **The Kings Arms,** with nine rooms, manages to keep its historic Cotswolds character while still feeling fresh and modern

in all the right ways (Sb-£60, Db-£75–110, higher prices are for weekends, steep stairs, off-street parking, Market Square, tel. 01451/830-364, www.thekingsarmsstow.co.uk, info@thekings armsstow.co.uk). Jo, Peter, and Sam run the hotel and Peter's brother Thomas cooks—see "Eating in and near Stow," later.

$$$ The Old Stocks Hotel, facing the town square, is a good value, even though the building itself is classier than its 18 big, simply furnished rooms. It's friendly and family-run, yet professional as can be. Beware the man-killer beams (Sb-£45–55, standard Db-£90, refurbished "superior" Db-£110, Tb-£120, family deals, ground-floor rooms, attached bar and restaurant, garden patio, off-street parking, The Square, tel. 01451/830-666, fax 01451/870-014, www.oldstockshotel.co.uk, info@oldstockshotel.co.uk).

$$ Number Nine has three large, bright, recently refurbished, and tastefully decorated rooms. This 200-year-old home comes with watch-your-head beamed ceilings and old wooden doors (Db-£60–70, free Internet access and Wi-Fi, 9 Park Street, tel. 01451/870-333, mobile 07779-006-539, www.number-nine.info, enquiries@number-nine.info, James and Carol Brown).

$$ Chipping House B&B is a fine, warm, old place with three rooms and a welcoming lounge—it feels like a visit to auntie's house (Db-£60–70, cash only, Park Street, tel. 01451/831-756, chippinghouse@tesco.net, dog-lovers Merv and Carolyne Oliver).

$$ Cross Keys Cottage offers four smallish but smartly updated rooms with bright floral decor and modern bathrooms. Kindly Margaret and Roger Welton take care of their guests in this 350-year-old beamed cottage (Sb-£55–65, Db-£65–70, cash discount, free Wi-Fi, Park Street, tel. & fax 01451/831-128, rogxmag@hotmail.com).

$ The Pound is the quaint 500-year-old, slanty, cozy, and low-beamed home of Patricia Whitehead. She offers two bright, inviting, twin-bedded rooms and a classic old fireplace lounge (D-£50–60, T-£85, cash only, downtown on Sheep Street, tel. & fax 01451/830-229, patwhitehead1@live.co.uk).

$ West Deyne B&B has two grandmotherly rooms, a garden, a fountain, and a small conservatory overlooking the countryside (D-£50–60, T-£85, cash only, Lower Swell Road, tel. 01451/831-011, run by Joan Cave).

$ Tall Trees B&B, on the Oddington Road 100 yards outside of Stow, comes with horses and chickens on four acres of land. Run by no-nonsense Jennifer, the six contemporary rooms are in an old-style building (Sb-£40–50, Db-£60–70, family room-£100, cash only, two ground-floor rooms, off-street parking, tel. 01451/831-296, fax 01451/870-049, talltreestow@aol.com). She also rents a lovely cottage that sleeps six (£450–900/week, kitchenette, off-street parking).

$ *Hostel:* The **Stow-on-the-Wold Youth Hostel,** on Stow's main square, is the only hostel in the Cotswolds, with 48 beds in nine rooms. It has a friendly atmosphere, good hot meals, and a members' kitchen (dorm bed-£18, non-members-£3 extra, includes sheets, some family rooms with private bathrooms, evening meals, reception closed 10:00–17:00, Internet-£1/15 min, lockers, reserve long in advance, tel. 01451/830-497, fax 01451/870-102, www.yha.org.uk, stow@yha.org.uk, manager Rob). Anyone can eat here: Breakfast is £4.65 and dinner is £9.25.

Near Stow

$ **Little Broom B&B** hides out in the neighboring hamlet of Maugersbury, which enjoys the peace Stow once had. It rents three cozy rooms that share a fine garden and a pool (S-£30, Sb-£45, D-£50, Db-£55–70, apartment Db-£70 for two people plus £10–15 for each extra person, cash only, tel. & fax 01451/830-510, mobile 07989-832-714). Brenda keeps racehorses just beyond her pool, which hides in a low-lying greenhouse to keep it warm throughout the summer (guests welcome). It's an easy eight-minute walk from Stow: Head east on Park Street, taking the right fork to Maugersbury, then turn right on the road marked *No Through Road*.

Eating in and near Stow

In Stow

These places are all within a five-minute walk of each other, either on the main square or downhill on Queen and Park Streets.

Restaurants and Pubs

Stow Lodge is a formal but friendly bar serving fine £8–10 lunches and a popular £24 three-course dinner. This is the choice of the town's proper ladies (daily 12:00–14:00 & 19:00–20:30, smoke-free, veggie options, good wines, also has pricier restaurant, just off main square).

The Old Stocks Hotel Restaurant, which might at first glance seem like a tired and big hotel dining room, is actually a classy place to dine. With attentive service and an interesting menu, they provide tasty and well-presented food. If they're not too busy, you can order more economically from the bar menu, and sit in the fancy dining room enjoying views of the square. In good weather, the garden out back is a hit (£8–15 meals, nightly 18:30–20:30, Fri–Sat until 21:00, reservations recommended on weekends, tel. 01451/830-666).

The Kings Arms has two floors, both serving traditional English fare. Downstairs, you'll find pub food; upstairs has an "English-with-a-twist" menu in a once-medieval, now-classy ambience (£10–12 pub food, £13–18 meals, daily 12:00–14:30 & 19:00–21:30, sandwiches available all day, reserve for dinner, tel. 01451/830-364).

The Queen's Head faces the Market Square, next to the Stow Lodge. With a classic pub vibe, it's a great place to bring your dog, eat pub grub, and drink the local Cotswold brew, Donnington Ale (£9–19 plates, daily 12:00–14:30 & 18:30–21:00).

The Eagle and Child is more of a hotel restaurant than a pub, with delicious food and indifferent service (meals available daily 12:00–14:30 & 18:00–21:00, afternoon tea available Fri–Sun, Park Street, tel. 01451/830-670).

Eating Cheap

Head to the grassy triangle where Digbeth hits Sheep Street; there, you'll find take-out fish-and-chips and Indian and Chinese food. You can picnic at the triangle or on the benches by the stocks on Market Street.

Greedy's Fish and Chips, on Park Street, is a favorite with locals for take-out (Mon–Sat 12:00–14:00 & 16:30–21:00, closed Sun).

The Prince of India offers good Indian food in a delightful setting, to take out or eat in (nightly 18:00–23:30, Park Street, tel. 01451/830-099).

The Coffee House provides a nice break from the horses-and-hounds traditional cuisine found elsewhere, though the service can be slow (£6–10 soups and salads, good coffee, Mon–Sat 9:30–17:00, Sun 10:00–16:00, Church Street, tel. 01451/870-802).

Even Cheaper: Small grocery stores face the main square, and a big **Tesco** supermarket is 200 yards north of town. The youth hostel (see "Sleeping in and near Stow," earlier) welcomes non-hostelers for breakfast (£4.65) or its evening family-style meal (£9.25, drop by early to confirm time and book a spot).

Pub Dinner Hike from Stow

From Stow, consider taking a half-hour scenic countryside walk past the old Roman Well to the village of Broadwell. (At the end of the hike at the road, turn right—downhill—to get to Broadwell.) There, **The Fox Inn** serves good pub dinners and draws traditional ales (food served Mon–Sat 11:30–13:30 & 18:30–21:00, Sun 12:00–14:00 only, on the village green, tel. 01451/870-909).

Great Country Pubs near Stow

These three places—known for their great £10 meals and fine settings—are very popular. Arrive early or phone in a reservation. (If you show up at 20:00, it's unlikely that they'll be able to seat you for dinner if you haven't called first.) These pubs allow "well-behaved children" and are practical only for those with a car. The first two (in Oddington, two miles from Stow) are more trendy and fresh, yet still in a traditional pub setting. The Plough (in Ford, a few miles farther away) is your jolly olde dark pub.

The Horse and Groom Village Inn in Upper Oddington is a smart place with a sea-grass-green carpet in a 16th-century inn, serving modern English and Mediterranean food with a good wine list (32 wines by the glass) and serious beer (daily 12:00–14:00 & 18:30–21:00, tel. 01451/830-584).

The Fox Inn, a different Fox Inn than the one listed above, is old but fresh and famous among locals for its quality cooking (daily 12:00–14:00 & 18:30–22:00, in Lower Oddington, tel. 01451/870-555). They also rent three rooms (Db-£68–95, www.foxinn.net).

The Plough Inn fills a fascinating old building, once an old coaching inn and later a courthouse. Ask the bar staff for some fun history—like what "you're barred" means. Eat from the same traditional English menu in the restaurant, bar, or garden. They are serious about both their beer and—judging by the extensive list of homemade temptations—their desserts (£12–18 meals,  food served daily 12:00–14:00 & 18:00–21:00, 4 miles from Stow on Tewkesbury Road in hamlet of Ford, reservations smart, tel. 01386/584-215).

Near Stow-on-the-Wold

These sights are all south of Stow: Some are very close (Bourton-on-the-Water, the Slaughters, and Northleach) and one is 20 miles away (Cirencester).

▲Bourton-on-the-Water

I can't figure out whether they call this "the Venice of the Cotswolds" because of its quaint canals or its frequent miserable crowds. Either way, it's very pretty. This town—four miles south of Stow and a mile from the Slaughters—gets overrun by midday and weekend hordes. Surrounding Bourton's green are sidewalks jammed with disoriented tourists wearing nametags. If you can avoid them, it's worth a drive-through and maybe a short stop. Although it can be mobbed with tour groups during the day, it's pleasantly empty in the early evening and after dark.

Parking: Finding a spot here is predictably tough. Even during the busy business day, rather than park in the pay-and-display parking lot a five-minute walk from the center, drive right into town and wait for a spot on High Street just past the village green (there's a long row of free two-hour spots in front of the Edinburgh Woolen Mills Shop).

Tourist Information: The TI is just off Victoria Street (April–Oct Mon–Fri 9:30–17:00, Sat 9:30–17:30, closed Sun, closes one hour earlier Nov–March, tel. 01451/820-211, www.bourtoninfo .com).

Sights: Bourton has three sights worth considering. All are on High Street in the town center. In addition to these, families also enjoy Bourton's kid-perfect **leisure centre** (big pool and sauna, 5-min walk from town center, open daily, call for public hours, tel. 01451/824-024).

▲**Motor Museum**—This excellent, jumbled museum shows off a lifetime's accumulation of vintage cars, old lacquered signs, thread-bare toys, and prewar memorabilia. Wander the car-and-driver displays, from the automobile's early days to the stylish James Bond era. Talk to an elderly Brit who's touring the place for some personal memories (£4, Feb–Nov daily 10:00–18:00, closed Dec–Jan, in  the mill facing the town center, tel. 01451/821-255, www.cotswold -motor-museum.com).

Model Railway Exhibition—This exhibit of four model railway layouts is impressive only to train buffs (£2.50, June–Aug daily 11:00–17:00, Sept–May weekends only, limited Jan hours, located in the back of a hobby shop, tel. 01451/820-686, www.bourton modelrailway.co.uk).

Model Village—This light but fun display re-creates the town on a 1:9 scale in a tiny park, and has an attached room full of tiny models showing off various bits of British domestic life (£3.25 for the park, £1 more for the model room, daily 10:00–17:45, tel. 01451/820-467).

Lower and Upper Slaughter

Lower Slaughter is a classic village, with ducks, a working water mill, and usually an artist busy at her easel somewhere. Just behind the skippable Old Mill Museum, two kissing gates lead to the path that goes to nearby Upper Slaughter (a 10-minute walk or 2-minute drive away).

In **Upper Slaughter,** walk through the yew trees (sacred in pagan days) down a lane through the raised graveyard (a buildup of centuries of graves) to the peaceful church. In the back of the fine graveyard, the statue of a wistful woman looks over the tomb of an 18th-century rector (sculpted by his son).

By the way, "Slaughter" has nothing to do with lamb chops. It comes from the sloe tree (the one used to make sloe gin). These towns are an easy two-hour round-trip walk from Bourton. You could also walk from Bourton through the Slaughters to Stow. The small roads from Upper Slaughter to Ford and Kineton are some of England's most scenic. Roll your window down and joyride slowly.

▲Northleach

One of the "untouched and untouristed" Cotswold villages, Northleach is worth a short stop. The town's impressive main square and church attest to its position as a major wool center in the Middle Ages. Park in the square called The Green or the adjoining Market Place and pick up a free town map at the **TI,** located on The Green in the black-and-white-striped Fothergills Gallery shop (Tue–Fri 9:30–17:00, Sat 9:30–16:00, closed Sun–Mon, tel. 01451/860-135, www.northleach.gov.uk). If the TI is closed, maps are available at the post office on the Market Place (Mon–Fri 9:00–17:30, Sat 9:00–13:00, closed Sun and for lunch 13:00–14:00) and at other nearby shops. Northleach is nine miles south of Stow, down A429. Bus #855 connects it to Stow and Moreton (tel. 0871-200-2233—calls are 10p/min, www.traveline.org.uk).

▲Keith Harding's World of Mechanical Music—In 1962, Keith Harding, tired of giving ad-lib "living room tours," opened this delightful little one-room place. It offers a unique opportunity to listen to 300 years of amazing self-playing musical instruments. It's run by people who are passionate about the restoration work they do on these musical marvels. The curators delight in demonstrating about 20 of the museum's machines with each hour-long tour. You'll hear Victorian music boxes and the earliest polyphones (record players) playing cylinders and then discs—all from an age when music was made mechanically, without the help of electricity. The admission fee includes an essential hour-long tour (£8, daily 10:00–17:00, last entry at 15:45, tours go constantly—join one in progress, High Street, Northleach, tel. 01451/860-181, www.mechanicalmusic.co.uk).

Church of Saints Peter and Paul—This fine Perpendicular Gothic church has been called the "cathedral of the Cotswolds."

It's one of the Cotswolds' finest two "wool" churches (along with Chipping Campden's), paid for by 15th-century wool tycoons. Find the oldest tombstone. The brass plaques on the floor memorialize big shots, showing sheep and sacks of wool at their long-dead feet, and inscriptions mixing Latin and the old English.

▲Bibury

Six miles northeast of Cirencester, this village is a favorite with British picnickers fond of strolling and fishing. Bibury offers some relaxing sights, including a row of very old weavers' cottages, a trout farm, a stream teeming with fat fish and proud ducks, and a church surrounded by rosebushes, each tended by a volunteer of the parish. A protected wetlands area on the far side of the stream hosts newts and water voles— walk around to the old weavers' Arlington Row and back on the far side of the marsh, peeking into the rushes for wildlife.

For a closer look at the fish, cross the bridge to the 15-acre Trout Farm, where you can feed them—or catch your own (£3.50, fish food-50p; March–Oct Mon–Sat 9:00–18:00, Sun 10:00–18:00; Nov–Feb daily 10:00–16:00; catch-your-own only available March–Oct weekends and school holidays, tel. 01285/740-215, www.biburytroutfarm.co.uk).

Don't miss the scenic **Coln Valley drive** from A429 to Bibury via the enigmatic villages of Coln St. Dennis, Coln Rogers, Coln Powell, and Winson.

Sleeping in Bibury: If you'd like to spend the night in tiny Bibury, consider **$$ The William Morris B&B,** named for the 19th-century designer and writer (Db-£65–85, cheaper prices Mon–Thu, cash only, 2 rooms, 200 yards from the bridge at 11 The Street, tel. 01285/740-555, fax 01285/850-648, www.thewilliam morris.com, info@thewilliammorris.com).

▲▲Cirencester

Nearly 2,000 years ago, Cirencester (SIGH-ren-ses-ter) was the ancient Roman city of Corinium. It's 20 miles from Stow down A429, which was called Fosse Way in Roman times. In Cirencester, stop by the **Corinium Museum** to find out why they say, "If you scratch Gloucestershire, you'll find Rome" (£4.25, Mon–Sat 10:00–17:00, Sun 14:00–17:00, Park Street, tel. 01285/655-611, www.cirencester .co.uk/coriniummuseum). Cirencester's church is the largest of the Cotswolds "wool" churches. The cutesy New Brewery Arts crafts center entertains visitors with traditional weaving and potting, workshops, an interesting gallery, and a good coffee shop. Monday and Friday are general-market days, Friday features an antiques market, and a crafts market is held on the first and third Saturdays of the month. The **TI** is in the Corinium Museum shop (Mon–Sat 10:00–17:00, Sun 14:00–17:00, tel. 01285/654-180, cirencester vic@cotswold.gov.uk).

Moreton-in-Marsh

This workaday town—worth ▲—is like Stow or Chipping Campden without the touristy sugar. Rather than gift and antiques shops, you'll find streets lined with real shops: iron-mongers selling cottage nameplates and carpet shops strewn with the remarkable patterns that decorate B&B floors. A shin-kickin' traditional market of 100-plus stalls fills High Street each Tuesday, as it has for the last 400 years (8:00–16:00, handicrafts, farm produce, clothing, great people-watching, best if you go early). The Cotswolds has an economy aside from tourism, and you'll feel it here.

Orientation to Moreton-in-Marsh

(area code: 01608)
Moreton has a tiny, sleepy train station two blocks from High Street, lots of bus connections, and the best **TI** in the region (Mon 8:45–16:00, Tue–Thu 8:45–17:15, Fri 8:45–16:45, Sat 10:00–13:00, closed Sun, good public WC, 50p *Town Trail* leaflet for self-guided walk, rail and bus schedules, racks of fliers, tel. 01608/650-881).

Helpful Hints
Internet Access: It's free at the **TI** (see above) and at the errati-cally open **library** (down High Street where it becomes Stow Road, tel. 01608/650-780).

Laundry: The handy **launderette** is a block in front of the train station on New Road (daily 7:00–19:00, last wash at 18:00, £3.40 self-service wash, £2–3 self-service dry, or drop off Mon–Fri 8:00–17:00 for £2.50 extra and same-day service, tel. 01608/650-888).

Baggage Storage: Although there is no formal baggage storage in town, the Black Bear Inn (next to the TI) might let you leave bags there if you buy a drink.

Parking: It's easy—anywhere on High Street is fine any time, as long as you want, for free. On Tuesdays, when the market makes parking tricky, you can park at the Budgens supermarket for £3—refundable if you spend at least £5 in the store.

Bike Rental, Taxis, and Car Rental: See "Getting Around the Cotswolds" (page 266).

Sleeping in Moreton-in-Marsh

(£1 = about $1.60, country code: 44, area code: 01608)

$$$ Manor House Hotel is Moreton's big old hotel, dating from 1545 but sporting such modern amenities as toilets and electricity. Its 35 classy-for-the-Cotswolds rooms and its garden invite relaxation (Sb-£115–155, Db-£145–205, family suite-£210–250, includes breakfast, elevator, pay Wi-Fi, log fire in winter, attached restaurants—no kids under age 8, on far end of High Street away from train station, tel. 01608/650-501, fax 01608/651-481, www.cotswold-inns-hotels.co.uk, info@manorhousehotel.info).

$ Kymalton House has two bright, tastefully decorated rooms in a gracious modern house. With a pleasant garden, it's set back off of a busy street just outside the town center (Db-£65, cheaper for 3 or more nights, double beds only, cash only, closed Dec–Jan, tel. 01608/650-487, kymalton@uwclub.net, Sylvia and Doug Gould). It's a seven-minute walk from town (walk past Budgens supermarket, turn right on Todenham Road, look for house on the right). They'll happily pick up and drop off train travelers at the station.

$ Treetops B&B is plush, with seven spacious, attractive rooms, a sun lounge, and a three-quarter-acre backyard. Liz and Ben (the family dog) will make you feel right at home—if you meet their two-night minimum (large Db-£65, gigantic Db-£70, ground-floor rooms have patios, free Wi-Fi, set far back from the busy road, London Road, tel. & fax 01608/651-036, www.treetopscotswolds.co.uk, treetops1@talk21.com, Liz and Brian Dean). It's an eight-minute walk from town and the railway station (exit station, keep left, go left on bridge over train tracks, look for sign, then long driveway).

$ Warwick House, just down the road from Treetops, is where "half-American" Charlie Grant rents three rooms in a contemporary, casual house. It's on a noisy road, but the windows are triple-glazed. Charlie will do your laundry if you stay three or more nights (Sb-£38, Db-£60, Tb-£72, cash only, free Wi-Fi and loaner laptop, no kids under age 12, will pick up from train station, London Road, tel. 01608/650-773, www.snoozeandsizzle.com, whbandb@yahoo.com).

THE COTSWOLDS

Moreton-in-Marsh

1. Manor House Hotel
2. Kymalton House
3. Treetops B&B
4. Warwick House
5. The Marshmallow Restaurant
6. The Black Bear Inn
7. Hassan Balti Rest.
8. Tilly's Tea House & Mermaid Fish Shop
9. Ask Restaurant
10. Co-op & Tesco Express
11. Budgens Supermarket
12. Launderette
13. Toy Shop Bike Rental

Eating in Moreton-in-Marsh

A stroll up and down High Street lets you survey your small-town options.

The Marshmallow is relatively upscale but affordable, with a menu that includes traditional English dishes as well as lasagna and salads (£8–12 entrées, 15 fancy teas, Sun–Mon 10:00–17:00, Tue 10:00–16:00, Wed–Sat 10:00–20:00, reservations advised, shady back garden for summer dining, tel. 01608/651-536).

The Black Bear Inn offers traditional English food. As you enter, choose between the dining room on the left or the pub on the right (£5–10 meals and daily specials, restaurant open daily 12:00–14:00 & 18:30–21:00, pub open daily 11:00–23:00, tel. 01608/652-992).

Hassan Balti, with tasty Bangladeshi food, is a fine value for sit-down or take-out (£7–12 meals, Mon–Fri 18:00–23:30, Sat–Sun 12:00–14:00 & 18:00–23:30, High Street, tel. 01608/650-798).

Tilly's Tea House serves fresh soups, salads, sandwiches, and pastries for lunch in a cheerful spot on High Street across from the TI (£5 light meals, good cream tea-£5, Mon–Sat 9:00–16:30, closed Sun, tel. 01608/650-000).

Ask, a chain restaurant across the street, has decent pastas, pizzas, and salads, and a breezy, family-friendly atmosphere (£8–10 pizzas, daily 12:00–23:00, take-out available, tel. 01608/651-119).

Mermaid fish shop is popular for its take-out fish and tasty selection of traditional pies (Mon–Sat 12:00–14:00 & 17:00–22:30, closed Sun).

Picnic: There's a small **Co-op** grocery on High Street in the town center (Mon–Sat 7:00–20:00, Sun 8:00–20:00), and a **Tesco Express** one door down (Mon–Fri 6:00–23:00, Sat–Sun 7:00–23:00). The big **Budgens** supermarket is indeed super (Mon–Sat 8:00–22:00, Sun 10:00–16:00, far end of High Street). There are picnic tables across the busy street in pleasant Victoria Park.

Moreton-in-Marsh Connections

Moreton, the only Cotswolds town with a train station, is also the best base to explore the region by bus (see "Getting Around the Cotswolds," page 266).

From Moreton by Train to: London's Paddington Station (one-way-£27–29, round-trip after 8:15-£27, every 1–2 hrs, 1.5–1.75 hrs), **Bath** (hourly, 2–3 hrs, 1–3 transfers), **Oxford** (hourly, 40 min), **Ironbridge Gorge** (hourly, 2.75–3.5 hrs, 2–3 transfers; arrive Telford, then catch bus or cab 7 miles to Ironbridge Gorge—see next chapter). Train info: tel. 0845-748-4950, www.nationalrail.co.uk.

Near Moreton-in-Marsh

▲Chastleton House

This stately home, located about five miles southeast of Moreton-in-Marsh, was actually lived in by the same family from 1607 until 1991. It offers a rare peek into a Jacobean gentry house. (Jacobean, which comes from the Latin for "James," indicates the style from the time of King James I—the early 1600s.) Built, like most Cotswold palaces, with wool money, it gradually declined with the fortunes of its aristocratic family until, according to the last lady of the house, it was "held together by cobwebs." It came to the National Trust on condition that they would maintain its musty Jacobean ambience. Wander on creaky floorboards, many of them original, and chat with volunteer guides stationed in each room. It's an uppity place that doesn't encourage spontaneity. The docents are proud to play on one of the best croquet teams in the region (the rules of croquet were formalized in this house in 1868). Page through the early 20th-century family photo albums in the room just off the entry.

Cost, Hours, Location: £8.25; April–Sept Wed–Sat 13:00–17:00, closed Sun–Tue; Oct Wed–Sat 13:00–16:00, closed Sun–Tue; last entry one hour before closing; closed Nov–March; well signposted, 5-min hike to house from free parking lot, recorded info tel. 01494/755-560, www.nationaltrust.org.uk/chastleton. Only 175 visitors a day are allowed into the home (25 people every 30 min). You can reserve an entry time in advance by phone (tel. 01608/674-981, Mon–Fri 10:00–14:00). Reservations are not possible for same-day visits.

▲▲▲Blenheim Palace

Too many palaces can send you into a furniture-wax coma, but everyone should see Blenheim. The Duke of Marlborough's

home—the largest in England—is still lived in, which is wonderfully obvious as you prowl through it. Note: Americans who pronounce the place "blen-HEIM" are the butt of jokes. It's "BLEN-em."

Cost, Hours, Information: £17.50, family deals, mid-Feb–Oct daily 10:30–17:30, last tour departs at 16:45, park open but palace closed Nov–mid-Dec Mon–Tue and mid-Dec–mid-Feb, tel. 01993/811-091, recorded info tel. 0870-060-2080, www.blenheimpalace.com.

Getting There: Blenheim Palace sits at the edge of the cute cobbled town of Woodstock. The train station nearest the palace (Hanborough, 1.5 miles away) has no taxi or bus service. From the Cotswolds, your easiest train connection is from Morton-in-Marsh to Oxford, where you can catch the bus to Blenheim (bus #S3 to the palace gate departs from Oxford train station or Oxford's

Gloucester Green bus station—a 5-min walk from train station, Mon–Sat 2/hr, less frequent on Sun, 30 min; bus tel. 01865/772-250, www.stagecoachbus.com).

Background: John Churchill, first duke of Marlborough, beat the French at the Battle of Blenheim in 1704. A thankful Queen Anne built him this nice home, perhaps the finest Baroque building in England (designed by playwright-turned-architect John Vanbrugh). Ten dukes of Marlborough later, it's as impressive as ever. (The current, 11th duke considers the 12th more of an error than an heir, and what to do about him is quite an issue.) The 2,000-acre yard, well designed by Lancelot "Capability" Brown, is as majestic to some as the palace itself. The view just past the outer gate as you enter is a classic.

◑ Self-Guided Tour: The well-organized palace tour begins with a fine **Churchill exhibit,** centered on the bed in which Sir Winston was born in 1874 (prematurely...begun while his mother was at a Blenheim Palace party). Take your time in the Churchill exhibit, then catch the 45-minute guided tour (6/hr, included with ticket, last tour at 16:45). When the palace is really busy, they dispense with guided tours and go "free flow," allowing those with an appetite for learning to strike up conversations with docents in each room.

Your ticket also includes the modern 45-minute, multimedia "visitors' experience"—a tour called **Blenheim Palace: The Untold Story** (6/hr, included with ticket). You're guided through 300 years of history by a maid named Grace Ridley. (If you have limited time to spend at the palace, focus on Churchill instead.)

For a more extensive visit, follow up the general tour with a 30-minute guided walk through the actual **private apartments** of the duke. Tours leave at the top and bottom of each hour (£4.50, generally May–Sept daily 12:00–16:30, tickets are limited, tours don't run if the duke's home, buy from table in library or at Flagstaff info booth outside main gates, enter in corner of courtyard to left of grand palace entry).

Kids enjoy the **pleasure garden** (a tiny train takes you from the palace parking lot to the garden, but if you have a car, it's more efficient simply to drive there). A lush and humid greenhouse flutters with butterflies. A kid zone includes a few second-rate games and the "world's largest symbolic hedge maze." The maze is worth a look if you haven't seen one and could use some exercise.

Winston Churchill fans can visit his **tomb,** a short walk away in the Bladon town churchyard.

Sleeping near Blenheim Palace, in Woodstock: Blenheim nestles up against the two-road town of Woodstock, which offers walkable accommodations and a nice selection of eateries.

$$ Blenheim Guest House, 200 years old and charming, has six rooms in the town center. Literally next door to the palace's green gate, it's a five-minute walk from the palace (Sb-£50, Db-£60–75 depending on size, Wi-Fi, 17 Park Street, tel. 01993/813-814, fax 01993/813-810, www.theblenheim.com, the blenheim@aol.com).

$$ The Townhouse is a refurbished 18th-century stone house with five plush rooms (Sb-£55–70, Db-£75–90, includes breakfast, in town center at 15 High Street, tel. & fax 01993/810-843, www.woodstock-townhouse.com, info@woodstock-townhouse.com).

$$ Wishaw House B&B is grandmotherly and offers two rooms (Sb-£43, D-£56, Tb-£78, 2 Browns Lane, 5-min walk from palace, tel. 01993/811-343, Pat Hillier).

STRATFORD-UPON-AVON

To see or not to see? Stratford is Shakespeare's hometown, and is a must for every big-bus tour in England, and probably the single most popular side-trip from London. Sure, it's touristy. But nobody back home would understand if you skipped Shakespeare's house. A walking tour with a play's the thing to bring the Bard to life. And the town's riverside charm, coupled with its hardworking tourist industry, makes it a fun stop.

While you're in the area, explore Warwick, England's finest medieval castle, and stop by Coventry, a blue-collar town with a spirit that the Nazis' bombs couldn't destroy.

Planning Your Time

Stratford, Warwick, and Coventry are a made-to-order day for drivers connecting the Cotswolds with points north (such as Ironbridge Gorge or North Wales). While connections from the Cotswolds to Ironbridge Gorge are tough, Stratford, Warwick, and Coventry are well-served by public transportation.

If you're just passing through Stratford, it's worth a half-day, but to see a play, you'll need to spend the night or drive in from the nearby Cotswolds (30 min to the south; see previous chapter).

Warwick is England's single most spectacular castle. It's very touristy, but it's also historic and fun (worth three hours of your time). Have lunch in Warwick town. Coventry, the least important stop on a quick trip, is most interesting as a chance to see a real, struggling, Midlands industrial city (with some decent sightseeing).

If you're speedy, you can hit all three sights on a one-day drive-through. If you're more relaxed, see a play and stay in Stratford, then stop by Warwick and Coventry the following morning en route to your next destination.

Orientation to Stratford

(area code: 01789)

Stratford's old town is compact, with the TI and theater along the riverbank, and Shakespeare's birthplace a few blocks inland; you can walk easily to everything except Anne Hathaway's and Mary Arden's places. The river has an idyllic yet playful feel, with a park along both banks, paddleboats, hungry swans, and an old, crank-powered ferry.

Tourist Information

The TI is as central as can be, located where the main street hits the river. Although the office has been swallowed whole by gimmicky knickknacks and fliers—and corrupted by a sales-pitch fervor—the people here can still provide a little help. They sell discounted tickets for local and regional sights, including Warwick Castle and Blenheim Palace (April–Sept Mon–Sat 9:00–17:30, Sun 10:00–16:00; Oct–March Mon–Sat 9:00–17:00, Sun 10:00–15:00; free room-finding service, on Bridgefoot, toll tel. 0870-160-7930, www.shakespeare-country.co.uk).

Helpful Hints

Name That Stratford: If you're coming by train or bus, be sure to request a ticket for "Stratford-upon-Avon," not just "Stratford." Another Stratford—also known as Stratford Langthorne, just outside London—is the location for the 2012 Olympics, and is nowhere near where you're trying to go.

Festival: Every year on the weekend following Shakespeare's birthday (traditionally considered to be April 23—also the day he died), Stratford celebrates. The town hosts free events, including activities for children. In 2010, expect tours and hotels to be booked up long in advance surrounding the weekend of April 24–25.

Internet Access: Get online at **Cyber Junction** (£1.50/15 min, £4/hr, daily 10:00–18:00, sometimes later, 28 Greenhill Street, tel. 01789/263-400, www.thecyberjunction.co.uk) or the **library,** on Henley Street just a few doors down from Shakespeare's Birthplace (£5/hr, weekdays generally 9:00–17:30, shorter hours on weekends; if computers are all in use, reserve a time at the desk; tel. 01789/292-209, www.warwickshire.gov.uk).

Baggage Storage: Located directly behind the TI, the **Old Barn Shop** stores bags—but be back to pick them up before the store closes, or you're out of luck for the night (£3/bag, Mon–Sat 10:00–17:00, Sun 10:00–16:00, tel. 01789/269-567).

Laundry: Sparklean, a 10-minute walk from the city center, is near the Grove Road and Broad Walk B&Bs (daily 8:00–21:00, self-serve wash-£8.50, kindly Jane will do it for £10–12 in a few hours if you drop it off by 12:00, 74 Bull Street, tel. 01789/269-075).

Taxis: Try **007 Taxis** (tel. 01789/414-007) or the taxi stand on Woodbridge, near the intersection with High Street. To arrange for a private car and driver, contact **Platinum Cars** (£25/hr, tel. 01789/264-626, www.platinum-cars.co.uk).

Tours in Stratford

Stratford Town Walks—These entertaining, award-winning 90-minute walks introduce you to the town and its famous play-wright. Tours run daily year-round, rain or shine. Just show up at the Swan foun-tain (on the waterfront, opposite Sheep Street) in front of the Royal Shakespeare Theatre and pay the guide (£5, kids-£2, ticket stub offers good discounts to some sights, Mon–Wed at 11:00, Thu–Sun at 14:00, tel. 01789/292-478 or 07855/760-377, www.stratfordtownwalk.co.uk).  They also run an evening ghost walk led by a professional magician (£5, kids-£3, Mon, Thu, and Fri at 19:30, must book in advance).

City Sightseeing Bus Tours—Open-top buses constantly make the rounds, allowing visitors to hop on and off at all the Shakespeare sights. Given the far-flung nature of two of the Shakespeare sights, and the value of the fun commentary provided, this tour makes the town more manageable. The full circuit takes about an hour, and comes with a steady and informative commentary (£11, buy tickets on bus or as you board, buses leave from the TI every 20 min in high season 9:30–17:00, every 30 min off-season; buses alternate between tape-recorded commentary and live guides—for the best tour, wait for a live guide; tel. 01789/412-680, www.citysightseeing-stratford.com).

Shakespearean Sights

Fans of the Bard's work will want to visit at least a few of these sights. Shakespeare's Exhibition and Birthplace has the best historical introduction to the playwright (as well as a disappoint-ing house where he spent his early years). There are four other Shakespearean properties in and near Stratford, all run by the

Shakespeare Birthplace Trust. Each has a garden and helpful docents who love to tell a story.

Combo-Tickets: Admission to the Shakespeare Birthplace Trust sights in town requires one of two combo-tickets; no individual tickets are sold. Individual tickets are sold for Anne Hathaway's Cottage (£6.50) and Mary Arden's Farm (£8), but these make sense only if you visit just these two sights. If you're visiting only the sights in town—Shakespeare's Birthplace, Hall's Croft, and Nash's House—get the £12 **Shakespeare Birthplace combo-ticket.** To add the two sights outside of Stratford—Anne Hathaway's Cottage and Mary Arden's Farm (my favorite)—get the £17 **Shakespeare Five House combo-ticket.** If you've taken a walking tour with Stratford Town Walks (described under "Tours in Stratford," earlier), show your ticket stub to get the Shakespeare Five House combo-ticket for just £12. Tickets are sold at participating sights and the TI, and are good for one year. Shakespeare's grave isn't covered by either combo-ticket.

In Stratford

▲**Shakespeare Exhibition and Birthplace**—Touring this sight, you'll visit an excellent modern museum before seeing Shakespeare's place of birth (covered by £12 or £17 combo-ticket, daily April–Oct 9:00–17:00, Nov–March 10:00–16:00, in town center on Henley Street, tel. 01789/204-016, www.shakespeare .org.uk).

The **Shakespeare exhibition** provides a fine historical background, with actual historic artifacts. Linger in the museum rather than rushing to the old house, since the meat of your visit is here. It's the best introduction to the life and work of Shakespeare in Stratford, with an original 1623 First Folio of Shakespeare's work. Of the 700 printed, about 150 survive. (Most are in the US, but three are in Stratford.) Western literature owes much to this folio, which collects 36 of the 37 known Shakespeare's plays (*Pericles* missed out). It came with an engraving of the only portrait from living memory of Shakespeare, and likely the most accurate depiction of the great playwright.

The **birthplace,** a half-timbered Elizabethan building furnished as it was when young William was growing up, is filled with bits about his life and work. I found the old house disappointing—only the creaky floorboards feel authentic. After the Shakespeares moved out,

Stratford-upon-Avon

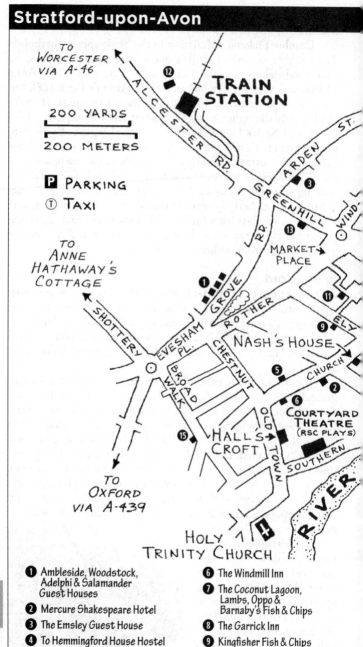

TO WORCESTER VIA A-46

ALCESTER RD.

⑫

TRAIN STATION

200 YARDS

200 METERS

🅿 PARKING

ⓣ TAXI

ARDEN ST.

GREENHILL RD.

③

⑬

WINDM...

MARKET PLACE

TO ANNE HATHAWAY'S COTTAGE

SHOTTERY

GROVE RD.

ROTHER

⑪

⑨

ELY

EVESHAM PL.

BROAD WALK

CHESTNUT

NASH'S HOUSE

⑤

CHURCH

②

⑥ COURTYARD THEATRE (RSC PLAYS)

OLD TOWN

SOUTHERN

⑮

HALL'S CROFT

TO OXFORD VIA A-439

RIVER

HOLY TRINITY CHURCH

① Ambleside, Woodstock, Adelphi & Salamander Guest Houses

② Mercure Shakespeare Hotel

③ The Emsley Guest House

④ To Hemmingford House Hostel

⑤ Russons Restaurant

⑥ The Windmill Inn

⑦ The Coconut Lagoon, Lambs, Oppo & Barnaby's Fish & Chips

⑧ The Garrick Inn

⑨ Kingfisher Fish & Chips

⑩ Marks & Spencer

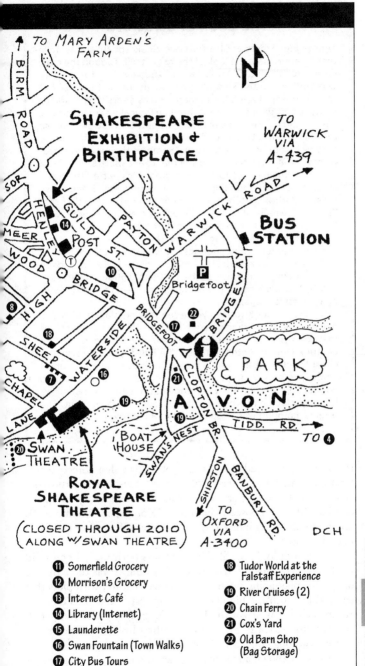

TO MARY ARDEN'S FARM

BIRM. ROAD

SHAKESPEARE EXHIBITION & BIRTHPLACE

TO WARWICK VIA A-439

WARWICK ROAD

BUS STATION

SOR

MEER

WOOD

HENLEY

GUILD ST.

PAYTON ST.

Post Office

BRIDGE

HIGH

⑩

⑭

Ⓣ

Ⓒ

P Bridgefoot

BRIDGEFOOT

BRIDGEWAY

⑰ ㉒

ⓘ

⑧

SHEEP

⑱

WATERSIDE

⑦ ⑯

⑲

⑳ SWAN THEATRE

BOAT HOUSE

SWAN'S NEST

㉑

⑲

CLOPTON BR.

A V O N

PARK

TIDD. RD.

TO ④

CHAPEL LANE

ROYAL SHAKESPEARE THEATRE
(CLOSED THROUGH 2010
ALONG W/SWAN THEATRE)

SHIPSTON RD.

BANBURY RD.

TO OXFORD VIA A-3400

DCH

⑪ Somerfield Grocery
⑫ Morrison's Grocery
⑬ Internet Café
⑭ Library (Internet)
⑮ Launderette
⑯ Swan Fountain (Town Walks)
⑰ City Bus Tours

⑱ Tudor World at the Falstaff Experience
⑲ River Cruises (2)
⑳ Chain Ferry
㉑ Cox's Yard
㉒ Old Barn Shop (Bag Storage)

The Look of Stratford

There's much more to Stratford than Shakespeare sights. Take time to appreciate the look of the town itself. Though the main street goes back to Roman times, the key date for the city was 1196, when the king gave the town "market privileges." Stratford was shaped by its marketplace years. The market's many "departments" were located on logically named streets, whose names still remain: Sheep Street, Corn Street, and so on. Today's street plan—and even the 57' 9" width of the lots—survives from the 12th century. (Some of the modern store-fronts in the town center are still that exact width.)

Starting in about 1600, three great fires gutted the town, leaving very few buildings older than that era. Since those fires, tinderbox thatch roofs were prohibited—the Old Thatch Tavern on Greenhill Street is the only remaining thatch roof in town, predating the law and grandfathered in.

The town's main drag, Bridge Street, is the oldest street in town, but looks the youngest. It was built in the Regency style—a result of a rough little middle row of wattle-and-daub houses being torn down in the 1820s to double the street's width. Today's Bridge Street buildings retain that early 19th-century style: Regency.

Throughout Stratford you'll see striking black-and-white, half-timbered buildings, as well as half-timbered structures that were partially plastered over and covered up in the 19th century. During Victorian times, the half-timbered style was considered low-class, but in the 20th century—just as tourists came, preferring the ye olde style—timbers came back into vogue, and the plaster was removed on many old buildings. But any black and white you see is likely modern paint. The original coloring was "biscuit yellow" and brown.

the building was used as a pub and a butcher's shop. Since its restoration in the 1800s, it feels like millions of visitors have rubbed it clean of anything original. The furnishings seem tacky and modern, but they're supposed to be true to 1575, when William was 11. The house becomes interesting only if you talk up the attendants in each room.

Although William Shakespeare was born in this house (in 1564), he spent most of his career in London. It was there that he taught his play-going public about human nature, with plots that entertained both the highest and the lowest minds. His tool was an unrivaled mastery of the English language. He retired—rich and famous—back in Stratford, spending his last five years at a house (now long gone) called New Place.

Little is known about Shakespeare the man. The scope of his

brilliant work, his humble beginnings, and the fact that no original Shakespeare manuscripts survive raise a few scholarly eyebrows. And though some wonder who penned all these plays, all serious scholars accept his authorship.

Hall's Croft—This former home of Shakespeare's daughter is in the Stratford town center. A fine old Jacobean house, it's the fanciest of the group (she married a doctor). It's worth a quick pop-in if you already have one of the Shakespearean combo-tickets; to make the exhibits on 17th-century medicine interesting, ask the docent for the 15- to 20-minute introduction, which helps bring the plague—and some of the bizarre remedies of the time—to life (covered by £12 or £17 combo-ticket, daily April–Oct 10:00–17:00, Nov–March 11:00–16:00, on-site tearoom, between Church Street and the river on Old Town Street, tel. 01789/292-107).

Nash's House—Built beside New Place (the house where Shakespeare retired), this is the least impressive and least inter-esting of the Shakespeare-related prop-erties. (Nash was the first husband of Shakespeare's granddaughter.) While Shakespeare's New Place is long gone (notice the foundation in the adjacent garden as you leave), Nash's house has survived. Your visit starts here with a five-minute guided intro in the parlor. The upper level hosts temporary exhibits (covered by £12 or £17 combo-ticket, same hours as Hall's Croft, Chapel Street).

You can get into the neighboring gardens for free, and cheapskates can get a nice view of Nash's House's gardens (included in the entry price to the house) just by walking behind it along Chapel Street.

Shakespeare's Grave—To see his final resting place, head to the riverside Holy Trinity Church (£1.50, not covered by either combo-ticket, free to view for churchgoers, April–Sept Mon–Sat 8:30–18:00, Sun 12:30–17:00, slightly shorter hours Oct–March, 10-min walk past the theater—see its graceful spire as you gaze down the river, tel. 01789/266-316, www.stratford-upon-avon.org). The church marks the ninth-century birthplace of the town, which was once a religious settlement.

Just Outside Stratford

▲▲**Mary Arden's Farm and Shakespeare Countryside Museum**—Along with the birthplace museum, this is my favorite of the Shakespearean sights. Famous as the girlhood home of William's mom, this homestead is in Wilmcote (about three miles from Stratford). Built around two historic farmhouses, it's an open-air folk museum depicting 16th-century farm life. It has many more domestic artifacts—and sees far fewer tourists—than the other Shakespeare sights (£8 or covered by £17 combo-ticket, daily April–Oct 10:00–17:00, Nov–March 10:00–16:00).

The first building, **Palmer's farm** (mistaken for Mary Arden's home for hundreds of years, and correctly identified in 2000), is furnished as it would have been in Shakespeare's day.

Mary Arden actually lived in the neighboring **farmhouse,** seemingly less impressive and covered in brick facade. Dorothy Holmes, who lived here until 1979, left it as a 1920s time warp, and that's just what you'll see today. Ask the docent about how they discovered that Palmer's farm was actually built a few years too late to be from Shakespeare's time.

At both buildings you'll see period interpreters in Tudor costumes. They'll likely be going through the day's chores as people back then would have done—activities such as milking the sheep and cutting wood to do repairs on the house. They're there to answer questions and provide fun, gossipy insight into what life was like at the time.

The grounds also host a 19th-century farming exhibit, as well as enjoyable and informative **falconry demonstrations** with lots of

mean-footed birds. Chat with the falconer about their methods for earning the birds' trust. The birds' hunger sets them to flight (a round-trip earns the bird a bit of food; the birds fly when hungry—but don't have the energy if they're *too* hungry). Like Katherine, the wife described as "my falcon" in *The Taming of the Shrew,* these birds are tamed and trained with food as a reward. If things are slow, ask if you can feed one.

Getting to Mary Arden's House: The most convenient way to get here is by car or the hop-on, hop-off bus tour, but it's also possible to reach by train. The Wilmcote train station is directly across the street from Mary Arden's House (£2 round-trip fare, one stop from Stratford-upon-Avon on Birmingham-bound train, 5-min trip, train runs about every hour, call London Midland to confirm departure time—tel. 0844-811-0133, www.londonmidland.com).

▲**Anne Hathaway's Cottage**—Located 1.5 miles out of Stratford (in Shottery), this home is a picturesque, thatched, 12-room farm-

house where the Bard's wife grew up. William courted Anne here—she was 26, he was only 18—and his tactics proved successful. (Maybe a little too much, as she was several months pregnant at their wedding.) They were married for 34 years, until his death in 1616 at age 52.

Stop in the first room for a fun eight-minute intro talk. (If the place shakes, a tourist has thunked his or her head on the low beams.) The Hathaway family lived here for 400 years, until 1912, and much of the family's 92-acre farm remains part of the sight. Though the house has little to do with Shakespeare, it offers an intimate peek at life in Shakespeare's day. Guides in each room do their best to lecture to the stampeding crowds. The garden comes with a prizewinning "traditional cottage garden," a yew maze (planted only in 2001, so not yet a challenge), a great photo-op statue of the British Isles, and a rotating exhibit, generally on a gardening theme (£6.50 or covered by £17 combo-ticket, daily April–Oct 9:00–17:00, Nov–March 10:00–16:00; a 30-min walk, a stop on the hop-on, hop-off tour bus, or a quick taxi ride from Stratford; well-signposted for drivers entering Stratford from any direction, easy and free parking).

Seeing a Shakespeare Play in Stratford

In 2008, the mighty Royal Shakespeare Company (RSC) down-sized, as its historic theater underwent a multiyear renovation (esti-mated reopening date: late 2010). Most performances are now held in the new Courtyard Theatre, a testing ground for the lights, seats, and structure of the multi-million-dollar renovation of the main theater. (While you're in Stratford, you also may see ads for RSC productions scattered in other smaller theaters around town.)

For the most up-to-date show times, check with the TI or the Royal Shakespeare Company's box office or website (see below).

▲▲Royal Shakespeare Company

The RSC, undoubtedly the best Shakespeare company on earth and a memorable experience, performs year-round in Stratford and in London (see page 122). If you're a Shakespeare fan, see if the

Stratford Thanks America

Residents of Stratford are thankful for the many contributions Americans have made to their city and its heritage. Along with pumping up the economy day in and day out with tourist visits, Americans paid for half the rebuilding of the Royal Shakespeare Theatre after it burned down in 1926. The Swan Theatre renovation was funded entirely by American aid. Harvard University inherited—you guessed it—the Harvard House, and it maintains the house today. London's much-loved theater, Shakespeare's Globe, was the dream (and gift) of an American. And there's even an odd but prominent "American Fountain" overlooking Stratford's market square on Rother Street, which was given in 1887 to celebrate the Golden Jubilee of the rule of Queen Victoria.

RSC schedule fits into your itinerary.

Tickets in Stratford range from £5 (standing) to £50 (Mon–Sat at 19:30, matinees vary, sporadic shows Sun). You'll probably need to buy your tickets ahead of time. Even if there aren't any seats available, you can sometimes buy a returned ticket on the evening of an otherwise sold-out show (box office window open Mon–Sat 9:30–20:00, ticket hotline open 24/7, tel. 0844-800-1100, www.rsc.org.uk). Because the RSC website is so user-friendly, it makes absolutely no sense to pay extra to book tickets through any other source. If you're feeling bold, buy a £5 standing ticket and then slip into an open seat as the lights dim—if there's not something available during the play's first half, chances are there will be plenty of seats after intermission.

Theaters

The Courtyard Theatre—This temporary theater, a two-minute walk down Southern Lane from the original Royal Shakespeare Theatre, seats 1,000 people, and is a prototype for the new Royal Shakespeare Theatre.

The Royal Shakespeare Theatre—The original theater was built in 1879 to honor the bard, but burned down in 1926. The big replacement building you see under construction today (facing the riverside park) was erected in 1932. During the design phase, no actors were consulted; as a result, they built the stodgy Edwardian "picture frame"–style stage, even though the more dynamic "thrust"-style stage—which makes it

easier for the audience to become engaged—is the actors' choice. (It would also have been closer in design to Shakespeare's Globe stage, which juts into the crowd.) The original ill-conceived design is the reason for the multiyear renovation. When the theater reopens, it will have an updated, thrust-style stage (the kind you'll see in the Courtyard Theatre).

The Swan Theatre—Adjacent to the RSC Theatre is the smaller, Elizabethan-style Swan Theatre, a galleried playhouse that opened in 1986. In the past, the Swan has hosted theater tours, but as part of the renovation of the main theater, the Swan shut its doors to visitors.

Non-Shakespearean Sights

Tudor World at the Falstaff Experience—While a bit gimmicky, this is about the best non-Shakespeare historical sight

in the town center. (It's named for a Shakespeare character, but the exhibit isn't about the Bard.) Filling Shrieve's House Barn with informative and entertaining exhibits, it sweeps through Tudor history from the plague to Henry VIII's privy chamber to a replica 16th-century tavern. If you're into ghost-spotting, their nightly ghost tours may be your best shot (museum-£5, daily 10:30–17:30; ghost tours-£7.50, daily at 18:00; Sheep Street, toll tel. 0870-350-2770, www.falstaffexperience.co.uk).

Avon Riverfront—The River Avon is a playground of swans and canal boats. The swans have been the mascots of Stratford since 1623, when, seven years after the Bard's death, a poem in his First Folio nicknamed him "the sweet swan of Avon." Join in the bird-scene fun and buy **swan food** (50p) to feed swans and ducks; ask at the ice-cream stand for details. Don't feed the Canada geese, which locals disdain (according to them, the geese are vicious and

have been messing up the eco-balance since they were imported by a king in 1665).

The **canal boats** saw their workhorse days during the short window of time between the start of the Industrial Revolution and the establishment of the railways. Today, they're mostly pleasure boats. The boats are long and

Stratford, the Birthplace of...
Teletubbies

The children's television series *Teletubbies* was first produced at a secret location somewhere around Stratford. Ragdoll, the local TV production company that made *Teletubbies,* became phenomenally successful, also creating the kids' series' *Rosie and Jim, Brum,* and *Boohbah. Teletubbies,* comprising 365 episodes, is no longer in production, but will likely continue to appear in reruns worldwide for years to come. Its creator, Ann Wood, has had quite a ride. Sales of her little stuffed animals went through the roof in Britain, thanks in part to American televangelist Jerry Falwell, who infamously declared that Tinky Winky, the purse-toting purple tubby with the triangle above his head, was gay; he issued an alert to parents stating that the Teletubbies were sinisterly promoting deviant lifestyles among preschoolers. At first, Mrs. Wood—a proper and decent English woman—was crushed to hear about his claim. Then sales skyrocketed, and she went on to become Britain's fifth wealthiest woman, the beneficiary of Falwell's homophobic paranoia. Stratford's Ragdoll shop, long a local fixture, closed in 2005, but hopes to eventually reopen in a bigger location (www.ragdoll.co.uk).

narrow, so two can pass in the slim canals. There are 2,000 miles of canals in England's Midlands, built to connect centers of industry with seaports and provide vital transportation during the early days of the Industrial Revolution. Stratford was as far inland as you could sail on natural rivers from Bristol; it was the terminus of the manmade Birmingham Canal, built in 1816. Even today, you can motor your canal boat all the way to London from here.

For a little bit of mellow river action, rent a **rowboat** (£4/hr per person) or, for more of a challenge, pole yourself around on a Cambridge-style **punt** (canal is poleable—only 4 or 5 feet deep; same price and more memories/ embarrassment if you do the punting—don't pay £16/hr for a waterman to do the punting for you). Take a short stop on your lazy tour of the English countryside, and moor your canal boat at Stratford's Canal Basin.

You can try a sleepy half-hour **river cruise** (£4, no commentary, Avon Boating, board boat in Bancroft Gardens near the RSC theater or at Swan's Nest Boathouse across the Tramway Bridge, tel. 01789/267-073, www.avon-boating.co.uk), or jump on the oldest surviving **chain ferry** (c. 1937) in Britain (50p), which shuttles people across the river just beyond the theater.

Cox's Yard, a riverside timber yard until the 1990s, is a rare physical remnant of the days when Stratford was an industrial port. Today, Cox's is a touristic entertainment center with pubs that have live music most nights (£5–15, schedule at tel. 01789/404-600 or www.coxsyard.co.uk).

Sleeping in Stratford

If you want to spend the night after you catch a show, options abound. Ye olde timbered hotels are scattered through the city center. Most B&Bs are on the fringes of town, right on the busy ring roads that route traffic away from the center. (The recommended places below generally have double-paned windows for rooms in the front.) The weekend after Shakespeare's birthday (April 24–25 in 2010) is particularly tight, but Fridays and Saturdays are busy throughout the season. This town is so reliant upon the theater for its business that some B&Bs have secondary insurance covering their loss if the Royal Shakespeare Company stops performing in Stratford for any reason.

On Grove Road

These accommodations are at the edge of town on busy Grove Road, across from a grassy park.

$$ Ambleside Guest House is run with quiet efficiency and attentiveness by owners Peter and Ruth. Each of the seven rooms has been completely renovated, including the small but tidy bathrooms. The place has a homey, airy feel, with none of the typical B&B clutter (S-£28–33, Db-£60–75, Tb-£85–105, Qb-£95–125, one ground-floor room, secure parking available, free Wi-Fi, 41 Grove Road, tel. 01789/297-239, fax 01789/295-670, www.ambleside guesthouse.com, ruth@amblesideguesthouse.com—include your phone number in your request, since they prefer to call you back to confirm).

$$ Woodstock Guest House is a friendly, frilly, family-run, and flowery place with five comfortable rooms (Sb-£35–40, Db-£60–70, family room-£75–90, cash only, deals for 2 or more nights, parking, 30 Grove Road, tel. 01789/299-881, www.wood stock-house.co.uk, jackie@woodstock-house.co.uk, owners Denis and bubbly Jackie).

$$ Adelphi Guest House has six rooms—two with four-poster beds—in a newly renovated B&B (S-£35–40, D-£75–80, 5 percent surcharge on credit cards, 10 percent discount in 2010

Sleep Code

(£1 = about $1.60, country code: 44, area code: 01789)
S = Single, **D** = Double/Twin, **T** = Triple, **Q** = Quad, **b** = bathroom, **s** = shower only. Unless noted otherwise, you can assume credit cards are accepted and breakfast is included.

To help you sort easily through these listings, I've divided the rooms into three categories based on the price for a standard double room with bath:

$$$ Higher Priced—Most rooms £90 or more.
  $$ Moderately Priced—Most rooms between £60–90.
    $ Lower Priced—Most rooms £60 or less.

if you mention this book when you reserve, free Wi-Fi, parking available if booked in advance, 39 Grove Road, tel. 01789/204-469, www.adelphi-guesthouse.com, info@adelphi-guesthouse.com, Martin and Ellen).

$ Salamander Guest House, run by gregarious Frenchman Pascal and his wife, Anna, rents seven well-priced but basic rooms (S-£30–35, Db-£50–60, Tb-£60–75, Qb-£80–90, free Wi-Fi, free on-site parking, 40 Grove Road, tel. & fax 01789/205-728, www.salamanderguesthouse.co.uk, p.delin@btinternet.com).

Elsewhere in Stratford

$$$ Mercure Shakespeare Hotel, located in a black-and-white building just up the street from Nash's House, has 74 central, spacious, and elegant rooms. Singles are cheaper on weekends, and doubles drop in price on Sunday and midweek—check website for special deals (Sb-£80, standard Db-£130, deluxe Db-£150, prices soft depending on demand—can be as low as £100 for a double, parking-£10/day, Wi-Fi in lobby, Chapel Street, tel. 01789/294-997, fax 01789/415-411, www.mercure.com, h6630-re@accor.com).

$$ The Emsley Guest House holds five bright rooms named after different counties in England, and has a homey and inviting atmosphere (Sb-£45–50, Db-£60–80, Tb-£90–120, Q-£120–160, 5-person family room-£150–200, families welcome, off-street parking, 4 Arden Street, tel. 01789/299-557, www.theemsley.co.uk, mel@theemsley.co.uk, Melanie and Ray Coulson).

$ *Hostel:* Hemmingford House, with 130 beds in 2- to 10-bed rooms, is a 10-minute bus ride from town (from £25 for non-members, includes breakfast; take bus #15, #18, or #18A two miles to Alveston; tel. 01789/297-093 or 0845-371-9661, stratford@yha.org.uk).

Eating in Stratford

Stratford's numerous eateries vie for your pre- and post-theater business, with special hours and meal deals. (Most offer light two- and three-course menus from 17:30 to 19:00.) You'll find many hard-working places lined up along Sheep Street and Waterside.

Russons Restaurant, which specializes in fresh fish and seafood, is probably the best place in town. It's cheery and chic, offering international cuisine in a woody, yellow candlelit ambience. Reserve in advance for evening meals (£10–15 plates, Tue–Sat 11:30–14:00 & 17:15–21:00, closed Sun–Mon, 8 Church Street, tel. 01789/268-822).

The Windmill Inn, across from Russons, serves modestly priced but elegant fare in a 17th-century inn. Order drinks and food at the bar, settle into a comfy chair, and wait for your meal to be served (£6–12 plates, Mon–Fri 12:00–19:00, Sat–Sun 12:00–17:00, Church Street, tel. 01789/297-687).

The Coconut Lagoon serves tasty, spicy nouveau–South Indian cuisine and offers pre-theater specials until 19:00: a £10.50 two-course deal or £13.25 for three courses (Tue–Sun 12:00–14:30 & 17:00–23:00, closed Mon, 21 Sheep Street, tel. 01789/293-546).

Lambs is an intimate place serving meat, fish, and veggie dishes with panache (£15 two-course special, £20 three-course special, Mon 17:00–22:00, Tue–Sat 12:00–14:00 & 17:00–22:00, Sun 12:00–14:00 & 18:00–21:00, 12 Sheep Street, tel. 01789/292-554). The related **Oppo Restaurant,** next door, is similar but less formal (Mon–Thu 12:00–14:00 & 17:00–21:30, Fri–Sat 12:00–14:00 & 17:00–23:00, Sun 18:00–21:00, tel. 01789/269-980).

The Garrick Inn bills itself as the oldest pub in town, and comes with a cozy, dimly lit restaurant vibe. They serve pricey but above-average pub cuisine (£11 or less, Mon–Sat 12:00–22:00, Sun 12:00–21:00, 25 High Street, tel. 01789/292-186).

Barnaby's is a greasy fast-food fish-and-chips joint near the waterfront—but it's convenient if you want to get takeout for the riverside park just across the street (daily 11:00–19:30, at Sheep Street and Waterside). For a better set of fish-and-chips, queue up with the locals at **Kingfisher** (Mon–Sat 11:30–13:45 & 17:00–21:30, closed Sun, a long block up at 13 Ely Street, tel. 01789/292-513).

Picnic: For groceries, you'll find **Marks & Spencer** on Bridge Street (Mon–Sat 9:00–18:00, Sun 10:30–16:30, small coffee-and-sandwiches café upstairs, tel. 01789/292-430), **Somerfield** in the Town Centre mall (Mon–Sat 8:00–19:00, Sun 10:00–16:00, tel. 01789/292-604), and a huge **Morrison's** next to the train station, a 10-minute walk from the city center (Mon–Sat 8:00–20:00, Sun

10:00–16:00, pharmacy, tel. 01789/267-675). To picnic, head to the canal and riverfront park between the Royal Shakespeare Theatre and the TI. Choose a bench with views of the river or of vacation houseboats, and munch your fish-and-chips while tossing a few fries into the river to attract swans. It's a fine way to spend a mid-summer night's eve.

Stratford Connections

Remember: When buying tickets or checking schedules, ask for "Stratford-upon-Avon," not just "Stratford" (which is a different town).

From Stratford-upon-Avon by Train to: London (every 2 hrs, 2.25 hrs, direct to Marylebone Station), **Warwick** (every 1–2 hrs, 30 min, **Coventry** (at least hourly, 1.75 hrs, change in Leamington Spa or Birmingham), **Oxford** (every 2 hrs, 1.25–2.5 hrs, change in Banbury). Train info: toll tel. 0845-748-4950, www.nationalrail.co.uk.

By Bus to: Chipping Campden (Mon–Sat 11 buses/day, none on Sun, 35 min, Johnsons Coach & Bus, tel. 01564/797-070, www.johnsonscoaches.co.uk), **Warwick** (hourly by bus, 20 min, tel. 01788/535-555, www.stagecoachbus.com), **Coventry** (hourly, 1.25 hrs, tel. 01788/535-555, www.stagecoachbus.com). Most intercity buses stop on Stratford's Bridge Street (a block up from the TI). For bus info that covers all the region's companies, call Traveline at toll tel. 0871-200-2233 (www.travelinemidlands.co.uk).

By Car: Driving is easy and distances are brief: **Stow-on-the-Wold** (22 miles), **Warwick** (8 miles), **Coventry** (19 miles).

Near Stratford

Warwick

The pleasant town of Warwick—home to England's finest medieval castle—goes about its business almost oblivious to the busloads of tourists passing through. From the castle, a lane leads into the old town center a block away, where you'll find the **TI** (daily 10:00–16:30, tel. 01926/492-212, www.warwick-uk.co.uk), plenty of eateries (including the Ask restaurant chain), and several minor attractions. The TI can also sell same-day tickets to Warwick Castle; there's no discount, but it can save you time in line at the castle.

Sights in Warwick

▲▲Warwick Castle

Almost *too* groomed and organized, this theme park of a castle gives its crowds of visitors a decent value for the stiff £20 entry

fee. The cash-poor but enterprising lord hired the folks at Madame Tussauds (now part of Merlin Entertainments, which also owns the London Eye and Legoland) to wring maximum tourist dollars out of his castle. The greedy feel of the place is a little annoying, considering the already-steep admission. But there just isn't a better medieval castle experience in England—especially for kids.

With a lush, green, grassy moat and fairy-tale fortifications, Warwick will entertain you from dungeon to lookout. Standing inside the castle gate, you can see the mound where the original Norman castle of 1068 stood. Under this "motte," the wooden stockade (or "bailey") defined the courtyard in the way the castle walls do today. The castle is a 14th- and 15th-century fortified shell, holding an 18th- and 19th-century royal residence, surrounded by another one of dandy "Capability" Brown's landscape jobs (like at Blenheim Palace).

Within the castle's mighty walls, there's something for every taste. The Great Hall and six lavish staterooms are the sumptu-

ous highlights. You'll also find a Madame Tussauds–mastered re-creation of a royal weekend party—an 1898 game of statue-maker (look for a young Winston Churchill). You can ponder the weapons in the fine educational armory, then see demonstrations outside of a trebuchet (like a catapult) and ballista (a type of giant slingshot). The "King Maker" exhibit (set in 1471, when the towns-folk are getting ready for battle) is highly promoted, but not quite as good as a Disney ride. From the classic ramparts, the tower is a one-way, no-return, 250-step climb, offering a fun perch from which to fire your imaginary longbow. A recently restored mill and engine house come with an attendant who explains how the castle was electrified in 1894. Surrounding everything is a lush, peacock-patrolled, picnic-perfect park, complete with a Victorian

Stratford Area

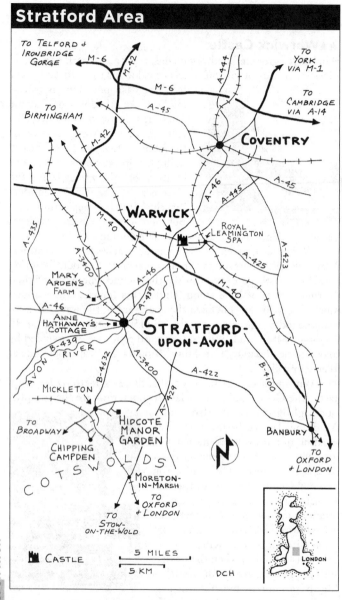

TO TELFORD &
IRONBRIDGE
GORGE

M-6

M-42

M-6

TO BIRMINGHAM

M-42

A-45

A-444

TO YORK VIA M-1

TO CAMBRIDGE VIA A-14

COVENTRY

A-46

A-445

A-45

A-435

M-40

WARWICK

ROYAL LEAMINGTON SPA

A-425

A-423

A-3400

A-46

A-439

MARY ARDEN'S FARM

ANNE HATHAWAY'S COTTAGE

A-46

B-439

AVON RIVER

B-4632

STRATFORD-UPON-AVON

M-40

A-3400

A-422

B-4100

A-429

MICKLETON

TO BROADWAY

CHIPPING CAMPDEN

HIDCOTE MANOR GARDEN

COTSWOLDS

MORETON-IN-MARSH

TO OXFORD & LONDON

TO STOW-ON-THE-WOLD

BANBURY

TO OXFORD & LONDON

🏰 CASTLE

5 MILES

5 KM

DCH

LONDON

rose garden. The castle grounds are often enlivened by a knight in shining armor on a horse that rotates with a merry band of musical jesters.

Cost, Hours, Location: Steep £20 entry fee (£12 for seniors), includes gardens and nearly all castle attractions—except the gory £7.50 dungeon, crazy pricing scheme varies based on anticipated crowds—may go down to £18 in slow periods, discounted tickets available on the castle's website and at the TI in Stratford. It's open daily April–Oct 10:00–18:00, Nov–March 10:00–17:00. Driving and parking tips are noted under "Warwick Connections—By Car," later. For train travelers, it's a 15-minute, one-mile walk from the Warwick train station to the castle (toll tel. 0870-442-2375, recorded info tel. 0870-442-2000, www.warwick-castle.com).

Audioguide: Three audioguides provide descriptions of the State Apartments, the Royal Weekend Party exhibit, and A Knight's Tale (£3 apiece, or all three for £6, can be combined

with online ticket purchase or rented upon arrival). The £5 guidebook gives you nearly the same script in souvenir-booklet form. Either is worthwhile if you want to understand the various rooms. If you tour the castle without help, pick the brains of the earnest and talkative docents.

Events: During summer, special events (great for kids) are scheduled every half-hour throughout the day (jousting, longbow demo, sword fights, jester acts, and so on). Pick up the daily events flier (which also lists kiosks that sell snacks) and plan accordingly.

Eating in Warwick

The castle has three main lunch options. **The Coach House** has cafeteria fare and grungy seating (located just before the turnstiles). **The Undercroft** offers the best on-site cooked food, and has a sandwich buffet line (located inside, in basement of palace); you can sit under medieval vaults or escape with your food and picnic outside. The **riverside pavilion** sells sandwiches and fish-and-chips, and has fine outdoor seating (in park just before the bridge, behind castle).

Literally a hundred yards from the castle turnstiles—through a tiny gate in the wall—is the workaday commercial district of the town of **Warwick,** with several much more elegant and competitive eateries that serve fine lunches at non-Tussauds prices. It's worth the walk.

Warwick Connections

From Warwick by Train to: London (3/hr, 2 hrs), **Stratford** (every 1–2 hrs, 30 min—buses are better, see below). Warwick's little train station is a 15-minute walk (or £3 taxi) from the castle. It has no official baggage check, but you can ask politely. The castle has a baggage-check facility. Train info: toll tel. 0845-748-4950, www.nationalrail.co.uk.

By Bus to: Stratford (hourly, 20 min, bus #X17, also slower #18), **Coventry** (10/day, 1 hour, bus #X17, www.stagecoachbus .com).

By Car: The main Stratford–Coventry road cuts right through Warwick. Coming from Stratford (8 miles to the south) you'll hit the castle parking lots first (£3.50; if these are full, lurk until a few cars leave and they'll let you in). The four castle lots are expensive, and three of them are a 10- to 15-minute walk from the actual castle; "premium" £6 parking lot next to the entrance, off Castle Lane. Consider continuing into the town center (on the main road). At the TI (near the big square church spire), grab any street-side parking (free for 2 hours). The castle is a block behind the TI.

Coventry

Coventry, a ▲ sight, was bombed to smithereens in 1940 by the Nazi Luftwaffe. From that point on, the German phrase for "to really blast the heck out of a place" was "to coventrate" it. But Coventry rose from its ashes, and its message to our world is one of forgiveness, reconciliation, and the importance of peace. Browse through Coventry, the closest thing to normal, everyday, urban England that most tourists  will ever see. Get a map at the **TI,** located at the cathedral ruins (Mon–Fri 9:30–17:00, Sat–Sun 10:00–16:30, shorter hours off-season, tel. 02476/227-264, www.visitcoventryandwarwickshire .co.uk, tic@cvone.co.uk).

The symbol of Coventry is the bombed-out hulk of its old **cathedral,** with the huge new one adjoining it. The inspirational complex welcomes visitors. Climb the tower (£2.50, daily 9:30–16:00, 180 steps, tel. 02476/225-616, www.coventrycathedral.org.uk).

According to legend, Coventry's most famous hometown girl, Lady Godiva, rode bareback and bare-naked through the town in the 11th century to help lower taxes. You'll see her bronze statue a block from the cathedral (near Broadgate). Just beyond that is the **Coventry Transport Museum,** which features the first, fastest, and most famous cars and motorcycles that came from this "British Detroit" (free, daily 10:00–17:00, tel. 02476/234-270, www.transport-museum.com).

St. Mary's Guildhall has 14th-century tapestries, stained glass, and an ornate ceiling (free, Easter–Sept Sun–Thu 10:00–16:00; closed Fri–Sat, during events, and off-season; www.coventry .gov.uk/stmarys).

Coventry Connections

From Coventry by Train to: Telford Central (near Ironbridge Gorge; 2/hr, 1.5 hrs, change in Birmingham or Wolverhampton), **Warwick** (hourly, 30 min, change in Leamington Spa), **Stratford-upon-Avon** (at least hourly, 1.75 hrs, change in Leamington Spa or Birmingham). Train info: toll tel. 0845-748-4950, www .nationalrail.co.uk.

Route Tips for Drivers: Stratford to Ironbridge Gorge via Warwick and Coventry

Entering Stratford from the Cotswolds, cross a bridge and pass the TI for the best parking. Veer right (following *Through Traffic, P,* and *Wark* signs), go around the block—turning right and right and right—and enter the multistory Bridgefoot garage (80p/hr, £20/6–24 hrs, you'll find no place easier or cheaper). The TI and City Sightseeing bus stop are a block away. Leaving the garage, circle to the right around the same block, but stay on "the Wark" (Warwick Road, A439). Warwick is eight miles away. The castle is just south of town on the right. (For parking advice, see "Warwick Connections—By Car," earlier.) When you're trying to decide whether to stop in Coventry, factor in Birmingham's rush hour— try to avoid driving the section described below between 14:00 and 20:00, if you can (see next chapter for tips).

If You're Including Coventry: After touring the castle, carry on through the center of Warwick and follow signs to Coventry (still A439, then A46). If you're stopping in Coventry, follow signs painted on the road to the *city centre,* and then to *cathedral parking.* Grab a place in the high-rise parking lot. Leaving Coventry, follow signs to *Nuneaton* and *M6 North* through lots of sprawl, and you're on your way. (See below.)

If You're Skirting Coventry: Take M69 (direction: Leicester) and follow M6 as it threads through giant Birmingham.

Once You're on M6: The highway divides into a free M6 and a toll M6 (designed to help drivers cut through the Birmingham traffic chaos). Take the toll road—£4 is a small price to pay to avoid all the nasty traffic.

When battling through sprawling Birmingham, keep your sights on M6. If you're heading for any points north—Ironbridge Gorge (Telford), North Wales, Liverpool, Blackpool, or the Lakes (Kendal for the South Lake District, Keswick for the North Lake District)—just stay relentlessly on M6 (direction: North West). Each destination is clearly signed directly from M6.

For Ironbridge Gorge, take the T8 exit (don't miss this exit, or you'll have to go all the way to T11 to turn around and back-track). Follow M54 heading toward Telford. Keep an eye out for *Ironbridge* signs and do-si-do through a long series of roundabouts until you're there.

IRONBRIDGE GORGE

The Industrial Revolution was born in the Severn River Valley. In its glory days, this valley (blessed with abundant deposits of iron ore and coal and a river for transport) gave the world its first iron wheels, steam-powered locomotive, and cast-iron bridge (begun in 1779). The museums in Ironbridge Gorge, which capture the flavor of the Victorian Age, take you back to the days when Britain was racing into the modern era and pulling the rest of the West with her.

Planning Your Time

Without a car, Ironbridge Gorge isn't worth the headache. Drivers can slip it in between the Cotswolds/Stratford/Warwick and points north (such as the Lake District or North Wales). Speed demons zip in for a midday tour of Blists Hill, look at the bridge, and speed out. For an overnight visit, arrive in the early evening to browse the town, and spend the morning and early afternoon touring the sights before driving on (10:00–Museum of the Gorge, which has a nice overview of the entire area; 11:00–Blists Hill Victorian Town for lunch and sightseeing; 15:30–Head to your next destination).

With more time—say, a full month in Britain—I'd spend two nights and a leisurely day: 9:30–Iron Bridge and the town; 10:30–Museum of the Gorge; 11:30–Coalbrookdale Museum of Iron; 14:30–Blists Hill; then dinner at Coalbrookdale Inn.

Orientation to Ironbridge Gorge

(area code: 01952)
The town is just a few blocks gathered around the Iron Bridge, which spans the peaceful, tree-lined Severn River. While the smoke-belching bustle is long gone, knowing that this wooded, sleepy river valley was the "Silicon Valley" of the 19th century makes wandering its brick streets almost a pilgrimage. The actual museum sites are scattered over three miles. The modern cooling towers (for coal, not nuclear energy) that loom ominously over these red-brick remnants seem strangely appropriate.

Tourist Information
The TI is in the tollhouse on the Iron Bridge (Mon–Fri 9:00–17:00, Sat–Sun 10:00–17:00, tel. 01952/884-391). The TI has lots of booklets for sale; hikers like the three booklets of nearby walks (£3–5).

Getting Around Ironbridge Gorge
On weekends from Easter through October, **Gorge Connect** buses link the museum sites (£0.50/ride, £2.50 day ticket, may be free with Museum Passport in 2010—described later, 1–2/hr, April–Oct Sat–Sun 9:00–18:00 only, no buses Mon–Fri, several morning and afternoon runs go to the Telford rail station—schedule on website, tel. 01952/200-005 or 01952/382-121, www .telfordtravelink.co.uk).

Sights in Ironbridge Gorge

▲▲Iron Bridge
While England was at war with her American colonies, this first cast-iron bridge was built in 1779 to show off a wonderful new building material. Lacking experience with cast iron, the builders erred on the side of sturdiness and constructed it as if it were made out of wood. Notice that the original construction used traditional timber-jointing techniques rather than rivets. (Any rivets are from later repairs.) The valley's centerpiece is free, open all the time,  and thought-provoking. Walk across the bridge to the tollhouse/ TI/gift shop/museum (free, see "Tourist Information," above). Read the fee schedule and notice the subtle slam against royalty. (England was not immune to the revolutionary sentiment brewing in the colonies at this time.) Pedestrians paid half a penny to cross;

Ironbridge Gorge

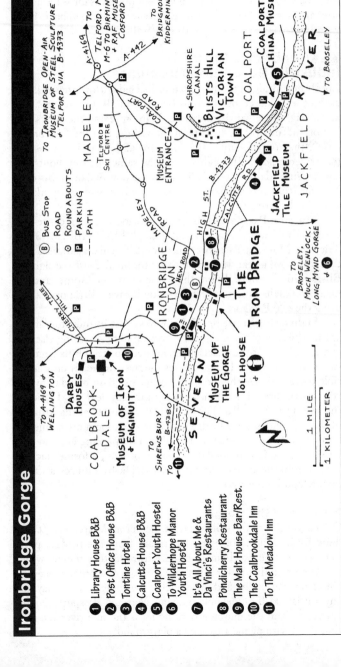

1. Library House B&B
2. Post Office House B&B
3. Tontine Hotel
4. Calcutts House B&B
5. Coalport Youth Hostel
6. To Wilderhope Manor Youth Hostel
7. It's All About Me & Da Vinci's Restaurants
8. Pondicherry Restaurant
9. The Malt House Bar/Rest.
10. The Coalbrookdale Inn
11. To The Meadow Inn

poor people crossed cheaper by coracle—a crude tub-like wood-and-canvas shuttle ferry (you'll see old photos of these upstairs in the TI). Cross back to the town and enjoy a pleasant walk downstream along the towpath. Where horses once dragged boats laden with Industrial Age cargo, locals now walk their dogs.

▲▲▲Ironbridge Gorge Industrial Revolution Museums

Locals take pride in the 10 museums located within a few miles of each other, focused on the Iron Bridge and all it represents. Not all the sights are worth your time. Plan on seeing the Blists Hill Victorian Town, the Museum of the Gorge, and the Coalbrookdale Museum of Iron, all using the £20 Museum Passport (described below). The sights share the same opening hours and contact info (daily 10:00–17:00, a few Coalbrookdale sights close Nov–March, tel. 01952/884-391, www.ironbridge.org.uk, tic @ironbridge.org.uk).

Museum Passport: This group of widely scattered sites has varied admission charges (usually £3–7; Blists Hill is £13.25). The £20 Museum Passport (families-£55) covers admission to everything for a year. If you're visiting the area's must-see sights—Blists Hill Victorian Town, the Museum of the Gorge, and the Coalbrookdale Museum of Iron—you'll save a little over £3 by using the £20 Passport.

Sightseeing Strategies: It helps to see the introductory movie at the Museum of the Gorge first, to help put everything else into context. A few of these museums, located up steep hills from the valley where the Iron Bridge crosses the river, are really only accessible by car. To see the most significant sights in one day by car, you'll park three times: Once either in the lot near the TI (across the river from the village) or in the pay lot located at the Museum of the Gorge (the Iron Bridge and Gorge Museum are connected by an easy, flat walk); once at the Blists Hill parking lot; and once outside of the Coalbrookdale Museum of Iron, a former factory, with Enginuity across the lot and the Darby Houses a three-minute uphill hike away.

Museum of the Gorge

Orient yourself to the valley here in the Severn Warehouse (£3.25, daily 10:00–17:00, 500 yards upstream from the bridge, parking-£1). See the excellent 11-minute introductory movie, which lays the groundwork for what you'll see in the other museums. Check out the exhibit and the model of the gorge in its heyday, and buy a Blists Hill guidebook and your Museum Passport. Farther upstream from the museum parking lot is the fine riverside Dale End Park, with picnic areas and a playground.

Blists Hill Victorian Town

Save most of your time and energy for this wonderful town—an immersive, open-air folk museum. You'll wander through 50 acres

of Victorian industry, factories, and a re-created community from the 1890s. Pick up the Blists Hill guidebook for a good step-by-step rundown (£13.25, closes at 16:00 in winter, tel. 01952/601-048).

The board by the entry lists which exhibits are staffed with lively docents in Victorian dress. Pop in to say hello to the lonely bankers—when the schoolchildren visit, the bankers lose the popularity contest to the "sweet shop" next door. It's OK to take photos.

Stop by the pharmacy and check out the squirm-inducing setup of the dentist's chair from the time—it'll make you appreciate the marvel of modern dental care. Down the street, kids like watching the candlemaker at work. Check the events in the barn across the path, where hands-on candle-making and other activities take place.

Just as in Victorian days, the village has a working pub, a greengrocer's shop, a fascinating squatter's cottage, and a snorty, slippery pigsty. Don't miss the explanation of the winding machine at the Blists Hill Mine (demos throughout the day, call for times). Located by the canal, a scale model made for a 2001 television program shows how the Iron Bridge was erected. Walk along the canal to the "inclined plane."

Grab lunch in The New Inn Pub or in the cafeteria near the children's old-time rides.

Coalbrookdale Museum of Iron

This museum does a fine job of explaining the original iron-smelting process. Compared to the fun and frolicking Blists Hill village, it is sleepy (£7.75, includes entry to the Darby Houses, listed later; £1 less in winter—when Darby Houses are closed for lack of light; opposite Darby's furnace).

The Coalbrookdale neighborhood is the birthplace of the Industrial Revolution, where locals like to claim that mass production was invented. Abraham Darby's blast furnace sits like a shrine inside a big glass pyramid (free), surrounded by evocative Industrial Age ruins. It was here that, in 1709, Darby first smelted iron, using coke as fuel. To me, "coke" is a drink, and "smelt" is the past tense of smell...but around here, these words recall the event that kicked off the modern Industrial Age.

All the ingredients of the recipe for big industry were here in abundance—iron ore, top-grade coal, and water for power and shipping. Wander around Abraham Darby's furnace. Before this furnace was built, iron ore was laboriously melted by charcoal. With huge waterwheel-powered bellows, Darby burned top-grade coal at super-hot temperatures (burning off the impurities to make "coke"). Local iron ore was dumped into the furnace and melted. Impurities floated to the top, while the pure iron sank to the bottom of a clay tub in the bottom of the furnace. Twice a day, the plugs were knocked off, allowing the "slag" to drain away on the top and the molten iron to drain out on the bottom. The low-grade slag was used locally on walls and paths. The high-grade iron trickled into molds formed in the sand below the furnace. It cooled into pig iron (named because the molds look like piglets suckling their mother). The pig-iron "planks" were broken off by sledgehammers and shipped away. The Severn River became one of Europe's busiest, shipping pig iron to distant foundries, where it was remelted and made into cast iron (for projects such as the Iron Bridge), or to forges, where it was worked like toffee into wrought iron.

Enginuity

Located across the parking lot from the Coalbrookdale Museum of Iron, Enginuity is a hands-on funfest for kids. Riffing on Ironbridge's engineering roots, this converted 1709 foundry is full of mesmerizing water contraptions, pumps, magnets, and laser games. Build a dam, try your hand at earthquake-proof construction, navigate a water maze, operate a remote-controlled robot, or power a turbine with your own steam (£7).

Darby Houses

The Darby family, Quakers who were the area's richest neighbors by far, lived in these two homes located just above the Coalbrookdale Museum.

The 18th-century Darby mansion, **Rosehill House,** features a collection of fine china, furniture, and trinkets from various family members. It's decorated in the way the family home would have been in 1850. If the gilt-framed mirrors and fancy china seem a

little ostentatious for the normally wealth-shunning Quakers, keep in mind that these folks were rich beyond reason. Docents assure visitors that, in another family's hands, Rosehill would have been completely over the top (included in £7.75 Coalbrookdale Museum of

Iron ticket, otherwise £4.15, closed Nov–Easter).

Skip the adjacent **Dale House.** Dating from the 1780s, it's older than Rosehill but almost completely devoid of interior furniture and exhibits.

Coalport China Museum, Jackfield Tile Museum, and Broseley Pipeworks

Housed in their original factories, these showcase the region's porcelain, decorated tiles, and clay tobacco pipes. These industries were developed to pick up the slack when the iron industry shifted away from the Severn Valley. Each museum features finely decorated pieces, and the china and tile museums offer low-energy workshops.

Ironbridge Open-Air Museum of Steel Sculpture

This park is a striking tribute to the region's industrial heritage. Stroll the 10-acre grounds and spot works by Roy Kitchin and other sculptors stashed in the forest and perched in rolling grasslands (£3, March–Nov Tue–Sun 10:00–17:00, closed Mon except Bank Holidays, closed Dec–Feb, 2 miles from Iron Bridge, Moss House, Cherry Tree Hill, Coalbrookdale, Telford, tel. 01952/433-152, www.go2.co.uk/steelsculpture).

Near Ironbridge Gorge

Skiing and Swimming—There's a small, brush-covered ski slope with two Poma lifts at Telford Snowboard and Ski Centre in Madeley, two miles from Ironbridge Gorge; you'll see signs for it as you drive into Ironbridge Gorge (£10.20/hr including gear, less for kids, open practice times Mon and Thu 10:00–20:00, Tue and Fri 12:00–22:00, Wed 10:00–19:00, Sat 16:00–18:00, Sun 10:00–16:00, tel. 01952/382-688, www.telford.gov.uk/skicentre). A public swimming pool is up the road on Court Street (Madeley Court Sports Centre, tel. 01952/382-770).

Royal Air Force (RAF) Museum Cosford—This Red Baron magnet displays more than 80 aircraft, from warplanes to rockets. Get the background on ejection seats and a primer on the principles of propulsion (free, daily 10:00–18:00, last entry at 17:00, Shifnal, Shropshire, on A41 near junction with M54, tel. 01902/376-200, www.rafmuseum.org.uk).

More Sights—If you're looking for reasons to linger in Ironbridge Gorge, these sights are all within a short drive: the medieval town of Shrewsbury, the abbey village of Much Wenlock, the scenic Long Mynd gorge at Church Stretton, the castle at Ludlow, and the steam railway at the river town of Bridgnorth. Shoppers like Chester (en route to points north).

Sleeping in Ironbridge Gorge

$$$ Library House is *Better Homes and Gardens* elegant. Located in the town center, a half-block downhill from the bridge, it's a classy, friendly gem that used to be a library. The Chaucer room, which includes a small garden, is a delight, but all three of the house's rooms are lovely. The complimentary drink upon arrival is a welcome touch (Sb-£65–75, Db-£75–100, DVD library, Wi-Fi, free parking just up the road or free pass for Ironbridge parking lot, 11 Severn Bank, Ironbridge Gorge, tel. 01952/432-299, www.libraryhouse.com, info@libraryhouse.com). Lizzie Steel—who's joined by her husband and daughters most weekends—will pick you up from the Telford train station if you request it in advance.

Two lesser places, right in the town center, overlook the bridge:

$$ Post Office House B&B is literally above the post office, where the postmaster's wife, Janet Hunter, rents three rooms. It's a shower-in-the-corner, old-fashioned place (Sb-£40–42, Db-£56–60, Tb-£66–90, family room available, discount for two or more nights, cash only, 6 The Square, tel. 01952/433-201, fax 01952/433-582, pohouseironbridge@yahoo.co.uk).

$$ Tontine Hotel is the town's big, 12-room, musty, Industrial Age hotel. Check out the historic photos in the bar (S-£25, Sb-£40, D-£40, Db-£56, en-suite rooms include breakfast—otherwise it's £5 extra, family rooms, 10 percent discount with this book through 2010, The Square, tel. 01952/432-127, fax 01952/432-094, www.tontine-hotel.com, tontinehotel@tiscali.co.uk).

Outside of Town

$$$ Calcutts House rents seven rooms in their 18th-century iron-master's home and adjacent coach house. Rooms in the main house are elegant, the coach-house rooms bright and modern. Ask the owners, Colin and Sarah Williams, how the rooms were named (Db-£52–85, price depends on room size, located on Calcutts Road, Gorge Connect Jackfield bus stop is across street, tel. 01952/882-631, www.calcuttshouse.co.uk, enquiries@calcuttshouse.co.uk).

$ Coalport Youth Hostel, plush for a hostel, fills an old factory at the China Museum in Coalport (£15–20 bunks in mostly 4-bed dorms, bunk-bed Db-£32–48, £3 more for non-members, includes sheets, kitchen, self-service laundry, tel. 01952/588-755, ironbridge@yha.org.uk). Don't confuse this hostel with the area's other hostel, Coalbrookdale, which is only available for groups.

$ Wilderhope Manor Youth Hostel, a beautifully remote 425-year-old manor house, is one of Europe's best hostels. On Wednesday and Sunday afternoons, tourists actually pay to see what hostelers get to sleep in (£19–23 bunks, under 18-£13.50, £3

Sleep Code

(£1 = about $1.60, country code: 44, area code: 01952)
S = Single, **D** = Double/Twin, **T** = Triple, **Q** = Quad, **b** = bathroom,
s = shower only. You can assume credit cards are accepted
unless noted otherwise.

To help you sort easily through these listings, I've divided
the rooms into three categories based on the price for a
standard double room with bath during high season:

$$$ Higher Priced—Most rooms £65 or more.
 $$ Moderately Priced—Most rooms between £40-65.
  $ Lower Priced—Most rooms £40 or less.

more for non-members, single-sex dorms, family rooms available,
reservations recommended, reception closed 10:00–17:00, restaurant open 17:30–20:00, tel. 01694/771-363, wilderhope@yha.org
.uk). It's in Longville-in-the-Dale, six miles from Much Wenlock
down B4371 toward Church Stretton.

Eating in Ironbridge Gorge

It's All About Me is an inviting café/bistro/wine bar in a prime
location near the river. On a sunny day, sit on their inviting back
patio, with peek-a-boo views of the Iron Bridge. Inside, this two-
story place has the same menu upstairs or down: Mediterranean
food, including £4 tapas-style small meals called "nibbly bits" (£11
for one course, £16 for two, Tue–Sat 12:00–14:30 & 18:00–21:30,
Sun 12:00–16:00 & 18:00–20:45, closed Mon, plenty of indoor/
outdoor seating, veggie options, 29 High Street, tel. 01952/432-
716).

Pondicherry, in a renovated former police station, serves
delicious Indian curries and a few British dishes to keep the less
adventurous happy. The mixed vegetarian sampler is popular
even with meat-eaters (£12–16 plates, Mon–Sat 17:00–23:00, Sun
17:00–21:30—starts to get hopping after 19:00, 57 Waterloo Street,
tel. 01952/433-055).

Da Vinci's serves good, though pricey, Italian food and has
a dressy ambience (£15–20 main courses, Tue–Sat 19:00–22:00,
closed Sun–Mon, 26 High Street, tel. 01952/432-250).

The Malt House, located in an 18th-century beer house,
offers an English menu with a European accent. This is a very
popular scene with the local twentysomething gang (£9–15 main
courses, bar menu at Jazz Bar, daily 12:00–21:30 except Sun until
22:00, near Museum of the Gorge, 5-min walk from center, The

Wharfage, tel. 01952/433-712). The Malt House is *the* vibrant nightspot in town, with live music and a fun crowd (generally Thu–Sat).

The Coalbrookdale Inn is filled with locals enjoying excellent ales and surprisingly good food. This former "best pub in Britain" has a tradition of offering free samples from a lineup of featured beers. Ask which real ales are available (Mon–Thu 17:00–23:30, Fri–Sun 12:00–23:30, food served 12:00–14:00 & 18:00–21:00, no food Sun evening, reservations unnecessary for the bar but a good idea for the fancier restaurant, lively ladies' loo, across street from Coalbrookdale Museum of Iron, 1 mile from Ironbridge Gorge, 12 Wellington Road, tel. 01952/433-953, www.coalbrookdaleinn .co.uk). Danny and Dawn Wood, the inn's owners, also rent three rooms above the restaurant for around £70.

The Meadow Inn would have appealed to Lawrence Welk. This local favorite serves prizewinning pub grub and has lovely riverside outdoor seating if the weather cooperates (£8–10 meals, Mon–Fri 12:00–14:30 & 18:00–21:30, Sat–Sun 12:00–21:30, can get crowded, no reservations taken, a pleasant 15-min walk from the center; head upstream, at Dale End Park take the path along the river, the inn is just after railway bridge; tel. 01952/433-193).

Ironbridge Gorge Connections

Ironbridge Gorge is five miles from Telford, which has the nearest train station. To get between Ironbridge Gorge and Telford, take bus #9, #39, #76, #77, or #99 (£3.60 "Day Saver" fare, 1–2/hr, 20–45 min, none on Sun) or a taxi (about £8). Although Telford's train and bus stations are an annoying 15-minute walk apart, you can connect them in five minutes on bus #44 (every 10 min, covered by "Day Saver") or #55 (every 15 min), or with a £3 cab ride. The Telford bus station is part of a large modern mall, an easy place to wait for the bus to Ironbridge Gorge. Buses are run by Arriva (www.arrivabus.co.uk), but you can also call Traveline for departure times and other information (toll tel. 0871-200-2233, www.traveline.org.uk).

The Gorge Connect bus service, which runs among Ironbridge Gorge sights on weekends, makes several morning and afternoon runs between Ironbridge Gorge and the Telford train station. For schedule information on the Gorge Connect, see page 326. If you need a **taxi** while in Ironbridge Gorge, call Central Taxis at tel. 01952/501-050.

By Train from Telford to: Birmingham (2/hr, 40–50 min), **Conwy** in North Wales (9/day, 2.5–3.25 hrs, some change in Chester or Shrewsbury), **Blackpool** (hourly, 2.75–3 hrs, usually 2–3 changes), **Keswick/Lake District** (every 1–2 hrs, 4–4.5

hrs; 3–3.25 hrs to Penrith with 1–2 changes, then catch a bus to Keswick, hourly except Sun 6/day, 40 min, www.stagecoachbus .com), **Edinburgh** (every 1–2 hrs, 4.5–5 hrs, 1–2 changes). Train info: tel. 0845-748-4950, www.nationalrail.co.uk.

By Car to Telford: Driving in from the **Cotswolds** and **Stratford,** take M6 through Birmingham, then exit T8 to M54 to the Telford/Ironbridge exit. Follow the brown *Ironbridge* signs through lots of roundabouts to Ironbridge Gorge. The traffic north through Birmingham is miserable from 14:00 to 20:00, especially on Fridays. From **Warwick,** consider the M40/M42/Kidderminster alternative, coming into Ironbridge Gorge on A442 via Bridgnorth to avoid the Birmingham traffic. (Note: On maps, Ironbridge Gorge is often referred to as either "Iron Bridge" or "Iron-Bridge.")

BLACKPOOL AND LIVERPOOL

These two bustling cities—wedged between serene North Wales and the even-more-serene Lake District—provide an opportunity to sample the "real" England, both at work (Liverpool) and at play (Blackpool). Scream down roller coasters and eat "candy floss" until you're deliriously queasy at fun-loving Blackpool. In Liverpool, experience industrial England and relive the early mop-top days of some famous Liverpudlians...meet the Beatles.

Blackpool

Blackpool is Britain's tacky, laid-back underbelly. It's one of England's most-visited attractions, the private domain of its working class, a faded and sticky mix of Coney Island, Las Vegas, and Denny's. Juveniles of any age love it. My kids declared it better than Disneyland.

Blackpool grew up with the Industrial Revolution. In the mid-1800s, entire mill towns would close down and take a two-week break here. They came to drink in the fresh air (much needed after a hard year in the mills) and—literally—the seawater. (Back then they figured it was healthy.) Supposedly, because it lies in a rain shadow, Blackpool has fewer rainy days than some other parts of England.

Blackpool's heyday is long past now, as more and more working people can afford the cheap charter flights to sunny

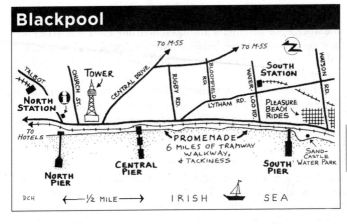

Spain. Recently, the resort has become popular for "stag" and "hen" (bachelor and bachelorette) parties—basically a cheap drunk weekend for the twentysomething crowd. Consequently, there are two Blackpools: the daytime Blackpool of kids riding roller coasters and grannies getting early-bird specials; and the drunken, debauched, late-night Blackpool of glass-dance-floor clubs and bars.

But Blackpool is beginning to reinvent itself to draw more visitors. A large overhaul of The Promenade has begun, as well as numerous renovations in the city center. No matter what, the town remains an accessible and affordable fun zone for the Flo and Andy Capps of northern England. People come year after year. They stay for a week, and they love it.

Most Americans don't even consider a stop in Blackpool. Many won't like it. It's an ears-pierced-while-you-wait, tipsy-toupee kind of place. Tacky, yes. Lowbrow, OK. More than a little run-down in parts, sure. But it's as English as can be, and that's what you're here for. An itinerary should feature as many facets of a culture as possible. Blackpool is as English as the queen—and considerably more fun.

Spend the day "muckin' about" the beach promenade of fortune-tellers, fish-and-chips joints, amusement piers, warped mirrors, and Englanders wearing hats with built-in ponytails. A million greedy doors try every trick to get you inside. Huge arcade halls advertise free toilets and broadcast bingo numbers onto the streets; the wind machine under a wax Marilyn Monroe blows at a steady gale; and the smell of fries, tobacco, and sugar is everywhere. Milk comes in raspberry or banana in this land where people under incredibly bad wigs look normal. If you're bored in Blackpool, you're just too classy.

Planning Your Time

Ideally, get to Blackpool around lunchtime for a free afternoon and evening of making bubbles in this cultural mud puddle. For full effect, it's best to visit during peak season: June through early November.

Blackpool's Illuminations, when much of the waterfront is decorated with lights, draws crowds in fall, particularly on weekends (Sept 3–Nov 7 in 2010). The early-evening light is great with the sun setting over the sea. Walk out along the peaceful North Pier at twilight.

Blackpool is easy by car or train. Speed demons with a car can treat it as a midday break (it's just off M6 on M55) and continue north. If you have kids, they'll want more time here (hey, it's cheaper than Disneyland). If you're into nightlife, this town delivers. If you're before or beyond kids and not into kitsch and greasy spoons, skip it. If the weather's great and you love nature, the lakes are just a few hours north. A visit to Blackpool sharpens the wonders of Windermere.

Orientation to Blackpool

(area code: 01253)

Everything clusters along The Promenade, a tacky, glittering six-mile-long beachfront good-time strip mall punctuated by three fun-filled piers reaching out into the sea. The Pleasure Beach rides are near the South Pier. Jutting up near the North Pier is Blackpool's stubby Eiffel-type tower. The most interesting shops, eateries, and theaters are inland from the North Pier. For a break from glitz, walk north along The Promenade or sandy beach—a residential neighborhood stretches for miles. When you've had enough, just hop on the tram or a bus for a quick ride back.

Tourist Information

A spiffy new TI sits about 50 yards inland from the North Pier (Mon–Sat 9:00–17:00, Easter–early Nov Sun 10:00–16:30, closed Sun off-season, 1 Clifton Street, tel. 01253/478-222—the same number gives recorded entertainment info after hours, www.visitblackpool.com). There you'll find a £1 city map, brochures on the amusement centers, and an extremely helpful staff. The free *What's On* booklet lists local events, and the TI can book shows for you for a £1.50 fee. If you're going to Sandcastle Waterpark, buy your tickets here to save a few pounds. The TI books rooms for no fee (but collects a 10 percent deposit, which hotels don't recoup; room-finding service closes at 16:30).

Arrival in Blackpool

The main (north) **train** station is three blocks from the town center (no maps given but one is posted, no ATM in station but many in town). There's no luggage storage in town, but if you're desperate, Pleasure Beach has a few lockers big enough for a backpack.

If arriving by **car,** the motorway funnels you down Yeadon Way into a giant parking zone. If you're just spending the day, head for one of the huge £6/day garages. If you're spending the night, drive to the waterfront and head north. My top accommodations are north on The Promenade (easy parking). Leaving Blackpool, to go anywhere, follow signs to *M55,* which starts at Blackpool and zips you to M6 (for points north or south).

Helpful Hints

Markets: At the indoor **Abingdon Street Market,** vendors sell baked goods, fruit, bras, jewelry, eggs, and more (Mon–Sat 9:00–17:00, closed Sun). The **Fleetwood Market,** eight miles north, is huge, with two buildings full of produce, clothes, and crafts spilling out onto the street (May–Oct Mon–Tue and Thu–Sat 8:00–17:00, closed Wed and Sun; Nov–April Tue and Fri–Sat only; catch tram marked *Fleetwood,* 30 min, £2.70 one-way).

Tipping: The pubs of Blackpool have a unique tradition of "and (name an amount) your own, luv." Say that here and your barmaid will add that amount to your bill and drop it into her tip jar. (Say it anywhere else and they won't know what you mean.)

Internet Access: The public library, in the big domed building on Queen Street, lets visitors stand and use its computers for 15 minutes (free, Mon and Fri 9:00–17:00, Tue and Thu 9:00–19:00, Wed and Sat 10:00–17:00, Sun 11:00–14:00, tel. 01253/478-111).

Post Office: The main P.O. is in the basement of the WH Smith store, at 12–16 Bank Hey Street (Mon–Sat 9:00–17:30, closed Sun).

Car Rental: In case you decide to tour the Lake District by car, you'll find plenty of rental agencies in Blackpool (closed Sat afternoon and Sun), including **Avis** (at the airport—just south of the South Pier, tel. 01253/408-003) and **Budget** (434 Waterloo Road—just north of the South Pier, tel. 01253/691-632).

Getting Around Blackpool

Laid-back **tram cars** trundle 13 miles up and down the waterfront, connecting all the sights. Trams come in all shapes and colors (some vintage, some modern, some dressed up like boats), but are all on the same system and take the same tickets. This electric tramway—the first in Europe—dates from 1885 (£1.60–2.70 depending on length of trip, pay conductor, trams come every 10–15 min or so year-round, run 6:00–23:15). Many **buses** also run along The Promenade—make sure you're not standing at a tram stop when you're waiting for a bus (similar prices, pay conductor, tel. 01253/473-001, www.blackpooltransport.com). For £6 you can purchase an all-day pass that covers both trams and buses; buy it on a tram or bus or at their office on Market Street.

City Sightseeing's one-hour, 16-stop **hop-on, hop-off bus** has a recorded commentary and leaves from the Blackpool Tower every 30 minutes (£7.50, first two weeks of April and June–early Nov daily from 9:00 until last departure at 19:00, mid-April–May Sat–Sun only, none off-season, tel. 01253/473-001, www.city -sightseeing.com).

Taxis are easy to snare in Blackpool, and three to five people travel cheaper by cab than by tram. Hotels can get you a taxi by phone within three minutes (no extra charge).

Sights in Blackpool

▲▲The Piers—Blackpool's famous piers were originally built for Victorian landlubbers who wanted to go to sea but were afraid of getting seasick. Each of the three amusement piers has its own personality and is a joy to wander. The sedate **North Pier** is most traditional and refreshingly uncluttered (open first Sat in March to first weekend in Nov, daily 10:00–23:00, £0.50 admission 10:00–17:30 includes discounts on an ice cream or drink and the carousel ride, free admission after 17:30). Dance down its empty planks at twilight to the early English rock playing on its speakers. Its **Carousel Bar** at the end is great for families—with a free kids' DJ nightly from 19:00 to 23:00 (parents drink good beer while the kids bunny-hop and boogie). The something-for-everyone **Central Pier** is lots of fun. Ride its great Ferris wheel for the best view in Blackpool (rich photography at twilight, get the operator to spin you as you bottom out). And check out the sadist running the adjacent Waltzer ride—just watch the miserably ecstatic people spinning. The rollicking **South Pier** is all rides.

From the far end of any pier, look out at the horizon to see the natural-gas drilling platforms in the Irish Sea. In the distance, off the North Shore, a castaway gaggle of wind turbines capture energy.

▲Blackpool Tower—This mini–Eiffel Tower is a 100-year-old vertical fun center. You pay £14 to get in (£11 for kids, family tickets available); after that, the fun is free. Work your way up from the bottom through layer after layer of noisy entertainment: a circus (two to three acts a day, runs Easter–first weekend in Nov), a 3-D cinema, an aquarium, and a wonderful old ballroom with barely live music and golden oldies dancing to golden oldies all day. Enjoy a break at the dance-floor-level pub or on a balcony perch. Kids love this place. (With a little marijuana, adults would, too.) Ride the glass elevator to the tip of the 500-foot-tall symbol of Blackpool for a smashing view, especially at sunset (Easter–June daily 10:00–17:00; July–early Nov daily 10:00–23:00; early Nov–Easter Wed 10:00–17:00, Sat–Sun 10:00–18:00; may be closed for events, top of tower closed when windy, toll tel. 0844-856-1111, www.theblackpooltower.co.uk). If you want to leave and return, request a hand stamp.

▲**Pleasure Beach**—Rated ▲▲▲ for roller coaster enthusiasts, these 42 acres across The Promenade from the beach attract nearly

six million visitors annually, and are littered with rides galore, an ice show, circus and illusion shows, and varied amusements. Many rides are tame enough for the under-10 set, but the top few offer some of the best thrills in Europe: the Pepsi Max Big One (with a peak of 235 feet and 85 mph, it's one of the world's fastest, highest, and steepest roller coasters), the Infusion (a twisty, loopy speed rush that you ride with feet dangling), and the IceBlast (which rockets you straight up before letting you bungee down). The Bling ride spins gondola riders in three different directions 100 feet above the ground at speeds of over 60 mph. Also memorable is the Steeplechase—carousel horses stampeding down a roller-coaster track (a dream come true for *National Velvet* and *Mary Poppins* fans). The Irn Bru Revolution speeds you over a steep drop and upside-down in a loop, then does it again backward. The Valhalla ride zips you on a Viking boat in watery darkness past scary Nordic things like lutefisk. With two 80-foot drops and lots of hype, first you're scared, then you're soaked, and—finally—you're just glad you survived. The park also offers several old wooden-framed rides full of historic charm—but brittle travelers will want to consider their necks and backs. The tame-looking Wild Mouse, built in 1958, is the jerkiest, and has no doubt kept generations of Blackpool chiropractors in the money.

Admission to Pleasure Beach is £5, which includes a few attractions, then you can pay individually for rides with your £1 tickets (2–7 tickets per ride), or get unlimited rides with a £25–30 armband (price varies with season and day of week, cheaper if purchased in advance on their website). If you haven't pre-purchased your pass, pay the £5 entry fee and have a look around (check to see how long lines are for the top rides)—once you've paid admission to the park, you can upgrade to the armband by paying the difference (daily Easter–early Nov, also open some weekends in winter, opens at about 10:30 and closes as early as 17:00 or as late as 21:30, depending on season, weather, and demand—check website; toll tel. 0871-222-1234, www.pleasure beachblackpool.com). Note: Pleasure Beach is about two miles (a 45-minute walk) south of the North Pier, so consider taking the tram or bus.

Sandcastle Waterpark—This popular indoor attraction, across the street from Pleasure Beach, has a big pool, long slides, a wave machine, and water, water, everywhere, at a constant temperature of 84 degrees. Featuring the longest tube waterslide in the world, this is a place where most kids could easily spend a day (£11 limited entry/£14 full admission, £9/£11.50 for kids, family passes, discount tickets online and at TI; roughly July–Aug daily 10:00–17:30; April–June and Sept–Oct Sat–Thu 10:00–17:00, Fri 13:30–20:00; Nov–March Sat–Sun only 10:00–16:30—confirm as hours may vary; last admission one hour before closing, tel. 01253/343-602, www.sandcastle-waterpark.co.uk).

▲▲▲**People-Watching**—Blackpool's top sight is its people. You'll see England here as nowhere else. Grab someone's hand and a big baton of "rock" (candy), and stroll. Grown men walk around with huge teddy bears looking for places to play "bowlingo," a short-lane version of bowling. Ponder the thought of actually retiring here and spending your last years, day after day, wearing plaid pants and a bad toupee, surrounded by Blackpool. This place puts people in a talkative mood. Ask someone to explain the difference between tea and supper. Back at your hotel, join in the chat sessions in the lounge.

▲**Illuminations**—Blackpool was the first town in England to "go electric" in 1879. Now, every fall, Blackpool stretches its tourist season by illuminating its six miles of waterfront with countless lights, all blinking and twinkling (Sept 3–Nov 7 in 2010). The American in me kept saying, "I've seen bigger, and I've seen better," but I stuffed his mouth with cotton candy and just had some simple fun like everyone else on my specially decorated tram. Look for the animated tableaux on North Shore.

St. Annes-on-Sea—Had enough greasy food and flashing lights? The seaside village of St. Annes is an easy 20-minute bus ride away to the south, and offers a welcome break (buses #7 and #11 run from the Blackpool Tower every 10 minutes, covered by the all-day tram/bus pass). Get off at St. Annes Square, which is the first stop after the bus turns left following the long, dune-side straightaway. The town's promenade and simple Victorian pier feel like a breath of sanity. The broad sand beach is perfect for flying a kite, building a sandcastle, or watching happy dogs play in the surf. Consider strolling the beach northward all the way to the southern edge of The Promenade (about 3 miles); if you max out on sand and sea before that, simply cross the dunes back to the seaside road and find the nearest bus stop.

Nightlife in Blackpool

▲**Showtime**—Blackpool always has a few razzle-dazzle music, dancing-girl, racy-humor, magic, and tumbling shows. Box offices around town can give you a rundown on what's available (£7–30 tickets). Your hotel has the latest. For something more highbrow, try the Opera House for musicals (booking toll tel. 0844-856-1111, info tel. 01253/625-252) and the Grand Theatre for drama and ballet (£15–25, tel. 01253/290-190, www.blackpoolgrand.co.uk). Both are on Church Street, a couple blocks behind the tower. For the latest in evening entertainment, see the window displays at the TI on The Promenade (www.blackpoollive.com).

▲▲**Funny Girls**—Blackpool's current hot bar is in a dazzling location a couple blocks from the train station. Most nights, from 20:00 to 23:30, Funny Girls puts on a "glam bam thank you ma'am" burlesque-in-drag show that delights footballers and grannies alike.

Get your drinks at the bar...unless the transvestites are dancing on it. The show, though racy, is not raunchy. The music is very loud. The crowd is young, old, straight, gay, very down-to-earth, and fun-loving. Go on a weeknight; Friday and Saturday are too jammed. While the area up front can be a mosh pit, there are more sedate tables in back, where service comes with a vampish smile.

There are two tiers of seats: sitting and standing (Sun £4 to stand, £14 to sit; Tue–Thu £3.50 to stand, £11 to sit; Fri £6 to stand, £17.50 to sit; Sat £8 to stand, £19.50 to sit; no shows Mon). Getting dinner here before the show runs about £16 (dinner reservations required, must be 18 to enter, 5 Dickson Road, TI sells tickets; to reserve in advance, call 01253/624-901, or visit box office at 44 Queen Street—open 9:30–17:15, www.funnygirls showbar.co.uk).

Other Nightspots—Blackpool's clubs and discos are cheap, with live bands and an interesting crowd (nightly 22:00–2:00 in the morning). With all the stag and hen parties, the late-night streets can be clotted with rude rowdies.

Sleeping in Blackpool

(area code: 01253)

Blackpool's 140,000 people provide 120,000 beds in 3,500 mostly dumpy, cheap, nondescript hotels and B&Bs. Remember, this town's in the business of accommodating the people who can't afford to go to Spain. Most have the same design—minimal character, maximum number of springy beds—and charge £15–25 per person. Empty beds abound except from September through early November, and on summer weekends. It's only really tight on Illuminations weekends (when everyone bumps up prices). I've listed regular high-season prices. With the huge number of hotels in town, prices get really soft in the off-season. There's likely a launderette within a five-minute walk of your hotel; ask your host or hostess.

North of the Tower

These listings are on or near the waterfront in the quiet area they call "the posh end," a mile or two north of Blackpool Tower, with easy parking and easy access to the center by tram or bus. The first two listings have classy extras you wouldn't expect in Blackpool, and aren't too far from the North Pier. The last two are B&Bs with welcoming owners and lots of stairs, a short tram ride or approximately 35-minute walk from the North Pier.

$$$ Barceló Imperial Hotel is where the queen would stay in Blackpool. (They boast that every prime minister since they opened has visited their bar.) With dark-paneled Old World elegance, this splurge has all the comforts at its posh address (standard Db-£115–168 depending on size of room, season, and day of week—Sun and Mon are cheapest; request standard with view—if none is available it's £60 extra for "premium" or "deluxe" room with sea view, rates much lower in slow times, check website for deals but call front desk for best standard room available, children stay free, no air-con, parking-£2.50/day, tram stop: Imperial Hotel, North Promenade, tel. 01253/623-971, fax 01253/751-784, www .barcelo-hotels.co.uk, imperialblackpool@barcelo-hotels.co.uk).

$$$ I know, staying at the **Hilton Hotel** in Blackpool is like wearing a tux to eat falafel. But if you need a splurge, this is a grand place with lots of views, a pool, sauna, gym, and comfortable rooms (Db-£110–170, "club deal" Db with lots of extras-£25 more, ask if there are any "special rates" being advertised, best deals online, call front desk to request room with view for no extra charge, air-con, tram stop: Warley Road, North Promenade, tel. 01253/623-434, fax 01253/627-864, www.hilton.com).

$$$ Carlton Hotel, a Best Western, rents business-class rooms at rack rates too high for what you get—check for more

Sleep Code

(£1 = about $1.60, country code: 44)
S = Single, **D** = Double/Twin, **T** = Triple, **Q** = Quad, **b** = bathroom,
s = shower only. You can assume credit cards are accepted
unless otherwise noted.

To help you sort easily through these listings, I've divided
the rooms into three categories based on the price for a
standard double room with bath:

  $$$ **Higher Priced**—Most rooms £90 or more.
    $$ **Moderately Priced**—Most rooms between £45-90.
     $ **Lower Priced**—Most rooms £45 or less.

reasonable rates online (Sb-£50–70, Db-£80–110, can be a little
higher during Illuminations, sea-view rooms about £10 extra, a
long block closer to town from the Imperial, tram stop: Pleasant
Street, North Promenade, tel. 01253/628-966, fax 01253/752-587,
www.carltonhotelblackpool.co.uk, mail@carltonhotelblackpool
.co.uk).

$$ Beechcliffe Private Hotel has seven clean rooms run by
a friendly couple, Ken and Carol Selman. The rooms are tight, but
this place has a homey touch, and the decor is being updated (Sb-
£25, Db-£54–60, kids half-price, home-cooked dinner-£8, tram
stop: Cabin; turn left from tram stop, then right at Shaftesbury
Avenue, and walk a block away from beach; 16 Shaftesbury
Avenue, North Shore, tel. 01253/353-075, www.beechcliffe.co.uk,
info@beechcliffe.co.uk). Ken offers rides to or from the train sta-
tion for no charge.

$$ Robin Hood Hotel is a cheery place with a big, welcoming living room, a family underfoot, and nine spacious rooms
with big beds and sea views (especially rooms 1, 5, and 9). Run
by nutritionist and therapist Kathy, it also serves as a diet retreat
center (Sb-£25–27, Db-£50–54, discount for kids, under 6 free,
various facial and massage treatments available, tram stop: St.
Stephen's Avenue and walk a block north, 1.5 miles north of tower
across from a peaceful stretch of beach, 100 Queens Promenade,
North Shore, tel. 01253/351-599, www.robinhoodhotel.co.uk, info
@robinhoodhotel.co.uk).

Near the Train Station

$$ Valentine Private Hotel is a handy and adequate 13-room
place. It's run with care by on-site owner Anthony and manager
Steve, with a plush red bar/sitting room and comfortable rooms.
It's just two blocks from the train station and one block from the

Central Blackpool

BLACKPOOL
NORTH
TRAIN
STN.

To M-55

NOT TO SCALE
NORTH PIER TO CENTRAL PIER
IS ABOUT ½ MILE (800 METERS)

+ TROLLEY LINE
P PARKING

BUS
STN.

KING

CHURCH STREET

MARKET

DICKSON

LIBRARY

ABINGDON

SPRINGFIELD ROAD

QUEEN ST.

TALBOT

CLIFTON STREET

CHEAPSIDE

ROAD

CORPORATION ST.

MARKET ST.

CHURCH ST.

POST

Opera House +
Winter Gardens

CORONATION STREET

VICTORIA ST.

ALBERT RD.

CENTRAL DRIVE

CHAPEL

TO
M-55

TO
SOUTH
PIER

TOWER

P R O M E N A D E

TO

R BEACH

R BEACH

R

NORTH PIER

I R I S H   S E A

CENTRAL PIER

DCH

1 Valentine Private Hotel
2 To Hotels North of the Tower
3 Kwizeen Restaurant
4 Harry Ramsden's
5 The Mitre Pub

6 Abingdon Barbeque
7 Rocco's Restaurant
8 Marks & Spencer
9 Funny Girls (Bar & Show)
10 Funny Girls (Box Office)

Funny Girls bar, in a neighborhood that's not exactly upscale, but safe and convenient (Sb-£30, Db-£50–60 depending on room, bunk-bed family deals—kids half-price, free Wi-Fi; 2 blocks from station: with back to tracks, exit station far right, go up Springfield 2 blocks to Dickson and turn right, 35 Dickson Road; tel. 01253/622-775, www.valentinehotelblackpool.co.uk, anthony @anthonypalmer.orangehome.co.uk).

Eating in Blackpool

Your hotel may serve a cheap early-evening meal. Generally, food in the tower and along The Promenade is terrible. The following places are all just a few minutes' walk from the Blackpool Tower and the North Pier.

Kwizeen is an elegant bistro away from the beach that serves good Mediterranean and modern British dishes with a focus on local produce. Popular with the natives, they've racked up awards for their locally sourced and creatively prepared food. Don't worry—it's a lot classier inside than it looks from the outside

(£13–17 main dishes, £13 two-course and £16 three-course early-bird specials 18:00–19:00, open Mon–Fri 12:00–13:30 & 18:00–21:00, Sat 18:00–21:00, closed Sun, 47–49 King Street, tel. 01253/290-045).

"World Famous" **Harry Ramsden's** will remind you of an English version of Denny's (it's the original location of a now UK-wide chain). This is *the* place for mushy peas, fish-and-chips, and a chance to get goofy with waiters—call the place *Henry* Ramsden's and see what happens (£6–10 meals, order a side of mushy peas, Sun–Thu 11:30–21:00, Fri–Sat 11:30–22:00, off-season until 20:00, 60–63 The Promenade, tel. 01253/294-386).

The Mitre Pub serves light lunches (weekdays 12:00–14:15) and beers in a truly rare, old-time Blackpool ambience. Drop in any time to survey the fun photos of old Blackpool and for the great people scene (daily 11:00–23:00, Fri–Sat until 24:00, 3 West Street, tel. 01253/623-718).

Abingdon Barbeque, with its expansive deli counter, is mobbed with hungry locals at lunch, munching on cheap roasted chicken and meat pies. Get a whole chicken and some sides, and you've got lunch for four for less than £10 (daily 7:00–17:00, take-away only, 44 Abingdon Street, tel. 01253/621-817).

Clifton Street: This street is lined with decent ethnic-food eateries, including Indian and Chinese. For Italian, try **Rocco's** (£10 three-course early-bird specials Sun–Thu 17:30–20:00, daily 17:30–23:00, Fri–Sat until 23:30, 36 Clifton Street, tel. 01253/627-440).

Supermarket: **Marks & Spencer** has a big supermarket in its basement (Mon–Wed and Fri 9:00–18:00, Thu 9:00–19:00, Sat 8:30–18:00, Sun 10:30–16:30, near recommended eateries, on Coronation Street and Church Street). Go picnic at the beach.

Blackpool Connections

If you're heading to (or from) Blackpool by train, you'll usually need to transfer at **Preston** (5/hr, 30 min). The following trains leave from Blackpool's main (north) station.

From Blackpool to: Liverpool (hourly, 1.5 hrs), **Keswick/Lake District** (roughly hourly, allow at least 3.5 hrs total for journey: transfer in Preston—30 minutes away, then 1 hr to Penrith, then catch a bus to Keswick, hourly except Sun 8/day, 40 min), **Conwy** in North Wales (roughly hourly, 3–4 hrs, 2–3 transfers),

Edinburgh (roughly hourly, 3–3.5 hrs, transfer in Preston), **Glasgow** (1–3/hr, 3 hrs, transfer in Preston), **York** (hourly, 3 hrs, more with change in Manchester), **Moreton-in-Marsh** in the Cotswolds (roughly hourly, 4.5 hrs, 2–3 transfers), **Bath** (hourly, 4.5 hrs, 3 transfers), **London**'s Euston Station (hourly, 3 hrs, transfer at Preston). Train info: toll tel. 0845-748-4950, www.nationalrail .co.uk.

Liverpool

Liverpool, a large, bustling city with a downtown full of shopping malls, is a fascinating stop for Beatles fans and those who would like to look urban Britain straight in the eye. The city is becoming a favorite holiday spot for Brits, who enjoy its lively atmosphere and cultural and historical sights. In 2008, Liverpool was one of the European Capitals of Culture; to prepare for the honor, the  city rode a wave of new construction and architectural face-lifts.

Planning Your Time

If you're a casual Beatles fan, make Liverpool an afternoon pit-stop: Spend most of your time at the Albert Dock, popping in to see The Beatles Story, having lunch at the Tate's lunchtime café (and appreciating the art upstairs), and visiting the Maritime Museum. Consider getting a ticket to ride the ferry across the Mersey, which leaves from the docks north of the Albert Dock.

Beatles Blitz: If the Fab Four are what brought you to Liverpool, arrive the night before and follow this more ambitious, all-day sightseeing plan (which follows the Beatles' lives in roughly chronological order):

9:00–Visit the TI to book a seat on the 10:00 National Trust minibus tour to John and Paul's childhood homes, if you haven't pre-booked a time slot already (see reservations info on page 352). Note that this tour does not run on Mondays and Tuesdays (and not at all Dec–Feb).

9:50–Arrive at the Jurys Inn (just south of the Albert Dock) for the 2.5-hour minibus tour of John and Paul's childhood homes (departs at 10:00 sharp).

12:30–Return to the city center. Walk over to Mathew Street

for a quick pop-in to the original (but unimpressive) Cavern Club. (Skip this walk if you're taking the "Magical Mystery" bus tour—explained below—which ends at the club.)

13:00–Walk 15 minutes down to the Albert Dock (or take a bus or taxi). Enjoy lunch in one of my recommended eateries (listed under "Eating in Liverpool").

14:00–Choose between the bus and minivan tours (the "Magical Mystery" bus tour leaves the Albert Dock at 14:30) or The Beatles Story exhibit. Since the tours cover some of the same ground as the National Trust tour, an hour or two at The Beatles Story will satisfy all but the most die-hard fan.

For those who just can't get enough, it's possible to do an afternoon "Magical Mystery" bus tour and also see The Beatles Story (the tour ends at the Cavern Club around 16:15, and The Beatles Story allows a last entry at 17:00).

Orientation to Liverpool

(area code: 0151)

Tourist Information

Liverpool's main TI is on **Whitechapel Street,** a six-minute walk downhill from Lime Street Station. Ignore the pavilion with the information symbol on it—the real TI is a glossy silver storefront on this main shopping street (Mon and Wed–Sat 9:00–18:00, Tue 10:00–18:00, Sun 11:00–16:00, tel. 0151/233-2008, www.visitliverpool.com). Get the free, small map (also available at train station for £1). Walking tours about local history are sometimes offered on Sundays. There's another TI at **Albert Dock** (daily 10:00–17:00, inland from The Beatles Story, tel. 0151/707-0729), and a third at the **airport** (daily 9:00–18:00, tel. 0151/907-1057).

Arrival in Liverpool

From the Lime Street **train** station to the Albert Dock, it's about a 20-minute walk, a short ride on bus #C4 (£1.60 one-way, £3.30 all-day ticket, runs daily every 20 min until 21:00), or a £4 taxi trip. For public-transportation information, visit the Merseytravel center at the main bus center, between Lime Street Station and the TI (Mon–Sat 9:00–17:30, Sun 10:30–16:30, Queen Square, toll tel. 0871-200-2233, www.merseytravel.gov.uk). Regional trains also arrive at the much smaller Central Station, which is essentially a subway stop, located just a few blocks south.

From **Liverpool John Lennon Airport,** take bus #500 to the city center (£2.60, 2/hr).

Drivers approaching Liverpool follow signs to *City Center* and *Albert Dock,* where you'll find a huge car park at the dock.

Liverpool

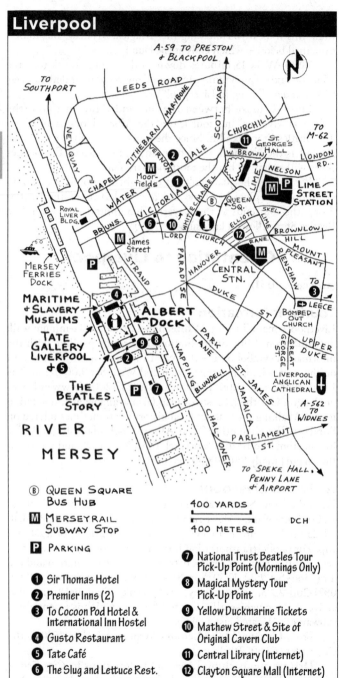

A-59 TO PRESTON & BLACKPOOL

TO SOUTHPORT

LEEDS ROAD

TO M-62

CHURCHILL

St. GEORGE'S HALL

W. BROWN

NELSON

LONDON RD.

TO LIME STREET STATION

Moorfields

Royal LIVER BLDG.

QUEEN SQ.

SKEL.

ELLIOTT

BROWNLOW

MOUNT PLEASANT

RENSHAW

MERSEY FERRIES DOCK

James Street

LORD CHURCH

CENTRAL STN.

HILL

MARITIME & SLAVERY MUSEUMS

ALBERT DOCK

HANOVER

DUKE

TO LEECE

TATE GALLERY LIVERPOOL

THE BEATLES STORY

WAPPING

PARK LANE

BLUNDELL

ST. JAMES

JAMAICA

BOMBED-OUT CHURCH

GEORGE ST.

GREAT UPPER DUKE

LIVERPOOL ANGLICAN CATHEDRAL

A-562 TO WIDNES

RIVER

MERSEY

CHALONER

PARLIAMENT ST.

TO SPEKE HALL, PENNY LANE & AIRPORT

B QUEEN SQUARE BUS HUB

M MERSEYRAIL SUBWAY STOP

P PARKING

400 YARDS

400 METERS

DCH

1 Sir Thomas Hotel

2 Premier Inns (2)

3 To Cocoon Pod Hotel & International Inn Hostel

4 Gusto Restaurant

5 Tate Café

6 The Slug and Lettuce Rest.

7 National Trust Beatles Tour Pick-Up Point (Mornings Only)

8 Magical Mystery Tour Pick-Up Point

9 Yellow Duckmarine Tickets

10 Mathew Street & Site of Original Cavern Club

11 Central Library (Internet)

12 Clayton Square Mall (Internet)

Helpful Hints

Internet Access: The Business and Technology department of the **Central Library** lets visitors use computers for free (Mon–Fri 9:00–18:00, Sat 9:00–17:00, Sun 10:00–16:00, boots you off after 30 min but OK to log in again if needed, on William Brown Street, just behind the grand colonnaded building that's across from Lime Street Station, tel. 0151/233-5829). Or get online at the **Le Boulevard Internet Café** (50p–£3/hr, price varies with demand, 20 coin-op terminals, second floor of Clayton Square shopping mall, Mon–Sat 9:00–18:00, Thu until 20:00, Sun 11:00–17:00, between train station and Albert Dock on Ranelagh Street).

Baggage Storage: Look for storage services on the train station's main concourse (£7/item for 24 hrs, open Mon–Thu 7:00–21:00, Fri–Sun 7:00–23:00). Most bus tours and private minivan/car tours are able to accommodate people with luggage (of "reasonable" size).

Tours in Liverpool

Beatles Tours

▲Lennon and McCartney Homes—John and Paul's boyhood homes have both been restored to how they looked during their 1950s childhoods. This isn't Graceland—you won't find an over-the-top rock-and-roll extravaganza here. And if you don't know the difference between John and Paul, you'll likely be bored. But for die-hard Beatles fans who want to get a glimpse into the time and place that created these musical masterminds, this tour is worth ▲▲▲.

Because the houses are in residential neighborhoods—and in both cases, still share walls with neighbors—the National Trust runs only four tours per day in summer (Wed–Sun only) with 14 Beatlemaniacs each, ending before 17:00. Just 7,000 people pass through these doors each year. While some Beatles bus tours stop here for photo ops, only the National Trust tour gets you inside the homes. And don't try to simply show up and stroll right in—you have to be on the tour to be allowed inside.

Cost and Information: £17, recorded info toll tel. 0844-800-4791, www.nationaltrust.org.uk/beatles.

Tour Options: From mid-March to October, tours run four times per day Wed–Sun (no tours Mon–Tue). Plan to arrive 10 minutes before the tour departure time. **Morning tours** (at 10:00 and 10:50) are better, as they follow a more scenic route that includes a quick pass by Penny Lane. They're also easier to reach, as they depart from the Jurys Inn at the Albert Dock (south of and visible from The Beatles Story). **Afternoon tours** (at 14:30 and 15:00) leave from Speke Hall, an out-of-the-way National Trust property located eight miles southeast of Liverpool. Allow 30 minutes to drive from the city center to Speke Hall—follow the brown *Speke Hall* signs through dozens of roundabouts, heading in the general direction of the airport (ample and free parking at the site). If you don't have a car, it takes at least 45 minutes to reach Speke Hall by bus and foot (airport bus #500, 2/hr, 20 min; or slower bus #80A, 4/hr, 40–50 min, direction: Airport; ask driver to let you off at the stop closest to Speke Hall, then walk a well-signed half-mile).

Off-Season: From early to mid-March and in Nov, tours leave Wed–Sun at 10:00, 12:30, and 15:00, and all depart from the handy Jurys Inn at the Albert Dock. No tours run Dec–Feb.

Reservations: Because only 14 people are allowed on each tour, it's smart to make a reservation ahead of time, especially for the morning tours. You can reserve online (www.nationaltrust.org.uk/beatles) or by calling 0151/427-7231. If you haven't reserved ahead, you can try to book a same-day tour by calling 0151/707-0729. The afternoon tours generally don't fill up, but remember that it takes 30 minutes (by car) to at least 45 minutes (without a car) to reach the tour's starting point from central Liverpool.

Guides: Each home has a live-in caretaker who will act as your guide. These folks give an entertaining, insightful-to-fans 20- to 30-minute talk, and then leave you time (10–15 minutes) to wander through the house on your own. Ask lots of questions if their spiel peters out early—the docents are a wealth of information. You can take photos of the outside of the house after they give their talk, but not before. They ask you to turn off your mobile phones, and not to bring big bags.

Mendips (John Lennon's Home): Even though he sang about being a working-class hero, John grew up in the suburbs of Liverpool, surrounded by doctors, lawyers, and—beyond the back fence—Strawberry Field (he added the "s" for the song).

This was the home of John's Aunt Mimi, who raised him in this house from the time he was five years old and once told him, "A guitar's all right, John, but you'll never earn a living by it." John moved out at age 23, but his first wife, Cynthia, bunked here for a while when John made his famous first trip to America. Yoko Ono bought the house in 2002, and gave it as a gift to the National Trust (generating controversy among the neighbors). The stewards, Colin and Sylvia, make this place come to life.

On the surface, it's just a 1930s house carefully restored to how it would have been in the past. But delve deeper. It's been lovingly cared for—restored to be the tidy, well-kept place Mimi would have recognized (down to her apron hanging in the kitchen). It's a lucky quirk of fate that the house's interior remained mostly unchanged after the Lennons left—the bachelor who owned it for the previous decades didn't upgrade much, so even the light switches are true to the time.

If you're a John Lennon fan, it's fun to picture him as a young boy drawing and imagining at his dining room table. It also makes for an interesting comparison to Paul's humbler home, which is the second part of the tour.

20 Forthlin Road (Paul McCartney's Home): In comparison to Aunt Mimi's house, the home where Paul grew up is sim-

pler, much less "posh," and even a little ratty around the edges. Michael, Paul's brother, wanted it that way—their mother, Mary (famously mentioned in "Let It Be"), died when the boys were young, and it never had the tidiness of a woman's touch. It's been intentionally scuffed up around the edges to preserve the historical accuracy. Notice the differences—Paul has said that John's house was vastly different and more clearly middle class; at Mendips, there were books on the bookshelves.

Over a hundred Beatles songs were written in this house (including "I Saw Her Standing There") during days Paul and John spent skipping school. The photos from Michael, taken in this house, help make the scene of what's mostly a barren interior much more interesting.

There's no blue plaque identifying the house from the outside—those are only awarded once the person's been dead for 20 years, or when it's been 100 years since their birth, whichever comes first. In fact, Paul hasn't been back inside the house since it was turned into a museum; he knocked on the door twice, but both times the custodian was out...an idea that might give you some comfort if you're not able to get inside yourself.

More Beatles Tours—The "sights" covered by the tours below are basically houses where the Fab Four grew up (exteriors only), places they performed, and spots made famous by the lyrics of their hits ("Penny Lane," "Strawberry Fields," the

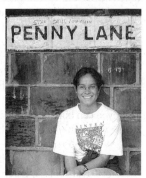

Eleanor Rigby graveyard, and so on). While boring to anyone not into the Beatles, fans will enjoy the commentary and seeing the shelter on the roundabout, the fire station with the clean machine, and the barber who shaves another customer.

Beatles fans may want to invest a couple hours taking the **"Magical Mystery" bus tour,** which hits the lads' homes (from the outside), Penny Lane, and so on (£15, 1.75 hours; July–Aug departs daily from the Albert Dock at 12:00 and 14:30; Easter–June and Sept Mon–Fri at 12:00, Sat–Sun at 12:00 and 14:30; Oct–Easter Sat–Sun at 12:00, no tours Mon–Fri; often fills up—book ahead by calling or stopping by any TI, leaves from Gower Street stop at southern end of dock—inland from The Beatles Story, ends at the Cavern Club, tel. 0151/236-9091, www.cavernclub.org).

For something more extensive, fun, and intimate, consider a four-hour minibus Beatles tour from **Phil Hughes.** It's longer because it includes information on historic Liverpool, along with the Beatles stuff. Phil organizes his tour to fit your schedule and will do his best to accommodate you (£15.50/person, £80/private group tour, can coordinate times with National Trust tour of Lennon and McCartney homes, 8-seat minibus, mobile 07961-511-223, tel. 0151/228-4565, www.tourliverpool.co.uk, tourliverpool @hotmail.com).

Jackie Spencer also hits the highlights and does private tours—just say when and where you want to go (up to four people in her minivan-£140, 2.5 hours, longer tours available, will pick you up at hotel or train station, mobile 0799-076-1478, www .beatleguides.com, jackie@beatleguides.com).

Beware of cheaper private-taxi tours promoted by some hotels—kickbacks, not quality, motivate concierges to recommend these tours.

Other Tours

City Bus Tour—The City Sightseeing bus is a hop-on, hop-off bus tour with a canned soundtrack, but considering the size of the city center, it's a quick way to get an overview that links all the major sights in 55 breezy minutes (£8, buy ticket from driver, valid for 24 hours, daily March–Oct 10:00–17:00, Jan–Feb 10:00–16:30, runs every 30 min, tel. 0151/203-3920, www.city-sightseeing.com).

Ferry Cruise—Mersey Ferries offers narrated cruises departing from Mersey Dock, an easy five-minute walk from the Albert Dock. The 50-minute cruise makes two brief stops on the other side of the river; you can hop off and catch the next boat back (£6.30, year-round, Mon–Fri 10:00–15:00, Sat–Sun 10:00–18:00, leaves at top of hour, café, WCs onboard, tel. 0151/330-1444, www.merseyferries.co.uk).

Harbor and City Tour—The Yellow Duckmarine runs wacky tours of Liverpool's waterfront, city, and docks by land and by sea in its amphibious WWII-era tourist assault vehicles. Be prepared to quack (£12, or £10 midweek and off-peak, family deals, one hour, buy tickets at office on the Albert Dock near The Beatles Story, departs from the Albert Dock every 30 min daily 10:30–17:00, more frequently with demand, tel. 0151/708-7799, www .theyellowduckmarine.co.uk).

Sights in Liverpool

At the Albert Dock

All of these sights are at the Albert Dock. Opened in 1852 by Prince Albert, and enclosing seven acres of water, the Albert Dock is surrounded by five-story brick warehouses. In its day, Liverpool was England's greatest seaport, but at the end of the 19th century, the port wasn't deep enough for the big new ships; trade declined after 1890, and by 1972 it was closed entirely. Like Liverpool itself, the docks have enjoyed a renaissance. Today, they contain the city's main attractions. A half-dozen trendy eateries are lined

up here, out of the rain, and padded by lots of shopping mall–type distractions. There's plenty of parking.

▲**Merseyside Maritime Museum/International Slavery Museum**—These museums tell the story of Liverpool, once the second city of the British Empire. The port prospered in the 18th century as one corner of a commerce triangle with Africa and America. The British shippers profited greatly through exploitation: About 1.5 million enslaved African people passed through Liverpool's docks (if you have African ancestors who arrived in America as slaves, chances are high they came through here). From Liverpool, the British exported manufactured goods to Africa in exchange for enslaved Africans; the slaves were then shipped to the Americas, where they were traded for raw material (cotton, sugar, and tobacco); and the goods were then brought back to Britain. Although the merchants on all three sides made money, the big profit came home to England. As Britain's economy boomed, so did Liverpool's. Not all the money made was above-board—a new gallery discusses the profitable business of smuggling.

Three galleries on the third floor make up the International Slavery Museum. They describe life in West Africa, enslavement and the Middle Passage to America, and the legacy of slavery. At the music desk, you can listen to over 300 songs from many different genres that were influenced by African music.

After participation in the slave trade was outlawed in Britain in the early 1800s, Liverpool kept its port busy as a transfer point for emigrants. If your ancestors came from Scandinavia, Ukraine, or Ireland, they likely left Europe from this port. Between 1830 and 1930, nine million emigrants sailed from Liverpool to find their dreams in the New World. Awe-inspiring steamers such as the *Lusitania* called this port home. One exhibit shows footage and artifacts of three big Liverpool-related shipwrecks: the *Lusitania*, the *Empress of Ireland,* and the *Titanic* (free, daily 10:00–17:00, café, tel. 0151/478-4499, www.liverpoolmuseums.org.uk).

Tate Gallery Liverpool—This prestigious gallery of modern art is near the Maritime Museum. It won't entertain you as much as its London sister, the Tate Modern, but if you're into modern art, any Tate's great (free but £3 suggested donation, £6–8 for special exhibits; Tue–Sun 10:00–17:50, closed Mon except in July–Aug; tel. 0151/702-7400, www.tate.org.uk/liverpool). The Tate has a nice, inexpensive café (recommended later, under "Eating in Liverpool").

▲**The Beatles Story**—It's sad to think the Beatles are stuck in a museum (and their music turned into a Las Vegas show). Still,

though this exhibit is overpriced and not very creative, the story's fascinating, and even an avid fan will pick up some new information.

Listen to the included audioguide while you study the knickknacks. Cynthia Lennon, John's first wife, still marvels at the manic power of Beatlemania, while the narrator reminds listeners of all that made the group earth-shattering—and even a little edgy—at the time. For example, performing before the Queen Mother, John Lennon famously quips: "Will the people in the cheaper seats clap your hands? And the rest of you, if you'll just rattle your jewelry." The audioguide captures the Beatles' charm and cheekiness in the way the stuffy wax mannequins can't.

The last few rooms trace the members' solo careers (mostly John and Paul's), and the last few steps are reserved for reverence about John's peace work, including a re-creation of the white room he used while writing "Imagine" (£12.50, includes audioguide, daily 9:00–19:00, last admission two hours before closing, tel. 0151/709-1963, www.beatlesstory.com). The shop has an impressive pile of Beatles buyables.

Sleeping in Liverpool

(£1 = about $1.60, country code: 44, area code: 0151)
B&Bs are a rarity in urban Liverpool. Your best budget options are the boring, predictable, and central chain hotels. Many hotels, including the ones listed below, charge more on weekends, especially when Liverpool's soccer team plays a home game. Rates shoot up even higher two weekends a year: during Beatles Week at the end of August and during the Grand National horse race (April 8–10 in 2010)—avoid these times if you can.

$$ Sir Thomas Hotel is a centrally located hotel that was once a bank—and feels like it. The 39 recently renovated rooms are comfortable, and deluxe rooms are outfitted with stately, heavy decor (Db-£55–70 midweek, £75–100 on non-event weekends, 10-min walk from station, 24 Sir Thomas Street at the corner of Victoria Street, tel. 0151/236-1366, fax 0151/227-1541, www .sirthomashotel.co.uk, reservations@sirthomashotel.co.uk).

$$ Premier Inn, which has pleasant, American-style rooms and a friendly staff, is right on the Albert Dock (Db-£67, mediocre breakfast costs £8 extra—try good cafés nearby instead, next to The Beatles Story, toll tel. 0870-990-6432, www.premierinn.com, liverpool.albert.pti@whitbread.com). There's a second, downtown **$$ Premier Inn** as well. Though it's a much less desirable location than the Albert Dock branch, it's just a 10-minute walk from the Lime Street train station (Db-£65, Vernon Street, just off Dale Street, tel. 0151-242-7650).

$$ Cocoon Pod Hotel, in the basement of the hostel (next listing), offers 32 no-nonsense, modern rooms with your choice of two twins or a king. As all the rooms are underground, there are no windows—but at least it's quiet (Sb or Db-£43 Sun–Thu, £53 Fri–Sat, 1- to 3-bedroom apartments from £65, free Wi-Fi, breakfast not included but café next door—with £1/30 min Internet access, laundry, same location and contact info as hostel below, www.cocoonliverpool.co.uk).

$ International Inn Hostel, run by the daughter of the Beatles' first manager, rents 100 budget beds in a former Victorian warehouse. Most nights, the hostel puts on fun, free food-themed events for guests—traditional Liverpudlian stew one night, pancakes the next, and even the occasional chocolate fountain (Db-£36–45, bed in 4- to 10-bed room-£15–20, includes sheets and towels, all rooms have bathrooms, free toast and tea/coffee, £1/30 min Internet access in adjacent café, free Wi-Fi, laundry room, games in lobby, TV lounge, video library, 24-hour reception, café, 4 South Hunter Street, tel. & fax 0151/709-8135, www.inter nationalinn.co.uk, info@internationalinn.co.uk). From the Lime Street Station, it's an easy 15-minute walk: Follow Lime Street south, which then becomes Renshaw Street, then ends at the bombed-out church. That puts you at the start of Leece Street—walk up three blocks (where it becomes Hardman Street) and hang a left onto South Hunter Street. Or take bus #80A or #86A (3–6/hr, direction: Liverpool Airport or Garston), and get off two stops after the bus veers left at the bombed-out church. If you take a taxi, tell them it's on South Hunter Street near Hardman Street.

Eating in Liverpool

Your best bet is to dine at the Albert Dock (my first two listings, below). Here you'll find a slew of trendy restaurants that come alive with club energy at night, but are sedate and pleasant in the afternoon and early evening.

Gusto, a chain restaurant that doesn't seem like one, serves local businesspeople, travelers, and families alike in its cavernous but classy and fun space (£9 weekday lunch deals, £9 pastas and pizzas, £13–18 meat and fish dishes, children's menu available, daily 11:00–24:00, free Wi-Fi, Albert Dock, tel. 0151/708-6969).

Tate Café, in the Tate Gallery, serves soups, salads, and light lunches in a bright room that feels like its own gallery (£5–8 lunches, daily 10:00–17:30 except closed Mon Oct–March, Albert Dock, tel. 0151/702-7580.)

The Slug and Lettuce, located in the city center, is another chain restaurant/bar. It mostly caters to the after-hours office crowd, who are more interested in drinking than eating, but it'll do in a pinch (£9 plates, Mon–Sat 10:00–22:00, Sun 11:00–22:00, 16 North John Street, tel. 0151/236-8820).

Liverpool Connections

By Train

From Liverpool by Train to: Blackpool (hourly, 1.5 hrs), **Lake District** (train to Penrith—roughly hourly with change at Wigan or Preston, 2 hrs; then bus to Keswick—hourly except Sun 8/day, 40 min), **York** (hourly, 2.25 hrs), **Edinburgh** (roughly hourly, 3.5–4 hrs, 1–2 changes), **Glasgow** (1–2/hr, 3.5 hrs Mon–Fri, change in Wigan or Preston), **London**'s Euston Station (hourly, 2 hrs), **Crewe** (2/hr, 45 min), **Chester** (2/hr, 45 min). Train info: toll tel. 0845-748-4950, www.nationalrail.co.uk.

By Ferry

By Ferry to Dublin, Republic of Ireland: It's a seven-hour trip between Liverpool and Dublin by boat. Both ferry companies require you to check in one to two hours before the sailing time—call to confirm the details. Ferries sail daily from both companies at 22:00, with an additional trip at 10:00 Tue–Sat. P&O Irish Sea Ferries runs a car ferry only—no foot passengers (prices vary, roughly £85–100, 20-min drive north of the city center at Liverpool Freeport—Gladstone dock, toll tel. 0871-664-4777, www.po irishsea.com). On foot or by car, you can use Norfolkline Irish Sea Ferry Services from nearby Birkenhead (£20 for foot passengers on daytime ferries, £20–30 more for overnight ferries, sleeper cabins extra; book online at least one day ahead to avoid £10 phone/in-person booking fee and £20 day-of-sailing fee, Birkenhead Port, toll tel. 0844-499-0007, www.norfolkline-ferries.co.uk). Birkenhead's dock is a 15-minute walk from Hamilton Square Station on Merseyrail's Wirral Line. You can also take a ferry to Dublin via the Isle of Man (www.steam-packet.com).

By Ferry to Belfast, Northern Ireland: Norfolkline Irish Sea Ferry Services sails most mornings (Tue–Sun) at 10:30, and every evening at 22:30 year-round (8 hrs, toll tel. 0844-499-0007, www .norfolkline-ferries.co.uk). You can also take a ferry to Belfast via the Isle of Man (www.steam-packet.com).

Route Tips for Drivers

From Liverpool to Blackpool: Leaving Liverpool, drive north along the waterfront, following signs to *M58* (Preston). Once on M58 (and not before), follow signs to *M6,* and then *M55* into Blackpool.

THE LAKE DISTRICT

In the pristine Lake District, Wordsworth's poems still shiver in trees and ripple on ponds. This is a land where nature rules and humanity keeps a wide-eyed but low profile. Relax, recharge, take a cruise or a hike, and maybe even write a poem. Renew your poetic license at Wordsworth's famous Dove Cottage.

The Lake District, about 30 miles long and 30 miles wide, is nature's lush, green playground. Explore it by foot, bike, bus, or car. While not impressive in sheer height (Scafell Pike, the tallest peak in England, is only 3,206 feet), there's a walking-stick charm about the way nature and the culture mix. Locals are fond of declaring that their mountains are older than the Himalayas and were once as tall, but have been worn down by the ages. Walking along a windblown ridge or climbing over a rock fence to look into the eyes of a ragamuffin sheep, even tenderfeet get a chance to feel very outdoorsy. The tradition of staying close to the land remains true—albeit in an updated form—in the 21st century; you'll see restaurants serving organic foods as well as stickers advocating for environmental causes in the windows of local homes.

Dress in layers, and expect rain mixed with brilliant "bright spells" (pubs offer atmospheric shelter at every turn). Drizzly days can be followed by delightful evenings.

Plan to spend the majority of your time in the unspoiled North Lake District. In this chapter, I focus on the town of Keswick, the lake called Derwentwater, and the vast, time-passed Newlands Valley. The North Lake District works great by car or by bus (with easy train access via Penrith), and is manna to nature-lovers, with good accommodations to boot.

The South Lake District—famous primarily for its Wordsworth and Beatrix Potter sights—is closer to London and gets the promotion, the tour crowds, and the tackiness that comes with them. I strongly recommend that you skip the South Lake District, and enter the region from the north via Penrith. Make your home base in or near Keswick, and side-trip from here into the South Lake District only if you're interested in the Wordsworth and Beatrix Potter sights.

Planning Your Time

On a three-week trip to Britain, I'd spend two days and two nights in this area. Penrith is the nearest train station, just 40 minutes by bus or car from Keswick. Those without a car will use Keswick as a springboard: Cruise the lake and take one of the many hikes in the Catbells area. Nonhikers can hop on a minibus tour. If great scenery is commonplace in your life, the Lake District can be more soothing (and rainy) than exciting. If you're rushed, you could make this area a one-night stand—or even a quick drive-through.

Two-Day Driving Plan: Here's the most exciting way for drivers coming from the south—who'd like to visit South Lake District sights en route to the North Lake District—to pack their day of arrival: On **Day 1,** get an early start, aiming to leave the motorway at Kendal by 10:30; drive along Windermere and through Ambleside; 11:30–Tour Dove Cottage; 12:30–Backtrack to Ambleside, where a small road leads up and over the dramatic Kirkstone Pass (far more scenic northbound than southbound, get out and bite the wind) and down to Glenridding on Lake Ullswater. You could catch the 15:00 boat. Hike six miles (3–4 hours, roughly 15:30–19:00) from Howtown back to Glenridding. Drive to your farmhouse B&B near Keswick, with a stop as the sun sets at Castlerigg Stone Circle. On **Day 2,** make the circular drive from Keswick through the Newlands Valley, Buttermere, Honister Pass, and Borrowdale, and do the Catbells High Ridge Hike. Return to the same farmhouse B&B for the evening.

Getting Around the Lake District

With a Car

Nothing is very far from Keswick and Derwentwater. Pick up a

good map, get off the big roads, and leave the car, at least occasionally, for some walking. In summer, the Keswick–Ambleside–Windermere–Bowness corridor (A591) suffers from congestion.

Keswick Motor Company rents cars in Keswick (from £32/ day with insurance, Mon–Sat

8:30–17:15, closed Sun, ages 25–70 only, must have an International Driving Permit and passport, Lake Road, a block from Moot Hall in town center, tel. 017687/72064).

Parking is tight throughout the region. It's easiest to just park in the pay-and-display lots (gather small coins, as most machines don't make change). If you're parking free on the roadside, don't block the vital turnouts. Where there are double yellow lines, you must be beyond them.

Without a Car

Those based in Keswick without a car manage fine.

By Bus: Keswick has no real bus station; all buses stop at a turnout in front of the Booths Supermarket. Local buses take you quickly and easily (if not always frequently) to all nearby points of interest. Check the schedule carefully to make sure you can catch the last bus home. The exhaustive *Cumbria & Lakes Rider* bus brochure (50 pages, free, at TI or on any bus) explains the schedules (note that some buses don't run during the winter). Onboard, you can purchase one-day Explorer passes (£10) or get one-day passes for certain routes. A four-day pass is available at the Keswick TI/ National Park Visitors Centre. For bus and rail info, call 0871-200-2233 (costs 10p/min) or visit www.traveline.org.uk.

Buses **#X4** and **#X5** connect Penrith train station to Keswick (hourly Mon–Sat, 8/day Sun, 40 min, £5.50).

Bus **#77/#77A**, the Honister Rambler, makes the gorgeous circle from Keswick around Derwentwater, over Honister Pass, through Buttermere, and down the Whinlatter Valley (4/day clockwise, 4/day "anticlockwise," daily Easter–Oct, weekends only in Nov, 1.5-hour loop, £6.50 Honister Dayrider all-day pass).

Bus **#78**, the Borrowdale Rambler, goes topless in the summer, affording a wonderful sightseeing experience in and of itself, heading from Keswick to Lodore Hotel, Grange, Rosthwaite, and Seatoller at the base of Honister Pass (hourly, 2/hr mid-July–Aug, 8/day on Sun, 25 min each way, £5.75 Borrowdale Dayrider all-day pass).

Bus **#108** runs between Penrith and Glenridding, stopping in Pooley Bridge (daily 4–6/day, no Sun service Sept–Easter, 40 min, £14 Ullswater Bus & Boat day pass covers this bus route as well as steamers on Ullswater).

Bus **#208** runs between Keswick and Glenridding (5/day mid-July–Aug, Sat–Sun only late May–mid-July, 45 min).

Bus **#505**, the Coniston Rambler, connects Windermere with Hawkshead (daily Easter–Oct, hourly, 35 min).

Bus **#517**, the Kirkstone Rambler, runs between Windermere and Glenridding (3/day mid-July–Aug, Sat–Sun only Easter–mid-July, 1 hr).

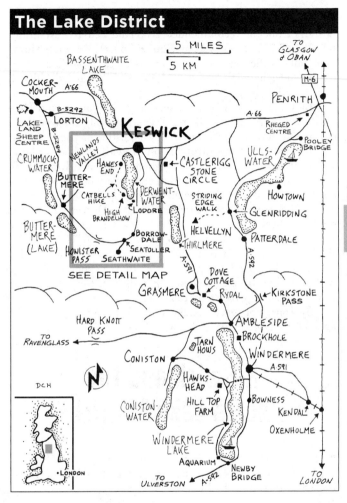

The Lake District

Buses **#555** and **#556** connect Keswick with the south (hourly, 1 hr to Windermere).

Bus **#599,** the open-top Lakes Rider, runs along the main Windermere corridor, connecting the big tourist attractions in the south (3/hr daily Easter–Aug, 50 min each way, £6.50 Central Lakes Dayrider all-day pass, route: Grasmere and Dove Cottage–Rydal Mount–Ambleside–Brockhole–Windermere–Bowness Pier.

By Bike: Several shops rent bikes in Keswick. **Keswick Mountain Bikes** has the largest selection (mountain bikes-£15–20/day depending on model, includes helmet and toolkit, Mon–Sat 9:00–17:30, Sun 10:00–17:30, can recommend guided bike tours; several locations, including right off the town square, upstairs from the recommended Lakeland Pedlar Restaurant; tel. 017687/75202, www.keswickbikes.co.uk). **Keswick Motor Company** in the town center also rents bikes (£10/4 hours, £15/day, includes helmet). Keswick Mountain Bikes and the TI sell various cycling maps.

By Boat: A circular boat service glides you around Derwentwater, with several hiker-aiding stops along the way (for a cruise/hike option, see the Derwentwater listing on page 368).

By Foot: Hiking information is available everywhere. Consider buying a detailed map (good selection at Keswick TI and at the outdoor gear stores that cram every block; or borrow one from your B&B). For easy hikes, pick up the helpful fliers at TIs and B&Bs that describe routes. The Lake District's TIs advise hikers to check the weather before setting out (for an up-to-date weather report, ask at TI or call toll tel. 0870-055-0575), wear suitable clothing and footwear, and bring a map. Plan for rain. It's wise to watch your footing. Fatalities aren't uncommon—every year, several people die while hiking in the area (some from overexertion; others are blown off ridges).

By Tour: For organized bus tours that run the roads of the Lake District, see "Tours in Keswick," later.

Keswick and the North Lake District

As far as touristy Lake District towns go, Keswick (KEZ-ick, population 5,000) is far more enjoyable than Windermere, Bowness, or Ambleside. Many of the place names around Keswick have Norse origins, inherited from the region's 10th-century settlers. An important mining center for slate, copper, and lead through the Middle Ages, Keswick became a resort in the 19th century. Its fine Victorian buildings recall those Romantic days when  city slickers first learned about "communing with nature." Today, the compact town is lined with tearooms, pubs, gift shops, and hiking-gear shops. Lake Derwentwater is a pleasant 10-minute walk from the town center.

Orientation to Keswick

(area code: 017687)

Keswick is an ideal home base, with plenty of good B&Bs, an easy bus connection to the nearest train station at Penrith, and a prime location near the best lake in the area, Derwentwater. In Keswick, everything is within a 10-minute walk of everything else: the pedestrian town square, the TI, recommended B&Bs, two grocery stores, the municipal pitch-and-putt golf course, the main bus stop, a lakeside boat dock, the post office (with Internet access), and a central parking lot. Thursdays and Saturdays are market days in the town square, but the square is lively every day throughout the summer (no Thu market Jan–Feb).

Keswick town is a delight for wandering. Its centerpiece, Moot Hall (meaning "meeting hall"), was a 16th-century copper warehouse upstairs with an arcade below (closed after World War II). "Keswick" means "cheese farm"—a legacy from the time when the town square was the spot to sell cheese. The town square recently went pedestrians-only, and locals are all abuzz about people tripping over the curbs. (The British, seemingly thrilled by ever-present danger, are endlessly warning visitors to "watch your head," "watch the step," and "mind the gap.")

Keswick and the Lake District are popular with British holiday-makers who prefer to bring their dogs with them on vacation. The town square in Keswick can look like the Westminster Dog Show, and the recommended Dog and Gun pub, where "well-behaved dogs are welcomed," is always full of patient pups. If you're shy about connecting with local people, pal up to a British pooch—you will often find they are happy to introduce you to their owners.

Tourist Information

The TI/National Park Visitors Centre is in Moot Hall, right in the middle of the town square (daily Easter–Oct 9:30–17:30, Nov–Easter 9:30–16:30, tel. 017687/72645, www.lake-district.gov .uk and www.keswick.org). The staff are pros at advising you about hiking routes. They'll also help you figure out public transportation to outlying sights, and book rooms (you'll pay a £4 booking fee; it's cheaper to call B&Bs direct).

The TI sells the £22 four-day bus pass (but not one-day passes, which you buy onboard), theater tickets, Keswick Launch tickets (at a £1.20 discount), fishing licenses, and brochures and maps that outline nearby hikes (60p–£1.80, including a very simple driver-friendly £1.60 *Lap Map* featuring sights, walks, and a mileage chart). The TI also has books and maps for hikers, cyclists, and drivers (more books are sold at the nearby store that contains the post office).

Keswick

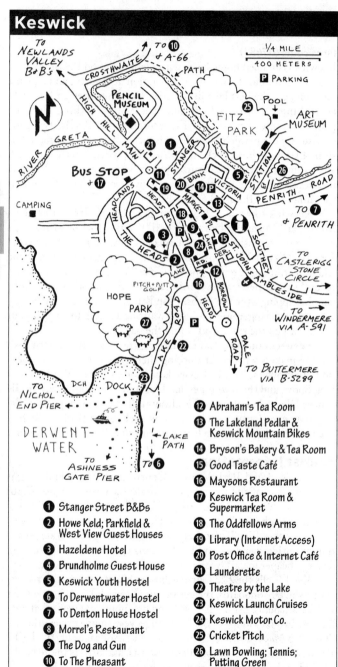

1 Stanger Street B&Bs

2 Howe Keld; Parkfield & West View Guest Houses

3 Hazeldene Hotel

4 Brundholme Guest House

5 Keswick Youth Hostel

6 To Derwentwater Hostel

7 To Denton House Hostel

8 Morrel's Restaurant

9 The Dog and Gun

10 To The Pheasant

11 Star of Siam

12 Abraham's Tea Room

13 The Lakeland Pedlar & Keswick Mountain Bikes

14 Bryson's Bakery & Tea Room

15 Good Taste Café

16 Maysons Restaurant

17 Keswick Tea Room & Supermarket

18 The Oddfellows Arms

19 Library (Internet Access)

20 Post Office & Internet Café

21 Launderette

22 Theatre by the Lake

23 Keswick Launch Cruises

24 Keswick Motor Co.

25 Cricket Pitch

26 Lawn Bowling; Tennis; Putting Green

27 Photo Fun with Sheep

THE LAKE DISTRICT

Check the "What's On Locally" boards (inside the TI's foyer) for information about walks, talks, and entertainment. The daily weather forecast is posted just outside the front door (weather toll tel. 0870-055-0575). Pop upstairs for a series of short videos about the history of Keswick and the Lake District (free). For information about the TI's guided walks, see "Tours in Keswick," below.

Helpful Hints

Book in Advance: Keswick hosts a variety of festivals and conventions, especially during the summer, so it's smart to book ahead. Please honor your bookings—the B&B proprietors here lose out on much-needed business if you don't show up.

A sampling of events for 2010: The Keswick Jazz Festival mellows out the town in mid-May, followed immediately by the new Mountain Festival, then a beer festival in early June (June 4–5 in 2010). The Keswick Religious Convention packs the town with 4,000 evangelical Christians the last three weeks in July.

Several Bank Holiday Mondays in spring and summer (May 3, May 31, and Aug 30 in 2010) draw vacationers from all over the island for three-day weekends.

If you have trouble finding a room (or a B&B that accepts small children), try www.keswick.org to search for available rooms.

Internet Access: Located above the store that contains the post office, **U-Compute** provides Internet access (£2/30 min, £3/hr, unused time valid for 2 weeks, daily May–mid-Sept 8:30–21:00, mid-Sept–April 9:00–17:30, 16 terminals and Wi-Fi—same price, corner of Main and Bank Streets, tel. 017687/75127). The **library** has 10 terminals (£2/hr, 50p/15-min minimum charge, Mon and Wed 10:00–19:00, Tue and Fri 10:00–17:00, Thu and Sat 10:00–12:30, closed Sun, tel. 017687/72656). The **launderette** listed next also has Wi-Fi (£2/hr).

Laundry: It's around the corner from the bus station on Main Street, next to the Co-op grocery (self-service Mon–Fri 8:00–19:00, Sat–Sun 9:00–18:00, £6/load wash and dry, change machine and coin-op soap dispenser; £8 full service; tel. 017687/75448).

Tours in Keswick

Guided Walks—Walks of varying levels of difficulty depart from the TI several times a week at 10:00. They're led by local guides, leave regardless of the weather, and sometimes incorporate a bus ride into the outing (£10, Easter–Oct, no tours during religious convention in July, wear suitable clothing and footwear, bring lunch and water, return by 17:00, tel. 017687/72645, www.keswick rambles.org.uk). TIs throughout the region also offer free walks led by "Voluntary Rangers" (generally from Keswick on Sun and Wed in summer, ask for the *National Park Visitor Guide*).

Bus Tours—These are great for people with bucks who'd like to wring maximum experience out of their limited time and see the area without lots of hiking or messing with public transport. For a cheaper alternative, take public buses.

Edwin Jackson of **Helm Wind Tours** can take you around Derwentwater and Buttermere on Fridays (£18, 9:30–12:30) or around Bassenthwaite and Caldbeck on Tuesdays (£16.50, 9:45–12:45; both tours leave from the Keswick bus stop, book at Keswick TI, mobile 07801-928-503). **Show Me Cumbria** runs personalized tours all around the area, and charges per tour, not per person (first hour-£35, otherwise £25/hr, tel. 01768/866-880, mobile 0780-902-6357, www.showmecumbria.co.uk, andy@showmecumbria.co.uk).

Mountain Goat Tours is the region's dominant tour company. Unfortunately, they run their minibus tours out of Windermere, with pick-ups in Ambleside and Grasmere, but not Keswick—adding about an extra hour of driving, round-trip, for those based in Keswick (£24/half-day, £34/full day, year-round if there are sufficient sign-ups, minimum 4 to a maximum of 16 per hearty bus, book in advance by calling 015394/45161, www.mountain-goat.com).

Sights in Keswick

▲**Derwentwater**—One of Cumbria's most photographed and popular lakes, Derwentwater has four islands, good circular boat service, plenty of trails, and the pleasant town of Keswick at its north end.
The roadside views aren't much, so hike or cruise. You can walk around the lake (fine trail, floods in heavy rains, 9 miles, 4 hours) or cruise it (1 hour). I suggest a hike/cruise combo. The Lodore Walk and the Catbells High Ridge Hike (both described later, under "Hikes and Drives in the North Lake District") start from Derwentwater docks.

Boating—Keswick Launch runs boats from mid-March to October (2/hr—alternating clockwise and "anticlockwise"—daily 10:00–16:30, July–Aug until 17:30, in winter 5/day weekends only, at end of Lake Road, tel. 017687/72263, www.keswick-launch .co.uk). Boats make seven stops on each one-hour round-trip.

The boat trip costs £9 per circle (£1.20 less if you book through TI) with free stopovers, or £1.85 per segment. Stand on the pier Gilligan-style, or the boat may not stop. Keswick Launch also rents pricey **rowboats** for two (£8/30 min, £12/hr).

Keswick Launch's **evening cruise** is a delightful little trip that comes with a glass of wine and a mid-lake stop for a short commentary (£9.50, £21 family ticket, 1 hour, mid-July–Aug at 19:30 every evening—weather permitting and if enough people show up). You're welcome to bring a picnic dinner and munch scenically as you cruise.

▲**Pencil Museum**—Graphite was first discovered centuries ago in Keswick. A hunk of the stuff proved great for marking sheep in the 15th century. In 1832, the first crude Keswick pencil factory opened, and the rest is history (which is what you'll learn about here). Although you can't actually tour the 150-year-old factory where the famous Derwent pencils are made, you can enjoy the smell of thousands of pencils getting sharpened for the first time. The adjacent charming and kid-friendly museum is a good way to pass a rainy hour; you may even catch an artist's demonstration. Take a look at the "war pencils" made for WWII bomber crews (filled with tiny maps and compasses) and relax for 10 minutes watching *The Humble Pencil* video in the theater, followed by a sleepy animated-snowman short (£3.25, daily 9:30–17:00, last entry at 16:00, humble café on-site, 3-min walk from the town center, signposted off Main Street, tel. 017687/73626, www.pencilmuseum.co.uk).

Fitz Park—An inviting grassy park stretches alongside Keswick's tree-lined, duck-filled River Greta. There's plenty of room for kids to burn off energy. Consider an after-dinner stroll on the footpath. You may catch men in white (or frisky schoolboys in uniform) playing a game of cricket. There's the serious bowling green (where you're welcome to watch the experts play), and the public one where tourists are welcome to give lawn bowling a go (£3). You can try tennis on a grass court (£6.50/hr for 2 people, includes rackets) or enjoy the putting green (£2). Find the rental pavilion across the road from the art gallery (open daily 9:30–19:45 or until dusk).

▲**Golf**—A lush nine-hole pitch-and-putt golf course near the gardens in Hope Park separates the town from the lake and offers a classy, cheap, and convenient chance to golf near the birthplace of the sport (£3.50 for 9 holes, £2 for putting, £2.30 for 18 tame holes of "obstacle golf," daily 9:30–19:45 or dusk, may close Nov–Easter, tel. 017687/73445).

Swimming—Although the Leisure Centre doesn't have a serious adult pool, it does have an indoor pool kids love, with a huge water slide and wave machine (pool-£4.75, kids-£3.75, family-£14, Mon–Tue 11:00–15:00, Wed 11:00–16:00, Thu 11:00–18:00, Fri 11:00–17:00, Sat–Sun 10:00–17:00, shorter hours off-season, longer during school break, no towels or suits for rent, lockers-£1 deposit, 10-min walk from town center, follow Station Road past Fitz Park and veer left, tel. 017687/72760).

Near Keswick

▲▲**Castlerigg Stone Circle**—For some reason, 70 percent of England's stone circles are here in Cumbria. This one's the best, and one of the oldest, in Britain. The circle—90 feet across and 5,000 years old—has 38 stones mysteriously laid out on a line between the two tallest peaks on the horizon. They served as a celestial calendar for ritual celebrations. Imagine the ambience here, as ancient people filled this clearing in spring to celebrate fertility, in late summer to

commemorate the harvest, and in the winter to celebrate the winter solstice and the coming renewal of light. Festival dates were dictated by how the sun rose and set in relation to the stones. The more that modern academics study this circle, the more meaning they find in the placement of the stones. The two front stones face due north, toward a cut in the mountains. The rare-for-stone-circles "sanctuary" lines up with its center stone to mark where the sun rises on May Day. (Party!) For maximum "goose pimples" (as they say here), show up at sunset (free, open all the time, 3 miles east of Keswick—follow brown signs, 3 min off A66, easy parking).

▲**Lakeland Sheep and Wool Centre**—If you have a car, this is worth a stop to watch working sheepdogs in action. Catch a dem-

onstration, see the 20 or so different breeds of sheep in Britain, and learn why each is bred. (If you knead the wool of the Merino sheep, you'll understand why it's so popular for sweaters.) You'll also see the quintessential sheepdog—the border collie—at work. At the end, you can pet whatever is still on stage: dogs, cows, sheep, sometimes a goose...if you can catch one. While the Visitors Centre and shop are free (daily 9:30–17:30), it's not really worth the trip unless you catch a sheep show (£5 for demo; March–Oct Sun–Thu at 10:30, 12:00, 14:00, and 15:30; no shows Fri–Sat and Nov–Feb, 13 miles west of Keswick on A66, just south of A5086 roundabout in Cockermouth, tel. 01900-822-673, www.sheep-woolcentre.co.uk).

THE LAKE DISTRICT

Rheged Centre—This shopping mall, just off a highway round-about (near Penrith, on A66 a mile west of the Keswick exit 40 off M6), has an IMAX theater that shows a rotating schedule of movies throughout the day, including the one-hour *Rheged: The Lost Kingdom,* which tells the story of the region's original Celtic inhabitants (£5 for any movie, £1.50 outdoor playground, daily 10:00–17:30, call ahead to check movie times, the #X4 and #X5 Keswick–Penrith buses stop here, tel. 01768/868-000, www .rheged.com).

Hikes and Drives in the North Lake District

From Keswick

The first four hikes (Lodore, Catbells, Latrigg, and Walla Crag) originate in Keswick; the rest require a car or public transportation to get to the trailhead and/or views.

Lodore Walk—The best hour-long lakeside walk is the 1.5-mile path between the docks at High Brandelhow and Hawes End in Keswick. Continue on foot along the lake back into Keswick or—better yet—go on to Lodore.

Lodore is a good stop for two reasons: Lodore Falls is a 10-minute walk from the dock (behind Lodore Hotel), and Shepherds Crag (a cliff overlooking Lodore) was made famous by pioneer rock climbers. (Their descendants hang from little ridges on its face today.) This is serious climbing (with several fatalities a year).

For a great lunch, or tea and cakes, drop into the much-loved High Lodore Farm Café, where sheep farmer Martin is busy feeding hikers and day-trippers. Eggs come from "the happy hen" (Easter–Oct daily 9:00–17:00, closed Nov–Easter; from the dock, walk up the road, turn right over bridge uphill to café; tel. 017687/77221).

▲▲Catbells High Ridge Hike—For a great "king of the moun-tain" feeling, sweeping views, and a close-up look at the weather blowing over the ridge, hike about two hours from Hawes End in Keswick up along the ridge to Catbells (1,480 feet) and down to High Brandelhow (moderate difficulty). From there, you can catch the boat or take the easy path along the shore of Derwentwater to your Hawes End starting point. (Extending the hike to Lodore takes you to a waterfall, rock climbers, a fine café, and another boat dock for a convenient return to Keswick.) Catbells is probably the most dramatic family walk in the area (but wear sturdy shoes, bring a raincoat, and watch your foot-ing). From Keswick, the lake, or your farmhouse B&B, you can see silhouetted stick figures hiking along this ridge. Drivers can

Derwentwater and Newlands Valley

THE LAKE DISTRICT

Legend:

- Ⓑ 78 — BUS ROUTES
- ── ROAD
- 🅿 PARKING
- ⋯ BOAT
- ‒‒‒ PATH

▲ PEAK
■ POINT OF INTEREST

Newlands Valley

1. Uzzicar Farm
2. Ellas Crag Guest House
3. Gill Brow Farm B&B
4. Keskadale Farm B&B
5. To Dancing Beck B&B

Derwentwater

6. Keswick Launch Pier
7. Ashness Gate Pier
8. Lodore Pier
9. High Brandelhow Pier
10. Low Brandelhow Pier
11. Hawes End Pier
12. Nichol End Pier

DCH

park free at Hawes End. The Keswick TI sells a *Catbells* brochure about the hike (60p).

Catbells is just the first of a series of peaks all connected by a fine ridge trail. Hardier hikers continue up to nine miles along this same ridge, enjoying valley and lake views as they arc around the Newlands Valley toward (and even down to) Buttermere. After High Spy, you can descend an easy path into Newlands Valley. An ultimate, very full day-plan would be to bus to Buttermere, climb Robinson, and follow the ridge around to Catbells and back to Keswick.

▲▲**More Hikes from Keswick**—The area is riddled with wonderful hikes. B&Bs all offer good advice, but consider these as well:

From downtown Keswick, you can walk the seven-mile **Latrigg** trail, which includes the Castlerigg Stone Circle described earlier (pick up 60p map/guide from TI).

From your Keswick B&B, a fine two-hour walk to **Walla Crag** offers great fell (mountain) walking and a ridge-walk experience without the necessity of a bus or car. Start by strolling along the lake to Great Wood parking lot, and head up Cat Ghyl (where "fell runners"—trail-running enthusiasts—practice) to Walla Crag. You'll be treated to great panoramic views over Derwentwater and surrounding peaks. You can do a shorter version of this walk from the parking lot at Ashness Bridge.

Beyond Keswick

▲▲**Easy Hikes**—For a very short hike and the easiest mountain-climbing sensation around, drive to the **Underscar** parking lot just north of Keswick, and hike 20 minutes to the top of the 1,200-foot-high hill for a commanding view of the town and lake.

From the parking lot at Newlands Pass, at the top of Newlands Valley, an easy one-mile walk to **Knottrigg** from Newlands Pass probably offers more TPCB (thrills per calorie burned) than any walk in the region.

▲▲**Buttermere Hike**—The ideal little lake with a lovely, circular four-mile stroll offers nonstop, no-sweat Lake District beauty. If you're not a hiker (but kind of wish you were), take this walk. If you're very short on time, at least stop here and get your shoes dirty.

Buttermere is connected with Borrowdale and Derwentwater by a great road that runs over rugged Honister Pass. From Easter through October and on November weekends, bus #77/#77A makes a 1.5-hour round-trip loop between Keswick and Buttermere over Honister Pass. The two-pub hamlet of Buttermere has a pay-and-display parking lot, but many drivers park free along the side of the road. You're welcome to leave your car at the Fish Hotel if you eat in their pub (recommended). There's also a pay parking lot at the Honister Pass end of the lake (at Gatesgarth Farm, £3). The Syke Farm (in the hamlet of Buttermere) is popular for its homemade ice cream (tel. 01768/770-277).

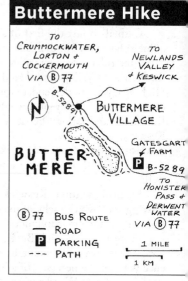

▲▲Car Hiking from Keswick —Distances are short, roads are narrow and have turnouts, and views are rewarding. Get a good map and ask your B&B host for advice. Two miles south of Keswick on the lakeside Borrowdale Valley Road (B5289), take the small road left (signposted *Ashness Bridge, Watendlath*) for a half-mile to the Ashness Packhorse Bridge (a quintessential Lake District scene, parking lot just above on right). A half-mile farther (parking lot on left) and you're startled by the "surprise view" of Derwentwater (great for a lakes photo op).

Continuing from here, the road gets extremely narrow en route to the hamlet of Watendlath, which has a tiny lake and lazy farm animals. Return down to Borrowdale Valley Road and back to Keswick, or farther south to scenic Borrowdale and over dramatic Honister Pass to Buttermere.

▲▲Scenic Circle Drive South of Keswick—This hour-long drive, which includes Newlands Valley, Buttermere, Honister Pass, and Borrowdale, is demanding. But it's also filled with the best scenery you'll find in the North Lake District. (To do a similar route without a car from Keswick, take loop bus #77/#77A.)

From Keswick, head west on the Cockermouth Road (A66). Take the second Newlands Valley exit (through Braithwaite) and

THE LAKE DISTRICT

follow signs up the majestic **Newlands Valley.** If the place had a lake, it would be packed with tourists. But it doesn't—and it isn't.

The valley is dotted with 500-year-old family-owned farms. Shearing day is reason to rush home from school. Sons get school out of the way ASAP and follow their dads into the family business. Neighbor girls marry those sons and move in. Grandparents retire to the cottage next door. With the price of wool depressed, most of the wives supplement the family income by running B&Bs (virtually every farm in the valley rents rooms). The road has one lane, with turnouts for passing. From the Newlands Pass summit, notice the glacial-shaped wilds, once forested, now not. There's an easy hike from your car to a little waterfall (or a thrilling one to Knottrigg, described earlier).

After Newlands Pass, descend to **Buttermere** (scenic lake, tiny hamlet with a pub and ice-cream store), turn left, and climb over rugged **Honister Pass**—strewn with glacial debris, remnants from the old slate mines, and curious, shaggy Swaledale sheep (looking more like goats with their curly horns). The valleys you'll see are textbook examples of those carved out by glaciers. Look high on the hillsides for "hanging valleys"—small glacial-shaped scoops cut off by the huge flow of the biggest glacier, which swept down the main valley. England's last still-functioning **slate mine,** at the summit of Honister Pass, gives tours (£10, 90-min tour; departures daily at 10:30, 12:30, 14:00, and 15:30; Dec–Jan 12:30 tour only, tel. 017687/77230, smart to book ahead, worthwhile slate-filled shop, nice WCs, www.honister.com).

After stark and lonely Honister Pass, drop into sweet and homey **Borrowdale,** with a few lonely hamlets and fine hikes from Seathwaite (get specifics on walks here from your B&B or the TI). Circling back to Keswick past Borrowdale, you pass a number of popular local attractions (climb stairs to the top of the house-sized Bowder Stone—signposted, a few minutes walk off the main road), the postcard-pretty Ashness Bridge and "surprise view" (described earlier, turnout signposted), and the rock climbers above Lodore. After that, you're home. A short detour before returning to Keswick takes you to the Castlerigg Stone Circle.

Nightlife in Keswick

▲▲**Theatre by the Lake**—Keswickians brag they enjoy "London-theater quality at Keswick prices." Their theater offers events year-round and a wonderful rotation of four to six plays through the summer (plays vary throughout the week, with music concerts on Sun). There are two stages: The main one seats 400, and the smaller "studio" theater seats 100 (and features edgier plays with rough language and nudity, £10–15). Attending a play here is a fine opportunity to do something completely local (£10–23, box office open from 9:30 until curtain time, discounts for old and young, 20:00 shows in summer, usually 19:30 in spring and fall, 19:00 in winter, café, smart to book ahead, parking at the adjacent lot is free after 18:30, tel. 017687/74411, book at TI or www.theatrebythelake.com).

▲▲**Evenings in Keswick**—For a small, remote town, Keswick has lots of great things to do in the evening. Remember, at this latitude it's light until 22:00 in midsummer. You can **golf** (fine course, pitch-and-putt, goofy golf, or just enjoy the putting green) or **walk** among the grazing sheep in Hope Park as the sun gets ready to set (between the lake and the golf course, access from just above the beach, great photo ops on a balmy eve).

To socialize with locals, head to a pub for one of their special evenings: There's **quiz night** at The Dog and Gun (21:30 on most Thu; £1, proceeds go to Keswick's Mountain Rescue team, which rescues hikers and the occasional sheep). At a quiz night, tourists are more than welcome. Drop in, say you want to join a team, and you're in. If you like trivia, it's a great way to get to know people here. Nearby, The Oddfellows Arms has free **live music** most nights.

Join Bob, the **Town Crier**, when he does his routine many summer Tuesday evenings (£2.50, 90 min, usually starts at 19:30, weekly late May–early July, details at TI). Catch a **movie** at the Alhambra Cinema, a restored old-fashioned movie theater a few minutes' walk from the town center. An **evening lake cruise** is perfect for an extremely scenic and relaxing picnic dinner (mid-July–Aug at 19:30).

Sleeping in Keswick

The Lake District abounds with attractive B&Bs, guest houses, and hostels. It needs them all when summer hordes threaten the serenity of this Romantic mecca.

Reserve your room in advance in high season. From October through April, you should have no trouble finding a room. But to get a particular place (especially on Saturdays), call ahead. If you're using public transportation, you should sleep in Keswick. If you're driving, staying outside Keswick is your best chance for a remote farmhouse experience. Lakeland hostels offer £20 beds and come with an interesting crowd of all ages.

In Keswick, I've featured B&Bs on two streets, each within three blocks of the bus station and town square. Stanger Street, a bit humbler but quiet and handy, has smaller homes and more moderately priced rooms. "The Heads" is a classier area lined with proud Victorian houses, close to the lake and theater, overlooking a golf course.

Many of my Keswick listings charge extra for a one-night stay.

Sleep Code

(£1 = about $1.60, country code: 44, area code: 017687)
S = Single, **D** = Double/Twin, **T** = Triple, **Q** = Quad, **b** = bathroom, **s** = shower only. You can assume credit cards are accepted unless otherwise noted, and all B&B stays include breakfast.

To help you sort easily through these listings, I've divided the rooms into three categories based on the price for a double room with bath:

$$$ Higher Priced—Most rooms £70 or more.
$$ Moderately Priced—Most rooms between £30-70.
$ Lower Priced—Most rooms £30 or less.

Most won't book one-night stays on weekends (but if you show up and they have a free bed, it's yours) and don't welcome children under 12 (unless extremely well-behaved). Owners are enthusiastic about offering plenty of advice to get you on the right walking trail. Most accommodations have inviting lounges with libraries of books on the region and loaner maps. Take advantage of these lounges to transform your humble B&B room into a suite.

This is still the countryside—expect huge breakfasts (often with big selections, including vegetarian options), no phones in the rooms, and shower systems that might need to be switched on to get hot water. Parking is pretty easy (park either in congested little private lots or on the street) except on Saturdays, when you may need to hunt for a little while.

On Stanger Street

This street, quiet but just a block from Keswick's town center, is lined with B&Bs situated in Victorian slate townhouses. Each of these places is small, family-run, and accepts cash only. They are all good, offering comfortably sized rooms.

$$$ Ellergill Guest House has five spick-and-span rooms with an airy, contemporary feel—several with views (D-£60, Db-£70, 2-night minimum, 22 Stanger Street, tel. 017687/73347, www.ellergill.co.uk, stay@ellergill.co.uk, run by Clare and Robin Pinkney and dog Tess).

$$ Dunsford Guest House rents four rooms decorated with a Victorian feel at a good price. Stained glass and wooden pews give the blue-and-cream breakfast room a country-chapel vibe (Db-£63, this price promised with this book in 2010, no children under age 16, free Wi-Fi, parking, 16 Stanger Street, tel. 017687/75059, www.dunsford.net, enquiries@dunsford.net, accommodating Richard and Linda).

$$ Heckberry House's two light, airy rooms are both on the first floor (D with big private bath just outside-£60, Db-£64, 2-night minimum, no children, will pick up from bus station, 12 Stanger Street, tel. 017687/71277, www.heckberry.co.uk, enquiries @heckberry.co.uk, friendly Judith and David).

$$ Badgers Wood B&B, at the top of the street, has six modern, bright, unfrilly view rooms, each named after a different tree (Sb-£36, Db-£68, 2-night minimum, no children under age 12, special diets accommodated, 30 Stanger Street, tel. 017687/72621, www.badgers-wood.co.uk, enquiries@badgers-wood.co.uk, Andrew and Anne).

$$ Abacourt House, with a daisy-fresh breakfast room, has five pleasant doubles (Db-£65, no children, 26 Stanger Street, tel. 017687/72967, www.abacourt.co.uk, abacourt.keswick@btinternet .com, John and Heather).

On The Heads

All of these B&Bs are in an area known as The Heads. Most have good mountain views.

$$$ Howe Keld has the polished feel of a boutique hotel, but offers all the friendliness of a B&B. Completely renovated in 2008, its 14 contemporary-posh rooms are decked out in native woods and slate. It's warm, welcoming, and family-run, with a wide variety of breakfast selections (Sb-£45–50, standard Db-£80, superior Db-£90–102, cash preferred, 2 ground-floor rooms, family deals, free Wi-Fi, toll-free tel. 0800-783-0212 or 017687/72417, www.howekeld.co.uk, david@howekeld.co.uk, run with care by David and Valerie Fisher).

$$$ Parkfield Guest House, thoughtfully run and decorated by John and Susan Berry, is a big Victorian house. Its seven bright pastel rooms have fine views (Sb-£50, Db-£78 with this book through 2010, Db suite-£98, 2-night minimum, no children under age 16, fresh fruit salads at breakfast, off-street parking available, tel. 017687/72328, www.parkfield-keswick.co.uk, susanberrypark field@hotmail.com).

$$$ West View Guest House, next to the Parkfield, has eight cheery rooms, a relaxing old-school lounge, and a "borrow box" for those desperate for walking gear. Ask Paul or Dawn about the cabinet in the lounge dedicated to pharmaceutical history (Sb-£50, Db-£72, tel. 017687/73638, www.westviewkeswick.co.uk, info @westviewkeswick.co.uk).

$$$ Hazeldene Hotel, on the corner of The Heads, has spacious, bright rooms. The carpeting is dated, but you'll hardly notice because the views are fantastic (Db-£70–80 depending on view, huge Db suite with grand view-£90–95, Tb-£105, £5 extra for one-

night stay, free Wi-Fi, tel. 017687/72106, www.hazeldene-hotel
.co.uk, Helen).

$$ Brundholme Guest House has three bright, comfy
rooms, all with grand views—especially from the front side—
and a friendly and welcoming atmosphere (Db-£62, cash only,
tel. 017687/73305, www.brundholme.co.uk, barbara@brundholme
.co.uk, Barbara and Paul Motler).

Hostels in and near Keswick

The Lake District's inexpensive hostels, mostly located in great old
buildings, are handy sources of information and social fun. The first
two hostels—both part of the Youth Hostels Association (www
.yha.org.uk)—are former hotels, offering Internet access, laundry
machines, and three cheap meals daily; at these, non-members pay
about £3 extra a night, or buy a £16 membership.

$ Keswick Youth Hostel, with 85 beds in a converted old
mill overlooking the river, has a great riverside balcony and plenty
of handy facilities. Travelers of all ages feel at home here, but
book ahead—beds here can be hard to come by from July through
September (£20–22 beds, mostly 3- to 4-bed rooms, D-£44,
café, bar, center of town just off Station Road before river, tel.
017687/72484, keswick@yha.org.uk).

$ Derwentwater Hostel, in a 200-year-old mansion on the
shore of Derwentwater, is two miles south of Keswick and has
88 beds (£16–18 beds in 4- to 22-bed rooms, family rooms, 23:00
curfew, follow B5289 from Keswick, look for sign 100 yards after
Ashness exit, tel. 017687/77246, derwentwater@yha.org.uk).

$ Denton House is Keswick's *other* hostel—it's independent
(not YHA), spartan, grimy, and institutional, but usually has spaces
available (£13–15 beds in 4- to 14-bed dorm rooms, lockers-£1–2,
breakfast-£3 extra and offered only when hostel is full—which is
most weekends, kitchen, tel. 017687/75351, www.vividevents.co.uk,
sales@vividevents.co.uk). From the town square, walk several blocks
uphill along Station Street. Just before the bridge over the river, turn
right onto Penrith Road; from there it's a seven-minute riverside
walk—the hostel is on the right, not long after the fire station.

West of Keswick, in the Newlands Valley

If you have a car, drive 10 minutes past Keswick down the majestic
Newlands Valley (described earlier, under "Scenic Circle Drive
South of Keswick"). This valley is studded with 500-year-old
farms that have been in the same family for centuries, and now
rent rooms to supplement the family income. The rooms are plainer
than the B&Bs in town, and come with steep and gravelly roads,
plenty of dogs, and an earthy charm. Traditionally, farmhouses

lacked central heating, and while they are now heated, you can still request a hot-water bottle to warm up your bed.

Getting to the Newlands Valley: Leave Keswick heading west on the Cockermouth Road (A66). Take the second Newlands Valley exit through Braithwaite, and follow signs through Newlands Valley (drive toward Buttermere). All of my recommended B&Bs are on this road: Uzzicar Farm (under the shale field, which local boys love hiking up to glissade down), Ellas Crag Guest House, then Gill Brow Farm, and finally—the last house before the stark summit—Keskadale Farm (about four miles before Buttermere). The one-lane road has turnouts for passing. Each place offers easy parking, grand views, and perfect tranquility. These are listed in geographical order, the first being a 10-minute drive from Keswick and the last being at the top of the valley (about a 15-min drive from Keswick).

$$$ Uzzicar Farm is a big, rustic place with a comfy B&B in a low-ceilinged, circa-1550 farmhouse—watch out for ducks (S-£45, D or Db-£70, discount for longer stays, family deals, cash only, tel. 017687/78026, www.uzzicarfarm.co.uk, stay@uzzicarfarm.co.uk, Helen).

$$ Ellas Crag Guest House, with three rooms—each with a great view—is more of a comfortable stone house than a farm. This homey B&B offers a good mix of modern and traditional decor, including beautifully tiled bathrooms (Ss-£45, Sb-50, Ds-£60, Db-£64, these prices guaranteed with this book through 2010, cash only, 2-night minimum, local free-range meats and eggs for breakfast, sack lunches available, huge DVD library, laundry-£10, tel. 017687/78217, www.ellascrag.co.uk, info@ellascrag.co.uk, Jane and Ed Ma and their children).

$$ Gill Brow Farm is a rough-hewn, working farmhouse where Anne Wilson and her delightful teenage daughter, Laura, rent two simple but fine rooms (D or Db-£54, 10 percent discount with this book and 3-night stay in 2010, tel. 017687/78270, www.gillbrow-keswick.co.uk, wilson_gillbrow@hotmail.com).

$$ Keskadale Farm is another good farmhouse experience, with Ponderosa hospitality. One of the valley's oldest, the house is made from 500-year-old ship beams. Though the two rooms for rent are dark and have dated decor, this working farm is an authentic slice of Lake District life and is your chance to get to know lots of curly-horned sheep and the dogs who herd them. Now that her boys are old enough to help dad in the fields, Margaret Harryman runs the B&B (Sb-£40, Db-£60–70, £2 extra for one-night stays, cash only, closed Dec–Feb, tel. 017687/78544, fax 017687/78150, www.keskadalefarm.co.uk, info@keskadalefarm.co.uk). They also rent a two-bedroom apartment (£400/week).

West and Southwest of Keswick, in Buttermere and Lorton

$$$ Bridge Hotel, just beyond Newlands Valley at Buttermere, offers 21 beautiful rooms—most of them quite spacious—and a classic Old World countryside-hotel experience that includes a fancy dinner (Sb-£89, standard Db-£180–182, superior Db-£198, suite-like Db-£198, £40 less without dinner, free Wi-Fi in lobby, tel. 017687/70252, fax 017687/70215, www.bridge-hotel .com, enquiries@bridge-hotel.com). There are no shops within 10 miles—only peace and quiet a stone's throw from one of the region's most beautiful lakes. The hotel has a dark-wood pub/ restaurant on the ground floor.

$$$ The Old Vicarage, with a lovely, genteel feeling, is in what once was the clergyman's house in this tiny village. It has six rooms in the main late-1800s house, and two more in the coach house. The owners, Jane and Peter Smith, offer an optional £21 two-course meal or a £25 three-course meal, with dishes such as rack of lamb (Sb-£75–80, Db-£110–120, one ground-floor room, Church Lane, Lorton, tel. 01900/85656, www.oldvicarage.co.uk, enquiries@oldvicarage.co.uk).

$ Buttermere Hostel, a quarter-mile south of Buttermere village on Honister Pass Road, has good food, 70 beds, family rooms, and a peacefully rural setting (£20 beds in 4- to 6-bed rooms, £2 cheaper midweek, includes breakfast, inexpensive lunches and dinners, laundry, office open 8:30–10:00 & 17:00–22:30, 23:00 curfew, toll tel. 0845-371-9508, buttermere@yha.org.uk).

North of Keswick, Toward Bassenthwaite Lake

This area has gorgeous views looking down the Newlands Valley, and is still near Keswick.

$$$ Dancing Beck B&B is a newly renovated but very traditional-feeling 1850 house. Its three light-filled rooms come with views and good-sized bathrooms. The "Squirrel Room" looks out on nest boxes hung for endangered red squirrels—you may spot some babies (Sb-£35–40, Db-£65–70, cash only; about two miles from Keswick—take A591, turn right at sign for *Millbeck* and *Applethwaite*, second house on the left; tel. 017687/74781, www .dancingbeck.co.uk, lyn.edmondson@btinternet.com, Lynne).

South of Keswick, near Borrowdale

$$$ Seatoller Farm B&B is a rustic 17th-century house in a five-building hamlet where Christine Simpson rents three rooms. The old windows are small, but the abundant flower boxes keep things bright (Db-£70, less for 2 or more nights, tel. 017687/ 77232, www.seatollerfarm.co.uk, info@seatollerfarm.co.uk).

Several restaurants are located about a mile away.

$ Borrowdale Hostel, in secluded Borrowdale Valley just south of Rosthwaite, is a well-run place surrounded by many ways to immerse yourself in nature. The hostel serves cheap dinners, offers sack lunches, and keeps the pantry well-stocked (86 beds, £18–22 beds in 2- to 8-bed dorms, D-£44, £3 more for non-members, family rooms, pay Internet access and Wi-Fi, laundry machines, 3 cheap meals daily, 23:00 curfew, toll tel. 0845-371-9624, borrowdale@yha .org.uk). To reach this hostel from Keswick by bus, take #78, the "Borrowdale Rambler" (hourly, 2/hr mid-July–Aug; last bus from Keswick at 17:40 most of year, at 18:00 mid-July–Aug).

Eating in Keswick

Keswick has a huge variety of eateries catering to its many visitors. Most restaurants stop serving by 21:00. Here's a selection of favorites.

Morrel's Restaurant is the top Keswick choice for a splurge. It's simple yet elegant, serving famously good and creative modern English cuisine (£11–17 meals, £14 two-course meals and £16 three-course meals on Sun, Tue–Sun 17:30–21:00, closed Mon, reservations recommended; tell them if you're going to the theater, otherwise expect a relaxed dinner; all meals cooked to order, 34 Lake Road, tel. 017687/72666).

The Dog and Gun serves good pub food, but mind your head and tread carefully: Low ceilings and wooden beams loom overhead, while paws poke out from under tables below, as Keswick's canines patiently wait for their masters to finish their beer (£6–10 meals, daily 12:00–21:00, goulash, no chips and proud of it, 2 Lake Road, tel. 017687/73463).

The Pheasant is a bit of a walk outside town, but locals make the trek regularly for the food. The menu offers local pub standards (fish pie, Cumbrian sausage, guinea fowl), as well as lighter, more inventive choices. Check the walls for caricatures of pub regulars, sketched at these tables by a local artist (£9–12 meals, daily 12:00–14:00 & 18:00–21:00, light meals served between lunch and dinner, Crosthwaite Road, tel. 017687/72219). From the town square, it's a 15-minute walk: Follow Main Street past the Pencil Museum, then hang a right onto Crosthwaite Road and walk for 10 minutes; the pub is opposite the Esso station. For a more scenic route, cross the river into Fitz Park, and go left along the riverside path until it ends at the gate to Crosthwaite Road; turn right here and walk for five minutes.

Star of Siam serves authentic Thai dishes in a tasteful dining room (£8–10 plates, daily 12:00–14:30 & 17:30–22:30, 89 Main Street, tel. 017687/71444).

Abraham's Tea Room, popular with locals, may be the best lunch deal in town. It's tucked away on the first floor of the giant George Fisher outdoor store (£4–6 soups and sandwiches, Mon–Fri 10:00–17:00, Sat 9:30–17:00, Sun 10:30–16:30, on the corner where Lake Road turns right).

The Lakeland Pedlar, a wholesome, pleasant café (with a bike shop upstairs), serves freshly baked vegan and vegetarian fare, including soups, organic bread, and daily specials. Their interior is cute. Outside tables face a big parking lot (£7 meals, daily 9:00–17:00, Thu–Sat until 21:00 in summer, Hendersons Yard, find the narrow walkway off Market Street between pink Johnson's sweet shop and The Golden Lion, tel. 017687/74492).

Bryson's Bakery and Tea Room has an enticing ground-floor bakery, with sandwiches and light lunches. The upstairs is a popular tearoom. Order lunch to go from the bakery, or for a few pence more, eat there, either sitting on stools or at a couple of sidewalk tables (£4–8 meals, Mon–Sat 8:30–17:30—tearoom opens at 9:30, Sun 9:30–17:00, 42 Main Street, tel. 017687/72257). Consider their £16 two-person Cumberland Cream Tea, which is like afternoon tea in London, but cheaper, and made with local products. Sandwiches, scones, and little cakes are served on a three-tiered platter with tea.

Good Taste has a small café space but a huge following, and is known for its fresh ingredients and its chef's expertise. Stop by for a light snack of homemade muffins and an espresso, or try a wild boar burger (Mon–Sat 8:30–16:30, closed Sun, 19 Lake Road, tel. 017687/75973).

Maysons Restaurant, with Californian ambience, is fast and easy, with a buffet line of curry, Cajun, and vegetarian options. The food is cooked fresh on the premises, but it's nothing fancy: You point, and they dish up and microwave (£6–8 plates, cash only; April–Oct daily 11:30–20:45; Nov–March Mon–Thu 11:45–17:00, Fri–Sun 11:45–20:30; family-friendly, also take-out—great for evening cruise picnic, 33 Lake Road, tel. 017687/74104).

Keswick Tea Room, next to Booths supermarket (described next), is popular with locals, and features cheap and cheery regional specialties (Mon–Sat 8:00–18:00, Sun 10:00–16:00).

Picnic: The fine **Booths supermarket** is right where all the buses arrive (Mon–Sat 8:00–21:00, Sun 10:00–16:00, The Headlands). The recommended **Bryson's Bakery** does good sandwiches to go (described earlier). **The Keswickian** serves up old-fashioned fish-and-chips to go (daily 11:00–23:30, on the town square). Just around the corner, **The Cornish Pasty** offers an enticing variety of fresh meat pies to go (£2–3 pies, daily 9:30–17:30 or until the pasties are all gone, across from The Dog and Gun on Borrowdale Road).

In the Newlands Valley

The farmhouse B&Bs of Newlands Valley don't serve dinner, so their guests have two good options: Go into Keswick, or take the lovely 10-minute drive to Buttermere for your evening meal at the **Fish Hotel Pub,** which has indoor and outdoor seating, but takes no reservations (£7 meals, daily 12:00–14:00 & 18:00–21:00, family-friendly, good fish and daily specials with fresh vegetables, tel. 017687/70253). The neighboring **Bridge Hotel Pub** is a bit cozier, but less popular (£6–7 meals, daily 12:00–21:30, tel. 017687/70252).

Keswick Connections

The nearest train station to Keswick is in Penrith, with a ticket window (Mon–Sat 5:30–21:00, Sun 11:30–21:00) but no lockers. For train and bus info, check at a local TI, visit www.traveline.org.uk, or call 0845-748-4950 (for train), or 0871-200-2233 (10p/min). Most routes run less frequently on Sundays.

From Keswick by Bus: For connections, see page 362.

From Penrith by Bus to: Keswick (Mon–Sat roughly hourly 7:20–22:45, only 8/day on Sun, 40 min, £5.50, pay driver, Stagecoach buses #X4 and #X5), **Ullswater** and **Glenridding** (6/day, 45 min, bus #108). The Penrith bus stop is just outside the train station (bus schedules posted inside and outside station).

From Penrith by Train to: Blackpool (roughly hourly, 1.75 hrs, change in Preston), **Liverpool** (roughly hourly, 2 hrs, change in Wigan or Preston), **Birmingham**'s New Street Station (roughly hourly, 2.5–3 hrs, some with change in Preston), **Durham** (1–2/hr, 2.5–3.5 hrs, change in Carlisle and Newcastle), **London**'s Euston Station (10/day, 3–3.5 hrs), **Edinburgh** (8/day to Penrith—some via Carlisle, 1.75 hrs), **Glasgow** (10/day, 1.5–2 hrs), **Oban** (2/day, morning train 5.75 hrs, evening 6.75 hrs, both require changing stations in Glasgow—see page 587, evening train requires additional change in Carlisle).

Route Tips for Drivers

Coming from (or Going to) the West: Only 1,300 feet above sea level, Hard Knott Pass is still a thriller, with a narrow, winding, steeply graded road. Just over the pass are the scant but evocative remains of the Hard Knott Roman fortress. The great views can come with miserable rainstorms, and it can be very slow and frustrating when the one-lane road with turnouts is clogged by traffic. Avoid it on summer weekends.

From Points South (such as Blackpool, Liverpool, or North Wales) to the Lake District: The direct, easy way to Keswick is to leave M6 at Penrith, and take the A66 highway for 16 miles to Keswick. For the scenic sightseeing drive through the south lakes to Keswick, exit M6 on A590/A591 through the towns of Kendal and Windermere to reach Brockhole National Park Visitors Centre. From Brockhole, the A road to Keswick is fastest, but the high road—the tiny road over Kirkstone Pass to Glenridding and lovely Ullswater—is much more dramatic.

Near Keswick: Ullswater

▲▲Ullswater Hike and Boat Ride

Long, narrow Ullswater, which some consider the loveliest lake in the area, offers eight miles of diverse and beautiful Lake District  scenery. You can drive it or cruise it, but I'd ride the boat from the south tip halfway up (to Howtown—which is nothing more than a dock) and hike back. Or walk first, then enjoy an easy ride back. Old-fashioned "steamer" boats (actually diesel-powered) leave **Glenridding** regularly for Howtown (£5.50 one-way, £9 round-trip, covered by £14 Ullswater Bus & Boat day pass, family rates, June–Aug daily 9/day 9:45–16:45, April–May and Sept 6/day 9:45–15:50, fewer off-season, 35 min one-way, drivers can use safe pay-and-display parking lot—£2/2 hrs, £4/12 hrs; take bus #108 from Penrith, bus #208 from Keswick, or bus #517 from Windermere; café at dock, brochure shows walking route, tel. 017684/82229, www.ullswater -steamers.co.uk).

From Howtown, spend three to four hours hiking and dawdling along the well-marked path by the lake south to Patterdale, and then along the road back to Glenridding. This is a serious seven-mile walk with good views, varied terrain, and a few bridges and farms along the way. For a shorter hike from Howtown Pier, consider a three-mile loop around Hallin Fell. A rainy-day plan is to ride the covered boat up and down the lake to Howtown and back, or to Pooley Bridge at the northern tip of the lake (£12 round-trip, 2–5/day, 2 hrs). Boats don't run in really bad weather—call ahead if it looks iffy.

Helvellyn

Considered by many the best high-mountain hike in the Lake District, this breathtaking round-trip route from Glenridding includes the spectacular Striding Edge—about a half-mile along the ridge. Be careful; do this six-hour hike only in good weather, since the wind can be fierce. While it's not the shortest route, the Glenridding ascent is best. Get advice from the Keswick TI, which has a helpful *Helvellyn from Glenridding* leaflet on the hike (60p).

South Lake District

The South Lake District has a cheesiness similar to other popular English resort destinations, such as Blackpool. Here, piles of low-end vacationers eat ice cream and get candy floss caught in their hair. The area around Windermere is worth a drive-through if you're a fan of Wordsworth or Beatrix Potter; otherwise, spend the majority of your Lake District time (and book your accommodations) up north.

Getting Around

By Car: This is your best option to see the small towns and sights clustered in the South Lake District; consider combining your drive with the bus trip mentioned below.

If you're coming to or leaving the South Lake District from the west, you could take the Hard Knott Pass for a scenic introduction to the area.

By Bus: Buses are a fine way to lace together this gauntlet of sights in the congested Lake Windermere neighborhood. The open-top Lakes Rider bus #599 stops at Bowness Pier (lake cruises), Windermere (train station), Brockhole (National Park Visitors Centre), Ambleside, Rydal Mount, and Grasmere (Dove Cottage). Consider leaving your car at Grasmere and enjoying the breezy, extremely scenic ride, hopping off and on as you like (3/hr daily Easter–Aug, 50 min each way, Central Lakes Dayrider all-day pass–£6.50—buy from driver). Buses #555 and #556 also run between Windermere and Keswick.

Sights in the South Lake District

Wordsworth Sights

William Wordsworth was one of the first writers to reject fast-paced city life. During Britain's Industrial Age, hearts were muzzled and brains ruled. Science was in, machines were taming nature, and factory hours were taming humans. In reaction to these brainy ideals, a rare few—dubbed Romantics—began to embrace untamed nature and undomesticated emotions.

Back then, nobody climbed a mountain just because it was there—but Wordsworth did. He'd "wander lonely as a cloud" through the countryside, finding inspiration in "plain living and high thinking." He soon attracted a circle of like-minded creative friends.

The emotional highs the Romantics felt weren't all natural. Wordsworth and his poet friends Samuel Taylor Coleridge and Thomas de Quincey got stoned on opium and wrote poetry,

Wordsworth at Dove Cottage

William Wordsworth (1770–1850) was a Lake District home-boy. Born in Cockermouth (in a house now open to the public), he was schooled in Hawkshead. In adulthood, he married a local girl, settled down in Grasmere and Ambleside, and was buried in Grasmere's St. Oswald's churchyard.

But the 30-year-old man who moved into Dove Cottage in 1799 was not the carefree lad who'd roamed the district's lakes and fields. At Cambridge University, he'd been a C student, graduating with no job skills and no interest in a nine-to-five career. Instead, he and a buddy hiked through Europe, where Wordsworth had an epiphany of the "sublime" atop Switzerland's Alps. He lived a year in France, watching the Revolution rage. It stirred his soul. He fell in love with a Frenchwoman who bore his daughter Caroline. But lack of money forced him to return to England, and the outbreak of war with France kept them apart.

Pining away in London, William hung out in the pubs and coffeehouses with fellow radicals, where he met poet Samuel Taylor Coleridge. They inspired each other to write, edited each other's work, and jointly published a groundbreaking book of poetry.

In 1799, his head buzzing with words and ideas, William and his sister (and soul mate) Dorothy moved into the white-washed, slate-tiled former inn now known as Dove Cottage. He came into a small inheritance, and dedicated himself to poetry full time. In 1802, with the war over, William returned to France to finally meet his daughter. (He wrote of the rich experience: "It is a beauteous evening, calm and free.../Dear child! Dear Girl! that walkest with me here,/If thou appear untouched by solemn thought,/Thy nature is not therefore less divine.")

Having achieved closure, Wordsworth returned home to marry a former kindergarten classmate, Mary. She moved into Dove Cottage, along with an initially jealous Dorothy. Three of their five children were born here, and the cottage was also home to Mary's sister, the family dog Pepper (a gift from Sir Walter Scott; see Pepper's portrait), and frequent house-guests who bedded down in the pantry: Scott, Coleridge, and Thomas de Quincey, the Timothy Leary of opium.

After nearly nine years here, Wordsworth's family and social status had outgrown the humble cottage. They moved first to a house in Grasmere before settling down in Rydal Hall. Wordsworth was changing. After the Dove years, he would write less, settle into a regular government job, quarrel with Coleridge, drift to the right politically, and endure criticism from old friends who branded him a sellout. Still, his poetry—most of it written at Dove—became increasingly famous, and he died honored as England's Poet Laureate.

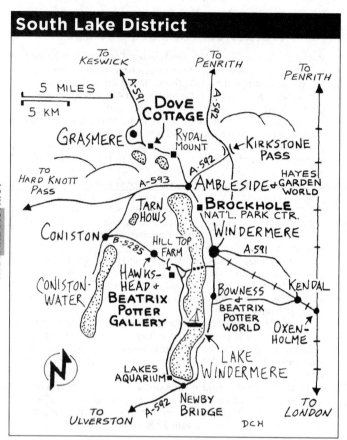

South Lake District

combining their generation's standard painkiller drug with their tree-hugging passions. Today, opium is out of vogue, but the Romantic movement thrives as visitors continue to inundate the region.

▲▲**Dove Cottage and Wordsworth Museum**—The poet whose appreciation of nature and a back-to-basics lifestyle put this area on the map spent his most productive years (1799–1808) in this well-preserved stone cottage on the edge of Grasmere. After functioning as the Dove and Olive Bow pub for nearly 200 years, it was bought by his family. This is where Wordsworth got married, had kids, and wrote much of his best poetry. The furniture, still owned by the Wordsworth family, was his, and the place comes with some amazing artifacts, including the poet's passport and suitcase (he packed light). Even during his lifetime, Wordsworth was famous, and Dove Cottage was turned into a museum in 1891—predating even the National Trust, which protects the house today.

Wordsworth's Poetry at Dove

At Dove Cottage, Wordsworth was immersed in the beauty of nature and the simple joy of his young, growing family. It was here that he reflected on both his idyllic childhood and his troubled twenties. The following are select lines from two well-known poems from this fertile time.

Ode: Intimations of Immortality

There was a time when meadow, grove, and stream,
The earth, and every common sight, to me did seem
Apparelled in celestial light, the glory and the freshness
   of a dream.
It is not now as it hath been of yore; turn wheresoe'er I
   may, by night or day,
The things which I have seen I now can see no more.
Now while the birds thus sing a joyous song...
To me alone there came a thought of grief...
Whither is fled the visionary gleam?
Where is it now, the glory and the dream?
Our birth is but a sleep and a forgetting:
The Soul...cometh from afar...
Trailing clouds of glory do we come
From God, who is our home.

I Wandered Lonely as a Cloud

I wandered lonely as a cloud
That floats on high o'er vales and hills,
When all at once I saw a crowd,
A host, of golden daffodils;
Beside the lake, beneath the trees,
Fluttering and dancing in the breeze...
For oft, when on my couch I lie
In vacant or in pensive mood,
They flash upon that inward eye
Which is the bliss of solitude;
And then my heart with pleasure fills,
And dances with the daffodils.

Today, Dove Cottage is a must-see for any Wordsworth admirer. Even if you're not a fan, Wordsworth's appreciation of nature, his Romanticism, and the ways his friends unleashed their creative talents with such abandon are appealing. The 30-minute cottage **tour** (departures on the hour and half-hour) and adjoining **museum**—with lots of actual manuscripts handwritten by Wordsworth and his illustrious friends—are both excellent. In dry weather, the garden where the poet was much inspired is worth a wander. (Visit this before leaving the cottage, and pick up the description at the back door.) Allow at least an hour for this two-part attraction (£7.50, daily Feb–Dec 9:30–17:30, last entry at 17:00, last tour at 16:50, closed Jan, bus #555 or #556 from Keswick, tel. 015394/35544, www.wordsworth.org.uk). Parking is free and easy in the Dove Cottage lot facing the main road (A591).

Poetry Readings: On Tuesday evenings in summer, the Wordsworth Trust puts on poetry readings, where national poets read their own works. They're hoping to continue the poetry tradition of the Lake District. Readings are held at the St. Oswald's Church in Grasmere Village (every other Tue at 18:45, runs May–mid-Oct only, two 45-min sessions followed by an optional dinner, £7 at the door or £6 pre-booked, £15 pre-booked dinner, tel. 015394/35544).

Rydal Mount—Wordsworth's final, higher-class home, with a lovely garden and view, lacks the charm of Dove Cottage. It feels like a B&B. He lived here for 37 years, and his family repurchased it in 1969 (after a 100-year gap). His great-great-great-grand-daughter still calls it home on occasion, as shown by recent family photos sprinkled throughout some rooms. Located just down the road from Dove Cottage, it's worthwhile only for Wordsworth

fans (£6; March–Oct daily 9:30–17:00; Nov–Dec and Feb Wed–Sun 11:00–16:00, closed Mon–Tue; closed Jan, 1.5 miles north of Ambleside, well-signed, free and easy parking, bus #555 or #556 from Keswick, tel. 015394/33002, www.rydalmount.co.uk).

Beatrix Potter Sights

Of the many Beatrix Potter commercial ventures in the Lake District, there are two serious Beatrix Potter sights: her farm (Hill Top Farm); and her husband's former office, which is now the Beatrix Potter Gallery, filled with her sketches and paintings. Both sights are in or near Hawkshead, a 20-minute drive south of Ambleside. If you're coming over from Windermere, catch the cute little 15-car ferry (runs constantly except when it's extremely windy, 10-min trip, £3.50 car fare includes all passengers). Note that both of the major sights are closed on Friday.

Hill Top Farm—A hit with Beatrix Potter fans, this farm was left just as it was when she died in 1943. While there's no informa-tion here (you'll need to buy the £3.50 guidebook for details on what you see), the dark and intimate cottage, swallowed up in the inspirational and rough nature around it, provides an enjoyable if quick experience (£6.50, tickets often sell out by 14:00, April–Oct Sat–Thu 10:30–16:30, mid-Feb–March Sat–Thu 11:00–15:30, closed Fri and Nov–mid-Feb, last entry 30 min before closing, in

Beatrix Potter
(1866–1943)

As a girl growing up in London, Beatrix Potter vacationed in the Lake District, where she became inspired to write her

popular children's books. Unable to get a publisher, she self-published the first two editions of *The Tale of Peter Rabbit* in 1901 and 1902. When she finally landed a publisher, sales of her books were phenomenal. With the money she made, she bought Hill Top Farm, a 17th-century cottage, and fixed it up, living there from 1905 until she married in 1913. Potter was more than a children's book writer; she was a talented artist, an avid gardener, and a successful farmer. She married a lawyer and put her knack for business to use, amassing a 4,000-acre estate. An early conservationist, she used the garden-cradled cottage as a place to study nature. She willed it—along with the rest of her vast estate—to the National Trust, which she enthusiastically supported. The events of Potter's life were dramatized in the 2007 movie *Miss Potter,* starring Renée Zellweger as Beatrix.

THE LAKE DISTRICT

Near Sawrey village, 2 miles south of Hawkshead, bus #525 from Hawkshead, tel. 015394/36269, www.nationaltrust.org.uk/beatrix potter). Drivers can park and buy tickets 150 yards down the road, and then walk back to tour the place.

▲▲**Beatrix Potter Gallery**—Located in the cute but extremely touristy town of Hawkshead, this gallery fills her husband's former law office with the wonderful intimate drawings and watercolors that Potter did to illustrate her books. The best of the Potter sights, the gallery has plenty of explanation about her life and work. Even non-Potter fans find her art surprisingly interesting. Of about 700 works in the gallery's possession, a rotation of about 40 are shown at any one time (£4.50, tiny discount with Hill Top Farm, same hours as Hill Top Farm, bus #505 from Windermere, Main Street, drivers use the nearby pay-and-display lot and walk 200 yards to the town center, tel. 015394/36355, www.nationaltrust.org.uk/beatrixpotter).

Hawkshead—The town of Hawkshead is engulfed in Potter tourism, and the extreme quaintness of it all is off-putting. Just across from the pay-and-display parking lot is the interesting Hawkshead Grammar School Museum, founded in 1585, where William Wordsworth studied from 1779 to 1787. It shows off old school benches and desks whittled with penknife graffiti (£2 includes guided tour; April–Sept Mon–Sat 10:00–13:00 & 14:00–17:00, Sun 13:00–17:00; Oct Mon–Sat 10:00–13:00 & 14:00–15:30, Sun 13:00–15:30; closed Nov–March; bus #505 from Windermere, tel. 015394/36735, www.hawksheadgrammar.org.uk).

The World of Beatrix Potter—This tour, a hit with children, is a gimmicky exhibit with all the history of a Disney ride. The 45-minute experience features a five-minute video trip into the world of Mrs. Tiggywinkle and company, a series of Lake District tableaux starring the same imaginary gang, and an all-about-Beatrix section, with an eight-minute video biography (£7, kids-£3.50, daily Easter–Sept 10:00–18:00, Oct–Easter 10:00–17:00, last entry 30 min before closing, in Bowness near Windermere town, tel. 015394/88444, www.hop-skip-jump.com).

More Sights at Lake Windermere

▲**Brockhole National Park Visitors Centre**—Set in a nicely groomed lakeside park, the center offers a free 15-minute slide show on life in the Lake District (played upon request), an information desk, organized walks (see the park's free *Visitor Guide*), exhibits, a bookshop (excellent selection of maps and guidebooks), a fine cafeteria, gardens, nature walks, and a large parking lot. Check the events board as you enter (free entry but steep £4 parking fee—coins only, or buy ticket at the Visitors Centre 100 yards away from parking lot; mid-Feb–Oct daily 10:00–17:00, closed Nov–mid-Feb, bus #555 from Keswick, buses #505 and #599 from Windermere, tel. 015394/46601, www.lake-district.gov.uk). It's in a stately old lakeside mansion between Ambleside and Windermere on A591. For a joyride around famous Windermere, catch the Brockhole "Green" cruise (£7, hourly April–Oct, more sailings mid-July–Aug, 45-min circle, scant narration).

Lakes Aquarium—This aquarium gives a glimpse of the natural history of Cumbria. Exhibits describe the local wildlife living in lake and coastal environments, including otters, eels, pike, sharks, and the "much maligned brown rat." Experts give various talks throughout the day (£9, kids under 15-£6, family deals, daily 9:00–18:00, until 17:00 in winter, last entry one hour before closing, in Lakeside, by Newby Bridge, at south end of Lake Windermere, tel. 015395/30153, www.lakesaquarium.co.uk).

Hayes Garden World—This extensive gardening center, a popular weekend excursion for locals, offers garden supplies, a bookstore, a playground, and gorgeous grounds. Gardeners could wander this place all afternoon. Upstairs is a fine cafeteria-style restaurant (Mon–Sat 9:00–18:00, Sun 11:00–17:00, at south end of Ambleside on main drag, see *Garden Centre* signs, located at north end of Lake Windermere, tel. 015394/33434, www.hayesgardenworld.co.uk).

YORK

Historic York is loaded with world-class sights. Marvel at the York Minster, England's finest Gothic church. Ramble The Shambles, York's wonderfully preserved medieval quarter. Enjoy a walking tour led by an old Yorker. Hop a train at Europe's greatest railway museum, travel to the 1800s in the York Castle Museum, and head back a thousand years to Viking York at the Jorvik exhibit. And to get a taste of some scenically desolate countryside, side-trip to the North York Moors.

York has a rich history. In A.D. 71, it was Eboracum, a Roman provincial capital—the northernmost city in the empire. Constantine was actually proclaimed emperor here in A.D. 306. In the fifth century, as Rome was toppling, a Roman emperor sent a letter telling England it was on its own, and York became Eoforwic, the capital of the Anglo-Saxon kingdom of Northumbria.

Locals built a church here in 627, and the town became an early Christian center of learning. The Vikings later took the town, and from the 9th through the 11th centuries, it was a Danish trading center called Jorvik. The invading and conquering Normans destroyed then rebuilt the city, fortifying it with a castle and the walls you see today.

Medieval York, with 9,000 inhabitants, grew rich on the wool trade and became England's second city. Henry VIII used the city's Minster as his Anglican Church's northern capital. (In today's Anglican Church, the Archbishop of York is second only to the Archbishop of Canterbury.)

In the Industrial Age, York was the railway hub of northern England. When it was built, York's train station was the world's largest. Today, York's leading industry is tourism.

Planning Your Time

York is the best sightseeing city in England after London. On even a 10-day trip through Great Britain, York deserves two nights and a day. For the best 36 hours, follow this plan: Catch the 18:45 free city walking tour on the evening of your arrival (evening tours offered mid-June–Aug). The next morning, be at the Castle Museum when it opens (at 10:00 or 9:30, depending on the day)—it's worth a good two hours. Then browse and sightsee the rest of town. Train buffs love the National Railway Museum, and scholars give the Yorkshire Museum an "A." Tour the Minster at 16:00 before catching the 17:15 evensong service (16:00 on Sun, usually none on Mon). Finish your day with an early-evening stroll along the wall, and perhaps through the abbey gardens. This schedule assumes you're here in the summer (when the evening orientation walk is going) and that there's an evensong on. Confirm your plans with the TI.

The North York Moors (described at the end of this chapter) are not worth going out of your way to visit, but you'll enjoy zipping through that area if you're traveling between York and Durham.

Orientation to York

(area code: 01904)

York has about 190,000 people; about 1 in 10 is a student. But despite the city's size, the sightseer's York is small. Virtually everything is within a few minutes' walk: sights, train station, TI, and B&Bs. The longest walk a visitor might take (from a B&B across the old town to the Castle Museum) is 20 minutes.

Bootham Bar, a gate in the medieval town wall, is the hub of your York visit. (In York, a "bar" is a gate and a "gate" is a street. Go ahead—blame the Vikings.) At Bootham Bar and on Exhibition Square you'll find the starting points for most walking tours and bus tours, handy access to the medieval town wall, a public WC, and Bootham Street—which leads to the recommended B&Bs. To find your way around York, use the Minster's towers as a navigational landmark, or follow the strategically placed green signposts, which point out all places of interest to tourists.

Tourist Information

The **Museum Street** TI sells a £1 *York Map and Guide*. Ask for the free monthly *What's On* guide and the *York MiniGuide*, which includes a map and some discounts (April–Oct Mon–Sat 9:00–18:00, Sun 10:00–17:00; Nov–March Mon–Sat 9:00–17:00, Sun 10:00–16:00; 1 Museum Street, tel. 01904/550-099, www.visityork.org). The TI books rooms for a £4 fee. The **train station** TI is smaller but provides all the same information and services (same hours as main TI). Their chalkboard lists "Today's Events in Town."

York and Yorkshire Pass: The TI sells an expensive pass that covers most York sights and a lot of other major sights in the region, and gives you discounts on the City Sightseeing hop-on, hop-off bus tours. You'd have to be a very busy sightseer to make this pass worth it, however, and most will want to skip it (£28/1 day, £38/2 days, £44/3 days, £68/6 days, www.yorkpass.com).

Arrival in York

By Train: The train station is a 10-minute walk from town. Day-trippers can store baggage at platform 1 (£5/24 hrs, Mon–Sat 8:00–20:30, Sun 9:00–20:30). To walk downtown from the station, turn left down Station Road and follow the crowd toward the Gothic towers of the Minster. After the bridge, a block before the Minster, you'll come upon the TI on your right.

My recommended B&Bs are a 10-minute walk or a £5 taxi ride from the station. To take a shortcut to the B&B area from the train station, exit the station to the left on Station Road. When the road swings right and goes through the old gate, turn left onto the busy street (Leeman Road). Just before that street goes under the rail bridge, turn right and follow the walkway along the tracks. Cross the bridge over the river and continue into the big parking lot. From here, to reach B&Bs on St. Mary's Street, stay to the left as you cross the lot; to reach the Coach House, Hazelwood, or Ardmore, cross the lot to the right. To reach B&Bs on Sycamore, Queen Annes Road, Bootham Terrace, or Grosvenor Terrace, duck through the pedestrian walkway under the tracks (on the left).

By Car: As you near York (and your B&B), you'll hit the A1237 ring road. Follow this to the A19/Thirsk roundabout (next to river on northeast side of town). From the roundabout, follow signs for *York City,* traveling through Clifton into Bootham. All recommended B&Bs are four or five blocks before you hit the medieval city gate (see neighborhood map on page 418). If you're approaching York from the south, take M1 until it becomes A1M, exit at junction 45 onto A64, and follow it for 10 miles until you reach York's ring road (A1237), which allows you to avoid driving through the city center. If you have more time, A19 from Selby is a slower, more scenic route into York.

Helpful Hints

Festivals: The Viking Festival features *lur* horn-blowing, warrior drills, and re-created battles (Feb 17–22 in 2010). The Late Music Festival is in early June...if it starts on time (www.latemusicfestival.org.uk). The Early Music Festival (medieval minstrels, Renaissance dance, and so on) zings its strings in

York

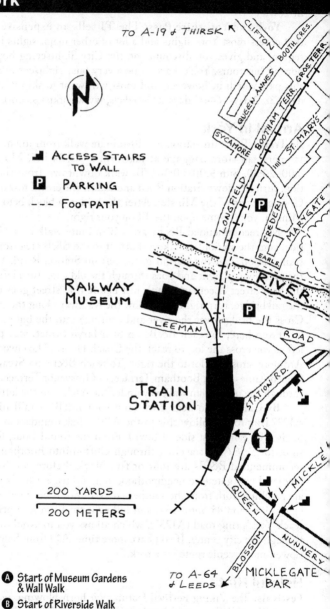

TO A-19 & THIRSK

CLIFTON

BOOTH. CRES.

QUEEN ANNES

SYCAMORE

BOOTHAM TERR.

GROS. TERR.

ST. MARYS

LONGFIELD

FREDERIC

EARLS

MARYGATE

P

◢ ACCESS STAIRS
  TO WALL

P PARKING

--- FOOTPATH

RIVER

RAILWAY
MUSEUM

LEEMAN

P

ROAD

STATION RD.

TRAIN
STATION

ℹ

QUEEN

MICKLE

NUNNERY

200 YARDS

200 METERS

BLOSSOM

TO A-64
& LEEDS

MICKLEGATE
BAR

Ⓐ Start of Museum Gardens
   & Wall Walk

Ⓑ Start of Riverside Walk
   or Bike Ride

YORK

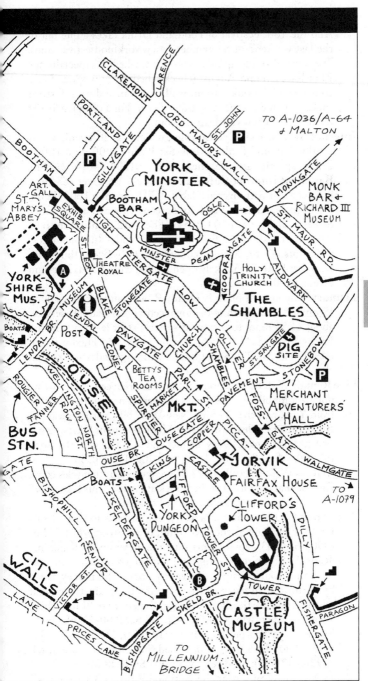

mid-July (July 9–17 in 2010, www.ncem.co.uk/yemf.shtml). And the York Festival of Food and Drink takes a bite out of the last weekend of September (www.yorkfoodfestival.com). The town also fills up on horse-race weekends, especially the Ebor Races in mid-August (check schedules at www.yorkrace course.co.uk). Book a room well in advance during festival times and on weekends any time of year. For a complete list of festivals, see www.yorkfestivals.com.

Internet Access: Evil Eye Lounge, which has 10 terminals, is creaky, hip, and funky (Mon–Sat 10:00–23:00, Sun 11:00–23:00, upstairs at 42 Stonegate, tel. 01904/640-002). **The Basement Internet Café-Bar** overlooks the river (£3/hr, a little cheaper with flyer available at TI, Tue–Sun 11:00–18:00, 9 terminals, basement of City Screens Cinema, at 13 Coney Street, toll tel. 0871-704-2054). The **York Public Library**'s reference desk, on the first floor up, provides Internet access to visitors (£1/hr, Mon–Wed and Fri 9:00–19:45, Thu 9:00–17:15, Sat 9:30–15:45, likely open longer, closed Sun, Museum Street, tel. 01904/552-828).

Laundry: The nearest place is **Haxby Road Launderette,** a long 15-minute walk north of the town center (£8/load self-service, about £1.50 more for drop-off service; start last loads Mon–Fri by 16:30, Sat by 15:45, Sun by 14:45; 124 Haxby Road, tel. 01904/623-379). Some B&Bs will do laundry for a small charge.

Bike Rental: With the exception of the pedestrian center, the town's not great for biking. But there are several fine countryside rides from York, and the riverside New Walk bike path is pleasant. **Bob Trotter Cycles,** just outside Monk Bar, rents bikes and has free cycling maps (£15/day, helmet and map free with this book in 2010, Mon–Sat 9:00–17:30, Sun 10:00–16:00, 13–15 Lord Mayor's Walk, tel. 01904/622-868, www.bobtrottercycles.com). **Europcar** at platform 1 at the train station also rents bikes (£6/5 hrs, £10/day, includes helmet, tel. 01904/656-181).

Taxi: From the train station, taxis zip new arrivals to their B&Bs for £5. Queue up at the taxi stand, or call 01904/623-332 or 01904/638-833; cabbies don't start the meter until you get in.

Car Rental: If you're nearing the end of your trip, consider dropping your car upon arrival in York. The money saved by turning it in early nearly pays for the train ticket that whisks you effortlessly to London. In York you'll find these agencies: **Avis** (Mon–Fri 8:00–18:00, Sat 8:00–13:00, closed Sun, 3 Layerthorpe, tel. 01904/610-460); **Hertz** (Mon–Fri 8:00–18:00, Sat 9:00–13:00, closed Sun, at train station, tel. 01904/612-586); **Budget** (Mon–Fri 8:00–18:00, Sat 8:00–13:00, closed Sun, near the National Railway Museum at 75

Leeman Road, tel. 01904/644-919); and **Europcar** (Mon–Fri 8:00–18:00, Sat until 16:00, closed Sun, train station platform 1, tel. 01904/656-181, central reservations toll tel. 0870-607-5000). Beware: Car-rental agencies close early on Saturday afternoons, and all close on Sundays—when dropping off is OK, but picking up is impossible.

Tours in York

▲▲▲Walking Tours

Free Walks with Volunteer Guides—Charming locals give energetic, entertaining, and free two-hour walks through York (daily at 10:15 all year, plus 14:15 April–Oct, plus 18:45 mid-June–Aug, depart from Exhibition Square in front of the art gallery). These tours often go long because the guides love to teach and tell stories. You're welcome to cut out early—but say so or they'll worry, thinking they lost you.

YorkWalk Tours—These are more serious 1.5-hour walks with a history focus. They do three different walks: Essential York, Roman York, and York's Snickelways (£5.50 each, Feb–Nov daily at 10:30 and 14:15, Dec–Jan weekends only, depart from Museum Gardens Gate, just show up, tel. 01904/622-303, www.yorkwalk .co.uk—check website, TI, or call for schedule). Tours go rain or shine with as few as two participants.

Haunted Walks—Numerous ghost tours, all offered after dusk, are more fun than informative. "Haunted Walk" relies a bit more on storytelling and history than on masks and surprises (£4, Easter–Oct nightly at 20:00, weekends only Nov–Easter, 1.5 hours, just show up, depart from Exhibition Square in front of the art gallery, end in The Shambles, tel. 01904/621-003).

Local Guide—**Julian Cripps** offers good private walking tours (£25/hr, tel. 01904/709-755, travellersintime@googlemail .com).

▲City Bus Tours

Two companies run hop-on, hop-off bus tours circling York. Though you can hop on and off all day, these have no real transportation value because York is so compact. If taking a bus tour, catch either one at Exhibition Square (near Bootham Bar) and ride it for an orientation all the way around. Consider getting off at the National Railway Museum, skipping the last five minutes.

City Sightseeing: This outfit's half-enclosed, bright-red, double-decker buses take tourists past secondary York sights the city walking tours skip—the mundane perimeter of town. They offer two one-hour routes: Route A sticks more or less to the outline of the town wall; Route B traces the same path, except where it

York at a Glance

▲▲▲**York Minster** York's pride and joy, and one of England's finest churches, with stunning stained-glass windows, text-book Decorated Gothic design, and glorious evensong services. **Hours:** Open for worship daily from 7:00 and for sightseeing Mon–Sat from 9:00, Sun from 12:30; flexible closing time (roughly May–Oct at 18:30, earlier off-season); shorter hours for tower and undercroft; evensong services Tue–Sat 17:15, Sun 16:00, occasionally on Mon, sometimes no services mid-July–Aug. See page 403.

▲▲▲**York Castle Museum** Excellent, far-ranging collection displaying everyday objects from Victorian times to the present. **Hours:** Daily 10:00–17:00, often opens at 9:30. See page 409.

▲▲**National Railway Museum** Train buff's nirvana, tracing the history of all manner of rail-bound transport. **Hours:** Daily 10:00–18:00. See page 411.

▲▲**Yorkshire Museum** Sophisticated archaeology museum with York's best Viking exhibit, plus Roman, Saxon, Norman, and Gothic artifacts. **Hours:** Closed for renovation, likely until Aug 2010; when open, probably daily 10:00–17:00. See page 412.

▲**The Shambles** Atmospheric old butchers' quarter, with colorful, tipsy medieval buildings. **Hours:** Always open. See page 409.

▲**Jorvik** Cheesy, crowded, but not-quite-Disney-quality exhibit/ride exploring Viking lifestyles and artifacts. **Hours:** Daily April–Oct 10:00–17:00, Nov–March 10:00–16:00. See page 410.

▲**Fairfax House** Glimpse into an 18th-century Georgian house, with enjoyably chatty docents. **Hours:** Mon–Thu and Sat 11:00–16:30, Sun 13:30–16:30, Fri by tour only at 11:00 and 14:00. See page 412.

makes a foray out to minor sights south of town. Buses that leave Exhibition Square at the top and bottom of each hour usually have live guides (£10, £12.50 combo-ticket with boat cruise through YorkBoat, pay driver cash, can also buy tickets from TI with credit card; April–Oct buses run 9:15–17:00, Route A every 10 min, Route B 4/day; less frequent off-season; tel. 01904/655-585, www.yorktourbuses.co.uk).

York Pullman Bus Tours: These classic old-time buses are slightly less expensive, with fewer stops, live guides, and two overlapping routes (£8, departs 6/hr from Exhibition Square daily 9:20–17:15, 4/hr Nov–mid-June, 45 min, enclosed bus used when raining, tel. 01904/622-992, www.yorkpullmanbus.co.uk).

Boat Cruise

YorkBoat does a lazy, narrated 45-minute lap along the River Ouse (£7, £12.50 combo-ticket with City Sightseeing bus tours—see above, 4/day Feb–Nov 10:30–17:00 or later; runs every 30 min April–Oct; leaves from Lendal Bridge and King's Staith landing, near Skeldergate Bridge, tel. 01904/628-324, www.yorkboat.co.uk).

Self-Guided Walk

Museum Gardens and Wall

Get a taste of Roman and medieval York on this easy stroll along a segment of York's wall.

• *Start just inside the Museum Gardens Gate (near the river, where Lendal Street hits Museum Street; gate closes at 20:00). About 20 yards to the right of the gate stands...*

Abbey Hospital: The 13th-century facade of the Abbey hospital is interesting mostly because of the ancient Roman tombs stacked just under its vault. These were buried outside the Roman city and discovered recently while building a new train line.

• *Continue into the garden. About 50 yards ahead (on the right) is another remnant of ancient Rome, the...*

Multangular Tower: This 12-sided tower (A.D. 300) was likely a catapult station built to protect the town from enemy river traffic. The red ribbon of bricks was a Roman trademark—both structural and decorative. The lower stones are Roman, while the upper, bigger stones are medieval. After Rome fell, York suffered through two centuries of a dark age. Then the Vikings ruled from 780. They built with wood, so almost nothing from that period remains. The Normans came in 1066 and built in stone, generally atop Roman structures (like this wall). The Roman wall that defined the ancient garrison town worked for the Norman town, too. From the 1600s on no such fortified walls were needed in England's interior.

• *Continue about 100 yards (past the Neoclassical building holding the fine Yorkshire Museum on right—likely closed for renovation through Aug 2010, but otherwise worth a visit and described on page 412) to York's ruined...*

St. Mary's Abbey: This abbey dates to the age of William the Conqueror—whose harsh policies of massacres and destruction in this region (called the "Harrowing of the North") made him unpopular. His son Rufus, who tried to improve relations in the

12th century, established a great church here. The church became an abbey that thrived from the 13th century until the Dissolution of the Monasteries in the 16th century. The Dissolution, which came with the Protestant Reformation and break with Rome, was a power play by Henry VIII. He took over the land and riches of the monasteries. Upset with the pope, he wanted his subjects to pay him taxes rather than give the Church tithes. (For more information, see the "England's Anglican Church" sidebar, later.)

As you gaze at this ruin, imagine magnificent abbeys like this scattered throughout the realm. Henry VIII destroyed most of them, taking the lead from their roofs and leaving the stones to scavenging townsfolk. Scant as they are today, these ruins still evoke a time of immense monastic power. The one surviving wall was the west half of a very long, skinny nave. The tall arch marked the start of the transept. Stand on the plaque that reads *Crossing beneath central tower,* and look up at the air that now fills the space where a huge tower once stood.

• *Now, backtrack about 50 yards and turn left, walking between the museum and the Roman tower. Continuing between the abbot's palace and the town wall, you're walking along a "snickelway"—a small, characteristic York lane or footpath. The snickelway pops out onto...*

Exhibition Square: With the Dissolution, the Abbot's Palace became the **King's Manor** (from the snickelway, make a U-turn to the left and through the gate). Today it's part of the University of York. Because the northerners were slow to embrace the king's reforms, Henry VIII came here to enforce the Dissolution. He stayed 17 days in this mansion and brought along a thousand troops to make a statement of his determination. You can wander into the grounds and building. The Refectory Café serves cheap cakes, soup, and sandwiches to students, professors, and visitors like you (Mon–Fri 9:30–15:30, closed Sat–Sun).

Exhibition Square is the departure point for various walking and bus tours. You can see the towers of the **Minster** in the distance. (Travelers in the Middle Ages could see the Minster from miles away as they approached the city.) Across the street is a public WC and **Bootham Bar**—one of the fourth-century Roman gates in York's wall—with access to the best part of the city walls (free, walls open 8:00–dusk).

• *Climb up and...*

Walk the Wall: Hike along the top of the wall behind the Minster to the first corner. York's 12th-century walls are three miles long. Norman kings built the walls to assert control over northern England. Notice the pivots in the crenellations (square notches at the top of a medieval wall), which once held wooden hatches to provide cover for archers. At the corner with the benches—Robin Hood's Tower—you can lean out and see the moat outside. This was originally the Roman ditch that surrounded the fortified garrison town. Continue walking for a fine view of the Minster (better when the scaffolding comes down in 2014), with its truncated main tower and the pointy rooftop of its chapter house.

• *Continue on to the next gate, **Monk Bar** (skip the tacky museum in the tower house). Descend the wall at Monk Bar and step past the portcullis to emerge outside the city's protective wall. Lean against the last bollard and gaze up at the tower, imagining 10 archers behind the arrow slits. Keep an eye on the 12th-century guards, with their stones raised and primed to protect the town. Return through the city wall and go left at the fork in the road to follow Goodramgate a couple of blocks into the old town center. Hiding off Goodramgate on the right is...*

Holy Trinity Church: This church holds rare box pews atop a floor that is sinking as bodies rot and coffins collapse (open Tue–Sun 10:00–16:00, closed Mon). The church is built in the late Perpendicular Gothic style, with lots of clear and precious stained glass from the 13th to 15th centuries. Enjoy the peaceful picnic-friendly gardens.

• *Goodramgate dead ends at...*

King's Square: This lively people-watching zone with its inviting benches is prime real estate for buskers and street performers. Just beyond (crossing the square diagonally) is the most characteristic and touristy street in old York: The Shambles (described on page 409). Our walk ends here, at the midpoint between York's main sights.

YORK

Sights in York

▲▲▲York Minster

The pride of York, this, the largest Gothic church north of the Alps (540 feet long, 200 feet tall), brilliantly shows that the

High Middle Ages were far from dark. The word "minster" comes from the Old English for "monastery," but is now simply used to imply that it's an important church. As it's the seat of a bishop, York Minster is also a cathedral. Though Henry VIII destroyed England's great abbeys, this was not part of a monastery and was therefore left standing. It seats 2,000 comfortably; on Christmas and Easter, at least 4,000 worshippers pack the place. Today, more than 250 employees and 300 volunteers work to preserve its heritage, and welcome the half-million visitors each year.

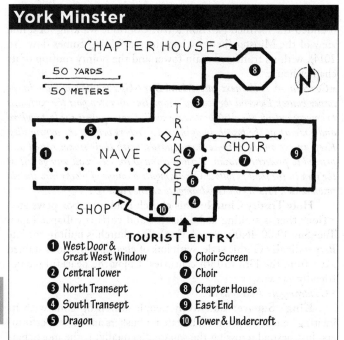

York Minster

CHAPTER HOUSE

50 YARDS
50 METERS

TRANSEPT

NAVE

CHOIR

SHOP

TOURIST ENTRY

1. West Door & Great West Window
2. Central Tower
3. North Transept
4. South Transept
5. Dragon
6. Choir Screen
7. Choir
8. Chapter House
9. East End
10. Tower & Undercroft

YORK

Cost, Hours, Tours: The cathedral opens for worship daily at 7:00 and for sightseeing Mon–Sat from 9:00 and Sun from 12:30, when they begin charging £6 admission (you can always worship for free—at the entry simply tell them you're coming for a service). There's no charge for admission after about 17:30—come late to enjoy the quiet church for a free hour or so. Closing time flexes with the season (roughly May–Oct at 18:30, earlier off-season— check the day's closing time posted outside the church, or call for details, tel. 01904/557-216, www.yorkminster.org). The tower and undercroft (£4 apiece) have shorter hours, typically opening a half-hour later and closing at 17:00 (18:00 for the tower). Two combo-ticket options save you money: £8 includes Minster entry and either the tower or the undercroft; £9.50 gets you all three.

After buying your ticket, go directly to the welcome desk, pick up the worthwhile *Welcome to the York Minster* flier, and ask when the next free guided **tour** departs (roughly 2/hr, Mon–Sat 10:30–15:00, one hour, they go even with just one or two people; you can join one in progress, or if none is scheduled, request a departure). The helpful Minster guides, wearing blue armbands, are happy to answer your questions.

Evensong and Church Bells: To experience the cathedral in musical and spiritual action, attend an evensong (Tue–Sat at

17:15, Sun at 16:00, visiting choirs occasionally perform on Mon, 45 min). When the choir is off on school break (mid-July–Aug), visiting choirs usually fill in (confirm at church or TI). Arrive 10 minutes early and wait just outside the choir in the center of the church. You'll be ushered in and can sit in one of the big wooden stalls.

If you're a fan of church bells, you'll experience ding-dong ecstasy daily except Monday (Sun morning about 10:00, Tue practice 19:30–21:30, and Tue–Sat at 16:45 to announce evensong). These performances are especially impressive, as the church now holds a full carillon of 35 bells (it's the only English cathedral to have such a range). Stand in front of the church's west portal and imagine the gang pulling on a dozen ropes (halfway up the right tower—you can actually see the ropes through a little window) while one talented carilloneur plays 22 more bells with a baton-keyboard and foot pedals. On special occasions, you might even catch them playing a Beatles tune.

➲ **Self-Guided Tour:** Upon entering, head left, to the back (west end) of the church. Stand in front of the grand **west door** (used only on Sundays) on the *Deo Gratias 627–1927* plaque—a place of worship for 1,300 years, thanks to God. Flanking the door, the list of bishops goes unbroken back to the 600s. The statue of Peter with the key and Bible is a reminder that the church is dedicated to St. Peter, and the key to heaven is found through the word of God. While the Minster sits on the remains of a Romanesque church (c. 1100), today's church was begun in 1220 and took 250 years to complete.

Grab a chair and enjoy the nave. Looking down the church, your first impression might be the spaciousness and brightness of the nave (built 1280–1360). The nave—from the middle period of Gothic, called "Decorated Gothic"—is one of the widest Gothic naves in Europe. Rather than risk a stone roof, builders spanned the space with wood. Colorful shields on the arcades are the coats of arms of nobles who helped the tall, formidable Edward I, known as "Longshanks," fight the Scots in the 13th century.

The coats of arms in the clerestory (upper-level) glass represent the nobles who helped his son, Edward II, in the same fight. There's more medieval glass in this building than in the rest of England combined. This precious glass survived World War II—hidden in stately homes throughout Yorkshire.

Walk to the very center of the church, under the **central tower.** Look up. Look down. Ask a Minster guide about how gifts and skill saved this tower—which weighs the equivalent of 40 jumbo jets—from collapse. (The first tower collapsed in 1407.) Although the tower is 197 feet tall, it was intended to be much taller. Use the neck-saving mirror to marvel at it.

England's Anglican Church

The Anglican Church (a.k.a. the Church of England) came into existence in 1534 when Henry VIII declared that he, and not Pope Clement VII, was the head of England's Catholics. The pope had refused to allow Henry to divorce his wife to marry his mistress Anne Boleyn (which Henry did anyway, resulting in the birth of Elizabeth I). Still, Henry regarded himself as a faithful Catholic—just not a *Roman* Catholic—and made relatively few changes in how and what Anglicans worshipped.

Henry's son, Edward VI, instituted many of the changes that Reformation Protestants were bringing about in continental Europe: an emphasis on preaching, people in the pews actually reading the Bible, clergy being allowed to marry, and a more "Protestant" liturgy in English from the revised Book of Common Prayer (1549). The next monarch, Edward's sister Mary I, returned England to the Roman Catholic Church (1553), earning the nickname "Bloody Mary" for her brutal suppression of Protestant elements. When Elizabeth I succeeded Mary (1558), she soon broke from Rome again. Today, many regard the Anglican Church as a compromise between the Catholic and Protestant traditions.

Is York's Minster the leading Anglican church in England? Yes and no (but mostly no). After a long feud, the archbishops of Canterbury and York agreed that York's bishop would have the title "Primate of England" and Canterbury's would be the "Primate of All England," directing Anglicans on the national level.

From here you can survey many impressive features of the church:

In the **north transept,** the grisaille windows—dubbed the "Five Sisters"—are dedicated to British women who died in all wars. Made in 1260 (before colored glass was produced in England), these contain more than 100,000 pieces of glass.

The **south transept** features the tourists' entry, where stairs lead down to the undercroft. The new "bosses" (carved medallions decorating the point where the ribs meet on the ceiling) are a reminder that the roof of this wing of the church was destroyed by fire in 1984. Some believe the fire was God's angry response to a new bishop, David Jenkins, who questioned the literal truth of Jesus' miracles. Others blame an electricity box hit by lightning. Regardless, the entire country came to York's aid. *Blue Peter* (England's top kids' show) conducted a competition among their young viewers to design new bosses. Out of 30,000 entries, there were six winners (the blue ones—e.g., man on the moon, feed the children, save the whales).

Look back at the west end to marvel at the **Great West Window,** especially the stone tracery. While its nickname is the

"Heart of Yorkshire," it represents the sacred heart of Christ, meant to remind people of his love for the world.

Find the **dragon** on the right of the nave (two-thirds of the way up). While no one is sure of its purpose, it pivots and has a hole through its neck—so it was likely a mechanism designed to raise a lid on a baptismal font.

The **choir screen** is an ornate wall of carvings separating the nave from the choir. It's lined with all the English kings from

William I (the Conqueror) to Henry VI (during whose reign it was carved, 1461). Numbers indicate the years each reigned. To say "it's slathered in gold leaf" sounds impressive, but the gold's very thin...a nugget the size of a sugar cube is pounded into a sheet the size of a driveway.

Step into the **choir** (or "quire"), where a daily service is held. All the carving was redone after an 1829 fire, but its tradition of glorious evensong services (sung by choristers from the Minster School) goes all the way back to the eighth century.

In the **north transept,** the 18th-century astronomical clock is worth a look (a sign to its left helps you make sense of it). It's dedicated to the heroic Allied aircrews from bases here in northern England who died in World War II (as Britain kept the Nazis from invading in its "darkest hour"). The Book of Remembrance below the clock contains 18,000 names.

A corridor that functions as a small church museum leads to the Gothic, octagonal **Chapter House,** the traditional meet-

ing place of the governing body (or chapter) of the Minster. Above the doorway, the Virgin holds Baby Jesus while standing on the devilish serpent. Look for the panel of stained glass that is often on display here (it may also be in the

undercroft). The panel is exquisitely detailed—its minute features would be invisible from the floor of the church and therefore "for God's eyes only."

The Chapter House, without an interior support, is remarkable (almost frightening) for its breadth. The fanciful carvings decorating the canopies above the stalls date from 1280 (80 percent are originals) and are some of the Minster's finest. Stroll around the entire room slowly, imagining the tiny sculpted heads are a

14th-century parade—a fun glimpse of medieval society. Grates still send hot air up robes of attendees on cold winter mornings. A model of the wooden construction illustrates the impressive 1285 engineering.

The Chapter House was the site of an important moment in England's parliamentary history. Fighting the Scots in 1295, Edward I (the "Longshanks" we met earlier) convened the "Model Parliament" here, rather than down south, in London. (The Model Parliament is the name for its early version, back before the legislature was split into the Houses of Commons and Lords.) The government met here through the 20-year reign of Edward II, before moving to London during Edward III's rule in the 14th century.

The church's **east end** is square, lacking a semicircular apse, typical of England's Perpendicular Gothic style (15th century). Monuments (almost no graves) were once strewn throughout the church, but in the Victorian Age, they were gathered into the east end, where you see them today.

The **Great East Window,** the size of a tennis court, is currently behind scaffolding. In the meantime, an interesting display explains the ongoing work. Also, a chart (on the right as you face the window) highlights the core Old Testament scenes in this masterpiece (hard to read from below, even when you can actually see the window). Because of the window's immense size, there's an extra layer of supportive stonework, parts of it wide enough to walk along. In fact, for special occasions, the choir sings from the walkway halfway up the window.

The **tower** and **undercroft** are two extra sights to consider, both accessed from the south transept. One gets you exercise and a view; the other is a basement full of history. You can scale the 275-step tower for the panoramic view (£4, last entry at 18:00 in summer and at 16:00 in winter, not good for kids or acrophobes). The **undercroft** consists of the crypt, treasury, and foundations (£4, last entry at 17:00). The crypt is an actual bit of the Romanesque church, featuring 12th-century Romanesque art, excavated in modern times. The foundations give you a chance to climb down—archaeologically and physically—through the centuries to see the roots of the much smaller, but still huge, Norman (Romanesque) church from 1100 that stood on this spot and, below that, the Roman excavations. Today's Minster stands upon the remains of a Roman fort. Peek also at the modern concrete save-the-church foundations.

Outside the Minster entrance, you'll find the **Roman Column.** Erected in 1971, this column commemorates the 1,900th anniversary of the Roman founding of Eboracum (later renamed York). Across the street is a statue of Constantine, who was in York when his father died. The troops declared him the Roman emperor in A.D. 306 at this site, and six years later he went to Rome to claim his throne. In A.D. 312, Constantine legalized Christianity, and in A.D. 314, York got its first bishop.

More Sights in York

▲**The Shambles**—This is the most colorful old street in the half-timbered, traffic-free core of town. Walk to the midway point, at

the intersection with Little Shambles. This 100-yard-long street, next to the old market, was once the "street of the butchers" (the name is derived from *shammell*—a butcher's cutting block). In the 16th century, it was busy with red meat. On the hooks under the eaves once hung rabbit, pheasant, beef, lamb, and pigs' heads. Fresh slabs were displayed on the fat sills.

People lived above—as they did even in Roman times. All the garbage was flushed down the street to a mucky pond at the end—a favorite hangout for the town's cats and dogs. Tourist shops now fill the fine 16th-century, half-timbered Tudor buildings. Look above the modern crowds and storefronts to appreciate the classic old English architecture. The soil here wasn't great for building. Notice how things settled in the absence of a good soil engineer.

Little Shambles leads to the frumpy Newgate Market (popular for cheap produce and clothing), created in the 1960s with the demolition of a bunch of lanes as colorful as The Shambles. Return to The Shambles a little farther

along, through a covered lane (or "snickelway"). Study the 16th-century oak carpentry—mortise and tenon joints with wooden plugs rather than nails.

For a cheap lunch, consider the cute, tiny **St. Crux Parish Hall**. This medieval church is now used by a medley of charities selling tea, homemade cakes, and light meals. They each book the church for a day, often a year in advance. Chat with the volunteers (Mon–Sat 10:00–16:00, closed Sun, on the left at bottom end of The Shambles, at intersection with Pavement).

▲▲▲**York Castle Museum**—Truly one of Europe's top museums, this is a Victorian home show, the closest thing to a time-tunnel experience Britain has to offer. Even a speedy museumgoer will want a couple hours here. Stroll down the museum's two re-created streets: Kirkgate, from the Victorian era, with roaming

YORK

live guides in period dress; and a fun street that re-creates the spirit of the swinging 1960s—"a time when the cultural changes were massive but the cars and skirts were mini."

The "From Cradle to Grave" clothing exhibit and fine costume collection are also impressive. The one-way plan assures you'll see everything: re-created rooms from the 17th to 20th centuries, prison cells with related exhibits, the domestic side of World War II, giant dollhouses from 1715 and 1895, Victorian toys, and a century of swimsuit fashions. The museum's £4 guidebook isn't necessary, but it makes a fun souvenir. The museum proudly offers no audioguides, as its roaming, costumed guides are enthusiastic about talking—engage them (£8, ticket good for one year, £10 combo-ticket with Yorkshire Museum when it reopens in Aug 2010, daily 10:00–17:00, opens at 9:30 when school's in session, cafeteria midway through museum, tel. 01904/687-687, www.yorkcastlemuseum.org.uk; at the bottom of the hop-on, hop-off bus route; museum can call a taxi for you—worthwhile if you're hurrying to the National Railway Museum).

Clifford's Tower—Located across from the Castle Museum, this ruin is all that's left of York's 13th-century castle, the site of an 1190 massacre of local Jews (read about this at base of hill). If you climb inside, there are fine city views from the top of the ramparts (not worth the £3.50, daily April–Sept 10:00–18:00, Oct 10:00–17:00, Nov–March 10:00–16:00, last entry 30 min before closing).

▲**Jorvik**—Take the "Pirates of the Caribbean," sail them north and back 1,000 years, and you get Jorvik—more a ride than a museum. Innovative 20 years ago, the commercial success of Jorvik (YOR-vik) inspired copycat ride/museums all over Great Britain. Some love this attraction; others call it a gimmicky rip-off. If you're looking for a grown-up museum, skip Jorvik and head instead to the Viking exhibit at the Yorkshire Museum (closed until Aug 2010). If you're thinking Disneyland with a splash of history, Jorvik's fun. To me, Jorvik is a commercial venture designed for kids, with nearly as much square footage devoted to its shop as to the museum. You'll ride a little Disney-type people-mover for 20 minutes through the re-created Viking street of Coppergate. It's the year 975, and you're in the village of Jorvik. Next, your little train takes you through the actual excavation site that inspired the reconstructed village. Everything is true to the dig—even the faces of the models are derived by computer from skulls dug up here. Finally, you'll browse through an impressive gallery of Viking shoes, combs, locks, and other intimate glimpses of that redheaded culture. Over 40,000 artifacts were dug out of the peat bog here in the 1970s. The exhibit on bone archaeology is fascinating (£8.50, £11.50 combo-ticket with Dig—see below, daily April–Oct 10:00–17:00, Nov–March 10:00–16:00, these are last admission times, tel. 01904/615-505, www.vikingjorvik.com).

Dig—This kid-oriented archaeological site gives young visitors an idea of what York looked like during Roman, medieval, Viking, and Victorian eras. Sift through "dirt" (actually shredded tires), reconstruct Roman wall plaster, and have a look at what archaeologists have dug up recently (£5.50, £11.50 combo-ticket with Jorvik, daily 10:00–17:00, last entry one hour before closing, St. Saviour's Church, Saviourgate, tel. 01904/543-402, www.digyork.co.uk).

▲▲**National Railway Museum**—If you like model railways, this

is train-car heaven. The thunderous museum shows 200 illustrious years of British railroad history. Fanning out from a grand roundhouse is an array of historic cars and engines, including Queen Victoria's lavish royal car and the very first "stagecoaches on rails," with a crude steam engine from 1830. A working steam engine is sliced open, showing cylinders, driving wheels, and smoke box in action. You'll trace the evolution of steam-powered transportation to the era of the aerodynamic Mallard, famous as the first train to travel at a startling two miles per minute (a marvel back in 1938). There's much more, including exhibits on dining cars, post cars, sleeping cars, train posters, and videos. At the Works section, you can see live train switchboards. And don't miss the English Channel Tunnel video (showing the first handshake at the breakthrough). Purple-shirted "explainers" are everywhere, eager to talk trains. This biggest and best railroad museum anywhere is interesting even to people who think "Pullman" means "don't push" (free, £2.50 audioguide with 60 bits of railroad lore is worthwhile for train buffs, daily 10:00–18:00, tel. 01904/621-261, www.nrm.org.uk).

Getting There: It's about a 15-minute walk from the Minster (southwest of town, behind the train station). A cute little "street train" shuttles you more quickly between the Minster and the Railway Museum (£2 each way, runs daily Easter–Oct, leaves Railway Museum every 30 min 11:00–16:00 at the top and bottom of the hour; leaves the town—from Duncombe Place, 100 yards in front of the Minster—at 15 and 45 min after the hour).

▲▲**Yorkshire Museum**—Located in a lush, picnic-perfect park next to the stately ruins of St. Mary's Abbey, Yorkshire Museum is the city's forgotten, serious "archaeology of York" museum. Unfortunately, it's closed for the first half of 2010 for extensive renovations—but if you're here after it reopens (likely Aug 2010), it's worth a stop.

The museum holds York's best Viking artifacts. While the hordes line up at Jorvik, this museum has no crowds and provides a better historical context. The Roman collection includes slice-of-life exhibits from Roman gods and goddesses and the skull of a man killed by a sword blow to the head. (The latter makes it graphically clear that the struggle between Romans and barbarians was a violent one.) A fine eighth-century Anglo-Saxon helmet shows a bit of barbarian refinement; you'll notice that the Vikings wore some pretty decent shoes, and actually combed their hair.

The Middleham Jewel, an exquisitely etched 15th-century pendant, is considered the finest piece of Gothic jewelry in Britain. The noble lady who wore this on a necklace believed that it helped her worship and protected her from illness. The back of the pendant, which rested near her heart, shows the nativity. The front shows the Holy Trinity crowned by a sapphire (which people believed put their prayers at the top of God's to-do list).

The 20-minute video about the creation of the abbey plays continuously, and is worth a look. Kids will enjoy the interactive "Fingerprints of Time" exhibit (prices and times may change post-renovation, but likely: museum entry-£6, ticket good for one year, £10 combo-ticket includes York Castle Museum, daily 10:00–17:00, within Museum Gardens, tel. 01904/687-687, www.yorkshiremuseum.org.uk). Before leaving, enjoy the evocative ruins of St. Mary's Abbey in the park (described on page 401).

▲**Fairfax House**—This well-furnished building is perfectly Georgian inside, with wonderfully pleasant docents eager to talk with you. Built in 1740, and furnished as if it were 1762, the house is compact and bursting with insights into aristocratic life in 18th-century England (£6, Mon–Thu and Sat 11:00–16:30, Sun 13:30–16:30, Fri by tour only at 11:00 and 14:00—the tours are

worthwhile, on Castlegate, near Jorvik, tel. 01904/655-543, www
.fairfaxhouse.co.uk).

Traditional Tea—York is famous for its elegant teahouses. Drop
into one around 16:00 for tea and cakes. Ladies love **Bettys Café
Tea Rooms,** where you pay £8 for a Yorkshire Cream Tea (tea
and scones with clotted Yorkshire cream and strawberry jam) or
£16 for a full traditional English afternoon tea (tea, delicate sandwiches, scones, and sweets). Your table is so full of doily niceties
that the food is served on a little three-tray tower. You'll pay a
little extra here (and the food's nothing special), but the ambience and people-watching are hard to beat. If there's a line, it
moves quickly (except at dinnertime). Wait for a seat by the
windows on the ground level rather than sit in the much bigger
basement (daily 9:00–21:00, piano music nightly 18:00–21:00, tel.
01904/659-142, St. Helen's Square, fine view of street scene from
a window seat on the main floor). Near the WC downstairs is a
mirror signed by WWII bomber pilots—read the story.

Riverside Walk or Bike Ride—The New Walk is a mile-long,
tree-lined riverside lane created in the 1730s as a promenade for
York's dandy class to stroll, see, and be seen—and a lovely place
for today's visitors to walk or bike. This hour-long walk along a
bike path is a great way to enjoy a dose of countryside away from
York. It's clearly described in the TI's *New Walk* flier (60p). Start
from the riverside under Skeldergate Bridge (near the York Castle
Museum), and walk away from town for a mile until you hit the
modern Millennium Bridge (check out its thin modern, stainless-
steel design). Cross the river and walk back home, passing through
Rowntree Park (a great Edwardian park with lawn bowling for
the public, plus family fun including a playground and adventure
rides for kids). Energetic bikers can continue past the Millennium
Bridge 18 miles to the market town of Selby.

Honorable Mentions

York has a number of other sights and activities (described in TI brochures) that, while interesting, pale in comparison to the biggies.

Merchant Adventurers' Hall—Claiming to be the finest medieval guildhall in Europe (from 1361), it's basically a vast half-
timbered building with marvelous exposed beams and 15 minutes'
worth of interesting displays about life and commerce back in
the days when York was England's second city (£3; April–Sept
Mon–Thu 9:00–17:00, Fri–Sat 9:00–15:30, Sun 12:00–16:00; Oct–
March Mon–Sat 9:00–15:30, closed Sun; south of The Shambles
off Piccadilly, tel. 01904/654-818, www.theyorkcompany.co.uk).

Richard III Museum—This goofy exhibit is like seeing a high
school history project. It's interesting only for Richard III enthusiasts (£2.50, daily March–Oct 9:00–17:00, Nov–Feb 9:30–16:00,

longer hours possible in summer, filling the top floors of Monk Bar, tel. 01904/634-191, www.richardiiimuseum.co.uk).

York Dungeon—It's gimmicky, but if you insist on papier-mâché gore, it's better than the London Dungeon (£14, daily 10:00–17:30, shorter hours off-season, 12 Clifford Street, tel. 01904/632-599, www.thedungeons.com).

Lawn Bowling Green—Visitors are welcome to watch the action—best in the evenings—at the green on Sycamore Place (near recommended B&Bs). Buy a pint of beer and tell them which B&B you're staying at. Another green is in front of the Coach House Hotel Pub on Marygate.

Near York

Several worthwhile attractions dot the countryside outside York. If you have some extra time here, don't miss the North Yorkshire chapter (next).

Shopping in York

With its medieval lanes lined with classy as well as tacky little shops, York is a hit with shoppers. I find the **antiques malls** interesting. Three places within a few blocks of each other are filled with stalls and cases owned by antiques dealers from the countryside. The malls sell the dealers' bygones on commission. Serious shoppers do better heading for the countryside, but York's shops are a fun browse: The **Antiques Centre York** (Mon–Sat 9:00–17:30, Sun 9:00–16:00, 41 Stonegate, tel. 01904/635-888, www.theantiquescentreyork.co.uk), the **York Antique Centre** (Mon–Fri 10:00–17:00, Sat 10:00–18:00, Sun 10:30–17:00, 2 Lendal, tel. 01904/641-445), and the **Red House Antiques Centre** (Mon–Fri 9:30–17:30, Sat 9:30–18:00, Sun 10:30–17:30, a block from Minster at Duncombe Place, tel. 01904/637-000, www.redhouseyork .co.uk).

You'll find **thrift shops** run by various charity organizations from the beginning of Goodramgate by the wall to just past Deangate. Good deals abound on clothing, purses, accessories, children's toys, books, CDs, and even guitars. If you buy something, you're getting a bargain and at the same time helping the poor, elderly, or even a pet in need of a vet (Mon–Sat 9:30–17:00, Sun 11:00–16:00). On Goodramgate alone you'll find shops run by the British Heart Foundation, Save the Children, and Oxfam (selling donated items as well as free-trade products such as coffee, tea, culinary goods, stationery items, and jewelry made in developing countries and purchased directly from the producers and artisans).

Nightlife in York

Theatre Royal—A full variety of dramas, comedies, and works by Shakespeare entertain the locals in either the main theater or the little 100-seat theater-in-the-round (£10–20, usually Tue–Sat at 19:30, tickets easy to get, on St. Leonard's Place near Bootham Bar and a 5-min walk from recommended B&Bs, booking tel. 01904/623-568, www.yorktheatreroyal.co.uk). Those under 25 and students of any age get tickets for only £5.

Ghost Tours—You'll see flyers, signs, and promoters hawking a variety of not-so-spooky after-dark tours; of these, I'd go for the "Haunted Walks" (for details, see "Tours in York," earlier).

Pubs—Atmospheric, half-timbered pubs abound. Two of my favorites for old-school York ambience are **The Royal Oak** (in the center of town, described under "Eating in York," later) and **The Blue Bell,** a tiny, traditional establishment with a time-warp Edwardian interior. This smallest pub in York serves no food. It has two distinct little rooms—each as cozy as can be—and the owners only recently allowed women to enter (near the east end of town at 53 Fossgate).

Movies—The centrally located City Screens Cinema is right on the river, playing both art-house and mainstream flicks (13 Coney Street, toll tel. 0870-758-3219).

Sleeping in York

I've listed peak-season, book-direct prices. Don't use the TI. Outside of July and August, some prices go soft. B&Bs will often charge £10 more for weekends and sometimes turn away one-night bookings, particularly for peak-season Saturdays. (York is worth two nights anyway.) Prices spike up for horse races and Bank Holidays (about 20 nights a season). Remember to book ahead during festival times (mid-Feb, early June, early July, mid-Aug, and late Sept—see "Helpful Hints" on page 395) and weekends year-round.

B&Bs and Small Hotels

These B&Bs are all small and family-run. They come with plenty of steep stairs (and no elevators) but no traffic noise. For a good selection, call well in advance. B&B owners will generally hold a room with a phone call, and work hard to help their guests sightsee and eat smartly. Most have permits to lend for street parking.

Near Bootham Bar

These recommendations are in the handiest B&B neighborhood, a quiet residential area just outside the old town wall's Bootham

Sleep Code

(£1 = about $1.60, country code: 44, area code: 01904)
S = Single, **D** = Double/Twin, **T** = Triple, **Q** = Quad, **b** = bathroom, **s** = shower only. You can assume credit cards are accepted unless otherwise noted.

To help you sort easily through these listings, I've divided the rooms into three categories based on the price for a standard double room with bath (during high season):

$$$ Higher Priced—Most rooms £90 or more.
$$ Moderately Priced—Most rooms between £60–90.
$ Lower Priced—Most rooms £60 or less.

gate, along the road called Bootham. All are within a 10-minute walk of the Minster and TI, and a 10- to 15-minute walk or taxi ride (£3–5) from the station. If driving, head for the cathedral and follow the medieval wall to the gate called Bootham Bar. The street called Bootham leads away from Bootham Bar.

$$$ The Hazelwood, my most hotelesque listing in this neighborhood, is plush and more formal than a B&B (there's always someone at reception). This spacious house has 14 beautifully decorated rooms with modern furnishings and lots of thoughtful touches (Db-£80/90/110 depending on room size, two ground-floor rooms, free Internet access and Wi-Fi, laundry service-£7, free parking, light breakfast option; a fridge, ice, and travel library in the pleasant basement lounge; 24 Portland Street, tel. 01904/626-548, www.thehazelwoodyork.com, reservations @thehazelwoodyork.com, Ian and Carolyn). Ask about their bright top-floor two-bedroom apartment, great for families and those with strong legs (continental breakfast only).

$$ Number 23 St. Mary's B&B is extravagantly decorated. Chris and Julie Simpson have done everything just right and offer nine spacious and tastefully comfy rooms, a classy lounge, and all the doily touches (Sb-£48–55, Db-£80–95 depending on room size and season, discount for longer stays, family room, DVD library and DVD players, free Wi-Fi, 23 St. Mary's, tel. 01904/622-738, www.23stmarys.co.uk, stmarys23@hotmail.com).

$$ Crook Lodge B&B, with seven tight but elegantly charming rooms, serves breakfast in an old Victorian kitchen (Db-£74–80, cheaper off-season, one ground-floor room, free Wi-Fi, parking, quiet, 26 St. Mary's, tel. 01904/655-614, www.crooklodge .co.uk, crooklodge@hotmail.com, Brian and Louise Aiken).

$$ Abbey Guest House is a peaceful refuge overlooking the River Ouse, with five cheerful, beautifully updated rooms and a cute little garden (Db-£75–80, four-poster Db with river view-£80, ask for Rick Steves discount when booking, free Wi-Fi, free parking, £7 laundry service, 13–14 Earlsborough Terrace, tel. 01904/627-782, www.abbeyghyork.co.uk, info@abbeyghyork.co.uk, delightful couple Gill—pronounced "Jill"—and Alec Saville, and a dog aptly named Loofah).

$$ Abbeyfields Guest House has eight comfortable, bright rooms. This doily-free place, which lacks the usual B&B clutter, has been designed with care (Sun–Thu: Sb-£45, Db-£72; Fri–Sat: Sb-£49, Db-£82; doesn't price-gouge during races, free Wi-Fi, 19 Bootham Terrace, tel. 01904/636-471, www.abbeyfields.co.uk, enquire@abbeyfields.co.uk, charming Al and Les).

$$ At **St. Raphael Guesthouse,** young, creative, and energetic Dom and Zoe understand a traveler's needs. You'll be instant friends. Dom's graphic design training brings a dash of class to their seven comfy rooms, each themed after a different York street, and each lovingly accented with a fresh rose (Db-£76 Sun–Thu, £88 Fri–Sat, free drinks in their guests' fridge, family rooms, free Internet access and Wi-Fi, 44 Queen Annes Road, tel. 01904/645-028, www.straphaelguesthouse.co.uk, info@straphaelguesthouse.co.uk).

$$ Airden House rents nine simple rooms (Db-£70–78, this price with 2-night minimum and this book in 2010, lounge, free parking, 1 St. Mary's, tel. 01904/638-915, www.airdenhouse.co.uk, info@airdenhouse.co.uk).

$$ Arnot House, run by a hardworking mother-and-daughter team, is homey and lushly decorated with Victorian memorabilia. The three well-furnished rooms have little libraries with books and DVDs (Db-£70–80 depending on size of room, 2-night minimum stay unless it's last-minute, no children, free Wi-Fi, 17 Grosvenor Terrace, tel. 01904/641-966, www.arnothouseyork.co.uk, kim.robbins@virgin.net, Kim).

$$ Hedley House Hotel, well-run by a wonderful family, has 30 clean and spacious rooms. The outdoor hot tub is a relaxing way to end your day (Sb-£45–70, Db-£70–90, ask for a deal with stay of 2 or more nights, family rooms, 3-course evening meals-£18, free Wi-Fi, parking, 3 Bootham Terrace, tel. 01904/637-404, www.hedleyhouse.com, greg@hedleyhouse.com, Greg and Louise Harrand).

$$ Alcuin Lodge has five relaxing rooms with comfy sofas and solid-wood furnishings (one small top-floor D-£60, Db-£68–74, family room-£80–100, discount for longer stays, laundry-£4–5, free Wi-Fi, free parking, 15 Sycamore Place, tel. 01904/632-222, www.alcuinlodge.com, info@alcuinlodge.com, Pete and Issy).

$$ The Coach House Hotel is a labyrinthine, well-located 17th-century coach house. Facing a bowling green and the abbey

York Accommodations

1. The Hazelwood
2. Number 23 St. Mary's B&B
3. Crook Lodge B&B
4. Abbey Guest House
5. Abbeyfields Guest House
6. St. Raphael Guesthouse
7. Airden House
8. Arnot House
9. Hedley House Hotel
10. Alcuin Lodge
11. The Coach House Hotel & Rest.
12. Ardmore Guest House
13. The Sycamore
14. Bootham Guest House
15. Number 34 & Amber House
16. Queen Annes Guest House
17. Dean Court Hotel
18. Travelodge York Central
19. Premier Inn
20. Ace Budget Hotel York
21. To Launderette
22. Internet Cafés (2)
23. Library (Internet)
24. Bike Rental

TO A-19 & THIRSK

CLIFTON
BOOTH. CRES.
QUEEN ANNES
BOOTHAM TERR.
GROS. TERR.
ST. MARY'S
SYCAMORE
LONGFIELD
FREDERIC
EARLS
MARYGATE

RAILWAY MUSEUM

RIVER

LEEMAN

ROAD

TRAIN STATION

STATION RD.

MICKLE

QUEEN

NUNNERY

BLOSSOM

MICKLEGATE BAR

TO A-64 & LEEDS

ACCESS STAIRS TO WALL

P   PARKING

--- FOOTPATH

200 YARDS

200 METERS

YORK

walls, it offers 14 huge beam-ceilinged rooms, some with views of the Minster (Sb-£50, Db-£77–81, family room for £130–150 sleeps up to 6, one ground-floor room, free parking, 20 Marygate, tel. 01904/652-780, www.coachhousehotel-york.com, info @coachhousehotel-york.com). This is also a fine place for a cozy pub dinner.

$$ Ardmore Guest House is a lovely little four-room place enthusiastically run by Irishwoman Vera, who's given it a green theme. It's about a 15-minute walk from the station, but only five minutes from Bootham Bar (Sb-£40, Db-£60–70, Tb-£70, discount for 3 or more nights, cash only, 31 Claremont Terrace, tel. 01904/622-562, mobile 079-3928-3588).

$$ The Sycamore is a fine value, with six homey rooms at the end of a quiet street opposite a fun-to-watch bowling green. A little cramped and funky, it's friendly and well-run (Db-£60–65, Tb-£90–96, Qb-£110, lower price is for weekdays, these are special prices with this book in 2010, may be cheaper off-season, free Wi-Fi, 19 Sycamore Place off Bootham Terrace, tel. 01904/624-712, www.thesycamore.co.uk, mail@thesycamore .co.uk, accommodating Elizabeth and Spiros freely dispense sightseeing advice).

$ Bootham Guest House features gregarious Emma, who welcomes you to her eight simple but cheery and thoughtfully renovated rooms (S-£35, D-£56, £60 Fri–Sat; Db-£60, £70 Fri–Sat; request 5 percent Rick Steves discount with this guidebook in 2010, free Wi-Fi, 56 Bootham Crescent, tel. 01904/672-123, www .boothamguesthouse.com, boothamguesthouse1@hotmail.com).

$ Number 34, run by hardworking Amy and Jason, has four somewhat stark but light, airy rooms at fair prices (May–Oct: Sb-£45, Db-£56, Tb-£78; Nov–April: Sb-£35, Db-£50, Tb-£70, free Wi-Fi, 34 Bootham Crescent, tel. 01904/645-818, www .number34york.co.uk, enquiries@number34york.co.uk).

$ Amber House is a small place with three breezy and well-tended rooms. Their red Oriental Room is worth asking for (Db-£60 Sun–Thu, £68 Fri–Sat; Tb-£80, mention Rick Steves when booking, free Wi-Fi, 36 Bootham Crescent, tel. 01904/620-275, www.amberhouse-york.co.uk, amberhouseyork@hotmail.co.uk, John and Linda).

$ Queen Annes Guest House has six very basic rooms at the best prices in the neighborhood. If you're looking for plush beds and rich decor, look elsewhere. If you'd like an affordable, clean place to sleep, this is it (high season: D-£46, Db-£52; off-season: D-£40, Db-£46; prices promised with this book through 2010, family room, ground-floor room, free Wi-Fi, lounge, 24 Queen Annes Road, tel. 01904/629-389, www.queen-annes-guesthouse .co.uk, info@queen-annes-guesthouse.co.uk, Jason).

Hotels in the Center and Big-Budget Hotel Options

$$$ Dean Court Hotel, a Best Western facing the Minster, is a big, stately hotel with classy lounges and 37 comfortable rooms (Ss/Sb-£104, small Db-£135, standard Db-£160, superior Db-£190, spacious deluxe Db-£210, cheaper midweek and off-season, elevator to most rooms, free Wi-Fi, bistro, restaurant, Duncombe Place, tel. 01904/625-082, fax 01904/620-305, www.deancourt-york.co.uk).

$$ Travelodge York Central offers 93 identical, affordable rooms near the Castle Museum. If you book long in advance on their website, this can be amazingly cheap (last year, as low as £9 for a room). River views make some rooms slightly less boring—after booking online, call the front desk to arrange a view (Db and Tb-£70 Sun–Thu, £85 Fri–Sat, often much lower with Internet deals, kids' bed free, breakfast £4.50 extra, pay Internet access and Wi-Fi, 90 Piccadilly, central reservations toll tel. 08719-848-484, front desk tel. 01904/651-852, www.travelodge.co.uk).

$$ Premier Inn is a 200-room hotel that I hate to recommend, but York has few budget options. This place has no character (you enter through a chain coffee shop) but offers industrial-strength efficiency and straight bargain pricing (Db-£74 Sun–Thu, £79 Fri–Sat, up to 2 kids stay free, breakfast-£8 extra, pay Internet access and Wi-Fi, free parking, 5-min walk to train station, 20 Blossom Street, toll tel. 0870-990-6594, www.premierinn.com, yorkcitycentre.pi@premierinn.com).

Hostel

$ Ace Budget Hotel York is a newly renovated hostel providing a much-needed option for backpackers. They rent 130 beds in two- to 14-bed rooms, most with great views and all with private bathrooms and thoughtful touches such as reading lights for each bed. They also offer fancier, hotel-quality doubles (£19–30/bed depending on size of dorm, Db-£105, family room, laundry-£3, pay Internet access and Wi-Fi, TV lounge, bar, lockers, 10 minutes' walk from the train station at 88 Mickelgate, tel. 01904/627-720, reception@ace-hotelyork.co.uk, www.ace-hotelyork.co.uk).

Eating in York

York is bursting with inviting eateries. There seems to be a pub serving grub on every corner. And in the last decade or so, the city has become a hot spot for the new British cuisine—every year seems to bring another bistro serving classy dishes made with fresh, local ingredients. Here are five of my favorites: Café Concerto, Café No. 8, The Blue Bicycle, J. Baker's, and Melton's Too. Each place is

York Restaurants

1. St. William's Tea Rooms
2. Bettys Café Tea Rooms
3. York Hogroast & Siam House
4. Petergate Fisheries
5. Café Concerto
6. El Piano Restaurant
7. Ask Restaurant
8. The Royal Oak Pub
9. Bengal Brasserie & Caesars
10. The Viceroy of India
11. Little Italy
12. Café No. 8
13. The Coach House
14. Mamma Mia
15. Sainsbury's
16. The Blue Bicycle
17. J. Baker's
18. Melton's Too
19. The Blue Bell

TO A-19 & THIRSK

RAILWAY MUSEUM

RIVER

TRAIN STATION

LEEMAN

ROAD

STATION RD.

QUEEN

MICKLE

BLOSSOM

NUNNERY

TO A-64 & LEEDS

MICKLEGATE BAR

⊿ ACCESS STAIRS TO WALL

P PARKING

--- FOOTPATH

200 YARDS

200 METERS

romantic, laid-back, and popular with locals (so reservations are wise for dinner). All have several creative vegetarian options on the menu. Main courses at these places cost about £15–20—not exorbitant by British standards, but not cheap either.

Fortunately, picnic and light-meals-to-go options abound, and it's easy to find a churchyard, bench, or riverside perch upon which to munch for cheap. On a sunny day, perhaps the best picnic spot in town is under the evocative 12th-century ruins of St. Mary's Abbey in the Museum Gardens (near Bootham Bar).

Just Lunch

St. William's Tea Rooms, signed as the "York Minster Tea Rooms," are nestled just behind the Great East Window of the Minster in a wonderful half-timbered 15th-century building (read the history on the menu). They serve quick, tasty lunches. Eat outside (with a scaffolded Minster view), inside (cafeteria under timbers), or in the peaceful cobbled courtyard (tea and pastries served daily 10:30–17:00, £7–8 lunches served daily 12:00–15:00, College Street, tel. 01904/634-830).

Bettys Café Tea Rooms, a favorite among local ladies, is popular for its traditional English afternoon tea (which works as a meal—£16 for tea, delicate sandwiches, scones, and sweets; for details, see page 413).

York Hogroast is a fixture, serving its delicious £3 hearty pork sandwiches with a choice of traditional fillings—try the apple (take-away only, Mon–Fri 11:00–16:00, Sat–Sun 11:00–17:00, 82 Goodramgate). Grab a sandwich and munch in the yard at the nearby Holy Trinity Church (to your left as you exit, peaceful) or in King's Square (to your right as you exit, lively with buskers).

Petergate Fisheries is about the only traditional chippie left in the center (eat in or take out, daily 11:00–18:00, at corner of Goodramgate and Low Petergate at 95 Low Petergate).

Near the Minster

Café Concerto, a casual bistro with a fun menu, wholesome food, and a charming musical theme, has an understandably loyal following (soup, sandwich, and salad meals-£9–10; fancier dinners-£14–20; daily 10:00–22:00, smart to reserve for dinner, also offers take-away, facing the Minster, 21 High Petergate, tel. 01904/610-478).

El Piano Restaurant, a few blocks from the Minster on charming Grape Lane, is a popular veggie option that serves only vegan, gluten-free, and low-sodium dishes in tapas-style portions. The dishes have Indian/Asian/Middle Eastern flavors, and the inside ambience is bubble gum with blinking lights. They also have a pleasant patio out back. If eating family-style, three or four plates serve two. Save money at the take-away window (£3–4 to-go "bamboo boats," Mon–Sat 11:00–23:00, Sun 11:00–17:00, between Low Petergate and Swinegate at 15–17 Grape Lane, tel. 01904/610-676).

Ask Restaurant is a cheap and cheery Italian chain, stuffed with happy diners slurping pasta and slicing pizza. Found in historic buildings all over England, York's version lets you dine in the majestic marble-columned yellow hall of its Grand Assembly Rooms. The food may be Italian-chain dull—but the atmosphere is 18th-century deluxe (£8–9 pizza and pastas, daily, Blake Street, tel. 01904/637-254).

Along Goodramgate

Goodramgate is lined with a fun variety of competitive eateries dishing up everything from fish-and-chips and pub grub to tastes of Thailand, India, and Italy. Strolling this lane, you'll find plenty of good options. Working roughly from the center to the medieval gate, Monk Bar, these are my favorites.

Siam House serves creative Thai food popular with locals (£7 lunches, £11–13 dinners, Sun–Fri 18:00–22:00, Wed–Fri also 12:00–14:00, Sat 12:00–23:00, 63a Goodramgate, tel. 01904/624-677).

The Royal Oak, a traditional, mellow 16th-century English pub with three cozy rooms, is a York institution. Despite having recently changed owners, the pub should still be serving up hearty dishes and hand-pulled ale—like most of York, they take their ale seriously (a block inside Monk Bar at 18 Goodramgate).

Bengal Brasserie is a local favorite for Indian cuisine (Sun–Fri 18:00–24:00, Sat 12:00–24:00, 21 Goodramgate, tel. 01904/613-131). I also like the **Viceroy of India,** just outside Monk Bar and therefore outside the tourist zone (£6–11 plates, daily 18:00–24:00, out Monk Bar to 26 Monkgate, tel. 01904/622-370).

Two popular (if not quite elegant) Italian places along Goodramgate offer pizzas and pastas for £8: **Little Italy** is a little more intimate (Mon–Fri 11:00–14:30 & 17:00–22:00 except Fri until 22:30, Sat 12:00–23:00, Sun 12:00–21:30, at #12, tel. 01904/623-539), whereas **Caesars** is bright and boisterous (Mon–Fri 12:00–14:30 & 17:30–23:00, Sat–Sun 12:00–23:00, at #27, tel. 01904/670-914).

Near Bootham Bar and Recommended B&Bs

Café No. 8 is a local favorite and your best bistro choice on Gillygate, serving modern European and veggie options. Grab one of eight tables inside or enjoy a shaded little garden out back if the weather's good. No. 8 feels like Café Concerto (described earlier) but is more romantic, with jazz, modern art, candles, and hardworking Martin bringing it all together. Chef Chris Pragnell uses what's fresh in the market to shape his menu. The food is simple, elegant, and creative—with appetizers such as figs with local bleu cheese (£6–10 lunches, £13–17 dinners, Mon–Fri 11:00–22:00, Sat 10:00–22:00, Sun 10:00–17:00, 8 Gillygate, tel. 01904/653-074).

The Coach House serves good-quality fresh food, with veggie options and homemade sweets, in a cozy atmosphere (£8–11, nightly 18:00–21:00, attached to a classic old guest house recommended in "Sleeping in York," 20 Marygate, tel. 01904/652-780).

Mamma Mia is the locals' choice for affordable Italian. The casual eating area features a tempting gelato bar, and in nice weather the back patio is *molto bella* (£8 pizza and pasta, daily 11:30–14:00 & 17:30–23:00, 20 Gillygate, tel. 01904/622-020).

Sainsbury's grocery store is handy and open late (daily 7:00–23:00, 50 yards outside Bootham Bar, on Bootham).

At the East End of Town

This neighborhood is across town from my recommended B&Bs, but still central (and a short walk from the Castle Museum). All three of these places are worth the longer after-dinner stroll.

The Blue Bicycle is no longer a brothel (but if you explore downstairs, you can still imagine when the tiny privacy snugs needed their curtains). Today it is passionate about fish. The energy of its happy eaters, its charming canalside setting, and its location just beyond the tourist zone make it worth the splurge. Of my recommended York restaurants, this wins the Best Ambience award. It's a velvety, hardwood scene, a little sultry but fresh...like its fish. Reservations are a must (£10 starters, £20 main dishes, vegetarian and meat options, nightly 18:00–21:30, Thu–Sun also 12:00–14:30, 34 Fossgate, tel. 01904/673-990).

J. Baker's, one of York's newer restaurants, has quickly gained popularity for turning local produce into highbrow versions of classic dishes. At lunchtime, their "grazing menu" makes it affordable to sample several dishes (available à la carte, or £12 for three courses). At dinnertime, the two earth-toned dining rooms—one downstairs, one upstairs—tend to fill up fast, so reservations are smart (£24 two-course meals, £28.50 three-course meals, Tue–Sat 12:00–14:30 & 18:00–22:00, closed Sun–Mon, near the end of The Shambles at 7 Fossgate, tel. 01904/622-688). Across the street is the recommended Blue Bell pub.

Melton's Too is a fun and casual place to eat. This homey, spacious, youthful restaurant serves up elegantly simple meals and a nice a selection of tapas, all with a focus on local ingredients (£10–12 main courses, Mon–Sat 10:30–22:30, Sun 10:30–21:30, just past Fossgate at 25 Walmgate, tel. 01904/629-222, Nick).

YORK

York Connections

From York by Train to: Durham (3–4/hr, 45 min), **London** King's Cross Station (2/hr, 2 hrs), **Bath** (2/hr, 4–4.5 hrs, 1–2 changes in Birmingham, Bristol, and/or London), **Cambridge** (hourly, 2.5 hrs, change in Peterborough), **Birmingham** (2/hr, 2–2.5 hrs), **Keswick** (hourly, with transfers to Penrith then bus, 4.5 hrs), **Edinburgh** (2/hr, 2.5 hrs). Train info: toll tel. 0845-748-4950.

    Connections with London's Airports: Heathrow (at least hourly, allow 3 hrs minimum; from airport take Heathrow Express train to London's Paddington Station, transfer via tube to King's Cross, train to York—2/hr, 2 hrs; for details on cheaper but slower tube or bus option from airport to London see page 159), **Gatwick** (at least hourly, allow 3 hrs minimum; from Gatwick catch First Capital Connect train to London's St. Pancras Station; from there, walk to neighboring King's Cross Station, and catch train to York—2/hr, 2 hrs).

Near York: North York Moors

In the lonesome North York Moors, sheep seem to outnumber people. In this high, desolate-feeling plateau, with a spongy and inhospitable soil, bleating flocks jockey for position against scrubby heather for control of the terrain. You can almost imagine the mysterious Heathcliff (from *Wuthering Heights*, which was set here) plodding across this terrain. As you pass through this haunting landscape, crisscrossed by only a few roads, notice how the gloomy brown heather—which blooms briefly with purple flowers at summer's end—is actually burned back by wardens to clear the way for new growth. The vast, undulating expanses of nothingness are punctuated by greener, sparsely populated valleys called dales. Park your car and take a hike across the moors on any small road. You'll come upon a few tidy villages and maybe even old Roman roads.

    Drivers can consider The Moors Centre; nondrivers can take the steam train; and most people might want to stop in Goathland.

The Moors Centre

This visitor facility near Danby provides the best orientation for exploring North York Moors National Park. (Unfortunately, it's at the northern end of the park—not as convenient if you're coming from York.) This grand old lodge, fully renovated in 2007, offers exhibits, shows, nature walks, an information desk, plenty of books and maps, brass rubbing, a cheery cafeteria, and brochures on several good walks that start right outside the front door.

    Cost and Hours: Free entry but £2 parking fee; April–Oct daily 10:00–17:00; March and Nov–Dec daily 10:30–15:30; Jan–Feb Sat–Sun 10:30–15:30, closed Mon–Fri; café, tel. 01439/772-737, www.visitnorthyorkshiremoors.co.uk.

Getting There: It's three-fourths of a mile from Danby in Esk Valley, in the northern part of the park (follow signs from Danby, which is a short drive from A171 running along the northern edge of the park).

▲North Yorkshire Moors Railway

This 18-mile, one-hour steam-engine ride between Pickering and Grosmont (GROW-mont) runs nearly hourly through some of the best parts of the moors. Sometimes the train continues from Grosmont on to the seaside town of Whitby; otherwise, you might be able to transfer in Grosmont to another, nonsteam train to reach Whitby (check schedules before you plan your trip). Once in Whitby, you can use the bus to connect along the coast, or to go back to York. Drivers find Pickering—the train line's starting point—right on A169 north of York (en route to the coast). Or you can catch Coastliner bus #840 from York to Pickering (every 1–2 hrs Mon–Sat, fewer on Sun, 1.25 hrs, www.yorkshiretravel.net).

Even with the small, dirty windows (try to wipe off the outside of yours before you roll), and with the track situated mostly in a scenic gully, it's a good ride. You can stop along the way for a walk on the moors (or at the appealing village of Goathland—described next) and catch the next train (£15 round-trip to Grosmont, or £20 round-trip to Whitby, includes hop-on, hop-off privileges; runs daily late-March–Oct, weekends Nov–Dec, no trains Jan–late-March, schedule flexes with the season but generally the first train departs Pickering at 9:00, last train departs Grosmont about 18:20; trip takes about one hour one-way to Grosmont, allow about 2.75 hours round-trip to come back on the same train; tel. 01751/472-508 or 01751/473-799, www.nymr.co.uk). You can't leave luggage at any stop on the steam-train line—pack light if you decide to hike.

Goathland

This tranquil village, huddled along a babbling brook, is worth considering for a sleepy stopover, either on the steam-train trip or for drivers (it's an easy detour from A169, which cuts through the moors). Movie buffs will enjoy Goathland's train station, which was used to film scenes at "Hogwarts Station" for the early Harry Potter movies (for more on Harry Potter sights, see page 726). But Brits know and love Goathland as the setting for the beloved, long-running TV series *Heartbeat,* about a small Yorkshire town in the 1960s. You'll see TV sets intermingled with real buildings, and some shops are even labeled "Aidensfield," for the TV town's fictional name.

DURHAM AND NORTHEAST ENGLAND

Northeast England harbors some of the country's best historical sights. Go for a Roman ramble at Hadrian's Wall, a reminder that Britain was an important Roman colony 2,000 years ago. Make a pilgrimage to Holy Island, where Christianity gained its first toehold in Britain. At Durham, marvel at England's greatest Norman church, and enjoy an evensong service. At the Beamish Museum, travel back in time to the year 1913.

Planning Your Time

For train travelers, Durham is the most convenient overnight stop in this region. If you like Roman ruins, visit Hadrian's Wall (doable with transfers, easiest Easter–Oct). The Beamish Museum is an easy day trip from Durham (25 min by car, one hour by bus). If you're traveling by train, note that it's problematic to visit Durham en route to another destination, because there's no baggage storage in Durham. Either stay overnight or do Durham as a day trip from York.

By car, you can easily visit Beamish Museum, Hadrian's Wall, Bamburgh Castle, and Holy Island. Spend a night in Durham and a night near Hadrian's Wall.

For the best quick visit, arrive in Durham by mid-afternoon in time to tour the cathedral and enjoy the evensong service (Tue–Sat at 17:15, Sun at 15:30). Sleep in Durham. Visit Beamish (25 min north of Durham by car, or 1 hr by bus) the next morning before continuing on to your next destination.

Durham

Without its cathedral, Durham would hardly be noticed. But this magnificently situated cathedral is hard to miss (even if you're zooming by on the train). Seemingly happy to go nowhere, Durham sits along its river, and below its castle and famous cathedral. It has a medieval, cobbled atmosphere and a scraggly peasant's indoor market just off the main square. While Durham is the home to England's third-oldest university, the town feels working-class, surrounded by recently closed coal mines, and filled with tattooed and pierced people in search of job security and a good karaoke bar. Yet Durham has a youthful vibrancy and a small-town warmth that shines—especially on sunny days, when most everyone is licking ice-cream cones.

Orientation to Durham

(area code: 0191)

As it has for a thousand years, tidy little Durham clusters everything safely under its castle, within the protective hairpin bend of the River Wear. The longest walk you'll make will be a 20-minute jaunt from the train station to the cathedral.

Tourist Information

The TI books rooms and local event tickets, and provides train times (Mon–Sat 9:30–17:30, Sun 11:00–16:00, WC, café; 1 block north of Market Place, past St. Nicholas Church, in Gala Theatre building; tel. 0191/384-3720, www.durhamtourism.co.uk, tourist info@durhamcity.gov.uk).

Arrival in Durham

From the **train station,** follow the road downhill and take the second pedestrian turnoff (within sight of railway bridge), which leads almost immediately over a bridge above the busy road called Alexander Crescent. Then take North Road into town or to the first couple of B&Bs (take Alexander Crescent to the other B&Bs). Or you can just hop on the convenient Cathedral Bus at the train station (described later, under "Getting Around Durham").

Drivers simply surrender to the wonderful 400-space Prince Bishops parking lot (at the roundabout at the base of the old town). It's perfectly safe, and an elevator deposits you right in the heart of Durham (£2/2 hrs, £3.20/4 hrs, a short block from Market Place, tel. 0191/383-9592).

Durham

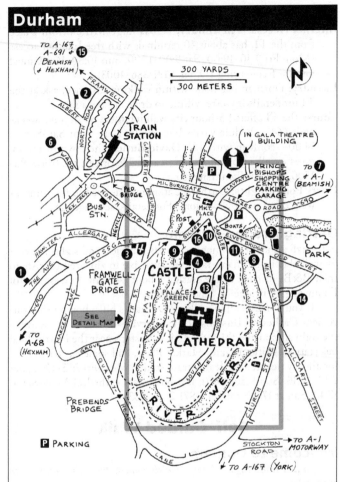

300 YARDS
300 METERS

TO A-167
A-691 &
(BEAMISH
& HEXHAM)

FRAMWELL

ALBERT ROAD

NORTH ROAD

WADD

GATE PETH

TRAIN
STATION

(IN GALA THEATRE
BUILDING)

PED.
BRIDGE

MILBURNGATE

FREEMAN'S PL.

PRINCE
BISHOP'S
SHOPPING
CENTRE
PARKING
GARAGE

To
& A-1
(BEAMISH)

CLAYPATH

LEAZES ROAD

A-690

BUS
STN.

NEVILLE ST.

NORTH ROAD

ALEX. CRES.

POST

MKT.
PLACE

SILVER

BOATS!

ELVET BRIDGE

ALLERGATE

HAW. TER

CROSSGATE

SADDLER

NEW ELVET

OLD ELVET

PARK

FRAMWELL-
GATE
BRIDGE

A-690

THE AVE.

MARGERY LANE

SOUTH ST.

SOUTH PATH

CASTLE

PALACE
GREEN

NORTH BAILEY

SEE
DETAIL MAP

TO
A-68
(HEXHAM)

GROVE

QUARRY HEADS

CATHEDRAL

SOUTH BAILEY

CHURCH STREET

HALLGARTH STREET

RIVER WEAR

PREBENDS
BRIDGE

P PARKING

LANE

STOCKTON
ROAD

TO A-1
MOTORWAY

TO A-167 (YORK)

DURHAM

❶ Farnley Tower B&B
❷ Victorian Town House B&B
❸ Castleview Guest House
❹ Durham Castle Rooms
❺ Durham Marriott Hotel
   Royal County
❻ Kingslodge Hotel & Rest.
❼ To Travelodge Durham
❽ Melanzana Restaurant

❾ Café Rouge & Bella Italia
❿ Bimbi's Fish & Chips
⓫ Hide Café
⓬ Shaheen's Restaurant
⓭ The Almshouses
⓮ The Court Inn Pub
⓯ To Bistro 21
⓰ Marks & Spencer

Helpful Hints

Internet Access: The **library,** across huge Millennium Place from the TI, has about 40 terminals with free Internet access (Mon–Fri 9:30–19:00, Sat 9:00–17:00, Sun 10:30–16:30, must join for free—bring ID, tel. 0191/386-4003).

Laundry: Durham has none within walking distance; ask at the TI for details if you're willing to drive or take a taxi.

Tours: The TI offers 1.5-hour city walking tours on summer weekends (£4, schedule varies but usually May–Sept Sat–Sun at 14:00—confirm with TI). **David Butler,** the town historian, gives excellent private tours (reasonable prices, tel. 0191/386-1500, dhent@dhent.fsnet.co.uk).

Harry Potter Sights: Durham Cathedral was used in the films, as were other nearby locations. For details, see page 728.

Getting Around Durham

Although all my recommended hotels, eateries, and sights are easily walkable in Durham, taxis are available to zip tired tourists to their B&Bs or back to the station (about £4, wait on west side of Framwellgate Bridge on Silver Street).

If you don't feel like walking Durham's hills, hop on the convenient **Cathedral Bus** (also called Service 40) that runs between the train station and the cathedral, with stops near the North Road bus station, Millburngate, Market Place, and some car parks (50p for all-day ticket, 3/hr, leaves train station Mon–Fri 7:55–17:30, Sat 9:10–17:30, Sun 9:50–16:50; last bus leaves cathedral Mon–Sat at 17:40, Sun at 17:00; toll tel. 0871-200-2233).

Self-Guided Walk

Welcome to Durham

• *Begin at Framwellgate Bridge (which connects the train station with the center).*

Framwellgate Bridge was a wonder when it was built in the 12th century—much longer than the river is wide and higher than seemingly necessary. It was well-designed to connect stretches of solid high ground, and to avoid steep descents to the marshy river. Note how elegantly today's Silver Street (which leads toward town) slopes into the Framwellgate Bridge. (Imagine that as late as the 1970s, this people-friendly lane was congested with traffic and buses.)

• *Follow Silver Street up the hill to the town's main square.*

Durham's **Market Place** retains the same platting the Prince Bishop gave it when he moved villagers here in about 1100. Each plot of land was the same width (about 8 yards). Find today's distinctly narrow buildings (Thomas Cook, Whittard, and the optician shop)—they still fit the 800-year-old plan. The rest of the buildings fronting the square are multiples of that first shop width. Plots were long and skinny, maximizing the number of shops that could have a piece of the Market Place action.

Examine the square's **statues.** Coal has long been the basis of this region's economy. The statue of Neptune was part of an

ill-fated attempt by a coal baron to bribe the townsfolk into embracing a canal project that would make the shipment of his coal more efficient. The statue of the fancy guy on the horse is Charles Stewart Vane, the Third Marquess of Londonderry. A general in Wellington's army, he was an Irish aristocrat who married a local coal heiress. A clever and aggressive businessman, he managed to create a vast business empire controlling every link in the coal business chain—mines, railroads, boats, harbors, and so on.

In the 1850s throughout England, towns were moving their markets off squares and into Industrial Age iron-and-glass market halls. Durham was no exception, and today its **indoor market** (which faces Market Place) is a funky 19th-century delight to explore (Mon–Sat 9:00–17:00). There are also outdoor markets in Market Square (Sat retail market 9:00–16:30, farmer's market third Thu of each month, 8:30–15:30, tel. 0191/384-6153, www.durhammarkets .co.uk).

Do you enjoy the sparse traffic in Durham's old town? It was the first city in England to institute a "congestion fee." Look where traffic enters the old town on the downhill side of the square. The bollard (series of short posts) is up, blocking traffic Monday through Saturday 10:00–16:00. Anyone can drive in...but it costs £2 to get out. This has cut downtown traffic by more than 50 percent. Locals brag that London (which now has a similar congestion fee) was inspired by their success.

• *Head up to the cathedral along Saddler Street. On the left, you'll see a bridge.*

A 12th-century construction, **Elvet Bridge** led to a town market over the river. Like Framwellgate, it was very long (17 arches) to avoid river muck and steep inclines. Even today, Elvet Bridge leads to an unusually wide road—a reminder that it was once swollen to accommodate the market action. Shops lined the right-hand side of Elvet Bridge in the 12th century as they do today. An alley separated the bridge from the buildings on the left. When the bridge was widened, it met the upper stories of the buildings on the left, which became "street level."

Central Durham

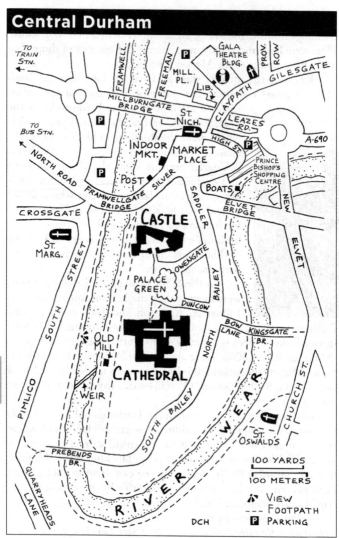

TO TRAIN STN.

TO BUS STN.

NORTH ROAD

CROSSGATE

ST. MARG.

PIMLICO

QUARRYHEADS LANE

FRAMWELL.

FREEMAN

MILL. PL.

P

GALA THEATRE BLDG.

PROV. ROW

GILESGATE

LIB.

MILLBURNGATE BRIDGE

ST. NICH.

CLAYPATH

LEAZES RD.

HIGH ST.

A-690

INDOOR MKT.

MARKET PLACE

PRINCE BISHOP'S SHOPPING CENTRE

POST

SILVER

FRAMWELLGATE BRIDGE

BOATS

ELVET BRIDGE

ELVET

NEW

CASTLE

SADDLER

OWENGATE

PALACE GREEN

DUNCOW

NORTH BAILEY

SOUTH STREET

OLD MILL

CATHEDRAL

BOW LANE

KINGSGATE BR.

WEIR

SOUTH BAILEY

RIVER WEAR

CHURCH ST.

ST. OSWALD'S

PREBENDS BR.

100 YARDS
100 METERS

↑ VIEW
--- FOOTPATH
P PARKING

DCH

The Scots were on the rampage in the 14th century. After their victory at Bannockburn in 1314, they pushed farther south and actually burned part of Durham. With this new threat, Durham's **city walls** were built. Because people settled within the walls, the population density soared. Soon open lanes were covered by residences, becoming tunnels (called "vennels"). A classic vennel leads to Saddlers Yard, a fine little 16th-century courtyard (immediately opposite Elvet Bridge). While these are cute today, centuries ago they were Dickensian nightmares...the filthiest of hovels.

The History of Durham

Durham's location, tucked inside a tight bend in the River Wear, was ideal for easy fortifications. But it wasn't settled until A.D. 995, with the arrival of St. Cuthbert's body (buried in Durham Cathedral). Shortly after that, a small church and fortification were built upon the site of today's castle and church to house the relic. The castle was a classic "motte-and-bailey" design (with the "motte," or mound, providing a lookout tower for the stockade encircling the protected area, or "bailey"). By 1100, the Prince Bishop's bailey was filled with villagers—and he wanted everyone out. This was *his* place! He provided a wider protective wall, and had the town resettle below, around today's Market Place. But this displaced the townsfolk's cows, so the Prince Bishop constructed a fine stone bridge (today's Framwellgate) connecting the new town to grazing land he established across the river. The bridge had a defensive gate, with a wall circling the peninsula and the river serving as a moat.

• *Continue up Saddler Street. Between the two* Georgian Window signs, *go through the purple door to see a bit of the medieval wall incorporated into the brickwork of a newer building and a turret from an earlier wall. Back on Saddler Street, you can see the ghost of the old wall. (It's exactly the width of the building now housing the Salvation Army.) Veer right at Owengate as you continue uphill, until you reach...*

The **Palace Green** was the site of the original 11th-century Saxon town, filling this green between the castle and an earlier church. Later the town made way for 12th-century Durham's defenses, which now enclose the green. With the threat presented by the Vikings, it's no wonder people found comfort in a spot like this.

The **castle** still stands—as it has for a thousand years—on its motte (man-made mound). The castle is now part of Durham University. Like Oxford and Cambridge, Durham U. is a collection of colleges scattered throughout the town. And, like Oxford and Cambridge, the town has a youthful liveliness because of its university. Look into the old courtyard from the castle gate. It traces the very first and smallest bailey. As future bishops expanded the castle, they left their coats of arms as a way of "signing" the wing they built. Because the Norman kings appointed the Prince Bishops here to rule this part of their realm, Durham was the seat of power for much of northern England. The bishops had their own army, and even minted their own coins (castle entrance by guided tour only, £5, 45 min, call ahead for schedule, 24-hr info tel. 0191/334-3800, www.dur.ac.uk/university.college/tours).

DURHAM

• *This walk ends at Durham's stunning* **cathedral**, *which is described next.*

Sights in Durham

▲▲▲Durham's Cathedral

Built to house the much-venerated bones of St. Cuthbert from Lindisfarne, Durham's cathedral offers the best look at Norman architecture in England. ("Norman" is British for "Romanesque.") In addition to touring the cathedral and its attached sights, try to fit in an evensong service.

Cost and Hours: Entry to the cathedral itself is free, though a £4 donation is requested. You must pay to enter its several interior sights: the climbable tower (£4), relic-filled treasury (£2.50), Monk's Dormitory (£1), and boring AV show (£1). It's open mid-July–Aug daily 9:30–20:00; Sept–mid-July Mon–Sat 9:30–18:00, Sun 12:30–17:30; opens daily at 7:30 for worship and prayer, tel. 0191/386-4266, www.durham cathedral.co.uk. A bookshop, cafeteria, and WC are tucked away in the cloisters. No photos, videos, or mobile phones are allowed inside the cathedral.

Tours: The cathedral offers regular tours in summer. If one's already in session, you're welcome to join (£4; late July–late Sept Mon–Sat at 10:30, 11:00, and 14:30; tours also possible near Easter and during school vacations in May and Oct, call or check website to confirm schedule, tel. 0191/386-4266).

Evensong: For a thousand years, this cradle of English Christianity has been praising God. To really experience the cathedral, go for an evensong service. Arrive early and ask to be seated in the choir. It's a spiritual Oz, as 40 boys sing psalms—a red-and-white-robed pillow of praise, raised up by the powerful pipe organ. If you're lucky and the service goes well, the organist will run a spiritual musical victory lap while the congregation breaks up (Tue–Sat at 17:15, Sun at 15:30, 1 hour, sometimes sung on Mon; visiting choirs nearly always fill in when choir is off on school break during mid-July–Aug; tel. 0191/386-4266).

Organ Recitals: During July and August on Wednesday evenings, you can catch a recital at the cathedral (£8, 19:30).

❍ **Self-Guided Tour:** Begin your visit outside the cathedral. From the Palace Green, notice how this fortress of God stands boldly opposite the Norman keep of Durham's fortress of man. The **exterior** of this awe-inspiring cathedral—if you look

Durham's Cathedral

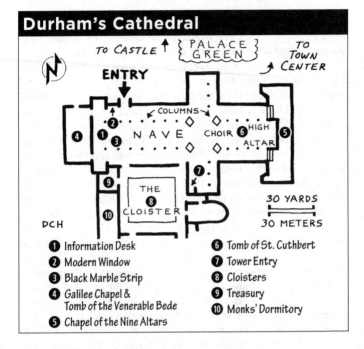

TO CASTLE ↑ { PALACE GREEN }   TO TOWN CENTER

ENTRY

← COLUMNS →

N A V E   CHOIR

HIGH ALTAR

THE CLOISTER

DCH

30 YARDS

30 METERS

❶ Information Desk
❷ Modern Window
❸ Black Marble Strip
❹ Galilee Chapel & Tomb of the Venerable Bede
❺ Chapel of the Nine Altars

❻ Tomb of St. Cuthbert
❼ Tower Entry
❽ Cloisters
❾ Treasury
❿ Monks' Dormitory

closely—has a serious skin problem. In the 1770s, as the stone was crumbling, workers crudely peeled it back a few inches. The scrape marks give the cathedral a bad complexion to this day. For proof of this odd "restoration," study the masonry 10 yards to the right of the door. The L-shaped stones in the corner would normally never be found in a church like this—they only became L-shaped when the surface was cut back.

At the cathedral **door,** the big, bronze, lion-faced knocker (a replica of the 12th-century original—now in the treasury) was used by criminals seeking sanctuary (read the explanation).

Immediately inside, at the **information desk,** church attendants are standing by, ready to answer your questions. Ideally, follow a church tour. The £1 pamphlet, *A Short Guide to Durham Cathedral,* is informative but dull.

Notice the **modern window** with the novel depiction of the Last Supper (above and to the left of the entry door). It was given to the church by a local department store in 1984. The shapes of the apostles represent worlds and persons of every kind, from the shadowy Judas to the brightness of Jesus. This window is a good reminder that the cathedral remains a living part of the community.

Near the info desk, the **black marble strip** on the floor was as close to the altar as women were allowed in the days when this was a Benedictine church (until 1540). Sit down (ignoring the black line) and let the fine proportions of England's best Norman nave—and arguably Europe's best Romanesque nave—stir you. Any frilly woodwork and stonework were added in later centuries.

The architecture of the **nave** is particularly harmonious because it was built in a mere 40 years (1093–1133). The round arches and zigzag carved decorations are textbook Norman. The church was also proto-Gothic, built by well-traveled French masons and architects who knew the latest innovations from Europe. Its stone and ribbed roof, pointed arches, and flying buttresses were revolutionary in England. Notice the clean lines and simplicity. It's not as cluttered as other churches for several reasons: Out of respect for St. Cuthbert, for centuries no one else was buried here; during Reformation times, sumptuous Catholic decor was cleaned out; and subsequent fires and wars destroyed what Protestants didn't.

Enter the **Galilee Chapel** (late Norman, from 1175) in the back of the nave. The paintings of St. Cuthbert and St. Oswald (seventh-century king of Northumbria) on the side walls of the side altar niche are rare examples of Romanesque (Norman) paintings. Facing this altar, look above to your right to see more faint paintings on the upper walls above the columns. Near the center of the chapel, the upraised tomb topped with a black slab contains the remains of the Venerable Bede, an eighth-century Christian scholar who wrote the first history of England. The Latin reads, "In this tomb are the bones of the Venerable Bede."

Back in the main church, stroll down the nave to the center, under the highest **bell tower** in Europe (218 feet). Gaze up. The ropes turn wheels upon which bells are mounted. If you're stirred by the cheery ringing of church bells, tune in to the cathedral on Sunday (9:15–10:00 & 14:30–15:30) or Thursday (19:30–21:00 practice, trained bell ringers welcome), when the resounding notes tumble merrily through the entire town.

Continuing east (all medieval churches faced east), you enter the **choir.** Monks worshipped many times a day, and the choir in the center of the church provided a cozy place to gather in this vast, dark, and chilly building. Mass has been said daily here in the heart of the cathedral for 900 years. The fancy wooden chairs are from the 17th century. Behind the altar is the delicately carved stone Neville Screen from 1380 (made of Normandy stone in London, shipped to Newcastle by sea, then brought here by wagon). Until the Reformation, the niches contained statues of 107 saints. Exit the choir from the far right side (south). Look for the stained-glass window (to your right) commemorating the church's 1,000th anniversary in 1995. The colorful scenes depict England's history, from coal miners to cows to computers.

Step down behind the high altar into the east end of the church, which contains the 13th-century **Chapel of the Nine**

Altars. Built later than the rest of the church, this is Gothic—taller, lighter, and relatively more extravagant than the Norman nave.

Climb a few steps to the **tomb of St. Cuthbert.** An inspirational leader of the early Christian Church in north England, St. Cuthbert lived in the Lindisfarne monastery on Holy Island (100 miles north of Durham). He died in 687. Eleven years later, his body was exhumed and found to be miraculously preserved. This stoked the popularity of his shrine, and pilgrims came in growing numbers. When Vikings raided Lindisfarne in 875, the monks fled with his body (and the famous illuminated *Lindisfarne Gospels,* now in the British Library in London). In 995, after 120 years of roaming, the monks settled in Durham on an easy-to-defend tight bend in the River Wear. This cathedral was built over Cuthbert's tomb.

Throughout the Middle Ages, a shrine stood here and was visited by countless pilgrims. In 1539, during the Reformation—whose proponents advocated focusing on God rather than saints—the shrine was destroyed. But pilgrims still come, especially on St. Cuthbert's feast day—March 20.

Other Cathedral Sights: The entry to the **tower** is in the south transept; the view from the tower will cost you 325 steps and £4 (Mon–Sat 10:00–16:00, closes at 15:00 in winter, last entry 20 min before closing; closed Sun, during events, and in bad weather; must be at least 4'3" tall, no backless shoes). The following sights are within the cloisters: The **treasury,** filled with medieval bits and holy pieces (including Cuthbert's coffin, vestments, and cross), fleshes out this otherwise stark building. The actual relics from St. Cuthbert's tomb are at the far end (treasury well worth the £2.50 admission, Mon–Sat 10:00–16:30, Sun 14:00–16:30). The **Monks' Dormitory,** now a library with an original 14th-century timber roof filled with Anglo-Saxon stones, is worth its £1 admission (likely Mon–Sat 10:00–16:00, Sun 12:30–16:00). Skip the unexceptional **AV show** about St. Cuthbert in the unexceptional undercroft (£1, Mon–Sat 10:00–15:00, no showings Sun, off-season also no showings Fri, closed Nov–early Jan).

Near the treasury you'll find the **WCs,** the **bookshop** (in the old kitchen), and the fine **Undercroft** cafeteria (daily 10:00–16:30, tel. 0191/386-3721).

Activities

Riverside Path—For a 20-minute woodsy escape, walk Durham's riverside path from busy Framwellgate Bridge to sleepy Prebends Bridge.

Boat Cruise and Rental—Hop on the *Prince Bishop* for a relaxing one-hour narrated cruise of the river that nearly surrounds

DURHAM

Durham (£6, Easter–Oct, for schedule call 0191/386-9525, check at TI, or go down to dock at Brown's Boat House at Elvet Bridge, just east of old town, www.princebishoprc.co.uk). Sailings vary based on weather and tides. For some exercise with the same scenery, you can rent a rowboat at the same pier (£4/hr per person, £10 deposit, Easter–Sept daily 10:00–18:00, last boat rental one hour before dusk, tel. 0191/386-3779).

Sleeping in Durham

(area code: 0191)

B&Bs

$$$ **Farnley Tower,** a luxurious B&B, has 13 large rooms with all the comforts. On a quiet street at the top of a hill, it's a 10-minute hike from the town center (Sb-£65, Db-£85, superior Db-£95, family room-£120, some rooms have views, paying with credit card costs 2 percent extra, phones in rooms, easy parking, inviting yard, evening meals at their adjacent, wildly inventive Gourmet Spot restaurant, The Avenue, tel. 0191/375-0011, fax 0191/383-9694, www.farnley-tower.co.uk, enquiries@farnley-tower.co.uk, Raj and Roopal Naik).

$$ **Victorian Town House B&B** offers three spacious, tastefully updated rooms in an 1853 townhouse in a nice residential area just down the hill from the train station (Sb-£50–60, Db-£80–85, family room-£85–105, cash only, 2 Victoria Terrace, 5-min walk from train or bus station, tel. 05601/459-168, www.durham bedandbreakfast.com, stay@durhambedandbreakfast.com, friendly Jill and Andy).

$$ **Castleview Guest House** rents six airy, restful rooms in a classy, well-located house close to Silver Street (Sb-£55, Db-£80, cash only, 4 Crossgate, tel. 0191/386-8852, www.castle-view.co.uk, castle_view@hotmail.com, Mike and Anne Williams).

$$ *Student Housing Open to Anyone:* **Durham Castle,** a student residence actually on the castle grounds facing the cathedral, rents rooms during the summer break (generally end of June–Sept only). Request a room in the stylish main building, or you may get one of the few bomb shelter–style modern dorm rooms (S-£28.50, Sb-£40, D-£51, Db-£70, fancier Db-£180, elegant breakfast hall, parking-£5 on Palace Green or free with voucher from reception, University College, The Castle, Palace Green, tel. 0191/334-4108 or 0191/334-4106, fax

Sleep Code

(£1 = about $1.60, country code: 44)
S = Single, **D** = Double/Twin, **T** = Triple, **Q** = Quad, **b** = bathroom,
s = shower only. You can assume credit cards are accepted
unless otherwise noted.

    To help you sort easily through these listings, I've divided
the rooms into three categories based on the price for a
standard double room with bath (during high season):

  $$$ **Higher Priced**—Most rooms £85 or more.
   $$ **Moderately Priced**—Most rooms between £50-85.
    $ **Lower Priced**—Most rooms £50 or less.

0191/374-7470, www.dur.ac.uk/university.college, durham.castle
@durham.ac.uk).

Hotels

$$$ Durham Marriott Hotel Royal County scatters its 150 posh,
four-star rooms among several buildings sprawling along the river
near the city center. The Leisure Club has a pool, sauna, Jacuzzi,
and fitness equipment (Db-£150, £30 less on weekends, includes
breakfast, 2 restaurants, bar, parking, Old Elvet, tel. 0191/386-
6821 or toll tel. 0870-400-7286, fax 0191/386-0704, www
.marriott.co.uk).

    $$ Kingslodge Hotel & Restaurant, a renovated lodge with
charming terraces, an attached restaurant, a pub, and a champagne
and oyster bar, is a cushy option convenient to the train station
(Sb-£60, Db-£75, family room-£95, includes breakfast, parking, Waddington Street, Flass Vale, tel. 0191/370-9977, www
.kingslodge.info, kingslodgehotel@yahoo.co.uk).

    $$ Travelodge Durham's 57 simple rooms are in a converted
1844 train station, with the former waiting room now housing
the reception desk (Db-£55–65 but check website for deals, cold
breakfast delivered to room—not worth price, half-mile northeast
of cathedral, off A690 at Station Lane, Gilesgate, toll tel. 0871-
984-6136, fax 0191/386-5461, www.travelodge.co.uk).

Eating in Durham

Durham is a university town with plenty of lively, inexpensive eateries. Stroll down North Road, across Framwellgate Bridge, through
Market Place, and up Saddler Street, and consider these places.

    Melanzana, just over Elvet Bridge on the other side of town,
is a popular Italian restaurant, with £8–11 pizzas and pastas and

DURHAM

£11–19 dinners in an inviting setting (Mon–Sat 11:00–22:00, Sun 11:00–21:00, even cheaper during happy hour, 96 Elvet Bridge, tel. 0191/384-0096).

Café Rouge, a chain restaurant with French-bistro food and decor, is just east of Framwellgate Bridge (21 Silver Street, tel. 0191/384-3429). **Bella Italia,** next door and down the stairs, is another chain, with surprisingly good food (20 Silver Street, tel. 0191/386-1060).

Bimbi's, on Market Place, is a standby for fish-and-chips (Mon–Sat 11:00–18:30, Sun 12:00–18:30).

Saddler Street, leading from Market Place up to the cathedral, is lined with eateries. The hip **Hide Café,** with youthful, jazz-filled ambience, serves the best modern continental cuisine in the old town (£6–10 lunches, £8–14 meals, Mon–Sat 12:00–15:00 & 18:00–21:00, Sun 12:00–15:00, reservations smart, 39 Saddler Street, tel. 0191/384-1999).

Shaheen's is the place for good Indian cuisine (£6–10 meals, Tue–Sat 17:00–21:30, closed Sun–Mon, 48 North Bailey Street, just past turnoff to cathedral, tel. 0191/386-0960).

The Almshouses, on the Palace Green across from the cathedral, serves tasty, light meals in a cheap cafeteria setting (£6–7 plates, daily July–Aug 9:00–20:00, Sept–June 9:00–17:00, tel. 0191/386-1054).

The Court Inn, on the outskirts of town, is a local favorite for traditional pub grub (£7–10 meals, daily 11:00–22:20, 5-min walk east of old town over Elvet Bridge, Court Lane, tel. 0191/384-7350).

Bistro 21, with modern French/Mediterranean fare and good seafood, works well for drivers looking for a non-touristy splurge (£15–22 main dishes, £15–18 two- or three-course dinner specials Mon–Thu 18:00–22:00, Fri–Sat 18:00–19:00; open Mon–Sat 12:00–14:00 & 18:00–22:00, Sun 12:00–15:00, 1.5 miles northwest of town, Aykley Heads, tel. 0191/384-4354).

Supermarket: **Marks & Spencer** is in the old town, just off the main square (Mon–Sat 9:00–18:00, Sun 11:00–17:00, 4 Silver Street, across from post office). You can **picnic** in Market Square, sitting around the tiered stone base of the horseman's statue, or on the benches and grass outside the cathedral entrance (but not on the Palace Green, unless the park police have gone home).

Durham Connections

From Durham by Train to: York (3–4/hr, 45 min), **Lake District** (train to Penrith—1–2/hr, 2.5–3.5 hrs, change in Carlisle and Newcastle; then bus to Keswick—hourly Mon–Sat, Sun 8/day, 40 min), **London** (2/hr, 3 hrs), **Hadrian's Wall** (take train to

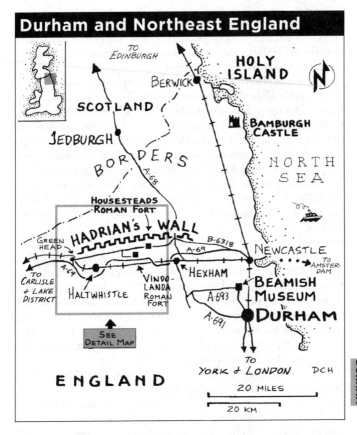

Durham and Northeast England

TO EDINBURGH

HOLY ISLAND

BERWICK

SCOTLAND

JEDBURGH

BAMBURGH CASTLE

B O R D E R S

A-68

NORTH SEA

HOUSESTEADS ROMAN FORT

HADRIAN'S WALL

GREEN HEAD

B-6318

A-69

NEWCASTLE

TO AMSTER-DAM

TO CARLISLE + LAKE DISTRICT

A-69

HEXHAM

VINDO-LANDA ROMAN FORT

HALTWHISTLE

A-693

BEAMISH MUSEUM

A-691

DURHAM

SEE DETAIL MAP

TO YORK & LONDON

DCH

E N G L A N D

20 MILES

20 KM

N

DURHAM

Newcastle—1–4/hr, 15 min, then a bus or a train/bus combination to Hadrian's Wall), **Edinburgh** (at least hourly, 1.75 hrs), **Bristol** (near Bath, 2/hr, 5 hrs). Train info: toll tel. 0845-748-4950.

Near Durham: Beamish Museum

This huge 300-acre open-air museum, which re-creates the years 1825 and 1913 in northeast England, takes at least three hours to explore. Vintage trams and cool circa-1910 double-decker buses shuttle visitors to the four stations: Colliery Village, The Town, Pockerley Manor/Waggonway, and Home Farm. Tram routes are more plentiful than bus routes, but attendants on both are helpful and knowledgeable. Signs on the trams advertise a variety of 19th-century products, from "Borax, for washing everything" to "Murton's Reliable Travelling Trunks." This isn't a wax museum. If you touch the exhibits, they may smack you. Attendants at each stop happily explain everything. In fact, the place is only really interesting if you talk to the attendants. In 2008, the "Westoe netty"—a circa 1890 men's public WC—was acquired and rebuilt near the 1913 railway station. The loo became famous in 1972 as the subject in a painting by a local artist.

Cost and Hours: £16, £11 with bus receipt, £6 in winter, choose the Beamish Unlimited Pass at no extra charge for a 2-day visit; Easter–Oct open daily 10:00–17:00; Nov–Easter only The Town, Colliery Village, and Tramway are open, Tue–Thu and Sat–Sun 10:00–16:00, closed Mon and Fri and most of Dec; check events schedule as you enter, last tickets sold at 15:00 year-round, tel. 0191/370-4000, www.beamish.org.uk, museum@beamish.org.uk.

Getting There: By **car,** the museum is five minutes off the A1/M1 motorway (one exit north of Durham at Chester-le-Street/ Junction 63, well signposted, 12 miles and a 25-min drive north-west of Durham). To get to Beamish from Durham by public transportation, catch **bus** #21 or #X1 from the bus station (3–4/ hr, 1 hr, £3.30 day pass; transfer at Chester-le-Street to bus #X8, #28, or #28A at central bus kiosk a half-block away, get handy bus schedule at Durham TI, toll tel. 0871-200-2233, www.traveline .org.uk). When you get off the bus at Beamish, the museum is a five-minute walk down the hill. Show your bus receipt for the £5 museum discount. To catch the bus leaving Beamish, the bus stop for bus #X8 is on the side of the street near the pub; the stop for #28 and #28A is on the opposite side of the street.

◐ **Self-Guided Tour:** Start with the **Colliery Village** (com-pany town around a coal mine), with a school, a church, miners' homes, and a fascinating—if claustrophobic—20-minute tour into the Mahogany drift mine. Your guide will tell you about beams collapsing, gas exploding, and flooding; after that cheerful speech, you'll don a hard hat as you're led into the mine.

The Town is a bustling street featuring a 1913 candy shop (the chocolate room in back is worth a stop for chocolate fans), a dentist's office, a Masonic hall, a garage, a working pub (The Sun Inn, Mon–Sat 11:00–16:30, Sun 12:00–16:30), Barclays Bank, and a hardware store featuring a variety of "toilet sets" (not what you think). For lunch, try the Tea Rooms cafeteria (upstairs, daily 10:30–16:30). If the weather is good, picnic on the grassy pavilion next to the tram stop.

Pockerley Manor and the Waggonway has an 1820s manor house with attendants who have plenty to explain. Enjoy the lovely view from the gardens behind the manor, then enter through the kitchen, where they bake bread several times a week. Ask for a sample if you have a taste for tough rye. Adjacent is the re-created first-ever passenger train from 1825, which takes modern-day visitors for a spin on 1825 tracks—a hit with railway buffs. **Home Farm** is the least interesting section.

DURHAM

Hadrian's Wall

This is one of England's most thought-provoking sights. In about A.D. 122, during the reign of Emperor Hadrian, the Romans built

this great stone wall. Its actual purpose is still debated. Although Rome ruled Britain for 400 years, it never quite ruled its people. The wall may have been used for any number of reasons: to define the northern edge of the empire, to protect Roman Britain from invading Pict tribes from the north (or at least cut down on pesky border raids), to monitor the movement of people, or to simply give an otherwise bored army something to do. (Emperors understood that nothing's more dangerous than a bored army.) Stretching 73 miles coast to coast across the narrowest stretch of northern England, it was built and defended by nearly 20,000 troops. Not just a wall, this was a military complex that included forts, ditches, settlements, and a road on the south side. At every mile of the wall, a castle guards a gate, and two turrets stand between each castle. The mile castles are numbered—80 of them cover the 73 miles, because a Roman mile was slightly shorter than our mile.

Today, several chunks of the wall, ruined forts, and museums thrill history buffs. About a dozen Roman sights cling along the wall's route; the best are Housesteads Roman Fort and Vindolanda. Housesteads shows you where the Romans lived; Vindolanda's museum shows you how they lived.

The Hadrian's Wall National Trail runs 84 miles, following the wall's route from coast to coast (for details, see www.national trail.co.uk/HadriansWall).

Portions of the wall are in Northumberland National Park. The **Once Brewed National Park Visitor Centre** is located along the Hadrian's Wall bus route and has walking guides to the wall and information on the area (Easter–Oct daily 9:30–17:00, Nov– Easter 10:00–15:00 Sat–Sun only, pay parking lot, Military Road, Bardon Mill, tel. 01434/344-396, www.northumberlandnational park.org.uk, tic.oncebrewed@nnpa.org.uk).

Getting to Hadrian's Wall

Hadrian's Wall is anchored by Newcastle on the east and Carlisle on the west. Driving is the most convenient way to see Hadrian's Wall; if you're coming by train, consider renting a car for the day at either Newcastle or Carlisle.

DURHAM

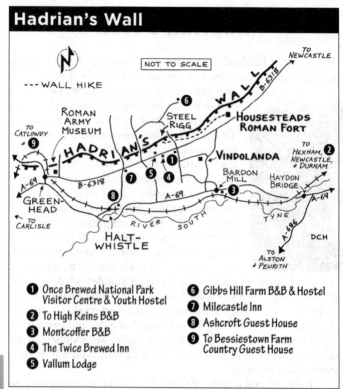

Hadrian's Wall

NOT TO SCALE

--- WALL HIKE

1. Once Brewed National Park Visitor Centre & Youth Hostel
2. To High Reins B&B
3. Montcoffer B&B
4. The Twice Brewed Inn
5. Vallum Lodge
6. Gibbs Hill Farm B&B & Hostel
7. Milecastle Inn
8. Ashcroft Guest House
9. To Bessiestown Farm Country Guest House

DURHAM

Public transportation has improved, but the train only gets you *near* the wall. You still need to take a local bus to the Roman sights. If you want to see everything—or even hike part of the wall—stay overnight in a nearby town.

The free "Great Days Out" pamphlet, available at local visitor centers and train stations, has information on how to do the wall, including bus and train timetables, suggested itineraries, and more.

You can also call Haltwhistle's helpful **TI** for schedule information (Easter–Oct Mon–Sat 9:30–13:00 & 14:00–17:00, Sun 13:00–17:00; Nov–Easter Mon–Sat 9:30–12:00 & 13:00–15:30, closed Sun; tel. 01434/322-002, www.hadrians-wall.org).

If you're just passing through for the day on the bus, it's almost impossible to stop and see all the sights—you'll need to study the bus schedule carefully and prioritize. It's also hard to bring your luggage with you. Store your luggage in Newcastle or Carlisle if you're day-tripping (see train information below). If you must travel with luggage, visit Housesteads Roman Fort or Vindolanda, where you can leave baggage at the entrance while exploring.

If you want to walk the wall, **Hadrians Haul** baggage-courier service will send your luggage ahead (£5/bag per pick-up, mobile 07967-564-823, www.hadrianshaul.com).

By Car

Take B6318; it parallels the wall and passes several viewpoints, minor sights, and "severe dips." (If there's a certified nerd or bozo in the car, these road signs add a lot to a photo portrait.) Buy a good local map to help you explore this interesting area more easily and thoroughly.

By Train and Bus

During the peak season, one bus conveniently links all the sights to Newcastle and Carlisle. During the off-season, you will have to take a train and then either a local bus or a taxi to visit the wall.

Between Easter and October, take **Hadrian's Wall bus #AD122** to get to all the Roman sights (£8 day pass, tel. 01434/322-002, www.hadrians-wall.org). The bus runs between Carlisle and Newcastle, stopping at the important Roman sights. Several buses a day have onboard guides on part of the trip (noted on the schedule). For travelers spending the night, this bus also stops near the Once Brewed Youth Hostel, which is about two blocks from The Twice Brewed Inn (both recommended under "Sleeping and Eating near Hadrian's Wall," later).

From Newcastle by Bus #AD122: The bus leaves Newcastle Central Train Station daily at 9:00. If you miss the bus, you will need to take the train to Hexham or Haltwhistle, which has more frequent bus service to the wall.

From Newcastle by Train to: Hexham (Mon–Fri 2/hr, Sat–Sun hourly, 30 min), **Haltwhistle** (Mon–Fri hourly, Sat–Sun almost hourly, 1 hr). Catch bus #AD122 in either town to visit the wall. You can store luggage at the Newcastle train station.

From Carlisle by Bus #AD122: Leaves from English Street outside Carlisle Train Station (Mon–Sat 8/day, Sun 5/day).

From Carlisle by Train to: Hexham (Mon–Sat hourly, Sun 10/day, 45 min), **Haltwhistle** (Mon–Sat hourly, Sun 11/day, 30 min). Catch bus #AD122 in either town to visit the wall. Next to the Carlisle train station, you can store your luggage at **Bar Solo** (£2/bag per day, Mon–Sat 9:00–23:00, opens at 11:00 on Sun, tel. 01228/631-600).

Off-Season Options: If you're traveling off-season (Nov–Easter), you can take a train/bus or a train/taxi combination. For the train/bus option, take a train to Haltwhistle, then bus #185 to the Roman Army Museum, or bus #681 to Vindolanda and Housesteads Roman Fort.

If you're staying near the wall, your B&B host can arrange

a taxi (Turnbull tel. 01434/320-105, one-way about £10 from Haltwhistle to Housesteads Roman Fort, arrange for return pickup or have museum staff call a taxi).

Sights at Hadrian's Wall

▲▲**Housesteads Roman Fort**—With its tiny museum, powerful scenery, and the best-preserved segment of the wall, this is your best single stop at Hadrian's Wall. All Roman forts were the same rectangular shape and design you see here, containing a commander's headquarters, barracks, and latrines (lower end); this fort even has a hospital. The fort was built right up to the wall, which is on the far side. From the parking lot and gift shop, it's a half-mile, mostly uphill walk to the entrance of the sprawling fort and minuscule museum (£4.50 for sight and museum—pay up at fort, not at gift shop; daily Easter–Sept 10:00–18:00, Oct–Easter closes at 16:00 or dusk, parking-£3, tel. 01434/344-363, www.english-heritage.org.uk/housesteads). At the car park are WCs, a snack bar, and a gift shop. You can leave your luggage at the gift shop (same hours as fort, tel. 01434/344-525).

▲▲**Hiking the Wall**—From Housesteads, hike west along the wall speaking Latin. For a good, craggy, three-mile walk along the wall, hike between Housesteads and Steel Rigg (free guides available at Once Brewed Visitor Centre). You'll pass a castle sitting in a nick in a crag (milecastle #39, called Castle Nick). There's a parking lot near Steel Rigg (take the little road up from the Twice Brewed Inn). East of Steel Rigg you'll see the "Robin Hood Tree," a large symmetrical tree

(in a little roller-coaster gap) that was featured in the movie *Robin Hood: Prince of Thieves* (with Kevin Costner, 1991).

▲**Vindolanda**—This larger Roman fort (which actually predates the wall by 40 years) and museum are just south of the wall. Although Housesteads has better ruins and the wall, Vindolanda has the better museum, revealing intimate details of Roman life. It's an active dig—from Easter through September, you'll see the work in progress (usually daily, weather permitting). Eight forts were built on this spot. The Romans, by carefully sealing the foundations from each successive fort, left modern-day archaeologists with seven yards of remarkably well-preserved artifacts to excavate: keys, coins, brooches, scales, pottery, glass, tools, leather shoes, bits of cloth, and even a wig. Impressive examples of early Roman writing were recently discovered here. And though the actual letters—written on thin pieces of wood—are in London's British Museum, see the interesting video here and read the translations, including the first known example of a woman writing to a woman (an invitation to a birthday party). These varied letters, about parties held, money owed, and sympathy shared, bring Romans to life in a way that stones alone can't.

From the free parking lot, you'll pay at the entrance, then walk 500 yards of grassy parkland decorated by the foundation stones of the Roman fort and a full-size replica chunk of the wall. At the far side are the museum, gift shop, and cafeteria.

Cost and Hours: £5.20, £8 combo-ticket includes Roman Army Museum, daily April–Sept 10:00–18:00, mid-Feb–March and Oct–mid-Nov 10:00–17:00, mid-Nov–mid-Feb 10:00–16:00, last entry 45 min before closing, can leave luggage at entrance, tel. 01434/344-277, www.vindolanda.com.

Roman Army Museum—This museum, a few miles farther west at Greenhead, is redundant if you've seen Vindolanda. Its film offers a good eagle-eye view of a portion of the wall (£4.20, or buy £8 combo-ticket that includes Vindolanda, same hours as Vindolanda, but closed mid-Nov–mid-Feb, tel. 016977/47485).

Sleeping and Eating near Hadrian's Wall

(£1 = about $1.60, country code: 44)

Near Hexham
(area code: 01434)

$$ High Reins offers four rooms in a stone house built by a shipping tycoon in the 1920s (Sb-£45, Db-£66, cash only, ground-floor bedrooms, lounge, 1 mile west of train station on the western outskirts of Hexham, Leazes Lane, tel. 01434/603-590, www.high reins.co.uk, pwalton@highreins.co.uk, Jan and Peter Walton).

In Bardon Mill
(area code: 01434)

$$ Montcoffer, a restored country home, is decorated with statues, old enameled advertising signs, and other artifacts collected by owner John McGrellis and his wife, Dehlia, whose textile art is displayed in and around your room (Sb-£48, Db-£78, includes hearty breakfasts, ground-floor bedrooms, 2 miles from Vindolanda, Bardon Mill, tel. 01434/344-138, mobile 07912-209-992, www.montcoffer.co.uk, john-dehlia@talk21.com).

$$ The Twice Brewed Inn, two miles west of Housesteads and a half-mile from the wall, rents 14 rooms and serves real ales and decent pub grub all day (pub open daily 11:00–23:00, food served daily 12:00–21:00). It's a friendly pub that serves as the community gathering place (S-£32, D-£55, Db-£70–80, free Internet access for hotel guests, otherwise £1/30 min, Military Road, Bardon Mill, tel. 01434/344-534, www.twicebrewedinn .co.uk, info@twicebrewedinn.co.uk).

$ Once Brewed Youth Hostel is a comfortable place near the Twice Brewed Inn and right next door to the Once Brewed National Park Visitor Centre (£16–19/bed with sheets in 4- to 8-bed room, £3 extra for non-members, breakfast-£4.65, packed lunch-£5, dinner-£9, reception open daily 8:00–10:00 & 16:00–22:00, hostel closed Dec–Jan, Military Road, Bardon Mill, tel. 01434/344-360, fax 01434/344-045, www.yha.org.uk, oncebrewed@yha.org.uk). The Hadrian's Wall bus #AD122 stops here several times a day.

Other B&Bs include **$$ Vallum Lodge** (Db-£75–80, Military Road, tel. 01434/344-248, www.vallum-lodge.co.uk) and **$$ Gibbs Hill Farm B&B and Hostel** (Db-£60–70, 5-min drive from Housesteads and Vindolanda, tel. 01434/344-030, www .gibbshillfarm.co.uk).

Milecastle Inn cooks up all sorts of exotic game and offers the best dinner around, according to hungry national park rangers (daily 12:00–20:30, smart to reserve, North Road, tel. 01434/ 321-372).

In Haltwhistle
(area code: 01434)

$$ Ashcroft Guest House, a former vicarage, is 400 yards from the Haltwhistle train station and 200 yards from a Hadrian's Wall bus stop. The family-run B&B has nine rooms, pleasant gardens, and views from the comfy lounge (Sb-£38, Db-£76, four-poster Db-£88, ask about family deals and two-bedroom suite, free Wi-Fi, 1.5 miles from the wall, Lanty's Lonnen, tel. 01434/320-213, www.ashcroftguesthouse.co.uk, info@ashcroftguesthouse .co.uk, Geoff and Christine James).

Near Carlisle
(area code: 01228)

$$$ Bessiestown Farm Country Guest House, located northwest of the Hadrian sights, is convenient for drivers connecting the Lake District and Scotland. It's a quiet, soothing stop in the middle of sheep pastures (Sb-£57, Db-£98, family room-£99–110, fancier suites-£130, discounts for 3-night stays; in Catlowdy, midway between Gretna Green and Hadrian's Wall just north of Carlisle; tel. 01228/577-219, fax 01228/577-019, www.bessiestown .co.uk, info@bessiestown.co.uk, Margaret Sisson).

Holy Island and Bamburgh Castle

This area is worthwhile only for those with a car.

▲Holy Island

Twelve hundred years ago, this "Holy Island" was Christianity's toehold on England. It was the home of St. Cuthbert. We know it today for the *Lindisfarne Gospels*, decorated by monks in the seventh century with some of the finest art from Europe's "Dark Ages" (now in the British Museum). It's a pleasant visit—a quiet town with a striking castle (not worth touring) and an evocative priory.

Lindisfarne Priory: The museum in the priory is tiny but instructive. It's adjacent to the ruined abbey (£4.50; April–Sept daily 9:30–17:00; Oct daily 9:30–16:00; Nov–Jan Mon and Sat–Sun 10:00–14:00, closed Tue–Fri; Feb–March daily 10:00–16:00; tel. 01289/389-200, www.english-heritage.org.uk/LindisfarnePriory). You can wander the abbey grounds and graveyard, and pop in to the church without paying.

Holy Island is reached by a two-mile causeway that's cut off daily by high tides. Tidal charts are posted, warning you when this holy place becomes Holy Island—and you become stranded.

For TI and tide information, check with the **Berwick TI** (generally May–Sept Mon–Sat 10:00–17:00, Sun 11:00–15:00; Oct–April Mon–Sat 10:00–16:00, closed Sun; tel. 01289/330-733, berwicktic@northumberland.gov.uk). Park at the pay-and-display lot and walk five minutes into the town.

▲▲Bamburgh Castle

About 10 miles south of Holy Island, this grand castle dominates the Northumbrian countryside and overlooks Britain's loveliest beach. The place was bought and passionately refurbished by Lord Armstrong, a Ted Turner–like industrialist and engineer in the 1890s. Its interior, lined with well-described history, feels lived-in because it still is—with Armstrong family portraits and aristocratic-yet-homey knickknacks hanging everywhere. Take advantage of the talkative guides posted throughout the castle.

DURHAM

The included **Armstrong Museum** features the inventions of the industrial family that has owned the castle through modern times (£7.50, daily March–Oct 10:00–17:00, last entry at 16:00, closed Nov–Feb, tel. 01668/214-515, www.bamburghcastle.com). Rolling dunes crisscrossed by walking paths lead to a vast sandy beach and lots of families on holiday.

WALES

WALES

Wales, a country the size of Massachusetts, is located on a peninsula on the west coast of the Isle of Britain, facing the Irish Sea. Longer than it is wide (170 miles by 60 miles), it's shaped somewhat like a miniature Britain. The north is mountainous, rural, and sparsely populated. The south, with a less-rugged topography, is where two-thirds of the people live (including the capital, Cardiff, pop. 320,000). The country has 750 miles of scenic, windswept coastline and is capped by Mount Snowdon, which, at 3,560 feet, is taller than any mountain in England.

Despite centuries of English imperialism, the Welsh language (or Cymraeg, pronounced kum-RAH-ig) remains alive and well...

better than its Celtic cousins of Gaelic in Scotland or Cornish in Cornwall, which survive only on the fringe or on life-support. Though everyone in Wales speaks English, one in five can also speak the native tongue. In the northwest, well over half the population is fluent in Welsh, and uses it in everyday life. Listen in.

Most certainly *not* a dialect of English, the Celtic Welsh tongue sounds to foreign ears like the Middle Earth languages from *The Lord of the Rings*. One of Europe's oldest languages, Welsh has been written down since about A.D. 600, and was spoken 300 years before French or German. Today, the Welsh language and those who speak it are protected by law, the country is officially bilingual, and signs always display both languages (e.g., Cardiff/Caerdydd). In schools it's either the first or the required second language; in many areas, English isn't used in classes at all until middle school.

Though English has been the dominant language in Wales for many years (and most newspapers and media are in English), the Welsh people cherish their linguistic heritage as something that sets them apart. In fact, a line of the Welsh national anthem goes, "Oh, may the old language survive!"

Speaking Welsh

Welsh pronunciation is tricky. The common "ll" combination sounds roughly like "thl" (pronounced as if you were ready to make an "l" sound and then blew it out). As in Scotland, "ch" is a soft, guttural k, pronounced in the back of the throat. The Welsh "dd" sounds like the English "th," f = v, ff = f, w = the "u" in "push," y = i. Non-Welsh people often make the mistake of trying to say a long Welsh name too fast, and inevitably trip themselves up. A local tipped me off: Slow down and say each syllable separately, and it'll come out right. For example, Llangollen is thlang-GOT-hlen.

Although there's no need to learn any Welsh (because everyone also speaks English), make friends and impress the locals by learning a few polite phrases:

Hello	**Helo**	hee-LOH
Goodbye	**Hwyl**	hoo-il
Please	**Os gwelwch yn dda**	os GWELL-uck UN thah
Thank you	**Diolch**	dee-olkh
Wales	**Cymru**	KUM-ree
England	**Lloegr**	THLOY-ger

In a pub, toast the guy who just bought your drink with *Diolch* and *Yeach-hid dah* (YECH-id dah, "Good health to you").

Wales has some traditional foods worth looking for, particularly lamb dishes and leek soup *(cawl)*. In fact, the national symbol is the leek, ever since medieval warriors—who wore the vegetable on their helmets in battle—saved the land from Saxon invaders. Cheese on toast is known as "Welsh rarebit" (or "Welsh rabbit"; the name is a throwback to a time when the poor Welsh couldn't afford much meat in their diet). At breakfast you might get some "Welsh cakes," basically a small squashed scone. Cockles and seaweed bread were once common breakfast items—but don't expect your hotel to serve them.

Wales' three million people are mostly white and Christian (Presbyterian, Anglican, or Catholic). Like their UK counterparts, they enjoy football (soccer), but rugby is the unofficial Welsh sport, more popular in Wales than in any country outside of New Zealand. Other sports are cricket and snooker (similar to billiards).

The Welsh love their choirs. Every town has a choir (men's or mixed) that practices weekly. Visitors are usually welcome to observe, and very often they follow the choir down to the pub afterward for a good old-fashioned beer-lubricated sing-along.

WALES

Take in a weekly choir practice at one of the following towns in North Wales (note that some towns have more than one choir, and schedules are subject to change—confirm the schedule with a local TI or your B&B before making the trip, or go to www.home comingwales.com and click the "Choirs" tab): **Ruthin** (mixed choir Thu 20:00 except Aug at Tabernacle Church, tel. 01824/703-757), **Llangollen** (two men's choirs: Fri 19:30 except Jan at Hand Hotel, 21:00 pub singsong afterward, hotel tel. 01978/860-303; the other choir meets Wed 20:00 at Neuadd Goffa on High Street, tel. 01691/600-242), **Denbigh** (men's choir Tue 19:30–21:30 at the Eirianfa Centre, tel. 01824/790-524, www.denbigh-choir.co.uk), **Llandudno** (men's choir rehearsals Mon and Wed 19:30–21:00 except Aug, near Conwy, tel. 01248/681-159), and **Caernarfon** (Tue 20:00 in the gallery at Victoria Dock, no practice in Aug, tel. 01286/672-633, www.cormeibioncaernarfon.org). Additionally, many of these groups regularly perform concerts—inquire for the latest schedule.

The Welsh flag features a red dragon on a field of green and white. The dragon has been a symbol of Wales since at least the ninth century (maybe even from Roman days). According to legend, King Arthur's men carried the dragon flag to battle.

Welsh history stretches back into the mists of prehistoric Britain. The original Celtic tribes were conquered by the Romans, who built forts and cities, and (later) introduced Christianity. As Rome fell, Saxon tribes like the Angles from Germany conquered "Angle-land" (England) but failed to penetrate Wales. Brave Welsh warriors, mountainous terrain, and the 177-mile man-made ditch-and-wall known as Offa's Dyke helped preserve the country's unique Celtic/Roman heritage. In 1216, Wales' medieval kingdoms unified under Llywelyn Fawr ("the Great").

This brief unification ended in 1282, however, when King Edward I of England invaded and conquered, forever ending Wales' sovereignty. To solidify his hold on the country, Edward built a string of castles (at Caernarfon, Conwy, and many other places— see sidebar on page 474). He then named his son and successor the "Prince of Wales," starting the tradition (which continues to today's Prince Charles) of England's heir to the throne bearing that ceremonial title. Despite an unsuccessful rebellion in 1400, led by Owen Glendower (Owain Glyndwr), Wales has remained under English rule since 1282. In 1535, the annexation was formalized under Henry VIII.

By the 19th century, Welsh coal and iron stoked the engines of Britain's Industrial Revolution, and its slate was exported to shingle roofs throughout Europe. The stereotype of the Welsh as poor, grimy-faced miners continued into the 20th century. They began the slow transition from mining, factories, and sheep-farming to the service-and-software economy of the global world.

In recent decades the Welsh have consciously tried to preserve their local traditions and language. In 1999, Wales was granted its own parliament, the National Assembly, with powers to distribute the national budget. Though still ruled by the UK government in London, Wales now has a measure of independence and self-rule.

Less urbanized and less wealthy than England, Wales consists of miles of green land where sheep graze (because the soil is too poor for crops). Because it's a cheap weekend destination spot, the country is becoming popular for English drinkers who pour over the border to drink the cheap beer, before stumbling home on Sunday. This can make some Welsh border towns surprisingly rowdy on Saturday nights.

I've focused my coverage of Wales on the north, which has the highest concentration of castles, natural beauty, and attractions. A few South Wales sights that are convenient to visit from Bath are covered in the Near Bath chapter.

Try to fit a rare bit of Welsh sights into your itinerary. Clamber over a castle, eat a leek, count sheep in a field, catch a rugby match, or share a pint of bitter with a baritone. Open your ears to the sound of words as old as the legendary King Arthur. "May the old language survive!"

NORTH WALES

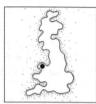

Wales' top historical, cultural, and natural wonders are found in the northern part of the country. From towering Mount Snowdon to lush forests to desolate moor country, North Wales is a poem written in landscape. For sightseeing thrills and diversity, North Wales is Britain's most interesting slice of the Celtic crescent. But be careful not to be waylaid by the many gimmicky sights and bogus "best of" lists. The region's economy is poor, and they're wringing every possible pound out of the tourist trade. Sort through your options carefully.

Planning Your Time

On a three-week Britain trip, give North Wales two nights and a day. It'll give you mighty castles, a giant slate mine, and some of Britain's most beautiful scenery. Many visitors are charmed and decide to stay an extra day.

By Public Transportation: Use Conwy as a home base, and skip Ruthin. From Conwy, you can get around Snowdonia and Caernarfon by bus, train, or private driving tour.

By Car: Drivers interested in a medieval banquet should set up in Ruthin and do this ambitious loop: 9:00–Drive over Llanberis mountain pass to Caernarfon (with possible short stops at Trefriw Woolen Mills, Betws-y-Coed, Pen-y-Gwryd Hotel Pub, and Llanberis); 12:00–Caernarfon Castle (catch the noon tour and 13:00 movie in Eagle Tower, and climb to the top for the view); 13:30–Browse through Caernarfon town and have lunch; 14:30–Drive the scenic road (A4085) to Blaenau Ffestiniog; 15:30–Tour Llechwedd Slate Mine; 17:30–Drive home to Ruthin;

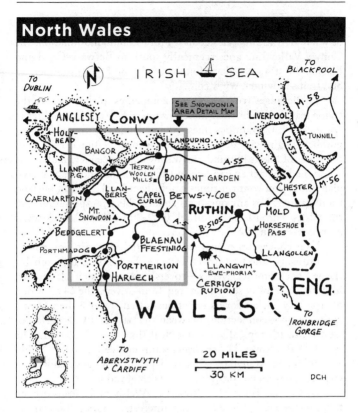

North Wales

19:00–Arrive home; 19:30–Arrive for 19:45 medieval banquet at castle (if you didn't already do it on the night of your arrival). For all the details, see "One-Day North Wales Blitz Tour from Ruthin" on page 499.

With a second day, slow down and take the train up Mount Snowdon. With more time and a desire to hike, consider using the mountain village of Beddgelert as your base.

If you have no interest in the castle banquet, skip Ruthin and shorten your drive time by spending two nights in Conwy or Beddgelert.

Getting Around North Wales

By Public Transportation: North Wales (except Ruthin) is surprisingly well-covered by a combination of buses and trains (though you'll want to get an early start to allow ample time to visit several destinations).

A main **train** line runs along the north coast from Chester to Holyhead via Llandudno Junction, Conwy, and Bangor, with hourly departures (toll tel. 0845-748-4950, www.nationalrail.co.uk or www.arrivatrainswales.co.uk). From Llandudno Junction, the Conwy Valley line goes scenically south to Betws-y-Coed and Blaenau Ffestiniog (5/day Mon–Sat, 3/day on Sun in summer, no Sun trains in winter, www.conwy.gov.uk/cvr).

Public **buses** (run by various companies) pick up where the trains leave off. Get the *Public Transport Information* booklet at any local TI. Certain bus lines—dubbed "Sherpa" routes (the bus numbers begin with #S)—circle Snowdonia National Park with the needs of hikers in mind (www.snowdoniagreenkey.co.uk).

Schedules get sparse late in the afternoon and on Sundays; plan ahead and confirm times carefully at local TIs and bus and train stations. For any questions about public transportation, call the Wales Travel Line at toll tel. 0871-200-2233, or check www.traveline-cymru.info.

Your choices for money-saving public-transportation **passes** are confusing. The Red Rover Ticket—the simplest and probably the best bet for most travelers—covers all buses west of Llandudno, including Sherpa buses (£5/day, buy from driver). The £4 Snowdon Sherpa Day Ticket covers select buses that traverse the national park—but not connections between the park and Caernarfon or Conwy, so it's typically a worse deal than the Red Rover. The North Wales Rover Ticket covers trains and certain buses within a complex zone system (£7–22/day, depending on how many zones you need; buy on bus or train, www.taith.gov.uk).

By Private Tour: Mari Roberts, a Welsh guide, leads driving tours of the area tailored to your interests. Tours in her car are generally out of Conwy, but she will happily pick you up in Ruthin or Holyhead (£15/hr, 4-hour minimum, tel. 01824/702-713, marihr @talktalk.net).

Ruthin

Ruthin (RITH-in; "Rhuthun" in Welsh) is a low-key market town whose charm is in its ordinary Welshness. The people are the sights, and admission is free if you start the conversation. The market square, castle, TI, bus station, and in-town accommodations are all within five blocks of each other. Ruthin is Welsh as can be, makes a handy base for drivers doing  North Wales, and serves up an interesting medieval banquet.

Orientation to Ruthin

(area code: 01824)
Ruthin (pop. 5,000) is situated atop a gentle hill surrounded by undulating meadows. Simple streets branch out from the central roundabout (at the former medieval marketplace, St. Peter's Square) like spokes on a wheel.

Tourist Information

Ruthin does not have its own TI. Inquiries for this area are handled by the TI in nearby Llangollen (see page 466).

Internet Access: You'll find two terminals and Wi-Fi at Crown House Café, which also serves up drinks and thoughtfully prepared light lunches in an inviting indoor-or-out ambience (Internet-£3/hr, £3–4 sandwiches, Mon 9:00–16:00, Tue–Fri 9:00–17:00, Sat 9:30–16:00, closed Sun, 11 Well Street, tel. 01824/704-516, www.crownhousecatering.co.uk).

Sights in Ruthin

▲▲**Ruthin Castle Welsh Medieval Banquet**—English, Scottish, Irish, and Welsh medieval banquets are all variations

on the same touristy theme. This one, while growing more tired and tacky each year, remains fun and more culturally justifiable (if that's necessary) than most. The hefty £40-per-person price tag stings slightly less when you consider that you're paying both for a huge, good meal and an evening of entertainment.

You'll be greeted with a chunk of bread dipped in salt, which, the maiden explains, will "guarantee your safety." Your medieval master of ceremonies then seats you, and the candlelit evening of food, drink, and music rolls gaily on. You'll enjoy harp music, angelic singing, jokey stories and poems, and lots of other entertainment. With fanfare (and historical explanation), wenches serve mead, spiced wine, and four hearty traditional courses (pace yourself). Drink from a pewter goblet, wear a bib, and eat with your fingers and a dagger. Food and mead are unlimited—just ask for more. The hardworking actors—who go for it with gusto, and are really quite talented—kick up their energy even more if the audience reacts loudly. For the most entertaining experience, don't hesitate to clap, holler, stamp your feet, or pound the table. Yes, I know it's cheesy—but just enjoy it and

NORTH WALES

Ruthin

RIVER CLWYD

ROAD

TROED Y RHIW (ROAD)

TESCO

PARK ROAD

SCHOOL ROAD

PRIOR ST

CHURCH

MARKET SQUARE

MOUNT ST

MARKET ST

WYNNSTAY ST

STATION RD.

WERNFECHAN ROAD

TO CHESTER VIA MOLD

RUTHIN GAOL

STREET

UPPER CLWYD

CLWYD

NANTCLWYD HOUSE

CASTLE ST

WELL ST

RECORD ST

STREET

RHOS ST

A-494

LLANFAIR ST.

CASTLE

CORWEN ST

DOG LANE

DCH

TO CERRIGYDRUDION

PARKING

TO LLANGOLLEN, LLANFAIR

1. Manorhaus Hotel & Rest.
2. Castle Hotel
3. Wynnstay Arms Rooms & Restaurants
4. Gorphwysfa Guest House
5. To Eyarth Station B&B
6. To Bryn Awel B&B
7. On the Hill Restaurant
8. Leonardo's Delicatessen
9. Finn's Fish-and-Chips
10. Ruthin Castle (Banquet)
11. Crown House Café (Internet)
12. To Offa's Dyke Path

go along for the ride (starts at 19:45, arrive 15–30 min early, lasts about 2.5 hours, runs several nights per week year-round depending upon demand—most likely on weekends, vegetarian options, call for reservations, easy doorstep parking, down Castle Street from town square, tel. 01824/702-664, www.ruthincastle.co.uk). Ask to be seated with other readers of this book to avoid being stuck amidst a dreary tour group. They also run murder-mystery dinners—see their website for details.

▲**Ruthin Gaol**—Get a glimpse into crime and punishment in 17th- to early-20th-century Wales in this 100-cell prison. Explore the "dark" and condemned cells, give the dreaded hand-crank a whirl, and learn about the men, women, and children who did time here before the prison closed in 1916. The included audioguide—partly narrated by a jovial "prisoner" named Will—is very good, informative, and engaging. You'll find out why prison kitchens came with a cat, why the bathtubs had a severe case of ring-around-the-tub, how they got prisoners to sit still for their mug shots (and why these photos often included the prisoners' hands), and why the prison was renovated into the "panopticon" style in the late 19th century (£3.50, family-£10; March–Oct daily 10:00–17:00; Nov–Feb Sat–Sun and school holidays only 10:00–17:00; last entry one hour before closing, Clwyd Street, tel. 01824/708-281, www.ruthingaol.co.uk).

Nantclwyd House—This Elizabethan-era "oldest timbered townhouse in Wales"—a white-and-brown half-timbered house between the castle and the market square—recently underwent an award-winning £600,000 renovation (funded partly by the EU) to convert it into a museum. Seven decorated rooms give visitors a peek into the history of the house, which was built in 1435 (£3.60, April–Sept Fri–Sun 10:00–17:00, last entry 45 min before closing, closed Mon–Thu and Oct–March, Castle Street, tel. 01824/709-822, www.nantclwydydre.co.uk).

Walks—For a scenic and interesting one-hour walk, try the Offa's Dyke Path to Moel Famau (the "Jubilee Tower," a 200-year-old war memorial on a peak overlooking stark moorlands). The trail-head is a 10-minute drive east of Ruthin on A494.

▲▲**Welsh Choir**—The mixed choir performs weekly at the Tabernacle Church Chapel (Thu 20:00 except Aug, tel. 01824/703-757).

Sleeping in Ruthin

(area code: 01824)

For cheap sleeps, you'll have to stay at the youth hostels in Conwy or Caernarfon. Or, if you're driving, keep an eye out for rustic hostel-like "bunkhouses" that dot the North Wales countryside.

$$$ Manorhaus rents the classiest rooms in Ruthin. Its eight rooms are impeccably appointed with artsy-contemporary decor, and the halls serve as gallery space for local artists. Guests enjoy use of the sauna, steam room, fitness room, library, and mini-cinema in the cellar (Sb-£70–95, "compact" Db with lower ceilings-£95, standard Db-£110, superior Db-£130, pricier Db suite-£150, free Wi-Fi, recommended restaurant, Well Street, tel. 01824/704-830, fax 01824/707-333, www.manorhaus.com, post@manorhaus.com).

$$$ The **Castle Hotel,** not to be confused with the hotel at Ruthin Castle, is a modern but faded 18-room hotel on the town square (Sb-£50, Db-£100, family suites-£120–129, prices vary

Sleep Code

(£1 = about $1.60, country code: 44)
S = Single, **D** = Double/Twin, **T** = Triple, **Q** = Quad, **b** = bathroom, **s** = shower only. You can assume credit cards are accepted unless otherwise noted. Few of my accommodations in North Wales have elevators.

To help you sort easily through these listings, I've divided the rooms into three categories based on the price for a standard double room with bath:

$$$ Higher Priced—Most rooms £70 or more.
 $$ Moderately Priced—Most rooms between £45-70.
  $ Lower Priced—Most rooms £45 or less.

with demand, deals on website, front rooms are larger and overlook the square, back rooms are quieter—especially on weekends, 4 uneven funhouse floors with no elevator, St. Peter's Square, tel. 01824/702-479, fax 01824/703-488, www.castle-hotel-ruthin .co.uk, reception@castle-hotel-ruthin.co.uk).

$$$ Wynnstay Arms is a pub renting seven nicely updated rooms upstairs. As it's a dining pub rather than a rowdy drinking pub, noise isn't much of a problem (Sb-£45-55, Db-£70-90, Db suite-£95-105, depends on size and day, family room, special rates for B&B plus dinner, Wall Street, tel. 01824/703-147, www .wynnstayarms.com, reservations@wynnstayarms.com).

$$ Gorphwysfa Guest House ("Resting Place") is in a cozy 16th-century Tudor townhouse between the castle and the town square, next door to Ruthin's oldest house. The three rooms are huge, comfortable, and modern, while the public spaces are grand and Elizabethan—with wattle-and-daub construction, a library, a grand piano, and a breakfast room with a gigantic fireplace (Db-£60, Tb-£70, Qb-£80, less for 2-night stays, cash only, 8a Castle Street, tel. 01824/707-529, marg@gorphwysfa.fsnet.co.uk, Margaret O'Riain).

Near Ruthin

These places, just outside of town, are better for drivers.

$$$ Eyarth Station, an old railway station converted to a country B&B, rents six rooms in the scenic Vale of Clwyd, about a mile outside Ruthin. Jen loves to dole out travel advice and can suggest one-day driving routes for seeing North Wales (Sb-£50, Db-£72, family room-£86-96, all rooms on ground floor, closed Jan–Feb, beautiful sunroom for breakfast, swimming pool, Llanfair D.C., tel. 01824/703-643, www.eyarthstation.co.uk, stay@eyarth station.com).

$$ Bryn Awel, a traditional and charming farmhouse B&B with two rooms and a paradise garden, is run by chatty Beryl and John Jones in the hamlet of Bontuchel, just outside of Ruthin. Beryl, a prizewinning quilter, is helpful with travel tips and key Welsh words (Db-£55, 2-night minimum, use credit card for deposit but must pay in cash, parking, tel. 01824/702-481, beryljjones@msn.com). From Ruthin, take A494 (toward Bala) past the Ruthin Gaol, then the B5105/Cerrigydrudion road. Turn right after the little white church, at the *Bontuchel/Cyffylliog* sign. Look for the B&B sign on the right, 1.8 fragrant miles down a narrow road.

Eating in Ruthin

On the Hill serves hearty £3–6 lunches and £10–15 dinners—mostly made with fresh local ingredients—to an enthusiastic crowd. The Old World decor complements the good cuisine (Tue-Sat 12:00–14:00 & 18:30–21:00, closed Sun–Mon, 1 Upper Clwyd Street, tel. 01824/707-736).

The **Wynnstay Arms** pub on Well Street, two blocks below the main square, has two different restaurants, both classy and new-feeling. **Fusion Brasserie** serves modern European cuisine (£13–15 Sun brunch; open Wed–Sat 19:00–21:00, Sun 12:00–14:00, closed Mon–Tue). **Bar W** serves pub food (£5–6 sandwiches, £8–15 main dishes, food served Mon–Fri 12:00–14:00 & 17:30–21:30, Sat 12:00–21:30, Sun 12:00–19:30, tel. for both: 01824/703-147).

Manorhaus is the town splurge in a recommended hotel (described earlier), with updated Welsh and British dinners served in a mod art-gallery space (£24 for two courses, £30 for three courses, food served daily 18:30–21:00, reservations recommended, Well Street, tel. 01824/704-830).

Leonardo's Delicatessen is *the* place to buy a top-notch gourmet picnic. They have £3–4 made-to-order sandwiches and a small salad bar (Mon–Sat 9:30–17:30, closed Sun, 4 Well Street, just off the main square, tel. 01824/707-161).

Finn's is the local favorite for take-away fish-and-chips (£3, daily 11:00–22:00, in winter may close 14:00–16:00, near Ruthin Gaol at the bottom of Clwyd Street, at #45A, tel. 01824/704-737).

Ruthin Connections

Ruthin has poor connections to just about everywhere. Skip it unless you have a car.

From Ruthin: The following bus connections are sparse and irregular—get local help figuring out the best trip for your itinerary. Note that bus frequency (including the Ruthin–Corwen bus crucial for the first two connections) dwindles to near nothing on

Sundays: to **Llangollen** (Mon–Sat hourly, 1/day on Sun, 1.25 hrs, transfer in Corwen or Wrexham), **Betws-y-Coed** (hourly, 1.75–3 hrs, 1–3 transfers), **Conwy** (hourly, 2.25 hrs, 2–3 transfers on bus-and-train combo), **Chester** in England (2/hr, 1.5–2.25 hrs, 1–2 transfers; or take a 40-min taxi ride for around £35, set price up front).

Near Ruthin

▲▲Ewe-Phoria Sheepdog Show

Despite the goofy name, this really is a fun and fascinating peek into the world of sheep farmers and their frantically loyal, well-trained border collies. Aled Owen's working farm has diversified, turning traditional farming methods into an enjoyable, educational show. Drop in for the one-hour dog-and-sheep demo (Easter–Sept Wed and Fri at 13:00, also Sun at 13:00 in Aug only). First, you'll head into

the barn, where trained sheep enter one at a time to show the different breeds, followed by a sheep-shearing demonstration. Then you'll go outside to see the dogs rounding up the sheep. The shepherd guides the dog with nothing but whistles (£4.50; farm open Easter–Sept Wed, Fri, and Sun 12:00–15:00; closed Oct–Easter; café, just off A5 midway between Betws-y-Coed and Llangollen in Llangwm, tel. 01490/460-369, www.adventure-mountain.co.uk). They also have "rally carting" (go-carts on a gravel track) and "quad biking" (ATV treks into the hills)—see website for details.

Llangollen

Worth a stop if you have a car, Llangollen (thlang-GOTH-lehn) is a red-brick riverside town that's equal parts blue collar and touristy. The town is famous for its **International Musical Eisteddfod,** a very popular and crowded festival of folk songs and

dance (July 6–11 in 2010, tel. 01978/862-001, www .international-eisteddfod .co.uk). Two men's choirs practice weekly: one on Friday nights (19:30 except Jan at the Hand Hotel, 21:00 pub singsong afterward, hotel tel. 01978/860-303) and another on Wednesday nights (20:00 at Neuadd Goffa on High Street, tel. 01691/600-242).

The enthusiastic **TI** has the details on these events, the scenic steam-train trips, and other attractions (daily 9:30–17:30, Nov–March until 17:00, tel. 01978/860-828, www.llangollen.org.uk). They also serve as the TI for nearby Ruthin.

Llangollen's most interesting attraction is its **canal**, a narrow, shallow waterway up the hill and across the bridge from the town center. You can stroll along the canal or take one of two different boat rides from Llangollen Wharf: a horse-drawn boat down to the Cistercian abbey (£5, Easter–Oct, 45 min, hourly from 11:00 in summer, less off-season, tel. 01978/860-702, www.horsedrawnboats .co.uk), or a longer, motorized canal-boat trip over the remarkable Pontcysyllte aqueduct (£11, daily at 12:15 and 14:00, 2 hrs).

If you take a walk or the horse-drawn canal trip, you'll reach the lovely 13th-century Cistercian **Valle Crucis Abbey** (£2.70, April–Oct daily 10:00–17:00, last entry one hour before closing, free access to grounds Nov–March, tel. 01978/860-326, www .llangollen.com/valle.html). An even older cross, **Eliseg's Pillar,** is nearby.

Sleeping in Llangollen: **$$ Glasgwm B&B** rents four spacious rooms in a Victorian townhouse (Sb-£35, Db-£55–65, Abbey Road, tel. 01978/861-975, glasgwm@llangollen.co.uk, John and Heather).

Llangollen Connections: Llangollen is a 30-minute drive from Ruthin. You can take the bus to **Ruthin** (Mon–Sat hourly, 1/day on Sun, 1 hr, transfer in Corwen or Wrexham). From Llangollen, bus #X6 runs to **Betws-y-Coed** (Mon and Wed–Sat 3/day, Tue 2/day, none on Sun, 1 hr). Llangollen is also connected by bus with train stations at **Ruabon** (4/hr, 15 min) and **Wrexham** (4/hr, 35 min).

Conwy

Along with the Conwy Castle, this garrison town was built in the 1280s to give Edward I an English toehold in Wales. What's left today are the best medieval walls in Britain, surrounding a humble

town, crowned by the bleak and barren hulk of a castle that was awesome in its day (and still is). Conwy's charming High Street leads down to a fishy harbor that permitted Edward to restock his castle safely. Because the highway was tunneled under the town, a strolling ambience has returned to Conwy. Beyond the castle, the mighty Telford suspension bridge is a 19th-century slice of English imperialism, built in 1826 to better connect (and control) the route to Ireland.

Orientation to Conwy

(area code: 01492)
Conwy is an enjoyably small community of 4,000 people. The walled old town center is compact and manageable. Lancaster Square marks the center, where you'll find the bus "station" (a blue-and-white shelter), the unstaffed train station (the little white hut at the end of a sunken parking lot), and the start of the main drag, High Street—and my self-guided walk.

Tourist Information

The TI shares a building with the castle's ticket office and gift shop (April–Oct daily 9:00–17:00; Nov–March Mon–Sat 9:30–16:00, Sun 11:00–16:00; tel. 01492/592-248, www.visitconwy.org.uk). Because Conwy's train and bus stations are unstaffed, ask at the TI about train or bus schedules for your departure. The TI sells books and maps on the area, such as *The Ascent of Snowdon* (£3). The TI also reserves rooms for a £2 fee and makes theater bookings.

Don't confuse the TI with the tacky "Conwy Visitors Centre," a big gift shop near the station with a goofy little £1 video show.

Helpful Hints

Trains: When taking the train to Conwy, tell the conductor as you get on that Conwy's where you want to get off; when catching a train in Conwy, you'll need to flag one down or it won't stop. Train schedules are posted above the train platforms at either end of the bridge. The nearest "real" train station is in **Llandudno Junction,** visible a mile away beyond the bridges, and a safer bet for more regular trains. Make sure to ask for trains that stop at Llandudno Junction, and not Llandudno proper, which is a seaside resort farther from Conwy.

Internet Access: Get online at the **library** at the bottom of High Street (free, Mon and Thu–Fri 10:00–17:30, Tue 10:00–19:00, Sat 10:00–13:00, closed Wed and Sun, tel. 01492/596-242). **Coffi Conway** has free Wi-Fi for paying customers (reasonable sandwiches and desserts, Easter–Oct daily 10:00–17:00, shorter hours in winter, tel. 01492/596-436).

Car Rental: A dozen car-rental agencies in the city of Llandudno (1.5 miles away, north of Llandudno Junction) offer cars for about £40 per day and can generally deliver to you in Conwy; the Conwy TI has a list. The closest is **Avis,** a 10-minute walk from Conwy (Conwy Road, Llandudno Junction, toll tel. 0870-608-6388).

Medieval Festivals: The town is eager emphasize its medieval history, with several events and festivals planned for 2010—ask at the TI or at your B&B to see what's going on during your visit. Festival or no, if you're in the market for a battle axe or perhaps some chain mail, pop into **The Knight Shop,** located across the street from the castle, near the bridge.

Self-Guided Walk

Welcome to Conwy

This brief orientation walk leads you through the heart of Conwy: Down its main street, then along its harborfront. It takes about 30 minutes. Begin at the top of High Street, at the center of the old town, on...

Lancaster Square: The square's centerpiece is a **column** honoring the town's founder, the Welsh prince Llywelyn the Great. Looking past the blue-and-white bus stop, find the cute pointed archway built into the medieval wall so the train could get through.

Side-trip up the lane called York Place (past Alfredo Restaurant) to a wall of **slate memorials** from the 1937 coronation of King George (his wife, the Queen Consort Elizabeth, was the late Queen Mum). Notice the Welsh-language lesson here: the counties (shires, or *sir*), months (only *mai* is recognizable), days, numbers, and alphabet with its different letters.

• *Go back out to the square and head down to the harborfront on Conwy's main drag...*

High Street: Wander downhill, enjoying the slice-of-Welsh-life scene: tearooms, bakery, butcher, newsstand, old-timers, and maybe even suds in the fountain. **Plas Mawr** (on the left), the first Welsh house built within the town walls, dates from the time of Henry VIII (well worth touring). Opposite Castle Hotel, a lane leads to the **Carmel Church,** a fine example of stark Methodist "statement architecture": stern, with no frills, and typical of these churches built in the early 20th century.

Aberconwy House marks the bottom of High Street. One of the oldest houses in town, it's a museum (not worth touring). Conwy was once a garrison town filled with half-timbered buildings just like this one. From here **Berry Street** leads left. Originally called "burial street," it was a big ditch for mass burials during a 17th-century plague.

• *Continue downhill, crossing under the wall to the harborfront.*

Harborfront: The stones date from the 13th century, when the harbor served Edward's castle and town. (The harborfront

NORTH WALES

Conwy

1. Castle Hotel & Dawson's Cuisine
2. Gwynfryn B&B
3. The Town House B&B
4. Castle View B&B
5. The Bridge Inn & Pub
6. Castlebank Hotel
7. Bryn B&B
8. Llys Llywelyn B&B
9. To Conwy Hostel
10. To Glan Heulog Guest House, Bryn Derwen & Fishermore B&Bs
11. To Whinward House B&B
12. Bistro Bach
13. Amélie's Bistro
14. Alfredo Restaurant
15. Conwy Pantry & Pen-y-Bryn Tea Room
16. Anna's Tea Rooms & Conwy Outdoor Shop
17. Raj Indian Restaurant
18. The Galleon Fish-and-Chips
19. Fisherman's Fish-and-Chips
20. Spar Grocery
21. Coffi Conwy (Wi-Fi)
22. The Knight Shop
23. Bus Stop

NORTH WALES

street is still called "King's Quay.") Conwy was once a busy slate port. Slate, barged downstream to here, was loaded onto big three-mast ships and transported to the Continent. Back when much of Europe was roofed with Welsh slate, Conwy was a boomtown. In 1900, it had 48 pubs. All the mud is new—the modern bridge caused this part of the river to silt up.

Conwy's harbor is now a laid-back area locals treat like a town square. In fact, the town recently constructed a handy promenade to make this space even more inviting. On summer evenings, the action is on the quay. The scene is mellow, multigenerational, and

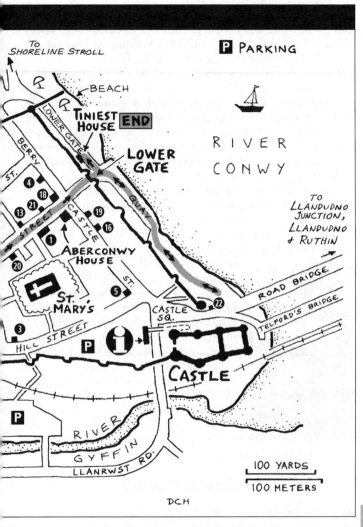

To SHORELINE STROLL

P PARKING

BEACH

Lower Gate

TINIEST HOUSE | END

LOWER GATE

RIVER CONWY

BERRY ST.

LOWER GATE

QUAY

4

18

21

13

CASTLE STREET

19

1

16

ABERCONWY HOUSE

20

ST. MARY'S

5

ST.

22

TO LLANDUDNO JUNCTION, LLANDUDNO & RUTHIN

ROAD BRIDGE

TELFORD'S BRIDGE

CASTLE SQ.

3

HILL STREET

P

i

CASTLE

P

RIVER GYFFIN

LLANRWST RD.

100 YARDS

100 METERS

DCH

perfectly Welsh. It's a small town and everyone is here enjoying the local cuisine—"chips," ice cream, and beer—and savoring that great British pastime: torturing little crabs.

• *Let's join the Conwy people-parade by walking a little loop along the harbor. Start by strolling to the right—to the end of the harbor next to Conwy's top sight, its* **castle**.

Near the castle, the harbormaster's house fills the former customs building. The **lifeboat house** welcomes visitors. Each coastal town has a house like this one, outfitted with a rescue boat suited to the area—in the shallow waters around Conwy, inflatable boats work best. You'll see *Lifeboats* stickers around town, marking homes of people who donate to the valuable cause of the Royal National Lifeboat Institution (RNLI)—Britain's all-volunteer and totally donation-funded answer to the Coast Guard.

• *Head back toward the gate where you emerged onto this promenade.*

Mussels, historically a big "crop" for Conwy, are processed "in the months with an r" by the **Mussels Museum.** In the other months, it's open to visitors (free, Easter–Aug daily 10:30–16:30). Also check out the striking new sculpture on the quay—a giant clump of mussels carved from dark-gray limestone. The benches are great for a picnic (two recommended fish-and-chips shops are back through the gate) or a visit with the noisy gulls.

The **Liverpool Arms pub** was built by a captain who ran a ferry service to Liverpool in the 19th century, when the North Wales coast was discovered by English holiday-goers. Today it remains a salty and characteristic hangout. Nearby, the **Queen Victoria tour boat** departs from here (£5, lazy 30-min cruise, nearly hourly 11:00–17:00 depending on tides, pay on boat, tel. 07917/343-059).

It's easy to miss **The Smallest House in Great Britain,** but don't. It's red, 72 inches wide, 122 inches high, and worth £1 to pop in and listen to the short audioguide tour. No WC—but it did have a bedpan (April–Oct roughly Mon–Sat 10:00–17:30, Sun 11:00–16:30, closed Nov–March, tel. 01492/593-484).

• *Our tour is finished. From this quay, there's a peaceful half-mile shoreline stroll along the harbor promenade (from the tiny house, walk through the wall gate and keep going).*

Sights in Conwy

▲**Conwy Castle**—Dramatically situated on a rock overlooking the sea with eight linebacker towers, this castle has an interesting story to tell. Built in just four years, it had a water gate that allowed safe entry for English boats in a land of hostile Welsh subjects (£4.70, or £7 combo-ticket with Plas Mawr; April–Oct daily 9:00–17:00; Nov–March Mon–Sat 9:30–16:00, Sun 11:00–16:00; last entry 30 min before closing, tel. 01492/592-358, www.cadw .wales.gov.uk). Guides wait

inside to take you on a one-hour, £1.50 tour. They usually depart about once per hour (no set schedule). If the guide booth is empty, look for the group and join it, or check the clock to see when the next tour departs.

▲**City Wall**—Much of the wall, with its 22 towers and castle and harbor views, can be walked for free. Start at Upper Gate (the highest point) or Berry Street (the lowest), or do the small section at the castle entrance. In the evening, some of the entry stairs up to the wall may be gated and locked.

▲**Plas Mawr**—A rare house from 1580, this was built during the reign of Elizabeth I. It was the first Welsh home to be built within Conwy's walls. (The Tudor family had Welsh roots—and therefore relations between Wales and England warmed.) Billed as "the oldest house in Wales," Plas Mawr offers a delightful look at 16th-century domestic life, but you must be patient enough to spend an hour following the excellent included audioguide. Historically accurate household items bring the rooms to life, as does the refreshing lack of velvet ropes—you're free to wander as you imagine life in this house. As a bonus, one display explains the long process involved in restoring historic buildings (this house was restored in the 1990s). Docents, who are posted in some rooms, are happy to point out what's original and chat about how the restoration was done.

Visitors stepping into the house in the 16th century were wowed by the heraldry over the fireplace. This symbol, now repainted in its original bright colors, proclaimed the family's rich lineage and princely stock. The kitchen came with all the circa-1600 conveniences: hay on the floor to add a little warmth and soak up spills; a hanging bread cage to keep food away from wandering critters; and a good supply of fresh meat in the pantry (take a whiff). Upstairs, the lady of the house's bedroom doubled as a sitting room—with a finely carved four-poster bed and a foot warmer by the chair. At night the bedroom's curtains were drawn to keep in warmth. In the great chamber next door, hearty evening feasting was followed by boisterous gaming, dancing, and music. And fixed above all of this extravagant entertainment was...more heraldry, pronouncing those important—if unproven—family connections and leaving a powerful impact on impressed guests. On the same floor is a well-done exhibit on health and hygiene in medieval Britain—you'll be grateful that you were born a few centuries later (£5.10, or £7 combo-ticket with Conwy Castle, April–Sept Tue–Sun 9:30–17:00, last entry 45 min before closing, closed Mon and Oct–March, tel. 01492/580-167, www.cadw.wales.gov.uk).

St. Mary's Parish Church—Sitting lonely in the town center, Conwy's church was the centerpiece of a Cistercian abbey that stood here a hundred years before the town. The Cistercians were French

King Edward's Castles

In the 13th century, the Welsh, unified by two great princes named Llywelyn, created a united and independent Wales. The English king Edward I fought hard to end this Welsh sovereignty. In 1282, Llywelyn the Last was killed (and went to where everyone speaks Welsh). King Edward spent the next 20 years building or rebuilding 17 great castles to consolidate his English foothold in troublesome North Wales. The greatest of these

(such as Conwy Castle) were masterpieces of medieval engineering, with round towers (tough to undermine by tunneling), castle-within-a-castle defenses (giving defenders a place to retreat and wreak havoc on the advancing enemy...or just wait for reinforcements), and sea access (safe to restock from England).

These castles were English islands in the middle of angry Wales. Most were built with a fortified grid-plan town attached, and were filled with English settlers. (With this blatant abuse of Wales, you have to wonder, where was Greenpeace 700 years ago?) Edward I was arguably England's best monarch. By establishing and consolidating his realm (adding Wales to England), he made his kingdom big enough to compete with the other rising European powers.

monks who built their abbeys in lonely places, "far from the haunts of man." Popular here because they were French and *not* English, the Cistercians taught locals farming and mussel-gathering techniques. Edward moved the monks 12 miles upstream but kept the church for his town. Notice the tombstone of a victim of the 1805 Battle of Trafalgar just left of the north transept. On the other side of the church, a tomb containing seven brothers and sisters is marked "We Are Seven." It inspired William Wordsworth to write his poem of the same name. The slate tombstones look new even though many are hundreds of years old; slate weathers better than marble (cemetery always open, church may be staffed June–Aug Mon–Fri 10:00–12:00 & 14:00–16:00, tel. 01492/593-402).

Near Conwy

Llandudno—This genteel Victorian beach resort, a few miles away, is bigger and better-known than Conwy. It was built after the advent of the railroads, which made the Welsh seacoast easily accessible to the English industrial heartland. In the 1800s,

NORTH WALES

Castle-lovers will want to tour each of Edward's five great-est castles (see map on page 490). With a car and two days, this makes one of Europe's best castle tours. I'd rate them in this order:

Caernarfon is the most entertaining and best presented.

Conwy is attached to the cutest medieval town, and has the best public transport.

Harlech is the most dramatically situated, on a hilltop (£3.60, tel. 01766/780-552, TI open March–Oct, www.harlech.com).

Beaumaris, surrounded by a swan-filled moat, is the last, largest, and most romantic (£3.60, tel. 01248/810-361).

Criccieth (KRICK-ith), built in 1230 by Llywelyn and later renovated by Edward, is also dramatic and remote (£3, tel. 01766/522-227).

All the above castles have the same opening hours: April–Oct daily 9:00-17:00; Nov–March Mon–Sat 9:30-16:00, Sun 11:00-16:00; last entry 30 min before closing (with one exception: Criccieth is closed Mon–Thu in winter).

CADW, the Welsh version of the National Trust, sells a three-day Explorer Pass that covers many sights in Wales. If you're planning to visit at least three of the above castles, the pass will probably save you money (three-day pass: £11.50 for 1 person, £18.50 for 2 people, £26.50 for a family; seven-day pass for about £6 more per person; available at castle ticket desks). For photos and more information on the castles, as well as information on Welsh historic monuments in general, check www.cadw .wales.gov.uk.

the notion that bathing in seawater was good for your health was trendy, and the bracing sea air was just what the doctor ordered. These days, Llandudno remains popular with the English, but you won't see many other foreigners strolling its long pier and line of old-time hotels.

Hill Climb—For lovely views across the bay to Llandudno, take a pleasant walk (40 min one-way) along the footpath up Conwy Mount (follow Sychnant Pass Road past the Bryn B&B, look for fields on the right and a sign with a stick figure of a walker).

Sleeping in Conwy

(£1 = about $1.60, country code: 44, area code: 01492)
Conwy's hotels are overpriced, but its B&Bs include some good-value gems. Nearly all have free parking (ask when booking), and most are happy to accommodate dietary needs in their breakfast offers (the local butcher, who supplies many of these B&Bs, even makes gluten-free sausages). There's no launderette in town.

NORTH WALES

Inside Conwy's Walled Old Town

$$$ Castle Hotel, along the main drag, rents 28 elegant rooms where Old World antique furnishings mingle with modern amenities. Peter and Bobbi Lavin, who co-own the hotel with chef Graham Tinsley, are eager to make your stay comfortable (Sb-£70–80, premium Sb-£90–99, Db-£115–145, premium Db-£125–165, deluxe Db-£140–185, posh Jacuzzi suite-£225–265, rates vary with season and room size, 10 percent discount if you show this book at check-in in 2010, free Wi-Fi, High Street, tel. 01492/582-800, fax 01492/582-300, www.castlewales.co.uk, mail@castlewales.co.uk). The hotel has a recommended restaurant and a bar.

$$$ The Town House B&B is a colorful place renting five tidy, bright, updated rooms—some with views—between the train station and the castle (S-£45, D-£65, Db-£70, Tb-£100, discount with this book for 2 or more nights—not valid with other discounts, cash only, no children under 12, vegetarian breakfast available, free Wi-Fi, 18 Rosehill Street, tel. 01492/596-454, mobile 07974-650-609, www.thetownhousebb.co.uk, thetownhousebb@aol.com, friendly Alan and Elaine Naughton and shy sheepdog Glenn).

$$ Gwynfryn B&B rents five recently renovated bright, airy rooms, each with eclectic decor, a DVD player, and access to a DVD library. The location is dead-center in Conwy, and out back there's a tiny patio for pleasant breakfasts in good weather (D-£60–65, Db-£65–80, price depends on season and room size, S/Sb possible for £5 less, no children under 12, free Internet access and Wi-Fi, fridge, 4 York Place, on the lane off Lancaster Square just past Alfredo Restaurant, tel. & fax 01492/576-733, www.gwynfrynbandb.co.uk, info@gwynfrynbandb.co.uk, energetic Monica and Colin). They also rent a renovated two-bedroom fisherman's cottage with castle views (£300–500/week).

$$ Castle View B&B, just inside the city wall near the waterfront, rents two cozy, pleasant rooms and has an upper "secret garden" out back. Front stoop aside, you won't see the castle from here; the name comes from a pub that used this building long ago (Db-£55, Tb-£75, cash only, call ahead, 3 Berry Street, tel. 01492/596-888, elainepritchard156@hotmail.com, warm Elaine and Ernest Pritchard). Ernest is a huuuuge *Lord of the Rings* fan.

$$ The Bridge Inn rents five fine but forgettable (and forgotten) rooms above its pub. Check in at the bar for these somewhat stuffy accommodations. While the floor just above the pub can be noisy, particularly on weekend nights, the top floor is quieter (Sb-£45, Db-£65, family room-£85, possible discount for 2-night stay, some views, Wi-Fi, separate entrance from pub, intersection of Rosehill and Castle Streets, tel. 01492/573-482, www.bridge-conwy.com).

NORTH WALES

Just Outside the Wall

The first three options are a two-minute walk from Conwy's old town wall; the hostel is about 10 minutes uphill beyond those.

$$$ Castlebank Hotel is a small hotel with nine spacious rooms, a small bar, and an inviting lounge with a wood-burning fireplace that makes the Welsh winter cozy. Owners Jo and Henrique are doing a heroic job of rehabilitating a formerly dumpy hotel—and onetime Ministry of Agriculture building—into a dolled-up and comfortable home away from home. This place is well-equipped for families (S with private b down the hall-£40, Sb-£55–80, Db-£80–95, depends on season, 10 percent discount with this book for 2 or more nights through 2010—except on Bank Holiday weekends, family rooms, free Internet access, pay Wi-Fi, dinner available with advance reservation, easy parking, just outside town wall at Mount Pleasant, tel. 01492/593-888, www.castle bankhotel.co.uk, bookings@castlebankhotel.co.uk).

$$ Bryn B&B offers four large, clutter-free rooms with castle or mountain views in a big 19th-century house with the city wall literally in the backyard. Owner Alison Archard is justly proud of her fresh, organic breakfasts and is a pro at catering to special diets. This popular place books up quickly—reserve early (Sb-£50, Db-£70, Tb-£90, £5 extra for 1-night stays, ground-floor room available, free Wi-Fi, parking, on the right just outside upper gate of wall on Sychnant Pass Road, tel. 01492/592-449, www.bryn.org .uk, stay@bryn.org.uk).

$$ Llys Llywelyn B&B has five modest rooms, but the humor and pleasant nature of Alan Hughes—in his 70s and still a top-notch ski instructor—helps compensate (Sb-£35, Db-£50–55, 10 percent discount with this book in 2010, cooked breakfast-£2–5, pay Internet access, easy parking, ramp from parking lot allows access to first-floor rooms, next to Castlebank Hotel, Mount Pleasant, tel. 01492/593-257).

$ The well-run Conwy Hostel, welcoming travelers of any age, has super views from all 24 of its rooms (including eight doubles), and a spacious garden. Each room is equipped with either two, four, or six bunk beds and a shower; toilets are down the hall. The airy dining hall and glorious rooftop deck make you feel like you're in the majestic midst of Wales (beds in 4- to 6-bed rooms-£15–22 per person, Db-£40–50, depends on season and age—under 18 is cheaper, non-members pay £3 more, book in advance for doubles, breakfast-£5, Internet access, pay Wi-Fi, laundry, lockers, lunches and dinners, bar, elevator, parking, no lock-out times but office closed 10:00–14:00, Sychnant Pass Road, in Larkhill, tel. 01492/593-571, fax 01492/593-580, www.yha.org .uk, conwy@yha.org.uk). It's a 10-minute uphill walk from the upper gate of Conwy's wall: After passing Bryn B&B on your right, follow the road past several smaller streets and uphill as it bends a bit to the left.

Beyond the Old Town, on Llanrwst Road

These options are set high above Llanrwst Road, which skirts the south side of Conwy's old town wall on its way to Bodnant Garden, Trefriw Woolen Mills, and Betws-y-Coed. They're a longer walk from town than the rest of my listings (except the hostel), but offer a countryside experience close to town. To find them from the train station, exit the station from its farthest and lowest corner, go through the gate in the city wall to busy Llanrwst Road, and turn right. Glan Heulog and Bryn Derwen are about a six-minute walk from town (they share a huge Victorian house set back from the road and up a high bank—which allows for great first-floor views; look for signs at road level). The Fishermore is about eight minutes beyond that.

$$ Glan Heulog Guest House offers seven fresh, bright rooms and a pleasant enclosed sun porch. Practice speaking Welsh with your host, Stanley (Sb-£35–40, Db-£56–65, Tb-£75–80, family deals, price depends on room size, ask about healthy breakfast option, free Internet access and Wi-Fi, will pick up from train station, tel. 01492/593-845, www.snowdoniabandb.co.uk, info @snowdoniabandb.co.uk, Stan and Viv Watson-Jones).

$$ Bryn Derwen rents six airy, light-filled, newly refurbished rooms with what might be the town's nicest bedcovers (Sb-£32–37, Db-£54–58, family room-£68–79, cash only, free Wi-Fi, tel. 01492/596-134, www.conwybrynderwen.co.uk, info@conwy brynderwen.co.uk, Andrew and Gill).

$$ Fishermore B&B, a 15-minute walk from Conwy, is good for drivers and families. It's in a large house with a sprawling yard, a sweet garden patio, and three tidy if outdated rooms with flowery bedspreads (Db-£50–56, cash only, closed Oct–Easter, free Internet access, parking, 0.75-mile south of Conwy on Llanrwst Road, tel. 01492/592-891, www.northwalesbandb.co.uk, dyers @tesco.net, helpful Cath and Peter Dyer). After passing the first two B&Bs on Llanrwst Road, follow the road when it bends left (just after the school) and continue uphill, watching for the *B&B* sign on the right.

West of Town

$$$ Whinward House, a half-mile west of Conwy's town walls, works well for drivers, though the place is pricey. Because their three rooms lack any B&B formality—and because Chris and Janis quickly make you feel at home—staying here feels like sleeping in the spare room of old friends. Guests are encouraged to relax in the sunlit living room and the large garden. Hiking trails, two pubs, a marina, and a golf course are all within a short walk (Db-£70, free Internet access and Wi-Fi, Whinacres, tel. 01492/573-275, http://whinwardhouse.thefoxgroup.co.uk, whinwardhouse@aol .com). From the north gate in Conwy's town wall, head straight out along Bangor Road; after a minute's drive (or a 10-minute walk), turn right immediately before an overhead railroad bridge. Turn immediately right again onto Whinacres; the B&B is on the left (look for the sign on the gate). Chris and Janis are happy to pick up nondrivers at the train station.

Eating in Conwy

All of these places are inside Conwy's walled old town. For dinner, consider strolling down High Street, comparing the cute teahouses and workaday pubs.

The busy **Bistro Bach,** tucked away on Chapel Street, serves freshly prepared modern and traditional Welsh cuisine in a cozy wood-floor-and-candlelight setting. The menu (with tasty daily specials) is inventive, and the food must be the best in town (£13–16 meals with vegetables, potato, and salad; open Tue–Sat 18:30–21:00, closed Sun–Mon, reservations a must, tel. 01492/596-326).

Dawson's Cuisine, with dishes from award-winning chef Graham Tinsley, is a hit with locals and worth the splurge (£10–15 main dishes, food served daily 12:00–21:30, Fri–Sat until 22:00, reservations smart—especially weekends, at recommended Castle Hotel on High Street, tel. 01492/582-800). The hotel bar has the same menu (Mon–Sat 11:30–23:00, Sun 11:30–22:30).

Amélie's, named for the French film, is a bistro with great food in a relaxed loft overlooking High Street (£4–8 lunches, £11–16 dinners, Tue–Sat 11:00–14:15 & 18:00–21:15, closed Sun–Mon, 10 High Street, tel. 01492/583-142).

Alfredo Restaurant, a family-friendly place right on Lancaster Square, serves good, reasonably priced Italian food (£7–9 pizzas, £8–10 pastas, £12–18 main dishes, nightly from 18:00, last orders at 22:00, reservations recommended on weekends, York Place, tel. 01492/592-381, Christine).

Conwy Pantry dishes up cheap, hearty daily lunch specials, salads, and homemade sweets in a cheery setting (£4–6 lunches, daily 9:00–17:00, until 16:30 in winter, 26 High Street, tel. 01492/596-445). The same owners run the **Pen-y-Bryn** tea room next door (daily 10:00–17:00, 28 High Street, tel. 01492/596-445).

Anna's Tea Rooms, a frilly, doily, very feminine-feeling eatery located upstairs in the masculine-feeling Conwy Outdoor Shop, is popular with locals (£3–6 main dishes and teas, also sells lunches to go, daily 10:00–17:00, 9 Castle Street, tel. 01492/580-908).

Raj, on the main square, has good Indian food. Consider

NORTH WALES

take-out—service is slow and ambience is nonexistent (£5–8 main dishes, daily 17:30–22:30, 6 Lancaster Square, tel. 01492/572-747).

Fish-and-Chips: At the bottom of High Street, on the intersecting Castle Street, are two chippies—**The Galleon** (daily, generally mid-March–Oct 11:30–15:00, mid-July–mid-Sept until 19:00, closed Nov–mid-March) and **Fisherman's** (daily generally 11:30–18:30, until 21:00 July–Aug). Both brag that they're the best (Fisherman's probably is). Consider taking your fish-and-chips down to the harbor and sharing it with the noisy seagulls.

Pub Grub: The recommended **Bridge Inn,** right near the castle at the intersection of Rosehill and Castle Streets, is a great spot to rub elbows with chatty locals and dine on decent meals (£6–10 meals, food served daily 12:00–14:30 & 18:00–20:30, tel. 01492/573-482).

Picnic Fixings: The **Spar** grocery is conveniently located and well-stocked (daily 7:00–22:00, middle of High Street). Several other shops on High Street—including the bakery and the butcher nearby—sell meat pies and other microwaveables that can quickly flesh out a sparse picnic.

Conwy Connections

Whether taking the bus or train, you need to tell the driver or conductor you want to stop at Conwy. Consider getting train times and connections for your onward journey at a bigger station before you come here. For train info in town, ask at the TI, call toll tel. 0871-200-2233, or see www.traveline-cymru.info. If you want to depart Conwy by train, flag it down; for more frequent trains, go to Llandudno Junction (catch the bus, take a £4 taxi, or walk a mile). Remember, all of these connections are less frequent on Sundays.

From Conwy by Bus to: Llandudno Junction (4/hr, 5–20 min), **Caernarfon** (1–2/hr direct, more with change in Bangor, 1.25 hrs), **Betws-y-Coed** (at least hourly, 45 min), **Blaenau Ffestiniog** (hourly Mon–Sat, 4/day on Sun, 1.25 hrs, transfer in Llandudno Junction to bus #X1, also stops in Betws-y-Coed; train is better— see below), **Beddgelert** (9/day Mon–Sat, 5/day on Sun, 1.75 hrs total, transfer in Caernarfon), **Llangollen** (2/day, 2 hrs, transfer in Llanrwst).

From Conwy by Train to: Llandudno Junction (nearly hourly, 3 min), **Chester** (nearly hourly, 50 min), **Holyhead** (nearly hourly, 1 hr), **London's Euston Station** (8/day, 3.25 hrs, transfer in Chester or Crewe).

From Llandudno Junction by Train to the Conwy Valley: Take the train to Llandudno Junction, where you'll board the scenic little Conwy Valley line, which runs up the pretty Conwy River Valley to **Betws-y-Coed** and **Blaenau Ffestiniog** (5/day

Mon–Sat, 3/day on Sun, none on Sun in winter, 45 min to Betws-y-Coed, 1.25 hrs to Blaenau Ffestiniog, www.conwyvalleyrailway.co.uk). If your train from Conwy to Llandudno Junction is late and you miss the Conwy Valley connection, tell a station employee at Llandudno Junction, who can arrange a taxi for you. Your taxi is free, as long as the missed connection is the Conwy train's fault *and* the next train doesn't leave for more than an hour (common on the infrequent Conwy Valley line).

From Llandudno Junction by Train to: Chester (2–3/hr, 1 hr), **Birmingham** (1–2/hr, 2.5–3 hrs, 1–3 transfers), **London's Euston Station** (2/hr, 3 hrs, most with 1–2 changes).

Near Conwy

These two attractions are south of Conwy, on the route to Betws-y-Coed and Snowdonia National Park. Note that Bodnant Garden is on the east side of the Conwy River, on A470, and Trefriw is on the west side, along B5106. To see them both, you'll have to cross the river (most convenient at Tal-y-Cafn).

▲Bodnant Garden

This sumptuous 80-acre display of floral color six miles south of Conwy is one of Britain's best gardens. Originally the private gar-den of the stately Bodnant Hall, this lush landscape was donated by the Bodnant family (who still live in the house) to the National Trust in 1949. The map you receive upon entering suggests a handy walking route. The highlight for many is the famous "Laburnum Arch"—a 180-foot-long canopy made

of bright-yellow laburnum, hanging like stalactites over the heads of garden-lovers who stroll beneath it (blooms mid-May through early June). The garden is also famous for its magnolias, rhodo-

dendrons, and camellias, and the way that the buildings of the estate complement the carefully planned landscaping. The wild English-style plots seem to spar playfully with the more formal, Italian-style gardens (£8, mid-Feb–mid-Nov daily 10:00–17:00 except closes at 16:00 in Nov, closed off-season, last entry 30 min before closing, café, WCs in parking lot and inside garden, best in spring, phone message tells what's blooming, tel. 01492/650-460, www.bodnant-garden .co.uk).

Getting There: To reach it by public transportation from Conwy, first head to Llandudno Junction and catch bus #25 (hourly Mon–Sat, 3/day on Sun) toward Eglwysbach, which will take you right to the garden in about 20 minutes.

Trefriw Woolen Mills

The mill in Trefriw (TREV-roo), five miles north of Betws-y-Coed, lets you peek into a working woolen mill. It's surprisingly interesting and rated ▲ if the machines are running (weekdays Easter–Oct). Various parts of the mill show off different processes and have different hours—but everything's free.

This mill buys wool from local farmers, and turns it into scarves, sweaters, bedspreads, caps, and more. You can peruse the finished products in the **shop** (June–Sept Mon–Sat 9:30–17:30, Sun 10:00–17:30; Oct–May Mon–Sat 10:00–17:00, Sun 11:00–17:00; café closes 30 min before shop, tel. 01492/640-462, www.t-w-m .co.uk). The whole complex creates its own hydroelectric power; the **"turbine house"** in the cellar lets you take a peek at the enormous, fiercely spinning turbines, dating from the 1930s and 1940s, powered by streams that flow down the hillside above the mill (same hours as shop). The **weaving looms,** with bobbin-loaded shuttles flying to and fro, allow you to watch a bedspread being created before your eyes (year-round Mon–Fri 10:00–13:00 & 14:00–17:00). But the highlight is the **"working museum,"** which follows the 11 stages of wool transformation: blending, carding, spinning, doubling, hanking, spanking, warping, weaving, and so on. Follow a matted glob of fleece on its journey to becoming a fashionable cap or scarf. It's impressive that this Rube Goldberg–type process could have been so ingeniously designed and coordinated in an age before computers (mostly the 1950s and 1960s)—each machine seems to "know" how to do its rattling, clattering duty with amazing precision (some but not all machines are likely running at any one time; Easter–Oct Mon–Fri 10:00–13:00 & 14:00–17:00, closed Sat–Sun, closed Nov–Easter because they don't heat it in winter). In the summer, the **hand-spinning house** (next to the WC) has a charming spinster and a petting cupboard filled with all the various kinds of raw wool that can be spun into cloth (June–Sept only, Tue–Thu 10:00–17:00, closed Fri–Mon).

The grade school next door is rambunctious with Welsh-speaking kids—fun to listen to at recess. The woolen mill at Penmachno (also near Betws-y-Coed) is smaller and much less interesting.

NORTH WALES

Conwy or Caernarfon?

Trying to decide between these two walled towns and their castles? Here are some comparisons:

The town of Conwy is more quaint, with a higgledy-piggledy medieval vibe and a modern workaday heart and soul—both of which feel diluted in busier, although more Welsh-feeling, Caernarfon. Conwy also has more accommodations and good eateries than Caernarfon. All of this makes it the better home base, which also means its castle is more convenient to see. Conwy's castle is a bit more ruined and less slickly presented than Caernarfon's—with fewer fancy exhibits—but some think that makes it more evocative.

Caernarfon's castle is the best in Wales—beautifully maintained, and with a more diverting set of attractions inside.

If I had to pick one, it'd be Conwy...but if you have a healthy appetite for castles, doing both is a great option.

Getting There: Buses #19 and #19A go from Conwy and Llandudno Junction right to Trefriw (2/hr Mon–Sat, 1/hr on Sun, 30 min).

Caernarfon

The small, lively little town of Caernarfon (kah-NAR-von) is famous for its striking castle—the place where the Prince of Wales

is "invested" (given his title). Like Conwy, it has an Edward I garrison town marching out from the castle; it still follows the original, medieval grid plan laid within its well-preserved ramparts. Caernarfon lacks Conwy's quaintness—but its polished castle is Wales' best.

Caernarfon is mostly a 19th-century town. At that time, the most important thing in town wasn't the castle but the area—now a parking lot—that sprawls below the castle. This was once a booming slate port, shipping tidy bundles of slate from North Wales mining towns to roofs all over Europe.

The statue of local boy David Lloyd George looks over the town square. A member of Parliament from 1890 to 1945, he was the most important politician Wales ever sent to London, and ultimately became Britain's prime minister during the last years

NORTH WALES

of World War I. Young Lloyd George began his career as a noisy nonconformist Liberal advocating Welsh rights. He ended up an eloquent spokesperson for the notion of Great Britain, convincing his slate-mining constituents that only as part of the Union would their industry boom.

Caernarfon bustles with shops, cafés, and people. Market-day activities fill its main square on Saturdays year-round; a smaller, sleepier market yawns on Monday from late May to September. The charming town is worth a wander.

Orientation to Caernarfon

(area code: 01286)
The small, walled old town of Caernarfon spreads out from its waterfront castle, its outer flanks fringed with modern sprawl (pop. 10,000). The main square, called Castle Square ("Y Maes" in Welsh), is fronted by the castle (with the TI across from its entry) and a post office. Public WCs are off the main square, on the road down to the riverfront and parking lot, where you'll find a bike-rental shop.

Tourist Information

The TI, facing the castle entrance, has a wonderful free town map/guide (with a good self-guided town walk) and train and bus schedules. They cheerfully dispense tips about all of the North Wales attractions, sell hiking books, and book rooms here and elsewhere for a £2 fee (daily April–Oct 9:30–16:30, Nov–March 10:00–16:00, tel. 01286/672-232, www.caernarfon.com).

Arrival in Caernarfon

If you arrive by **bus,** walk straight ahead a few steps to Bridge Street, turn left, and walk two short blocks until you hit the main square and the castle. **Drivers** can park in the lot along the river-front quay below the castle (£4/day July–Sept, cheaper rates rest of year).

Helpful Hints

Internet Access: Get wired at the public **library** (£1/30 min for terminals, free Wi-Fi; Mon–Tue and Thu–Fri 9:30–19:00, Wed and Sat 9:30–13:00, closed Sun; just around the corner from Bridge Street—between the castle and the recommended Celtic Royal Hotel, tel. 01286/679-463, www.gwynedd.gov .uk/library).

Laundry: Pete's **Launderette** hides at the end of Skinner Street, a narrow lane branching off the main square (same-day full-service-£7/load, Mon–Thu 9:00–18:00, Fri–Sat 9:00–17:30,

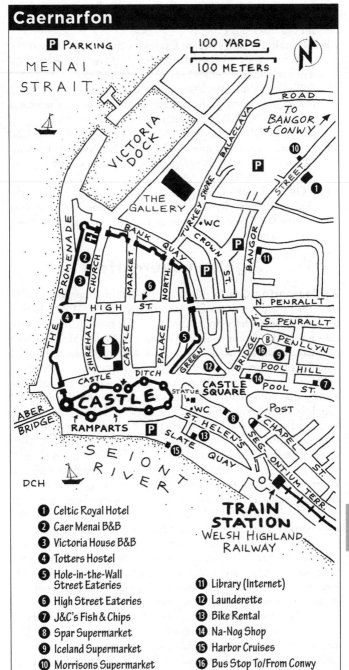

Caernarfon

P PARKING

100 YARDS
100 METERS

MENAI STRAIT

VICTORIA DOCK

THE GALLERY

ROAD
TO BANGOR & CONWY

BALACLAVA

TURKEY SHORE

WC

CROWN ST.

BANK QUAY

NORTH.

THE PROMENADE

CHURCH

MARKET

HIGH ST.

ST.

CASTLE

PALACE

GREEN.

SHIREHALL

CASTLE

DITCH

ABER BRIDGE

CASTLE

RAMPARTS

STATUE

WC

ST. HELEN'S

SLATE QUAY

BANGOR ST.

N. PENRALLT

S. PENRALLT

BRIDGE ST.

PENLLYN

POOL ST.

HILL

POOL ST.

CASTLE SQUARE

Post

CHAPEL ST.

SEIONT TERR.

SEIONT RIVER

DCH

TRAIN STATION
WELSH HIGHLAND RAILWAY

1 Celtic Royal Hotel
2 Caer Menai B&B
3 Victoria House B&B
4 Totters Hostel
5 Hole-in-the-Wall Street Eateries
6 High Street Eateries
7 J&C's Fish & Chips
8 Spar Supermarket
9 Iceland Supermarket
10 Morrisons Supermarket
11 Library (Internet)
12 Launderette
13 Bike Rental
14 Na-Nog Shop
15 Harbor Cruises
16 Bus Stop To/From Conwy

NORTH WALES

Sun 11:00–16:00, tel. 01286/678-395; Pete, Monica, and Yogi the big black dog).

Bike Rental: Try **Beics Menai Cycles** on the riverfront, near the start of a handy bike path (£12/2 hrs, £14/4 hrs, £16/6 hrs, £19/ day, includes helmet and map of suggested routes, Mon–Sat 9:30–17:00, Sun 10:00–16:00, closed Sun–Mon in winter, 1 Slate Quay—across the parking lot from the lot's payment booth, tel. 01286/676-804, mobile 07770-951-007).

A Taste of Welsh: For a store selling all things Welsh—books, movies, music, and more—check out **Na-Nog** on the main square (Mon–Sat 9:00–17:00, closed Sun, 16 Castle Square, tel. 01286/676-946).

Local Guide: Donna Goodman leads private day trips of North Wales (£180/day, book in advance, tel. 01286/677-059, mobile 07946-163-906, www.turnstone-tours.co.uk, info@turnstone -tours.co.uk).

Sights in Caernarfon

▲▲**Caernarfon Castle**—Edward I built this impressive castle 700 years ago to establish English rule over North Wales. Rather than being purely defensive, it also had elements of a palace—where Edward and his family could stay on visits to Wales. Modeled after the striped, angular walls of ancient Constantinople, the castle, though impressive, was never finished and never really used. From the inner courtyard you can see the notched walls ready for more walls—that were never built. Its fame derives from its physical grandeur and its association with the Prince of Wales. The English king got the angry Welsh to agree that if he presented them with "a prince, born in Wales, who spoke not a word of English," they would submit to the Crown. In time, Edward had a son born in Wales (here in Caernarfon), who spoke not a word of English, Welsh, or any other language—as an infant. In modern times, as another political maneuver, the Prince of Wales has been "invested" (given his title) here. This "tradition" actually dates only from the 20th century, and only two of 21 Princes of Wales have taken part.

Despite its disappointing history, it's a great castle to explore. An essential part of any visit is the £2 guided tour (50-min tours leave on the hour—and occasionally, with demand, on the half-hour—from the courtyard steps just beyond the ticket booth; if you're late, ask to join one in progress).

In the huge **Eagle Tower** (on the seaward side, to the far right as you enter), see the ground-floor "Prospect of Caernarfon" history exhibit (look for the model of the original castle); watch the 23-minute movie (*The Eagle and the Dragon*, a broad mix of Welsh legend and history enthusiastically enacted by an elfin narrator, shown upstairs on the hour and half-hour); and climb the tower for a great view. The nearby **Chamberlain's Tower** and **Queen's Tower** (ahead and to the right as you enter) house the mildly interesting "Museum of the Royal Welsh Fusiliers"—a military branch made up entirely of Welshmen. The museum shows off medals, firearms, uniforms, and information about various British battles and military strategies. The **northeast tower,** at the opposite end of the castle (to the left as you enter), has a "Princes of Wales" exhibit highlighting the investiture of Prince Charles in 1969.

Cost and Hours: £5.10; April–Oct daily 9:00–17:00; Nov–March Mon–Sat 9:30–16:00, Sun 11:00–16:00; last entry 30 min before closing, tel. 01286/677-617, www.cadw.wales.gov.uk. Martin de Lewandowicz gives mind-bending tours of the castle (tel. 01286/674-369).

Distractions—The Welsh Highland Railway **steam train** billows through the countryside from Caernarfon to Porthmadog via Rhyd Ddu on the slopes of Mount Snowdon (£17.50 round-trip to Rhyd Ddu, 2.75 hours; about £30 round-trip to Porthmadog, about 6 hrs; 2–5/day mid-March–Oct, tel. 01766/516-000, www.festrail .co.uk). At Porthmadog, you can change to the Ffestiniog Railway steam train, and ride it to Blaenau Ffestiniog (see page 497).

Narrated **harbor cruises** on the *Queen of the Sea* run daily in summer (£6, May–Oct 11:30 or 12:30 until 18:00 or 19:00, depending on weather, tides, and demand, 40 min, castle views, tel. 01286/672-772, mobile 07979-593-483).

The **Segontium Roman Fort,** dating from A.D. 77, is the westernmost Roman fort in Britain. It was manned for more than 300 years to keep the Welsh and the coast quiet. Little is left but foundations (free, Tue–Sun 12:30–16:30, closed Mon, small museum, 20-min walk from town, tel. 01286/675-625, www.segontium .org.uk).

To ride a pony or horse, try **Snowdonia Riding Stables** (£17/1 hr, longer times available, 3 miles from Caernarfon, off the road to Beddgelert, bus #S4 from Caernarfon, tel. 01286/650-342, www .snowdonia2000.fsnet.co.uk, riding@snowdonia2000.fsnet.co.uk).

Welsh Choir—If you're spending a Tuesday night here, drop by the weekly practice of the local men's choir (Tue at 20:00 in the gallery at Victoria Dock, no practice in Aug, just outside the old town walls, tel. 01286/672-633, www.cormeibioncaernarfon.org).

Sleeping in Caernarfon

(£1 = about $1.60, country code: 44, area code: 01286)
$$$ Celtic Royal Hotel rents 110 large, comfortable rooms and includes a restaurant, gym, pool, hot tub, and sauna; some top-floor rooms have castle views. Its grand, old-fashioned look comes with

modern-day conveniences—but it's still overpriced (Db-£122–125, extra bed-£35 or £20 for kids, discounts for 2 or more nights, bar, restaurant; it's on Bangor Street, a 5-min walk from bus stop: go right on Bridge Street, which turns into Bangor Street; tel. 01286/674-477, fax 01286/674-139, www.celtic-royal.co.uk).

$$ Caer Menai B&B ("Fort of the Menai Strait") rents seven bright rooms one block from the harbor (Sb-£45–55, Db-£60–65, family room-£75–80, ask for seaview room, free Internet access and Wi-Fi, 15 Church Street, tel. 01286/672-612, www.caer menai.co.uk, info@caermenai.co.uk, John and Sandy Price). Church Street is two blocks from the castle and the TI; with your back to the TI, turn right at the nearest corner and walk down Shirehall Street, which becomes Church Street after one block.

$$ Victoria House B&B, next door to the Caer Menai, rents four airy, fresh, large-for-Britain rooms with nice natural-stone bathrooms and in-room fridges stocked with free soft drinks. Generous breakfasts are served in a pleasant, woody room (Db-£65–70, £5 discount per night when staying for 2 or more nights, ask for seaview room, free Internet access and Wi-Fi, 13 Church Street, tel. 01286/678-263, www.thevictoriahouse.co.uk, jan@thevictoriahouse .co.uk, friendly Jan Baker). For directions, see previous listing.

$ Totters Hostel is a creative little hostel well-run by Bob and Henriette. Book ahead if possible, as this place often fills up in summer (28 beds in 5 dorm rooms, £16/bed with sheets, includes continental breakfast, cash only, couples can have their own twin room when available-£36, beautiful and large top-floor Db-£45, open all day, lockers, welcoming cellar game room/lounge, kitchen, a block from castle and sea at 2 High Street—look for sign in window, tel. 01286/672-963, mobile 07979-830-470, www .totters.co.uk, totters.hostel@googlemail.com). They also own a three-bedroom house across the street (D-£36, Db-£45, entire house rents for £100/4 people, £125/6 people—perfect for families).

Eating in Caernarfon

The streets near Caernarfon's castle teem with inviting eateries. Rather than recommending a particular one, I'll point you in the direction of several good streets. Just follow your nose.

"Hole-in-the-Wall Street" (between Castle Square and TI) is lined with several charming cafés and bistros.

Nearby **High Street** has plenty of cheap and cheery sandwich shops and tearooms.

The pedestrianized but grubby **Pool Street** offers several budget options, including the popular **J&C's** fish-and-chips joint (£4, Mon–Sat 11:00–21:00, Sun 12:00–19:00, tel. 01286/678-605).

Picnic: For groceries, you'll find a small **Spar** supermarket on the main square, an **Iceland** supermarket near the bus stop, and a huge **Morrisons** supermarket a five-minute walk from the city center on Bangor Street (just past Celtic Royal Hotel; all of these are open long hours daily).

Caernarfon Connections

Caernarfon is a handy hub for buses into Snowdonia National Park (such as to Llanberis, Beddgelert, and Betws-y-Coed). Bus info: toll tel. 0871-200-2233, www.gwynedd.gov.uk/bwsgwynedd.

From Caernarfon by Bus to: Conwy (1–2/hr direct, more with change in Bangor, 1.25 hrs), **Llanberis** (2/hr, 25 min, bus #88), **Beddgelert** (9/day Mon–Sat, 5/day on Sun, 30 min, bus #S4), **Betws-y-Coed** (hourly, 1–1.5 hrs, 2 transfers), **Blaenau Ffestiniog** (at least hourly, 1.25 hrs, change in Porthmadog).

Snowdonia National Park

This is Britain's second-largest national park, and its centerpiece—the tallest mountain in Wales or England—is Mount Snowdon

(www.eryri-npa.co.uk). Each year, half a million people ascend one of seven different paths to the top of the 3,560-foot mountain. Hikes take from five to seven hours; if you're fit and the weather's good, it's an exciting day. Trail info abounds (local TIs sell the small £3 book *The Ascent of Snowdon,* by E. G. Bowland, which describes the routes). As you explore, notice the slate roofs—the local specialty.

Betws-y-Coed

The resort center of Snowdonia National Park, Betws-y-Coed (BET-oos-uh-coyd) bursts with tour buses and souvenir shops. This picturesque town is cuddled by wooded hills, made cozy by generous trees, and situated along a striking, waterfall-rippled stretch of the Conwy River. It verges on feeling overly

Snowdonia Area

CASTLE

IRISH SEA

5 MILES
5 KM

N

TO HOLYHEAD (FERRY TO IRELAND)

LLANDUDNO

LLANDUDNO JUNCTION

CONWY

BEAUMARIS

A-55

A-5

A-545

BANGOR

TO CHESTER & RUTHIN

B-5106

BODNANT GARDEN

LLANFAIR P.G.

A-470

TREFRIW WOOLEN MILLS

CAERNARFON

LLANBERIS

A-5

CAPEL CURIG

A-4086

PEN-Y-PASS

PEN-Y-GWRYD HOTEL PUB

A-4085

DINAS

A-487

MT. SNOWDON

A-498

BETWS-Y-COED

A-470

A-5

TO LLAMGWN, RUTHIN & LLANGOLLEN

BEDDGELERT

LLECHWEDD SLATE MINE

PORTH-MADOG

A-498

BLAENAU FFESTINIOG

CRICCIETH

FFESTINIOG

PORTMEIRION

A-496

HARLECH

TO ABERYSTWYTH

---

manicured, with uniform checkerboard-stone houses yawning at each other from across a broad central green. There's little to do here except wander along the waterfalls (don't miss the old stone bridge—just up the river from the green—with the best waterfall views), have a snack or meal, or go for a walk in the woods.

Stop by Betws-y-Coed's good **National Park Centre/TI,** which books rooms for a £2 fee and sells the handy £2 *Forest Walks* map, outlining five different walks you can do from here. They show a free 13-minute video with aerial views of the park (daily April–Oct 9:30–17:30, Nov–March 9:30–12:30 & 13:30–16:30, tel. 01690/710-426, www.snowdonia-npa.gov.uk). In summer there's sometimes live entertainment in the TI's courtyard.

Arrival in Betws-y-Coed: Drivers can follow signs for

National Park and *i* to find the main parking lot by the TI. **Trains** and **buses** arrive at the village green; with your back to the station, the TI is to the right of the green.

Nearby: If you drive west out of town on A5 (toward Beddgelert or Llanberis), after two miles you'll see the parking lot for scenic **Swallow Falls**, a pleasant five-minute walk from the road (£1.50 entry). A half-mile past the falls on the right, you'll see **The Ugly House**, built overnight to take advantage of a 15th-century law that let any quickie building avoid fees and taxes.

Eating and Sleeping in Betws-y-Coed

(£1 = about $1.60, country code: 44, area code: 01690)
$$ Bistro Betws-y-Coed serves tasty Welsh cuisine just up the river from the TI on the main drag, with indoor or outdoor seating (£5–8 lunches served daily from 11:00, £13–17 dinners served from 18:30, closed for dinner Mon–Tue Oct–April). They also rent two fine rooms upstairs (S-£33, Sb-£35, D-£45, Db-£50, Holyhead Road, tel. 01690/710-328, www.bistrobetws-y-coed.com, info @bistrobetws-y-coed.com).

Betws-y-Coed Connections

Betws-y-Coed is connected to **Llandudno Junction** near Conwy (north, 45 min) and **Blaenau Ffestiniog** (south, 30 min) by the Conwy Valley train line (5/day Mon–Sat, 3/day Sun, no Sun trains in winter). Buses connect Betws-y-Coed with **Conwy** (at least hourly, 45 min), **Llanberis** (hourly, 45–70 min, transfer at Pen-y-Pass), **Beddgelert** (7/day, 1–2 hrs, 1–2 changes), **Blaenau Ffestiniog** (Mon–Sat hourly 10:00–18:00; 6/day on Sun, 20–35 min; 20 min, usually bus #X1), **Caernarfon** (hourly, 1–1.5 hrs, 2 transfers), and **Llangollen** (Mon and Wed–Sat 3/day, Tue 2/day, none on Sun, 1 hr).

Beddgelert

This is the quintessential Snowdon village, rated ▲▲ and packing a scenic mountain punch without the tourist crowds (17 miles from Betws-y-Coed). Beddgelert (BETH-geh-lert) is a cluster of stone houses lining a babbling brook in the shadow of Mount Snowdon and her sisters. Cute as a hobbit, Beddgelert will have you looking

for The Shire around the next
bend. Thanks to the fine variety of hikes from its doorstep
and its decent bus service,
Beddgelert makes a good stop
for those wanting to experience the peace of Snowdonia.

There are no real "sights"
here, but locals can recom-
mend **walks.** You can follow the lane along the river (3 miles
round-trip); walk down the river and around the hill (3 hrs, 6
miles, 900-foot gain, via Cwm Bycham); hike along (or around)
Llyn Gwynant Lake and four miles back to Beddgelert (ride the
bus to the lake); or try the dramatic ridge walks on Moel Hebog
(Hawk Hill).

Orientation to Beddgelert

(area code: 01766)
Beddgelert clusters around its triple-arch stone bridge. The recommended B&Bs line up single-file along one side of the brook,
while the hotels, most eateries, and the TI are on the other side.
The **National Park Centre/TI** is at the far end of town on the
right, several blocks from the bridge. They can suggest tips for
walks and hikes (April–Oct daily 9:30–17:30; Nov–March Fri–Sun
9:30–16:30—but closes for lunch, closed Mon–Thu; tel. 01766/890-
615, www.snowdonia-npa.gov.uk or www.beddgelerttourism.com).
There's **Internet access** inside the TI (£2/hr). For **mountain-
bike rental,** try Beddgelert Bikes (2 miles from Beddgelert, tel.
01766/890-434, www.beddgelertbikes.co.uk).

Sleeping in Beddgelert

(£1 = about $1.60, country code: 44, area code: 01766)
The three recommended B&Bs all line up in a row at the bridge.
They're quite different from each other—each seems to fill its own
niche. The larger inn (listed first) is across the river.

$$$ Tanronnen Inn has seven hotelesque rooms above a pub
that's been beautifully renovated from its interior medieval timbers
to its exterior stone walls (Sb-£55, Db-£100, cheaper for longer
stays, tel. 01766/890-347, fax 01766/890-606, www.tanronnen
.co.uk, guestservice@tanronnen.co.uk).

$$$ Plas Tan y Graig Guest House is the best value in town:
seven thoughtfully updated, calming, uncluttered rooms run with care
and contemporary style by Tony and Sharon (Sb-£43–48, Db-£70–80
depending on season, often cheaper on winter weeknights, 2-night

minimum stay, fine lounge, free Wi-Fi, beautiful breakfast terrace overlooking the village, packed lunches offered, tel. 01766/890-310, www.plas-tanygraig.co.uk, plastanygraig@googlemail.com).

$$$ Plas Gwyn Guest House rents six rooms in a cozy, cheery, 19th-century townhouse with a comfy lounge. Friendly Brian Wheatley is happy to dispense travel tips (S-£35, Db-£70–80, 10 percent discount with this book, cash only, tel. 01766/890-215, mobile 07815-549-708, www.plas-gwyn.com, bandb@beddgelert.fsbusiness.co.uk).

$$ Colwyn Guest House has five tight but slick and new-feeling rooms (S-£30–35, D-£55–65, Db-£60–70, 10 percent discount with this book, cash only, free Internet access and Wi-Fi, tel. 01766/890-276, www.beddgelertguesthouse.co.uk, colwyn guesthouse@tiscali.co.uk, Colleen).

Near Beddgelert

Mountaineers note that this area was used by Sir Edmund Hillary and his men as they practiced for the first ascent of Mount Everest. They slept at **$$$ Pen-y-Gwryd Hotel Pub,** at the base of the road leading up to the Pen-y-Pass by Mount Snowdon, and today the bar is strewn with fascinating memorabilia from Hillary's 1953 climb. The 16 rooms, with dingy old furnishings and crampon ambience, are a poor value—aside from the impressive history (S-£40, Sb-£48, D-£80, Db-£96, old-time-elegant public rooms, some D rooms share museum-piece Victorian tubs and showers, natural pool and sauna for guests, £23 three-course dinners, £29 grand five-course dinners, tel. 01286/870-211, www.pyg.co.uk).

Eating in Beddgelert

Lyn's Café, just across the bridge from the B&Bs, serves nicely done home cookin' at good prices in a cozy one-room bistro (£3–8 lunches, £8–10 dinners, daily 9:00–20:00, Sat until 23:00, closes early off-season, so don't wait too late; tel. 01766/890-374).

The **Tanronnen Inn** serves up tasty food in an inviting pub setting, with several cozy, atmospheric rooms (£9–14 meals, cheaper snacks, tel. 01766/890-347).

And for Dessert: The **Glaslyn Homemade Ice Cream** shop (up the road from the Tanronnen Inn) offers good quality and selection.

Beddgelert Connections

Beddgelert is connected to **Caernarfon** by handy bus #S4 (9/day Mon–Sat, 5/day Sun, 30 min). Bus connections to **Betws-y-Coed** are much less convenient (7/day, 1–2 hrs, 1–2 changes). To reach

Conwy, it's generally easiest to transfer in Caernarfon (9/day Mon–Sat, 5/day Sun, 1.75 hrs total). Buses to **Blaenau Ffestiniog** involve one or two transfers (7/day Mon–Sat, 1–1.5 hrs; 2/day Sun, 2.25–3.25 hrs).

Llanberis

A town of 2,000 people with as many tourists on a sunny day, Llanberis (THLAN-beh-ris) is a popular base for Snowdon activities. Most people prefer to take the train from here to the summit, but Llanberis is also loaded with hikers, as it's the launchpad for the longest (five miles) but least-strenuous hiking route to the Snowdon summit. (Routes

from the nearby Pen-y-Pass, between here and Beddgelert, are steeper and even more scenic.)

Orientation to Llanberis

(area code: 01286)
Llanberis is a long, skinny, rugged, and functional town that feels like a frontier village. **Drivers** approaching Llanberis will find several parking lots, including one right by the Snowdon Mountain Railway, and a lakeside lot (marked with an *i*) across the road from the town center and TI.

Tourist Information

The TI, right on the colorful main street (High Street) in the center of the village, sells maps and offers tips for ascending Snowdon (Easter–Oct daily 9:30–16:30; Nov–Easter Fri–Mon 10:30–15:00, closed Tue–Thu; 41B High Street, tel. 01286/870-765, www.visitsnowdonia.info).

Sights in Llanberis

▲▲**Snowdon Mountain Railway**—This is the easiest and most popular ascent of Mount Snowdon. You'll travel 4.5 miles from Llanberis to the summit on Britain's only rack-and-pinion railway (from 1896), climbing a total of 3,500 feet. On the way up you'll hear a constant narration on legends, geology, and history. A new mountaintop visitors center includes a café. On the way down there's only engine noise (£25 round-trip, 2.5 hrs, includes 30-min stop at top, train departs from station along the main road at the

NORTH WALES

south end of Llanberis town center, toll tel. 0870-458-0033, www .snowdonrailway.co.uk). Drivers should avoid the Royal Victoria Hotel's parking lot, which is pricey; instead turn right after the station onto Victoria Terrace (£4/day).

The first departure is often at 9:00. While the schedule flexes with weather and demand, they try to run several trips each day mid-March through October (up to 2/hr in peak season). On sunny summer days—especially in July and August—trains fill up fast. It's smart to reserve ahead by calling toll tel. 0871-720-0033 (£3.50 reservation fee per party, ask about half-price discount with advance booking for 9:00 departure). Otherwise, show up early— the office opens at 8:15, and on very busy days, tickets can be sold out by midmorning; even if you get one, you may have to wait until afternoon for your scheduled departure time. Off-season trains often stop short of the summit (due to snow and high winds). If the train isn't running all the way to the summit, tickets are sold at a reduced rate.

Don't confuse this with the Llanberis Lake Railway, a different (and far less appealing) steam train that runs to the end of Padarn Lake and back.

▲**Welsh Slate Museum**—Across the lake from Llanberis yawns a giant slate quarry. To learn more, venture across to this free museum. The well-presented exhibit, displayed around the workshop that was used until 1969 to support the giant slate mine above, explains various aspects of this local industry. In addition to a giant water wheel and the slate-splitting demo, the museum has a little row of modest quarrymen's houses from different eras, offering a thought-provoking glimpse into their hardy lifestyle. While not as in-depth (literally) as the Llechwedd Slate Mine in Blaenau Ffestiniog, this is interesting and convenient (free entry but £3 parking; Easter–Oct daily 10:00–17:00; Nov–Easter Sun-Fri 10:00–16:00, closed Sat; tel. 01286/870-630, www.museum wales.ac.uk/en/slate).

Electric Mountain—This attraction offers visits into a power plant burrowed into the mountain across the lake from town (£7.50; frequent tours daily Easter–Oct, otherwise call ahead; open daily June–Aug 9:30–17:30, Sept–May 10:00–16:30; café, tel. 01286/870-636, www.electricmountain.co.uk).

Sleeping in Llanberis

(£1 = about $1.60, country code: 44, area code: 01286)
$$ Dolafon Guest House ("River Meadows") is a beautiful 1860s Victorian building with seven traditionally furnished rooms (Db-£56–75, depends on size, garden, High Street, tel. & fax 01286/870-993, www.dolafon.com, sandra@dolafon.com).

Llanberis Connections

Llanberis is easiest to reach from **Caernarfon** (2/hr, 25 min, bus #88) or **Betws-y-Coed** (hourly, 45–70 min, transfer at Pen-y-Pass); from **Conwy,** transfer in one of these towns (Caernarfon is generally best). While it's a quick 30-minute drive from Llanberis to **Beddgelert,** the bus connection is more complicated, requiring a transfer at Pen-y-Pass, on the high road around Mount Snowdon (hourly, 50–75 min).

Blaenau Ffestiniog

Blaenau Ffestiniog (BLEH-nigh FES-tin-yog) is a quintessential Welsh slate-mining town, notable for its slate-mine tour and its old steam train. The town—a dark, poor place—seems to struggle on, oblivious to the tourists who nip in and out. Though it's tucked amidst a pastoral Welsh landscape, Blaenau Ffestiniog is surrounded by a gun-metal gray wasteland of "tips," huge mountain-like piles of excess slate.

Take a walk. The shops are right out of the 1950s. Long rows of humble "two-up and two-down" houses (four rooms) feel a bit grim. The train station, bus stop, and parking lot all cluster along a one-block stretch in the heart of town. There's no TI.

Getting There: Blaenau Ffestiniog is conveniently connected to **Betws-y-Coed** and **Conwy** both by the Conwy Valley train line (5/day Mon–Sat, 3/day Sun, none on Sun in winter, 30 min to Betws-y-Coed, 1.25 hrs to Conwy with transfer in Llandudno Junction) and by bus #X1 (hourly Mon–Sat, 4/day Sun, 20 min to Betws-y-Coed, 1 hr to Llandudno Junction near Conwy). To connect with **Beddgelert,** you must make one or two transfers (7/day Mon–Sat, 1–1.5 hrs; 2/day Sun, 2.25–3.25 hrs).

Sights in Blaenau Ffestiniog

▲▲Llechwedd Slate-Mine Tour

Slate mining played a blockbuster role in Welsh heritage, and this working slate mine on the northern edge of Blaenau Ffestiniog does a fine job of explaining the mining culture of Victorian Wales.

The Welsh mined and split most of the slate roofs of Europe. For every ton of usable slate found, 10 tons were mined. The exhibit has a free section and two expensive tours. It's free to enter the tiny Victorian mining town (with a miners' pub and a view from "The Top of the Tip," free and worthwhile but closed Oct–Easter).

The cool slate-splitting demonstration, which is at the end of the tramway tour, is also free to the public but occurs only at certain times (likely at 12:00, 14:00, and 16:00—check the posted schedule and plan your visit around it).

For a more in-depth visit, you'll have to pay for one or both of two different tours (each about 45 min): The **"tramway"** tour is a level train ride with three stops, not much walking, and a live guide. It focuses on working life and traditional mining techniques. The **"deep mine"** tour descends deep into the mountain for an audiovisual dramatization of social life and a half-mile of walking with lots of stairs and some uneven footing. The tours overlap slightly, but the combo-ticket makes doing both worth considering (£10 for 1 tour, £16 for both tours, daily March–Sept 10:00–18:00, Oct–Feb 10:00–17:00, 2–6 tours per hour depending on demand, last tour starts 45 min before closing, cafeteria, tel. 01766/830-306, www.llechwedd-slate-caverns .co.uk). Dress warmly—I mean it. You'll freeze underground without a sweater. Lines are longer when rain drives in the hikers.

Getting There: The slate mine is about a mile from the town center. Each arriving train on the Ffestiniog Railway from Porthmadog (described next) is met by bus #X1, which takes you to the mine (fewer buses on Sun). Unfortunately, buses don't meet the more useful Conwy Valley train line from Llandudno Junction and Betws-y-Coed, but you can walk 30 minutes to the mine, or take a taxi (about £5, reserve in advance, tel. 01766/831-781 or 01766/830-082).

Near Blaenau Ffestiniog

▲**Ffestiniog Railway**—This 13-mile narrow-gauge train line was built in 1836 for small horse-drawn wagons to transport the slate from the Ffestiniog mines to the port of Porthmadog. In the 1860s, horses gave way to steam trains. Today, hikers and tourists enjoy these tiny titans (£18.50 round-trip, 2–8/day depending on day and season, 2.75 hours round-trip, first-class observation cars cost £8 extra, limited service in winter, tel. 01766/516-000, www.festrail.co.uk). This is a novel steam-train experience, but the full-size Conwy Valley Line from Llandudno to Blaenau Ffestiniog is more scenic and works a little better for hikers (see page 480).

Serious train enthusiasts will want to continue from Porthmadog all the way to Caernarfon, along the Welsh Highland Railway (see page 487 for details).

NORTH WALES

Portmeirion—Ten miles southwest of Blaenau Ffestiniog, this "Italian Village" was the life's work of a rich local architect who began building it in 1925. Set idyllically on the coast just beyond the poverty of the slate-mine towns, this flower-filled fantasy is extravagant. Surrounded by lush Welsh greenery and a windswept mudflat at low tide, the village is an artistic glob of palazzo arches, fountains, gardens, and promenades filled with cafés, tacky shops, a hotel, and local tourists who always wanted to go to Italy. Fans of the cultish British 1960s TV series *The Prisoner*, which was filmed here, will recognize the place (www.portmeirion.com).

North Wales Connections

Two major transfer points out of (or into) North Wales are Crewe and Chester. Figure out your complete connection at www.nationalrail.co.uk.

From Crewe by Train to: London Euston Station (2/hr, 1.75 hrs), **Bristol,** near Bath (2/hr, 2.5–3 hrs), **Cardiff** (hourly, 2.75 hrs), **Holyhead** (hourly, 2–2.5 hrs), **Blackpool** (hourly, 1.5 hrs), **Keswick** in the Lake District (nearly hourly, 1.75–2.75 hrs to Penrith, some via Oxenholme or Manchester; then catch a bus to Keswick, hourly except Sun 8/day, 40 min, allow 3.5 hrs total), **Glasgow** (nearly hourly, 3–4 hrs, some via Lancaster or Preston).

From Chester by Train to: London Euston Station (2/hr, 2 hrs), **Liverpool** (2/hr, 45 min), **Birmingham** (2/hr, 1.75 hrs); points in North Wales including **Conwy** (nearly hourly, 50 min).

Ferry Connections Between North Wales and Ireland

Two companies make the crossing between Holyhead (in North Wales, beyond Caernarfon) and Ireland. Some boats go to Dublin, while others head for Dublin's southern suburb of Dun Laoghaire (pronounced "Dun Leary"). Stena Line sails from Holyhead to Dublin (2/day, 3.25 hrs, plus 2 overnight) and also to Dun Laoghaire (1/day, 2 hrs; one-way walk-on fare for either crossing-£25, cheaper if booked in advance, extra to use credit card, reserve by phone or online—they book up long in advance on summer weekends, British toll tel. 0870-570-7070, or book online at www.stenaline.co.uk). Irish Ferries sails to Dublin (3/day—1 slow, 2 fast; plus 1 slow overnight sailing; slow boat 3.25 hrs, fast boat 2 hrs; one-way walk-on fare for either crossing-£25; extra to use credit card, reserve online for best fares; Britain toll tel. 08705-300-200, for Irish number dial 00-353-818-300-400 from Britain, www.irishferries.co.uk).

Sleeping near Holyhead Dock: The fine **$$ Monravon B&B** has seven rooms a 15-minute uphill walk from the dock (Sb-£35, Db-£50, family deals, £4 breakfast, free Wi-Fi, Porth-Y-Felin

NORTH WALES

Road, tel. & fax 01407/762-944, www.monravon.co.uk, monravon @yahoo.co.uk). **$$ Celyn Villa B&B** is a lovely mid-19th-century house with views of the Dee estuary (Sb-£40, Db-£56–60, twin and family rooms available, 2-night minimum July–Aug, dinner available, Carmel Road, tel. 01352/710-853, www.celynvilla.co.uk, celynvilla@btinternet.com, Paulene and Les).

Route Tips for Drivers
One-Day North Wales Blitz Tour from Ruthin
Ruthin to Caernarfon (56 miles) to Blaenau Ffestiniog (34 miles) back to Ruthin (35 miles): This route connects the top sights with the most scenic routes. From Ruthin, take B5105 (steepest road off main square) and follow signs to *Cerrigydrudion*. Then follow A5 into Betws-y-Coed, with a possible quick detour to the Trefriw Woolen Mills (5 miles north on B5106, well-signposted). Climb west on A5 through Capel Curig, then take A4086 over the rugged Pass of Llanberis, under the summit of Mount Snowdon (to the south, behind those clouds), and on to Caernarfon. Park under the castle in the harborside parking lot.

Leaving Caernarfon, take lovely A4085 southeast through Beddgelert to Penrhyndeudraeth. (Make things even more beautiful by taking the little B4410 road from Garreg through Rhyd.) Then take A487 toward What Maentwrog and A496 to Blaenau Ffestiniog. Go through the dark and depressing mining town of Blaenau Ffestiniog on A470, continue over hills of slate, and turn right into the Llechwedd Slate Mine.

After the mine, continue uphill on A470, snapping photos north through Dolwyddelan (passing a fine old Welsh castle ruin) and back to A5. For a high, desolate detour, return to Ruthin on curvy A543. Go over the stark moors to the Sportsman's Arms Pub (the highest pub in Wales, good food), continue through Denbigh, and then go home.

Reaching and Departing North Wales
From Points South in England to North Wales
To Ruthin: Drive to Wales on A5 through Shrewsbury, crossing into Wales and following A5 to Llangollen. Cross the bridge in Llangollen, turn left, and follow A542 and A525 past the romantic Vale Crucis Abbey, over the scenic Horseshoe Pass, and into Ruthin.

To Conwy and the North Coast: Driving to Conwy is faster via Wrexham and then A55, but more scenic if you stay on A5 from Llangollen to Betws-y-Coed and then zip north to Conwy from there.

From North Wales to Points North in England
From North Wales to Liverpool (40 miles): From Ruthin or A55,

follow signs to the town of *Mold,* then *Queensferry,* then *Manchester M56,* then *Liverpool M53,* which tunnels under the Mersey River (£1.40).

From North Wales to Blackpool, Skipping Liverpool (100 miles): From A55, follow the blue signs to the motorway. (From Ruthin, you can reach A55 by taking A494 through the town of Mold). The M56 road zips you to M6, where you'll turn north toward Preston and Lancaster (don't miss your turnoff). A few minutes after Preston, take the not-very-clearly signed next exit (#32, M55) into Blackpool, and drive as close as you can to the stubby Eiffel-type tower in the town center.

SCOTLAND

SCOTLAND

 The country of Scotland makes up about a third of Britain's geographical area (30,400 square miles), but has less than a tenth of its population (just over five million). This sparsely populated chunk of land stretches to Norwegian latitudes. Its Shetland Islands, at about 60°N (similar to Anchorage, Alaska), are the northernmost point in Britain.

The southern part of Scotland, called the Lowlands, is relatively flat and urbanized. The northern area—the Highlands—features a wild, severely undulating terrain, punctuated by lochs (lakes) and fringed by sea lochs (inlets) and islands. The Highland Boundary Fault that divides Scotland geologically also divides it culturally. Historically, there was a big difference between grizzled, kilt-wearing Highlanders in the northern wilderness, and the more refined Lowlanders in the southern flatlands and cities. The Highlanders talk and act like "true Scots," while the Lowlanders often seem more "British" than Scottish. Although this division has faded over time, some Scots still cling to it today—city slickers  down south think that Highlanders are crude and unrefined, and those who live at higher latitudes grumble about the soft, pampered urbanites in the Lowlands.

The Lowlands are dominated by a pair of rival cities: Edinburgh, the old royal capital, teems with Scottish history and is the country's best tourist attraction. Glasgow, once a gloomy industrial city, is becoming a hip, laid-back city of today, known for its modern architecture. The medieval university town and golf mecca of St. Andrews, the whisky village of Pitlochry, and the historic city of Stirling round out the Lowlands' top sights.

The Highlands provide your best look at traditional Scotland. The sights are subtle, but the warm culture and friendly people are engaging. There are a lot of miles, but they're scenic, the roads are good, and the traffic is light. Generally, the Highlands are

Scotland

••• FERRY ROUTES (NOT ALL SHOWN)

ATLANTIC OCEAN

ORKNEY
STROMNESS • KIRKWALL
THURSO • JOHN O'GROATS

50 MILES
30 KM

LEWIS
ULLAPOOL
NORTH UIST
KYLE OF LOCHALSH
MORAY FIRTH
SOUTH UIST
CULLODEN
PORTREE • **INVERNESS**
SKYE
RUM
LOCH NESS
ABERDEEN •
MALLAIG
▲ BEN NEVIS
COLL
FT. WILLIAM
PITLOCHRY
NORTH SEA
TIREE
GLENCOE
PERTH
DUNDEE
MULL
OBAN
LOCH LOMOND
ST. ANDREWS
IONA
← EAST NEUK
STIRLING
JURA
FIRTH OF FORTH
BANNOCK BURN
ISLAY
GLASGOW
EDINBURGH
CAMPBELTOWN •
• TROON
BERWICK-UPON-TWEED
ARRAN
AYR
LOWLANDS
CAIRNRYAN
ENGLAND
STRANRAER
CARLISLE
NORTHERN IRELAND
HADRIAN'S WALL
NEW-CASTLE
LARNE
BELFAST •
IRISH SEA
TO ↓ DUBLIN
TO LAKE DISTRICT ↓
TO YORK & LONDON ↓
DCH
HIGHLANDS
CALEDONIAN CANAL

hungry for the tourist dollar, and everything overtly Scottish is exploited to the kilt. You'll need more than a quick visit to get away from that. But if two days is all you have, you can get a feel for the area with a quick drive to Oban, through Glencoe, then up the Caledonian Canal to Inverness. With more time, the islands of Iona and Mull (an easy day trip from Oban), the Isle of Skye, and countless brooding countryside castles will flesh out your Highlands experience.

The Highlands are more rocky and harsh than other parts of the British Isles. It's no wonder that most of the scenes around Hogwarts in the Harry Potter movies were filmed in this moody, sometimes spooky landscape. Though Scotland's "hills" are technically too short to be called "mountains," they do a convincing imitation. Scotland has 284 hills over 3,000 feet. A list of these was compiled in 1891 by Sir Hugh Munro, and to this day the Scots still call their high hills "Munros." According to the Scottish Mountaineering Club,  more than 4,300 intrepid hikers can brag that they've climbed all of the Munros.

In this northern climate, cold and drizzly weather isn't uncommon—even in midsummer. The blazing sun can quickly be covered over by black clouds and howling wind. Scots warn visitors to prepare for "four seasons in one day." Because the Scots feel personally responsible for bad weather, they tend to be overly optimistic about forecasts. Take any Scottish promise of "sun by the afternoon" with a grain of salt—and bring your raincoat.

In the summer, the Highlands swarm with tourists...and midges. These miniscule mosquitoes—called "no-see-ums" in some parts of the US—are bloodthirsty and determined. Depending on the weather, you'll be covered with them between mid-June and late August. Hot sun or a stiff breeze blows the tiny buggers away, but they thrive in damp, shady areas. Locals suggest blowing or brushing them off, rather than swatting them—since killing them only seems to attract more (likely because of the smell of fresh blood). Scots say, "If you kill one midge, a million will come to his funeral." Even if you don't usually travel with bug spray, consider bringing or buying some for a summer visit—or your most vivid memory of your Scottish vacation might be itchy arms and legs.

Keep an eye out for another uniquely Scottish animal: shaggy Highland cattle, with their hair falling in their eyes. Dubbed

"hairy coos," these adorable beasts will melt your heart. With a heavy coat to keep them insulated, hairy coos graze on sparse vegetation that other animals ignore.

The major theme of Scottish history is the drive for independence, especially from England. (Scotland's rabble-rousing national motto is *Nemo me impune lacessit*—"No one provokes me with impunity.") Like Wales, Scotland is a country of ragtag Celts sharing an island with wealthy and powerful Anglo-

Saxons. Scotland's Celtic culture is a result of its remoteness—the invading Romans were never able to conquer this rough-and-tumble people, and even built Hadrian's Wall to lock off this distant corner of their empire. The Anglo-Saxons, and their descendants the English, fared little better than the Romans did. Even King Edward I—who so successfully dominated Wales—was unable to hold on to Scotland for long, largely thanks to the relentlessly rebellious William Wallace (a.k.a. "Braveheart").

Failing to conquer Scotland by the blade, England eventually absorbed it politically. In 1603, England's Queen Elizabeth I died without an heir, so Scotland's King James VI took the throne, becoming King James I of England. It took another century or so of battles, both military and diplomatic, but the Act of Union in 1707 definitively (and controversially) unified the Kingdom of Great Britain. In 1745, Bonnie Prince Charlie attempted to reclaim the Scottish throne on behalf of the deposed Stuarts, but his army was trounced at the Battle of Culloden (described in the Inverness and the Northern Highlands chapter). This cemented English rule over Scotland, and is seen by many Scots as the last gasp of the traditional Highlands clan system.

Scotland has been joined—however unwillingly—to England ever since, and the Scots have often felt oppressed by their English countrymen (see "British, Scottish, and English" on page 524). During the Highland Clearances in the 18th and 19th centuries, landowners (mostly English) decided that vast tracks of land were more profitable as grazing land for sheep, than as farmland for people. Many Highlanders were forced to abandon their traditional homes and lifestyles and seek employment elsewhere. Large numbers ended up in North America, especially parts of eastern Canada, such as Prince Edward Island and Nova Scotia (literally, "New Scotland").

Today, Americans and Canadians of Scottish descent enjoy coming "home" to Scotland. If you're Scottish, your surname will tell you which clan your ancestors likely belonged to. The prefix "Mac" (or "Mc") means "son of"—so "MacDonald" means the same thing as "Donaldson." Tourist shops everywhere are happy

to help you track down your clan's tartan, or distinctive plaid pattern—many clans have several.

Is Scotland really a country? It's not a sovereign state, but it is a "nation" in that it has its own traditions, ethnic identity, languages (Gaelic and Scots, described below), and football league. To some extent, it even has its own government: Over the past several years, Scotland has enjoyed its greatest measure of political autonomy in centuries—a trend called "devolution." In 1998, the Scottish parliament opened its doors in Edinburgh for the first time in almost 300 years. Though the Scottish parliament's powers are limited (most major decisions are still made in London), the Scots are enjoying the refreshing breeze of increased independence. The Scottish Nationalists held more seats than any other party as of the 2007 elections. Today's politicians are poised to ask the EU to recognize Scotland as a separate country.

Scotland even has its own currency. While Scots use the same coins as England, Scotland also prints its own bills (with Scottish rather than English people and landmarks). Just to confuse tourists, three different banks print Scottish pound notes, each with a different design. In the Lowlands (around Edinburgh and Glasgow), you'll receive both Scottish and English pounds from ATMs and in change. But in the Highlands, you'll almost never see English pounds. Though most merchants in England accept Scottish pound notes, a few might balk—especially at the rare one-pound note, which their cash registers don't have a slot for. (They are, however, legally required to accept your Scottish currency.)

The Scottish flag—a diagonal, X-shaped white cross on a blue field—represents the cross of Scotland's patron saint, the Apostle Andrew (who was crucified on an X-shaped cross). You may not realize it, but you see the Scottish flag every time you look at the Union Jack: England's flag (the red St. George's cross on a white field) superimposed on Scotland's (a blue field with a white diagonal cross). The diagonal red cross (St. Patrick's cross) over Scotland's white one represents Northern Ireland. (Wales gets no love on the Union Jack.)

Scots are known for their inimitable burr, but they are also proud of their old Celtic language, Scottish Gaelic (pronounced "gallic"; Ireland's closely related Celtic language is spelled the same but pronounced "gaylic"). Gaelic thrives only in the remotest corners of Scotland. In major towns and cities, virtually nobody speaks Gaelic every day, but the language is kept on life-support by a Scottish population keen to remember their heritage. New Gaelic schools are opening all the time, and Scotland recently passed a law to replace road signs with new ones listing both English and Gaelic spellings (e.g., Edinburgh/Dùn Èideann).

Scotland has another language of its own, called Scots (a.k.a. "Lowland Scots," to distinguish it from Gaelic). Aye, you're likely already a wee bit familiar with a few Scots words, ye lads and lassies. As you travel, you're sure to pick up a bit more (see sidebar). Many linguists argue that Scots is technically an ancient dialect of English, rather than a distinct language. These linguists

Scottish Words

Scotch may be the peaty drink the bartender serves you, but the nationality of the bartender is **Scots** or **Scottish.** Here are some other Scottish words that may come in handy during your time here:

aye	yes
auld	old
ben	mountain
blether	talk
bonnie	beautiful
brae	slope, hill
burn	creek or stream
cairn	pile of stones
close	an alley leading to a courtyard or square
craig	rock, cliff
firth	estuary
innis	island
inver	mouth of a river
ken	to know
kirk	church
kyle	strait
loch	lake
nae	no (as in "nae bother"—you're welcome)
neeps	turnips
ree	king, royal ("righ" in Gaelic)
tattie	potato
wee	small
wynd	tight, winding lane connecting major streets

A sharp intake of breath (like a little gasp), sometimes while saying "aye," means "yes."

have clearly never heard a Scot read aloud the poetry of Robert Burns, who wrote in unfiltered (and often unintelligible) Scots. (Opening line of "To a Louse": *Ha! Whaur ye gaun, ye crowlin ferlie?*) Fortunately, you're unlikely to meet anyone quite that hard to understand; most Scots speak Scottish-accented standard English, peppered with their favorite Scots phrases. If you have a hard time understanding someone, ask them to translate—you may take home some new words as souvenirs.

Scottish cuisine is down-to-earth, often with an emphasis on local produce. Both seafood and "land food" (beef and chicken) are common. One Scottish mainstay—eaten more by tourists than by Scots these days—is the famous haggis, a rich assortment of oats and sheep organs stuffed into a chunk of sheep intestine, liberally seasoned and boiled. Usually served with "neeps and tatties" (turnips and potatoes), it's tastier than it sounds and worth trying... once.

The "Scottish Breakfast" is similar to the English version, but they add a potato scone (like a flavorless, soggy potato pancake) and occasionally haggis (which is hard enough to get down at dinnertime).

Breakfast, lunch, or dinner, the Scots love their whisky—and touring one of the country's many distilleries is a sightseeing treat. The Scots are fiercely competitive with the Irish when it comes to this peaty spirit. Scottish "whisky" is distilled twice, whereas Irish "whiskey" adds a third distillation (and an extra *e*). Grain here is roasted over peat fires, giving it a smokier flavor than its Irish cousin. Also note that what we call "scotch"—short for "scotch whisky"—is just "whisky" here. I've listed several of the most convenient and interesting distilleries to visit, but if you're a whisky connoisseur, make a point of tracking down and touring your favorite.

Another unique Scottish flavor to sample is the soft drink called Irn-Bru (pronounced "Iron Brew"). This bright-orange beverage tastes not like orange soda, but like bubblegum with a slightly bitter aftertaste. (The diet version is even more bitter.) While Irn-Bru's appeal eludes non-Scots, it's hugely popular here, even outselling Coke. Be cautious sipping it—as the label understates, "If spilt, this product may stain."

Whether toasting with beer, whisky, or Irn-Bru, enjoy meeting the Scottish people. Many travelers fall in love with the irrepressible spirit and beautiful landscape of this faraway corner of Britain.

EDINBURGH

Edinburgh is the historical and cultural capital of Scotland. Once a medieval powerhouse sitting on a lava flow, it grew into Europe's first great grid-planned modern city. The colorful hometown of Robert Louis Stevenson, Sir Walter Scott, and Robert Burns, Edinburgh is Scotland's showpiece and one of Europe's most entertaining cities. Historic, monumental, fun, and well-organized, it's a tourist's delight—especially in August, when the Edinburgh Festival takes over the town.

Promenade down the Royal Mile through Old Town. Historic buildings pack the Royal Mile between the grand castle (on the top) and the Palace of Holyroodhouse (on the bottom). Medieval skyscrapers stand shoulder to shoulder, hiding peaceful courtyards connected to High Street by narrow lanes or even tunnels. This colorful jumble is the tourist's Edinburgh.

Edinburgh (ED'n-burah) was once the most crowded city in Europe—famed for its skyscrapers and filth. The rich and poor lived atop one another. In the Age of Enlightenment, a magnificent Georgian city (today's New Town) was laid out to the north, giving Edinburgh's upper class a respectable place to promenade. Georgian Edinburgh—like the city of Bath—shines with broad boulevards, straight streets, square squares, circular circuses, and elegant mansions decked out in colonnades, pediments, and sphinxes in the proud Neoclassical style of 200 years ago.

While the Georgian city celebrated the union of Scotland and England (with streets and squares named after English kings and emblems), "devolution" is the latest trend. For the past several centuries, Scotland was ruled from London, and Parliament had not met in Edinburgh since 1707. But in a 1998 election, the Scots

EDINBURGH

Greater Edinburgh

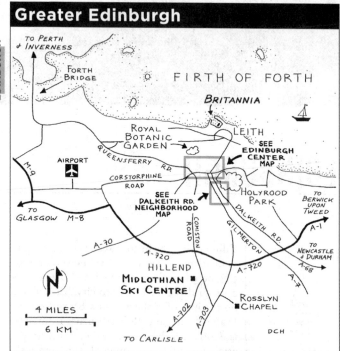

voted to gain more autonomy and bring their Parliament home. In 1999, Edinburgh resumed its position as home to the Scottish parliament (although London still calls the strategic shots). A strikingly modern new Parliament building, which opened in 2004, is one more jewel in Edinburgh's crown. Today, you'll notice many references to the "nation" of Scotland.

Planning Your Time

While the major sights can be seen in a day, on a three-week tour of Britain, I'd give Edinburgh two days and three nights.

Day 1: Tour the castle (open from 9:30). Then consider catching one of the city bus tours for a one-hour loop (departing from a block below the castle at The Hub/Tolbooth Church; you could munch a sandwich from the top deck if you're into multitasking). Back at the castle, catch the 14:15 Mercat Tours walk (1.5 hours, leaves from Mercat Cross on the Royal Mile). Spend the remainder of your day enjoying the Royal Mile's shops and museums, or touring the Palace of Holyroodhouse (at the bottom of the Mile).

Day 2: Visit the Museum of Scotland. After lunch, stroll through the Princes Street Gardens and the National Gallery of Scotland. Then tour the good ship *Britannia*.

Evenings: Options include various "haunted Edinburgh" walks, literary pub crawls, or live music in pubs. Sadly, traditional folk shows are just about extinct, surviving only in excruciatingly schmaltzy variety shows put on for tour-bus groups. Perhaps the most authentic local evening out is just settling down in a pub to sample the whisky and local beers while meeting the natives... and attempting to understand them through their thick Scottish accents.

Orientation to Edinburgh

(area code: 0131)

The center of Edinburgh, a drained lake bed, holds the Princes Street Gardens park and Waverley Bridge, where you'll find the TI, Princes Mall, train station, bus info office (starting point for most city bus tours), National Gallery, and a covered dance-and-music pavilion. Weather blows in and out—bring your sweater and be prepared for rain. Locals say the bad weather is one of the disadvantages of living so close to England.

You might notice the city is pretty dug up. Skeptical residents seem to regret the huge investment they've made in their new tram system even before its 2011 opening date.

Tourist Information

The crowded TI is as central as can be atop the Princes Mall and train station (Mon–Sat 9:00–17:00, Sun 10:00–17:00, July–Aug daily until 19:00, tel. 0845-225-5121). The staff is knowledgeable and eager to help, but much of their information—including their assessment of museums and even which car-rental companies "exist"—is skewed by tourism payola. There's another TI (which I find more helpful) at the airport.

Pick up a free map or buy the excellent £4.50 *Collins Discovering Edinburgh* map (which comes with opinionated commentary and locates almost every major shop and sight). If you're interested in late-night music, ask for the free monthly entertainment *Gig Guide*. (The best monthly entertainment listing, *The List*, sells for a few pounds at newsstands.) The free *Essential Guide to Edinburgh*, while not truly essential, lists additional sights and services (when it's in stock). The TI also sells the mediocre Edinburgh Pass, which provides unlimited travel on Lothian buses (includes the airport) and entry to dozens of B-list sights (£25/1 day, £37/2 days, £49/3 days, doesn't include Edinburgh Castle, www.edinburghpass.org).

Book your room direct, using my listings (the TI charges you a £4 booking fee, and also takes a 10 percent cut, which means that B&Bs end up charging more for rooms booked this way). Browse the racks—tucked away in the hallway at the back of the

TI—for brochures on the various Scottish folk shows, walking tours, regional bus tours, and other touristic temptations.

Connect@edinburgh, a small Internet café, is beyond the brochure racks.

Arrival in Edinburgh

By Train: Arriving by train at Waverley Station puts you in the city center and below the TI. Taxis queue almost trackside; the ramp they come and go on leads to Waverley Bridge. If there's a long line for taxis, I hike up the ramp and hail one on the street. From the station, *Way Out–1–Princes Street* signs lead up to the TI and the city bus stop (for bus directions from here to my recommended B&Bs, see below). For picnic supplies, a **Marks & Spencer Simply Food** is near platform 2.

By Bus: Both Scottish Citylink and National Express buses use the bus station (with luggage lockers) in the New Town, two blocks north of the train station on St. Andrew Square.

By Plane: Edinburgh's slingshot of an airport is located 10 miles northwest of the center. Airport flight info: tel. 0870-040-0007, www.edinburghairport.com.

Taxis between the airport and the city center are pricey (£20, 20 min to downtown or to Dalkeith Road B&Bs). Fortunately, the airport is well-connected to central Edinburgh by the convenient, frequent, cheap Lothian **Airlink bus #100** (£3.50, 6/hr, 30 min, buses run all day and more sporadically through the night, tel. 0131/555-6363, www.flybybus.com). The bus drops you at the center of Waverley Bridge. From here, to reach my recommended B&Bs near Dalkeith Road, you can either take a taxi (about £7), or hop on a bus at St. Andrew Square (walk along Waverley Bridge toward Princes Street, turn right, then immediately left onto St. Andrew Street; after one block, cross the street toward the park). Ride bus #14, #30, #33, or #48, and get off at the first or second stop after the bus makes a right turn onto Dalkeith Road (£1.30, have coins ready—drivers don't make change, buses leave frequently, confirm specific directions with your B&B).

If you're headed *to* the airport, you can take the same Airlink bus described above. To reach the Airlink bus stop from the Dalkeith Road B&Bs, ride the bus to the end of North Bridge and hop out just after the bus turns left at the grand Balmoral Hotel; exit the bus to your right and walk a short distance down Princes Street to the next bridge, Waverley, where you'll find the Airlink bus stop. (Rather than taking a £20 taxi all the way to the airport, consider taking a £7 taxi to this stop, then hopping the bus to the airport.)

By Car: If you're arriving from the north, rather than drive through downtown Edinburgh to the recommended B&Bs, circle the city on the A720 City Bypass road. Approaching Edinburgh on M9, take M8 (direction: Glasgow) and quickly get onto A720 City Bypass (direction: Edinburgh South). After four miles, you'll hit a roundabout. Ignore signs directing you into *Edinburgh North* and stay on A720 for 10 more miles to the next and last roundabout, named *Sheriffhall*. Exit the roundabout on the first left (A7 Edinburgh). From here it's four miles to the B&B neighborhood. After a while, A7 becomes Dalkeith Road. If you see the huge construction zone for the swimming pool, you've gone a couple of blocks too far (avoid this by referring to the map on page 554).

If you're driving in on A68 from the south, take the A7 Edinburgh exit off the roundabout and follow the directions above.

Helpful Hints

Festivals: August is a crowded, popular month to visit Edinburgh because of the multiple festivals hosted here, including the official Edinburgh Festival (Aug 13–Sept 5 in 2010). Book ahead if you'll be visiting during this month, and expect to pay significantly more for your accommodations. For all the details, see page 548.

Sunday Activities: Many Royal Mile sights close on Sunday (except during August and the Festival), but other major sights are open. Sunday is a good day to catch a guided walking tour along the Royal Mile or a city bus tour (buses go faster in light traffic). Arthur's Seat is lively with locals on weekends.

Internet Access: Get online at the central **Connect@edinburgh** (£1/30 min, in the TI, Mon–Sat 9:00–17:00, Sun 10:00–17:00, July–Aug daily until 19:00); the atmospheric **Elephant House Café** (Mon–Fri 8:00–23:00, Sat–Sun 9:00–23:00, 4 stations, 24 George IV Bridge, off top of Royal Mile, also described on page 560); or **E-Corner Internet Café and Call Shop,** a funky little place just off the Royal Mile, next to the Smart City Hostel (£1/30 min, Mon–Fri 9:00–21:30, Sat–Sun 10:00–21:30, in winter daily 10:00–21:00, packed with fast terminals and digital services, 54 Blackfriars Street, tel. 0131/558-7858).

Baggage Storage: At the train station you'll find pricey, high-security luggage storage near platform 2 (£7/24 hrs, daily 7:00–23:00). It's cheaper to use the lockers at the bus station on St. Andrew Square, just a five-minute walk from the train station (£4–6 depending on size—even smallest locker is plenty big, station open Mon–Sat 6:00–20:00, Sun 8:00–20:00).

Laundry: Ace Cleaning Centre launderette is located near the recommended B&Bs (Mon–Fri 8:00–20:00, Sat 9:00–17:00, Sun 10:00–16:00, self-service or drop-off; along the bus route to the city center at 13 South Clerk Street, opposite Queens Hall; tel. 0131/667-0549). For a small extra fee, they collect and drop off laundry at the neighborhood B&Bs.

Car Rental: Most of these places have offices both in the town center and at the airport: **Avis** (5 West Park Place, tel. 0844-544-6059, airport tel. 0844-544-6004), **Europcar** (24 East London Street, tel. 0131/557-3456, airport tel. 0131/333-2588), **Hertz** (10 Picardy Place, tel. 0870-846-0013, airport tel. 0870-846-0009), and **Budget** (airport only, tel. 0844-544-4605). Some downtown offices are closed on Sunday, but the airport locations tend to be open daily—call ahead to confirm. If you're going to rent a car, pick it up on your way out of Edinburgh—you won't need it in town.

Bike Rental: The laid-back crew at **Cycle Scotland** is happy to recommend some good bike routes (£10/3 hrs, £15/day, £20/24 hrs, daily 10:00–18:00, just off Royal Mile at 29 Blackfriars Street, tel. 0131/556-5560).

Blue Badge Local Guides: All of these guides charge the same rates for private tours, except where noted (£80/half-day, £120/day). **Ken Hanley** wears his kilt as if pants didn't exist, knows all the stories, and loves sharing his passion for Edinburgh and Scotland (extra charge if he uses his car—which fits up to 6, tel. 0131/666-1944, mobile 0771-034-2044, www.small -world-tours.co.uk, k.hanley@blueyonder.co.uk). Other good guides include **Jean Blair** (£140 extra per day with car, tel. 0150/682-5930, mobile 0798-957-0287, jean@travelthrough scotland.com), **Sergio La Spina** (an Argentinean who adopted Edinburgh as his hometown more than 20 years ago, tel. 0131/664-1731, mobile 0797-330-6579, sergiolaspina@aol .com), and **Anne Doig** (mobile 0777-590-1792, annedoig2 @hotmail.com).

Getting Around Edinburgh

Nearly all of Edinburgh's sights are within walking distance of each other.

City **buses** are handy, and run from about 6:00 to 23:00 (£1.30/ride, buy tickets on bus, Lothian Buses transit office at Old Town end of Waverley Bridge has schedules and route maps, tel. 0131/555-6363, www.lothianbuses.com). Tell the driver where you're going, have change handy (buses require exact change—you lose any extra you put in), take your ticket as you board, and ping the bell as you near your stop. Double-deckers come with fine views upstairs. Two companies handle the city routes: Lothian (which dominates) and First. Day passes sold by each company are valid only on their buses (£3, buy from driver).

The 1,300 **taxis** cruising Edinburgh's streets are easy to flag down (a ride between downtown and the B&B neighborhood costs about £7). They can turn on a dime, so hail them in either direction.

Tours in Edinburgh

Royal Mile Walking Tours—**Royal Mile Tours** is your best basic historical walk (without all the ghosts and goblins). The staff of committed local guides heads out as long as there are enough tourists to make a group. It's a gentle two-hour downhill stroll from the castle to the palace (£9, daily at 10:00, meet outside Gladstone's Land, near the top of the Royal Mile—see map on page 530, call to confirm and reserve, tel. 0131/443-0548, mobile 0794-847-2828, www.edinburghtourguides.com).

Mercat Tours offers 1.5-hour guided walks of the Mile, which are more entertaining than intellectual (£8.50, daily at 14:15, leaves from Mercat Cross on the Royal Mile, tel. 0131/225-5445, www.mercattours.com). The guides, who enjoy making a short story long, ignore the big sights and take you behind the scenes with piles of barely historical gossip, bully-pulpit Scottish pride, and fun but forgettable trivia. These tours can move quickly, scaling the steep hills and steps of Edinburgh—wear good shoes. They also offer several ghost tours, as well as one focused on Edinburgh's literary history.

The **Voluntary Guides Association** offers free two-hour walks, but only during the Edinburgh Festival. You don't need a reservation, but it's a good idea to call or drop by the TI to double-check details, such as departure point and time (daily at about 10:00 and 14:00, generally depart from Cannonball House at Castle Esplanade, tel. 0131/669-8263 or 0131/441-1373).

Evening **ghost walks** and **pub tours** are described later, under "Nightlife in Edinburgh."

Edinburgh Bus Tours—Four different one-hour hop-on, hop-off bus tours circle the town center, stopping at the major sights.

You can hop on and off at any stop all day with one ticket (pick-ups about every 10–15 min). All tours are narrated. Two of the tours have live guides: **Mac Tours' City Tour** (focuses on Old Town, most comprehensive, live Mon–Fri with "vintage buses") and **Edinburgh Tour** (focuses on the wider city, more panoramic, always live). Avoid the **City Sightseeing Tours,** which have a recorded narration (better for non-English speakers). The tours all have virtually the same route, cost, and frequency, except the **Majestic Tour,** whose regular route is longer and includes a stop at the *Britannia* and the Royal Botanic Garden (£12/tour, £15 for all four tours, tickets give small discounts on most sights along the route, valid 24 hours, buy on bus, tel. 0131/220-0770, www.edinburghtour.com). Buses run daily year-round; in peak season, they leave Waverley Bridge every

Edinburgh at a Glance

▲▲▲**Edinburgh Castle** Iconic 11th-century hilltop fort and royal residence complete with crown jewels, Romanesque chapel, memorial, and fine military museum. **Hours:** Daily April–Oct 9:30–18:00, Nov–March 9:30–17:00. See page 520.

▲▲▲**Royal Mile** Historic road—good for walking—stretching from the castle down to the palace, lined with museums, pubs, and shops. **Hours:** Always open, but best during business hours. Walking tours daily, generally at 10:00 and 14:15. See page 528.

▲▲▲**National Museum of Scotland** Intriguing, well-displayed artifacts from prehistoric times to the 20th century. **Hours:** Daily 10:00–17:00. See page 540.

▲▲**Gladstone's Land** Sixteenth-century Royal Mile merchant's residence. **Hours:** Daily July–Aug 10:00–18:30, April–June and Sept–Oct 10:00–17:00, closed Nov–March. See page 530.

▲▲**St. Giles' Cathedral** Preaching grounds of Calvinist John Knox, with spectacular organ, Neo-Gothic chapel, and distinctive crown spire. **Hours:** May–Sept Mon–Fri 9:00–19:00, Sat 9:00–17:00, Sun 13:00–17:00; Oct–April Mon–Sat 9:00–17:00, Sun 13:00–17:00. See page 533.

▲▲**Scottish Parliament Building** Controversial new headquarters for the recently returned Parliament. **Hours:** Mon–Fri 10:00–17:30, until 16:30 Oct–March, Sat 11:00–17:30 year-round, closed Sun. See page 538.

▲▲**Georgian New Town** Elegant 1776 subdivision spiced with trendy shops, bars, and eateries. **Hours:** Always open. See page 543.

▲▲**Georgian House** Intimate peek at upper-crust life in the late 1700s. **Hours:** Daily July–Aug 10:00–18:00, April–June and Sept–Oct 10:00–17:00, March 11:00–16:00, Nov 11:00–15:00, closed Dec–Feb. See page 544.

▲▲**National Gallery of Scotland** Choice sampling of European masters and Scotland's finest. **Hours:** Daily 10:00–17:00, Thu until 19:00. See page 544.

▲▲*Britannia* The royal yacht with a history of distinguished passengers, a 15-minute trip out of town. **Hours:** Daily July–Aug 9:30–16:00, April–June and Sept–Oct 10:00–16:00, Nov–March 10:00–15:30 (these are last entry times). See page 547.

▲**Writers' Museum at Lady Stair's House** Tribute to Scottish literary triumvirate: Robert Burns, Sir Walter Scott, and Robert Louis Stevenson. **Hours:** Mon–Sat 10:00–17:00, closed Sun except during Festival 14:00–17:00. See page 531.

▲**Museum of Childhood** Five stories of historic fun. **Hours:** Mon–Sat 10:00–17:00, Sun 12:00–17:00. See page 537.

▲**John Knox House** Reputed 16th-century digs of the great reformer. **Hours:** Mon–Sat 10:00–18:00, closed Sun except in July–Aug 12:00–18:00. See page 537.

▲**Cadenhead's Whisky Shop** Sample whisky straight from the distilleries. **Hours:** Mon–Sat 10:30–17:30, closed Sun except possibly in Aug 12:30–17:30. See page 537.

▲**People's Story** Proletarian life from the 18th to 20th centuries. **Hours:** Mon–Sat 10:00–17:00, closed Sun except during Festival 12:00–17:00. See page 538.

▲**Museum of Edinburgh** Historic mementos, from the original National Covenant inscribed on animal skin to early golf balls. **Hours:** Mon–Sat 10:00–17:00, closed Sun except during Festival 12:00–17:00. See page 538.

▲**Palace of Holyroodhouse** The Queen's splendid home away from home, with lavish rooms, 12th-century abbey, and gallery with rotating exhibits. **Hours:** Daily April–Oct 9:30–18:00, Nov–March 9:30–16:30. See page 539.

▲**Sir Walter Scott Monument** Climbable tribute to the famed novelist. **Hours:** April–Sept daily 9:00–19:00; Oct–March Mon–Sat 9:00–15:00, Sun 10:00–15:00. See page 545.

EDINBURGH

Edinburgh

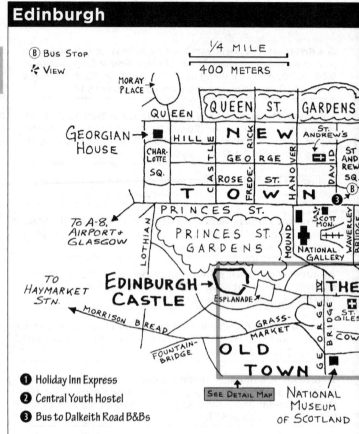

ⓑ BUS STOP
☇ VIEW

¼ MILE
400 METERS

MORAY PLACE

GEORGIAN HOUSE →

QUEEN

NEW

QUEEN ST. GARDENS

HILL

CHARLOTTE SQ.

CASTLE

GEO RGE

ROSE ST.

FREDERICK

ST. ANDREW'S

HANOVER

DAVID

ST AND REW SQ.

TOWN

ⓑ ❸

To A-8, AIRPORT + GLASGOW

PRINCES ST.

LOTHIAN

PRINCES ST. GARDENS

MOUND

NATIONAL GALLERY

SCOTT MON.

WAVERLEY BRIDGE

To HAYMARKET STN.

EDINBURGH CASTLE →

ESPLANADE

THE

GEORGE IV BRIDGE

ST. GILES

MORRISON B READ

GRASSMARKET

COW

FOUNTAINBRIDGE

OLD TOWN

SEE DETAIL MAP

NATIONAL MUSEUM OF SCOTLAND

❶ Holiday Inn Express
❷ Central Youth Hostel
❸ Bus to Dalkeith Road B&Bs

day between around 9:15 and 19:00 (mid-June–early Sept; hours shrink off-season). On sunny days they go topless (the buses), but come with increased traffic noise and exhaust fumes. All of these companies are actually run by Lothian Buses (which has to splinter its offerings this way because of local antimonopoly laws).

Busy sightseers might want to get the **Royal Edinburgh Ticket** (£37), which covers two days of unlimited travel on Lothian city buses—including all four tour buses, as well as admission to Edinburgh Castle (usually £12–14), the Palace of Holyroodhouse (£10), and the *Britannia* (£10.50). If you plan to visit all these sights and to use a tour bus both days, the ticket will save you a few pounds (and, in the summer, help you bypass any lines). You can buy these tickets from the TI, or from the staff at the tour-bus pick-up point on Waverley Bridge. If your main interest is seeing the *Britannia*, you'll save money by taking a regular bus instead (see page 547).

Day Trips from Edinburgh

Many companies run a variety of day trips to regional sights. Study the brochures at the TI's rack.

Highlands Tours—By far the most popular tour is the all-day Highlands trip. The standard Highlands tour gives those with limited time a chance to experience the wonders of Scotland's wild and legend-soaked Highlands in a single long day (about £35–40, roughly 8:30–20:30). You'll generally see the vast and brutal Rannoch Moor; Glencoe, still evocative with memories of the clan massacre; views of Britain's highest mountain, Ben Nevis; Fort Augustus on Loch Ness (some tours have a 1.5-hour stop here with an optional £9 boat ride); and a 45-minute tea or pub break in the fine town of Pitlochry. You learn about the Loch Ness monster, and a bit about Edinburgh to boot as you drive in and out.

Various competing companies run these tours, including **Timberbush Highland Tours** (£37, 7- to 36-seat air-con buses, reliable, depart from entrance to Edinburgh Castle, tel. 0131/226-6066, www.timberbushtours.com); **Gray Line** (£38, tel. 0131/555-5558, www.graylinescotland.com); **Rabbie's Trail Burners** (£30–43 depending on tour and time of year, maximum 16 per tour, guaranteed departures, depart from High Street and Cockburn Street, 207 High Street, tel. 0131/226-3133, www.rabbies.com); and **Heart of Scotland Tours** (£37, £3 discount with this book in 2010, departures daily at 8:00, leaves from bus stand E on Waterloo Place near Waverley Station, tel. 01828/627-799, www.heartofscotlandtours.co.uk, run by Nick Roche). As Heart of Scotland is a small company, they may need to cancel if the requisite six people don't sign up. Be sure to leave a contact number so you can be notified. A final decision is made by 18:00 the night before.

Haggis Adventures runs cheap and youthful tours on 16- to 39-seat buses with a very Scottish driver/guide. Their day trips (£27–33) include a distillery visit and the northern Highlands, or Loch Lomond and the southern Highlands. Their overnight trips are designed for young backpackers, but they welcome travelers of any age who want a quick look at the countryside (£105/3 days, £175/5 days, £285/7 days—plus about £18/night for hostel beds; office hours: Mon–Sat 9:00–18:00 in summer, until 17:00 in winter; Sun 9:00–16:00, often closed Sun in winter; 60 High Street, at Blackfriars Street, tel. 0131/557-9393, www.haggisadventures.com).

Glasgow—Scotland's biggest city is a happening cultural center and a mecca for those interested in architecture (particularly the Art Nouveau designs of Charles Rennie Mackintosh). Only 50 minutes away by train from Edinburgh (4/hr, £10.50 same-day round-trip if leaving after 9:15 or on a weekend), it makes an interesting day trip. For details, see the Glasgow chapter.

Sights in Edinburgh

▲▲▲Edinburgh Castle

The fortified birthplace of the city 1,300 years ago, this imposing symbol of Edinburgh sits proudly on a rock high above you. While the castle has been both a fort and a royal residence since the 11th century, most of the buildings today are from its more recent use as a military garrison. This fascinating and multifaceted sight deserves several hours of your time.

Edinburgh Castle

PRINCES ST. GARDENS

CLIFFS

CLIFFS

GARDENS

MIDDLE WARD

WALLS

CROWN SQUARE

SHOP

ESPLANADE

DITCH

START

ENTRY GATE

TO → ROYAL MILE

WC

DITCH

DCH

50 YARDS

50 METERS

➡ ROUTE FROM ENTRY GATE TO CROWN SQUARE

▨ MAIN BUILDINGS

☐ OTHER BUILDINGS

↗ VIEW

☶ STAIRS

Tour
- ❶ Crown Jewels
- ❷ Royal Palace
- ❸ Scottish National War Memorial
- ❹ St. Margaret's Chapel
- ❺ National War Museum Scotland

Other
- ❻ Ticket Booth
- ❼ Red Coat Café & Jacobite Room
- ❽ Queen Anne Café
- ❾ One O' Clock Gun
- ❿ Dog Cemetery

Cost, Hours, Information: £12–14 depending on time of year, daily April–Oct 9:30–18:00, Nov–March 9:30–17:00, last entry 45 min before closing, National War Museum Scotland closes 15 min before rest of castle, tel. 0131/225-9846, www.edinburghcastle.gov.uk.

Tours: Twenty-minute guided introductory tours are free with admission (2–4/hr, depart from entry gate, see clock for next departure; fewer tours off-season). The excellent audioguide provides a good supplement to the live guided tour, offering four hours of quick-dial digital descriptions of the sights, including the National War Museum Scotland (£3.50, slightly cheaper if purchased with entry ticket, pay at the ticket booth and pick it up at the entry gate).

Services: The clean WC at the entry routinely wins "British Loo of the Year" awards. For lunch, you have two choices. **The Red Coat Café and Jacobite Room**—located within Edinburgh Castle—is a big, bright, efficient cafeteria with great views (£6

William Wallace
(c. 1270–1305)

In 1286, Scotland's king died without an heir, plunging the prosperous country into a generation of chaos. As Scottish nobles bickered over naming a successor, the English King Edward I—nicknamed "Longshanks" because of his height—invaded and assumed power (1296). He placed a figurehead on the throne, forced Scottish nobles to sign a pledge of allegiance to England (the "Ragman's Roll"), moved the British parliament north to York, and carried off the highly symbolic 336-pound Stone of Scone to London, where it would remain for the next seven centuries.

A year later, the Scots rose up against Edward, led by William Wallace (nicknamed "Braveheart"). A mix of history and legend portrays Wallace as the son of a poor-but-knightly family that refused to sign the Ragman's Roll. Exceptionally tall and strong, he learned Latin and French from two uncles, who were priests. In his teenage years, his father and older brother were killed by the English. Later, he killed an English sheriff to avenge the death of his wife, Marion. Wallace's rage inspired his fellow Scots to revolt.

In the summer of 1297, Wallace and his guerrillas scored a series of stunning victories over the English. On September 11, a large, well-equipped English army of 10,000 soldiers and 300 horsemen began crossing Stirling Bridge. Half of the army had made it across when Wallace's men attacked. In the chaos, the bridge collapsed, splitting the English ranks in two, and the ragtag Scots drove the confused English into the river. The Battle of Stirling Bridge was a rout, and Wallace was knighted and appointed Guardian of Scotland.

All through the winter, King Edward's men chased Wallace, continually frustrated by the Scots' hit-and-run tactics. Finally, at the Battle of Falkirk (1298), they drew Wallace's men out onto the open battlefield. The English with their horses and archers easily destroyed the spear-carrying Scots. Wallace resigned in disgrace and went on the lam, while his successors negotiated truces with the English, finally surrendering unconditionally in 1304. Wallace alone held out.

In 1305, the English tracked him down and took him to London, where he was convicted of treason and mocked with a crown of oak leaves as the "King of Scotland." On August 23, they stripped him naked and dragged him to the execution site. There he was strangled to near death, castrated, and dismembered. His head was stuck on a stick atop London Bridge, while his body parts were sent on tour around the realm to spook would-be rebels. But Wallace's martyrdom only served to inspire his countrymen, and the torch of independence was picked up by Robert the Bruce (see sidebar on page 526).

quick, healthy meals). Punctuate the two parts of your castle visit (the castle itself and the impressive National War Museum Scotland) with a smart break here. The **Queen Anne Café,** in a building right across from the crown jewels, serves sit-down meals in its small, tight space (last orders 30 min before castle complex closes).

Getting There: Regular city buses drop you a little below the castle entry (at the top of the Royal Mile, near the Camera Obscura); taxis take you right to the esplanade, in front of the gate.

➲ **Self-Guided Tour:** Start at the entry gate, where you can pick up your audioguide and enjoy the droll 20-minute introductory tour with a live guide. (It'd be a shame to miss this included and charmingly entertaining intro tour.) The castle has five essential stops: the crown jewels, Royal Palace, Scottish National War Memorial, St. Margaret's Chapel (with a city view), and the excellent National War Museum Scotland. The first four are at the highest and most secure point—on or near the castle square, where your introductory guided tour ends (and the sights described below begin). The separate National War Museum Scotland is worth a serious look—allow at least a half-hour (50 yards below the cafeteria and big shop).

❶ **Crown Jewels:** There are two ways to get to the jewels. You can go in directly from the top palace courtyard, Crown Square, but there's often a line. To avoid the line, head to the left as you're facing the building and find the entrance near the WCs. This route takes you through the "Honors of Scotland" exhibition—an interesting, if Disney-esque, series of displays (which often moves at a very slow shuffle) telling the story of the crown jewels and how they survived the harrowing centuries.

Scotland's **crown jewels,** though not as impressive as England's, are older and treasured by the locals. Though Oliver Cromwell destroyed England's jewels, the Scots managed to hide theirs. Longtime symbols of Scottish nationalism, they were made in Edinburgh—in 1540 for a 1543 coronation—out of Scottish diamonds, gems, and gold...some say the personal gold of King Robert the Bruce. They were last used to crown Charles II in 1651. When the Act of Union was forced upon the Scots in 1707—dissolving Scotland's parliament into England's to create the United Kingdom—part of the deal was that the Scots could keep their jewels locked up in Edinburgh. The jewels remained hidden for more than 100 years. In 1818, Sir Walter Scott and a royal commission rediscovered them intact. In 1999, for the first time in nearly three

British, Scottish, and English

Scotland and England have been tied together for 300 years, since the Act of Union in 1707. For a century and a half afterward, Scottish nationalists rioted for independence in Edinburgh's streets and led rebellions in the Highlands. In this controversial union, history is clearly seen through two very different filters.

If you tour a British-oriented sight, such as the National War Museum Scotland, you'll find things told in a "happy union" way, which ignores the long history of Scottish resistance—from the ancient Picts through the time of Robert the Bruce. The official line: In 1706–1707, it was clear to England and some of Scotland (especially landowners from the Lowlands) that it was in their mutual interest to dissolve the Scottish government and fold it into Britain, to be ruled from London.

But talk to a cabbie or your B&B host, and you may get a different spin. In a clever move by England to deflate the military power of its little sister, Scottish Highlanders were often sent to fight and die for Britain—in disproportionately higher numbers than their English counterparts. Poignant propaganda posters in the National War Museum Scotland show a happy lad with the message, "Hey, look! Willie's off to Singapore with the Queen's Own Highlanders."

Scottish independence is still a hot-button issue today. In 2007, the Scottish National Party (SNP) won a major election, and now has the largest majority in the fledgling Scottish parliament. Alex Salmond, SNP leader and the First Minister of Scotland, is widely expected to push for Scotland to be recognized as an independent nation within the EU. (English leaders are obviously not in favor of breaking up the "united kingdom," though there's a like-minded independence movement in Wales, as well.)

The deep-seated rift shows itself in sports, too. While the English may refer to a British team in international competition as "English," the Scots are careful to call it "British." If a Scottish athlete does well, the English call him "British." If he screws up…he's a clumsy Scot.

centuries, the crown of Scotland was brought from the castle for the opening of the Scottish parliament (see photos on the wall where the "Honors of Scotland" exhibit meets the crown jewels room; a smiling Queen Elizabeth II presides over the historic occasion).

The **Stone of Scone** (a.k.a. the "Stone of Destiny") sits plain and strong next to the jewels. This big gray chunk of rock is the coronation stone of Scotland's ancient kings (ninth century). Swiped by the English, it sat under the coronation chair at Westminster Abbey from 1296 until 1996. Queen Elizabeth finally agreed to let the stone go home, on one condition: that it be returned to Westminster Abbey in London for all future coronations. With major fanfare, Scotland's treasured Stone of Scone returned to Edinburgh on Saint Andrew's Day, November 30, 1996. Talk to the guard for more details.

❷ **The Royal Palace:** Scottish royalty lived here only when safety or protocol required it (they preferred the Palace of Holyroodhouse at the bottom of the Royal Mile). The Royal Palace, facing the castle square under the flagpole, has two historic yet unimpressive rooms (through door marked "1566") and the Great Hall (separate entrance from opposite side of square; see below). Enter the **Mary, Queen of Scots room,** where in 1566 the queen gave birth to James VI of Scotland, who later became King James I of England. The Presence Chamber leads into **Laich Hall** (Lower Hall), the dining room of the royal family.

The **Great Hall** was the castle's ceremonial meeting place in the 16th and 17th centuries. In later times, it was a barracks and a hospital. Although most of what you see is Victorian, two medieval elements survive: the fine hammer-beam roof and the big iron-barred peephole (above fireplace on right). This allowed the king to spy on his subjects while they partied.

❸ **The Scottish National War Memorial:** This commemorates the 149,000 Scottish soldiers lost in World War I, the 58,000 who died in World War II, and the nearly 800 (and counting) lost in British battles since. Each bay is dedicated to a particular Scottish regiment. The main shrine, featuring a green Italian-marble memorial that contains the original WWI rolls of honor, sits—almost as if it were sacred—on an exposed chunk of the castle rock. Above you, the archangel Michael is busy slaying a dragon. The bronze frieze accurately shows the attire of various wings of Scotland's military. The stained glass starts with Cain and Abel on the left, and finishes with a celebration of peace on the right. To appreciate how important this place is, consider that Scottish soldiers died at twice the rate of other British soldiers in World War I.

❹ **St. Margaret's Chapel:** The oldest building in Edinburgh is dedicated to Queen Margaret, who died here in 1093 and was sainted in 1250. Built in 1130 in the Romanesque style of the Norman invaders, it's wonderfully simple, with classic Norman zigzags decorating the round arch that separates the tiny nave from the sacristy. It was used as a powder magazine for 400 years; very little survives. You'll see a facsimile of St. Margaret's 11th-century gospel book and small windows featuring St. Margaret, St. Columba (who brought Christianity to Scotland via Iona), and William Wallace (the brave-hearted defender of Scotland). The place is popular for weddings—and, as it seats only 20, it's particularly popular with brides' fathers.

Robert the Bruce
(1274–1329)

William Wallace's story (see sidebar on page 522) paints the Scottish fight for independence in black-and-white terms—the oppressive English versus the plucky Scots. But Scotland had to overcome its own divisiveness, and no one was more divided than Robert the Bruce. As Earl of Carrick, he was born with blood ties to England and a long-standing family claim to the Scottish throne.

When England's King Edward I ("Longshanks") conquered Scotland in 1296, the Bruce family welcomed it, hoping Edward would defeat their rivals and put Bruce's father on the throne. They dutifully signed the "Ragman's Roll" of allegiance...and then Edward chose someone else as king.

Twentysomething Robert the Bruce (the "the" comes from his original family name of "de Bruce") then joined William Wallace's revolt against the English. Legend has it that it was he who knighted Wallace after the victory at Stirling Bridge. When Wallace fell from favor, Bruce became co-Guardian of Scotland (caretaker ruler in the absence of a king) and continued fighting the English. But when Edward's armies again got the upper hand in 1302, Robert—along with Scotland's other nobles—diplomatically surrendered and again pledged loyalty.

In 1306, Robert the Bruce murdered his chief rival and boldly claimed to be King of Scotland. Few nobles supported him. Edward crushed the revolt and kidnapped Bruce's wife, the Church excommunicated him, and Bruce went into hiding on a distant North Sea island. He was now the king of nothing. Legend says he gained inspiration by watching a spider patiently build its web.

The following year, Bruce returned to Scotland and weaved alliances with both nobles and the Church, slowly gaining acceptance as Scotland's king by a populace chafing under English rule. On June 24, 1314, he decisively defeated the English (now led by Edward's weak son, Edward II) at the Battle of Bannockburn. After a generation of turmoil (1286–1314), England was finally driven from Scotland, and the country was united under Robert I, King of Scotland.

As king, Robert the Bruce's priority was to stabilize the monarchy and establish clear lines of succession. His descendants would rule Scotland for the next 400 years, and even today, Bruce blood runs through the veins of Queen Elizabeth II, Prince Charles, and princes William and Harry.

Mons Meg, in front of the church, is a huge and once-upon-a-time frightening 15th-century siege cannon that fired 330-pound stones nearly two miles. It was a gift from the Belgians, who shared a common enemy with the Scots—England—and were eager to arm Scotland.

Belly up to the banister (outside the chapel, below the cannon) to enjoy the grand view. Beneath you are the guns—which fire the one o'clock salute—and a sweet little line of doggie tombstones, marking the soldiers' pet cemetery. Beyond stretches the Georgian New Town (read the informative plaque).

Crowds gather for the 13:00 gun blast, a tradition that gives ships in the bay something to set their navigational devices by. (The frugal Scots don't fire it at high noon, as that would cost 11 extra rounds a day.)

❺ The National War Museum Scotland: This museum is a pleasant surprise, thoughtfully covering four centuries of Scottish military history. Instead of the usual musty, dusty displays of endless armor, this museum has an interesting mix of short films, uniforms, weapons, medals, mementos, and eloquent excerpts from soldiers' letters. Just when you thought your castle visit was about over, you'll likely find yourself lingering at this stop, which rivals any military museum you'll see in Europe (closes 15 min before rest of castle complex).

Here you'll learn the story of how the fierce and courageous Scottish warrior changed from being a symbol of resistance against Britain to being a champion of that same empire. Along the way, these military men received many decorations for valor and did more than their share of dying in battle. But even when fighting for—rather than against—England, Scottish regiments still promoted their romantic, kilted-warrior image.

Queen Victoria fueled this ideal throughout the 19th century. (She was infatuated with the Scottish Highlands and the culture's untamed, rustic mystique.) Highland soldiers, especially officers, went to great personal expense to sport all their elaborate regalia, and the kilted men fought best to the tune of their beloved bagpipes. For centuries the stirring drone of bagpipes accompanied Highland soldiers into battle—inspiring them, raising their spirits, and announcing to the enemy that they were about to meet a fierce and mighty foe.

This museum shows the human side of war, and the cleverness of government-sponsored ad campaigns that kept the lads enlisting. Two centuries of recruiting posters make the same pitch that still works today: a hefty signing bonus, steady pay, and job security with the promise of a manly and adventurous life—all spiked with a mix of pride and patriotism.

Leaving the Castle: As you exit, turn around and look back at the gate. There stand King Robert the Bruce (on the left, 1274–1329) and Sir William Wallace (Braveheart—on the right, 1270–1305). Wallace—now well-known to Americans, thanks to Mel Gibson—fought long and hard against English domination before being executed in London. Bruce beat the English at Bannockburn in 1314. Bruce and Wallace still defend the spirit of Scotland. The Latin inscription above the gate between them reads, more or less, "What you do to us...we will do to you."

▲▲▲The Royal Mile

The Royal Mile is one of Europe's most interesting historic walks. Consisting of a series of four different streets—Castlehill, Lawnmarket, High Street, and Canongate (each with its own set of street numbers)—the Royal Mile is actually 200 yards longer than a mile. And every inch is packed with shops, cafés, and lanes leading to tiny squares.

Start at the castle at the top and amble down to the palace. These sights are listed in walking order. Entertaining guided walks bring the legends and lore of the Royal Mile alive (described earlier, under "Tours in Edinburgh").

As you walk, remember that originally there were two settlements here, divided by a wall: Edinburgh lined the ridge from the castle at the top. The lower end, Canongate, was outside the wall until 1856. By poking down the many side alleys, you'll find a few surviving rough edges of an Old Town well on its way to becoming a touristic mall. Be glad you're here now; in a few years it'll be all tartans and shortbread, with tourists slaloming through the postcard racks on bagpipe skateboards.

Royal Mile Terminology: A "close" is a tiny alley between two buildings (originally with a door that closed it at night). A close usually leads to a "court," or courtyard. A "land" is a tenement block of apartments. A "pend" is an arched gateway. A "wynd" is a narrow, winding lane. And "gate" is from an old Scandinavian word for street.

Castle Esplanade—At the top of the Royal Mile, the big parking lot leading up to the castle was created as a military parade ground in 1816. It's often cluttered with bleachers for the Military Tattoo—a spectacular massing of the bands, filling the square nightly for most of August. At the bottom, on the left (where the square hits the road), a plaque above the tiny witches' fountain memorializes 300 women who were accused of witchcraft and burned here. Scotland burned more witches per capita than any other country—17,000 between 1479 and 1722. The plaque shows two witches: one good and one bad.

Walking downhill, you'll pass a touristy "Weaving Mill and Exhibition" that was once the Old Town's reservoir (you'll see the wellheads it served all along this walk). At Ramsey Lane, the street just before the Camera Obscura, turn left and walk one block. At the corner, enjoy a commanding **Edinburgh view:** Nelson's column stands atop Calton Hill with a Greek temple folly from 1822 (they ran out of money to finish this memorial to the British victory over France in the Napoleonic era). The big clock tower marks the Balmoral Hotel—built as a terminal hotel above Waverley Station in 1903. The lacy Neo-Gothic Sir Walter Scott Memorial is to the left. Below, two Neoclassical buildings—the National Gallery and Royal Scottish Academy—stand on The Mound.

Now head back out to the Mile.

Camera Obscura—A big deal when it was built in 1853, this observatory topped with a mirror reflected images onto a disc before the wide eyes of people who had never seen a photograph or captured image. Today, you can climb 100 steps for an entertaining 15-minute demonstration (3–4/hr). At the top, enjoy the best view anywhere of the Royal Mile. Then work your way down through three floors of illusions, holograms, and early photos. This is a big hit with kids, but sadly overpriced (£9, daily July–Aug 9:30–19:30, April–June and Sept–Oct 9:30–18:00, Nov–March 10:00–17:00, last demonstration one hour before closing, tel. 0131/226-3709).

Scotch Whisky Heritage Centre (a.k.a. "Malt Disney")— This gimmicky ambush is designed only to distill £11 out of your pocket. You kick things off with a little whisky-barrel train-car ride that goes to great lengths to make whisky production seem thrilling (things get pretty psychedelic when you hit the yeast stage). A presentation on whisky in Scotland includes sampling a wee dram, and the chance to stand amid the world's largest whisky collection. At the end, you'll find yourself in the bar, which is worth a quick look for its wall of unusually shaped whisky bottles. If you're visiting Oban, Pitlochry, or the Isle of Skye, you'll find cheaper, less hokey distillery tours there. People do seem to enjoy this place, but that might have something to do with the sample. Plus, I have to admit, it's fun to get a photo with the barrel man hustling business out front (daily July–Sept 10:00–18:30, Oct–June 10:00–18:00, last tour one hour before closing, tel. 0131/220-0441, www.whisky-heritage.co.uk). Serious connoisseurs of the Scottish firewater will want to pop into Cadenhead's Whisky Shop at the bottom of the Royal Mile (see page 537).

The Hub (Tolbooth Church)—This Neo-Gothic church (1844), with the tallest spire in the city, is now The Hub, Edinburgh's

Edinburgh's Royal Mile

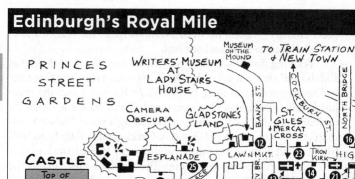

PRINCES STREET GARDENS

MUSEUM ON THE MOUND

TO TRAIN STATION & NEW TOWN

WRITERS' MUSEUM AT LADY STAIR'S HOUSE

CAMERA OBSCURA

GLADSTONE'S LAND

BANK ST.

COCKBURN ST.

NORTH BRIDGE

CASTLE

TOP OF ROYAL MILE

ESPLANADE

LAWN MKT.

ST. GILES

MERCAT CROSS

TRON KIRK

HIGH

16

12

23

JOHNSTON TERRACE

25

22

8

VICTORIA

GEORGE IV BR.

13

OLD PARLIAMENT HOUSE

14

3

21

26

6

15

GOOD RESTAURANTS & ANTIQUE SHOPS

GRASSMARKET

COWGATE

SOUTH BRIDGE

5

11

10

CHAMBERS

FOLK MUSIC PUBS

GREYFRIARS BOBBY STATUE

NATIONAL MUSEUM OF SCOTLAND

𝄢 VIEW

① MacDonald Hotel & Holiday Inn Express

② Jurys Inn

③ Ibis Hotel & Creelers Seafood Restaurant

④ Travelodge

⑤ Smart City Hostel

⑥ High Street Hostel

⑦ Royal Mile Backpackers Hostel

⑧ Castle Rock Hostel

⑨ Brodie's Hostels & The World's End Pub

⑩ The Elephant House

⑪ The Outsider Restaurant

⑫ Deacon Brodie's Tavern

Festival Ticket and Information Centre (for ticket information, see page 548). It also houses a handy café (£5–8 lunches).

▲▲**Gladstone's Land**—This is a typical 16th- to 17th-century merchant's house. "Land" means tenement, and these multi-story buildings—in which merchants ran their shops on the ground floor and lived upstairs—were typical of the time. (For an interesting comparison of life in the Old Town versus the New Town, also visit the Georgian House—described later.) Gladstone's Land comes complete with an almost-lived-in, furnished interior and guides in each room who love to talk. Keep this place in mind as you stroll the rest of

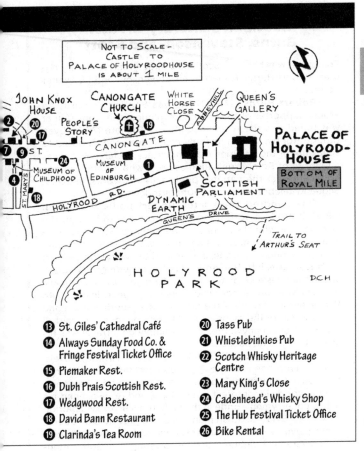

NOT TO SCALE -
CASTLE TO
PALACE OF HOLYROODHOUSE
IS ABOUT 1 MILE

JOHN KNOX HOUSE

CANONGATE CHURCH

WHITE HORSE CLOSE

QUEEN'S GALLERY

PEOPLE'S STORY

CANONGATE

PALACE OF HOLYROOD-HOUSE

BOTTOM OF ROYAL MILE

MUSEUM OF CHILDHOOD

MUSEUM OF EDINBURGH

ST. MARY'S

HOLYROOD RD.

SCOTTISH PARLIAMENT

DYNAMIC EARTH

QUEEN'S DRIVE

TRAIL TO ARTHUR'S SEAT

HOLYROOD PARK

DCH

13 St. Giles' Cathedral Café	20 Tass Pub
14 Always Sunday Food Co. & Fringe Festival Ticket Office	21 Whistlebinkies Pub
15 Piemaker Rest.	22 Scotch Whisky Heritage Centre
16 Dubh Prais Scottish Rest.	23 Mary King's Close
17 Wedgwood Rest.	24 Cadenhead's Whisky Shop
18 David Bann Restaurant	25 The Hub Festival Ticket Office
19 Clarinda's Tea Room	26 Bike Rental

the Mile, imagining other houses as if they still looked like this on the inside (£5.50, daily July–Aug 10:00–18:30, April–June and Sept–Oct 10:00–17:00, last entry 30 min before closing, closed Nov–March, no photos allowed, tel. 0844-493-2120).

For a good Royal Mile photo, climb the curved stairway outside the museum to the left of the entrance (or to the right as you're leaving). Notice the snoozing pig outside the front door. Just like every house has a vacuum cleaner today, in the good old days a snorting rubbish collector was a standard feature of any well-equipped house.

▲**Writers' Museum at Lady Stair's House**—This aristocrat's house, built in 1622, is filled with well-described manuscripts and knickknacks of Scotland's three greatest literary figures: Robert Burns, Sir Walter Scott, and Robert Louis Stevenson. Edinburgh's high society would gather in homes like this in the 1780s to hear

Scotland's Literary Greats: Burns, Stevenson, and Scott

Edinburgh was home to Scotland's three greatest literary figures: Robert Burns, Robert Louis Stevenson, and Sir Walter Scott.

Robert Burns (1759–1796) was Scotland's bard. An ardent supporter of the French Revolution, this poor farmer was tuned into the social inequities of the late 1700s. Even though Robby, as he's lovingly called even today, dared to speak up for the common man and attack social rank, he was a favorite of Edinburgh's high society, who'd gather in fine homes to hear the national poet recite his works. In 2009, Scotland celebrated Burns' 250th birthday.

One hundred years later, **Robert Louis Stevenson** (1850–1894) also stirred the Scottish soul with his pen. An avid traveler who always packed his notepad, Stevenson created settings that are vivid and filled with wonder. Traveling through Scotland, Europe, and around the world, he distilled his adventures into Romantic classics, including *Kidnapped* and *Treasure Island* (as well as *The Strange Case of Dr. Jekyll and Mr. Hyde*). Stevenson, who spent his last years in the South Pacific, wrote, "Youth is the time to travel—both in mind and in body—to try the manners of different nations." He said, "I travel not to go anywhere...but to simply go." Travel was his inspiration and his success.

Sir Walter Scott (1771–1832) wrote the *Waverley* novels, including *Ivanhoe* and *Rob Roy*. He's considered the father of the Romantic historical novel. Through his writing, he generated a worldwide interest in Scotland, and re-awakened his fellow countrymen's pride in their inheritance. An avid patriot, he wrote, "Every Scottish man has a pedigree. It is a national prerogative, as unalienable as his pride and his poverty." Scott is so revered in Edinburgh that his towering Neo-Gothic monument dominates the city center. With his favorite hound by his side, Sir Walter Scott overlooks the city that he inspired, and that inspired him.

The best way to learn about and experience these literary greats is to visit the Writers' Museum at Lady Stair's House (see page 531) and to take Edinburgh's Literary Pub Tour (see page 550).

the great poet Robby Burns read his work. Burns' work is meant to be read aloud rather than to oneself. In the Burns room, you can hear his poetry—worth a few minutes for anyone, and essential for fans (free, Mon–Sat 10:00–17:00, closed Sun except during Festival 14:00–17:00, tel. 0131/529-4901).

Wander around the courtyard here. Edinburgh was a wonder in the 17th and 18th centuries. Tourists came here to see its skyscrapers, which towered 10 stories and higher. No city in Europe was as densely populated—or polluted—as "Auld Reekie."

Deacon Brodie's Tavern—Read the "Doctor Jekyll and Mister Hyde" story of this pub's notorious namesake on the wall facing Bank Street. Then, to see his spooky split personality, check out both sides of the hanging signpost.

Deacon Brodie's Tavern lies at the intersection of the Royal Mile and George IV Bridge. At this point, you may want to con-

sider several detours. If you head down the street to your right, you'll reach some recommended eateries (The Elephant House and The Outsider), as well as the excellent National Museum of Scotland, the famous Greyfriars Bobby statue, and the photogenic Victoria Street, which leads to the fun pub-lined Grassmarket square (all described later in this chapter). To your left, down Bank Street, is the Museum on the Mound (free exhibit on banking history, described later). All are a five-minute walk from here.

Heart of Midlothian—Near the street in front of the cathedral, a heart-shaped outline in the brickwork marks the spot of a gallows and the entrance to a prison (now long gone). Traditionally, locals stand on the rim of the heart and spit into it. Hitting the middle brings good luck. Go ahead...do as the locals do.

Across the street is a seated green statue of hometown boy **David Hume** (1711–1776)—one of the most influential thinkers not only of the Scottish Enlightenment, but in all of Western philosophy. (Fun fact: Born David *Home*, he changed his name after getting tired of hearing the English say it without the correct Scottish pronunciation.)

Look around to understand Royal Mile plumbing. About 65 feet uphill is a **wellhead** (the square stone with a pyramid cap). This was the neighborhood well, served by the reservoir up at the castle before buildings had plumbing. Imagine long lines of people in need of water standing here, until buildings were finally retrofitted with water pipes—the ones you see running outside of buildings.

▲▲St. Giles' Cathedral—This is Scotland's most important church. Its ornate spire—the Scottish crown steeple from 1495—is a proud part of Edinburgh's skyline. As the church functions as a kind of Westminster Abbey of Scotland, the interior is fascinating.

Cost and Hours: Free but donations encouraged, £2 to take photos; May–Sept Mon–Fri 9:00–19:00, Sat 9:00–17:00, Sun 13:00–17:00; Oct–April Mon–Sat 9:00–17:00, Sun 13:00–17:00; tel. 0131/225-9442, www.stgilescathedral.org.uk.

Concerts: St. Giles' busy concert schedule includes organ recitals and visiting choirs (frequent free events at 12:15, £7–10 concerts often Wed at 20:00 and Sun at 18:00, see schedule or ask for the *Music at St. Giles'* pamphlet).

➲ **Self-Guided Tour:** Today's facade is 19th-century Neo-Gothic, but most of what you'll see inside is from the 14th and 15th centuries. You'll also find cathedral guides trolling around, hoping you'll engage them in conversation. You'll be glad you did.

Just inside the entrance, turn around to see the modern stained-glass **Robert Burns window,** which celebrates Scotland's favorite poet. It was made in 1985 by the Icelandic artist Leifur Breidfjord. The green of the lower level symbolizes the natural world—God's creation. The middle zone with the circle shows the brotherhood of man—Burns was a great internationalist. The top is a rosy red sunburst of creativity, reminding Scots of Burns' famous line, "My love is like a red, red rose"—part of a song near and dear to every Scottish heart.

To the right of the Burns window is a fine **Pre-Raphaelite window.** Like most in the church, it's a memorial to an important patron (in this case, John Marshall). From here stretches a great swath of war memorials.

As you walk along the north wall, find **John Knox's statue.** (Warning: They move him around like a six-foot-tall bronze chess piece.) Look into his eyes for 10 seconds from 10 inches away, and think of the Reformation struggles of the 16th century. Knox, the great Reformer and founder of austere Scottish Presbyterianism, first preached here in 1559. His insistence that every person should be able to read the word of God gave Scotland an educational system 300 years ahead of the rest of Europe (for more on Knox, see "The Scottish Reformation" on page 575). Thanks partly to Knox, it was Scottish minds that led the way in math, science, medicine, and engineering. Voltaire called Scotland "the intellectual capital of Europe."

Knox preached Calvinism. Consider that the Dutch and the Scots both embraced this creed of hard work, frugality, and strict ethics. This helps explain why Scots are so different from the English (and why the Dutch and the Scots—both famous for their thriftiness and industriousness—are so much alike).

The oldest parts of the cathedral—the **four massive central pillars**—date from 1120. After the English burned the cathedral, in 1385, it was rebuilt bigger and better than ever, and in 1495 its famous crown spire was completed. During the Reformation—when Knox preached here (1559–1572)—the place was simplified and whitewashed. Before this, when the emphasis was on holy services provided by priests, there were lots of little niches. With the new focus on sermons rather than rituals, the grand pulpit took center stage. Knox even had the church's fancy medieval glass windows replaced with clear glass, but 19th-century Victorians took them out and installed the brilliantly colored ones you see today.

Cross over to the **organ** (1992, Austrian-built, one of Europe's finest) and take in its sheer might. For a peek into the realm of the organist, duck around back to look through the glass panel.

Immediately to the right of the organ (as you're facing it) is a tiny chapel for silence and prayer. The dramatic **stained-glass**  **window** above (c. 1570) shows the commotion that surrounded Knox when he preached. Bearded, fiery-eyed Knox had a huge impact on this community. Notice how there were no pews back then. The church was so packed, people even looked through clear windows from across the street. With his hand on the holy book, Knox seems to conduct divine electricity to the Scottish faithful.

Between this window and the organ is a copy of the **National Covenant.** It was signed in blood in 1638 by Scottish heroes who refused to compromise their religion for the king's. Most who signed were martyred (their monument is nearby in Grassmarket).

Head toward the east (back) end of the church, and turn right to see the Neo-Gothic **Chapel of the Knights of the Thistle** and its intricate wood carving. Built in two years (1910–1911), entirely with Scottish materials and labor, it is the private chapel of the Knights of the Thistle, the only Scottish chivalric order. It's used about once a year to inaugurate new members. Scotland recognizes its leading citizens by bestowing upon them a membership. The Queen presides over the ritual from her fancy stall, marked by her Scottish coat of arms—a heraldic zoo of symbolism. Are there bagpipes in heaven? Find the tooting angel at a ceiling joint to the left of the altar.

Downstairs is an inviting café (see page 560 St. Gile's listing,) and handy public toilets.

Just outside, behind the church, is the **burial spot of John Knox**—with appropriate austerity, he's under the parking lot, at spot 23. The statue among the cars shows King Charles II riding to a toga party back in 1685.

• Near parking spot 15, enter the...

Old Parliament House—Step in (through security) to see the grand hall, with its fine 1639 hammer-beam ceiling and stained glass. This space housed the Scottish parliament until the Act of Union in 1707. Find the big stained-glass depiction of the initiation of the first Scottish High Court in 1532. Just under it, you'll find a history exhibition explaining the Scottish parliament. The building now holds the civil law courts and is busy with wigged and robed lawyers hard at work in the old library (peek through the door) or pacing the hall deep in discussion. Look for the "Box Corridor," a hallway filled with haphazard mailboxes for attorneys (the white dot indicates which lawyers have email). The friendly doorman is helpful (free, public welcome Mon–Fri 9:00–16:30, closed Sat–Sun, enter behind St. Giles' Cathedral; open-to-the-public trials are just across the street at the High Court—doorman has day's docket). The cleverly named Writz Café, in the basement, is literally their supreme court's restaurant (cheap, Mon–Fri 9:00–14:00, closed Sat–Sun).

Mary King's Close—For an unusual peek at Edinburgh's past, join a costumed guide on a trip through recently excavated underground streets and courtyards. Tours cover the standard goofy, crowd-pleasing ghost stories, but also provide authentic and interesting historical insight. It's best to book ahead—even though tours leave every 20 minutes, groups are small and the sight is popular (£10.50; Aug daily 9:00–21:00; April–July and Sept–Oct daily 10:00–21:00; Nov–March Sun–Fri 10:00–17:00, Sat 10:00–21:00; these are last tour times, no kids under 5, tel. 0845-070-6244, www.realmarykingsclose.com).

Mercat Cross—This chunky pedestal, on the downhill side of St. Giles', holds a slender column topped with a white unicorn. Royal proclamations have been read at this market cross since the 14th century. In 1952 a town crier heralded the news that Britain had a new queen—three days (traditionally the time it took for a horse to speed here from London) after the actual event. Today, Mercat Cross is the meeting point of various walking tours—both historic and ghostly.

• *A few doors downhill is the...*

Police Information Center—This center provides a pleasant police presence (say that three times) and a little local law-and-order history to boot (free, daily May–Aug 10:00–21:30, until 18:00 in winter). Ask the officer on duty about the grave-robber William Burke's skin and creative poetic justice, Edinburgh-style. Seriously—drop in and discuss whatever law-and-order issue piques your curiosity.

Along this stretch of Royal Mile, which is traffic-free most of the day (notice the bollards that raise and lower for permitted traffic), you'll see the Fringe Festival office (at #180), street musicians, and another wellhead (with horse "sippies," dating from 1675).

Cockburn Street—This street was cut through High Street's dense wall of medieval skyscrapers in the 1860s to give easy access to the Georgian New Town and the train station. Notice how the sliced buildings were thoughtfully capped with facades in a faux-16th-century Scottish baronial style. In the Middle Ages, only tiny lanes (like the Fleshmarket Lane just uphill from Cockburn Street) interrupted the long line of Royal Mile buildings.

• *Continue downhill 100 yards to the...*

▲**Museum of Childhood**—This five-story playground of historical toys and games is rich in nostalgia and history (free, Mon–Sat 10:00–17:00, Sun 12:00–17:00, last entry 30 min before closing). Just downhill is a fragrant fudge shop offering delicious free samples.

▲**John Knox House**—Intriguing for Reformation buffs, this fine 16th-century house offers a well-explained look at the life

of the great reformer. Although most contend he never actually lived here, preservationists called it "Knox's house" to save it from the wrecking ball in 1850. On the top floor, there's a fun cape, hat, and feather pen photo op (£3.50, Mon–Sat 10:00–18:00, closed Sun except in July–Aug 12:00–18:00, 43 High Street, tel. 0131/556-9579).

The World's End—For centuries, a wall halfway down the Royal Mile marked the end of Edinburgh and the beginning of Canongate, a community associated with Holyrood Abbey. Today, where the Mile hits St. Mary's and Jeffrey Streets, High Street becomes Canongate. Just below the John Knox House (at #43), notice the hanging sign showing the old gate. At the intersection, find the brass bricks that trace the gate (demolished in 1764). The cornerside Tass Pub is a great venue for live traditional music—pop in and see what's on tonight. Look down St. Mary's Street about 200 yards to see a surviving bit of that old wall.

• *Entering Canongate, you leave what was Edinburgh and head for...*

▲**Cadenhead's Whisky Shop**—The shop is not a tourist sight. Founded in 1842, this firm prides itself on bottling good malt whisky from casks straight from the best distilleries, without all the compromises that come with profitable mass production (coloring with sugar to fit the expected look, watering down to lessen the alcohol tax, and so on). Those drinking from Cadenhead-bottled whiskies will enjoy the pure product as the distilleries owners themselves do, not as the sorry public does.

If you want to learn about whisky—and perhaps pick up a bottle—chat up Mark and Alan, who love to talk. To buy whisky here, ask for a sample first. Sip once. Consider the flavor. Add a little water and sip again. Buy a small bottle of your favorite (£12 for about 7 ounces) and enjoy it in your hotel room night after night. Unlike wine, it has a long shelf life after it's opened. If you want to savor it post-trip, keep in mind that customs laws prohibit you from shipping whisky home, so you'll have to pack it in your checked luggage. Fortunately, the bottles are extremely durable—just ask Mark or Alan to demonstrate (Mon–Sat 10:30–17:30, closed Sun except possibly in Aug 12:30–17:30, 172 Canongate, tel. 0131/556-5864, www.wmcadenhead.com, chws@wmcadenhead.com).

▲**People's Story**—This interesting exhibition traces the conditions of the working class through the 18th, 19th, and 20th centuries (free, Mon–Sat 10:00–17:00, last entry 15 min before closing, closed Sun except during Festival 12:00–17:00, tel. 0131/529-4057). Curiously, while this museum is dedicated to the proletariat, immediately around the back (embedded in the wall of the museum) is the tomb of Adam Smith—the author of *Wealth of Nations* and the father of modern free-market capitalism (1723–1790).

▲**Museum of Edinburgh**—Another old house full of old stuff, this one is worth a look for its early Edinburgh history and handy ground-floor WC. Don't miss the original copy of the National Covenant (written in 1638 on an animal skin), sketches of pre-Georgian Edinburgh (which show a lake, later filled in to become Princes Street Gardens when the New Town was built), and early golf balls. A favorite Scottish say-it-aloud joke: "Balls," said the queen. "If I had two, I'd be king." The king laughed—he had to (free, same hours as People's Story—listed above, tel. 0131/529-4143).

White Horse Close—Step into this 17th-century courtyard (bottom of Canongate, on the left, a block before the Palace of Holyroodhouse). It was from here that the Edinburgh stagecoach left for London. Eight days later, the horse-drawn carriage would pull into its destination: Scotland Yard.

• *Across the street is the new...*

▲▲**Scottish Parliament Building**—Scotland's parliament originated in 1293 and was dissolved by England in 1707. In 1998 it was decided that "there shall be a Scottish parliament guided by justice, wisdom, integrity, and compassion," and in 1999 it was formally reopened by Queen Elizabeth. Except for matters of defense, foreign policy, and taxation, Scotland now enjoys home rule. The current government, run by the Scottish Nationalist Party, is pushing for more independence.

In 2004 the Parliament moved into its striking new home. Although its cost ($800 million) and perceived extravagance made it controversial from the start, an in-person visit wins most people over. The eco-friendly building, by the Catalan architect Enric Miralles, mixes wild angles, lots of light, bold windows, oak, and local stone into a startling complex that would, as he envisioned, "arise from the sloping base of Arthur's Seat and arrive into the city as if almost surging out of the rock."

Since it celebrates Scottish democracy, the architecture is not a statement of authority. There are no statues of old heroes. There's not even a grand entry. You feel like you're entering an office park. The building is people-oriented. Signs are written in both English and Gaelic (the Scots' Celtic tongue). Anyone is welcome to attend the committee meetings (viewable by live video hookups throughout the nation's libraries).

For a peek at the new building and a lesson in how the Scottish parliament works, drop in, pass through security, and

find the visitors' desk. You're welcome into the public parts of the building, including the impressive "Debating Chambers" (free, Mon–Fri 10:00–17:30, until 16:30 Oct–March, Sat 11:00–17:30 year-round, last entry 30 min before closing, closed Sun, schedule can change when Parliament is in session). Worthwhile hour-long tours by proud locals are offered about every 20 minutes (free, call for times and details or check www.scottish.parliament.uk). Or you can sign up online to witness the Scottish parliament's debates—best on Thursdays at noon, when the First Minister is on the hot seat and has to field questions from members across all parties (usually Wed 14:15–18:00, Thu 9:30–12:30 & 14:30–17:30, tel. 0131/348-5200).

▲**Palace of Holyroodhouse**—Since the 14th century, this palace has marked the end of the Royal Mile. The Queen spends a week in the palace each summer. An abbey—part of a 12th-century Augustinian monastery—originally stood in its place. It was named for a piece of the cross brought here as a relic by Queen (and later Saint) Margaret. Because Scotland's royalty preferred living at Holyroodhouse to the blustery castle on the rock, the palace evolved over time.

Consider touring the interior (£10 includes a quality audioguide, £14 combo-ticket includes Queen's Gallery—listed below, daily April–Oct 9:30–18:00, Nov–March 9:30–16:30, last entry one hour before closing, tel. 0131/556-5100, www .royalcollection.org.uk). The palace is closed when the Queen is at home—generally for a week around July 1—and whenever a prince or someone else important drops by (Prince Charles has a habit of showing up in May). The building, rich in history and decor, is filled with elegantly furnished rooms and a few darker, older rooms with glass cases of historic bits and Scottish pieces that locals find fascinating.

Bring the palace to life with the included one-hour **audio-guide.** You'll learn which of the kings featured in the 110 portraits lining the Great Gallery are real and which are fictional, what touches were added to the bedchambers to flatter King Charles II, and why the exiled Comte d'Artois took refuge in the palace. You'll also hear a goofy reenactment of the moment when conspirators—dispatched by Mary, Queen of Scots' jealous second husband—stormed into the queen's chambers and stabbed her male secretary. Royal diehards can pick up a palace guidebook for £4.50.

After exiting, you're free to stroll through the ruined abbey (destroyed by those dastardly English during the time of Mary, Queen of Scots, in the 16th century) and the queen's gardens (closed in winter). Hikers: Note that the wonderful trail up Arthur's Seat starts just across the street from the gardens (see page 546 for details).

Queen's Gallery—This small museum features rotating exhibits of artwork from the royal collection. For more than five centuries, the royal family has amassed a wealth of art treasures. While the Queen keeps most in her many private palaces, she shares an impressive load of it here, with exhibits changing about every six months. Though the gallery occupies just a few rooms, it can be exquisite. The entry fee includes an excellent audioguide, written and read by the curator (£5.50, £14 combo-ticket includes Palace of Holyroodhouse, daily  April–Oct 9:30–18:00, Nov–March until 16:30, last entry one hour before closing, on the palace grounds, to the right of the palace entrance).

Sights Just Off the Royal Mile

▲▲▲**National Museum of Scotland**—This huge museum has amassed more historic artifacts than every other place I've seen in Scotland combined. It's all wonderfully displayed with fine descriptions offering a best-anywhere hike through the history of Scotland. Start in the basement and work your way through the story: prehistoric, Roman, Viking, the "birth of Scotland," Edinburgh's witch-burning craze, clan massacres, all the way to life in the 20th century. Free audioguides offer a pleasant description of various rooms and exhibits, and even provide mood music for your wanderings (free entry, daily 10:00–17:00; free 1-hour "Highlights" tours daily at 11:30 and 13:30, themed tours at 14:30—confirm

tour schedule at info desk; 2 long blocks south of Royal Mile from St. Giles' Cathedral, Chambers Street, off George IV Bridge, tel. 0131/247-4422, www.nms.ac.uk).

The **Kingdom of the Scots** exhibit shows evidence of a vibrant young nation. While largely cut off from Europe by hos-

tilities with England, Scotland connected with the Continent through trade, the Church, and their monarch, Mary, Queen of Scots. Throughout Scotland's long, underdog struggle with England, its people found inspiration from romantic (and almost legendary) Scottish leaders, including Mary. Educated and raised in France during the Renaissance, Mary brought refinement to the Scottish throne. After she was imprisoned and then executed by the English, her countrymen rallied each other by invoking her memory. Pendants and coins with her portrait stoked the irrepressible Scottish spirit. Near the replica of Mary's tomb are tiny cameos, pieces of jewelry, and coins with her image.

The industry exhibit explains how (eventually) the Scots were tamed, and the union with England brought stability and investment to Scotland. Powered by the Scottish work ethic and the new opportunities that came from the Industrial Revolution, the country came into relative prosperity. Education and medicine thrived. Cast iron and foundries were huge, and this became one of the most industrialized places in Europe. With the dawn of the modern age came leisure time, the concept of "healthful sports," and golf—a Scottish invention. The first golf balls, which date from about 1820, were leather stuffed with feathers.

On the museum's top floor, the upscale **Tower restaurant** serves a two-course lunch/early-dinner special (£13, available daily 12:00–18:30) and fancy £15–£25 meals (open daily 12:00–23:00—later than the museum itself, tel. 0131/225-3003).

The **Royal Museum,** next door, fills a fine iron-and-glass Industrial Age building (built to house the museum in 1851) with all the natural sciences as it "presents the world to Scotland." It's great for school kids, but of no special interest to foreign visitors (closed until 2011).

Greyfriars Bobby—This famous statue of Edinburgh's favorite

dog is across the street from the National Museum of Scotland. Every business nearby, it seems, is named for this terrier, who stood by his master's grave for 14 years and was immortalized in a 1960s Disney flick.

Grassmarket—Once Edinburgh's site for hangings (locals rented out their windows—above the rudely named "Last Drop" pub—for the view), today Grassmarket is being renovated into a people-friendly

piazza. It was originally the city's garage, a depot for horses and cows (hence the name). It's rowdy here at night—a popular place for "hen" and "stag" parties. During the day, the literary pub tour departs from here. Budget shoppers might want to look at Armstrongs, a fun secondhand-clothing store. Victoria Street, built in the Victorian Age and lined with colorful little shops and eateries, was built to connect Grassmarket and High Street.

Hiding in the blur of traffic is a monument to the "Covenanters." These strict 17th-century Scottish Protestants were killed for refusing to accept the king's Episcopalian prayer book. To this day, Scots celebrate their emphatically democratic church government. Rather than big-shot bishops (as in the Anglican or Roman Catholic churches), they have a low-key "moderator" who's elected each year.

Museum on the Mound—Located in the basement of the grand Bank of Scotland building (easily spotted from a distance), this exhibit tells the story of the bank, which was founded in 1695 (making it only a year younger than the Bank of England). Featuring displays on cash production, safe technology, and bank robberies, this museum struggles mightily, with some success, to make banking interesting (the case holding £1 million is cool). It's worth popping in if you have some time or find the subject appealing. But no matter how well the information is presented, it's still about... yawn...banking (free, Tue–Fri 10:00–17:00, Sat–Sun 13:00–17:00, closed Mon, down Bank Street from the Royal Mile—follow the street around to the left and enter through the gate, tel. 0131/243-5464, www.museumonthemound.com).

Dynamic Earth—Located about a five-minute walk from the Palace of Holyroodhouse, this immense exhibit tells the story of

our planet, filling several underground floors under a vast Gore-Tex tent. It's pitched, appropriately, at the base of the Salisbury Crags. The exhibit is designed for younger kids and does the same thing an American science exhibit would do—but with a charming Scottish accent. Standing in a time tunnel, you watch the years rewind from Churchill to dinosaurs to the Big Bang. After viewing several short films on stars, tectonic plates, and ice caps, you're free to wander past salty pools, a re-created rain forest, and various TV screens. End your visit with a 12-minute video finale (£9.50; April–Oct daily 10:00–17:00, July–Aug until 18:00; Nov–March Wed–Sun 10:00–17:00, closed Mon–Tue; last ticket sold 70 min before closing, on Holyrood Road, between the palace and mountain, tel. 0131/550-7800, www.dynamicearth.co.uk). Dynamic Earth is a stop on the hop-on, hop-off bus route.

Bonnie Wee Sights in the New Town

▲▲**Georgian New Town**—Cross Waverley Bridge and walk through the Georgian New Town. According to the 1776 plan, the New Town was three streets (Princes, George, and Queen) flanked by two squares (St. Andrew and Charlotte), woven together by alleys (Thistle and Rose). George Street—20 feet wider than the others (so a four-horse carriage could make a U-turn)—was the main drag. And, while Princes Street has gone down-market, George Street still maintains its old grace. The entire elegantly planned New Town—laid out when George III was king—celebrated the hard-to-sell notion that Scotland was an integral part of the United Kingdom. The streets and squares are named after the British royalty (Hanover was the royal family surname). Even Thistle and Rose Streets (the national flowers of Scotland and England, respectively) are emblems of the two happily paired nations. Mostly pedestrianized Rose Street is famous for its rowdy pubs; where it hits St. Andrew Square, the street is flanked by the venerable Jenners department store and a Sainsbury's supermarket. Sprinkled with popular restaurants and bars, the stately New Town is turning trendy.

Princes Street—Edinburgh's main drag will likely be torn up for tram construction during your visit. If it's patched up, it'll be busy with buses and taxis (and trams, if running). Jenners department store is an institution. Notice how statues of women support the building—just as real women support the business. The arrival of new fashions here was such a big deal that they'd announce it by flying flags on the Nelson Monument. Step inside. The central space—filled with a towering tree at Christmas—is classic Industrial Age architecture. The Queen's coat of arms high on the wall indicates she shops here.

St. Andrew Square—This green space bookends the Georgian New Town opposite Charlotte Square. In the early 19th century, there were no shops around here—just fine residences. And this was a private garden for the fancy people living here. Newly opened to the public, the square is now a popular lunch hangout for local workers. The Melville Monument honors a powermonger Member of Parliament who, for four decades (around 1800), was nicknamed the "uncrowned king of Scotland."

St. Andrew's and St. George's Church—Designed as part of the New Town in the 1780s, the church is a product of the Scottish Enlightenment. It has an elliptical plan (the first in Britain) so that all can focus on the pulpit. A fine leaflet tells the story of the church, and a handy cafeteria downstairs serves cheap and cheery lunches (see page 563).

▲▲Georgian House—This refurbished Georgian house, set on Edinburgh's finest Georgian square, is a trip back to 1796. It recounts the era when a newly gentrified and well-educated Edinburgh was nicknamed the "Athens of the North." A volunteer guide in each of the five rooms shares stories and trivia—from the kitchen in the basement to the fully stocked medicine cabinet in the bedroom. Start your visit in the basement and view the interesting 16-minute video, which shows the life of one family who owned this property and touches on the architecture of the Georgian period (£5.50, daily July–Aug 10:00–18:00, April–June and Sept–Oct 10:00–17:00, March 11:00–16:00, Nov 11:00–15:00, last entry 30 min before closing, closed Dec–Feb, 7 Charlotte Square, tel. 0131/226-3318, www.nts.org.uk). A walk down George Street after your visit here can be fun for the imagination.

▲▲National Gallery of Scotland—The elegant Neoclassical building has a delightfully small but  impressive collection of European masterpieces, from Raphael, Titian, and Peter Paul Rubens to Thomas Gainsborough, Claude Monet, and Vincent van Gogh. A highlight (along with guards in plaid trousers) is Canova's exquisite *Three Graces*, and it offers the best look you'll get at Scottish paintings (in the basement). There's no audioguide, but each painting is well-described (free, daily 10:00–17:00, Thu until 19:00, tel. 0131/624-6200, www.nationalgalleries.org). The skippable **Royal Scottish Academy,** next door, hosts temporary art exhibits and is connected to the National Gallery at the garden level (underneath the gallery) by the Weston Link building (same hours as the gallery, fine café and restaurant).

Two other museums are associated with the National Gallery, but are outside the downtown core: the Scottish National Portrait Gallery (closed until August 2011) and the Scottish National Gallery of Modern Art.

The Mound—The National Gallery sits upon what's known as "The Mound." When the lake was drained and the Georgian New Town was built, rubble from the excavations was piled into The Mound (c. 1770) to allay Old Town merchant concerns about being disconnected from the future heart of the city. The two fine Neoclassical buildings here (which house museums) date from the 1840s. From The Mound you can enjoy fine views of "Auld Reekie" (medieval Edinburgh), with its 14-story "skyscrapers."

Princes Street Gardens—The grassy park, a former lakebed, separates Edinburgh's New and Old Towns and offers a wonderful escape from the bustle of the city. Once the private domain of wealthy locals, it was opened to the public around 1870—not as a democratic gesture, but because it was thought that allowing the public into the park would increase sales for the Princes Street department stores. Join the local office workers for a picnic lunch break, or see the oldest floral clock in the world. In summer you can also watch Scottish country dancing in the park (£3, May-Aug Mon and sometimes Tue 19:30–21:30, at Ross Bandstand, tel. 0131/228-8616).

The big lake, Nor' Loch, was drained around 1800 as part of the Georgian expansion of Edinburgh. Before that, the lake was the town's sewer, water reservoir, and handy place for drowning witches. Much was written about the town's infamous stink (a.k.a. the "flowers of Edinburgh"). The town's nickname, "Auld Reekie," referred to both the smoke of its industry and the stench of its squalor.

Although the loch is now long gone, memories of the countless women drowned as witches remain. With their thumbs tied to their ankles, they'd be lashed to dunking stools. Those who survived the ordeal were considered "aided by the devil" and burned as witches. If they died, they were innocent and given a good Christian burial. Until 1720, Edinburgh was Europe's witch-burning mecca—any perceived "sign," including a small birthmark, could condemn you.

▲**Sir Walter Scott Monument**—Built in 1840, this elaborate Neo-Gothic monument honors the great author, one of

Edinburgh's many illustrious sons. When Scott died in 1832, it was said that "Scotland never owed so much to one man." To all of Western literature, he's considered the father of the Romantic historical novel. The 200-foot monument shelters a marble statue of Scott and his favorite pet, Maida, a deerhound who was one of 30 canines this dog-lover owned during his lifetime. They're surrounded by busts of 16 great Scottish poets and 64 characters from his books. Climbing the tight, stony spiral staircase of 287 steps earns you a peek at a tiny museum midway, a fine city view at the top, and intimate encounters going up and down (£3; April–Sept daily 9:00–19:00—call ahead to confirm summer closing time; Oct–March Mon–Sat 9:00–15:00, Sun 10:00–15:00; last entry one hour before closing, tel. 0131/529-4068).

Activities

▲▲**Arthur's Seat Hike**—A 45-minute hike up the 822-foot remains of an extinct volcano (surrounded by a fine park overlooking Edinburgh) starts from the Palace of Holyroodhouse. You can run up like they did in *Chariots of Fire,* or just stroll—at the summit you'll be rewarded with commanding views of the town and surroundings. On May Day, be on the summit at dawn and wash your face in the morning dew to commemorate the Celtic holiday of Beltaine, the celebration of spring. (Morning dew is supposedly very good for your complexion.)

From the parking lot below the Palace of Holyroodhouse, there are two trailheads. Take the wide path on the left (easier grade, through the abbey ruins and "Hunter's Bog"). After making the summit, you can return along the other path (to the right, with the steps), which skirts the base of the cliffs.

Those staying at my recommended B&Bs can enjoy a pre-breakfast or late-evening hike starting from the other side (in June, the sun comes up early, and it stays light until nearly midnight). From the Commonwealth Pool, take Holyrood Park Road, turn right on Queen's Drive, and continue to a small parking lot. From here it's a 20-minute hike.

If you have a car, you can drive up most of the way from behind (follow the one-way street from palace, park safely and for free by the little lake, and hike up).

Brush Skiing—If you like skiing, but not all that pesky snow, head a little south of town to Hillend, where the Midlothian Snowsports Centre has a hill with a chairlift, two slopes, a jump slope, and rentable skis, boots, and poles. It feels like snow-skiing on a slushy day, even though you're schussing over what seems like a million toothbrushes. Beware: Local doctors are used to treating an ailment called "Hillend Thumb"—thumbs dislocated when people fall here and get tangled in the brush. Locals say skiing here is "like falling on a carrot grater" (£9.30/first hour, then £4/hr, includes gear, beginners must take a lesson, Mon–Fri 9:30–21:00, Sat–Sun 9:30–19:00, Lothian bus #4 from Princes Street—garden side, tel. 0131/445-4433, www.midlothian.gov.uk). Ironically, it closes if it snows.

More Hikes—You can hike along the river (called Water of Leith) through Edinburgh. Locals favor the stretch between Roseburn and Dean Village, but the 1.5-mile walk from Dean Village to the Royal Botanic Garden is also good. For more information on these and other hikes, ask at the TI for the free *Walks In and Around Edinburgh* one-page flier (if it's unavailable, consider their £2 guide to walks).

Prestonfield Golf Club—Just a mile and a half from town, the Prestonfield Golf Club has golfers feeling like they're in a country estate (£32–38/person plus £10 for clubs, 6 Priestfield Road North, tel. 0131/667-9665, www.prestonfieldgolf.com).

Shopping—The streets to browse are Princes Street (the elegant old Jenners department store is nearby on Rose Street, at St. Andrew Square), Victoria Street (antiques galore), Nicolson Street (south of the Royal Mile, line of interesting secondhand stores), and the Royal Mile (touristy but competitively priced). Shops are usually open from 9:00 to 17:30 (later on Thu, some closed Sun).

Near Edinburgh

▲▲Britannia—This much-revered vessel, which transported Britain's royal family for more than 40 years and 900 voyages before being retired in 1997, is permanently moored at the Ocean Terminal Shopping Mall in Edinburgh's port of Leith. It's open to the public and worth the 15-minute bus or taxi ride from the center. Explore the museum, filled with engrossing royal-family-afloat history. Then, armed with your included audioguide, you're welcome aboard.

This was the last in a line of royal yachts that stretches back to 1660. With all its royal functions, the ship required a crew of more than 200. The captain's bridge feels like it's been preserved from the day it was launched in 1953. Queen Elizabeth II, who enjoyed the ship for 40 years, said, "This is the only place I can truly relax." The sunny lounge just off the back Veranda Deck was the queen's favorite, with teak from Burma (now Myanmar, in Southeast Asia) and the same phone system she was used to in Buckingham Palace.

The back deck was the favorite place for outdoor entertainment. Ronald Reagan, Boris Yeltsin, Bill Clinton, and Nelson

Mandela all sipped champagne here with the Queen. When she wasn't entertaining, the Queen liked it quiet. The crew wore sneakers, communicated in hand signals, and (at least near the Queen's quarters) had to be finished with all their work by 8:00 in the morning.

The dining room, decorated with gifts given by the ship's many noteworthy guests, enabled the Queen to entertain a good-size crowd. The silver pantry was just down the hall. The drawing room, while rather simple, was perfect for casual relaxing among royals. Princess Diana played the piano, which is bolted to the deck. Royal family photos evoke the fine times the Windsors enjoyed on the *Britannia*.

Cost, Hours, Information: £10.50, daily July–Aug 9:30–16:00, April–June and Sept–Oct 10:00–16:00, Nov–March 10:00–15:30, these are last entry times, tel. 0131/555-5566, www.royal yachtbritannia.co.uk.

Getting There: From central Edinburgh, catch Lothian bus #1, #11, #22, #34, or #35 at Waverley Bridge. If you're doing a city bus tour, consider the Majestic Tour, which includes transportation to the *Britannia* (see page 515).

Rosslyn Chapel—Founded in 1446 by the Knights Templar, this church became famous for its role in the final scenes of *The Da Vinci Code* (£7.50, Mon–Sat 9:30–18:00, until 17:00 Oct–March, Sun 12:00–16:45 year-round, last entry 30 min before closing, located in Roslin Village, www.rosslynchapel.org.uk). To get to the chapel by bus, ride Lothian bus #15 from the station at St. Andrew Square (1–2/hr). By car, take A701 to Penicuik/Peebles, and follow signs for *Roslin;* once you're in the village, you'll see signs for the chapel.

Royal Botanic Garden—Britain's second-oldest botanical garden (after Oxford) was established in 1670 for medicinal herbs, and is now one of Europe's best (gardens free, greenhouse admission-£4, daily April–Sept 10:00–19:00, March and Oct 10:00–18:00, Nov–Feb 10:00–16:00, 1-hour tours April–Oct daily at 11:00 and 14:00 for £3, a mile north of the city center at Inverleith Row; take Lothian bus #8, #23, or #27; Majestic Tour stops here—see page 515, tel. 0131/552-7171, www.rbge.org.uk).

Experiences in Edinburgh

Edinburgh Festival

One of Europe's great cultural events, Edinburgh's annual festival turns the city into a carnival of the arts. There are enough music, dance, drama, and multicultural events to make even the most jaded traveler giddy with excitement. Every day is jammed with formal and spontaneous fun. A riot of festivals—official, fringe, book, and jazz and blues—rages simultaneously for about three weeks each August, with the Military Tattoo starting a week earlier (the best overall website is www.edinburghfestivals .co.uk). Many city sights run on extended hours, and those along the Royal Mile that are normally closed on Sunday are open in the afternoon. It's a glorious time to be in Edinburgh—if you have (and can afford) a room.

The official **Edinburgh International Festival** (Aug 13–Sept 5 in 2010) is the original, more formal, and most likely to get booked up. Major events sell out well in advance. The ticket office is at **The Hub,** located in the former Tolbooth Church, near the top of the Royal Mile (tickets-£5–55, booking from April, office open Mon–Sat 10:00–17:00 or longer, in Aug until 19:30 plus Sun 10:00–19:30, tel. 0131/473-2000). You can also book online at www.eif.co.uk.

Call and order your ticket through The Hub with your credit-card number. Pick up your ticket at the office on the day of the show or at the venue before showtime. Several publications—including the festival's official schedule, the *Edinburgh Festivals Guide Daily, The List,* the *Fringe Program,* and the *Daily Diary*—list and evaluate festival events.

The less-formal **Fringe Festival,** featuring "on the edge" comedy and theater, is huge—with 2,000 shows—and desperate for an audience (Aug 6–30 in 2010, ticket/info office just below St. Giles' Cathedral on the Royal Mile, 180 High Street, tel. 0131/226-0026, bookings tel. 0131/226-0000, can book online from mid-June on, www.edfringe.com). Tickets are usually available at the door.

The **Military Tattoo** is a massing of bands, drums, and bagpipes, with groups from all over the former British Empire. Displaying military finesse with a stirring lone-piper finale, this grand spectacle fills the Castle Esplanade nightly except Sunday, normally from a week before the festival starts until a week before it finishes (Aug 6–28 in 2010, Mon–Fri at 21:00, Sat at 19:30 and 22:30, £15–50, booking starts in Dec, Fri–Sat shows sell out first, all seats generally sold out many months ahead, some scattered same-day tickets may be available; office open Mon–Fri 10:00–16:30, during Tattoo open until show time and Sat 10:00–22:30, closed Sun; 33 Market Street, behind Waverley Station, tel. 0131/225-1188, www.edinburgh-tattoo.co.uk). The last day is broadcast as a big national television special.

The **Festival of Politics,** a new dimension to Edinburgh's festival action, is held in late August in the new Scottish Parliament building. It's a busy four days of discussions and lectures on environmentalism, globalization, terrorism, gender, and other issues (www.festivalofpolitics.org.uk).

Other summer festivals cover jazz and blues (early August,

tel. 0131/467-5200, www.edinburghjazzfestival.co.uk), film (mid-June, tel. 0131/228-4051, www.edfilmfest.org.uk), and books (late August, tel. 0131/718-5666, www.edbookfest.co.uk).

If you do manage to hit Edinburgh during a festival, book a room far in advance and extend your stay by a day or two. Once you know your dates, reserve tickets to any show you really want to see.

Nightlife in Edinburgh

▲▲**Literary Pub Tour**—This two-hour walk is interesting even if you think Sir Walter Scott was an Arctic explorer. You'll follow the witty dialogue of two actors as they debate whether the great literature of Scotland was high art or the creative re-creation of fun-loving louts fueled by a love of whisky. You'll wander from the Grassmarket, over the Old Town to the New Town, with stops in three pubs as your guides share their takes on Scotland's literary greats. The tour meets at The Beehive pub on Grassmarket (£10, book online and save £1, May–Sept nightly at 19:30, March–April and Oct Thu–Sun, Nov–Feb Fri only, call 0800-169-7410 or 0131/226-6665 to confirm, www.edinburghliterarypubtour.co.uk).

▲**Ghost Walks**—These walks are an entertaining and cheap night out (offered nightly, usually around 19:00 and 21:00, easy socializing for solo travelers). The theatrical and creatively staged **Witchery Tours,** the most established outfit, offers two different walks: "Ghosts and Gore" (1.5 hours) and "Murder and Mystery" (1.25 hours). The former is better-suited for kids than the latter (either tour £7.50, leave from top of Royal Mile near Castle Esplanade, reservations required, tel. 0131/225-6745, www.witcherytours.com).

Auld Reekie Tours offers a scary array of walks daily and nightly (£7–10, 50–75 min, leaves from front steps of the Tron Kirk building on Cockburn Street, pick up brochure or visit www.auldreekietours.com). Auld Reekie is into the paranormal, witch covens, and pagan temples, taking groups into the "vaults" under the old bridges "where it was so dark, so crowded, and so squalid that the people there knew each other not by how they looked, but by how they sounded, felt, and smelt. If you had a candle, you weren't poor enough to live in the vaults. Then the great fire came. They crowded in, thinking that a brick refuge like this wouldn't burn...and they all roasted. To this day, creepy things happen in the haunted vaults of Edinburgh." If you want more, there's plenty of it (complete with screaming Gothic "jumpers").

Scottish Folk Evenings—These £35–40 dinner shows, generally for tour groups intent on photographing old cultural clichés,

Try Whisky

While pub-hopping tourists generally think in terms of beer, many pubs are just as enthusiastic about serving whisky. If

you are unfamiliar with whisky (what Americans call "Scotch"), it's a great conversation-starter. Many pubs (including Leslie's, described on next page) have lists of dozens of whiskies available. Lists include descriptions of their personalities (peaty, heavy iodine finish, and so on), which are much easier to discern than most wine flavors. A glass generally costs around £2.50. Let a local teach you how to drink it "neat," then add a little water. Learn how to swish it around and let your gums taste it, too. Keep experimenting until you discover "the nurse's knickers."

---

are held in the huge halls of expensive hotels. (Prices are bloated to include 20 percent commissions.) Your "traditional" meal is followed by a full slate of swirling kilts, blaring bagpipes, and Scottish folk dancing with an "old-time music hall" emcee. If you like Lawrence Welk, you're in for a treat. But for most travelers, these are painfully cheesy variety shows. You can sometimes see the show without dinner for about two-thirds the price. The TI has fliers on all the latest venues.

Prestonfield House offers its kitschy Scottish folk evening—a plaid fantasy of smiling performers accompanied by electric keyboards—with or without dinner Sunday to Friday. For £40 you get the show with two drinks and a wad of haggis (20:00–22:00); £51 buys you the same, plus a four-course meal and wine (be there at 18:45). It's in the stables of "the handsomest house in Edinburgh," which is now home to the recommended Rhubarb Restaurant (Priestfield Road, a 10-min walk from Dalkeith Road B&Bs, tel. 0131/225-7800).

Theater—Even outside of festival time, Edinburgh is a fine place for lively and affordable theater. Pick up *The List* for a complete rundown of what's on (sold at newsstands for a few pounds).

▲**Live Music in Pubs**—Edinburgh used to be a good place for traditional folk music, but in the last few years, pub owners—out of economic necessity—are catering to college-age customers more interested in beer-drinking. Pubs that were regular venues for folk music have gone pop. Rather than list places likely to change their format in a few months, I'll simply recommend the monthly *Gig Guide* (free at TI, accommodations, and various pubs, www .gigguide.co.uk). This simple little sheet lists eight or ten places each night that have live music. Listings are divided by genre (pop, rock, world, and folk).

Pubs in the Old Town: The **Grassmarket** neighborhood (below the castle) bustles with live music and rowdy people spilling out of the pubs and into what was (once upon a time) a busy market square. It's fun to just wander through this area late at night and check out the scene at pubs such as Finnegans Wake, Biddy Mulligan, and White Hart Inn. Thanks to the music and crowds, you'll know where to go...and where not to. Have a beer and follow your ear.

Pubs on the Royal Mile: Several bars here feature live folk music every night. **Tass Pub** is a great and accessible little place with a love of folk and traditional music and free performances nearly every night from 21:00. Drop by during your sightseeing—as you walk the lower part of the Royal Mile—and ask what's on tonight (across from World's End, #1 High Street, tel. 0131/556-6338). **Whistlebinkies** is famous for live music (rock, pop, blues, South Bridge, tel. 0131/557-5114, www.whistlebinkies.com).

Pubs in the New Town: All the beer-drinkers seem to head for the pedestrianized Rose Street, famous for having the most pubs per square inch anywhere in Scotland—and plenty of live music.

Pubs near Dalkeith Road B&Bs: The first three listed below are classic pubs (without a lot of noisy machines and rowdy twentysomethings). Located near the Dalkeith Road B&B neighborhood, they cluster within 100 yards of each other around the intersection of Duncan Street and Causewayside.

Leslie's Pub, sitting between a working-class and an upperclass neighborhood, has two sides. Originally, the gang would go in on the right to gather around the great hardwood bar, glittering with a century of *Cheers* ambience. Meanwhile, the more delicate folks would slip in on the left, with its discreet doors, plush snugs (cozy private booths), and ornate ordering windows. Since 1896, this Victorian classic has been appreciated for both its "real ales" and its huge selection of fine whiskies (listed on a six-page menu). Dive into the whisky mosh pit on the right, and let them show you how whisky can become "a very good friend." (Leslie's is a block downhill from the next two pubs, at 49 Ratcliffe Terrace.)

The Old Bell Inn, with a nostalgic sports-bar vibe, serves only drinks after 19:00 (see "Scottish Grub and Pubs" on page 565).

Swany's Pub, perhaps a little less welcoming than the others, is a quintessential hangout for the working-class boys of the neighborhood—with some fun characters to get to know.

A few blocks away, you'll find **Bierex,** a much younger and noisier scene. It's a favorite among young people for its cheap drinks (132 Causewayside, see "Scottish Grub and Pubs" on page 565).

Sleeping in Edinburgh

The advent of big, inexpensive hotels has made life more of a struggle for B&Bs. Still, book ahead, especially in August, when the annual festival fills Edinburgh. Conventions, rugby matches, school holidays, and weekends can make finding a room tough at almost any time of year. For the best prices, book direct rather than through the TI, which charges a higher room fee and levies a £4 booking fee. "Standard" rooms, with toilets and showers a tissue-toss away, save you £10 a night.

B&Bs off Dalkeith Road

South of town near the Royal Commonwealth Pool, these B&Bs— just off Dalkeith Road—are nearly all top-end, sporting three or four stars. While pricey, they come with uniformly friendly hosts and great cooked breakfasts, and are a good value for people with enough money. At these not-quite-interchangeable places, character is provided by the personality quirks of the hosts.

Most listings are on quiet streets and within a two-minute walk of a bus stop. Though you won't find phones in the rooms, most have Wi-Fi and several offer Internet access. Most can provide triples or even quads for families.

The quality of all these B&Bs is more than adequate. Prices listed are for most of peak season; if there's a range, prices slide up with summer demand. *Unless otherwise noted, the highest prices in the range provided are for August; B&Bs also do not accept bookings for one-night stays during this time.* Conversely, in winter, when there's no demand, prices get really soft (less than what's listed here). These prices are for cash; expect a 3–5 percent fee for using your credit card.

Near the B&Bs, you'll find plenty of great eateries (see "Eating in Edinburgh," later) and several good, classic pubs (see "Nightlife in Edinburgh," earlier). A few places have their own private parking spots; others offer access to easy, free street parking, though the neighborhood is supposed to convert to metered parking, possibly in 2010 (ask about it when booking—better yet, don't rent a car for your time in Edinburgh).

If you bring in take-out food, your host would probably prefer you eat it in the breakfast area rather than muck up your room— ask. The nearest launderette is Ace Cleaning Centre (which picks up and drops off; see page 513).

EDINBURGH

Edinburgh's Dalkeith Road Neighborhood

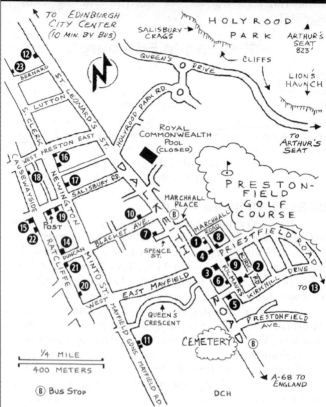

1 Hotel Ceilidh-Donia

2 Airdenair Guest House

3 Dunedin Guest House

4 Ard-Na-Said B&B

5 AmarAgua Guest House

6 Kenvie Guest House

7 Gil Dun Guest House

8 Dorstan House

9 Priestville Guest House

10 Belford Guest House

11 23 Mayfield Guest House & Glenalmond House

12 Blonde Restaurant

13 To Rhubarb Restaurant & Prestonfield House

14 The New Bell & The Old Bell Inn

15 Bierex Pub

16 Reverie Bar, Metropole Café & Wild Elephant Thai Restaurant

17 Il Positano Ristorante

18 Hewat's Restaurant & Hanedan Turkish Restaurant

19 Hellers Kitchen

20 Leslie's Pub

21 Swany's Pub

22 Tesco Express Supermarket

23 Launderette

Sleep Code

(£1 = about $1.60, country code: 44, area code: 0131)
S = Single, **D** = Double/Twin, **T** = Triple, **Q** = Quad, **b** = bathroom,
s = shower only. You can assume credit cards are accepted
unless otherwise noted.

To help you sort easily through these listings, I've divided
the rooms into three categories based on the price for a
standard double room with bath (during high season):

$$$ Higher Priced—Most rooms £80 or more.

$$ Moderately Priced—Most rooms between £60–80.

$ Lower Priced—Most rooms £60 or less.

Getting There: This comfortable, safe neighborhood is a
10-minute bus ride from the Royal Mile. From the train station,
TI, or Sir Walter Scott Monument, the nearest place to catch the
bus is at St. Andrew Square, one block away. (If you're here after
the Princes Street construction is finished, use the bus stop in front
of the H&M store.) Buses also stop on North Bridge (£1.30, use
exact change; catch Lothian bus #14, #30, #33, or #48, or First
bus #86). Tell the driver your destination is Dalkeith Road; about
10 minutes into the ride, after following South Clerk Street for
a while, the bus makes a left turn, then a right—depending on
where you're staying, you'll get off at the first or second stop after
the turn. Ping the bell and hop out. These buses also stop at the
corner of North Bridge and High Street on the Royal Mile. Buses
run from 6:00 (9:00 on Sun) to 23:00. Taxi fare between the train
station or Royal Mile and the B&Bs is about £7. Taxis are easy to
hail on Dalkeith Road if it isn't raining.

$$$ Hotel Ceilidh-Donia rents 17 tricked-out rooms with a
pleasant back deck, a quiet bar, a DVD lending library, and the only
restaurant—open to the public—in the immediate area (Sb-£35–55,
Db-£72–100 special with this book in 2010, £15–20 more in Aug,
less off-season, includes breakfast, free Internet access and Wi-Fi
for guests and diners, 14–16 Marchhall Crescent, tel. 0131/667-
2743, www.hotelceilidh-donia.co.uk, reservations@hotelceilidh
-donia.co.uk, Max, Annette, Alan, and Struan).

$$ Airdenair Guest House, offering views and a friendly
welcome, has five attractive rooms on the second floor with a lofty
above-it-all feeling. Homemade scones are a staple here, and Jill's
dad regularly makes batches of "tablet"—a Scottish delicacy that's
sweet as can be (Sb-£35–45, Db-£56–75, Tb-£75–90, free Wi-Fi,
29 Kilmaurs Road, tel. 0131/668-2336, www.airdenair.com, jill
@airdenair.com, Jill and Doug McLennan).

$$ Dunedin Guest House (dun-EE-din) is a fine value: bright, plush, and elegantly Scottish, with seven airy rooms and a spacious breakfast room (S with private b on hall-£35–50, Db-£64–74, or £110 in Aug, family rooms for up to five, free Wi-Fi, 8 Priestfield Road, tel. 0131/668-1949, www.dunedinguesthouse.co.uk, reservations@dunedinguesthouse.co.uk, David and Irene Wright).

$$ Ard-Na-Said B&B is an elegant 1875 Victorian house with a comfy lounge. It offers thoughtful touches and luxurious modern bathrooms in seven bright and spacious rooms—including one ground-floor room with a pleasant patio (Sb-£35–50, Db-£60–80, huge four-poster Db-£70–100, Tb-£110–120, prices depend on size of room as well as season, family room, free Wi-Fi, DVD players, free parking, 5 Priestfield Road, tel. 0131/667-8754, www.ardnasaid.co.uk, jim@ardnasaid.co.uk, Jim and Olive Lyons).

$$ AmarAgua Guest House is an inviting Victorian home away from home, with seven rooms and a Japanese garden. It's given a little extra sparkle by its energetic young proprietors, Dawn-Ann and Tony Costa (S with private b on hall-£35–42, Db-£64–84, fancy four-poster Db-£74–94, free Internet access and Wi-Fi, 10 Kilmaurs Terrace, tel. 0131/667-6775, www.amaragua.co.uk, reservations@amaragua.co.uk).

$$ Kenvie Guest House, expertly run by Dorothy Vidler, comes with six basic rooms (one small twin-£54, D-£56–62, Db-£64–72, these prices with cash and this book through 2010—must claim when you reserve, family deals, free Internet access and Wi-Fi, 16 Kilmaurs Road, tel. 0131/668-1964, www.kenvie.co.uk, dorothy@kenvie.co.uk).

$$ Gil Dun Guest House, with eight rooms on a quiet cul-de-sac just off Dalkeith Road, is comfortable, pleasant, and managed with care by Gerald McDonald and Bill (Sb-£35–40, Db-£70–80, or £120 in Aug, Tb-£90–100, or £120 in Aug, family deals, free Wi-Fi, pleasant garden, 9 Spence Street, tel. 0131/667-1368, www.gildun.co.uk, gildun.edin@btinternet.com).

$$ Dorstan House is more hotelesque with a few extra comforts—but still friendly and relaxed. Several of its 14 thoughtfully decorated rooms are on the ground floor (S-£25–50, Sb-£30–60, Ds-£40–80, Db-£50–90, Tb-£70–120, family rooms and suites available, free Wi-Fi, lounge, laundry service, 7 Priestfield Road, tel. 0131/667-6721, www.dorstan-hotel.demon.co.uk, reservations@dorstan-hotel.demon.co.uk, Richard and Maki Stott).

$ Priestville Guest House is homey, with a high, skylit ceiling, sunny breakfast room, and cozy charm—not fancy, but an exceptional value. The six rooms have Wi-Fi, VCRs, and a free video library (D-£44–60, Db-£48–68, Q-£96–120, discount for 2 or more nights, free Internet access on downstairs computer with this book in 2010, 10 Priestfield Road, tel. 0131/667-2435, www.priestville.com, bookings@priestville.com, Trina and Colin Warwick and their "rescue dog" Torrie).

$ The **Belford Guest House** is a tidy, homey place offering three basic rooms and a warm welcome. The two en-suite rooms are twins; the lone double has its own bathroom outside the room (Db-£54–60, around £70 in Aug, cheaper for longer stays, cash only, free parking, 13 Blacket Avenue—no sign out front, tel. 0131/667-2422, fax 0131/667-7508, www.belfordguesthouse.com, tom@belfordguesthouse.com, Tom Borthwick).

Guest Houses on Mayfield Gardens

These two very-well-run B&Bs are set back from a busy four-lane highway. They come with a little street noise, but are bigger buildings with more spacious rooms, finer public lounges, and nice comforts (such as iPod-compatible bedside radios).

$$ At **23 Mayfield Guest House**, Ross and Kathleen (and Grandma Mary) rent nine thoughtfully appointed rooms in an outstanding house. Every detail has been chosen with care, from the historically accurate paint colors to the "James Bond bathrooms." Being travelers themselves, they know the value of little extras, offering a wide breakfast selection and a comfy lounge with cold soft drinks at an "honesty bar" (Sb-£50–55, Db-£60–80, bigger Db-£70–100, 4-poster Db-£80–110, about £10–15 more/person during Festival, family room for up to 5, free Internet access and Wi-Fi, swap library, free parking, 23 Mayfield Gardens, tel. 0131/667-5806, www.23mayfield.co.uk, info@23mayfield.co.uk).

$$ **Glenalmond House**, run by Jimmy and Fiona Mackie, has 10 gorgeous rooms with fancy modern bathrooms (Db-£70–80, bigger 4-poster Db up to £95, Tb-£75–105, Qb-£80–120, mention Rick Steves when booking for £2/person-per-night discount, less off-season, discount for longer stays, rooms about £20–30 more during Festival, free Internet access and Wi-Fi, free parking, 25 Mayfield Gardens, tel. 0131/668-2392, www.glenalmondhouse .com, enquiries@glenalmondhouse.com).

Big, Modern Hotels

The first listing's a splurge. The next four are cheaper than most of the city's other chain hotels, and offer more comfort than character. In each case I'd skip the institutional breakfast and eat out. To locate these hotels, see the maps on pages 518 and 530. You'll generally pay £10 a day to park near these hotels.

$$$ **MacDonald Hotel**, my only fancy listing, is an opulent four-star splurge, with 156 rooms up the street from the new Parliament building. With its classy marble-and-wood decor, fitness center, and pool, it's hard to leave. On a gray winter day in Edinburgh, this could be worth it. Prices can vary wildly

(Db-£110–150, breakfast extra, near bottom of Royal Mile, across from Dynamic Earth, Holyrood Road, tel. 0131/550-4500, book online for better deals at www.macdonaldhotels.co.uk).

$$$ Jurys Inn offers a more enjoyable feeling than the Ibis and Travelodge (listed next). A cookie-cutter place with 186 dependably comfortable and bright rooms, it is capably run and well-located a short walk from the station (Sb/Db/Tb-£85, less on weekdays, much cheaper off-season and for online bookings, 2 kids sleep free, breakfast-£10, some views, pub/restaurant, on quiet street just off Royal Mile and just above the train station, 43 Jeffrey Street, tel. 0131/200-3300, www.jurysinns.com).

$$$ Ibis Hotel, at the middle of the Royal Mile, is well-run and perfectly located. It has 98 soulless but clean and comfy rooms drenched in prefab American "charm." Room rates vary widely—book online to get their best offers (Db in June–Sept-£80–100, up to £135 during Festival, less off-season, lousy continental breakfast-£6 extra, 6 Hunter Square, tel. 0131/240-7000, fax 0131/240-7007, www.ibishotels.com, h2039@accor.com).

$$$ Edinburgh City Center Holiday Inn Express rents 160 rooms with stark modern efficiency in a fine location, a five-minute walk from the train station. You can add up to two adults for £10 each, so two couples or a family can find a great deal here (Db-£80–130 depending on day, generally most expensive on Fri–Sat, for best rates book online, includes continental breakfast, just down Leith Street from the station at 16 Picardy Place, tel. 0131/558-2300, www.hiexpress.co.uk). There's another location just off the Royal Mile (Db-£75–150 depending on season and day of week, much more during Festival, free Wi-Fi, 300 Cowgate, tel. 0131/524-8400).

$$ Travelodge has 193 well-located, no-nonsense rooms, all decorated in dark blue. All rooms are the same and suitable for two adults with two kids, or three adults. While sleepable, it has a cheap feel with a quickly revolving staff (Sb/Db/Tb-£60–70, weekend Db-£70–85, Aug Db-£150, cheaper off-season and when booked on the Web in advance, breakfast-£8 extra, 33 St. Mary's Street, a block off Royal Mile, tel. 0871-984-8484, www.travelodge.co.uk). Travelodge's website offers a great £9–50 per room "super-saver" deal for a limited number of midweek bookings.

Hostels

Edinburgh has two new five-star hostels with dorm beds for about £20, slick modern efficiency, and careful management. They offer the best cheap beds in town. These places welcome families—travelers of any age feel comfortable here. Anyone on a tight budget wanting a twin room should think of these as simple hotels. The alternative is one of Edinburgh's scruffy bohemian hostels, each of which offers a youthful, mellow ambience and beds for around £15.

$–$$ Edinburgh Central Youth Hostel rents 300 beds in rooms with one to eight beds (all with private bathrooms and lockers). Guests can eat cheap in the cafeteria or cook for the cost of groceries in the members' kitchen. Prices include sheets but no towels (£20/person in 4- to 8-bed rooms, Sb-£36–42, Db-£54–68, Qb-£90–110, non-members pay £1 extra per night, single-sex dorms, £5 cooked breakfast, open 24/7, 10-min walk to Waverley Station, Lothian bus #22 from station, 9 Haddington Place off Leith Walk, tel. 0131/524-2090. www.syha.org.uk).

$–$$ Smart City Hostel is a godsend for backpackers and anyone looking for simple, efficient rooms in the old center for cheap. You'll pay £13–22 (depends on season) for a bed in an austere, industrial-strength 5- to 12-bed dorm—each with its own private bathroom. But it can get crazy with raucous weekend stag and hen parties. The Smart City Café in the basement has an inviting lounge with cheap meals. Half of the rooms function as a university dorm during the school year, becoming available just in time for the tourists (620 beds, Db-£50–65, bunky Qb-£60–120, £5 cooked breakfast, some female-only rooms, lockers, kitchen, lots of modern and efficient extras, free Wi-Fi, coin-op laundry, 50 Blackfriars Street, tel. 0131/524-1989, www.smartcityhostels.com, info@smartcityhostels.com).

Cheap and Scruffy Bohemian Hostels in the Center: These first three sister hostels—popular crash pads for young, hip backpackers—are beautifully located in the noisy center (£13.50–18 depending on time of year, twin D-£40–55, www.scotlandstop hostels.com): **High Street Hostel** (laundry-£2.50, kitchen, 8 Blackfriars Street, just off High Street/Royal Mile, tel. 0131/557-3984); **Royal Mile Backpackers** (dorms only—no private rooms, 105 High Street, tel. 0131/557-6120); and **Castle Rock Hostel** (just below the castle and above the pubs, 15 Johnston Terrace, tel. 0131/225-9666). **Brodie's Hostels,** somewhere between spartan and dumpy in the middle of the Royal Mile, rents 70 cheap beds in four- to eight-bed dorms (lockers, kitchen, Internet access-£1/20 min, laundry, 93 High Street, tel. 0131/556-2223, www.brodies hostels.co.uk).

Eating in Edinburgh

Reservations for restaurants are a good idea in August and on weekends. All restaurants in Scotland are smoke-free.

Along the Royal Mile

Historic pubs and doily cafés with reasonable, unremarkable meals abound. Though the eateries along this most-crowded stretch of the city are invariably touristy, the scene is fun and competition makes a well-chosen place a good value. Here are some handy, affordable options for a good bite to eat (listed in downhill order; for locations, see map on pages 530–531). Sprinkled in this list are some places a block or two off the main drag offering better values—and correspondingly filled with more locals than tourists.

The first two restaurants are in a cluster of pleasant eateries happily removed from the Royal Mile melee. Consider stopping at one of these on your way to the National Museum of Scotland, which is a half-block away.

The Elephant House, two blocks out of the touristy zone with an unmarked front door, is a comfy neighborhood coffee shop  where locals browse newspapers in the stay-awhile back room, listen to soft rock, enjoy the castle vistas, and sip coffee or munch a light meal. During the day you'll pick up food at the counter and grab your own seat; after 18:00, the café switches to table service. It's easy to imagine J. K. Rowling annoying waiters with her baby pram while spending long afternoons here writing the first Harry Potter book (£5–7 plates, "gourmet" pizza, daily 8:00–23:00, 4 computers with cheap and fast Internet access, vegetarian options, 2 blocks south of Royal Mile near National Museum of Scotland at 21 George IV Bridge, tel. 0131/220-5355).

The Outsider, also without a hint of Royal Mile tourism, is a sleek spot serving creative and trendy cuisine (good fish and grilled meats and vegetables) in a minimalist, stylish, hardwood, candlelit castle-view setting. It's noisy with enthusiasm, and the service is crisp and youthful. As you'll be competing with local yuppies, reserve for dinner (£6 lunch plates, £10–13 main dishes, always a vegetarian course, good wines by the glass, daily 12:00–23:00, 30 yards up from Elephant House at 15 George IV Bridge, tel. 0131/226-3131).

Deacon Brodie's Tavern, at a dead-center location on the Royal Mile, is a sloppy pub on the ground floor with a sloppy restaurant upstairs serving basic £9 pub meals. While painfully touristy, it comes with a fun history (daily 10:00–22:00, hearty salads, kids' menu, kids welcome upstairs, tel. 0131/220-0317).

St. Giles' Cathedral Café, hiding under the landmark church, is *the* place for paupers to munch prayerfully. Stairs on the back side of the church lead into the basement, where you'll find simple, light lunches from 11:45 and coffee with cakes all day (Mon–Sat 9:30–17:00, Sun 11:00–16:30, open a little later during Festival).

Always Sunday Food Company is a tiny place with a wonderful formula. It's a flexible fantasy of Scottish and Mediterranean hot dishes, fresh salads, smoked salmon, sharp cheese, and homemade desserts. You're invited to mix and match at their user-friendly create-a-lunch buffet line. They use healthy ingredients and are sensitive to diet concerns. Sit inside or people-watch from Royal Mile tables outside (£6 lunches, Mon–Fri 8:00–18:00, Sat–Sun 9:00–18:00, 30 yards below St. Giles' Cathedral at 170 High Street, tel. 0131/622-0667).

Creelers Seafood Restaurant's Tim and Fran James have been fishing and feeding since 1995. This respected eatery creates a kind of rough, honest, unpretentious ambience with fresh seafood you'd expect from this salty part of Scotland (£15–20 mains, lunch and early dinner specials before 19:00, reservations smart, 30 yards off the Royal Mile at 3 Hunter Square, tel. 0131/220-4447).

Piemaker is a great place to grab a quick, cheap, and tasty meal, especially if you're in a hurry. Their meat pies and pastries—try the cherry—are "so fresh they'll pinch your bum and call you darlin'" (most everything under £3, Tue–Sat 9:00–24:00, Sun 11:00–18:00, Mon 9:00–19:00, about 100 yards off the Royal Mile at 38 South Bridge, tel. 0131/556-8566).

Dubh Prais Scottish Restaurant is a dressy nine-table place filling a cellar 10 steps and a world away from the High Street bustle. The owner-chef, James McWilliams, proudly serves Scottish "fayre" at its very best (including gourmet haggis). The daily specials are not printed, to guard against "zombie waiters." They like to get to know you a bit by explaining things (£27 dinners, open Tue–Sat 17:00–22:30, closed Sun–Mon, reservations smart, opposite Radisson SAS Hotel at 123 High Street, tel. 0131/557-5732).

Wedgwood Restaurant is romantic, contemporary, chic, and as gourmet as possible with no pretense. Paul Wedgwood cooks while his partner Lisa serves with appetizing charm. The cuisine: creative, modern Scottish with an international twist and a whiff of Asia. The pigeon and haggis starter is scrumptious. Paul and Lisa believe in making the meal the event of the evening—don't come here to eat and run. I like the ground level with the Royal Mile view, but the busy kitchen ambience in the basement is also fine (£10 two-course lunch, £7–9 starters, £17–24 mains, fine wine by the glass, daily from 12:00 and from 18:00, 267 Canongate on Royal Mile, tel. 0131/558-8737, www.wedgwoodthe restaurant.co.uk).

The World's End Pub, a colorful old place, dishes up hearty £8 meals from a creative menu in a fun, dark, and noisy space (daily 12:00–21:00, 4 High Street, tel. 0131/556-3628).

David Bann, just a three-minute walk off the Royal Mile, is a worthwhile stop for well-heeled vegetarians in need of a break from the morning fry. While vegetarian as can be, there's not a hint of hippie here. It's upscale (there's a cocktail bar), stylish (gorgeously presented dishes), serious about quality (David is busy in the kitchen), and organic—they serve polenta, tartlets, soups, and light meals (£6 starters, £11 mains, decadent deserts, daily 11:00–22:00, vegan options, 56–58 St. Mary's Street, tel. 0131/556-5888).

Clarinda's Tea Room, near the bottom of the Royal Mile, is charming and girlish—a fine and tasty place to relax after touring the Mile or the Palace of Holyroodhouse. Stop in for a £5 quiche, salad, and soup lunch. It's also great for tea and cake anytime (Mon–Sat 8:30–16:45, Sun 9:30–16:45, 69 Canongate, tel. 0131/557-1888).

In the New Town

While most of your sightseeing will be along the Royal Mile, it's important that your Edinburgh experience stretches beyond this happy tourist gauntlet. Just a few minutes away, in the Georgian town, you'll find a bustling world of office workers, students, and pensioners doing their thing. And at midday, that includes eating. Simply hiking over to one of these places will give you a good helping of modern Edinburgh. All these places are within a few minutes' walk of the TI and main Waverley Bridge tour-bus depot.

Le Café St. Honoré, tucked away like a secret in the Georgian New Town, is a pricey but charming place with walls lined by tempting wine bottles. It serves French-Scottish cuisine in tight, Old World, cut-glass elegance to a dressy local crowd (open Mon–Fri 12:00–14:15 & 17:15–22:00, Sat–Sun 12:00–14:15 & 18:00–22:00, reservations smart, down Thistle Street from Hanover Street, 34 Northwest Thistle Street Lane, tel. 0131/226-2211).

Café Royal is a movie producer's dream pub—the perfect *fin de siècle* setting for a coffee, beer, or light meal. (In fact, parts of *Chariots of Fire* were filmed here.) Drop in, if only to admire the 1880 tiles featuring famous inventors (daily 12:00–14:30 & 17:30–22:00, until 21:30 in winter, bar food available during the afternoon, 2 blocks from Princes Mall on West Register Street, tel. 0131/556-1884). There are two eateries here: the pub (with a "ladies' pub" atmosphere, basic £9 meals, 11:00–21:45) and the dressier restaurant, specializing in oysters, fish, and game (£20 plates, reserve for dinner—it's quite small and understandably popular).

The Dome Restaurant, in what was a fancy bank, serves decent meals around a classy bar and under the elegant 19th-century skylight dome. With soft jazz and chic, white-tablecloth ambience, it feels a world apart (£14 plates until 17:00, £15–20 dinners until 22:00, daily 10:00–22:00, modern international cuisine, open for a drink anytime under the dome or in the adjacent Art Deco bar, 14 George Street, tel. 0131/624-8634, reserve for dinner). As you leave, look up to take in the facade of this former

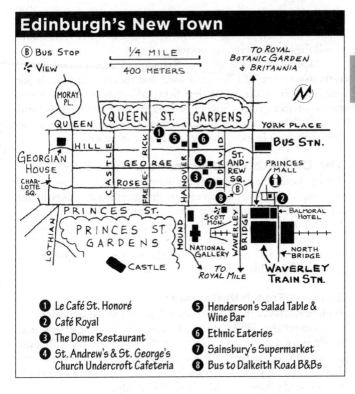

Edinburgh's New Town

Ⓑ Bus Stop
👁 View

¼ MILE
400 METERS

TO ROYAL
BOTANIC GARDEN
& BRITANNIA

MORAY PL.

QUEEN ST. GARDENS

YORK PLACE

QUEEN

HILL

GEORGIAN HOUSE

GEORGE

ROSE

CHARLOTTE SQ.

CASTLE

FREDERICK

HANOVER

DAVID

ST. ANDREW SQ.

BUS STN.

PRINCES MALL

PRINCES ST.

LOTHIAN

PRINCES ST. GARDENS

CASTLE

MOUND

SCOTT MON.

NATIONAL GALLERY

TO ROYAL MILE

WAVERLEY BRIDGE

BALMORAL HOTEL

NORTH BRIDGE

WAVERLEY TRAIN STN.

❶ Le Café St. Honoré
❷ Café Royal
❸ The Dome Restaurant
❹ St. Andrew's & St. George's Church Undercroft Cafeteria
❺ Henderson's Salad Table & Wine Bar
❻ Ethnic Eateries
❼ Sainsbury's Supermarket
❽ Bus to Dalkeith Road B&Bs

bank building—the pediment is filled with figures demonstrating various ways to make money, which they do with all the nobility of classical gods.

The **St. Andrew's and St. George's Church Undercroft,** in the basement of a fine old church, is the cheapest place in town for lunch—just £3.50 for sandwich and soup. Your tiny bill helps support the Church of Scotland (Mon–Fri 10:00–14:30, closed Sat–Sun, on George Street, just off St. Andrew Square, tel. 0131/225-3847).

Henderson's Salad Table and Wine Bar has fed a generation of New Town vegetarians hearty cuisine and salads. Even carnivores love this place for its delectable salads and desserts (two-course lunch for £9, Mon–Sat 8:00–22:45, closed Sun except in July–Aug 10:00–17:00, strictly vegetarian; pleasant live music nightly in wine bar—generally guitar or jazz; between Queen and George Streets at 94 Hanover Street, tel. 0131/225-2131). Henderson's two different seating areas use the same self-serve cafeteria line. For the same healthy food with more elegant seating and table service, eat at the attached **Henderson's Bistro** (daily 12:00–20:30, Thu-Sat until 21:30).

Fun Ethnic Eateries on Hanover Street: Hanover Street is lined with Thai, Greek, Turkish, Italian, and other restaurants. Stroll the block to eye your options.

Supermarket: The glorious **Sainsbury's** supermarket, with a tasty assortment of take-away food and specialty coffees, is just one block from the Sir Walter Scott Monument and the lovely picnic-perfect Princes Street Gardens (Mon–Sat 7:00–22:00, Sun 9:00–20:00, on corner of Rose Street on St. Andrew Square, across the street from Jenners, the classy department store).

The Dalkeith Road Area, near Your B&B

All of these places are within a 10-minute walk of my recommended B&Bs. Most are on or near the intersection of Newington Road and East Preston Street. Reserve on weekends and during the Festival. For locations, see the map on page 554. The nearest grocery store is **Tesco Express** (daily 6:00–23:00, 158 Causewayside). For a cozy drink after dinner, visit the recommended pubs in the area (see "Nightlife in Edinburgh," earlier).

Scottish/French Restaurants

Blonde Restaurant, with a modern Scottish and European menu, is less expensive, bigger, and more crowded than the others, with no set-price dinners. It's a bit out of the way, but a hit with locals (about £15–17 for two courses, Tue–Sun 12:00–14:30 & 18:00–22:00, open only for dinner on Mon, good vegetarian options, 75 St. Leonard's Street, tel. 0131/668-2917, Andy).

Rhubarb Restaurant is the hottest thing in Old World elegance. It's in "Edinburgh's most handsome house"—a riot of antiques, velvet, tassels, and fringes. The plush rhubarb color theme reminds visitors that this was the place where rhubarb was first grown in Britain. It's a 10-minute walk past the other recommended eateries behind Arthur's Seat, in a huge estate with big, shaggy Highland cattle enjoying their salads al fresco. While most spend a wad here (£25–30 plates), smart budget travelers time their visit to take advantage of the great off-hours two-course meal for £17 (arrive during these windows of time to get the deal: Sun–Thu 12:00–14:00 & 18:30–19:00, Fri–Sat 12:00–14:00 & 18:00–19:00, reserve in advance and dress up if you can, in Prestonfield House, Priestfield Road, tel. 0131/225-1333). For details on the Scottish folk evening offered here, see "Nightlife in Edinburgh," earlier.

The New Bell serves up filling modern Scottish fare, from steak and salmon to haggis, in a Victorian living-room setting above the lovable Old Bell Inn (see below). Along with wonderfully presented meals, you'll enjoy white tablecloths, Oriental carpets on hardwood floors, and a relaxing spaciousness under open beams (£13.50 two-course special until 18:45, £15 plates, open Sun–Thu 17:30–21:30, Fri–Sat 17:30–22:00, always a veggie option, 233 Causewayside, tel. 0131/668-2868).

Scottish Grub and Pubs

The Old Bell Inn, with an old-time sports-bar ambience—fishing, golf, horses—serves simpler £8 pub meals from the same fine kitchen as the fancier New Bell (which is just upstairs, described above). This is a classic snug pub, all dark woods and brass beer taps, littered with evocative knickknacks. It comes with fine sidewalk seating and a mixed-age crowd (open daily until 24:00; food served 12:00–14:30 & 17:30–19:00, until 19:30 Mon–Thu, opens at 12:30 on Sun, 233 Causewayside, tel. 0131/668-1573).

Bierex, a youthful pub, is the neighborhood favorite for modern dishes (£8 plates), camaraderie, and cheap booze. It's a spacious, bright, mahogany-and-leather place popular for its long and varied happy hours (daily until late, food served 12:00–15:00 and 16:30–21:00, Wi-Fi for customers, 132 Causewayside, tel. 0131/667-2335).

Hotel Ceilidh-Donia serves fish, meat, and vegetarian dishes in a flagstone-floored, high-ceilinged space with a small, friendly adjoining pub. The decor is likeable Scottish-castle-esque kitsch with attitude, and the garden seating is a delight. This is the only eatery in the immediate neighborhood of my recommended B&Bs (£10 plates with good vegetables, Mon–Sat dinner from 18:00, closed Sun, free Internet access for customers, 14–16 Marchhall Crescent, tel. 0131/667-2743).

Reverie Bar is just your basic, fun pub with a focus on food rather than drinking and free live music most nights from 21:00 (Sun-jazz, Tue-traditional, Thu-blues; £8–10 main dishes, dinner served daily 12:00–21:00, 3 Newington Road, tel. 0131/667-8870).

Hewat's Restaurant is new to the neighborhood but already a hit. Sample Scottish cuisine (locals recommend the steak) in this elegantly whimsical dining space (midweek dinner deals: £18.50 for two courses, £22.50 for three courses; open Wed–Sat 12:00–14:00 & 18:00–21:30, Fri–Sat until 22:30, Tue 18:00–21:30 only, closed Sun–Mon, 19 Causeway, tel. 0131/466-6660).

Hellers Kitchen is a casual blond-wood space specializing in dishes using local produce and fresh-baked breads and doughs. Check the big chalkboard to see what's on (£5 sandwiches, £9 pizzas, daily 10:00–21:00 or later, opens at 8:30 midweek, next to post office at 15 Salisbury Place, tel. 0130/667-4654).

Metropole Café is a fresh, healthy eatery with a Starbucks ambience, serving light bites for £4 and simple meals for £7 (daily 8:30–22:00, always a good vegetarian entrée, free Wi-Fi, 33 Newington Road).

Ethnic Options

Wild Elephant Thai Restaurant is a small, hardworking eatery that locals consider the best around for Thai (£9–11 main dishes, £13 three-course meal available 17:00–19:00, also does take-away, open daily 12:00–14:30 & 17:00–23:00, 21 Newington Road, tel. 0131/662-8822).

Il Positano Ristorante has a spirited Italian ambience, as manager Giuseppe Votta injects a love of life and food into his little restaurant. The moment you step through the door, you know you're in for good, classic Italian cuisine (£8 pizzas and pastas, £15 plates, Mon–Fri 12:00–14:00 & 17:00–23:00, Sat 12:00–23:00, Sun 14:00–22:00, 85 Newington Road, tel. 0131/662-9977).

Hanedan Turkish Restaurant is generating a huge buzz. This friendly, contemporary 10-table place serves great Turkish grills and vegetarian specials at a fine price (£9 two-course special anytime, £9 mains, open Tue–Sun from 12:00 and from 17:30, closed Mon, 41 West Preston Street, tel. 0131/667-4242, friendly Gürsel Bahar).

Edinburgh Connections

By Train or Bus

From Edinburgh by Train to: Glasgow (4/hr, 50 min), **St. Andrews** (train to Leuchars, 1–2/hr, 1 hr, then 10-min bus into St. Andrews), **Stirling** (2/hr, 50 min), **Pitlochry** (6/day direct, 2 hrs, more with change in Stirling or Perth), **Inverness** (every 2 hrs, 3.5–4 hrs, some with change in Stirling or Perth), **Oban** (3/day, 4.25 hrs, change in Glasgow), **York** (2/hr, 2.5 hrs), **London** (hourly, 4.5 hrs), **Durham** (at least hourly, 1.75 hrs), **Newcastle** (2/hr, 1.5 hrs), **Keswick/Lake District** (8/day to Penrith—some via Carlisle, then catch bus to Keswick, fewer on Sun, 3 hrs including bus transfer in Penrith), **Birmingham** (at least hourly, 4–5 hrs, some with change in York), **Crewe** (every 2 hrs, 3 hrs), **Bristol** near Bath (hourly, 6–6.5 hrs), **Blackpool** (roughly hourly, 3–3.5 hrs, transfer in Preston). Train info: tel. 0845-748-4950, www.thetrain line.com, or www.nationalrail.co.uk.

By Bus to: Glasgow (4/hr, 1.25 hrs, £6), **Oban** (7/day Mon–Sat, 4–5 hrs; 1 direct, rest with transfer in Glasgow, Perth, or Tyndrum), **Fort William** (7/day, 4–5 hrs, 1 direct, rest with change in Glasgow or Tyndrum), **Portree** on the Isle of Skye (3/day, 7.5–8 hrs, transfer in Inverness or Glasgow), **Inverness** (7/day, 3.5–4.5 hrs). For bus info, call Scottish Citylink (tel. 0870-550-5050, www .citylink.co.uk) or National Express (tel. 0871-781-8181). You can get info and tickets at the bus desk inside the Princes Mall TI.

Route Tips for Drivers

To Hadrian's Wall: It's 100 miles south from Edinburgh to Hadrian's Wall; to Durham it's another 50 miles. From Edinburgh, Dalkeith Road leads south and eventually becomes A68 (handy Cameron Toll supermarket with cheap gas is on the left as you leave Edinburgh Town, 10 min south of Edinburgh; gas and parking behind store). The A68 road takes you to Hadrian's Wall in two hours. You'll pass Jedburgh and its abbey after one hour. (For one last shot of Scotland shopping, there's a coach tour's delight just before Jedburgh, with kilt-makers, woolens, and a sheepskin shop.) Across from Jedburgh's lovely abbey is a free parking lot, a good visitors center, and public toilets (20p to pee). The England/Scotland border is a fun, quick stop (great view, ice cream, and tea caravan). Just after the turn for Colwell, turn right onto A6079, and roller-coaster four miles down to Low Brunton. Then turn right onto B6318, and stay on it by turning left at Chollerford, following the Roman wall westward. (For information on Hadrian's Wall, see the Durham and Northeast England chapter.)

ST. ANDREWS

For many, St. Andrews is synonymous with golf. But there's more to this charming town than its famous links. Dramatically situated at the edge of a sandy bay, St. Andrews is the home of Scotland's most important university—think of it as the Scottish Cambridge. And centuries ago, the town was the religious capital of the country.

In its long history, St. Andrews has seen two boom periods. First, in the early Middle Ages, the relics of St. Andrew made the town cathedral one of the most important pilgrimage sites in Christendom. The faithful flocked here from all over Europe, leaving the town with a medieval all-roads-lead-to-the-cathedral street plan that survives today. But after the Scottish Reformation, the cathedral rotted away and the town became a forgotten backwater. A new wave of visitors arrived in the mid-19th century, when a visionary mayor named (appropriately enough) Provost Playfair began to promote the town's connection with the newly-in-vogue game of golf. Most buildings in town date from this time (similar to Edinburgh's New Town).

Today St. Andrews remains a popular spot for both students and golf devotees (including professional golfers and celebrities such as Scotsman Sean Connery, often seen out on the links). With vast sandy beaches, golfing opportunities for pros and novices alike, a fun-loving student vibe, and a string of relaxing fishing villages nearby (the East Neuk), St. Andrews is an appealing place to take a vacation from your busy vacation.

Planning Your Time

St. Andrews, hugging the east coast of Scotland, is a bit off the main tourist track. But it's well-connected by train to Edinburgh (via nearby Leuchars), making it a worthwhile day trip from the capital. Better yet, spend a night (or more, if you're a golfer) to enjoy this university town after dark.

If you're not here to golf, this is a good way to spend a day: Stroll up Market Street past the TI to the cathedral, then head back along the waterfront street called The Scores, visiting the castle and St. Salvator's College quad en route to the golf courses. Dip into the Golf Museum, watch the golfers on the Old Course, and play a round at "the Himalayas" putting green. With more time, walk along the West Sands beach, backtrack up Market Street to tour the cute St. Andrews Preservation Trust Museum (open only late May–late Sept daily 14:00–17:00), or take a spin by car or bus to the nearby East Neuk.

Orientation to St. Andrews

(area code: 01334)

St. Andrews (pop. 14,000), situated at the tip of a peninsula next to a broad bay, retains its old medieval street plan: Three main roads (North Street, Market Street, and South Street) converge at the cathedral, which overlooks the sea at the tip of town. The middle of these streets—Market Street—has the TI and many handy shops and eateries. North of North Street, the seafront street called The Scores connects the cathedral with the golf scene, which huddles along the West Sands beach at the base of the old town. It's an enjoyably compact town: You can stroll across town—from the cathedral to the historic golf course—in about 10 minutes.

Tourist Information

St. Andrews' helpful TI is right on the central Market Street, about two blocks in front of the cathedral (July–Aug Mon–Sat 9:15–19:00, Sun 10:00–17:00; April–June and Sept–mid-Oct Mon–Sat 9:15–17:00, Sun 11:00–16:00; mid-Oct–March Mon–Sat 9:15–17:00, closed Sun; 70 Market Street, tel. 01334/472-021). Pick up their stack of brochures on the town and region, and ask about other tours (such as ghost walks or witches walks). They also have Internet access (£1/20 min) and can find you a room for a £4 fee.

Arrival in St. Andrews

By Train and Bus: The nearest train station is in the village of Leuchars, five miles away. From there a handy 10-minute shuttle bus brings you right into St. Andrews (£3.25; buses meet most

St. Andrews

1. Cameron House & Glenderran Guest House
2. Lorimer House
3. Doune House
4. Arran House
5. St. Andrews Tourist Hostel
6. New Hall
7. McIntosh Hall
8. The Doll's House Rest.
9. The Seafood Rest.
10. Aikmans Pub
11. The Central Pub
12. Ma Bells Pub
13. Greyfriars Pub
14. Fritto Fish-and-Chips
15. Fisher & Donaldson Pastries
16. B. Jannettas Ice Cream
17. Gregg's & Tesco (Groceries)
18. Swilken Burn (Bridge)

trains, see digital display for next bus to St. Andrews; while waiting at the Leuchars station's bus shelter, read the historical info under the nearby flagpole). St. Andrews' bus station is near the base of Market Street. To reach most B&Bs, turn left out of the station, then right at the roundabout, then look for Murray Park on the left. To reach the TI, turn right out of the station, then take the next left and head up Market Street. Taxis from Leuchars into St. Andrews cost about £12.

By Car: For a short stay, drivers can simply head into the town center and park anywhere along the street. Easy-to-use meters dispense stickers (85p/hr, monitored Mon–Sat 9:00–17:00). For longer stays, you can park free along certain streets near the center (such as along The Scores), or use one of the long-stay lots near the entrance to town.

Helpful Hints

Events: Every five years, St. Andrews is swamped with about 100,000 visitors when it hosts the British Open (called simply

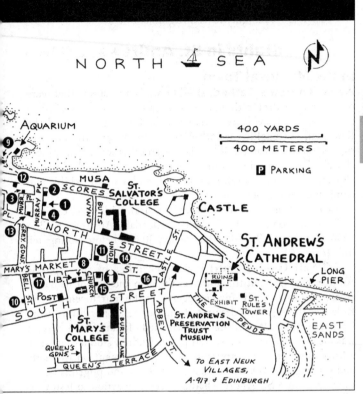

"The Open" around here)—and 2010 is one of those years (July 15–18). The town also fills up every year at the end of September (or the first week of October) for the Alfred Dunhill Links Championship. Unless you're a golf pilgrim, avoid the town at these times. If you are a golf pilgrim, expect room rates to skyrocket.

School Term: The University of St. Andrews has two terms: spring semester ("Candlemas"), from mid-February through May; and fall semester ("Martinmas"), from late September until mid-January. St. Andrews feels downright sleepy in summer, when most students leave and golfers take over the town.

Internet Access: You can get online for free at the **public library,** behind the church on South Street (Mon and Fri–Sat 9:30–17:00, Tue–Thu 9:30–19:00, closed Sun, tel. 01334/659-378). The TI also has an Internet terminal.

Walking Tour: June Riches offers good walking tours that bring St. Andrews' history to life. There's no set schedule, so call or email ahead to join a tour or arrange for one of your own (roughly £6/1.5 hours, prices vary by tour and group size, tel. 01334/850-638, june.riches@virgin.net).

Sights in St. Andrews

In the Medieval Town

▲▲**St. Andrew's Cathedral**—The walls and spires that were once the cathedral, although pecked away by centuries of scavengers, are still evocative. Between the Great Schism and the Reformation (roughly the 14th–16th centuries), St. Andrews was the ecclesiastical capital of Scotland—and this was its showpiece church. Today the site features the remains of the cathedral and cloister (free to explore), a graveyard, and a small exhibit and climbable tower (both covered by one ticket).

Cost, Hours, Information: Cathedral ruins-free; exhibit-£4.20, £7.20 combo-ticket includes castle; daily April–Sept 9:30–17:30, Oct–March 9:30–16:30, last entry 30 min before closing, tel. 01334/472-563.

◐ **Self-Guided Tour:** It was the relics of the Apostle Andrew that first put this town on the map and gave it its name. According to a (likely untrue) legend, in the fourth century, St. Rule was directed in a dream to bring the relics northward from Constantinople. When the ship wrecked offshore from here, it was clear that this was a sacred place. Andrew's bones (an arm, a knee, some fingers, and some teeth) were kept on this site, and starting in 1160, the cathedral was built and pilgrims began to arrive. Since St. Andrew had a direct connection to Jesus, his relics were believed to possess special properties, making them worthy of pilgrimages on par with St. James' relics in Santiago de Compostela, Spain (of Camino de Santiago fame). St. Andrew became Scotland's patron saint; in fact, the white "X" on the blue Scottish flag evokes the diagonal cross on which St. Andrew was crucified (he chose this type of cross because he felt unworthy to die as Jesus had).

You can stroll around the cathedral **ruins**—the best part of the complex—for free. First walk between the two tall ends of the church, which used to be the apse (at the sea end) and the main entry (at the town end). Visually trace the gigantic footprint of the former church in the ground, including the bases of columns—like giant sawed-off tree trunks. Plaques identify where elements of the church once stood. Looking at the one wall that's still standing, you can see the architectural changes over the 150 years the cathedral was built—from the rounded, Romanesque windows at the front, to the more highly decorated, pointed Gothic arches near the back. Mentally rebuild the church, and try to imagine it in its former majesty, when it played host to pilgrims from all over Europe. The church wasn't destroyed all at once, like all those ruined abbeys in England (demolished in a huff by Henry VIII when he broke with the pope). Instead, because the Scottish Reformation was more gradual, this church was slowly picked apart over time. First just the decorations were removed from inside the cathedral. Then the roof was pulled down to make use of its lead. Without a roof, the cathedral fell further and further into disrepair, and was quarried by locals for its handy precut stones (which you'll still find in the walls of many old St. Andrews homes).

The surrounding **graveyard,** dating from the post-Reformation Protestant era, is much more recent than the cathedral. In this golf-obsessed town, the game even infiltrates the cemeteries: Many notable golfers from St. Andrews are buried here (such as Young Tom—or "Tommy"—Morris, four-time British Open winner).

Go through the surviving wall into the former **cloister,** marked by a gigantic green square in the center. You can still see the cleats up on the wall, which once supported beams. Mentally reconstruct the cloister, and imagine its passages filled with strolling monks.

At the end of the cloister is a small **exhibit.** You'll have to pay to enter this relatively dull collection of old tombs and other carved-stone relics that have been unearthed on this site. Your ticket also includes entry to the surviving **tower of St. Rule's Church** (the rectangular tower beyond the cathedral ruins). If you feel like hiking up the 156 very claustrophobic steps for the view over St. Andrews' rooftops, it's worth the price. Up top, you can also look out to sea to find the pier where students traditionally walk out in their robes (see "Student Life in St. Andrews" sidebar).

▲**Castle**—The remains of St. Andrews' castle sit overlooking the sea. Another casualty of the Scottish Reformation, they're basically an evocative empty shell. Built by a bishop to entertain visiting diplomats in the late 12th century, the castle was home to the powerful bishops, archbishops, and cardinals of St. Andrews. In 1546, the cardinal burned a Protestant preacher at the stake in front of the castle. In retribution, Protestant Reformers took the castle and killed the cardinal. In 1547, the French came to attack the castle on behalf of their Catholic ally, Mary, Queen of Scots. During the ensuing siege, a young Protestant refugee named John Knox was captured and sent to France to row on a galley ship. Eventually he  traveled to Switzerland and met the Swiss Protestant ringleader, John Calvin. Knox brought Calvin's ideas back home and became Scotland's greatest Reformer.

Today's castle is the ruined post-Reformation version. You'll first walk through a colorful, well-presented exhibit about the history of the castle, then you'll head outside to explore the ruins. The most interesting parts are underground: the "bottle dungeon," where prisoners were sent never to return (peer down into it in the Sea Tower); and, around under the main drawbridge, the tight "mine" and even tighter "counter-mine" tunnels (you'll have to crawl to reach it all; go in as far as your claustrophobia allows). This shows how the besieging French army dug a mine to take the castle—but were followed at every turn by the Protestant counter-miners.

Cost, Hours, Information: £5.20, £7.20 combo-ticket includes cathedral exhibit, daily April–Sept 9:30–17:30, Oct–March 9:30–16:30, last entry 30 min before closing, tel. 01334/477-196.

Museum of the University of St. Andrews (MUSA)—Just down The Scores from the castle, this free museum is worth a quick stop. The first room has some well-explained medieval paraphernalia, but the highlight is the earliest-known map of the town, made in 1580—back when the town walls led directly to countryside and the cathedral was intact. Notice that the street plan within the walls has remained the same. The next room has some exhibits on student life; the rest is skippable (free; April–Sept Mon–Sat 10:00–17:00, Sun 12:00–16:00; Oct–March Thu–Sun 10:00–16:00, closed Mon–Wed; 7a The Scores, tel. 01334/461-660). For a great view of the West Sands (listed next), walk out and around to the back of the museum to the small cliff-top patio.

▲The West Sands—This broad sandy beach, stretching below the golf courses, is a wonderful place for a relaxing and invigorating walk. Or jog the beach, humming the theme to *Chariots of Fire* (this is the beach they run along in the iconic opening scene). Thanks to the drizzly weather, on any spring day you're likely to see rainbows over the sea.

▲University Buildings—Like Oxford and Cambridge, the University of St. Andrews is made up of several smaller colleges

The Scottish Reformation

It's easy to forget that during the 16th-century English Reformation—when King Henry VIII split with the Vatican and formed the Anglican Church (so he could get an officially recognized divorce)—Scotland was still its own independent nation. Like much of northern Europe, Scotland eventually chose a Protestant path, but it was more gradual and grassroots than Henry VIII's top-down, destroy-the-abbeys approach. While the English Reformation resulted in the Church of England (a.k.a. the Anglican Church, called "Episcopal" outside of England), with the monarch at its head, the Scottish Reformation created the Church of Scotland, with groups of elected leaders (called "presbyteries" in church jargon).

One of the leaders of the Scottish Reformation was John Knox (1514–1572), who learned at the foot of the great Swiss Reformer John Calvin. Returning to Scotland, Knox hopped from pulpit to pulpit, and his feverish sermons incited riots of "born-again" iconoclasts who dismantled or destroyed Catholic churches and abbeys (including St. Andrew's Cathedral). Knox's newly minted Church of Scotland gradually spread from the Lowlands to the Highlands. The southern and eastern part of Scotland, around St. Andrews—just across the North Sea from the Protestant countries of northern Europe—embraced the Church of Scotland long before the more remote and Catholic-oriented part of the country to the north and west. Today about 40 percent of Scots claim affiliation with the Church of Scotland, compared with 20 percent who are Catholic (still mostly in the western Highlands).

scattered around town. Many visitors (and even some students) don't realize how easy it is to visit some seemingly off-limits university buildings. Most are marked by blue doors and are open to the public. If the door's open, step in. There are two areas especially worth exploring:

St. Salvator's College is accessible from The Scores, via the narrow lane called (no joke) Butts Wynd. (For some strange reason, the street sign is often missing.) Explore the green quad. Under the tall tower is a chapel dating from 1450 that supposedly contains the pulpit of reformer John Knox. Step inside to enjoy the Gothic interior, with its wooden ceiling and 19th-century stained glass.

St. Mary's College, home of the university's School of Divinity (theology), is at the other end of town, on South Street. The peaceful quad has a gnarled tree purportedly planted by Mary, Queen of Scots.

▲**St. Andrews' Preservation Trust Museum and Garden**— This adorable museum, on Market Street just before the cathedral,

Student Life in St. Andrews

Although most people associate St. Andrews with golf, it's first and foremost a university town—the home of Scotland's most prestigious university. Founded in 1411, it's the third-oldest in the English-speaking world—only Oxford and Cambridge have been around longer.

The U. of St. A. has about 6,000 undergrads and 1,000 grad students. Though Scots attend for free, others (including students from England) must pay tuition. Some Scots resent the high concentration of upper-class English students (disparagingly dubbed "Yahs" for the snooty way they say "yes"), who treat St. Andrews as a "safety school" if rejected by Cambridge or Oxford. The school has even been called "England's northernmost university," because it has as many English students as Scottish ones. (Adding to the mix, about a quarter of the students come from overseas.) Its most famous recent graduate is Prince William (class of '05). Soon after he started here, the number of female applicants to study art history—his major—skyrocketed. (He later switched to geography.)

As with any venerable university, St. Andrews has its share of quirky customs—as if the university, like the town's street plan, insists on clinging to the Middle Ages. Most students own traditional red woolen academic "gowns" (woolen robes). Today these are only worn for special occasions (such as graduation), but in medieval times, students were required to wear them always—supposedly so they could be easily identified in brothels and pubs. (In a leap of faith, divinity students—apparently beyond temptation—wear black.) The way the robe is worn indicates the student's progress toward graduation: first-year students (called "bejants") wear them normally, on the shoulders; second-years

---

fills a 17th-century fishing family's house that was protected from developers. The house itself is of interest—it seems built for Smurfs, but once housed 20 family members. The museum is a time capsule of an earlier, simpler era. The ground floor features replicas of a grocer's shop and a chemist's, using original fittings from actual stores. Upstairs are temporary exhibits, and out back is a tranquil garden (dedicated to the memory of a beloved professor) with "great-grandma's washhouse," featuring an exhibit about the history of soap and washing. Lovingly presented, this quaint, humble house provides a nice contrast to the big-money scene around the golf course at the other end of town (free but donation requested, late May–late Sept daily 14:00–17:00, closed off-season, 12 North Street, tel. 01334/477-629, www.standrewspreservationtrust.co.uk).

St. Andrews Museum—This small, modest museum, which traces St. Andrews' history from A to Z, is an enjoyable way to pass time on a rainy day. It's situated in an old mansion in Kinburn ("semi-bejants") wear them slightly off the shoulders; third-years ("tertians") wear them off one shoulder (right shoulder for "scientists" and left shoulder for "artists"); and fourth-years ("magistrands") wear them off both shoulders.

There's no better time to see these robes than during the Pier Walk on Sunday afternoons during the university term. After church services (around noon), students clad in their gowns parade out to the end of the lonesome pier beyond the cathedral ruins. The tradition dates so far back that no one's sure how it started (either to commemorate a student who died rescuing victims of a shipwreck, or to bid farewell to a visiting dignitary). Today students participate mostly because it's fun to be a part of the visual spectacle of a long line of red robes flapping in the North Sea wind.

St. Andrews also clings to an antiquated family system, where underclassmen choose an "academic mother and father." In mid-November comes Raisin Monday, named for the raisins traditionally given as treats to one's "parents" (today students usually give wine to their "dad" and lingerie to their "mum"). After receiving their gifts, the upperclassmen dress up their "children" in outrageous costumes and parade them through town. The underclassmen are also obliged to carry around "receipts" for their gifts—often written on unlikely or unwieldy objects (e.g., plastic dinosaurs, microwave ovens, even refrigerators). Any upperclassmen they come across can demand a rendition of the school song (in Latin). The whole scene invariably turns into a free-for-all food fight in St. Salvator's quad (weapons include condiments, shaving cream, and, according to campus rumors, human entrails pilfered by med students).

Park, a five-minute walk from the old town (free, daily April–Sept 10:00–17:00, Oct–March 10:30–16:00, café, Doubledykes Road, tel. 01334/659-380).

Golf Sights on the Links

St. Andrews is the Cooperstown and Mount Olympus of golf, a mecca for the plaid-knickers-and-funny-hats crowd. Even if you're not a golfer, consider going with the flow and becoming one for your visit. While St. Andrews lays claim to founding the sport, nobody knows exactly where and when golf was born. In the Middle Ages, St. Andrews traded with the Dutch, and some historians believe they picked up a golf-like Dutch game on ice, and translated it to the bonny rolling hills of Scotland's east coast. Since the grassy beach-front strip just outside St. Andrews was too poor to support crops, it was used for playing the game—and, centuries later, it still is. Why do golf courses have 18 holes? Because that's how many fit at the Old Course in St. Andrews.

The Old Course and Other Golfing—The famous Old Course, golf's single most famous site, hosts the British Open every five years, including 2010. At other times it's open to the public for golfing. The course is watched over by the **Royal and Ancient Golf Club of St. Andrews** (or "R&A" for short), which is the world's governing body for golf (like the British version of the PGA). The R&A—the stately white building at the corner of the Old Course—is closed to the public, and only men can be members (which might be kind of quaint...if it weren't the 21st century). In fact, women can enter the R&A building only during the Women's British Open on St. Andrew's Day (Nov 30). Anyone can enter the shop nearby, which is a great spot to buy a souvenir for the golf-lover back home. Even if you're not golfing, watch the action for a while. Consider walking around to the low-profile stone bridge called Swilken Burn, with golf's single most iconic view: back over the 18th hole, the R&A, and Hamilton Hall (the red-sandstone building next to R&A). Hamilton Hall was supposedly built by an American who was upset over being declined membership to the R&A and hoped to upstage the exclusive club. Once a hotel, then a university dorm, the Hall is now being converted into expensive timeshares.

Fortunately for women golfers, the R&A doesn't actually own the golf course, which is public and managed by the **St. Andrews Links Trust.** Drop by their clubhouse, overlooking the beach near the Old Course (hours change frequently with the season—figure May–Aug daily 6:00–22:00, progressively shorter until 7:30–16:00 in Dec, www.standrews.org.uk). To reserve a tee time (explained below), call 01334/466-666 or email reservations@standrews.org.uk. Note that no advance reservations are taken on Saturdays, and the courses are closed on Sundays—which is traditionally the day when townspeople can walk the course.

The Old Course is golf's pinnacle. It's pricey (£130/person, less off-season), but accessible to the public—subject to lottery drawings for tee times and reserved spots by club members. You can play the Old Course only if you have a handicap of 24 (men) or 36 (women); bring along your certificate or card. If you don't know your handicap—or don't know what "handicap" means—then you're not good enough to play here (they want to keep the game moving, rather than wait for novices to spend 10 strokes on each hole). If you play, you'll do nine holes out, then nine more back in—however, all but four share the same greens. To ensure a specific tee time, it's smart to reserve a full year ahead. Otherwise, some tee times are determined each day by a lottery. Call or visit in person by 14:00 the day before to put your name in (2 players minimum, 4 players max)—then keep your fingers crossed when they post the results online at 16:00 (or call 01334/466-666 to see if you made it).

The trust manages six **other courses** (including two right next to the Old Course—the New Course and the Jubilee Course) that are cheaper and much easier to get a tee time for (£65 for New and Jubilee, £12–40 for others). It's usually possible to get a tee time for the same day or next day (if you want a guaranteed reservation, you'll need to make it at least 2 weeks in advance). The Castle Course has great views overlooking the town (but even more wind to blow your ball around).

If you're not serious about golf, but catch golf fever while here, consider...

▲**The Himalayas**—For less than the cost of a Coke, you can pretend you're Tiger Woods, stuck in a sand trap on the Old

Course with the British Open title on the line. Technically the "Ladies' Putting Green," this cute little patch of undulating grass presents the perfect opportunity for non-golfers (female or male) to say they've played the links at St. Andrews. Named for its dramatically hilly terrain, "The Himalayas" is basically a very classy (but still relaxed) game of minigolf. It's remarkable how the contour of the land can present even more challenging obstacles than the tunnels, gates, and distractions of a corny putt-putt course back home. Flat shoes are required (no high heels). You'll see it on the left as you walk toward the clubhouse from the R&A.

Cost and Hours: £2 for 18 holes. Except when it's open only to members, the putting green is open to the public June–July Mon–Sat 10:30–19:30; May and Aug Mon–Sat 10:30–19:00; April and Sept Mon–Sat 10:30–18:30. It's closed to the public (because members are using it) Mon–Tue and Thu–Fri 17:00–17:30, Wed 12:30–16:00, and Thu 10:00–11:00, plus all day Sun and Oct–March (tel. 01334/475-196).

British Golf Museum—This exhibit, which started as a small collection in the R&A across the street, is the best place in Britain to learn about the Scots' favorite sport. It's a bit tedious for those of us who reach for the remote when we see a golfer, but a must (and worth at least ▲▲) for golf-lovers. The compact, one-way exhibit reverently presents a meticulous survey of the game's history— from the monarchs who loved and hated golf (including the king who outlawed it because it was distracting men from church and archery practice), right up to the "Golden Bear" and a certain Tiger. A constant two-and-a-quarter-hour loop film shows highlights of the British Open from 1923 to the present, and other video screens show scratchy black-and-white highlights from the days before corporate sponsorship. At the end, find items donated by the golfers of today, including Tiger Woods' shirt, hat, and glove (£5.50, ticket good for 2 days and includes informative book about the history of golf; April–Oct Mon–Sat 9:30–17:00, Sun 10:00–17:00; Nov–March daily 10:00–16:00; last entry 45 min before closing; Bruce Embankment, in the blocky modern building squatting behind the R&A by the Old Course, tel. 01334/460-046, www.britishgolfmuseum.co.uk).

Sleeping in St. Andrews

Owing partly to the high-roller golf tourists flowing through the town, St. Andrews' accommodations are expensive. Solo travelers are at a disadvantage, as many B&Bs don't have singles—and charge close to the double price for one person (I've listed "S" or "Sb" below for those that actually have single rooms). But the quality at my recommendations is high, and budget alternatives—including a hostel—are workable. All of these, except the hostel, are on the streets called Murray Park and Murray Place, between North Street and The Scores in the old town. If you need to find a room on the fly, head for this same neighborhood, which has far more options than just the ones I've listed below. Keep in mind that during the British Open in mid-July, prices will skyrocket and last-minute rooms will be nearly impossible to come by.

$$$ Cameron House has five old-fashioned, paisley, masculine-feeling rooms (including two singles that share one bathroom) around a beautiful stained-glass atrium (S-£40, Db-£80, discount for longer stays, prices soft Nov–March, free Wi-Fi, 11 Murray Park, tel. 01334/472-306, www.cameronhouse-sta.co.uk, elizabeth@cameronhouse-sta.co.uk, Elizabeth and Leonard Palompo).

Sleep Code

(£1 = about $1.60, country code: 44, area code: 01334)

S = Single, **D** = Double/Twin, **T** = Triple, **Q** = Quad, **b** = bathroom, **s** = shower only. Unless otherwise noted, you can assume credit cards are accepted and breakfast is included.

To help you sort easily through these listings, I've divided the rooms into three categories based on the price for a standard double room with bath (during high season):

$$$ Higher Priced—Most rooms £75 or more.

$$ Moderately Priced—Most rooms between £60-75.

$ Lower Priced—Most rooms £60 or less.

$$$ Lorimer House has five comfortable, tastefully decorated rooms, including one on the ground floor (Db-£90–100 July–Sept, Db-£86–92 spring and fall, cheaper in winter, higher prices are for deluxe top-floor rooms, ask about discount for longer stays, free Internet access and Wi-Fi, 19 Murray Park, tel. 01334/476-599, www.lorimerhouse.com, info@lorimerhouse.com, Mick and Chris Cordner).

$$$ Doune House is golfer-friendly with six straightforward, comfy, plaid-heavy rooms. The helpful owners are happy to arrange early breakfasts and airport transfers (S-£40–47, Db-£80–94, price depends on season, cheaper off-season, cash only, free Internet access and Wi-Fi, 5 Murray Place, tel. 01334/475-195, www.dounehouse.com, info@dounehouse.com, Maria and Dell Roberts-Jones).

$$$ Arran House has nine modern rooms, including a single with a private bathroom across the hall. Golf portraits line the otherwise stark staircase (S-£50, Db-£80–90, three ground floor rooms, family room, free Wi-Fi, 5 Murray Park, tel. 01334/474-724, mobile 07768-718-237, www.arranhousestandrews.co.uk, jmgmcgrory@btinternet.com, Anne and Jim McGrory).

$$$ Glenderran Guest House offers plush golf-oriented rooms and a few nice breakfast extras (Sb-£35–40, Db-£85–90, free Internet access and Wi-Fi, same-day laundry-£6, 9 Murray Park, tel. 01334/477-951, www.glenderran.com, info@glenderran .com, Ray and Maggie).

Hostel: **$ St. Andrews Tourist Hostel** has 44 beds in colorful rooms about a block from the base of Market Street. The high-ceilinged lounge is a comfy place for a break, and the friendly staff is happy to recommend their favorite pubs (£14/bunk on weekends, £10/bunk during the week, no breakfast, free Wi-Fi, self-service laundry-£3.50, towels-£1, office open 8:00–22:00, office closed 15:00–18:00 outside of summer, St. Mary's Place, tel. 01334/479-911, www.standrewshostel.com, info@standrewshostel.com).

University Accommodations

In the summer (early June–early Sept), two of the University of St. Andrews' student-housing buildings are tidied up and rented out to tourists (website for both: www.discoverstandrews.com; pay when reserving). You have two options: **$$ New Hall** (more comfort, more expensive, less central) or **$$ McIntosh Hall** (less comfort, less expensive, more central). They rent singles for £35, but for couples they're best used as a last resort if no other rooms are available in town, since their dorm-bed twins without breakfast are about the same price as a B&B (Db-£60–72; New Hall—tel. 01334/467-000, new.hall@st-andrews.ac.uk; McIntosh Hall—tel. 01334/467-035, mchall@st-andrews.ac.uk).

Eating in St. Andrews

The Doll's House, part of a popular local chain, serves up reliably good international cuisine with a French flair. The two floors of indoor seating have a cozy, colorful, casual atmosphere; the sidewalk seating out front is across from Holy Trinity Church (£7–10 lunches, £9–16 dinners, £13 early-bird special 17:00–19:00, open daily 12:00–15:00 & 17:00–22:00, a block from the TI at 3 Church Square, tel. 01334/477-422). Also consider their sister restaurants, The Glass House (near the castle on North Street) and The Grill House (at St. Mary's Place).

The Seafood Restaurant is St. Andrews' favorite splurge. Situated in a modern glassy building overlooking the beach near the Old Course, it's like dining in an aquarium. The seafood is locally caught, the dining room wraps around the busy open kitchen, and dinner reservations are essential (£22 two-course lunch, £26 three-course lunch, £45 three-course dinner, daily 12:00–14:30 & 18:30–22:00, The Scores, tel. 01334/479-475).

On Market Street: In the area around the TI, you'll find a concentration of good restaurants—pubs, grill houses, coffee shops, Asian food, fish-and-chips (see below), and more...take your pick. A block down Market Street, you can stock up for a picnic at Gregg's and Tesco.

Pubs: There's no shortage in this college town. **Aikmans** features a cozy wood-table ambience and frequent live music (open-mic folk night once weekly, traditional Scottish music upstairs about twice per month, other live music generally Thu–Sat, £5–7 pub grub, open daily 11:00–24:00, 32 Bell Street, tel. 01334/477-425). **The Central** is a St. Andrews standby, with old lamps and lots of brass (£5 sandwiches, £7 burgers, Mon–Sat 11:00–24:00, Sun 12:30–24:00, food until 21:00, tel. 01334/478-296). **Ma Bells** is a sleek but friendly place that clings to its (pre-remodel) status as one of Prince William's favorites (£4–7 pub grub, pricier bistro meals, daily 11:00–24:00, a block from the Old Course and R&A at 40 The Scores, tel. 01334/472-622). **Greyfriars** is a classy, new, modern place near the Murray Park B&Bs (£5 light meals, £8–10 main dishes, daily 11:00–24:00, 129 North Street, tel. 01334/474-906).

Fish-and-Chips: **Fritto** is a local favorite for take-away fish-and-chips, centrally located on Market Street near the TI (£4 fish-and-chips, £3 burgers, daily 11:00–22:00, until 23:00 Fri–Sat, at the corner of Union and Market). Brave souls will order a can of Irn-Bru with their fish (warning: it doesn't taste like orange soda—see page 508). For what's considered the country's best chippies, head for the famous place in the East Neuk (described at the end of this chapter).

Dessert: **Fisher and Donaldson** is beloved for its rich, afford-able pastries and chocolates. Listen as the straw-hatted bakers chat with their regular customers, then try their Coffee Tower—like a giant cream puff filled with rich, lightly coffee-flavored cream (£1–2 pastries, Mon–Fri 6:00–17:15, Sat until 17:00, closed Sun, just around the corner from the TI at 13 Church Street, tel. 01334/472-201). **B. Jannettas** features a wide and creative range of tasty ice-cream flavors (£1 per scoop, daily 9:00–22:00, 31 South Street, tel. 01334/473-285).

St. Andrews Connections

Remember, trains don't go into St. Andrews—instead, use the Leuchars station (5 miles from St. Andrews, connected by a shuttle bus coordinated to meet most trains—see "Arrival in St. Andrews," page 569). The TI has useful train schedules, which also list shuttle-bus departure times from St. Andrews.

From Leuchars by Train: The southbound train runs once or twice per hour, and goes to **Edinburgh** (1 hr). For **Glasgow** or **Stirling,** transfer in Edinburgh (about 2 hrs total to either). For **Inverness,** take the faster route via Dundee (8/day, 3.5 hours, 1–2 changes) or the slower coastal route via Aberdeen (6/day, 4–4.5 hrs, 1–2 changes). Both trains run less frequently on Sundays (hourly to Edinburgh, 5/day for Inverness).

Near St. Andrews: The East Neuk

On the lazy coastline meandering south from St. Andrews, the cute-as-a-pin East Neuk (pronounced "nook") is a collection of

tidy fishing villages. While hardly earth-shattering, the East Neuk is a pleasant detour if you've got the time. The villages of Crail and Pittenweem have their fans, but Anstruther (described below) is worth most of your

attention. The East Neuk works best as a half-day side-trip (by either car or bus) from St. Andrews, though drivers can use it as a scenic detour between Edinburgh and St. Andrews.

Getting There: It's an easy **drive** from St. Andrews. For the scenic route, follow A917 south of town along the coast, past Crail, on the way to Anstruther and Pittenweem. For a shortcut directly to Anstruther, take B9131 across the peninsula (or return that way after driving the longer coastal route there). **Buses** connect St. Andrews to the East Neuk: Bus #95 goes hourly from St. Andrews to Crail and Anstruther (40 min total to Anstruther, catch bus at St. Andrews bus station or from Church Street, around the corner from the TI). The hourly bus #X60 goes directly to Anstruther, then on to Edinburgh (25 min to Anstruther, 2 hrs more to Edinburgh).

▲Anstruther

Stretched out along its harbor, colorful Anstruther (AN-stru-ther; pronounced ENT-ster by locals) is the centerpiece of the East Neuk. The main parking lot and bus stop are both right on the harbor, across from Anstruther's handy **TI,** which offers lots of useful information for the entire East Neuk area (April–Oct Mon–Sat 10:00–17:00, Sun 11:00–16:00, closed Nov–March, tel. 01333/311-073). Stroll the harborfront to the end, detouring inland around the little cove (or crossing the causeway at low tide) to reach some colorful old houses, including one encrusted with seashells.

Anstruther's main sight is the **Scottish Fisheries Museum,** which, true to its slogan, is "bigger than you think." The endearingly hokey exhibit sprawls through several harborfront buildings, painstakingly tracing the history of Scottish seafaring from primitive dugout dinghies to modern vessels. You'll learn the story of Scotland's "Zulu" fishing boats, and walk through vast rooms filled with boats. For a glimpse at humble fishing lifestyles, don't miss the Fisherman's Cottage, hiding upstairs from the courtyard (£5; April–Sept Mon–Sat 10:00–17:30, Sun 11:00–16:30; Oct–March Mon–Sat 10:00–16:00, Sun 12:00–16:00; last entry one hour before closing, Harbourhead, tel. 01333/310-628, www .scotfishmuseum.org).

Eating in Anstruther: Anstruther's claim to fame is its fish-and-chips, considered by many to be Scotland's best. Though there are several good "chippies" in town, the famous one is the **Anstruther Fish Bar,** facing the harbor just a block from the TI and Fisheries Museum. As you enter, choose whether you want to get takeout or dine in for a few pounds more. While more expensive than most chippies, the food here is good—so good the place has officially been named "UK's Fish and Chip Shop of the Year" multiple times, including in 2009 (£5–7 takeout, £7–9 to dine in, dine-in prices include bread and a drink, daily 11:30–21:30, until 22:00 for take-away, 42–44 Shore Street, tel. 01333/310-518).

GLASGOW

Glasgow (GLAS-goh), though bigger than Edinburgh, lives forever in the shadow of its more popular neighbor. Once a decrepit former port city, Glasgow—astride the River Clyde—has climbed out of its recession in recent years. Today, it's both a workaday Scottish city and a cosmopolitan destination with an energetic dining and nightlife scene. The city is also a pilgrimage site of sorts for architecture buffs, thanks to a cityscape packed with Victorian architecture, early-20th-century touches, and modern flair (unfortunately, it also has some truly drab recent construction). Most beloved are the works by hometown boy Charles Rennie Mackintosh, the visionary turn-of-the-20th-century architect who left his mark all over Glasgow.

Edinburgh, a short train-trip away, may have the royal aura, but Glasgow has an unpretentious appeal. As my cab driver said, "The people of Glasgow have a better time at a funeral than the people of Edinburgh have at a wedding." In Glasgow, there's no upper-crust history, and no one puts on airs. Locals call sanded and polished concrete "Glasgow marble." You'll be hard-pressed to find a souvenir shop in Glasgow—and that's just how the natives like it. In this newly revitalized city, visitors are a novelty, and locals do their best to introduce you to the fun-loving, laid-back Glaswegian (rhymes with "Norwegian") way of life.

Planning Your Time

For most visitors, a few hours are plenty to sample Glasgow. Focus on my self-guided walking tour in the city core, which includes Glasgow's two most interesting sights: Charles Rennie Mackintosh's Glasgow School of Art, and the time-warp Tenement

House. With more time, add some of the outlying sights, such as the cathedral area (to the
east), Kelvingrove Gallery and the West End
restaurant scene (to the west), and the Burrell
Collection (a few miles out of town).

Day Trip from Edinburgh: For a full day,
grab breakfast at your B&B in Edinburgh,
then catch the 9:30 train to Glasgow (morning
trains every 15 min; £10.50 same-day round-
trip if leaving after 9:15 or on weekend); it
arrives at Queen Street Train Station at 10:20.
Call to reserve tickets to tour the Glasgow
School of Art (aim for an early-afternoon
time slot, which leaves you time for lunch beforehand). Once in
Glasgow, take my self-guided walk to hit all the major sights,
making sure to reach the Tenement House by the last entry time
(16:30). For dinner, consider heading out to the thriving West
End restaurant scene, then hop the subway back to Queen Street
Station (use the Buchanan Street stop) and catch the 21:00 train
back to Edinburgh (evening trains every 30 min).

Orientation to Glasgow

(area code: 0141)
With a grid street plan, a downtown business zone, and more than
its share of boxy office buildings, Glasgow feels more like a midsized
American city than a big Scottish one—like Cleveland or Cincinnati
with shorter skyscrapers, more sandstone, and more hills. While
greater Glasgow is a sprawling city of 2.3 million people, the tourist's
Glasgow has just three main parts: the city center, a cluster of minor
sights near the cathedral (in the east), and the West End restaurant/
nightlife/shopping zone. The hilly but easily walkable city center has
two main drags, both lined with shops and crawling with shoppers:
Sauchiehall Street (pronounced "Sockyhall," running west to east)
and Buchanan Street (running north to south).

Tourist Information

The TI is opposite Queen Street Station in the southwest corner of
George Square (at #11). They hand out an excellent free map, the
informative *Essential Guide*, an events listing, and other Glasgow
brochures, and can book you a room for a £4 fee (Mon–Sat
9:00–18:00, until 19:00 in June, until 20:00 in July–Aug, Sun
10:00–18:00 year-round, tel. 0141/204-4400, www.seeglasgow
.com or www.visitscotland.com). Buses to the West End depart
from in front of the TI (see page 605), and the city bus tour leaves
from across the square.

GLASGOW

Mackintosh Trail Ticket: This ticket, sold by the TI and all Mackintosh sights, covers entry to all "Charles Rennie Mac" sights and public transportation to those outside the city limits (£12/day, www.crmsociety.com).

Arrival in Glasgow

By Train: Glasgow, a major Scottish transportation hub, has two main train stations, which are just a few blocks apart in the very heart of town: **Central Station** (with a grand, genteel interior) and **Queen Street Station** (more functional, with connections to Edinburgh, and closer to the TI—take the exit marked *George Square* and continue straight across the square). Both stations have pay WCs (30p) and baggage storage (Central Station—at the head of track 1, £7; Queen Street Station—near the head of track 7, £5–7 based on size). Unless you're packing heavy, it's easier to walk the five minutes between the stations than to take the roundabout "RailLink" bus #398 between them (75p, or free if you have a ticket for a connecting train).

By Bus: Buchanan Street Bus Station is at Killermont Street, just two blocks behind Queen Street Train Station.

By Car: The M8 motorway, which slices through downtown Glasgow, is the easiest way in and out of the city. Ask your hotel for directions to and from M8, and connect with other highways from there.

By Air: For information on Glasgow's two airports, see "Glasgow Connections," at the end of this chapter.

Helpful Hints

Safety: The city center, which is packed with ambitious career types during the day, can feel deserted at night. Avoid the area near the River Clyde entirely (hookers and thugs), and confine yourself to the streets north of Argyle Street if you're in the downtown quarter. The West End and the Merchant City (east of the train stations) bustle with crowded restaurants well into the evening and feel well-populated in the wee hours.

If you've picked up a football (soccer) jersey or scarf as a souvenir, don't wear it in Glasgow; local passions run very high, and most drunken brawls in town are between supporters of Glasgow's two rival soccer clubs: the Celtic in green and white, and the Rangers in blue and red. (For reasons no one can explain, the Celtic team name is pronounced "sell-tic"—the only place you'll find this pronunciation outside of Boston.)

Sightseeing: Glasgow's city-owned museums—including the sights near the cathedral, but not biggies like the Glasgow School of Art or Tenement House—are free (www.glasgow museums.com).

Internet Access: You'll see signs advertising Internet cafés all around the city core (near Central Station and Buchanan Street). A big **easyInternetcafé** is between Central and Queen Street stations, at 57–61 St. Vincent Street (enter through Caffè Nero; Mon–Sat 8:00–20:00, Sun 9:00–19:30).

Sunday Travel: Bus and train schedules are dramatically reduced on Sundays—most routes have only half the departure times they have during the week (though Edinburgh is still easily accessible). If you plan to leave Glasgow for a remote destination on Sunday, check the schedules carefully when you arrive. All trains run less frequently in the off-season; if you want to get to the Highlands by bus on a Sunday in winter, forget it.

Local Guide: Joan Dobbie, a native Glaswegian and registered Scottish Tourist Guide, will give you the insider's take on Glasgow's sights (£80/half-day, £120/day, tel. 01355/236-749, mobile 07773-555-151, joan.leo@lineone.net).

GLASGOW

Getting Around Glasgow

By City Bus: Various companies run Glasgow's buses, but most city-center routes are operated by First Glasgow (price depends on journey, £3.20 for any two single journeys, £3.50 for all-day ticket, exact change required). Buses run every few minutes down Glasgow's main thoroughfares (such as Sauchiehall Street) to the downtown core (train stations). If you're waiting at a stop and a bus comes along, ask the driver if he's headed to Central Station; chances are he'll say yes. (For information on buses to the West End, see page 605.)

By Hop-on, Hop-off Bus Tour: This tour connects Glasgow's far-flung historic sights in an 80-minute loop (£10, ticket valid for 2 days, daily starting at 9:30, July–Aug 4/hr until 17:00, spring 3/hr until 16:30, winter 2/hr until 16:00; stops in front of Central Station, George Square, and major hotels; tel. 0141/204-0444, www.scotguide.com). If there's a particular sight you want to see, confirm that it's on the route.

By Taxi: Taxis are affordable, plentiful, and often come with nice, chatty cabbies—all speaking in the impenetrable local accent. Just smile and nod. Most taxi rides in the downtown area will cost about £3; from the West End, a one-way trip is about £6. Use taxis or public transport to connect Glasgow's more remote sights; splurge for a taxi (for safety) any time you're traveling late at night.

By Subway: The claustrophobic, orange-line subway—nicknamed "Clockwork Orange"—runs in a loop around the edge of the city center. The "outer circle" runs clockwise, and the "inner circle" runs counterclockwise. (If you miss your stop, you can just wait it out—you'll come full circle in about 25 minutes. Or hop out and cross to the other side of the platform to go back the way you came.)

Though the subway is essentially useless for connecting city-center sightseeing (Buchanan Street is the only downtown stop), it's handy for reaching sights farther out, including the Kelvingrove Gallery (Kelvinhall stop) and West End restaurant/nightlife neighborhood (Hillhead stop; £1.20 single trip, £3.50 Discovery Ticket lets you travel all day after 9:30; subway runs Mon–Sat 6:30–23:30, but Sun only 11:00–18:00; www.spt.co.uk/subway).

Self-Guided Walk

Get to Know Glasgow

Glasgow isn't romantic, but it has an earthy charm, and architecture buffs love it. The trick to sightseeing here is to always look up—above the chain restaurants and mall stores, you'll see a wealth of imaginative facades, complete with ornate friezes and expressive sculptures. These buildings transport you to the heady days around the turn of the 20th century—when the rest of Great Britain was enthralled by Victorianism, but Glasgow set its own course, thanks largely to the artistic bravado of Charles Rennie Mackintosh and his friends (the "Glasgow Four"). This walking tour takes three to four hours, including one hour for Mackintosh's masterpiece, the Glasgow School of Art (in summer, consider calling ahead to reserve your tour there—see page 595).

• Begin at Central Station. Exit the train station straight ahead from the tracks (to the north, onto Gordon Street), turn right, and cross busy Renfield/Union Street. Continue one block, then turn right down Mitchell Street, and look up on the left side of the street to see a multi-story brick water tower topped by a rounded cap. Turn left down a small alley (Mitchell Lane) just in front of the tower. Within about 25 yards, you'll see the entrance to...

The Lighthouse

This facility, which houses the Scotland Center for Architecture and Design, is made of two parts: a water tower designed by

Charles Rennie Mackintosh in the early 1900s, and a new, modern glass-and-metal museum built alongside it. The Lighthouse is filled mostly with design exhibitions, lonely floors of conference rooms, and funny icons directing desperate men and women to the bathrooms (£4, free on Sat; open Mon and Wed–Sat 10:30–17:30, Tue 11:00–17:30, Sun 12:00–17:30, 11 Mitchell Lane, tel. 0141/221-6362, www.thelighthouse.co.uk). This sight is skippable for most,

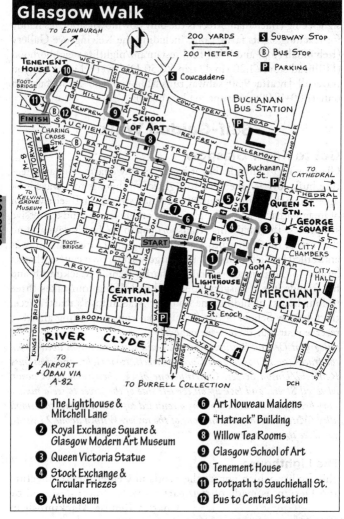

Glasgow Walk

TO EDINBURGH

S SUBWAY STOP
B BUS STOP
P PARKING

200 YARDS
200 METERS

TENEMENT HOUSE
FOOT-BRIDGE
Cowcaddens
School of Art
Buchanan Bus Station
Charing Cross Stn.
Finish
Queen St. Stn.
George Square
City Chambers
City Hall
Merchant City
Kelvin-Grove Museum
START
The Lighthouse
Central Station
GOMA
St. Enoch
River Clyde
Kingston Bridge
TO Airport & Oban VIA A-82
TO BURRELL COLLECTION
DCH

① The Lighthouse & Mitchell Lane
② Royal Exchange Square & Glasgow Modern Art Museum
③ Queen Victoria Statue
④ Stock Exchange & Circular Friezes
⑤ Athenaeum
⑥ Art Nouveau Maidens
⑦ "Hatrack" Building
⑧ Willow Tea Rooms
⑨ Glasgow School of Art
⑩ Tenement House
⑪ Footpath to Sauchiehall St.
⑫ Bus to Central Station

but it does offer a fine view over the city. Before you head up, be sure to request the free *View from the Top* pamphlet, which indicates the buildings you'll see in the panorama. You have two options for scaling the heights: Take the elevator to the sixth-floor windows, or (better) head to the third floor and climb the 135 spiral steps inside the water tower itself. At the top, you'll be able to walk out onto a wraparound balcony with 360-degree views. Also on the third floor of the Lighthouse, you'll find information about Mackintosh, with architectural plans and scale models. Linger here only if you're planning to skip the Glasgow School of Art.

• Exiting the Lighthouse, turn right down the alley, then turn left onto the bustling pedestrian shopping drag called Buchanan Street—Glasgow's outdoor mall. Take the second right onto Exchange Place and pass through the arch, emerging onto the...

Royal Exchange Square

This square—which marks the entrance to the shopping zone called Merchant City—is home to two interesting buildings. On your left as you enter the square is a stately Neoclassical bank-like building (today housing a Borders bookstore). This was once the **private mansion** of one of the tobacco lords, the super-rich businessmen who reigned here from the 1750s through the 1800s, stomping through the city with gold-tipped canes. During the port's heyday, these entrepreneurs helped make Glasgow Europe's sixth-biggest city.

In the middle of the square is the **Glasgow Modern Art Museum,** nicknamed GoMA. Walk around the GoMA building to the main entry (at the equestrian statue), and step back to take in the full Neoclassical facade. On the pediment (above the columns), notice the funky, mirrored mosaic—an example of how Glasgow refuses to take itself too seriously. The temporary exhibits inside GoMA are generally forgettable, but the  museum does have an unusual charter: It displays only the work of living artists (free, Mon–Wed and Sat 10:00–17:00, Thu 10:00–20:00, Fri and Sun 11:00–17:00, tel. 0141/287-3050).

• With the facade of GoMA behind you, turn left onto Queen Street. Within a block, you'll be at the southwest corner of...

George Square

Here, in the heart of the city, you'll find the TI (just to your right as you come to the square), Queen Street Train Station,  the Glasgow City Chambers (the big Neoclassical building to the east, not worth visiting), and—in front of that—a monument to Glaswegians killed fighting in the World Wars. The square is decorated with a *Who's Who* of statues depicting Glaswegians of note. Find James Watt (inventor of the steam engine), as well as Robert Burns and Sir Walter Scott (Scotland's two most famous poets). As you head north along the edge of the square, you'll see a statue of an idealized, surprisingly skinny **Queen Victoria** riding a horse. But you won't see a statue of King George III, for whom the square is named. The stubborn Scots are still angry at George for losing the colonies (i.e., us), and they never commissioned a statue of him.

• *Just past skinny Vic and Robert Peel, turn left onto West George Street and head for the tall church in the middle of the street. Cross Buchanan Street and go around the church on the left side, entering a little square called...*

Nelson Mandela Place

The area around this church features some interesting bits of architectural detail. First, as you stand along the left side of the church, look up and to the left (across from the church) to find the three circular friezes, on the first floor up, of the former **Stock Exchange** (built in 1875). These idealized heads, which were recently cleaned and restored, represent the industries that made Glasgow prosperous during its heyday: building, engineering, and mining.

Continue around to the back of the church and look to the right side of the street for the **Athenaeum** (the sandy-colored building at #8; notice the low-profile label over the door). Now a law office, this was founded in 1847 as a school and city library during Glasgow's golden age. (Charles Dickens gave the building's inaugural address.) Like Edinburgh, Glasgow was at the forefront of the 17th-century Scottish Enlightenment, a celebration of education and intellectualism. The Scots were known for their extremely practical brand of humanism; all members of society, including the merchant and working classes, were expected to be well-educated. (Tobacco lords, for example, often knew Latin and Greek.) Look above the door to find the symbolic statue of a reader sharing books with young children, an embodiment of this ideal.

• *Continue beyond the church and turn left onto West Nile Street; then, one block later, turn right onto...*

St. Vincent Street

We'll enjoy more architectural Easter eggs as we continue along this street toward the Glasgow School of Art. After a block, on the left side of the street (at #115), look up to the second floor to see sculptures of **Art Nouveau maidens.** Their elongated, melancholy faces and downcast eyes seem to reflect Glasgow's difficult recent past, decades of economic decline and urban decay. (They mirror similar faces in Art Nouveau paintings in the Glasgow School of Art, particularly in the artwork of Margaret MacDonald, Charles Rennie Mackintosh's wife and artistic partner.) Along this street, keep your eyes above street level to take in classic Glaswegian sandstone architecture and the Mackintosh-influenced modern takes on it.

Another block down on the right (at #144) is the slender building locals have nicknamed the **"Hatrack" Building.** At first glance it looks like most other sandstone buildings in the city. But look up at the very top, with an ornate rooftop that and elaborate ironwork (Glasgow had roaring iron forges back in the day). The Hatrack is a prime example of the adventurous turn-of-the-century Glaswegian architecture: The building's internal framework bears all the weight, so the facade can use very little load-bearing stone. This "curtain wall" method allows for architectural creativity—here the huge bay windows let in plenty of light and contrast nicely with the recessed arches, making the building both unusual and still quintessentially Glaswegian. (The same method gave Antoni Gaudí the freedom to create his fantastical buildings in Barcelona.) Above the left doorway as you face the building, notice the stained-glass ship in turbulent seas, another fitting icon for a city that's seen more than its share of ups and downs.

• *At the end of the block, turn right up...*

Wellington Street

Climb this street to the crest of the hill, where the two- and three-story buildings have a pleasing, uniform look. These sandstone structures were the homes of Glasgow's upper-middle class, the factory managers who worked for the city's barons (such as the titan who owned the mansion back on Royal Exchange Square). In the strict Victorian class structure, the people who lived here were distinctly higher on the social scale than the people who lived in the tenements (which we'll see at the end of this tour).

• *Turn left onto Bath Street, and then right onto West Campbell Street. It opens onto Sauchiehall, Glasgow's main commercial street. Turn left onto Sauchiehall. Half a block later, at #217 (on the left), you'll see a black-and-white Art Nouveau building with a sign reading...*

Willow Tea Rooms

Charles Rennie Mackintosh made his living from design commissions, including multiple tearooms for businesswoman Kate Cranston. (You might also see fake "Mockintosh" tearooms sprinkled throughout the city—ignore them.) A well-known control freak, Mackintosh designed everything here—down to the furniture, lighting, and cutlery. He took his theme for the café from the name of the street it's on—*saugh* is Scots for willow, and *haugh* for meadow.

In the design of these tearooms, there was a meeting of the (very modern) minds. Cranston wanted a place for women

Charles Rennie Mackintosh
(1868–1928)

During his lifetime, Charles Rennie Mackintosh brought an exuberant Art Nouveau influence to the architecture of his hometown. His designs challenged the city planners of this otherwise practical, working-class port city to create beauty in the buildings they commissioned. A radical thinker, he freely shared credit with his artist wife, Margaret MacDonald. (He once famously said, "I have the talent...Margaret has the genius.")

When Mackintosh was a young student at the Glasgow School of Art, the Industrial Age dominated life here. Factories belched black soot into the city as they burned coal and forged steel. Mackintosh and his circle of artist friends drew their solace and inspiration from nature (just as the Romantics had before them) and created some of the original Art Nouveau buildings, paintings, drawings, and furniture.

As a student traveling abroad in Italy, Mackintosh ignored the famous Renaissance paintings inside the museum walls, and set up his easel to paint the exteriors of churches and buildings instead. He rejected the architectural traditions of ancient Greece and Rome. In Venice and Ravenna, he fell under the spell of Byzantine design, and in Siena he saw a unified, medieval city design he would try to import—but with a Scottish flavor and Glaswegian palette—to his own hometown.

His first commission came in 1893, to design an extension to the Glasgow Herald building. More work soon followed, including the Glasgow School of Art and the Willow Tea Rooms 10 years later. Mackintosh envisioned a world without artistic borders, where an Islamic flourish could find its way onto a workaday building in a Scottish city. Inspired by the great buildings of the past and by his Art Nouveau peers, he in turn influenced others, such as painter Gustav Klimt and Bauhaus founder Walter Gropius. A century after Scotland's greatest architect set pencil to paper, his hometown is at last celebrating his unique vision.

to be able to gather while unescorted, in a time when traveling solo could give a woman a less-than-desirable reputation. An ardent women's rights supporter, Cranston requested that the rooms be bathed in white, the suffragists' signature color.

Enter the Willow Tea Rooms and make your way past the tacky jewelry and trinket store that now inhabits the bottom floor. On the open mezzanine level you'll find 20 crowded tables run like a diner from a corner kitchen, serving bland meals to middle-class people—just as this place has since it opened in 1903 (£2–3 teas, £4–7 breakfasts, £4–5 sandwiches, £7 salads and main dishes). Don't leave without poking your head into the almost-hidden Room de Luxe. Head up the stairs (following signs for the toilet) to see this peaceful tearoom space (unfortunately, you need a reservation to take tea here after 10:00). While some parts of the Room de Luxe are reproductions (such as the chairs and the doors, which were too fragile to survive), the rest is just as it was in Mackintosh's day (Mon–Sat 9:00–16:30, Sun 11:00–16:30, last orders 15 min before closing, 217 Sauchiehall Street, tel. 0141/332-0521, www.willow tearooms.co.uk).

• From here it's a five-minute, mostly uphill walk to the only must-see Mackintosh sight within the town center. Walk a block and a half west on Sauchiehall, and make a right onto Dalhousie Street; the big reddish-brown building on the left at the top of the hill is the Glasgow School of Art.

If you have time to kill before your tour starts, consider heading across the street for a cheap lunch at the recommended student café called **Where the Monkey Sleeps,** *or go around the corner and one block downhill to the recommended* **CCA Bar.** *Or, if you have at least an hour before your tour, you can head to the Tenement Museum (listed at the end of this walk, closed mornings and Nov–Feb), a preserved home from the early 1900s—right when Mackintosh was doing his most important work.*

▲Glasgow School of Art

A pinnacle of artistic and architectural achievement, the Glasgow School of Art presented a unique opportunity for Charles Rennie

Mackintosh to design a massive project entirely to his own liking, down to every last detail. These details—from a fireplace that looks like a kimono to windows that soar for multiple stories—are the beauty of the Glasgow School of Art.

Mackintosh loved the hands-on ideology of the Arts and Crafts movement, but he was also a practical Scot. Study the outside of the building. Those protruding wrought-iron brackets that hover outside the multipaned windows were a new invention during the time of the Industrial Revolution; they reinforce the big, fragile glass windows, allowing natural light to pour in to the school. Mackintosh brought all the most recent technologies to this work, and added them to his artistic palate—which also merged clean Modernist lines, Asian influences, and Art Nouveau flourishes.

Because the Glasgow School of Art is still a working school, the interior can only be visited by one-hour **guided tour.** Walk up the stairs into the main vestibule, and buy your tour ticket at the shop (£8, April–Sept tours generally depart daily at the top of the hour 10:00–17:00, Oct–March tours daily at 11:00 and 15:00, no tours for one week in early June during final exams; tip the starving students a pound or two if they give a good spiel). In the summer, tours are frequent, but they fill up quickly; it's smart to call the shop at 0141/353-4526 or email shop@gsa.ac.uk to confirm times and reserve a guided-tour ticket (shop open daily 9:30–18:30, leave call-back number if leaving a message, www.gsa.ac.uk). Several exhibition galleries in the school are free and open to the public, even if you don't go on a tour.

When the building first opened, it was modern and minimalist. Other elements were added later, such as the lobby's tile mosaics depicting the artistic greats, including mustachioed Mackintosh (who hovers over the gift shop). As you tour the building, you'll see how Mackintosh—who'd been a humble art student himself not too long before he designed this building—strove to create a space that was both artistically innovative and completely functional for students. The plaster replicas of classical sculptures lining the halls were part of Mackintosh's vision, to inspire students by the greats of the past. You'll likely see students and their canvases lining the halls. Do you smell oil paint?

Linking these useable spaces are clever artistic patterns and puzzles that Mackintosh embedded to spur creative thought. A resolute pagan in a very Protestant city, he romanticized the ideals of nature, and included an abstract icon of a spiral-within-a-circle rose design on many of his works. In some cases, he designed a little alcove just big enough for a fresh, single-stem rose and placed it next to one of his stained-glass roses—so students could compare reality with the artistic form. (You'll even find these roses on the swinging doors in the bathroom.)

Mackintosh cleverly arranged the school so that every one of the cellar studios is bathed in intense natural light. And yet, as you climb to the top of the building—which should be the brightest, most light-filled area—the space becomes dark and gloomy, and the stairwell is encumbered by a cage-like structure. Then, reaching the top floor, the professors' offices are again full of sunrays—a literal and metaphorical "enlightenment" for the students after slogging through a dark spell.

During the tour, you'll be able to linger a few minutes in the major rooms, such as the remarkable forest-like library and the furniture gallery (including some original tables and chairs from the Willow Tea Rooms). Walking through the GSA, remember that all of this work was the Art Nouveau original, and that Frank Lloyd Wright, the Art Deco Chrysler Building, and everything that resembles it came well after "Charles Rennie Mack's" time.

• *To finish this walk, we'll do a wee bit of urban "hillwalking" (a popular Scottish pastime). Head north from the Glasgow School of Art on Scott Street (from the shop's exit, turn left, then left again on to Renfrew Street; one block later, turn right onto Scott Street). Huff and puff your way over the crest of the hill, and make a left onto Buccleuch Street. The last house on the left is the...*

▲Tenement House

Packrats of the world, unite! A strange quirk of fate—the 10-year hospitalization of a woman who never redecorated—created this perfectly preserved middle-class residence. The Scottish Trust bought this otherwise ordinary row home, located in a residential neighborhood, because of the peculiar tendencies of Miss Toward. For five decades, she kept her home essentially unchanged. The kitchen calendar is still set for 1935, and canisters of licorice powder (a laxative) still sit on the bathroom shelf. It's a time-warp experience, where Glaswegian old-timers enjoy coming to reminisce about how they grew up.

Buy your ticket on the main floor, and poke around the little museum. You'll learn that in Glasgow, a "tenement" isn't a slum—it's simply a stone apartment house. In fact, tenements like these were typical for every class except the richest. But with the city's economic decline, tenements went the way of the dodo bird as the city's population shrank.

Then head upstairs to the apartment, which is staffed by caring volunteers. Ask them to demonstrate how to make the bed in the kitchen, or why the rooms still smell like natural gas. As you look through the rooms stuffed with lace and Victorian trinkets—such as the ceramic dogs on the living room's fireplace mantle—consider how different they are from Mackintosh's stark, minimalist designs from the same period (£5.50, £3.50 guidebook, no photos allowed, March–Oct 13:00–17:00, last admission 16:30, closed Nov–Feb, 145 Buccleuch Street at the top of Garnethill, toll tel. 0844-493-2197, www.nts.org.uk).

• *Exit the Tenement House to the left, and take another left down the hill. Follow the leafy footpath that slopes downhill along the highway. After about three minutes, you'll come out the other side of the small park. Go straight ahead one more block (passing the pedestrian bridge on your right) until you arrive back at the far end of Sauchiehall Street.*

To return to Central Station, turn left, walk to the first bus shelter, and take bus #44, #57, or #59 (every 10 min, other buses also go to station—ask the driver if another bus pulls up while you're waiting).

Taxis zip by on Sauchiehall; a ride to the station will cost you about £3.

To catch the bus from here straight out to the recommended restaurants in the West End (listed under "Eating in Glasgow," later), cross Sauchiehall Street and walk two blocks to Holland Street. Turn right and walk one short block to the bus stop on the corner of Holland and Bath streets, and wait for bus #16 (every 20 min, ask driver to let you off near the Hillhead subway stop).

More Sights in Glasgow

Away from the Center

▲**Kelvingrove Art Gallery and Museum**—Reopened in 2006 after a three-year, £28 million renovation, this museum is like a Scottish Smithsonian—with

everything from a pair of stuffed elephants to fine artwork by the great masters. The well-described collection is impressively displayed in an impressive 100-year-old Spanish Baroque–style building. It's divided into two sections. The "Life" section, in the West Court, features a menagerie of stuffed animals (including a giraffe, kangaroo, ostrich, and moose) with a WWII-era Spitfire fighter plane hovering overhead. Branching off are halls with exhibits ranging from Ancient Egypt to "Scotland's First Peoples" to weaponry ("Conflict and Consequence"), as well as several fine paintings (find Salvador Dalí's *Christ of St. John of the Cross*). The more serene "Expression" section, in the East Court, focuses on artwork, including Dutch, Flemish, French, and Italian paintings. It also has exhibits on "Scottish Identity in Art" and on Charles Rennie Mackintosh and the Glasgow School. The Kelvingrove claims to be one of the most-visited museums in Britain—presumably because of all the field-trip groups you'll see here. Watching all the excited Scottish kids—their imaginations ablaze—is as much fun as the collection itself (free, Mon–Thu and Sat 10:00–17:00, Fri and Sun 11:00–17:00, Argyle Street; subway to Kelvinhall stop, then 5-min walk; buses #9, #16, #18, #42, and #62 all stop nearby; tel. 0141/276-9599, www.glasgowmuseums.com).

▲**Burrell Collection**—This eclectic art collection of a wealthy local shipping magnate is one of Glasgow's top destinations, but it's three miles outside the city center. If you'd like to visit, plan to make an afternoon of it, and leave time to walk around the surrounding park, where Highland cattle graze. The diverse contents of this museum include sculptures (from Roman to Rodin),

stained glass, tapestries, furniture, Asian and Islamic works, and halls of paintings—starring Cézanne, Renoir, Degas, and a Rembrandt self-portrait (free, Mon–Thu and Sat 10:00–17:00, Fri and Sun 11:00–17:00, Pollok Country Park, 2060 Pollokshaws Road, tel. 0141/287-2550, www.glasgowmuseums.com). To get here from Central Station, take bus #45, #47, or #57 to Pollokshaws Road, or take a train to the Pollokshaws West train station; the entrance is a 10-minute walk from the bus stop and the train station. By car, follow M8 to exit at junction 22 onto M77 Ayr; exit junction 1 on M77 and follow signs.

Near the Cathedral, East of Downtown

To reach these sights from the TI on George Square, head up North Hanover Street, turn right on Cathedral Street, and walk about 10 minutes. All sights are free.

Glasgow Cathedral—This blackened, Gothic-to-the-extreme cathedral is a rare example of an intact pre-Reformation Scottish cathedral. Look up to see the wooden barrel-vaulted ceiling, and notice the beautifully decorated section over the choir ("quire"). Standing at the choir, turn around to look down the nave at the west wall, and notice how the right wall lists. (Don't worry; it's been standing for 800 years.) Peek into the lower church, and don't miss the Blacader Aisle (stairs down to the right as you face the choir), where you can look up to see the ceiling bosses—colorful carved demons, dragons, skulls, and more (April–Sept Mon–Sat 9:30–17:30, Sun 13:00–17:00; Oct–March until 16:30; near junction of Castle and Cathedral Streets, tel. 0141/552-6891, www.glasgowcathedral.org.uk).

Provand's Lordship—With low beams and medieval decor, this creaky home—supposedly the "oldest house in Glasgow"—displays the *Lifestyles of the Rich and Famous*...circa 1471. The interior shows off a few pieces of furniture from the 16th, 17th, and 18th centuries. Out back, explore the St. Nicholas Garden, which was once part of a hospital that dispensed herbal remedies. The plaques in each section show the part of the body each plant is used to treat (Mon–Thu and Sat 10:00–17:00, Fri and Sun 11:00–17:00, across the street from St. Mungo Museum at 3 Castle Street, tel. 0141/552-8819).

St. Mungo Museum of Religious Life and Art—This museum, next to the cathedral, aims to promote religious understanding. Taking an ecumenical approach, it provides a handy summary of major and minor world religions, showing how each faith handles various rites of passage through the human life span: birth, puberty, marriage, death, and everything in between (same hours as Provand's Lordship, cheap ground-floor café, 2 Castle Street, tel. 0141/276-1625).

Necropolis—Built to resemble Paris' Père Lachaise cemetery, Glasgow's huge burial hill has a similarly wistful, ramshackle appeal, along with an occasional deer. Its gravestones seem poised to slide down the hill (open erratic hours at the caretaker's whim, mostly 10:00–16:00 year-round; if main black gates are closed, walk around to the side and see if you can get in and out through a side alleyway).

Nightlife in Glasgow

Glasgow is a young city, and its nightlife scene is renowned. Walking through the city center, you'll pass at least one club or bar on every block. For the latest, pick up a copy of *The List* (sold at newsstands).

In the West End: **Òran Mòr,** a converted 1862 church overlooking a busy intersection, is one of Glasgow's most popular hangouts. In addition to hosting an atmospheric bar, outdoor beer garden, and brasserie, the building's former nave (now decorated with funky murals) has a nightclub featuring everything from rock shows to traditional Scottish music nights (brasserie serves £10–20 main dishes; pub with dressy conservatory or outdoor beer garden serves £7–10 pub grub; daily 9:00–very late, food served until 21:00 in pub or until 22:00 in brasserie, top of Byres Road at 731–735 Great Western Road, tel. 0141/357-6226, www.oran-mor.co.uk).

In the City Center: **The Pot Still** is an award-winning malt whisky bar from 1835 that boasts a formidable selection of more than 300 choices. You'll see locals of all ages sitting in its leathery interior, watching football (soccer) and discussing their drinks. They have whisky aged in sherry casks, whisky preferred by wine drinkers, and whisky from every region of Scotland. Give the friendly bartenders a little background on your beverage tastes, and they'll narrow down a good choice for you from their long list (whisky runs £2–250 a glass, average price £4–5, no food served, Mon–Wed 11:00–23:00, Thu–Sat 11:00–24:00, Sun 18:00–23:00, 154 Hope Street, tel. 0141/333-0980).

Sleeping in Glasgow

On Renfrew Street

B&Bs line Renfrew Street, a block away from the Glasgow School of Art. From here you can walk downhill into the downtown core in about 15 minutes (or take a £3–4 taxi). If approaching by car,

---

Sleep Code

(£1 = about $1.60, country code: 44, area code: 0141)

S = Single, **D** = Double/Twin, **T** = Triple, **Q** = Quad, **b** = bathroom, **s** = shower only. You can assume credit cards are accepted unless otherwise noted.

To help you sort easily through these listings, I've divided the rooms into two categories based on the price for a standard double room with bath (during high season):

$$ Higher Priced—Most rooms £50 or more.
$ Lower Priced—Most rooms less than £50.

---

you can't drive down one-way Renfrew Street from the city center. Instead, from busy Sauchiehall Street, go up Scott Street or Rose Street, turn left onto Buccleuch Street, and circle around to Renfrew Street.

$$ Rennie Mackintosh Hotel has 24 nice-enough rooms and public spaces inspired by Glasgow's favorite architect (slippery rates change with demand, but generally Sb-£35–45; Db-£50–55 Sun–Thu, £60–65 Fri–Sat; 218–220 Renfrew Street, tel. 0141/333-9992, fax 0141/333-9995, www.rmghotels.com, rennie@rmghotels.com).

$$ Victorian House Hotel is a crank-'em-out guest house with a friendly staff and 58 worn but workable rooms sprawling through several old townhouses (S-£32, Sb-£39, Db-£60, lots of stairs and no elevator, 212 Renfrew Street, tel. 0141/332-0129, fax 0141/353-3155, www.thevictorian.co.uk, info@thevictorian.co.uk).

Elsewhere in Central Glasgow

$$ Ibis Glasgow, part of the modern hotel chain, has 141 cookie-cutter rooms with blond wood and predictable comfort just three blocks downhill from the Renfrew Street B&Bs. It's a mostly level 10-minute walk from downtown (Sb/Db-£53–55 on weeknights, £59 on weekends, £85 "event rate" during festivals and in Aug, breakfast-£6, air-con, pay Internet access and Wi-Fi, elevator, restaurant, hiding behind a big Novotel at 220 West Regent Street, tel. 0141/225-6000, fax 0141/225-6010, www.ibishotel.com, h3139@ibishotel.com).

$$ Babbity Bowster, named for a traditional Scottish dance, is a pub and restaurant renting six basic rooms up top. It's located in the trendy Merchant City on the eastern fringe of downtown, near several clubs and restaurants (Sb-£45, Db-£60, lots of stairs and no elevator, 10-min walk from Central Station, 16–18 Blackfriars Street, tel. 0141/552-5055, babbity@btinternet.com).

Central Glasgow Hotels & Restaurants

The ground-floor pub serves £5–9 pub grub (sometimes closed Sun–Tue); the first-floor restaurant, run by a French chef, offers £15–18 main dishes (Tue–Sat 18:30–22:30, closed Sun–Mon).

$ **Euro Hostel** is the best bet for hostel beds in the city center. Part of a chain, this place is a lively hive of backpacker activity, with 365 beds on nine floors, plus pay Internet access, free Wi-Fi, a kitchen, a bar, and friendly staff (request a room on a higher floor and on the back for maximum quiet; very slippery rates, but figure Sb-£32–42, Db-£38–53, £14–20 bunk in 4- to 14-bed dorm with bathroom, couples should request a double or you'll get a bunk-bed, includes continental breakfast, elevator, laundry-£4/load, 318 Clyde Street, tel. 0141/222-2828, reservations@euro-hostels.co.uk, www.euro-hostels.co.uk). It's on the busy main thoroughfare past Central Station, along the River Clyde, near some seedy areas.

Eating in Glasgow

Many of Glasgow's fancier eateries serve "pre-theatre menus"—fixed-price meals at a good price served before 19:00.

200 YARDS
200 METERS

S SUBWAY STOP
P PARKING
B BUS STOP

1. Rennie Mackintosh & Victorian House Hotels
2. Ibis Glasgow
3. Babbity Bowster Rooms
4. Euro Hostel
5. Mussel Inn
6. Rogano Restaurant
7. Wagamama
8. CCA Bar
9. Where the Monkey Sleeps Cafeteria
10. To West End Eateries & Nightlife
11. The Pot Still Bar
12. easyInternetcafé
13. Bus to West End

GLASGOW

In the City Center

Mussel Inn offers light, good-value fish dinners and seafood plates in an airy, informal environment. The restaurant is a cooperative, owned and run by shellfish farmers. Their £10 "kilo pot" of Scottish mussels is popular with locals and big enough to share (£7 small grilled platters, £11–16 meals, Mon–Thu 12:00–14:30 & 17:00–22:00, Fri–Sat 12:00–22:00, Sun 17:00–22:00, 157 Hope Street, between St. Vincent and West George Streets, tel. 0141/572-1405).

Rogano is a time-warp Glasgow institution with essentially the same Art Deco interior it had when it opened in 1935. There are three parts: the bar in front, with outdoor seating (£6 lunch sandwiches, £9–10 meals); the fancy dining room in the back part of the main floor, which is like dining on the officers' deck of the *Titanic* (£22–35 meals with a focus on seafood); and a more casual yet still dressy bistro in the cellar, with a 1930s-Hollywood glamour (£10–17 meals, £15 high tea; daily 12:00–22:30, fancy restaurant closed 14:30–18:00, 11 Exchange Place—just before giant archway from Buchanan Street, reservations smart on weekends, tel. 0141/248-4055).

Wagamama is part of a reliably good UK chain that serves delicious Asian noodle dishes at a reasonable price (£6–10 main dishes, Mon–Sat 12:00–23:00, Sun 12:30–22:00, 97–103 West George Street, tel. 0141/229-1468).

And More: Dozens of restaurants line the main commercial areas of town: Sauchiehall Street, Buchanan Street, and the Merchant City area. Most are very similar, with trendy interiors, Euro disco-pop soundtracks, and dinner for about £15–20 per person.

Budget Options near the Glasgow School of Art

CCA Bar, located in the first floor of Glasgow's edgy contemporary art museum, has delicious designer food at art-student prices. An 18th-century facade, discovered when the site was excavated to build the museum, looms over the courtyard restaurant (£5 salads, £7 main courses, same prices for lunch or dinner; Tue–Thu 10:30–23:00, food served until 19:30; Fri–Sat 10:30–24:00, food served until 21:30; closed Sun–Mon, 350 Sauchiehall Street, tel. 0141/332-7959).

Where the Monkey Sleeps is a cheap student cafeteria across the street from the entrance to the Glasgow School of Art. This is a good spot for a subsidized lunch (open to the public, choice of two hot meals a day for £2–3, soups for £2, and sandwiches for £1–2). Nothing is ever more than £4. It's your chance to mingle with the city's next generation of artists and hear more of that lilting Glaswegian accent (Sept–June Mon–Fri 8:00–15:00, closed Sat–Sun, outside of the school year fewer foods to choose from, entrance is on the left as you face the multicolored windows, follow *refectory* signs, 167 Renfrew Street, tel. 0141/353-4728).

In the West End

The hip, lively residential neighborhood called the West End is worth exploring, particularly at dinnertime. A collection of fine and fun eateries line Ashton Lane, a small street just off bustling Byres Road (the scene continues north along Cresswell Lane). Before choosing a place, make a point of strolling the whole scene to comparison-shop.

Local favorites (all open long hours daily) include the landmark **Ubiquitous Chip** (with various pubs and restaurants sprawling through a deceptively large building; £5–7 pub grub, £8–20 restaurant meals, tel. 0141/334-5007) and **The Loft** (£7–9 pizzas and pastas in the lobby of Grosvenor Cinema, a grand old movie theater; tel. 0141/339-0686). Up at Cresswell Lane, consider **Café Andaluz,** which offers £4–7 tapas and sangria behind lacy wooden screens, as the waitstaff clicks past on the cool tiles (2 Cresswell

Lane, tel. 0141/339-1111). Back on Byres Road, **La Vallée Blanche** serves French cuisine with a Scottish twist, in a romantic dining area that resembles an upscale mountain lodge (£11–18 main dishes, closed Mon, 360 Byres Road, tel. 0141/334-3333). Also note that the church-turned-pub Òran Mòr—described earlier, under "Nightlife in Glasgow"—is a five-minute walk away (at the intersection of Byres and Great Western Road).

Getting to the West End: It's easiest to take the subway to Hillhead, which is a two-minute walk from Ashton Lane (exit the station to the left, then take the first left to find the lane). From the city center, you can also take a £5–6 taxi or catch bus #20 or #66 (stops just in front of the TI and on Hope Street, near recommended Renfrew Street hotels, runs every 10 min; get out when you reach Byres Road).

Glasgow Connections

Traveline Scotland has a journey planner that's linked to all of Scotland's train and bus schedule info. Go online (www .travelinescotland.com); call them at toll tel. 0871-200-2233; or use the individual websites listed below. If you're connecting with Edinburgh, note that the train is faster but the bus is cheaper.

From Glasgow's Central Station by Train to: Keswick in the Lake District (hourly, 1.5 hrs to Penrith, then catch a bus to Keswick, hourly except Sun 8/day, 40 min), **Stranraer** and ferry to Belfast (7/day, 2.5 hrs, some direct, others with change in Ayr, Troon, or Kilmarnock), **Troon** and ferry to Belfast (2/hr, 45 min), **Blackpool** (1–3/hr, 3 hrs, transfer in Preston), **Liverpool** (1–2/hr, 3.5 hrs, change in Wigan or Preston), **Durham** (1–2/hr, 3 hrs, may require change in Edinburgh), **York** (1–2/hr, 3.5 hrs), **London** (1–2 hr, 4.5–5 hrs direct). Train info: toll tel. 0845-748-4950 or www. nationalrail.co.uk.

From Glasgow's Queen Street Station by Train to: Oban (3/day, just 1/day Sun in winter, 3–3.25 hrs), **Inverness** (8/day, 3.5 hrs, 3 direct, the rest change in Perth), **Edinburgh** (3–4/hr, 50 min), **Stirling** (3/hr, 30–60 min), **Pitlochry** (9/day, 1.75 hrs, some with transfer in Perth).

From Glasgow by Bus to: Edinburgh (4/hr, 1.25 hr), **Oban** (buses #976 and #977, 7/day, 3 hrs, some with transfer in Tyndrum), **Fort William** (buses #914, #915, and #916; 8/day, 3 hrs), **Glencoe** (buses #914, #915, and #916; 8/day, 2.5 hrs), **Inverness** (every 2 hours, 4.5 hrs, transfer in Perth), **Portree** on the Isle of Skye (buses #915 and #916, 3/day direct, 6.5 hrs, 1 more with change in Fort William), **Pitlochry** (5/day, 2.25 hrs, transfer in Perth). Bus info: toll tel. 08705-505-050 or www.citylink.co.uk.

Glasgow International Airport: Located eight miles west of the city, this airport has currency-exchange desks, an information center, and ATMs (toll tel. 0844-481-5555, www.glasgowairport .com). Taxis connect downtown to the airport for about £20. Bus #500 runs to central Glasgow (daily at least 4/hr 5:00–23:00, then hourly through the night, £4.20/one-way, £6.20/round-trip, 15 min to both train stations, 25 min to the bus station).

Prestwick Airport: A hub for Ryanair (as well as the US military, which refuels planes here), this airport is about 30 miles southwest of the city center (toll tel. 0871-223-0700, ext. 1006, www.gpia.co.uk). A train connects the airport and Central Station (Mon–Sat 2/hr, 45 min). Buses run to and from Buchanan Street Station (£4–7, daily 1–2/hr, plus a few nighttime buses, 45 min, check schedules at airport TI or www.travelinescotland.com).

OBAN AND THE SOUTHERN HIGHLANDS

Oban • Mull • Iona • Glencoe • Fort William

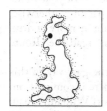

The area north of Glasgow offers a fun and easy dip into the southern part of the Scottish Highlands. Oban is a fruit crate of Scottish traditions, with a handy pair of wind-bitten Hebrides islands (Mull and Iona) just a hop, skip, and jump away. Nearby, the evocative "Weeping Glen" of Glencoe aches with both history and natural beauty. Beyond that, Fort William anchors the southern end of the Caledonian Canal, offering a springboard to more Highlands scenery—this is where Britain's highest peak, Ben Nevis, keeps its head in the clouds, and where you'll find a valley made famous by a steam train carrying a young wizard named Harry.

Planning Your Time

Oban is a smart place to spend the night on a blitz tour of central Scotland; with more time to linger (and an interest in a day trip to the islands), spend two nights—Iona is worthwhile but adds a day to your trip. If you have a third night to spare, you can sleep in Iona and give yourself time to roam around Mull. Glencoe is worth considering as a very sleepy, rural overnight alternative to Oban, or if you have plenty of time and want a remote village experience on your way north.

Oban works well if you're coming from Glasgow, or even all the way from England's Lake District (for driving tips, see the end of this chapter). Assuming you're driving, here's an ambitious two-day plan for the Highlands (some of these sights are described in the next three chapters).

Day 1: Morning: Drive up from the Lake District, or linger in Glasgow; 11:30–Depart Glasgow; 12:00–Rest stop on Loch Lomond, then joyride on; 13:00–Lunch in Inveraray; 16:00–Arrive in Oban, tour whisky distillery, and drop by the TI; 20:00–Dine in Oban.

Day 2: 9:00–Leave Oban; 10:00–Visit Glencoe museum and the valley's Visitors Centre; 12:00–Drive to Fort William and follow Caledonian Canal to Inverness, stopping at Fort Augustus to see the locks and along Loch Ness to search for monsters; 16:00–Visit the Culloden Battlefield (closes earlier off-season) near Inverness; 17:00–Drive south; 20:00–Arrive in Edinburgh.

While you'll see the Highlands this way, you'll whiz past them in a misty blur. With more time, head north from Fort William to the Isle of Skye, spend a night or two there, head over to Inverness via Loch Ness, and consider a stop in Pitlochry.

Getting Around the Highlands

By Car: Drivers enjoy flexibility and plenty of tempting stopovers. Barring traffic, you'll make great time on good, mostly two-lane roads. Be careful, but don't be too timid about passing; otherwise, diesel fumes and large trucks might be your main memory of driving in Scotland. For step-by-step instructions, read the "Route Tips for Drivers" at the end of this chapter.

By Public Transportation: Glasgow is the gateway to this region (so you'll most likely have to transfer there if coming from Edinburgh). The **train** zips from Glasgow to Fort William, Oban, and Kyle of Lochalsh in the west; and up to Stirling, Pitlochry, and Inverness in the east. For more remote destinations (such as Glencoe), the bus is better.

Buses are operated by Scottish Citylink (www.citylink.co.uk). Buy tickets at local TIs, pay the driver in cash when you board, or buy tickets in advance by calling 0870-550-5050. The nondescript town of Fort William serves as a hub for Highlands buses. Note that bus frequency is substantially reduced on Sundays and off-season—during these times, always carefully confirm schedules locally. Unless otherwise noted, I've listed bus information for summer weekdays.

These buses are particularly useful for connecting the sights in this book:

Buses **#976** and **#977** connect Glasgow with Oban (7/day, 3 hrs, some with transfer in Tyndrum).

Bus **#913** runs one daily direct bus from Edinburgh to this region—stopping at Glasgow, Stirling, and Glencoe on the way to Fort William (allow 4 hrs from Edinburgh to Fort William; 5 more/day with change in Glasgow on buses #900 and #914, 5 hrs). Bus **#978** connects Edinburgh with Oban, stopping in Stirling, but not Glencoe (1/day direct, 3.75 hrs; 6 more/day with changes in Glasgow and/or Tyndrum, 4.75 hrs). Bus **#914** goes from Glasgow to Fort William, stopping at Glencoe (5/day, 3 hrs).

Buses **#915** and **#916** follow the same route (Glasgow–Glencoe–Fort William), then continue all the way up to Portree on the Isle of Skye (3/day, 6.75 hrs for the full run).

Bus **#918** goes from Oban to Fort William, stopping en route at Ballachulish near Glencoe (3/day in summer, 2/day off-season, never on Sun; 1 hr to Ballachulish, 1.5 hrs total to Fort William).

Bus **#919** connects Fort William with Inverness (5/day, 2 hrs).

Seaplane service connects downtown Glasgow (on the River Clyde) and Oban Bay. While pricey—about £149 one-way—the trip takes only half an hour and provides a unique view of the Highlands you won't see any other way (on-demand morning or afternoon flights March–Nov, weather permitting, tel. 0870-242-1457, www.lochlomondseaplanes.com).

Oban

Oban (pronounced OH-bin) is called the "gateway to the isles." Equal parts functional and scenic, this busy little ferry-and-train

terminal has no important sights, but makes up the difference in character. It's a low-key resort, with a winding promenade lined by gravel beaches, ice-cream stands, fish-and-chip take-away shops, and a surprising diversity of fine restaurants. When the rain clears, you'll see sun-starved Scots

sitting on benches along The Esplanade, leaning back to catch some rays. Wind, boats, gulls, layers of islands, and the promise of a wide-open Atlantic beyond give Oban a rugged charm.

Orientation to Oban

(area code: 01631)

Oban's business action, just a couple of streets deep, stretches along the harbor and its promenade. (The island just offshore is Kerrera, with Mull looming behind it.) Everything in Oban is close together, and the town seems eager to please its many visitors. There's live music nightly in several bars and restaurants; wool and tweed are perpetually on sale (tourist shops stay open later than usual in summer—until 20:00—and many are even open on Sundays); and posters announce a variety of day tours to Scotland's wild and rabbit-strewn western islands.

Tourist Information

Oban's impressive TI, located in a former church, sells bus and ferry tickets and has a fine bookshop. Stop by to get brochures and information on everything from bike rental to golf courses to horseback riding to rainy-day activities and more. They also offer coin-operated Internet access and can book you a room for a £4 fee (flexible hours, generally July–Aug Mon–Sat 9:00–18:30, Sun 9:00–17:30; June and Sept Mon–Sat 9:00–17:30, Sun 10:00–17:00; April–May and Oct Mon–Sat 9:00–17:30, Sun 10:00–16:00; Nov–March Mon–Sat 10:00–17:00, Sun 12:00–16:00; on Argyll Square, just off harbor a block from train station, tel. 01631/563-122, www.oban.org.uk). Check the "What's On" board for the latest on Oban's small-town evening scene (free live entertainment year-round at the Great Western Hotel, Scottish Night generally every Thu, call for details, tel. 01631/563-101). Wander through their free exhibit on the area and pick up a few phones to hear hardy locals talk about their life on the wild western edge of Scotland.

Helpful Hints

OBAN

Internet Access: One option is at the **TI** (see above). **Fancy That** is a souvenir shop on the main drag with seven high-speed Internet terminals and Wi-Fi in the back room (£1/20 min, daily 9:30–17:00, until 22:00 July–Aug, 108 George Street, tel. 01631/562-996). To surf for free, get online at the **library** just above the ferry terminal; you can just show up, but it's smart to call ahead to book a 30-minute time slot (Mon and Wed 10:00–13:00 & 14:00–19:00, Thu until 18:00, Fri until 17:00, closed Sat afternoon and all day Tue and Sun, 77 Albany Street, tel. 01631/571-444, www.argyll-bute.gov.uk).

Baggage Storage: The train station has luggage lockers (£3–4 depending on bag size), but these have been known to close for security reasons. In this case, **West Coast Motors** has a pricey left-luggage service (£1/hr per piece, unsecured in main office, Mon–Fri 9:00–13:00 & 14:00–17:00, Sat 9:00–14:00, closed Sun, July–Aug open during lunch, can be sporadically closed Oct–May, next to Bowman's Tours at Queens Park Place).

Laundry: You'll find **Oban Quality Laundry** tucked a block behind the main drag, at the intersection of Stevenson and Tweedle Streets (£6–9 per load for same-day drop-off service, no self-service, Mon–Tue and Thu–Fri 9:00–17:30, Wed and Sat 9:00–13:00, closed Sun, tel. 01631/563-554). The **Oban Backpackers** and **IYHF** hostels have laundry service or facilities for guests.

Supermarket: **Tesco** is a five-minute walk from the TI (Mon–Sat 8:00–22:00, Sun 9:00–18:00, WC in front by registers,

Oban

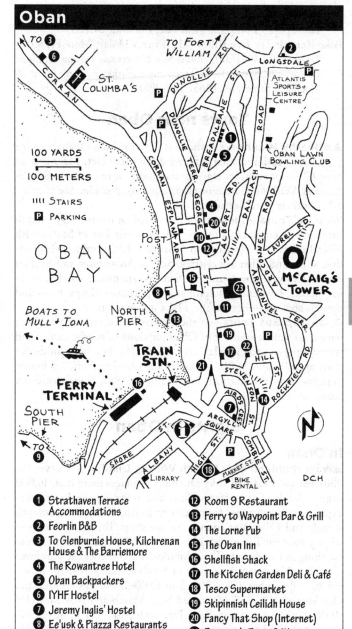

1. Strathaven Terrace Accommodations
2. Feorlin B&B
3. To Glenburnie House, Kilchrenan House & The Barriemore
4. The Rowantree Hotel
5. Oban Backpackers
6. IYHF Hostel
7. Jeremy Inglis' Hostel
8. Ee'usk & Piazza Restaurants
9. To The Seafood Temple
10. Coast Restaurant
11. Cuan Mòr Gastro-Pub
12. Room 9 Restaurant
13. Ferry to Waypoint Bar & Grill
14. The Lorne Pub
15. The Oban Inn
16. Shellfish Shack
17. The Kitchen Garden Deli & Café
18. Tesco Supermarket
19. Skipinnish Ceilidh House
20. Fancy That Shop (Internet)
21. Bowman's Tours & West Coast Motors (Bag Storage)
22. Laundry
23. Whisky Distillery

OBAN

inexpensive cafeteria, look for entrance to large parking lot a block past TI on right-hand side, Lochside Street).

Bike Rental: Try **Evo Bikes** (£10/4 hrs, £14/day, Mon–Fri 9:00–17:30, Sat 9:30–17:00, closed Sun but rentals can be arranged in advance, across from Tesco supermarket parking lot at 29 Lochside Street, tel. 01631/566-996).

Tours near Oban

▲▲**Nearby Islands**—For the best day trip from Oban, tour the islands of Mull and Iona (offered daily May–Oct, described on page 621)—or consider staying overnight on remote and beautiful Iona. With more time or other interests, consider one of many other options you'll see advertised.

Wildlife Tours—Those more interested in nature than church history will enjoy trips to the wildly scenic Isle of Staffa with Fingal's Cave. The journey to Treshnish Island brims with puffins, seals, and other sea critters. Sealife Adventures and SeaFari run whale-watching tours that feature rare minke whales, basking sharks, bottlenose dolphins, and porpoises. Departures and options abound—check at the TI for information.

Open-Top Bus Tours—If there's good weather and you don't have a car, take a spin out of Oban for views of nearby castles and islands, plus a stop at McCaig's Tower (£7, late May–mid-Oct daily at 11:00 and 14:00, no tours mid-Oct–late May, 2.5 hours, departs from rail station, tel. 01586/555-887, www.westcoast motors.co.uk).

Sights in Oban

In Oban

▲**West Highland Malt Scotch Whisky Distillery Tours**—The 200-year-old Oban Whisky Distillery produces more than 16,000 liters a week. They offer serious and fragrant one-hour tours explaining the process from start to finish, with a free, smooth sample and a discount coupon for the shop. This is the handiest whisky tour you'll see, just a block off the harbor and better than anything in Edinburgh. The exhibition that precedes the tour gives a quick, whisky-centric history of Scotland (£6; July–Sept Mon–Fri 9:30–19:30, Sat 9:30–17:00, Sun 10:00–17:00; Easter–June and Oct Mon–Sat 9:30–17:00, closed Sun; March and Nov Mon–Fri 10:00–17:00, closed Sat–Sun; Dec–Feb Mon–Fri 12:30–16:00, closed Sat–Sun; last tour one hour before closing, tel. 01631/572-004). In high season, these tours (which are limited to 15 people every 15 min) fill up quickly. Call or stop by early in the day to reserve your time slot.

Skipinnish Ceilidh House—On just about any night, you can stroll into Skipinnish on the main drag for Highland music and storytelling. This venue invests in talented musicians and puts on a good show, with live bands, songs sung in Gaelic, and Highland dancing. For many, the best part is the chance to learn some *ceilidh* dancing. These group dances are a lot of fun—wallflowers and bad dancers are warmly welcomed, and the staff is happy to give you pointers (£8 music session, pricier for concerts with visiting big-name *ceilidh* bands, nightly at 20:00, 2 hrs, sidewalk ticket stall open daily 10:00–19:30, 34–38 George Street, tel. 01631/569-599, www.skipinnish.com).

McCaig's Tower—The unfinished "colosseum" on the hill over-looking town was an employ-the-workers-and-build-me-a-fine-memorial project undertaken by an early Oban tycoon in 1900. While the structure itself is nothing to see close-up, a 10-minute hike through a Victorian residential neighborhood leads you to a peaceful garden and a mediocre view.

Atlantis Leisure Centre—This industrial-type sports center is a good place to get some exercise on a rainy day or let the kids run wild for a few hours. There's an indoor swimming pool with a big water slide, a rock-climbing wall, tennis courts, and two playgrounds (Mon–Fri 7:00–22:00, July–Aug until 21:00, Sat–Sun 8:30–18:30; pool hours vary by season— in summer roughly Mon–Fri 11:00–20:00, Sat 9:00–18:00, Sun 9:00–16:00, call or check online for exact times; pool entry: adults-£3.50, kids-£2.20, no rental towels or suits, lockers-20p, on the north end of Dalriach Road, tel. 01631/566-800, www.atlantisleisure.co.uk). The center's outdoor playground is free and open all the time; the indoor "soft play centre" for young children costs £2 per kid.

Oban Lawn Bowling Club—The club has welcomed visitors since 1869. This elegant green is the scene of a wonderfully British spectacle of old men tiptoeing wishfully after their balls. It's fun to watch, and—if there's no match and the weather's dry—for £4 each, anyone can rent shoes and balls and actually play (informal hours, but generally daily 10:00–16:00 & 17:00 to "however long the weather lasts," just south of sports center on Dalriach Road).

Near Oban

Kerrera—Just offshore from Oban, this stark but very green island offers a quick, easy opportunity to get that romantic island experience. Although Kerrera (KEH-reh-rah) dominates Oban's sea view, you'll have to head two miles south of town to catch the boat to the middle of the island (ferry-£5 round-trip, £1 for bikes, 5-min trip, first ferry Mon–Sat at 8:45, in summer 2/hr 10:30–17:00, last ferry at 18:00; in winter 5–7/day, last ferry Mon–Fri at 17:50, Sat–Sun at 17:00—but changes with demand; at Gallanach's dock,

OBAN

tel. 01631/563-665, if no answer contact Oban TI for info). The free shuttle service between Oban's North Pier and the Kerrera Marina is for customers of the Waypoint Bar & Grill (described on page 618), but you could always take a walk around the island after lunch.

Sleeping on Kerrera: To spend the night on the island, your only option is the **$ Kerrera Bunkhouse,** a converted 18th-century stable that has seven bunk beds in four compartments (£14 per person, £70 for the entire bunkhouse, cheaper for 2 nights or more, open year-round but book ahead in winter, kitchen, tel. 01631/570-223, ferry info at www.kerrerabunk house.co.uk, info@kerrerabunkhouse.co.uk, Marti and Paddy). They also run a tea garden (April–Sept Wed–Sun 10:30–16:30, closed Oct–March).

Isle of Seil—Enjoy a drive, a walk, some solitude, and the sea. Drive 12 miles south of Oban on A816 to B844 to the Isle of Seil (pronounced "seal"), connected to the mainland by a bridge (which, locals like to brag, "crosses the Atlantic"...well, maybe a small part of it).

Just over the bridge on the Isle of Seil is a pub called **Tigh-an-Truish** ("House of Trousers"). After a 1745 English law forbade the wearing of kilts on the mainland, Highlanders on the island used this pub to change from kilts to trousers before they made the crossing. The pub serves great meals and good seafood dishes to those either in kilts or pants (pub open daily April–Oct 11:00–23:00—food served 12:00–14:00 & 18:00–20:30, July–Aug all day until 21:00, Nov–March shorter hours and soup/sandwiches only, darts anytime, tel. 01852/300-242).

Five miles across the island, on a tiny second island and facing the open Atlantic, is **Easdale,** a historic, touristy, windy little slate-mining town—with a slate-town museum and incredibly tacky egomaniac's "Highland Arts" shop (shuttle ferry goes the 300 yards). An overpriced direct ferry runs from Easdale to Iona; but, at twice the cost of the Mull–Iona trip, the same time on the island, and very little time with a local guide, it's hardly worth it. For a better connection to Iona, see page 621.

Sleeping in Oban

(area code: 01631)

B&Bs

Oban's B&Bs offer a better value than its hotels. All of the places below are a very short walk from town except the Feorlin, which is a 10-minute uphill walk from the main action. None of these B&Bs accept credit cards.

Sleep Code

(£1 = about $1.60, country code: 44, area code: 01631)
S = Single, **D** = Double/Twin, **T** = Triple, **Q** = Quad, **b** = bathroom, **s** = shower only. Unless otherwise noted, you can assume credit cards are accepted at hotels and hostels—but not B&Bs—and breakfast is included.

    To help you sort easily through these listings, I've divided the rooms into three categories based on the price for a standard double room with bath (during high season):

  $$$ **Higher Priced**—Most rooms £70 or more.
   $$ **Moderately Priced**—Most rooms between £30-70.
    $ **Lower Priced**—Most rooms £30 or less.

On Strathaven Terrace

The following B&Bs line up on a quiet, flowery street that's nicely located two blocks off the harbor, three blocks from the center, and a 10-minute walk from the train station. By car, as you enter town, turn left after King's Knoll Hotel, and take your first right onto Breadalbane Street. ("Strathaven Terrace" is actually just the name for this row of houses on Breadalbane Street.) The alley behind the buildings has parking for all of these places.

$$ Sandvilla B&B rents six fine rooms—including one on the ground floor—with sleek contemporary decor (Db-£55, £65 in July–Aug, Tb-£83–95, at #4, tel. 01631/562-803, www.holiday-oban.co.uk, sandvilla@holidayoban.co.uk, Joyce and Scott).

$$ Gramarvin Guest House has five fresh, cheery, and clean rooms (Db-£50–60, £65 in Aug, Tb-£95, family deals, at #5, tel. 01631/564-622, www.gramarvin.co.uk, mary@gramarvin.co.uk, Mary).

$$ Raniven Guest House has four tastefully decorated rooms (Sb-£25, Db-£50–55, price depends on season, free Wi-Fi, at #1, tel. 01631/562-713, www.raniven.co.uk, info@raniven.co.uk, Moyra and Stuart).

$$ Tanglin B&B, with five Grandma's house–homey rooms, comes with lively, chatty hosts Liz and Jim Montgomery, who create an easygoing atmosphere (S-£23, tiny D-£42, Db-£48, flexible rates and family deals, free Wi-Fi, at #3, tel. 01631/563-247, jimtanglin@aol.com).

Uphill from Strathaven Terrace

$ Feorlin B&B isn't glamorous, but the price is right, and the welcome is warm. Lorna Campbell rents two homey rooms in a small house just uphill from the town center. Breakfast includes eggs from Lorna's own hens (Db-£45–50, closed Dec–Jan,

Longsdale Road, 01631/562-930, www.feorlin-oban.co.uk, feorlin@btinternet.com, Lorna). From Strathaven Terrace, continue uphill and follow the street as it curves to the right; the Feorlin is across the street and on your left as you head uphill.

Guest Houses and Small Hotels

These options are a step up from the B&Bs—in both amenities and price. The first three, which are along The Esplanade that stretches north of town (with beautiful bay views), are a five- to 10-minute walk from the center. The last one is on the main drag in town.

$$$ Glenburnie House, a stately Victorian home, has an elegant breakfast room overlooking the bay. Its 12 spacious, comfortable, classy rooms feel like plush living rooms (Sb-£40–50, Db-£80–95, price depends on size and view, cheaper off-season, closed mid-Nov–mid-March, free parking, The Esplanade, tel. & fax 01631/562-089, www.glenburnie.co.uk, graeme.strachan @btinternet.com, Graeme).

$$$ The Barriemore is the last place on Oban's grand waterfront esplanade. Its woody, bright front-facing rooms—some with bay views—are well-appointed, with furnishings that fit the house's grand Victorian feel. Rooms in the modern addition in the back have no views and bland furnishings, but are substantially cheaper (Sb-£45–70, Db-£75–99, Tb-£95–125, price depends on view and season, free Wi-Fi, The Esplanade, tel. 01631/566-356, fax 01631/571-084, www.barriemore-hotel.co.uk, reception @barriemore-hotel.co.uk, friendly Nic and Sarah Jones, and Mara the complacent Great Dane).

$$$ Kilchrenan House, the turreted former retreat of a textile magnate, has 13 tastefully renovated, large rooms, some with bay views (Sb-£45, Db-£70–90, 2-night minimum, higher prices are for seaview rooms in June–Aug, lower prices are for back-facing rooms and Sept–May, pleasant room #5 is worth the few extra pounds, welcome drink of whisky or sherry, different "breakfast special" every day, closed Dec–Jan, a few houses past the cathedral on The Esplanade, tel. 01631/562-663, www.kilchrenanhouse .co.uk, info@kilchrenanhouse.co.uk, Colin and Frances).

$$$ The Rowantree Hotel is a group-friendly place with a wood-and-flagstone lobby, 24 freshly renovated rooms reminiscent of a budget hotel in the US, and a central locale right on Oban's main drag (Sb-£45, Db-£90, prices may be soft for walk-ins and off-season, easy parking, George Street, tel. 01631/562-954, fax 01631/565-071).

Hostels

Oban offers plenty of cheap dorm beds. Your choice: easygoing, institutional (but with fantastic views), or New Age.

$ Oban Backpackers is the most central, laid-back, and fun, with a wonderful, sprawling public living room and 48 beds. The giant mural of nearby islands in the lobby is useful for orientation, and the staff is generous with travel tips (£12–15/bed, 6–12 bunks per room, breakfast-£2, Internet access, free Wi-Fi, £2.50 laundry service for guests only, 10-min walk from station, on Breadalbane Street, tel. 01631/562-107, www.obanbackpackers.com, info@oban backpackers.com, Peter). Their bunkhouse across the street has several basic but cheerful private rooms that share a kitchen (S-£19, D-£38, T-£57, family room-£58, same contact info as hostel).

$ The orderly **IYHF hostel,** on the scenic waterfront Esplanade, is in a grand building with 110 beds and smashing views of the harbor and islands from the lounges and all but one of the rooms. The smaller, private rooms—including several that can usually be rented as doubles—are in a separate newer building out back (£15–18/bed in 4- to 10-bed rooms, bunk-bed Db-£45–55, price varies with demand, also has 8-bed apartment with kitchen, disabled access, £1 cheaper for members, breakfast-£3, Internet access, great facilities and public rooms with cushy sofas, one laundry machine, tel. 01631/562-025, www.hihostels.com, oban@syha .org.uk).

$ Jeremy Inglis' Hostel has 30 beds located two blocks from the TI and train station. This loosely run place feels more like a commune than a youth hostel...and it's cheap (£15/bed, S-£22, cash only, free Wi-Fi, breakfast comes with Jeremy's homemade jam, 21 Airds Crescent, tel. 01631/565-065, jeremyinglis@mctavishs .freeserve.co.uk).

Eating in Oban

Restaurants

Ee'usk (a phonetic rendering of *iasg*, Scottish Gaelic for "fish") is a stylish, family-run place on the waterfront. It has tall tables, a casual-chic atmosphere, a bright and glassy interior, sweeping views, and fish dishes favored by both locals and tourists. Reservations are smart every day in summer and on weekends off-season; if you have to wait for a table, find a seat on one of the comfy sofas in the loft bar (£5–13 lunches, £13–20 dinners, daily 12:00–15:00 & 18:00–21:30, North Pier, tel. 01631/565-666, MacLeod family).

Piazza, next door and also run by the MacLeods, has similar decor but serves Italian cuisine and offers a more family-friendly ambience (£7–10 pizzas and pastas, daily 12:00–15:00 & 17:30–21:00, smart to reserve ahead July–Aug, tel. 01631/563-628).

The Seafood Temple is worth the 15-minute walk from the town center (follow the road past the ferry terminal, or take a £3 taxi ride). This small eatery is situated in a beautifully restored former public toilet building from the Victorian era (no joke), with panoramic views across the bay to the Isle of Kerrera. Owner/chef John—who also runs the shellfish shack at the ferry dock—prides himself on creating the best seafood dishes in town, listed on a limited, handwritten menu. Reservations are a must: To book a table, make a £10-per-person deposit at the shellfish shack, listed later (£12–21 meals, Thu–Sun seatings at 18:00 and 20:00, closed Mon–Wed, tel. 01631/566-000).

Coast proudly serves fresh local fish, meat, and veggies in a mod pine-and-candlelight atmosphere. As everything is prepared and presented with care by husband-and-wife team Richard and Nicola—who try to combine traditional Scottish elements in innovative new ways—come here only if you have time for a slow meal (£7–9 lunches, £12–17 dinners, daily 12:00–14:00 & 17:30–21:00, 104 George Street, tel. 01631/569-900).

Cuan Mòr is a "gastropub" that combines traditional Scottish with modern flair—both in its tasty cuisine and in its furnishings, made entirely of wood, stone, and metal scavenged from the beaches of Scotland's west coast (£6 lunches, £9–13 main dishes, food served daily 12:00–22:00, 60 George Street, tel. 01631/565-078).

Room 9 seats just 24 diners in one tiny light-wood room, and has a select menu of homemade nouvelle-cuisine dishes. It's owned and run with care by the chef (£5–10 lunches, £11–15 dinners, Mon–Sat 12:00–14:30 & 17:30–21:30, closed Sun, reservations smart Fri–Sat, 9 Craigard Road, tel. 01631/564-200).

Waypoint Bar & Grill, just across the bay from Oban, is a laid-back patio at the Kerrera Marina with a no-nonsense menu of grilled seafood. It's not fancy, but the food is fresh and inexpensive, and on a nice day the open-air waterside setting is unbeatable (£8–14 plates, £18 seafood platter, May–Sept daily 12:00–14:00 & 17:00–20:00, closed Oct–April, tel. 01631/565-333). A free-for-customers ferry to the marina leaves from Oban's North Pier, near the recommended Piazza restaurant, hourly at 10 minutes past each hour.

Pub Grub

The Lorne is a lively high-ceilinged pub known for its good grub and friendly service. After hours it becomes the most happening nightspot in town...which isn't saying much (£7–9, food served daily 12:00–14:30 & 17:30–21:00, outside seating, free Wi-Fi, tucked a couple of blocks off the main drag behind the stream at Stevenson Street, tel. 01631/570-020).

The Oban Inn, the oldest building in town, has a lived-in local vibe in its hole-in-the-wall downstairs bar and a quiet lounge

OBAN

upstairs. Enjoy the oak-beam ambience, stained-glass coats-of-arms, and comfy booth seating (£6–8 meals, food served 12:00–21:00, pub open "as late as the law allows," 1 Stafford Street).

Lunch

The green **shellfish shack** at the ferry dock is the best spot to pick up a seafood sandwich or snack (often free salmon samples, inexpensive coffee, meal-size £3 salmon sandwiches, picnic tables nearby, open daily from 10:00 until the boat unloads from Mull around 17:45). This is a good place to pick up a sandwich for your island day—or get a light, early dinner (or "appetizer") when you return from the isles. For a full meal, check out the same folks' Seafood Temple restaurant, described earlier.

The **Kitchen Garden** is fine for soup, salad, or sandwiches. It's a deli and gourmet-foods store with a charming café upstairs (£3 sandwiches to go, £5–11 dishes upstairs, Mon–Sat 8:45–17:30, Sun 11:00–17:00, closed Sun Jan–mid-Feb, 14 George Street, tel. 01631/566-332).

Oban Connections

OBAN

By Train from Oban: Trains link Oban to the nearest transportation hub in **Glasgow** (3/day, just 1/day Sun in winter, 3–3.25 hrs); to get to **Edinburgh,** you'll have to transfer in Glasgow (3/day, 4.25 hrs). To reach **Fort William** (a transit hub for the Highlands), you'll take the same Glasgow-bound train, but transfer in Crianlarich—the direct bus is easier (see below). Oban's small train station has limited hours (ticket window open Mon–Sat 7:15–18:00, Sun 10:45–18:00, same hours apply to lockers and free WC, train info tel. 08457-484-950, www.nationalrail.co.uk).

By Bus: Scottish Citylink bus #918 passes through Ballachulish—a half-mile from **Glencoe**—on its way to **Fort William** (3/day in summer, 2/day off-season, never on Sun; 1 hr to Ballachulish, 1.5 hrs total to Fort William). Take this bus to Fort William, then transfer to bus #919 to reach **Inverness** (3.75 hrs total, with a 20-min layover in Fort William) or **Portree** on the Isle of Skye (2/day, 4.5–5 hrs total). A different bus (#976 or #977) connects Oban with **Glasgow** (7/day, 3 hrs, some with transfer in Tyndrum), from where you can easily connect by bus or train to **Edinburgh** (figure 4–5 hrs total). Buses arrive and depart in front of the Caledonian Hotel, across from the train station (toll tel. 0871-200-2233, www.citylink.co.uk).

By Boat: Ferries fan out from Oban to the **southern Hebrides** (see information on the islands of Iona and Mull, later). Caledonian MacBrayne Ferry info: tel. 01631/566-688, free booking tel. 0800-066-5000, www.calmac.co.uk.

Between Glasgow and Oban

Drivers coming from the south can consider these stopovers, which are listed in order from Glasgow to Oban.

Loch Lomond

Leaving Glasgow on A82, you'll soon be driving along the scenic lake called Loch Lomond. The first picnic turnout has the best lake views, benches, a park, and a playground. Twenty-four miles long and speckled with islands, Loch Lomond is second in size only to Loch Ness. It's well-known mostly because of its easy proximity to Glasgow (about 15 miles away)—and also because its bonnie, bonnie banks inspired a beloved folk song: *Ye'll take the high road, and I'll take the low road, and I'll be in Scotland afore ye...* (You'll be humming that one all day. You're welcome.)

• *Halfway up the loch, at Tarbet, take the "tourist route" left onto A83, driving along Loch Long toward Inveraray.*

Rest-and-Be-Thankful Pass

A low-profile pull-out on A83 just west of A82 offers a pleasant opportunity to stretch your legs and get your first taste of that rugged Scottish countryside. The colorful name comes from the 1880s, when second- and third-class coach passengers got out and pushed the coach and first-class passengers up the hill.

Inveraray

Nearly everybody stops at this lovely, seemingly made-for-tourists castle town on Loch Fyne. Park near the pier and browse the wide selection of restaurants and tourist shops.

Inveraray's **TI** sells bus and ferry tickets, has Internet access, and offers a free mini-guide and an exhibit about the Argyll region (daily April–Oct 9:00–17:00, June–Aug until 18:00, Nov–March 10:00–16:00, tel. 01499/302-063). Public WCs are at the end of the nearby pier (20p).

The town's main "sight" is the **Inveraray Jail,** an overpriced, corny, but mildly educational former jail converted into a museum. This "living 19th-century prison" includes a courtroom where mannequins argue the fate of the accused. You'll have the opportunity to be locked up for a photo op by a playful guard (£8.50, daily Easter–Oct 9:30–18:00, Nov–Easter 10:00–17:00, last entry one hour before closing, Church Square, tel. 01499/302-381).

You'll spot the dramatic **Inveraray Castle** on the right as you cross the bridge coming from Glasgow. This impressive-looking stronghold of one of the more notorious branches of the Campbell clan is striking from afar but dull inside; save your time for better Highlands castles elsewhere.

• *To continue on to Oban, leave Inveraray through a gate (at the Woolen Mill) to A819, and go through Glen Aray and along Loch Awe. A85 takes you into Oban.*

Islands near Oban: Mull and Iona

For the easiest one-day look at two of the dramatic and historic Hebrides (HEB-rid-eez) Islands, take the Iona/Mull tour from Oban. (For a more in-depth look, head north to Skye—see next chapter.)

Here's the game plan: You'll take a ferry from Oban to Mull (40 min), ride a Bowman's bus across Mull (1.25 hours), then board a quick ferry from Mull to Iona. The total round-trip travel time is 5.5 hours (all of it incredibly scenic), plus about two hours of free time on Iona. Buy your set of six tickets—one for each leg—at the Bowman's office in Oban (£34, £2 discount with this book in 2010 for Iona/Mull tour, no tours Nov–Easter, book one day ahead in July–Sept if possible, bus tickets can sell out during busy summer weekends, office open daily 8:30–17:30, 1 Queens Park Place, a block from train station, tel. 01631/566-809 or 01631/563-221, www.bowmanstours.co.uk). For directions on how to buy individual tickets for various legs of this journey (for example, if you plan to sleep in Iona), see page 624.

You'll leave in the morning from the Oban pier on the huge Oban–Mull ferry run by Caledonian MacBrayne (boats depart Sun–Fri at 9:50, Sat at 9:30, board at least 10 min before departure; boats return daily around 17:45). As the schedule can change slightly from year to year, confirm your departure time carefully in Oban. The best seats on the ferry—with the biggest windows—are in the sofa lounge on the uppermost deck on the back end of the boat. (Follow signs for the toilets, and look for big staircase to the top floor; this floor also has its own small snack bar with £3 sandwiches and £4 box lunches.) On board, if it's a clear day, ask a local or a crew member to point out Ben Nevis, the tallest mountain in Great Britain. The ferry has a fine cafeteria and a bookshop (though guidebooks are cheaper in Oban). Five minutes before

Oban and the Southern Highlands

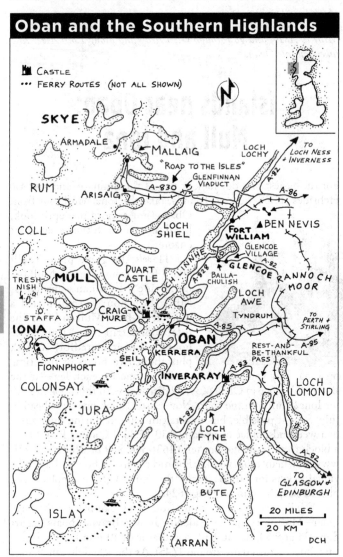

landing on Mull, you'll see the striking Duart Castle on the left.

Upon arrival in Mull, find your tour company's bus for the entertaining and informative ride across the Isle of Mull. All drivers spend the entire ride chattering away about life on Mull. They are hardworking local boys who make historical trivia fascinating—or at least fun. Your destination is Mull's westernmost ferry terminal (Fionnphort), where you'll board a small, rocking ferry for the brief ride to Iona. Unless you stay overnight, you'll have only about two hours to roam freely around the island before taking the ferry–bus–ferry ride in reverse back to Oban.

Mull

The Isle of Mull, the third-largest in Scotland, has 300 scenic miles of coastline and castles and a 3,169-foot-high mountain. Called

Ben More ("Big Mountain" in Gaelic), it was once much bigger. The last active volcano in northern Europe, it was 10,000 feet tall—making up the entire island of Mull—before it blew. It's calmer now, and, similarly, Mull has a notably laid-back population. My bus driver reported that there are no deaths from stress, and only a few from boredom.

With steep, fog-covered hillsides topped by cairns (piles of stones, sometimes indicating graves) and ancient stone circles, Mull has a gloomy, otherworldly charm. Bring plenty of rain protection and wear layers in case the sun peeks through the clouds. As my driver said, Mull is a place of cold, wet, windy winters and mild, wet, windy summers.

On the far side of Mull, the caravan of tour buses unloads at Fionnphort, a tiny ferry town. The ferry to the island of Iona takes about 200 walk-on passengers. Confirm the return time with your bus driver, then hustle to the dock to make the first trip over (otherwise, it's a 30-minute wait). There's a small ferry-passenger building/meager snack bar (and a pay WC). After the 10-minute ride, you wash ashore on sleepy Iona, and the ferry mobs that crowded your steps on the boat seem to disappear into Iona's back lanes.

The Mull and Iona Taxi service can also get you around these two islands (tel. 01681/700-507 or mobile 0788-777-4550, www .mullionataxi.com). They also do day tours of Mull, focusing on local history and wildlife (£35, minibus meets ferry arriving from Oban at 10:40 Tue–Fri; half-day tours cost £30 and leave from the Iona ferry dock; smart to book ahead, enquiries@mullionataxi .com). For directions on how to just buy ferry tickets to Mull and Iona (but not take the Bowman's bus tour), see "Staying Overnight on Iona," later.

OBAN

Iona

The tiny island of **Iona**, just 3 miles by 1.5 miles, is famous as the birthplace of Christianity in Scotland. You'll have about two hours here on your own before you retrace your steps (your driver will tell you which return ferry to take back to Mull—don't miss this boat); you'll dock back in Oban about 17:45. And though the day is spectacular when it's sunny, it's worthwhile in any weather.

A pristine quality of light and a thoughtful peace pervade the stark, car-free island and its tiny community. While the pres-

ent abbey, nunnery, and graveyard go back to the 13th century, much of what you'll see was rebuilt in the 19th century. It's free to see the ruins and the graveyard, but the abbey itself has an admission fee (£4.80, not covered by bus tour ticket, daily April–Sept 9:30–17:00, Oct–March 9:30–16:00, tel. 01681/700-512). It's worth the cost just to sit in the stillness of its lovely, peaceful interior courtyard. With buoyant clouds bouncing playfully off distant bluffs, sparkling white crescents of sand, and lone tourists camped thoughtfully atop huge rocks just looking out to sea, it's a place perfect for meditation. Climb a peak—nothing's higher than 300 feet above the sea.

The village, Baile Mòr, has shops, a restaurant/pub, enough beds, a meager heritage center, and no bank. The Finlay Ross Shop rents bikes (near ferry dock, £4.50/4 hrs, £8/day, £10 deposit per bike, tel. 01681/700-357). Iona's official website (www.isle-of-iona.com) has good information about the island.

Staying Overnight on Iona: For a chance to really experience peaceful, idyllic Iona, consider spending a night or two. Scots bring their kids and stay on this tiny island for a week. If you want to overnight in Iona, don't buy your tickets at Bowman's in Oban—they require a same-day return. Instead, buy each leg of the ferry–bus–ferry (and return) trip separately. Get your Oban–Mull ferry ticket in the Oban ferry office (one-way for walk-on passengers-£4.45, round-trip-£7.55). Once you arrive in Mull (Craignure), follow the crowds to the Bowman buses and buy a ticket directly from the driver (£10 round-trip). Once you arrive at the ferry terminal (Fionnphort), walk into the small trailer ferry office to buy a ticket to Iona (£4.10 round-trip, one-way tickets not available).

History of Iona

St. Columba, an Irish scholar, soldier, priest, and founder of monasteries, got into a small war over the possession of an

illegally copied psalm book. Victorious but sickened by the bloodshed, Columba left Ireland, vowing never to return. According to legend, the first bit of land out of sight of his homeland was Iona. He stopped here in 563, and established an abbey.

Columba's monastic community flourished, and Iona became the center of Celtic Christianity. Missionaries from Iona spread the gospel throughout Scotland and northern England, while scholarly monks established Iona as a center of art and learning. The *Book of Kells*—perhaps the finest piece of art from "Dark Ages" Europe—was probably made on Iona in the eighth century. The island was so important that it was the legendary burial place for ancient Scottish and even Scandinavian kings (including Shakespeare's Macbeth).

Slowly, the importance of Iona ebbed. Vikings massacred 68 monks in 806. Fearing more raids, the monks evacuated most of Iona's treasures to Ireland (including the *Book of Kells*, which is now in Dublin). Much later, with the Reformation, the abbey was abandoned, and most of its finely carved crosses were destroyed. In the 17th century, locals used the abbey only as a handy quarry for other building projects.

Iona's population peaked at about 500 in the 1830s. In the 1840s, a potato famine hit, and in the 1850s, a third of the islanders emigrated to Canada or Australia. By 1900, the population was down to 210, and today it's only around 100.

But in our generation, a new religious community has given the abbey fresh life. The Iona community is an ecumenical gathering of men and women who seek new ways of living the Gospel in today's world, with a focus on worship, peace and justice issues, and reconciliation.

OBAN

Sleeping and Eating on Iona

(£1 = about $1.60, country code: 44, area code: 01681)
$$$ Argyll Hotel, built in 1867, proudly overlooks the waterfront, with 15 rooms and pleasingly creaky hallways lined with bookshelves (Sb-£55, D-£65, Db-£91, seaview Db-£125, cheaper off-season, extra bed for kids-£15, Internet access, free Wi-Fi, closed Nov–Feb, tel. 01681/700-334, fax 01681/700-510, www.argyllhotel iona.co.uk, reception@argyllhoteliona.co.uk, Daniel and Claire).

Its restaurant is open to the public, and dinner is served (£12–16 main dishes) in an elegant white-linen dining room.

$$$ St. Columba Hotel, situated in the middle of a peaceful garden with picnic tables, has 27 pleasant rooms and spacious lodge-like common spaces (Sb-£55–70, Db-£90–120, huge view Db-£150, higher prices are for sea view but windows are small, prices include continental breakfast, discounts for stays of 2 or more nights, extra bed for kids-£15, next door to abbey on road up from dock, open Easter–Oct only, tel. 01681/700-304, fax 01681/700-688, www.stcolumba-hotel.co.uk, info@stcolumba-hotel.co.uk). Their fine 14-table restaurant, open to the public, overlooks the water (£10 lunches, £9–16 dinners, daily 12:00–14:30 & 18:30–20:00).

Glencoe

This valley is the essence of the wild, powerful, and stark beauty

of the Highlands. Along with its scenery, Glencoe offers a good dose of bloody clan history: In 1692, British Redcoats (led by a local Campbell commander) came to the valley, and were sheltered and fed for 12 days by the MacDonalds—whose leader had been late in swearing an oath to the British monarch. Then, the morning of February 13, the soldiers were ordered to rise up early and kill their sleeping hosts, violating the rules of Highland hospitality and earning the valley the name "The Weeping Glen." It's fitting that such an epic, dramatic incident should be set in this equally epic, dramatic valley, where the cliffsides seem to weep (with running streams) when it rains.

Orientation to Glencoe

(area code: 01855)
The valley of Glencoe is just off the main A828/A82 road between Oban and points north (such as Fort William and Inverness). The most appealing town here is the one-street Glencoe village, while the slightly larger and more modern town of Ballachulish (a half-mile away) has more services. Though not quite quaint, the very sleepy village of Glencoe is worth a stop for its folk museum and

its status as the gateway to the valley. The town's hub of activity is its **Spar** grocery store (daily 8:00–20:00).

Tourist Information

Your best source of information (especially for walks and hikes) is the **Glencoe Visitors Centre,** described later. The nearest **TI** is well-signed in Ballachulish (daily 9:00–17:00, opens at 10:00 on Sun in winter, bus timetables, free phone to call area B&Bs, café, shop, tel. 01855/811-866, www.glencoetourism.co.uk).

Sights in Glencoe

Glencoe Village

Glencoe village is just a line of houses. One is a tiny thatched early-18th-century croft house jammed with local history. The huggable **Glencoe and North Lorn Folk Museum** is filled with humble exhibits gleaned from the town's old closets and attics. When one house was being rethatched, its owner found a cache of 200-year-old swords and pistols hidden there from the British Redcoats after the disastrous battle of Culloden. Don't miss the museum's little door that leads out back, where you'll find more exhibits on the Glencoe Massacre, local slate, farm tools, and an infamous local murder that inspired Robert Louis Stevenson to write *Kidnapped* (£3, call ahead for hours—generally mid-May–Oct Mon–Sat 10:00–17:30, closed Sun and off-season except around Easter, tel. 01855/811-664).

In Glencoe Valley

▲▲Driving Through Glencoe Valley—If you have a car, spend an hour or so following A82 through the valley, past the Glencoe Visitors Centre (see next listing), into the desolate moor beyond, and back again. You'll enjoy grand views, flocks of "hairy coos" (shaggy Highland Cattle), and a chance to hear a bagpiper in the wind—roadside Highland buskers (most often seen on good-weather summer weekends). If you play the recorder (and no other tourists are there), ask to finger a tune while the piper does the hard work. At the end of the valley you hit the vast Rannoch
Moor—500 desolate square miles with barely enough decent land to graze a sheep.

Glencoe Visitors Centre—This modern facility, a mile into the dramatic valley on A82, is designed to resemble a *clachan*, or

OBAN

traditional Highlands settlement. The information desk inside the shop is your single best resource for advice (and maps or guidebooks) about local walks and hikes, some of which are described next. At the back of the complex you'll find a viewpoint with a handy 3-D model for orientation. There's also a pricey £5.50 exhibition about the surrounding landscape, local history, mountaineering, and conservation. It's worth the time to watch the more-interesting-than-it-sounds video on geology and the 14-minute film on the Glencoe Massacre, which thoughtfully traces the events leading up to the tragedy rather than simply recycling romanticized legends (Easter–Aug daily 9:30–17:30; Sept–Oct daily 10:00–17:00; Nov–Easter Thu–Sun 10:00–16:00, closed Mon–Wed; tel. 01855/811-307).

Walks—For a steep one-mile hike, climb the Devil's Staircase (trailhead just off A82, 8 miles east of Glencoe). For a three-hour hike, ask at the Visitors Centre about the Lost Valley of the MacDonalds (trailhead just off A82, 3 miles east of Glencoe). For an easy walk above Glencoe, head to the mansion on the hill (over the bridge, turn left, fine loch views). This mansion was built in 1894 by Canadian Pacific Railway magnate Lord Strathcona for his wife, a Canadian with First Nations (Native American) ancestry. She was homesick for the Rockies, so he had the grounds landscaped to represent the lakes, trees, and mountains of her home country. It didn't work, and they eventually returned to British Columbia. The house originally had 365 windows, to allow a different view each day.

Glencoe's Burial Island and Island of Discussion—In the loch just outside Glencoe (near Ballachulish), notice the burial island—where the souls of those who "take the low road" are piped home. (Ask a local about "Ye'll take the high road, and I'll take the low road.") The next island was the Island of Discussion—where those in dispute went until they found agreement.

Sleeping in Glencoe

(£1 = about $1.60, country code: 44, area code: 01855)

Glencoe is an extremely low-key place to spend the night between Oban or Glasgow and the northern destinations. These places are accustomed to one-nighters just passing through, but some people stay here for several days to enjoy a variety of hikes. All of these B&Bs are along the main road through the middle of the village, and all are cash-only.

$$ Inchconnal B&B is a cute house with a bonnie wee garden out front, renting two bright rooms—one frilly, the other woodsy (Db-£48, £50 July–Aug, tel. 01855/811-958, warm Caroline Macdonald).

$$ Heatherlea B&B, at the end of the village, has three pleasant, modern rooms and homey public spaces, and a big board-game collection (Sb-£25–26, Db-£48, £52 in July–Aug, closed Nov–Easter, tel. 01855/811-799, ivan-thea.heatherlea@tiscali.co.uk, friendly Ivan and Thea).

$$ Tulachgorm B&B has two spacious, comfortable rooms that share a bathroom in a modern house with fine mountain views (D-£40, tel. 01855/811-391, mellow Ann Blake).

Eating in Glencoe

The choices in and near Glencoe are slim—this isn't the place for fine dining. But three options offer decent food a short walk or drive away. For evening fun, take a walk or ask your B&B host where to find music and dancing.

In Glencoe: The best choice in Glencoe village is **The Carnoch,** with happy diners tucked into a small modern house a few steps off the main street (£9–10 main dishes; in summer Mon–Thu 11:00–16:00 & 17:00–21:00, Fri–Sun 12:00–21:00; closed Mon–Wed in winter, tel. 01855/811-140).

Near Glencoe: **Clachaig Inn** is a Highlands pub whose clientele is half locals and half tourists. This unpretentious place features billiards, jukeboxes, and pub grub (£5–13 main dishes, open daily for lunch and dinner, tel. 01855/811-252). Drive down the little road over the bridge at the end of Glencoe village, and follow it about five minutes until you reach the pub's big parking lot on the right.

In Ballachulish, near Glencoe: **Laroch Bar & Bistro,** in the next village over from Glencoe (toward Oban), is serene and family-friendly (£7–9 pub grub, tel. 01855/811-900). Drive into Ballachulish village, and you'll see it on the left.

Glencoe Connections

Unfortunately, buses don't actually drive down the main road through Glencoe village. Some buses (most notably those going between Glasgow and Fort William) stop near Glencoe village at a place called **"Glencoe Crossroads"**—a short walk into the village center. Other buses (such as those between Oban and Fort William) stop at the nearby town of **Ballachulish,** which is just a half-mile away (or a £3 taxi ride). Tell the bus driver where you're going ("Glencoe village") and ask to be let off as close to there as possible.

From **Glencoe Crossroads,** you can catch bus #914, #915, or #916 (8/day) to **Fort William** (30 min) or **Glasgow** (2.5 hrs).

From **Ballachulish,** you can take bus #918 (3/day in summer, 2/day off-season, never on Sun) to **Fort William** (30 min) or **Oban** (1 hr).

To reach **Inverness** or **Portree** on the Isle of Skye, transfer in Fort William. To reach **Edinburgh,** transfer in Glasgow.

Near Glencoe: Fort William

Laying claim to the title of "outdoor capital," Fort William is well-positioned between Oban, Inverness, and the Isle of Skye. This crossroads town is a transportation hub and has a pleasant-enough, shop-studded, pedestrianized main drag, but few charms of its own. Most visitors just pass through...and should. But while you're here, consider buying lunch and stopping by the TI to get your questions answered.

Tourist Information: The TI is at the top of the town's main square, Cameron Square (July–Aug Mon–Sat 9:00–18:00, Sun 9:30–17:00; Easter–June and Sept–Oct Mon–Sat 9:00–17:00, Sun 10:00–16:00; shorter hours and closed Sun off-season; Internet access, free public WCs behind building, toll tel. 0845-225-5121).

Sights in and near Fort William

Fort William has no real sights, aside from a humble-but-well-presented **West Highland Museum,** with exhibits on local history, wildlife, dress, and more (£3, guidebook-£2.50; June–Sept Mon–Sat 10:00–17:00, July–Aug also Sun 14:00–17:00; Oct–May Mon–Sat 10:00–16:00, closed Sun; next to TI on Cameron Square, tel. 01397/702-169, www.westhighlandmuseum.org.uk).

The appealing options described below lie just outside of town.

Ben Nevis

From Fort William, take a peek at Britain's highest peak, Ben Nevis (4,409 feet). Thousands walk to its summit each year. On a clear day, you can admire it from a distance. Scotland's only mountain cable cars—at the **Nevis Range Mountain Experience**—can take you to a not-very-lofty 2,150-foot perch for a closer look (£10, daily July–Aug 9:30–18:00, Sept–June 10:00–17:00, 15-min ride, shuts down in high winds—call ahead, signposted on A82 north of Fort William, tel. 01397/705-825).

Toward the Isle of Skye: The Road to the Isles and the Jacobite Steam Train

The magical steam train that scenically transports Harry Potter to the wizard school of Hogwarts runs along a real-life train line. The West Highland Railway Line runs 42 miles from Fort William west to the ferry port at Mallaig. Along the way, it passes the iconic **Glenfinnan Viaduct,** with 416 yards of raised track over 21 supporting arches. This route is also graced with plenty of loch-and-mountain views and, near the end, passes along a beautiful stretch of coast with some fine sandy beaches. While many people take the Jacobite Steam Train to enjoy this stretch of Scotland, it can be more rewarding to drive the same route—especially if you're headed for the Isle of Skye.

By Train: The **Jacobite Steam Train** (they don't actually call it the "Hogwarts Express") offers a small taste of the Harry Potter experience...but many who take this trip for that reason alone are disappointed. (For more Harry Potter sights in Britain, see page 726.) Doing the round-trip from Fort William takes the better part of a day to show you the same scenery twice. And, unfortunately for HP fans, the train company seems nearly oblivious to the Harry Potter connection—they make almost no effort to tie the trip to the films...so don't expect a theme ride. However, you can expect beautiful scenery. Along the way, the train stops for 20 minutes at Glenfinnan station (just after the Glenfinnan Viaduct), and then gives you way too much time (1.75 hours) to poke around the dull port town of Mallaig before heading back to Fort William (one-way—£22 adults, £13 kids; round-trip—£30 adults, £17 kids; 1/day Mon–Fri mid-May–mid-Oct, also Sat–Sun July–Aug, departs Fort William at 10:20 and returns at 16:00, about a 2-hour ride each way, www.steamtrain .info, tel. 01524/732-100).

Modern "Sprinter" trains follow the same line more frequently and off-season—consider taking the steam train one-way to Mallaig, then speeding back on a regular train to avoid the long Mallaig layover and slow return (1.25 hrs, book at least two days ahead July–Aug, tel. 08457-550-033, www.firstgroup.com/scotrail). Note that you can use this train to reach the Isle of Skye: Take the train to Mallaig, walk onto the ferry to Armadale (on Skye), then catch a bus in Armadale to your destination on Skye (tel. 08705-505-050, www.citylink.co.uk).

By Car: Although the train is time-consuming and expensive, driving the same **"Road to the Isles"** route (A830)—ideally on your way to Skye—can be a fun way to see the same famous scenery more affordably and efficiently. The key here is to be sure you leave enough time to make it to Mallaig before the Skye ferry departs—get timing advice from the Fort William TI. I'd allow at least 1 hour and 20 minutes to get from Fort William to the ferry landing in Mallaig (if you keep moving, with no stops en route)—and note that vehicles are required to arrive 30 minutes before the boat departs. As you leave Fort William on A830, a sign on the left tells you what time the next ferry will depart Mallaig. For more tips on the Mallaig–Armadale ferry, see "Getting to the Isle of Skye" on page 635.

OBAN

Sleeping in Fort William

These two B&Bs are on Union Road, a five-minute walk up the hill above the main pedestrian street that runs through the heart of town. Each place has three rooms, one of which has a private bathroom on the hall.

$$ Glenmorven Guest House is a friendly, flower-bedecked, family-run place renting three rooms with views of Loch Linnhe (Db-£60, Union Road, Fort William, tel. 01397/703-236, www.glenmorven.co.uk, glenmorven@yahoo.com, Anne Jamieson).

$$ Gowan Brae B&B ("Hill of the Big Daisy") has three antique-filled rooms in a hobbit-cute house. The breakfast room has a huge old-time radio and lots of other conversation-starters (Db-£64 in high season, £50 off-season, Union Road, tel. 01397/704-399, www.gowanbrae.co.uk, Jim and Ann Clark).

Eating in Fort William

All three places listed below are on the main walking street, near the start of town; the first two serve only lunch.

Hot Roast Company sells beef, turkey, ham, or pork sandwiches, topped with some tasty extras (£3 take-away, a bit more for sit-down service, Mon–Sat 9:30–15:30, closed Sun, 127 High Street, tel. 01397/700-606).

Café 115 features good food and modern decor (£5 sandwiches, £8 fish-and-chips, daily 10:30–16:30, Sun until 16:00, 115 High Street, tel. 01397/702-500).

The Grog & Gruel serves real ales, great pub grub, and even does take-out (£4–10 meals, food served daily 12:00–21:00, pub open later for drinks, Sun in winter 17:00–21:00 or sometimes closed, free Wi-Fi, 66 High Street, tel. 01397/705-078). Their upstairs restaurant features Tex-Mex and Cajun dishes, along with the usual alehouse standards (£10 meals, daily 17:00–21:00).

Fort William Connections

Fort William is a major transit hub for the Highlands, so you'll likely change buses here at some point during your trip.

From Fort William by Bus to: Glencoe (all Glasgow-bound buses—#914, #915, and #916; 8/day, 30 min), **Ballachulish** near Glencoe (Oban-bound bus #918, 3/day in summer, 2/day off-season, never on Sun, 30 min), **Oban** (bus #918, 3/day in summer, 2/day off-season, never on Sun, 1.5 hrs), **Portree** on the Isle of Skye (buses #915 and #916, 4/day, 3 hrs), **Inverness** (Citylink bus #919 or Stagecoach bus #19, 8/day, 2 hrs), **Glasgow** (buses #914, #915, and #916; 8/day, 3 hrs, some with change in Tyndrum),

Edinburgh (bus #913, 3/day in evening, 4 hrs, 1 direct, 2 with change in Tyndrum; more with transfer in Glasgow on buses #900 and #914/915, 5 hrs).

Route Tips for Drivers

From England's Lake District to Glasgow: From Keswick, take A66 for 18 miles to M6 and speed north nonstop (via Penrith and Carlisle), crossing Hadrian's Wall into Scotland. The road becomes M74 south of Glasgow. To slip through Glasgow quickly, leave M74 at Junction 4 onto M73, following signs to *M8/Glasgow*. Leave M73 at Junction 2, exiting onto M8. Stay on M8 west through Glasgow, exit on Junction 30, cross Erskine Bridge, and turn left on A82, following signs to *Crianlarich* and *Loch Lomond*. (For a scenic drive through Glasgow, take exit 17 off M8 and stay on A82 toward Dumbarton.)

From Oban to Glencoe and Fort William: From Oban, follow coastal A828 toward Fort William. After about 20 miles, you'll see the photogenic Castle Staulker marooned on a lonely island. At North Ballachulish, you'll reach a bridge spanning Loch Leven; rather than crossing the bridge, turn off and follow A82 into the Glencoe valley. After exploring the valley, make a U-turn and return through Glencoe. To continue on to Fort William, backtrack to the bridge at North Ballachulish and cross it, following A82 north. (For a scenic shortcut directly back to Glasgow or Edinburgh, head north only as far as Glencoe, and then cut to Glasgow or Edinburgh on A82 via Rannoch Moor and Tyndrum.)

From Fort William to Loch Ness and Inverness: Follow the Caledonian Canal north along A82, which goes through Fort Augustus (and its worthwhile Caledonian Canal Heritage Centre) and then follows the west side of Loch Ness on its way to Inverness. Along the way, A82 passes Urquhart Castle and two Loch Ness Monster exhibits in Drumnadrochit. These attractions are described in the Inverness and the Northern Highlands chapter.

From Fort William to the Isle of Skye: You have two options for this journey: Head west on A830 (the Road to the Isles), then catch the ferry from Mallaig to Armadale on the Isle of Skye (described on page 635); or head north on A82 to Invergarry, and turn left (west) on A87, which you'll follow (past Eilean Donan Castle) to Kyle of Lochalsh and the Skye Bridge to the island. Consider using one route one way, and the other on the return trip—for example, follow the "Road to the Isles" from Fort William to Mallaig, and take the ferry to Skye; later, leaving Skye, take A87 east from the Skye Bridge past Eilean Donan Castle to Loch Ness and Inverness.

OBAN

ISLE OF SKYE

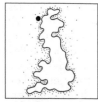

The rugged, remote-feeling Isle of Skye has a reputation for unpredictable weather ("Skye" means "cloudy" in Old Norse, and locals call it "The Misty Isle"). But it also offers some of Scotland's best scenery, and it rarely fails to charm its many visitors. Narrow, twisty roads wind around Skye in the shadows of craggy, black, bald mountains.

Skye seems to have more sheep than people; 200 years ago, many human residents were forced to move off the island to make room for more livestock during the Highland Clearances. The people who remain are some of the most ardently Gaelic Scots in Scotland. The island's Sleat Peninsula is home to a rustic but important Gaelic college. Half of all native island residents speak Gaelic (which they pronounce "gallic") as their first language. A generation ago, it was illegal to teach Gaelic in schools; today, Skye offers its residents the opportunity to enroll in Gaelic-only education, from primary school to college.

Set up camp in one of the island's home-base towns, Portree or Kyleakin. Then dive into Skye's attractions. Drive around the appealing Trotternish Peninsula, enjoying stark vistas of jagged rock formations with the mysterious Outer Hebrides looming on the horizon. Explore a gaggle of old-fashioned stone homes, learn about Skye's ancient farming lifestyles, and pay homage at the grave of a brave woman who rescued a bonnie prince. Climb the dramatic Cuillin Hills, and drive to a lighthouse at the end of the world. Visit a pair of castles—run-down but thought-provoking Dunvegan, and nearby but not on Skye, the photo-perfect Eilean Donan.

Planning Your Time

With a week in Scotland, Skye merits two nights, with a full day to hit its highlights (Trotternish Peninsula, Dunvegan Castle, Cuillin Hills, Talisker Distillery). Mountaineers enjoy extra time for hiking and hillwalking. Because it takes time to reach, Skye (the northernmost destination in this book) is skippable if you only have a few days in Scotland—instead, focus on Edinburgh and the more accessible Highlands sights near Oban.

Skye fits neatly into a Highlands itinerary between Oban/Glencoe and Loch Ness/Inverness. To avoid seeing the same scenery twice, it works well to drive the "Road to the Isles" from Fort William to Mallaig, then take the ferry to Skye; later, leave Skye via the Skye Bridge and follow A87 east toward Loch Ness and Inverness, stopping at Eilean Donan Castle en route.

Orientation to the Isle of Skye

The Isle of Skye is big (over 600 square miles), with lots of ins and outs—but you're never more than five miles from the sea. The island is punctuated by peninsulas and inlets (called "sea lochs"). Skye is covered with hills, but the most striking are the mountain-like Cuillin Hills in the south-central part of the island.

There are only about 11,000 people on the entire island, roughly a quarter of whom live in the main village, Portree. Other population centers include Kyleakin (near the bridge connecting Skye with the mainland) and Broadford (a tidy string of houses on the road between Portree and the bridge, with the biggest and handiest grocery store on the island). A few of the villages—including Broadford and Dunvegan—have TIs, but the most useful one is in Portree.

Getting to the Isle of Skye

By Car: Your easiest bet is the slick, free **Skye Bridge** that crosses from Kyle of Lochalsh on the mainland to Kyleakin on Skye (for more on the bridge, see page 646).

The island can also be reached from the mainland via a pair of **car ferry** crossings. The major ferry line connects the mainland town of Mallaig (west of Fort William along the "Road to the Isles" and the Harry Potter steam-train line—see page 630) to Armadale on Skye (£19.45/car, £3.65/passenger, 8/day each way, 6/day on Sun, late Oct–March very limited Sat–Sun connections, can be cancelled in rough weather, 30-min trip, operated by Caledonian MacBrayne, www.calmac.co.uk). A much smaller, proudly local "turntable" ferry crosses the short gap between the mainland Glenelg and Skye's Kylerhea (£10/car with up to 4 passengers, every 20 min 10:00–18:00, Easter–Oct only, sometimes no service on Sun, Skye Ferry, www.skyeferry.co.uk).

By Public Transportation: Skye is connected to the outside world by a series of Scottish CityLink **buses** (www.citylink.co.uk), which use Portree as their Skye hub. From Portree, buses connect to **Inverness** (bus #917, 2–3/day, 3.25 hrs, via Loch Ness), **Glasgow** (buses #915 and #916, 3/day, 7 hrs, also stops at **Fort William** and **Glencoe**), and **Edinburgh** (3/day, 7.5–8 hrs, transfer in Inverness or Glasgow).

There are also some more complicated connections possible for the determined: Take the train from Edinburgh, Glasgow, or Inverness to Fort William; transfer to the steam train to Mallaig; take the ferry across to Armadale; and catch a bus to Portree. Alternatively, you can take the train from Edinburgh or Glasgow to Inverness, take the train to Kyle of Lochalsh, then take the bus to Portree.

Getting Around the Isle of Skye

By Car: Once on Skye, you'll need a car to enjoy the island. (Even if you're doing the rest of your trip by public transportation, a car rental is worthwhile to bypass the frustrating public-transportation options; I've listed some car-rental options in Portree, page 648.) If you're driving, a good map is a must (look for a 1:130,000 map that covers the entire island with enough detail to point out side roads and attractions). You'll be surprised how long it takes to traverse this "small" island. Here are driving-time estimates for some likely trips: Kyleakin and Skye Bridge to Portree—45 min; Portree to Dunvegan—30 min; Portree to the tip of Trotternish Peninsula and back again—1.5–2 hours; Uig (on Trotternish Peninsula) to Dunvegan—45 min.

By Bus: Skye is frustrating by bus, especially on Sundays, when virtually no local buses run (except for a few long-distance buses to the ferry dock and mainland destinations). Portree is the hub for local bus traffic. Most Skye buses are operated by Stagecoach (www.stagecoachbus.com/highlands, timetable info from Traveline, toll tel. 0871-200-2233, www.traveline.org.uk). If you'll be using local buses a lot, consider a Skye Dayrider ticket (£6.50/1 day) or the Skye Megarider (£40/7 days, covers all of Skye plus trip to Eilean Donan). You can buy either of these tickets from any driver. From Portree you can go around the **Trotternish Peninsula** (Mon–Fri 6/day in each direction—clockwise and counterclockwise; fewer Sat) to **Dunvegan** (4–5/day, goes right to the castle, use the 10:35 or 12:35 to get to the castle in time to tour it) and to **Kyleakin** (at least hourly Mon–Fri, fewer Sat–Sun, possible transfer in Broadford). Remember, none of these buses runs on Sunday.

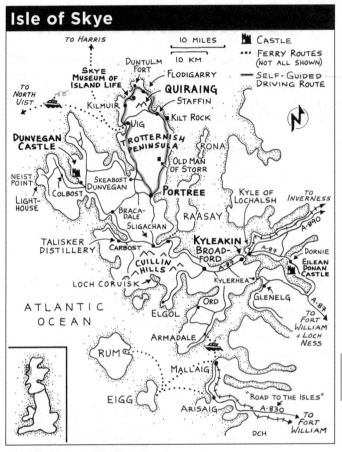

Isle of Skye

TO HARRIS

10 MILES

10 KM

🏰 CASTLE

••• FERRY ROUTES (NOT ALL SHOWN)

— SELF-GUIDED DRIVING ROUTE

DUNTULM FORT

SKYE MUSEUM OF ISLAND LIFE

FLODIGARRY

QUIRAING

STAFFIN

KILT ROCK

TO NORTH UIST

KILMUIR

UIG

TROTTERNISH PENINSULA

RONA

DUNVEGAN CASTLE

OLD MAN OF STORR

NEIST POINT

SKEABOST DUNVEGAN

PORTREE

KYLE OF LOCHALSH

TO INVERNESS

COLBOST

LIGHT-HOUSE

BRACA-DALE

SLIGACHAN

RAASAY

A-890

TALISKER DISTILLERY

CARBOST

KYLEAKIN

BROAD-FORD

A-87

DORNIE

EILEAN DONAN CASTLE

CUILLIN HILLS

KYLERHEA

A-87

LOCH CORUISK

ORD

GLENELG

TO FORT WILLIAM & LOCH NESS

ATLANTIC OCEAN

ELGOL

ARMADALE

RUM

MALLAIG

EIGG

ARISAIG

"ROAD TO THE ISLES"

A-830

TO FORT WILLIAM

DCH

ISLE OF SKYE

By Tour: If you're without a car, consider taking a tour. Several operations on the island take visitors to hard-to-reach spots on a half-day or full-day tour. Some are more educational, while others are loose and informal. Look for brochures around the island, or ask locals for tips. Local guide Dennis Briggs enthusiastically runs **Red Deer Tours** out of Portree, and will take you on tiny Skye back roads in his minibus (£25–60 depending on number of people on the tour, maximum of 7 people, tel. 01478/612-142 or book at the recommended Bayfield Backpackers hostel in Portree). The **Aros Centre** near Portree leads three-hour tours twice daily (£14, mid-April–mid-Oct Mon–Sat at 10:00 and 14:00, can pick you up in Portree, reserve ahead by calling 01478/613-649 or in person at the Portree TI).

The Trotternish Peninsula

This inviting peninsula north of Portree is packed with windswept castaway scenery, unique geological formations, and some offbeat sights. In good weather, a spin around Trotternish is the single best Skye activity (and you'll still have time to visit Dunvegan Castle or the Cuillin Hills later on).

Self-Guided Driving Tour

The following loop tour starts and ends in Portree, circling the peninsula counterclockwise. If you did it without stopping, you'd make it back to Portree within two hours—but it deserves the better part of a day.

Begin in the island's main town, Portree. (If you're heading up from Kyleakin, you'll enjoy some grand views of the Cuillin Hills on your way up—especially around the crossroads of Sligachan, described on page 642.) For sightseeing information on Portree—and the nearby Aros visitors center—see page 648.

• *Head north of Portree on A855, following signs for* Staffin. *About three miles out of town, you'll begin to enjoy some impressive views of the Trotternish Ridge. As you pass the small loch on your right, straight ahead is the distinctive feature called the...*

Old Man of Storr: This 160-foot-tall tapered volcanic plug stands proudly apart from the rest of the Storr. The lochs on your right have been linked together to spin the turbines at a nearby hydroelectric plant that once provided all of Skye's electricity.

• *After passing the Old Man, enjoy the scenery on your right, overlooking...*

Nearby Islands and the Mainland: Some of Skye's most appealing scenery isn't of the island itself, but of the surrounding terrain. In the distance, craggy mountains recede into the horizon. The long island in the foreground, a bit to the north, is called Rona. This military-owned island, and the channel behind it, were used to develop and test one of Margaret Thatcher's pet projects, the Sting Ray remote-control torpedo.

• *After about five miles, keep an eye out on the right for a large parking lot near a wee loch. Park and walk to the viewpoint to see...*

Kilt Rock: So named because of its resemblance to a Scotsman's tartan kilt, this 200-foot-tall sea cliff has a layer of volcanic rock with vertical lava columns that resemble pleats, sitting atop a layer of horizontal sedimentary rock.

• After continuing through the village of Staffin (whose name means "the pinnacle place"), you'll begin to see interesting rock formations high on the hill to your left. When you get to the crossroads, head left toward Quiraing (a rock formation). This crossroads is a handy pit stop—there's a public WC in the little white building behind the red phone box just up the main road.

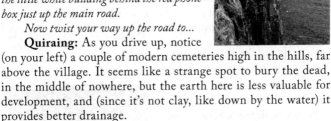

Now twist your way up the road to...

Quiraing: As you drive up, notice (on your left) a couple of modern cemeteries high in the hills, far above the village. It seems like a strange spot to bury the dead, in the middle of nowhere, but the earth here is less valuable for development, and (since it's not clay, like down by the water) it provides better drainage.

You'll enjoy fine views on the right of the jagged, dramatic northern end of the Trotternish Ridge, called the Quiraing—rated

▲▲. Each rock formation has a name, such as "The Needle" or "The Prison." As you approach the summit of this road, you'll reach a parking area on the left. This marks a popular trailhead for hiking out to get a closer look at the formations. If you've got the time, energy, and weather for a

sturdy 30-minute uphill hike, here's your chance. You can either follow the trail along the base of the rock formations, or hike up to the top of the plateau and follow it to the end (both paths are faintly visible from the parking area). Once up top, your reward is a view of the secluded green plateau called "The Table," which isn't visible from the road.

• You could continue on this road all the way to Uig, at the other end of the peninsula, but it's worth backtracking, then turning left onto the main road (A855), to see the...

Tip of Trotternish: A few miles north, you'll pass a hotel called **Flodigarry,** with a cottage on the premises that was once home to Bonnie Prince Charlie's rescuer, Flora MacDonald (for her story, read "Monument to Flora MacDonald," later; cottage not open to the public or worth visiting).

Soon after, at the top of the ridge at the tip of the peninsula, you'll see the remains of an old **fort**—not from the Middle Ages or the days of Bonnie Prince Charlie, but from World War II, when the Atlantic was monitored for U-boats from this position.

Then you'll pass (on the right) the remains of another fort, this one much older: **Duntulm Castle,** which was the first stronghold on Skye of the influential MacDonald clan. In the distance beyond, you can see the **Outer Hebrides**—the most rugged, remote, and Gaelic part of Scotland. (Skye, a bit closer to the mainland, belongs to the Inner Hebrides.)

• *A mile after the castle, you'll come to a place called Kilmuir. Watch for the turn-off on the left to the excellent...*

Skye Museum of Island Life: This fine little stand of seven thatched stone huts, organized into a family-run museum and

worth ▲▲, explains how a typical Skye family lived a century and a half ago (£2.50, Easter–Oct Mon–Sat 9:30–17:00, until 16:00 in Oct or when slow, closed Sun and Nov–Easter, tel. 01470/552-206, www.skyemuseum.co.uk). Though there are ample posted explanations, the £1.25 guidebook is worthwhile.

The three huts closest to the sea are original (more than 200 years old). Most interesting is the one called The Old Croft House, which was the residence of the Graham family until 1957. Inside you'll find three rooms: kitchen (with peat-burning fire) on the right, parents' bedroom in the middle, and a bedroom for the 12 kids on the left. Nearby, The Old Barn displays farm implements, and the Ceilidh House contains some dense but very informative displays about crofting (the traditional tenant-farmer lifestyle on Skye—explained later), Gaelic, and other topics.

The four other huts were reconstructed here from elsewhere on the island, and now house exhibits about weaving and the village smithy (which was actually a gathering place for villagers). As you explore, admire the smart architecture of these humble but deceptively well-planned structures. Rocks hanging from the roof keep the thatch from blowing away, and the streamlined shape of the structure embedded in the ground encourages strong winds to deflect around the hut rather than hit it head-on.

• *After touring the museum, drive out to the very end of the small road that leads past the parking lot, to a lonesome cemetery. The tallest Celtic cross at the far end of the cemetery (you can enter the gate to reach it) is the...*

Monument to Flora MacDonald: This local heroine supposedly rescued beloved Scottish hero Bonnie Prince Charlie at his darkest hour. After his loss at Culloden, and with a hefty price on his head, Charlie retreated to the Outer Hebrides. But the Hanover dynasty, which controlled the islands, was closing in.

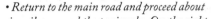

Flora MacDonald rescued the prince, disguised him as her Irish maid, Betty Burke, and sailed him to safety on Skye. (Charlie pulled off the ruse thanks to his soft, feminine features—hence the nickname "Bonnie," which means "beautiful.") The flight inspired a popular Scottish folk song: *Speed bonnie boat like a bird on the wing, / Onward, the sailors cry. / Carry the lad that's born to be king / Over the sea to Skye.* For more on Bonnie Prince Charlie, see page 668.

• *Return to the main road and proceed about six miles around the peninsula. On the right, notice the big depression.*

The Missing Loch: This was once a large loch, but it was drained in the mid-20th century to create more grazing land for sheep. If you look closely, you may see a scattering of stones in the middle of the field. Once an island, this is the site of a former monastery...now left as high, dry, and forgotten as the loch. Beyond the missing loch is Prince Charlie's Point, where the bonnie prince supposedly came ashore on Skye with Flora MacDonald.

• *Soon after the loch, you'll drop down over the town of...*

Uig: Pronounced "OO-eeg," this village is the departure point for ferries to the Outer Hebrides (North Uist and Harris islands, 3/day). It's otherwise unremarkable, but does have a café with good £3 sandwiches (follow *Uig Pier* signs into town, blue building with white *café* sign, next to ferry terminal at entrance to town).

• *Continue past Uig, climbing the hill across the bay. Near the top is a large parking strip on the right. Pull over here and look back to Uig for a lesson about Skye's traditional farming system.*

Crofting: You'll hear a lot about crofts during your time on Skye. Traditionally, arable land on the island was divided into

plots. If you look across to the hills above Uig, you can see strips of demarcated land running up from the water—these are crofts. Crofts were generally owned by landlords (mostly English aristocrats or Scottish clan chiefs, and later the Scottish government) and rented to tenant farmers. The crofters lived and worked under

very difficult conditions, and were lucky if they could produce enough potatoes, corn, and livestock to feed their families. Rights to farm the croft were passed down from father to son over generations, but always under the auspices of a wealthy landlord.

ISLE OF SKYE

Finally, in 1976, new legislation kicked off a process of privatization called "decrofting." Suddenly crofters could have their land decrofted, then buy it for an affordable price (£130 per quarter-hectare, or about £8,000 for one of the crofts you see here). Many decroftees would quickly turn around and sell their old family home for a huge profit, but hang on to most of their land and build a new house at the other end. In the crofts you see here, notice that some have a house at the top of a strip of land, and another house at the bottom. Many crofts (like most of these) are no longer cultivated, but a new law might require crofters to farm their land... or lose it. In many cases, families who have other jobs still hang on to their traditional croft, which they use to grow produce for themselves or to supplement their income.

• *Our tour is finished. From here, you can continue along the main road south toward Portree (and possibly continue from there on to the Cuillin Hills). Or, take the shortcut road just after Kensaleyre (B8036), and head west on A850 to Dunvegan and its castle (both options described later in this chapter).*

More Sights on the Isle of Skye

▲▲Cuillin Hills

These dramatic, rocky "hills" (which look more like mountains to me) stretch along the southern coast of the island, dominating Skye's landscape. More craggy and alpine than anything else you'll see in Scotland, the Cuillin seem to rise directly from the deep. You'll see them from just about anywhere on the southern two-thirds of the island, but no roads actually take you through the heart of the Cuillin—that's reserved for hikers and climbers, who love this area. To get the best views with a car, consider these options:

Near Sligachan: The road from the Skye Bridge to Portree is the easiest way to appreciate the Cuillin (you'll almost certainly drive along here at some point during your visit). As you approach, you'll clearly see that there are three separate ranges (from right to left): red, gray, and black. (The steep and challenging Black Cuillin are the most popular for serious climbers.) The crossroads of Sligachan, with an old triple-arched bridge and a landmark hotel (see page 649), is nestled at the foothills of the Cuillin, and is a popular launch pad for mountain fun. The 2,500-foot-tall cone-shaped hill looming over Sligachan, named Glamaig ("Greedy Lady"), is the site of an annual competition (likely July 17 in 2010; check date at www.carnethy.com): Speed hikers begin at the door of the Sligachan Hotel, race to the summit, run around a bagpiper, and scramble back down to the hotel. The record: 44 minutes (30 minutes up, 13 minutes down, 1 minute dancing a jig up top).

Elgol: For the best view of the Cuillin, locals swear by the drive from Broadford (on the Portree–Kyleakin road) to Elgol, at the tip of a small peninsula that faces the Black Cuillin head-on. While it's just 12 miles as the crow flies from Sligachan, give it a half-hour each way to drive into Elgol from Broadford. To get an even better Cuillin experience, take a boat excursion from Elgol into Loch Coruisk, a "sea loch" (fjord) surrounded by the Cuillin (various companies do the trip several times a day, few or no trips on Sun and off-season, generally 3 hours round-trip including 1.5 hours free time on the shore of the loch, figure £15–20 round-trip).

▲Dunvegan Castle

Perched on a rock overlooking a sea loch, this past-its-prime castle is a strange and intriguing artifact of Scotland's antiquated,

nearly extinct clan system. Dunvegan Castle is the residence of the MacLeod (pronounced "McCloud") clan—along with the MacDonalds, one of Skye's preeminent clans. Worth ▲▲▲ to people named MacLeod, and mildly interesting to anyone else, this is a good way to pass the time on a rainy day.

Cost and Hours: £7.50, April–mid-Oct daily 10:00–17:30, last entry 30 min before closing, mid-Oct–March open by appointment only, tel. 01470/521-206, www.dunvegancastle.com. Consider picking up the £2 guidebook by the late chief.

Getting There: It's near the small town of Dunvegan in the northwestern part of the island, well-signposted from A850. You can also get there by bus (the 10:35 or 12:35 departures from Portree get you there in time to tour the castle). As you approach Dunvegan on A850, the two flat-topped plateaus you'll see are nicknamed "MacLeod's Tables."

Background: In Gaelic, *clann* means "children," and the clan system was the traditional Scottish way of passing along power—similar to England's dukes, barons, and counts. Each clan traces its roots to an ancestral castle, like Dunvegan. The MacLeods (or, as they prefer, "MacLeod of MacLeod") have fallen on hard times. Having run out of male heirs in 1935, Dame Flora MacLeod of MacLeod became the 28th clan chief. Her grandson, John MacLeod of MacLeod, became the 29th chief after her death in 1976. Their castle is rough around the edges, and to raise money to fix the leaky roof, John MacL of MacL actually pondered selling

ISLE OF SKYE

the Black Cuillin ridge of hills (which technically belong to him) to an American tycoon for £10 million a few years back. The deal fell through, and the chief passed away in early 2007. Now his son Hugh Magnus MacLeod of MacLeod, in his mid-thirties, has become clan chief of the MacLeods.

◑ Self-Guided Tour: The interior feels a bit shoddy and run-down, but the MacLeods proudly display their family heritage—old photographs and portraits of former chiefs. You'll wander through halls, the dining room, the library, and past the dungeon's deep pit. In the **Drawing Room,** look for the tattered remains of the Fairy Flag, a mysterious swatch with about a dozen different legends attached to it (most say that it was a gift from a fairy, and somehow it's related to the Crusades). It's said that the clan chief can invoke the power of the flag three times, in the clan's darkest moments. It's worked twice before on the battlefield—which means there's just one use left.

The most interesting tidbits are in the **North Room.** The family's coat of arms (in the middle of the carpet) has a confused-looking bull and the clan motto, "Hold Fast"—recalling an incident where a MacLeod saved a man from being gored by a bull when he grabbed its horns and forced it to stop. In the case nearby, find the Dunvegan Cup and the Horn of Rory Mor. Traditionally, this horn would be filled with a half-gallon of claret (Bordeaux wine), which a potential heir had to drink without falling down to prove himself fit for the role. (The late chief, John MacLeod of MacLeod, bragged that he did it in less than two minutes...but you have to wonder if Dame Flora chug-a-lugged.) Other artifacts in the North Room include bagpipes and several relics related to Bonnie Prince Charlie (including a lock of his hair and several items belonging to Flora MacDonald).

At the end of the tour, you can wander out onto the **terrace** (overlooking a sea loch) and, in the cellar, watch a stuffy **video** about the clan. Between the castle and the parking lot are some enjoyable **gardens** to stroll through while pondering the fading clan system.

The flaunting of inherited wealth and influence in some English castles rubs me the wrong way. But here, seeing the rough edges of a Scottish clan chief's castle, I had the opposite feeling: sympathy and compassion for a proud way of life that's slipping into the sunset of history. You have to admire the way that they "hold fast" to this antiquated system (in the same way the Gaelic tongue is kept on life support). Paying admission here feels more like donating to charity than padding the pockets of a wealthy family. In fact, watered-down McClouds and McDonalds from America, eager to reconnect with their Scottish roots, help keep the Scottish clan system alive.

▲Neist Point and Lighthouse

To get a truly edge-of-the-world feeling, consider an adventure on the back lanes of the Duirinish Peninsula, west of Dunvegan. This

trip is best for hardy drivers looking to explore the most remote corner of Skye and undertake a strenuous hike to a lighthouse. (The lighthouse itself is a letdown, so do this only if you believe a journey is its own reward.) Although it looks close on the map, give this trip 30 minutes each way from Dunvegan, plus 30 minutes or more for the lighthouse hike.

Head west from Dunvegan, following signs for *Glendale*. You'll cross a moor, then twist around the Dunvegan sea loch, before heading overland and passing through rugged, desolate hamlets that seem like the setting for a BBC sitcom about backwater Britain. After passing through Glendale, carefully track *Neist Point* signs until you reach an end-of-the-road parking lot. The owner of this private property has signs on his padlocked gate stating that you enter at your own risk—which many walkers happily do. (It's laughably easy to walk around the unintimidating "wall.") From here you enjoy sheep and cliff views, but can't see the lighthouse itself unless you do the sturdy 30-minute hike (with a steep uphill return). After hiking around the cliff, the lighthouse springs into view, with the Outer Hebrides beyond.

It's efficient and fun to combine this trek with lunch or dinner at the recommended **Three Chimneys Restaurant,** on the road to Neist Point at Colbost (reservations essential; see page 651).

▲Talisker Distillery

Opened in 1830 and run by many of the same families today, Talisker is a Skye institution. If you've only tried mainland whisky, island whisky is worth a dram to appreciate the differences. Island whisky is known for having a strong smoky flavor, due to the amount of peat smoke used during the roasting of the barley. The Isle of Islay has the smokiest, and Talisker workers describe theirs as "medium smoky," which may be easier for non-connoisseurs to take. Talisker produces single-malt whisky only, so it's a favorite with whisky purists: On summer days, this tiny distillery down a tiny road in Carbost village swarms with visitors from all over the world (£5 for an hour-long tour and wee dram; April–Oct Mon–Sat 9:30–17:00, closed Sun except in July–Aug when it's open 12:00–17:00, last tour at 16:00; Nov–March by appointment only, last appointment at 15:30, call ahead; tel. 01478/614-308, www.taliskerwhisky.com).

Skye Bridge

Connecting Kyleakin on Skye with Kyle of Lochalsh on the mainland, the Skye Bridge severely damaged B&B business in the towns it connects. And environmentalists worry about the bridge disrupting the habitat for otters—keep an eye out for these furry native residents. But it's been a boon for Skye tourism—making a quick visit to the island possible without having to wait for a ferry.

The bridge, which was Europe's most expensive toll bridge when it opened in 1995, has stirred up a remarkable amount of controversy among island-dwellers. Here's the Skye natives' take on things: A generation ago, Lowlanders (city folk) began selling their urban homes and buying cheap property on Skye. Natives had grown to enjoy the slow-paced lifestyle that came with living life according to the whim of the ferry, but these new transplants found their commute into civilization too frustrating by boat. They demanded a new bridge be built. Finally a deal was struck to privately fund the bridge, but the toll wasn't established before construction began. So when the bridge opened—and the ferry line it replaced closed—locals were shocked to be charged upward of £5 per car each way to go to the mainland. A few years ago, the bridge was bought by the Scottish Executive, the fare was abolished, and the Skye natives were appeased...for now.

▲▲Near the Isle of Skye: Eilean Donan Castle

This postcard castle, watching over a sea loch from its island perch, is conveniently and scenically situated on the road between the

Isle of Skye and Loch Ness. Famous from such films as Sean Connery's *Highlander* (1986) and the James Bond movie *The World Is Not Enough* (1999), Eilean Donan might be Scotland's most photogenic countryside castle. Though it looks ancient, the castle is actually less than a century old. The original castle on this site (dating from 800 years ago) was destroyed in battle in 1719, then rebuilt between 1912 and 1932 by the MacRae family as their residence.

Even if you're not going inside, the castle warrants a five-minute photo stop. But the interior—with cozy rooms—is worth a peek if you have time. Walk across the bridge and into the castle complex, and make your way into the big, blocky keep. First you'll see the claustrophobic, vaulted Billeting Room (where soldiers had their barracks), then head upstairs to the inviting Banqueting Room. Docents posted in these rooms can tell you more. Another flight of stairs takes you to the circa-1930 bedrooms. Downstairs is the cute kitchen exhibit, with mannequins preparing a meal (read the recipes posted throughout). Finally, you'll head through a few more assorted exhibits to the exit.

Cost and Hours: £5.50, good £3 guidebook, mid-March–Oct daily 10:00–18:00, opens at 9:00 July–Aug, last entry one hour before closing, closed Nov–mid-March, tel. 01599/555-202, www.eileandonancastle.com).

Getting There: It's not actually on the Isle of Skye, but it's quite close, in the mainland town of Dornie. Follow A87 about 15 minutes east of Skye Bridge, through Kyle of Lochalsh and toward Loch Ness and Inverness. The castle is on the right side of this road, just after a long bridge.

Portree

Skye's main attraction is its natural beauty, not its villages. But among them, Portree (Port Righ, literally, "Royal Port") is the best home base. This village (with 3,000 people, too small to be considered a "town") is Skye's largest  settlement and the hub of activity and transportation.

Orientation to Portree

(area code: 01478)
This functional village has a small harbor and, on the hill above it, a tidy main square (from which buses fan out across the island and to the mainland). Surrounding the central square are just a few streets. Homes, shops, and B&Bs line the roads to other settlements on the island.

Tourist Information
Portree's helpful TI is a block off the main square, along Bridge Road. They can help you sort through bus schedules and can book you a room for a £4 fee (March–Sept Mon–Sat 9:00–18:00, Sun 10:00–16:00; Oct–Feb Mon–Fri 9:00–17:00, Sat 10:00–16:00,

ISLE OF SKYE

closed Sun; just south of Bridge Street, tel. 01478/612-137 or 0845-225-5121).

Helpful Hints

Internet Access: You can get online at the **library** in Portree High School (free, picture ID required, Mon–Fri 9:00–17:00, Tue and Thu until 20:00, Sat 10:00–16:00, closed Sun, Viewfield Road, tel. 01478/614-823).

Laundry: The **Independent Hostel,** just off the main square, has a self-service launderette down below (about £4 self-service, £8 full-service, sporadic hours, last load starts at 20:00, tel. 01478/613-737).

Bike Rental: Island Cycles rents bikes at the lower parking lot, along the water (£7.50/half-day, £14/24 hours, Mon–Sat 9:00–17:00, closed Sun, tel. 01478/613-121).

Car Rental: You can rent a car for the day at the **MacRae Dealership,** a 10-minute walk from downtown Portree on the road toward Dunvegan (£35–45/day, Mon–Fri 8:30–17:30, Sat 9:00–12:30, closed Sun, call one week in advance in summer, tel. 01478/612-554). Farther along the same road are two more options: **Jansvans** (£40–50/day, tel. 01478/612-087) and **Portree Coachworks** (£38/day, Mon–Fri 9:00–17:30, weekends by appointment, tel. 01478/612-688).

Sights in Portree

Harbor—There's little to see in Portree itself, other than to wander along the colorful harbor, where boat captains offer £10 90-minute excursions out to the sea-eagle nests and around the bay.

Aros Centre—This visitors center, a mile outside of town on the road to Kyleakin and Skye Bridge, offers a humble but earnest exhibit about the island's history and wildlife. Enjoy the movie with aerial photos of otherwise-hard-to-reach parts of Skye, and chat with the ranger. The exhibit also explains about the sea eagles that have been reintroduced to the Skye ecosystem, with a live webcam showing their nests nearby—or, if there are no active nests, a "greatest hits" video show of past fledglings (£4.50, daily 9:00–17:00, last entry 30 min before closing, a mile south of town center on Viewfield Road, tel. 01478/613-649, www.aros.co.uk).

Sleeping in Portree

(area code: 01478)

$$$ Almondbank Guest House, on the road into town from Kyleakin, works well for drivers. It has four tidy, homey rooms (two with sea views for no extra charge) run by friendly Effie Nicolson

(D-£64, Db-£70, free Wi-Fi, Viewfield Road, tel. 01478/612-696,
fax 01478/613-114, j.n.almondbank@btconnect.com).

$$ Braeside B&B has three rooms at the top of town, next
to the Bosville Hotel (Db-£55, cash only, closed Nov–Feb, steep
stairs, Stormyhill, tel. 01478/612-613, www.braesideportree.co.uk,
mail@braesideportree.co.uk, Judith and Philip Maughan and their
dog Midge).

$$ Bayview House has seven small, sterile, and basic rooms,
well-located on the main road just below the square (Db-£45–50,
no breakfast, tel. 01478/613-340, www.bayviewhouse.co.uk, info
@bayviewhouse.co.uk, Murdo and Alison). If there's no answer,
walk down the stairs to Bayfield Backpackers, described below.

$$ Marine House, run by sweet Skye native Fiona
Stephenson, has two simple, homey rooms (one with a private
bathroom down the hall) right at the harbor (S-£25–28, D or
Db-£60–65, cash only, 2 Beaumont Crescent, tel. 01478/611-557,
stephensonfiona@yahoo.com is checked at least once a week).

Hostel: **$ Bayfield Backpackers**—run by Murdo and Alison
from the Bayview House, above—is a modern-feeling, insti-
tutional, cinderblock-and-metal hostel with 24 beds in four- to
eight-bed rooms (£14 per bunk, kitchen, tel. 01478/612-231, www
.skyehostel.co.uk, info@skyehostel.co.uk).

Sleeping near Portree, in Sligachan

$$$ Sligachan Hotel—actually a compound of related sleep-
ing and eating options—is a local institution and a haven for
hikers. It's been in the Campbell family since 1913. The hotel's
21 recently renovated rooms are comfortable, if a bit simple for
the price, while the nearby campground and bunkhouse offer

ISLE OF SKYE

a budget alternative. The setting—surrounded by the mighty Cuillin Hills—is remarkably scenic (Db-£118 May–Sept, £98 Easter–April and Oct, closed Nov–Easter, campground-£5 per person, bunkhouse-£15 per person, on A87 between Kyleakin and Portree in Sligachan, tel. 01478/650-204, fax 01478/650-207, www.sligachan.co.uk, reservations@sligachan.co.uk).

Eating in Portree

Note that Portree's few eateries tend to close early (21:00 or 22:00), and during busy times, lines begin to form soon after 19:00. Eating early works best here.

On the Waterfront: A pair of good eateries vie for your attention along Portree's little harbor. **Lower Deck** feels like a salty sailor's restaurant, decorated with the names of local ships (£5–9 lunches, £12–18 dinners, daily 12:30–14:30 & 18:00–21:30, tel. 01478/613-611).

Sea Breezes, with a more contemporary flair, serves tasty cuisine with an emphasis on seafood (£6–8 lunches, £13–18 dinners, early-bird specials before 18:00, open daily 12:00–14:00 & 17:00–21:00, reserve ahead for dinner, tel. 01478/612-016).

Café Arriba tries hard to offer eclectic flavors in this small Scottish town. With an ambitious menu that includes local specialties, Mexican, Italian, and more, this youthful, colorful, easygoing eatery's hit-or-miss cuisine is worth trying. Drop in to see what's on the blackboard menu today (£4–6 lunches, £8–15 dinners, lots of vegetarian options, daily 7:00–17:00 & 18:00–22:00, Quay Brae, tel. 01478/611-830).

The Café, a few steps off the main square, is a busy, popular hometown diner serving good crank-'em-out food to an appreciative local crowd. The homemade ice-cream stand in the corner is a nice way to finish your meal (£7–9 lunches and burgers, £9–13 dinners, daily 8:30–15:30 & 17:30–21:00, tel. 01478/612-553).

The Bosville Hotel has, according to locals, the best of Portree's many hotel restaurants. There are two parts: the inexpensive, casual **bistro** (£5 lunch sandwiches, £9–16 lunches and dinners, June–Aug daily 12:30–22:00, shorter hours off-season), and the well-regarded formal **Chandlery Restaurant** (£32 two-course meal, £40 three-course meal, nightly 18:30–20:30). While pricey, it's a suitable splurge (just up from the main square, 9–11 Bosville Terrace, tel. 01478/612-846). Their 19 rooms, also expensive, are worth considering (Db-£128, www.bosvillehotel.co.uk).

ISLE OF SKYE

Eating Elsewhere on the Isle of Skye

In Sligachan

Sligachan Hotel (described earlier) has a restaurant and a micro-brew pub serving up mountaineer-pleasing grub in an extremely scenic setting nestled in the Cuillin Hills (traditional dinners in restaurant—£25 for three courses, served nightly 18:30–21:00; pub grub served until 22:00—£7–11; closed Nov–Feb, on A87 between Kyleakin and Portree in Sligachan, tel. 01478/650-204).

In Colbost, near Dunvegan

Three Chimneys Restaurant is your big-splurge-on-a-small-island meal. The high-quality Scottish cuisine, using local ingredients, earns rave reviews. Its 14 tables fill an old three-chimney croft house, with a stone-and-timbers decor that artfully melds old and new. It's cozy, classy, and candlelit, but not stuffy. Because of its remote location—and the fact that it's almost always booked up—reservations are absolutely essential, ideally several weeks ahead, although it's worth calling in case of last-minute cancellations (lunch: £27.50 for two courses, £35 for three courses; dinner: £55 for three courses, £70 for seven-course "tasting menu"; dinner served nightly from 18:15–21:45, lunch mid-March–Oct Mon–Sat 12:15–13:45, no lunch Sun or Nov–mid-March, closed for 3 weeks in Jan, tel. 01470/511-258, Eddie and Shirley Spear). They also rent six swanky, pricey suites next door (Db-£275, www.three chimneys.co.uk).

Getting There: It's in the village of Colbost, about a 15-minute drive west of Dunvegan on the Duirinish Peninsula (that's about 45 min each way from Portree). To get there, first head for Dunvegan, then follow signs toward *Glendale*. This road twists you through the countryside, over a moor, and past several dozen sheep before passing through Colbost. You can combine this with a visit to the Neist Point Lighthouse (described earlier), which is at the end of the same road.

ISLE OF SKYE

Kyleakin

Kyleakin (kih-LAH-kin), the last town in Skye before the bridge, used to be a big tourist hub...until the bridge connecting it to the mainland made it much easier for people to get to Portree and other areas deeper in the island. Today this unassuming little village with a ruined castle (Castle Moil), a cluster of lonesome fishing boats, and a forgotten ferry slip still works well as a home base.

Sleeping in Kyleakin

(£1 = about $1.60, country code: 44, area code: 01599)

$$$ MacKinnon Country House Hotel is my favorite countryside home base on Skye. It sits quietly in the middle of five acres of gardens just off the bustling Skye Bridge. Ian and the Tongs family have lovingly restored this old country home with 20 clan-themed rooms, an inviting overstuffed-sofa lounge, and a restaurant with garden views in nearly every direction (Sb-£50, Db-£100–135 depending on room size and amenities, 10 percent discount with this book in 2010, about 20 percent cheaper Oct–Easter, tel. 01599/534-180, www.mackinnonhotel.co.uk, info@mackinnonhotel.co.uk, a 10-minute walk from Kyleakin, at the turnoff for the bridge). Ian also serves a delicious dinner to guests and non-guests alike (see "Eating in Kyleakin," later).

$$$ White Heather Hotel, run by friendly and helpful Gillian and Craig Glenwright, has nine small but nicely decorated rooms with woody pine bathrooms right along the waterfront, across from the castle ruins (Sb-£50, Db-£70, family rooms, cheaper for stays longer than 2 nights, free Wi-Fi, closed Nov–mid-March, The Harbour, tel. 01599/534-577, fax 01599/534-427, www.whiteheatherhotel.co.uk, info@whiteheatherhotel.co.uk).

$$ Cliffe House B&B rents three rooms in a white house perched at the end of town. All of the rooms, and the breakfast room, enjoy wonderful views over the strait and the bridge (Db-£60, or £64 in July–Aug, cash only, tel. 01599/534-019, www.cliffehousebedandbreakfast.co.uk, i.sikorski@btinternet.com, Ian and Mary Sikorski).

Hostel: **$ Dun-Caan Hostel,** named for a dormant volcano on a nearby island, is mellow and friendly. With woody ambience and 15 beds in three rooms, it's quieter and cozier than most hostels—

enjoying a genuine camaraderie without an obnoxious party atmosphere (£15/bed, pleasant kitchen and lounge, free Wi-Fi, laundry service, The Pier Road, tel. 01599/534-087, www.skyerover.co.uk, info@skyerover.co.uk, Terry and Laila).

Eating in Kyleakin

A few hotels and pubs in little Kyleakin serve decent food—ask your B&B host for advice. For a nice dinner, head up to **MacKinnon Country House Hotel** (listed above; £25 three-course dinner, cheaper in winter, nightly 19:00–21:00, just outside Kyleakin at roundabout for bridge, tel. 01599/534-180). Or dine in **Portree**—with more appealing options than Kyleakin—or at the **Sligachan Hotel** on your way back from a busy sightseeing day (all described earlier in this chapter).

INVERNESS AND THE NORTHERN HIGHLANDS

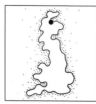

Filled with more natural and historical mystique than people, the northern Highlands are where Scottish dreams are set. Legends of Bonnie Prince Charlie linger around crumbling castles as tunes played by pipers in kilts swirl around tourists. Explore the locks and lochs of the Caledonian Canal while the Loch Ness monster plays hide-and-seek. Hear the music of the Highlands in Inverness and the echo of muskets at Culloden, where the English drove Bonnie Prince Charlie into exile and conquered his Jacobite supporters.

I've focused my coverage on the handy hub of Inverness, with several day-trip options into the surrounding countryside. For Highlands sights to the south and west, see the Oban and the Southern Highlands chapter; for the Isle of Skye off Scotland's west coast, see the previous chapter.

Planning Your Time

Though it has little in the way of sights, Inverness does have a workaday charm and is a handy spot to spend a night or two en route to other Highland destinations. One night here gives you time to take a quick tour of nearby attractions. With two nights, you can find a full day's worth of sightseeing nearby.

Note that Loch Ness is on the way toward Oban or the Isle of Skye. If you're heading to one of those places, it makes sense to see Loch Ness en route, rather than as a side trip from Inverness.

For a speedy itinerary through the Highlands that includes Inverness and Loch Ness, see page 607.

Getting Around the Highlands

With a car, the day trips around Inverness are easy. Without a car, you can get to Inverness by train (better from Edinburgh or Pitlochry) or by bus (better from Skye, Oban, and Glencoe), then side-trip to Loch Ness, Culloden, and other nearby attractions by public bus or with a package tour.

Inverness

The only city in the north of Scotland, Inverness is pleasantly situated on the River Ness at the base of a castle (now a courthouse, not a tourist attraction). Inverness' charm is its normalcy—it's a

nice, midsize Scottish city that gives you a palatable taste of the "urban" Highlands, and is well-located for enjoying the surrounding countryside sights. Check out the bustling pedestrian downtown or meander the picnic-friendly riverside paths where, after dark, couples hold hands while strolling along the water and over the many footbridges.

Orientation to Inverness

(area code: 01463)

Inverness, with about 70,000 people, is the fastest-growing city in Scotland. Marked by its castle, Inverness clusters along the River Ness. Where the main road crosses the river at Ness Bridge, you'll find the TI; within a few blocks (away from the river) are the train and bus stations and an appealing pedestrian shopping zone. The best B&Bs huddle atop a gentle hill behind the castle (a 10-minute mostly uphill walk, or a £3 taxi ride, from the city center).

Tourist Information

At the centrally located TI, you can pick up activity and day-trip brochures, the self-guided *Historic Trail* walking-tour leaflet, and the *What's On* events list for the latest theater, music, and film showings. The office also books rooms for a £4 fee and tours for a £1 fee (July–mid-Sept Mon–Sat 9:00–18:30, Sun 9:30–18:30, shorter hours off-season, closed Sun in winter, Internet access, free WCs behind TI, Castle Wynd, tel. 01463/234-353, www.visithighlands.com).

Inverness

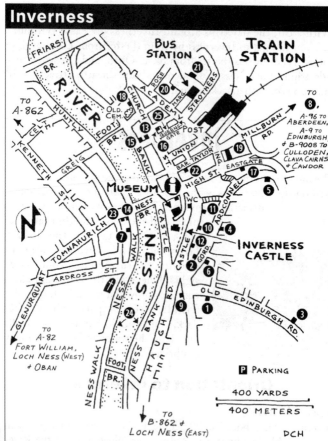

1. Melness Guest House
2. Craigside Lodge B&B
3. Dionard Guest House
4. Ardconnel House & Crown Hotel Guest House
5. Ryeford Guest House
6. The Redcliffe Hotel & Rest.
7. Inverness Palace Hotel & Spa
8. To Premier Inn Inverness Centre
9. Inverness Student Hotel & Bazpackers Hostel
10. Café 1
11. Number 27 Restaurant
12. La Tortilla Asesina Rest.
13. Hootananny Café/Bar
14. Rocpool Restaurant
15. The Mustard Seed Rest.
16. Rajah Indian Restaurant
17. Girvans Café & Délices de Bretagne Brasserie
18. Leakey's Bookshop & Café
19. Marks & Spencer (Groceries)
20. Scottish Showtime Experience (in Spectrum Centre)
21. Library (Internet)
22. Clanlan (Internet)
23. Launderette (Internet)
24. Riverside Paths
25. Bus Stop for Culloden & Cawdor

Helpful Hints

Internet Access: You can get online at the **TI** (£1/20 min), or for free at the Neoclassical **library** behind the bus station, though you'll be limited to a half-hour session (Mon and Fri 9:00–19:30, Tue and Thu 9:00–18:30, Wed 10:00–17:00, Sat 9:00–17:00, closed Sun, computers shut down 15 min before closing, tel. 01463/236-463). **Clanlan** is in the middle of town, between the train station and the river (£1/20 min, Sun–Fri 12:00–20:00, Sat 11:00–20:00, 22 Baron Taylor Street, tel. 01463/241-223). The launderette listed below also has Internet access (£1/30 min).

Laundry: New City Launderette is just across the Ness Bridge from the TI (self-service-£8, same-day full-service for £3.50 more, price calculated by weight, Internet access, Mon–Sat 8:00–18:00, until 20:00 Mon–Fri June–Oct, Sun 10:00–16:00, last load one hour before closing, 17 Young Street, tel. 01463/242-507).

Tours in Inverness

Walking Tour—Happy Tours offers guided historical walks in spring and summer. Keep an eye out for the guy in the kilt hanging around outside the TI (£10; April–Sept daily at 11:00, 13:00, and 15:00; one hour, arrange in advance in winter, mobile 0782-815-4683, www.happy-tours.biz, Cameron). They also do a "Crime and Punishment" tour nightly at 19:00 and 20:15.

Excursions from Inverness

While thin on sights of its own, Inverness is a great home base for day trips. The biggest attraction is Loch Ness, a 20-minute drive southwest. Tickets are available at the TI, and tours depart from somewhere nearby. It's smart to book ahead, especially in peak season.

Jacobite Tours—This outfit runs a variety of tours, from a one-hour basic boat ride to a six-hour extravaganza (£11–36, most tours run daily April–Sept). Their 3.5-hour "Sensation" tour includes a guided bus tour with live narration, a cruise of Loch Ness with recorded commentary, and an hour apiece at the Urquhart Castle and the better of the two Loch Ness exhibits (£25, includes admissions to both sights, departs at 10:30 from Bank Street, near the TI, tel. 01463/233-999, www.jacobite.co.uk).

Scottish Tours—Choose from several daylong tours, including one that focuses on the Isle of Skye, with stops along Loch Ness and at scenic Eilean Donan Castle. You'll get a few hours on Skye; unfortunately, it only takes you as far as the Sleat Peninsula at the island's southern end, rather than to the more scenic Trotternish Peninsula (£35, includes entry to Eilean Donan, departs from

Tattoos and the Painted People

In Inverness, as in other Scottish cities such as Glasgow and Edinburgh, hip pubs are filled with tattooed kids. In parts of Scotland, however, tattoos aren't a recent phenomenon—this form of body art has been around longer than the buildings and sights. Some of the area's earliest known settlers of the Highlands were called the Picts, dubbed the "Painted People" by their enemies, the Romans. The Picts, who conquered the northeast corner of Scotland (including Inverness), were believed to have ruled from the first century A.D. to approximately the ninth century, when they united with the Scots and were lost to written history.

Picts were known for their elaborate full-body tattoos. The local plant they used for their ink, called *woad*, had built-in healing properties, helping to coagulate blood (a property particularly handy in battle). The tattoos gave rise to a truly remarkable fighting technique: going to war naked. The Picts saw their tattoos as a kind of psychological armor, a combination of symbols and magical signs that would protect them more than any metal could. Imagine a Scottish hillside teeming with screaming, head-to-toe dyed-blue warriors, most with complex tattooed designs—and all of them buck naked.

Inverness TI at 9:30, returns at 18:30; mid-May–Sept runs daily; April–mid-May and Oct runs Sun, Wed, and Fri only; reservations recommended, tel. 0871-200-8008, www.scottishtours.co.uk). For more on the Isle of Skye, see the previous chapter.

More Options—Several companies host daily excursions to Culloden Battlefield, whisky distilleries, Cawdor Castle, and the nearby bay for dolphin-watching (ask at TI).

Sights in Inverness

"Imaginverness" Museum and Art Gallery—This free, likeable town museum is worth poking around on a rainy day to get a taste of Inverness and the Highlands. The ground-floor exhibits on geology and archaeology peel back the layers of Highland history: Bronze and Iron ages, Picts (including some carved stones), Scots, Vikings, and Normans. Upstairs you'll find the "social history" exhibit (everything from Scottish nationalism to hunting and fishing) and temporary art exhibits (free, Mon–Sat 10:00–17:00, closed Sun, cheap café, in the modern building behind the TI on the way up to the castle, tel. 01463/237-114).

Inverness Castle—Inverness' biggest nonsight has nice views from its front lawn, but the building itself isn't worth visiting.

The statue outside depicts Flora MacDonald, who helped Bonnie Prince Charlie escape from the English (see page 669). The castle is used as a courthouse, and when trials are in session, loutish-looking men hang out here, waiting for their bewigged barristers to arrive.

Folk Show—The **Scottish Showtime Experience** evening is a fun-loving, hardworking, Lawrence Welk–ish show giving you all the clichés in a clap-along two-hour package. I prefer it to the big hotel spectacles in Edinburgh (£12.50, kids-£7.50, usually June–Aug Mon–Thu at 20:30, no meals, next to the bus station in Spectrum Centre Theatre on Margaret Street, tel. 0800-015-8001 or 01349/830-930, www.scottishshowtime.com).

Sleeping in Inverness

(area code: 01463)

B&Bs on and near Ardconnel Street and Old Edinburgh Road

These B&Bs are popular; book ahead for July and August, and be aware that some require a two-night minimum during busy times. The rooms are all a 10-minute walk from the train station and town center. To get to the B&Bs, either catch a taxi (£3) or walk: From the train and bus stations, go left on Academy Street. At the first stoplight (the second if you're coming from the bus station), veer right onto Inglis Street in the pedestrian zone. Go up the Market Brae steps. At the top, turn right onto Ardconnel Street toward the B&Bs and hostels.

$$$ Melness Guest House has two country-comfy rooms, a tartan-bedecked lounge, and an adorable West Highland Terrier named Rogie (Db-£70, 2-night minimum in summer, free Wi-Fi, 8 Old Edinburgh Road, tel. 01463/220-963, www .melnessie.co.uk, joy@melnessie.co.uk, welcoming Joy Joyce).

$$$ Craigside Lodge B&B has five large, comfortable, cheery rooms recently remodeled with a tasteful modern flair. Guests share an inviting sunroom and a cozy lounge with a great city view (Sb-£35–40, Db-£65–70, prices depend on season, free Wi-Fi, just above Castle Street at 4 Gordon Terrace, tel. 01463/231-576, www.craigsideguesthouse.co.uk, enquiries@craig sideguesthouse.co.uk, Ewan and Amy).

$$$ Dionard Guest House, just up Old Edinburgh Road from Ardconnel Street, has cheerful blue-toned common spaces and four pleasant rooms, with two on the ground floor (Sb-£40, Db-£65–75 depending on size, no single-occupancy rate during high season, free Wi-Fi, in-room fridges, 39 Old Edinburgh Road,

Sleep Code

(£1 = about $1.60, country code: 44, area code: 01463)
S = Single, **D** = Double/Twin, **T** = Triple, **Q** = Quad, **b** = bathroom,
s = shower only. Unless otherwise noted, you can assume
credit cards are accepted at hotels and hostels—but not
B&Bs—and breakfast is included.

To help you sort easily through these listings, I've divided
the rooms into three categories based on the price for a
standard double room with bath (during high season):

$$$ Higher Priced—Most rooms £65 or more.
 $$ Moderately Priced—Most rooms between £30-65.
  $ Lower Priced—Most rooms £30 or less.

tel. 01463/233-557, www.dionardguesthouse.co.uk, enquiries
@dionardguesthouse.co.uk, welcoming Val and John).

$$$ Ardconnel House has six spacious and relaxing pastel rooms with lots of extra touches (Sb-£40, Db-£70, family room-£90, family deals but no children under 10, slightly cheaper off-season or for 2 or more nights, free Wi-Fi, 21 Ardconnel Street, tel. 01463/240-455, www.ardconnel-inverness.co.uk, ardconnel @gmail.com, John and Elizabeth—but may change hands in 2010).

$$ Crown Hotel Guest House has six clean, bright rooms and an enjoyable breakfast room (Sb-£35, Db-£60, family room-£80–90, 19 Ardconnel Street, tel. 01463/231-135, www.crown hotel-inverness.co.uk, gordon@crownhotel-inverness.co.uk, friendly Catriona—pronounced "Katrina"—Barbour).

$$ Ryeford Guest House is a great value, with six flowery rooms and plenty of teddy bears (Db-£58, Tb-£87, family deals, free Wi-Fi, vegetarian breakfast available, small room #1 in back has fine garden view, above Market Brae steps, go left on Ardconnel Terrace to #21, tel. 01463/242-871, www.scotland-inverness.co.uk /ryeford, joananderson@uwclub.net, Joan and George Anderson).

Hotels

The following hotels may have rooms when my recommended B&Bs are full.

$$$ The Redcliffe Hotel, which is actually in the midst of all the B&Bs described above, has recently renovated its 18 rooms with smooth contemporary style. Though a lesser value than the B&Bs, it's fairly priced for a small hotel (Sb-£50–60, Db-£80–100, Db suite-£100–130, depends on season, pay Wi-Fi, 1 Gordon Terrace, tel. & fax 01463/232-767, www.redcliffe-hotel.co.uk, enquiry@redcliffe-hotel.co.uk). They also have a good restaurant (listed later, under "Eating in Inverness").

$$$ Inverness Palace Hotel & Spa, a Best Western, is a fancy splurge with a pool, a gym, and 88 overpriced rooms. It's located right on the River Ness, across from the castle (Db-£199, but you can almost always get a much better rate—even half-price—if you book a package deal on their website, £70 last-minute rooms, prices especially soft on weekends, river/castle view rooms about £10 more than rest, breakfast extra, elevator, free Wi-Fi, free parking, 8 Ness Walk, tel. 01463/223-243, fax 01463/236-865, www.bw-invernesspalace.co.uk, palace@miltonhotels.com).

$$$ Premier Inn Inverness Centre, a half-mile east of the train station along busy and dreary Millburn Road, offers 55 modern, identical rooms in a converted distillery. While it feels like a freeway rest-stop hotel (nondrivers should skip it), it's fairly affordable, especially for families. The appealing onsite restaurant, Slice, offers steaks, salads, and more in a bright, contemporary atmosphere (Db for up to 2 adults and 2 kids-£75, cheaper in winter, continental breakfast-£5.25, full cooked breakfast-£7.50, B865/Millburn Road, just west of the A9 and A96 interchange, tel. 08701-977-141, fax 01463/717-826, www.premierinn.com).

Hostels on Culduthel Road

For inexpensive dorm beds near the center and the recommended Castle Street restaurants, consider these friendly side-by-side hostels, geared toward younger travelers. They're about a 12-minute walk from the train station.

$ Inverness Student Hotel has 57 beds in nine rooms and a cozy, inviting, laid-back lounge with a bay window overlooking the River Ness. The friendly staff accommodates groups doing the hop-on, hop-off bus circuit, but any traveler over 18 is welcome. Dorms come in some interesting shapes, and each bunk has its own playful name (£14 beds in 6- to 10-bed rooms, price depends on season, breakfast-£2, free tea and coffee, cheap Internet access, free Wi-Fi, full-service laundry for £2.50, kitchen, 8 Culduthel Road, tel. 01463/236-556, www.scotlands-top-hostels.com, inverness@scotlands-top-hostels.com).

$ Bazpackers Hostel, a stone's throw from the castle, has a pleasant common room and 34 beds in basic dorms (beds-£13–14, D-£35, cheaper Oct–May, linens provided, reception open 7:30–24:00, Internet access, laundry service, 4 Culduthel Road, tel. 01463/717-663).

Eating in Inverness

You'll find a lot of traditional Highland fare—game, fish, lamb, and beef. Reservations are smart at most of these places, especially on summer weekends.

INVERNESS

Near the B&Bs, on or near Castle Street

The first three eateries line Castle Street, facing the back of the castle. The last one is right in the middle of the B&B neighborhood.

Café 1 serves up high-quality modern Scottish and international cuisine with a trendy, elegant bistro flair. Despite a recent expansion of the eating area, this popular place still fills up on weekends, so it's smart to call ahead (£12–18 entrées, lunch and early-bird dinner specials 17:30–18:45, Mon–Sat 12:00–14:00 & 17:30–21:30, closed Sun, 75 Castle Street, tel. 01463/226-200).

Number 27, a local favorite, is the Scottish version of T.G.I. Friday's. The straightforward, crowd-pleasing menu offers something for everyone—salads, burgers, seafood, and more (£8–15 entrées, Sun–Fri 12:00–14:45 & 17:00–21:30, Sat 12:00–21:30, until 21:00 off-season, generous portions, noisy adjacent bar up front, quieter restaurant in back, 27 Castle Street, tel. 01463/241-999).

La Tortilla Asesina has Spanish tapas, including spicy king prawns (the house specialty). It's an appealing and vivacious dining option (£3–6 cold and hot tapas, a few make a meal, cheap three-course specials; July–Sept daily 12:00–23:00; Oct–June Sun–Thu 12:00–22:00, Fri–Sat until 23:00; 99 Castle Street, tel. 01463/709-809).

The Redcliffe Hotel's restaurant is conveniently located (right on the B&B street) and serves up good food in three areas: a bright and leafy sunroom, a pub, or an outdoor patio (£9–16 dinners, Mon–Sat 12:00–14:30 & 17:00–21:30, Sun 12:30–14:30 & 17:30–21:30, 1 Gordon Terrace, tel. 01463/232-767).

In the Town Center

Hootananny is a cross-cultural experience, combining a lively pub atmosphere, nightly live music (always Scottish traditional, plus rock, blues, and "bar music"), and Thai cuisine. It's got a great join-in-the-fun vibe at night (£6–7 Thai dishes, lunch deals, food served Mon–Sat 12:00–15:00 & 17:00–21:30, music begins every night at 21:30, closed Sun, 67 Church Street, tel. 01463/233-651, www.hootananny.co.uk). Upstairs is the Mad Hatter's nightclub, complete with a "chill-out room."

Rocpool Restaurant is a hit with locals and good for a splurge. Owner/chef Steven Devlin serves creative modern European food in a sleek—and often crowded—chocolate/pistachio dining room (£11 lunch specials, £13 pretheater special before 18:45, £12–18 dinners, daily 12:00–14:30 & 17:45–22:00, reserve or be sorry, across the Ness Bridge from TI at 1 Ness Walk, tel. 01463/717-274).

The Mustard Seed serves Scottish food with a modern twist and a view of the river in a lively-at-lunch, mellow-at-dinner atmosphere. It's pricey but worth considering for a nice meal. Ask for a seat on the balcony if the weather is cooperating (£10–15 meals,

INVERNESS

early-bird specials before 19:00, daily 12:00–15:00 & 17:30–22:00, reservations smart on weekends, on the corner of Bank and Fraser Streets, 16 Fraser Street, tel. 01463/220-220).

Rajah Indian Restaurant provides a tasty break from meat and potatoes, with vegetarian options served in a classy red-velvet, white-linen atmosphere (£8–13 meals, 10 percent less for take-out, Mon–Sat 12:00–23:00, Sun 15:00–22:30, last dine-in order 30 min before closing, just off Church Street at 2 Post Office Avenue, tel. 01463/237-190).

Girvans serves sandwiches and tempting pastries in an easy-going atmosphere (£5–9 meals, Mon–Sat 9:00–21:00, Sun 10:00–21:00, 2 Stephens Brae, at the end of the pedestrian zone nearest the train station, tel. 01463/711-900).

Délices de Bretagne, next door to Girvans, is a tiny French brasserie serving £5 croque sandwiches, £6 crêpes, and its share of tasty pastries in a lighthearted, Art Nouveau space (Mon–Sat 9:00–17:00, July–Aug until 20:00, closed Sun year-round, 4A/6 Stephens Brae, tel. 01463/712-422).

Leakey's Bookshop and Café, located in a 1649 converted church, has the best lunch deal in town. Browse through stacks of old books and vintage maps, warm up by the wood-burning stove, and climb the spiral staircase to the loft for hearty home-made soups, sandwiches, and sweets (£3–4 light lunches, Mon–Sat 10:00–16:30, bookstore stays open until 17:30, closed Sun, in Greyfriar's Hall on Church Street, tel. 01463/239-947, Charles Leakey).

Picnic: The **Marks & Spencer** food hall is best (you can't miss it—on the main pedestrian mall, near the Market Brae steps at the corner of the big Eastgate Shopping Centre; Mon–Wed and Fri–Sat 9:00–18:00, Thu 9:00–20:00, Sun 11:00–17:00, tel. 01463/224-844).

Inverness Connections

From Inverness by Train to: Pitlochry (every 2 hrs, 1.5 hrs), **Stirling** (every 1.5–2 hrs, 2.75–3 hrs, some transfer in Perth), **Kyle of Lochalsh** near Isle of Skye (4/day, 2.5 hrs), **Edinburgh** (every 2 hrs, 3.5–4 hrs, more with change in Perth), **Glasgow** (8/day, 3.5 hrs, most with change in Perth). ScotRail does a great sleeper service to **London** (generally £140–190 for first class/private compartment or £100–150 for standard class/shared compartment with breakfast, not available Sat night, www.firstscotrail.com). Consider dropping your car in Inverness and riding to London by train. Train info: tel. 0845-748-4950.

By Bus: To reach most destinations in western Scotland, you'll first head for **Fort William** (7/day Mon–Sat, 5/day Sun, 2 hrs). For connections onward to **Oban** (figure 4 hrs total) or **Glencoe** (3 hrs total), see the "Fort William Connections" on page 632. To reach **Portree** on the Isle of Skye, you can either take the direct bus (3/day in summer, 2/day in winter, 3.25 hrs direct), or transfer in Fort William. These buses are run by Scottish Citylink; for schedules, see www.citylink.co.uk. You can buy tickets in advance by calling Citylink at tel. 0870-550-5050 or stopping by the Inverness bus station (Mon–Sat 8:30–17:30, Sun 10:00–17:30, 50p extra for credit cards, daily baggage storage-£4–5/bag, 2 blocks from train station on Margaret Street, tel. 01463/233-371). For bus travel to England, check www.nationalexpress.com.

Route Tips for Drivers

Inverness to Edinburgh (150 miles, 3 hours minimum): Leaving Inverness, follow signs to A9 (south, toward Perth). If you haven't seen the Culloden Battlefield yet (described later), it's an easy detour: Just as you leave Inverness, head four miles east off A9 on B9006. Back on A9, it's a wonderfully speedy, scenic highway (A9, M90, A90) all the way to Edinburgh. If you have time, consider stopping en route in Pitlochry (just off A9; see the Between Inverness and Edinburgh chapter).

To Oban, Glencoe, or Isle of Skye: See the "Route Tips for Drivers" at the end of the Oban and the Southern Highlands chapter.

Near Inverness

Inverness puts you in the heart of the Highlands, within easy striking distance of a gaggle of famous and worthwhile sights: Squint across Loch Ness looking for Nessie—or, if you're a skeptic, just appreciate the majesty of Britain's largest body of water by volume. Commune with the Scottish soul at the historic Culloden Battlefield, where Scottish, English, and world history reached a turning point. Ponder three mysterious Neolithic cairns, reminding visitors that Scotland's history goes back even before Braveheart. And enjoy a homey country castle at Cawdor.

Loch Ness

I'll admit it: I had my zoom lens out and my eyes on the water. The local tourist industry thrives on the legend of the Loch Ness Monster. It's a thrilling thought, and there have been several

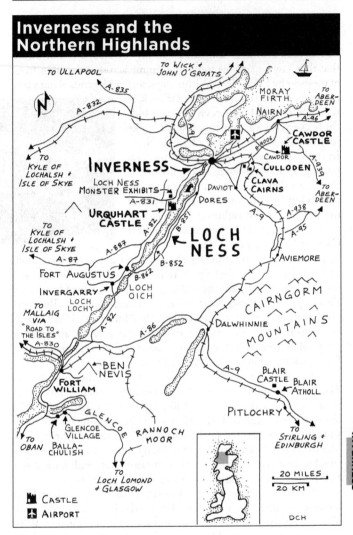

Inverness and the Northern Highlands

TO ULLAPOOL
TO WICK &
JOHN O'GROATS
A-835
A-832
MORAY
FIRTH.
TO ABER-
DEEN
NAIRN
A-9
A-96
CAWDOR
CASTLE
TO
KYLE OF
LOCHALSH &
ISLE OF SKYE
B-9006
Cawdor
CULLODEN
INVERNESS
LOCH NESS
MONSTER EXHIBITS
DAVIOT
CLAVA
CAIRNS
A-831
DORES
TO
ABER-
DEEN
**URQUHART
CASTLE**
A-92
B-851
A-938
TO
KYLE OF
LOCHALSH &
ISLE OF SKYE
A-87
A-887
**L O C H
N E S S**
A-95
FORT AUGUSTUS
B-862
B-852
AVIEMORE
INVERGARRY
LOCH
OICH
LOCH
LOCHY
C A I R N G O R M
TO
MALLAIG
VIA
"ROAD TO
THE ISLES"
A-830
A-92
A-86
DALWHINNIE
M O U N T A I N S
**BEN
NEVIS**
A-9
BLAIR
CASTLE
BLAIR
ATHOLL
**FORT
WILLIAM**
PITLOCHRY
GLENCOE
GLENCOE
VILLAGE
RANNOCH
MOOR
TO
STIRLING &
EDINBURGH
TO
OBAN
BALLA-
CHULISH
20 MILES
20 KM
TO
LOCH LOMOND
& GLASGOW
CASTLE
AIRPORT
DCH

INVERNESS

seemingly reliable "sightings" (monks, police officers, and sonar images). But even if you ignore the monster stories, the loch is impressive: 24 miles long, less than a mile wide, the third-deepest in Europe, and containing more water than in all the freshwater bodies of England and Wales combined.

Getting There: The Loch Ness sights are a quick drive southwest of Inverness. Various buses go from Inverness to Urquhart Castle in about a half-hour (8/day, various companies, ask at Inverness bus station or TI).

Sights on Loch Ness

Loch Ness Monster Exhibits—In July of 1933, a couple swore that they saw a giant sea monster shimmy across the road in front of their car by Loch Ness. Within days, ancient legends about giant

monsters in the lake (dating as far back as the sixth century) were revived—and suddenly everyone was spotting "Nessie" poke its head above the waters of Loch Ness. In the last 75 years, further sightings and photographic "evidence" have bolstered the claim that there's something mysterious living in this unthinkably deep and murky lake. (Most sightings take place in the deepest part of the loch, near Urquhart Castle.) Most witnesses describe a water-

bound dinosaur (resembling the real, but extinct, plesiosaur). Others cling to the slightly more plausible theory of a gigantic eel. And skeptics figure the sightings can be explained by a combination of reflections, boat wakes, and mass hysteria. The most famous photo of the beast (dubbed the "Surgeon's Photo") was later discredited—the "monster's" head was actually attached to a toy submarine. But that hasn't stopped various cryptozoologists from seeking photographic, sonar, and other proof.

And that suits the thriving local tourist industry just fine. The Nessie commercialization is so tacky that there are two different monster exhibits within 100 yards of each other, both in the town of Drumnadrochit. Each has a tour-bus parking lot and more square footage devoted to their kitschy shop than to the exhibit. The overpriced exhibitions are actually quite interesting—even though they're tourist traps, they'll appease that small part of you that knows the *real* reason you wanted to see Loch Ness.

The better option of the two—worth ▲—is the **Loch Ness Centre,** headed by a marine biologist who has spent more than 15 years researching lake ecology and scientific phenomena. With a 30-minute series of video bits and special effects, this exhibit explains the geological and historical environment that bred the monster story as well as the various searches that have been conducted. Refreshingly, it retains an air of healthy skepticism instead of breathless monster-chasing (£6.50, daily Easter–Oct 9:00–17:00, July–Aug until 18:00, Nov–Easter 10:00–15:30, in the big stone mansion right on the main road to Inverness, tel. 01456/450-573, www.lochness.com).

The other exhibit, called the **Loch Ness Visitor Centre** (up a side road closer to the town center, affiliated with a hotel), is less serious. It's basically a tacky high-school-quality photo report

The Caledonian Canal

The Highlands are cut in two by the impressive Caledonian Canal, which connects lakes (lochs) that lie in the huge depression created by the Great Glen Fault. The town of Fort William (described in the previous chapter) is located at the southwest end of the canal, and Inverness sits at its northeast end. The major sights—including the famous Loch Ness—cluster along the scenic 60-mile stretch between these two towns.

Three locks and a series of canals trace the fault. Oich, Loch, and Ness were connected in the early 1800s by the great British engineer Thomas Telford. Traveling between Fort William and Inverness, you'll follow Telford's work—20 miles of canals and locks between 40 miles of lakes, raising ships from sea level to 51 feet (Ness), 93 feet (Lochy), and to 106 feet (Oich).

While "Neptune's Staircase," a series of locks near Fort William, has been cleverly named to sound intriguing, the best

lock stop is midway, at Fort Augustus, where the canal hits the south end of Loch Ness. In Fort Augustus, the **Caledonian Canal Heritage Centre,** three locks above the main road, gives a good rundown on Telford's work (free, Easter–Oct daily 10:00–17:30, closed 30 min midday for lunch, tel. 01320/366-493). Stroll past several shops and eateries to the top of the locks for a fine view.

and a 30-minute *We Believe in the Loch Ness Monster* movie, which features credible-sounding locals explaining what they saw and a review of modern Nessie searches. (The most convincing reason for locals to believe: Look at the hordes of tourists around you.) There are also small exhibits on local history and on other "monsters" and hoaxes around the world (£5.50, daily May–Sept 9:00–18:00, Oct–April 9:00–17:00, tel. 01456/450-342).

▲Urquhart Castle—The ruins at Urquhart (UR-kurt), just up the loch from the Nessie exhibits, are gloriously situated with a view of virtually the entire lake. Its visitors center has a museum with castle artifacts and a good eight-minute film, but the castle itself is a relatively empty shell. Its previous owners blew it up to keep the Jacobites from taking it. As you walk toward the ruins, take

INVERNESS

a close look at the trebuchet (a working replica of one of the most destructive weapons of English King Edward I), and ponder how this giant slingshot helped Edward grab almost every castle in the country away from the native Scots (£7, guidebook-£4, daily April–Sept 9:30–18:00, Oct 9:30–17:00, Nov–March 9:30–16:30, last entry 45 min before closing, tel. 01456/450-551).

Culloden Battlefield

Jacobite troops under Bonnie Prince Charlie were defeated at Culloden (kuh-LAW-dehn) by supporters of the Hanover dynasty in 1746. This last major land battle fought on British soil spelled the end of Jacobite resistance and the beginning of the clan chiefs' fall from power. Wandering the desolate, solemn battlefield, you sense that something terrible occurred here. Locals still bring white roses and speak of "the '45" (as Bonnie Prince Charlie's entire campaign is called) as if it just happened. The battlefield at Culloden and its new high-tech Visitors Centre together are worth ▲▲▲.

Orientation to Culloden

Cost: £10, plus £2 for parking.

Hours: Daily April–Oct 9:00–18:00, Nov–March 10:00–16:00, possibly closed in Jan.

Information: £5 guidebook, tel. 01463/796-090, www.nts.org.uk/culloden.

Tours: Tours with live guides are included with your admission. Check for a schedule—there are generally 3–4/day, focusing on various aspects of the battle.

Audioguide: It's free, with good information tied by GPS to important sites on the battlefield; pick it up at the end of the indoor exhibit.

Getting There: It's a 15-minute drive east of Inverness. Follow signs to *Aberdeen*, then *Culloden Moor*, and B9006 takes you right there (well-signed on the right-hand side). Public buses leave from Inverness' Queensgate street and drop you off in the parking lot (bus #1 or #1A, hourly, 30 min, confirm that bus is going all the way to the battlefield).

Length of This Tour: Allow 2 hours.

Background: The Battle of Culloden

The Battle of Culloden (April 16, 1746) marks the end of the power of the Scottish Highland clans and the start of years of repression of Scottish culture by the English. It was the culmination of a year's worth of battles, known collectively as "the '45." At the center of it all was the charismatic, enigmatic Bonnie Prince Charlie (1720–1788).

Charles Edward Stuart, from his first breath, was raised with a single purpose—to restore his family to the British throne. His grandfather was King James II, deposed in 1688 by Parliament for his tyranny and pro-Catholic bias. In 1745, young Charlie crossed the Channel from exile in France to retake the throne for the Stuarts. He landed on the west coast of Scotland and rallied support for the "Jacobite" cause (from the Latin for "James"). Though Charles was not Scottish-born, he was the rightful heir directly down the line from Mary, Queen of Scots—and so many Scots joined the Stuart family's rebellion out of resentment at being ruled by a foreign king (English royalty of German descent).

Bagpipes droned, and "Bonnie" (handsome) Charlie led an army of 2,000 tartan-wearing, Gaelic-speaking Highlanders across Scotland, seizing Edinburgh. They picked up other supporters of the Stuarts from the Lowlands and from England. Now 6,000 strong, they marched south toward London, and King George II made plans to flee the country. But anticipated support for the Jacobites failed to materialize in the numbers they were hoping for (both in England and from France). The Jacobites had so far been victorious in their battles against the Hanoverian government forces, but the odds now turned against them. Charles retreated to the Scottish Highlands, where many of his men knew the terrain and might gain an advantage when outnumbered. The English government troops followed closely on his heels.

Against the advice of his best military strategist, Charles' army faced the Hanoverian forces at Culloden Moor on flat, barren terrain that was unsuited to the Highlanders' guerrilla tactics. The Scots—many of them brandishing only broadswords and spears—were mowed down by English cannons and horsemen. In less than an hour, the government forces routed the Jacobite army, but that was just the start. They spent the next weeks methodically hunting down ringleaders and sympathizers (and many others in the Highlands who had nothing to do with the battle), ruthlessly killing, imprisoning, and banishing thousands.

Charles fled with a £30,000 price on his head. He escaped to the Isle of Skye, hidden by a woman named Flora MacDonald (her grave is on the Isle of Skye, and her statue is outside Inverness Castle). Flora dressed Charles in women's clothes and passed him off as her maid. Later, Flora was arrested and thrown in the Tower of London before being released and treated like a celebrity.

INVERNESS

Charles escaped to France. He spent the rest of his life wandering Europe trying to drum up support to retake the throne. He drifted through short-lived romantic affairs and alcohol, and died in obscurity, without an heir, in Rome.

Though usually depicted as a battle of the Scottish versus the English, in truth Culloden was a civil war between two opposing dynasties: Stuart (Charlie) and Hanover (George). In fact, about one-fifth of the government's troops were Scottish, and several redcoat deserters fought along with the Jacobites. However, as the history has faded into lore, the battle has come to be remembered as a Scottish-versus-English standoff—or, in the parlance of the Scots, the Highlanders versus the Strangers.

The Battle of Culloden was the end of 60 years of Jacobite rebellions, the last major battle fought on British soil, and the final stand of the Highlanders. From then on, clan chiefs were deposed; kilts, tartans, and bagpipes became illegal paraphernalia; and farmers were cleared off their ancestral land, replaced by more-profitable sheep. Scottish culture would never recover from the events of the campaign called "the '45."

Self-Guided Tour

Culloden's new Visitors Centre, opened in spring 2008, is a state-of-the-art £10 million facility. The ribbon was cut by two young local men, each descended from soldiers who fought in the battle (one from either side). On the way up to the door, look under your feet at the memorial stones for fallen soldiers and clans, mostly purchased by their American and Canadian descendants.

The initial part of the exhibit provides you with some background. As you pass the ticket desk, note the **family tree** of Bonnie Prince Charlie ("Prince Charles Edward") and George II, who were essentially distant cousins. Next you'll come across the first of the exhibit's shadowy-figure **touchscreens,** which connect you with historical figures who give you details from both the Hanoverian and Jacobite perspectives. A **map** here shows the other power struggles happening in and around Europe, putting this fight for political control of Britain in a wider context. This battle was no simple local skirmish, but rather a key part of a larger struggle between Britain and its neighbors, primarily France, for control over trade and colonial power. In the display case are **medals** from the early 1700s, made by both sides as propaganda.

Your path through this building is cleverly designed to echo the course of the Jacobite army. Your short march gets underway as Charlie sails from France to Scotland, then finagles the support of Highland clan chiefs. As he heads south with his army to take London, you, too, are walking south. Along the way, maps show

INVERNESS

the movement of troops, and wall panels cover the build-up to the attack, as seen from both sides. Note the clever division of information: To the left and in red is the story of the "government" (a.k.a. Hanoverians/Whigs/English, led by the Duke of Cumberland); to right, in blue, is the Jacobites' perspective (Prince Charlie and his Highlander/French supporters).

But you, like Charlie, don't make it to London—in the dark room at the end, you can hear Jacobite commanders arguing over whether to retreat back to Scotland. Pessimistic about their chances of receiving more French support, they decide to U-turn, and so do you. Heading back up north, you'll get some insight into some of the strategizing that went on behind the scenes.

By the time you reach the end of the hall, it's the night before the battle. Round another bend into a dark passage and listen to the voices of the anxious troops. While the English slept soundly in their tents (recovering from celebrating the Duke's 25th birthday), the scrappy and exhausted Jacobite Highlanders struggled through the night to reach the battlefield (abandoning their plan of a surprise attack at Nairn and instead retreating back toward Inverness).

At last the two sides meet. An impressive four-minute **360° movie** puts you right in the center of the action (the violence is realistic; young kids should probably sit this one out). As you wait for the next showing to start, study the chart depicting how the forces were arranged on the battlefield.

Leave the movie, then enter the last room. Here you'll find **period weapons,** including ammunition found on the field, as well as **historical depictions** of the battle. You'll also find a section describing the detective work required to piece together the story from historical evidence. On the far end is a huge map, with narration explaining the combat you've just experienced while giving you a bird's-eye view of the field you're about to roam through. Collect your free battlefield **audioguide.** The doors in front of you lead out to the roof and then to the battlefield below.

From the **roof** of the Visitors Centre, survey the battlefield. In the foreground is a cottage used as a makeshift hospital during the conflict (it's decorated as it would have been then). To the east (south of the River Nairn) is the site that Lord George Murray originally chose for the action. In the end, he failed to convince Prince Charlie of its superiority, and the battle was held here—with disastrous consequences. Although not far from Culloden, the River Nairn site was miles away tactically, and things might have turned out differently for the Jacobites had the battle taken place there instead.

Head down to the **battlefield.** Your GPS guide knows where you are, and the attendant will give you directions on where to start. As you walk along the path, stop each time you hear the "ping" sound (if you keep going, you'll confuse the satellite). The basic audioguide will stop you 10 times on the battlefield—at the Jacobite front line, the Hanoverian front line, and more—taking a minimum of 30 minutes to complete the walking tour. Each stop has additional information on everything from the Brown Bess musket to who was standing on what front line—how long this part of the tour takes depends on how much you want to hear.

As you pass by the **mass graves,** realize that entire clans fought, died, and were buried together. The Mackintosh grave alone was 77 yards long.

Re-enter the hall, return your audioguide (before 17:50), then catch the last part of the exhibit, which covers the aftermath of the battle. As you leave the building, hang a left to see the wall of **protruding bricks,** each representing a soldier who died. The handful of Hanoverian casualties are on the left (about 50); the rest of the long wall's raised bricks represent the multitude of dead Jacobites (about 1,500).

If you're having trouble grasping the significance of this battle, play a game of "What if?" If Bonnie Prince Charlie had persevered on this campaign and taken the throne, he likely wouldn't have plunged Britain into the Seven Years' War with France (his ally). And increased taxes on either side of that war led directly to the French and American revolutions. So if the Jacobites had won...the American colonies might still be part of the British Empire today.

Clava Cairns

INVERNESS

Scotland is littered with reminders of prehistoric peoples—especially along the coast of the Moray Firth—but the Clava Cairns are among the best-preserved, most interesting, and easiest to reach. You'll find them nestled in the spooky countryside just beyond Culloden Battlefield. These "Balnauran of Clava" are Neolithic burial chambers dating from 3,000 to 4,000 years ago. Although they simply look  like giant piles of rocks in a sparsely forested clearing, they warrant a closer look to appreciate the prehistoric logic behind them. (The site is well-explained by informative plaques.) There are three structures: a central "ring cairn" with an open space in the center but no access to it, flanked by two "passage cairns," which were once covered. The entrance shaft in each passage cairn lines up with the setting sun at the winter solstice. Each cairn is surrounded by a stone circle, injecting this site with even more mystery.

Cost and Hours: Free, always open.

Getting There: Just after passing Culloden Battlefield on B9006 (coming from Inverness), signs on the right point to *Clava Cairns.* Follow this twisty road to the free parking lot by the stones. Skip it if you don't have a car.

Cawdor Castle

Homey and intimate, this castle is still the residence of the Dowager (read: widow) Countess of Cawdor, a local aristocratic

branch of the Campbell family. The castle's claim to fame is its connection to Shakespeare's *Macbeth,* in which the three witches correctly predict that the protagonist will be granted the title "Thane of Cawdor." The castle is not used as a setting in the play—which takes place in Inverness, 300 years before this castle was built—but the Shakespeare's dozen or so references to "Cawdor" are enough for the marketing machine to kick in. Today, virtually nothing tangibly ties Cawdor to the Bard or to the real-life Macbeth. But even if you ignore the Shakespeare lore, the castle is worth a visit.

The chatty, friendly docents (including Jean at the front desk, who can say "mind your head" in 42 different languages) give the castle an air of intimacy—most are residents of the neighboring village of Cawdor, and act as though they're old friends with the Dowager Countess (many probably are). Entertaining posted explanations—written by the countess' late husband, the sixth Earl of Cawdor—bring the castle to life, and make you wish you'd known the old chap. While many of today's castles are still residences for the aristocracy, Cawdor feels even more lived-in than the norm—you can imagine the Dowager Countess stretching out in front of the fireplace with a good book. Notice her geraniums in every room.

Stops on the tour include a tapestry-laden bedroom and a "tartan passage" speckled with modern paintings. In another bedroom (just before the stairs back down) is a tiny pencil sketch by Salvador Dalí. Inside the base of the tower, near the end of the tour, is the castle's proud symbol: a holly tree dating from 1372. According to the beloved legend, a donkey leaned against this tree to mark the spot where the castle was to be built—which it was, around the tree. (The tree is no longer alive, but its withered trunk is still propped up in the same position. No word on the donkey.)

The **gardens,** included with the ticket, are also worth exploring, with some 18th-century linden trees, a hedge maze (not open to the public), and several surprising species (including sequoia and redwood).

The nearby remote-feeling **village of Cawdor**—with a few houses, a village shop, and a tavern—is also worth a look if you've got time to kill.

Cost, Hours, Information: £8, good £3 guidebook explains the family and the rooms, May–mid-Oct daily 10:00–17:30, last entry at 17:00, gardens open until 18:00, closed mid-Oct–April, tel. 01667/404-401, www.cawdorcastle.com.

Getting There: It's on B9090, just off A96, about 10 miles east of Inverness (just beyond Culloden and the Clava Cairns). Without a car, you can either take a guided tour from Inverness (ask at the TI), or hop on public bus #1 or #1A—the same ones that go to Culloden—from central Inverness (hourly, 55 min, get on at Queensgate stop, check with driver that bus goes all the way to Cawdor, 15-min walk from Cawdor Church bus stop to castle, last bus back to Inverness around 18:45).

BETWEEN INVERNESS AND EDINBURGH

Pitlochry and Stirling

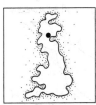

To break up the trip between Inverness and Edinburgh (3 hours by car, 3.5 hours by train), consider stopping over at one of these two worthwhile destinations. The town of Pitlochry, right on the train route, mixes whisky and hillwalking with a dash of countryside charm. Farther south, the historic city of Stirling boasts an impressive castle, a monument to a Scottish hero (William "Braveheart" Wallace), and one of the country's most important battle sites (Bannockburn).

Planning Your Time

Visiting both Pitlochry and Stirling on a one-day drive from Inverness to Edinburgh is doable but busy (especially since part of Pitlochry's allure is slowing down to taste the whisky).

Pleasant Pitlochry is well-located, a quick detour off of the main A9 highway from Inverness to Edinburgh (via Perth) or an easy stop for train travelers. The town deserves an overnight for whisky-lovers, or for those who really want to relax in small-town Scotland. Though many find the town of Pitlochry appealing, it lacks the rugged Highlands scenery and easy access to other major sights found in Oban and Glencoe.

Stirling, off the busy A9/M9 motorway between Perth and Edinburgh, is well worth a sightseeing stop, especially for historians and romantics interested in Scottish history. (If skipping Stirling, notice that you can take M90 due south over the Firth of Forth to connect Perth and Edinburgh.) Also note that Stirling is doable on a trip between Edinburgh and points west (such as Glasgow or Oban)—just take the northern M9/A80 route instead of more direct M8.

Between Inverness and Edinburgh

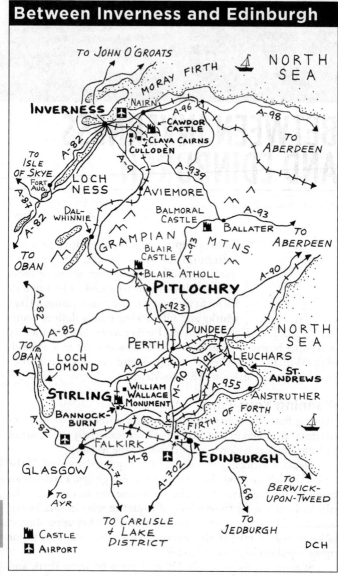

TO JOHN O'GROATS

NORTH SEA

MORAY FIRTH

NAIRN

INVERNESS

A-96

A-98

CAWDOR CASTLE

CLAVA CAIRNS

CULLODEN

TO ABERDEEN

A-82

A-9

A-939

TO ISLE OF SKYE

FORT AUG.

LOCH NESS

A-84

A-82

AVIEMORE

DAL-WHINNIE

BALMORAL CASTLE

A-93

BALLATER

TO ABERDEEN

GRAMPIAN

BLAIR CASTLE

MTNS.

A-93

TO OBAN

BLAIR ATHOLL

PITLOCHRY

A-90

A-82

A-923

A-85

DUNDEE

NORTH SEA

TO OBAN

LOCH LOMOND

PERTH

A-9

M-90

A-92

LEUCHARS

ST. ANDREWS

STIRLING

WILLIAM WALLACE MONUMENT

A-955

ANSTRUTHER

BANNOCK-BURN

FIRTH OF FORTH

A-82

FALKIRK

M-8

EDINBURGH

GLASGOW

M-74

M-8

A-702

TO AYR

TO CARLISLE & LAKE DISTRICT

TO JEDBURGH

A-68

TO BERWICK-UPON-TWEED

🏰 CASTLE

✈ AIRPORT

DCH

Pitlochry

This likable tourist town, famous for its whisky and its hillwalking (both beloved by Scots), makes an enjoyable overnight stop on the way between Inverness and Edinburgh. Just outside the craggy Highlands, Pitlochry is set amid pastoral rolling hills that offer plenty of forest hikes (brochures at TI). A salmon ladder climbs alongside the lazy river (free viewing area—best in May, 10-min walk from town).

Orientation to Pitlochry

(area code: 01796)
Plucky little Pitlochry (pop. 2,500) lines up along its tidy, tourist-minded main road, where you'll find the train station, bus stops, TI, and bike rental. The River Tummel runs parallel to the main road, a few steps away. Most distilleries are a short drive out of town, but you can walk to the two best; see my self-guided hill-walk, below. Navigate easily by following the black directional signs to Pitlochry's handful of sights.

Tourist Information
The helpful TI provides train schedules, books rooms for a £4 fee, and sells good maps for walks and scenic drives (July–mid-Sept Mon–Sat 9:00–19:00, Sun 9:30–17:30; mid-Sept–June Mon–Sat 9:30–17:30, Sun 10:00–16:00; exit from station and follow small road to the right with trains behind you, turn right on Atholl Road, and walk 5 min to TI on left, at #22; tel. 01796/472-215, pitlochry@visitscotland.com).

Helpful Hints
Bike Rental: Escape Route Bikes, located across the street and a block from the TI (away from town), rents a variety of bikes for adults and kids (£10/4 hours, £18/24 hours, price varies by type of bike and includes helmets and lock if you ask, Mon–Sat 9:00–17:30, Sun 10:00–16:00, shorter hours in winter, 3 Atholl Road, tel. 01796/473-859, www.escape-route.biz).

Self-Guided Hillwalk

Pitlochry Whisky Walk

If you were a hobbit in a previous life, spend an afternoon hill-walking from downtown Pitlochry to a pair of top distilleries. The entire loop trip takes two to three hours, depending on how long you linger in the distilleries (at least 45 minutes to an hour of walking each way). It's a good way to see some green rolling hills, especially if you've only experienced urban Scotland. The walk is largely uphill on the way to the Edradour Distillery; wear good shoes, bring a rain jacket just in case, and be happy that you'll stroll easily downhill *after* you've had your whisky samples.

At the TI, pick up the *Pitlochry Walks* brochure (50p). You'll be taking the **Edradour Walk** (marked on directional signs with the yellow hiker icons; on the map it's a series of yellow dots). Leave the TI and head left along busy A924. The walk can be done by going either direction, but I'll describe it counterclockwise.

Within 10 minutes, you'll come to **Bell's Blair Athol Distillery.** If you're a whisky buff, stop in here (described later, under "Sights in Pitlochry"). Otherwise, hold out for the much more atmospheric Edradour. After passing a few B&Bs and suburban homes, you'll see a sign (marked *Edradour Walk*) on the left side of the road, leading you up and off the highway. You'll come to a clearing, and as the road gets steeper, you'll see signs directing you 50 yards off the main path to see the "Black Spout"—a wonderful waterfall well worth a few extra steps.

At the top of the hill, you'll arrive in another clearing, where a narrow path leads along a field. Low rolling hills surround you in all directions. It seems like there's not another person around for miles, with just thistles to keep you company. It's an easy 20 minutes to the distillery from here.

Stop into the **Edradour Distillery** (described later, under "Sights in Pitlochry"). After the tour, leave the distillery, heading right, following the paved road (Old North Road). In about five minutes, there's a sign that seems to point right into the field. Take the small footpath that runs along the left side of the road. (If you see the driveway with stone lions on both sides, you've gone a few steps too far.) You'll walk parallel to the route you took getting to the distillery, and then you'll head back into the forest. Cross the footbridge and make a left (as the map indicates), staying on the wide road. You'll pass a B&B, and hear traffic noises as you emerge out of the

forest. The trail leads back to the highway, with the TI a few blocks ahead on the right.

Sights in Pitlochry

Distillery Tours—The cute **Edradour Distillery** (ED-rah-dower), the smallest in Scotland, takes pride in making its whisky with a minimum of machinery. Small white-and-red buildings are nestled in an impossibly green Scottish hillside. Wander through the buildings and take the £5 one-hour guided tour (3/hr in summer, 2/hr in winter). They offer a 10-minute A/V show and, of course, a free sample dram. Unlike the bigger distilleries, they allow you to take photos of the equipment. If you like the whisky, buy some here and support the local economy—this is one of the few independently owned distilleries left in Scotland (May–Oct Mon–Sat 10:00–17:00, Sun 12:00–17:00; Nov–April Mon–Sat 10:00–16:00, Sun 12:00–16:00, Jan–Feb closed Sun; last tour departs one hour before closing, tel. 01796/472-095, www.edradour.co.uk). Most come to the distillery by car (follow signs from the main road, 2.5 miles into the countryside), but you can also get there on a peaceful hiking trail that you'll have all to yourself (follow my "Pitlochry Whisky Walk," earlier).

The big, ivy-covered **Bell's Blair Athol Distillery** is more conveniently located (about a half-mile from the town center) and more corporate-feeling, offering £5 45-min tours with a wee taste at the end (Easter–Oct tours depart 2/hr Mon–Sat 9:30–17:00, June–Oct also Sun 12:00–17:00, last tour departs one hour before closing; Nov–Easter tours depart Mon–Fri at 11:00, 13:00, and 15:00, closed Sat–Sun; tel. 01796/482-003, www.discovering-distilleries.com).

Pitlochry Power Station—The station, adjacent to the salmon ladder, offers a mildly entertaining exhibit about hydroelectric power in the region (free, April–Oct Mon–Fri 10:00–17:00, closed Sat–Sun, July–Aug also open weekends, closed Nov–March, tel. 01796/473-152). Although walkers can reach this easily by crossing the footbridge from the town center (about a 15-min walk), drivers will head east out of town (toward Bell's Blair Athol Distillery), then turn right on Bridge Road, cross the river, and backtrack to the power station.

Theater—From May through October, the Pitlochry Festival Theatre presents a different play every night and concerts on some Sundays (both £15.50–22.50 Sun–Thu, £18–25 Fri–Sat, purchase tickets at TI or theater—same price, tel. 01796/484-626, www.pitlochry.org.uk). The Scottish Plant Hunters Garden adjacent to the theater is open for visits (£3, April–Oct daily 10:00–17:00, last entry at 16:30).

Sleep Code

(£1 = about $1.60, country code: 44, area code: 01796)
S = Single, **D** = Double/Twin, **T** = Triple, **Q** = Quad, **b** = bathroom,
s = shower only.

To help you sort easily through these listings, I've divided the rooms into two categories based on the price for a standard double room with bath (during high season):

$$ Higher Priced—Most rooms £50 or more.
$ Lower Priced—Most rooms less than £50.

Sleeping in Pitlochry

$$ Craigroyston House is a quaint, large Victorian country house with eight Laura Ashley–style bedrooms run by charming Gretta and Douglas Maxwell (Db-£60–80, less off-season, family room, cash only, above and behind the TI—small gate at back of parking lot—and next to the church at 2 Lower Oakfield, tel. & fax 01796/472-053, www.craigroyston.co.uk, reservations@craigroyston.co.uk). If they're full, Gretta can find you another B&B.

$ Pitlochry's fine **hostel** has 62 beds in 12 rooms, including some family rooms. It's on Knockard Road, well-signed from the town center, about a five-minute walk above the main drag (£15 bunks in 3- to 8-bed rooms, Db-£40; £1–2 more for non-members, Internet access, self-service laundry, office open 7:00–23:00, tel. 01796/472-308, www.syha.org.uk, pitlochry@syha.org.uk).

Eating in Pitlochry

Plenty of options line the main drag, including several bakeries selling picnic supplies. For a heartier meal, try **Victoria's** restaurant and coffee shop, located midway between the train station and the TI (lunch: £5–9 sandwiches, £9–12 mains; dinner: £9 pizzas, £11–20 mains; daily 9:30–21:00, patio seating, at corner of memorial garden at 45 Atholl Road, tel. 01796/472-670).

Pitlochry Connections

The train station is open daily 8:00–18:00 (maybe less in winter).

From Pitlochry by Train to: Inverness (every 2 hrs, 1.5 hrs), **Stirling** (every 1.5–2 hrs, 1.25–1.5 hrs, most transfer in Perth), **Edinburgh** (6/day direct, 2 hrs), **Glasgow** (10/day, 1.75–2 hrs, transfer in Perth). Train info: tel. 08457-484-950, www.nationalrail.co.uk.

Stirling

Once the Scottish capital, the quaint city of Stirling (pop. 41,000) is a mini-Edinburgh with lots of character and a trio of attractions: a dramatic castle, dripping with history and boasting sweeping views; the William Wallace Monument, honoring the real-life Braveheart; and the Bannockburn Heritage Centre, marking the site of Robert the Bruce's victorious battle.

Orientation to Stirling

(area code: 01786)
Stirling's old town is situated along a long, narrow, steep hill, with the castle at its apex. The **TI** is near the base of the old town (July–Aug Mon–Sat 9:30–17:30, Sun 10:00–16:00, shorter hours off-season, hours may change so call to confirm, closed Sun Oct–May, 41 Dumbarton Road, tel. 01786/475-019, www.visitscotland.com).

Getting Around Stirling

Stirling's three main sights (Stirling Castle, the Wallace Monument, and the Bannockburn Heritage Centre) are difficult to reach by foot, and there is currently no hop-on, hop-off tour bus (this bus service may resume, so check on arrival with the TI). If you lack a car, you can take a taxi to the sights from the train station. Or, to get near the Wallace Monument, take a local bus 10 minutes toward the university, then walk for 15 minutes. Ask at the TI about the various options, check www.travelinescotland .com, or call toll tel. 0871-200-2233.

Sights in Stirling

▲Stirling Castle

"He who holds Stirling, holds Scotland." These fateful words have proven, more often than not, to be true. Stirling Castle's strategic position—perched on a volcanic crag overlooking a bridge over the River Forth, the primary passage between the Lowlands and the Highlands—has long been the key to Scotland. This castle of the Stuart kings is one of Scotland's most historic and popular. Offering spectacular views over a gentle countryside, and a mildly interesting but steadily improving exhibit inside, Stirling is worth a look.

Cost and Hours: £9, daily April–Sept 9:30–18:00, Oct–March 9:30–17:00, last entry 45 min before closing, tel. 01786/450-000, www.historic-scotland.gov.uk.

Getting There: Similar to Edinburgh's castle, Stirling Castle sits at the very tip of a steep old town. If you enter Stirling by car, follow the *Stirling Castle* signs, twist up the mazelike roads to the esplanade, and park at the £2 lot just outside the castle gate. Without a car, it's a bit more complicated: From the train or bus station, you can either hike the 20-minute uphill route to the castle, or you can take a taxi (about £4 to castle).

Tours: Posted information is skimpy, so a tour or audioguide is important for bringing the site to life. You can take the included 45-minute guided tour (hourly April–June, 2/hr July–Sept, 4/day Oct–March, depart from the Castle Close just inside the entry) or rent the very good £2 audioguide from the kiosk near the ticket window. Knowledgeable docents posted throughout can tell you more.

Background: Stirling marks the site of two epic medieval battles where famous Scotsmen defeated huge English armies despite impossible odds: In 1297, William Wallace (a.k.a. "Braveheart") fended off an invading English army at the Battle of Stirling Bridge. And in 1314, Robert the Bruce won the battle of nearby Bannockburn. Soon after, the castle became the primary residence of the Stuart monarchs, who turned it into a showpiece of Scotland (and a symbol of one-upmanship against England). But when the Crown moved to London, Stirling's prominence waned. The military, which took over the castle during the Jacobite Wars of the 18th century, bulked it up and converted it into a garrison—damaging much of its delicate beauty. Since 1966, the fortress has been undergoing an extensive and costly restoration to bring it back to its glory days and make it, once again, one of Britain's premier castles.

❍ Self-Guided Tour: From the parking lot at the esplanade, go through the gate to buy your ticket (ask about tour times, and consider renting the audioguide), then head up into the castle through another gate. If you have time to kill before your tour, dip into the grassy courtyard on the left to reach an introductory **castle exhibition** about the history of the town and its fortress. Historians at Stirling are proud of the work they've done to rebuild the castle—and they're not shy about saying so.

Then head up through the main gateway into the **Outer Close.** Tours depart from just to your right, near the Grand Battery, which boasts cannon-and-rampart views. Down the hill along this wall is the Great Kitchens exhibit (where mannequin cooks oversee medieval recipes); below that the North Gate leads to the Nether Bailey (dating from the castle's later days as a military base). Back in the Outer Close, at the top of the courtyard (to your left as you enter), is a narrow passageway lined with exhibits about Stirling's medieval craftspeople.

Hike up into the **Inner Close,** where you're surrounded by Scottish history. Each of the very different buildings in this complex was built by a different monarch. Facing downhill, you'll see the Great Hall straight ahead. This grand structure—Scotland's biggest medieval banqueting hall—was built by the great Renaissance king James IV. Step inside the grand, empty-feeling space to appreciate its fine flourishes. The Chapel Royal, where Mary, Queen of Scots was crowned in 1543, is to your left and also worth a visit. To your right is the Palace (closed for restoration through 2011). And behind you is the King's Old Building, with a regimental (military) museum.

▲William Wallace Monument

Commemorating the Scottish hero better known to Americans as "Braveheart," this sandstone tower—built during a wave of Scottish nationalism in the mid-19th century—marks the Abbey Craig hill on the outskirts of Stirling. This is where Wallace gathered forces for his largest-scale victory against England's King Edward I, in 1297. To learn more about William Wallace, see page 522.

From the base of the monument, you can see the Stirling Bridge—a stone version that replaced the original wooden one. Looking out from the same vantage point as Wallace, imagine how the famous battle played out, and consider why the location was so important in the battle (explained in more detail inside the monument).

After entering the monument, pick up the worthwhile audioguide. You'll first encounter a passionate talking Wallace replica, explaining his defiant stand against Edward I. As you listen, ogle Wallace's five-and-a-half-foot-long broadsword (and try to imagine drawing it from a scabbard on your back at a dead run). Then take a spin through a hall of other Scottish heroes. Finally, climb the 246 narrow steps inside the tower for grand views. The stairways are extremely tight and require some maneuvering—claustrophobes be warned.

Cost, Hours, Information: £6.50, includes audioguide, daily July–Aug 10:00–18:00, April–June and Sept–Oct 10:00–17:00, Nov–March 10:30–16:00, last entry 45 min before closing, café and gift shop, tel. 01786/472-140, www.nationalwallacemonument .com.

Getting There: It's two miles northeast of Stirling on A8, signposted from the city center. From the Stirling train or bus station, you can take a taxi (about £5) or a public bus partway (see "Getting Around Stirling," earlier). From the parking lot's Visitors Pavilion, you'll need to hike (a very steep 10 min) or take a shuttle bus up the hill to the monument itself.

▲Bannockburn Heritage Centre

Just to the south of Stirling proper is the Bannockburn Heritage Centre, commemorating what many Scots view as their nation's most significant military victory over the invading English: the Battle of Bannockburn, won by a Scottish army led by Robert the Bruce against England's King Edward II in 1314.

In simple terms, Robert—who was first and foremost a politician—found himself out of political options after years of failed diplomatic attempts to make peace with the strong-arming English. Wallace's execution left a vacuum in military leadership, and eventually Robert stepped in, waging a successful guerrilla campaign that came to a head as young Edward's army marched to Stirling. Although the Scots were greatly outnumbered, their strategy and use of terrain at Bannockburn allowed them to soundly beat the English and drive Edward out of Scotland for good. For more about Robert the Bruce, read the sidebar on page 526.

This victory is so legendary among the Scots that the country's unofficial national anthem, "Flower of Scotland"—written 600 years after the battle—focuses on this one event. (CDs with a version of this song performed by The Corries can be purchased at the Heritage Centre. Buy one and learn the song, so you can sing along at a pub or sporting event.)

The Heritage Centre, though small, has excellent exhibits and a worthwhile film about the battle and events leading up to it. You can even try on a real chainmail shirt and helmet (£5.50, March–Oct daily 10:00–17:30, closed Nov–Feb, 2 miles south of Stirling on A872, tel. 0844/493-2139, www.nts.org.uk).

Stirling Connections

From Stirling by Train to: Edinburgh (2/hr, 50 min), **Glasgow** (3/hr, 30–45 min), **Pitlochry** (every 1.5–2 hrs, 1.25 hrs, most transfer in Perth), **Inverness** (every 1.5–2 hrs, 2.75–3 hrs, most transfer in Perth). Train info: tel. 08457-484-950, www.nationalrail.co.uk.

BRITISH HISTORY AND CULTURE

Britain was created by force and held together by force. This rich Victorian-era empire is really a nation of the 19th century—when it reached its financial peak. Its traditional industry, buildings, and the popularity of the notion of "Great" Britain are a product of its past wealth.

To best understand the many fascinating tour guides you'll encounter in your travels, you should have a basic handle on the sweeping story of this land. (Generally speaking, the wonderful and terrible stories are made up...and the boring ones are true.)

Basic British History for the Traveler

When Julius Caesar landed on the misty and mysterious isle of Britain in 55 B.C., England entered the history books. The primitive Celtic tribes he conquered were themselves invaders (who had earlier conquered the even more mysterious people who built Stonehenge). The Romans built towns and roads, establishing their capital at Londinium. The Celtic natives in Scotland and Wales—consisting of Gaels, Picts, and Scots—were not easily subdued. Even today, the Celtic language and influence are strongest in these far reaches of Britain. The Romans even built Hadrian's Wall near the Scottish border as protection against their troublesome northern neighbors.

As Rome fell, so fell Roman Britain, a victim of invaders and internal troubles. Barbarian tribes from Germany and Denmark, called Angles and Saxons, swept through the southern part of the island, establishing Angle-land. These were the days of the real King Arthur, possibly a Christianized Roman general who fought valiantly, but in vain, against invading barbarians. In 793 Britain was hit with the first of two centuries of savage invasions by barbarians from Norway, called the Vikings or Norsemen. The

Royal Families: Past and Present

Royal Lineage

802–1066	Saxon and Danish kings
1066–1154	Norman invasion (William the Conqueror), Norman kings
1154–1399	Plantagenet (kings with French roots)
1399–1461	Lancaster
1462–1485	York
1485–1603	Tudor (Henry VIII, Elizabeth I)
1603–1649	Stuart (civil war and beheading of Charles I)
1649–1653	Commonwealth, no royal head of state
1653–1659	Protectorate, with Cromwell as Lord Protector
1660–1714	Restoration of Stuart monarchy
1714–1901	Hanover (four Georges, Victoria)
1901–1910	Saxe-Coburg (Edward VII)
1910–present	Windsor (George V, Edward VIII, George VI, Elizabeth II)

The Royal Family Today

It seems you can't pick up a British newspaper without some mention of the latest scandal or oddity involving the royal family. Here is the cast of characters:

Queen Elizabeth II wears the traditional crown of her great-great grandmother, Victoria. Her husband is Prince Philip, who's not considered king.

Their son, Prince Charles (the Prince of Wales), is next in line to become king. In 1981, Charles married Lady Diana Spencer

island was plunged into 500 years of Dark Ages—wars, plagues, and poverty—lit only by the dim candle of a few learned Christian monks and missionaries trying to convert the barbarians. As a sightseer, you'll see little evidence of this Anglo-Saxon period.

To become a strong nation, England needed yet another invasion. William the Conqueror and his Norman troops crossed the English Channel from France in 1066. William crowned himself king in Westminster Abbey (where all subsequent coronations would take place), and began building the Tower of London. While his heirs eventually lost Normandy, they made forays into Ireland and took over a country to England's west—Wales. French-speaking Norman kings ruled England and Wales for two centuries, followed by two centuries of civil wars, with various noble families vying for the crown. In one of the most bitter feuds,

(Princess Di) who, after their bitter divorce, died in a car crash in 1997. Their two sons, William and Harry, are next in line to the throne after their father. In 2005, Charles married his longtime girlfriend, Camilla Parker Bowles, who is trying to gain respectability with the Queen and the public. But she's not allowed to call herself a princess yet—her current title is Duchess of Cornwall (she'll be Princess Consort—not "Queen"—if and when Charles becomes king).

Prince Charles' siblings are occasionally in the news: Princess Anne, Prince Andrew (who married and divorced Sarah "Fergie" Ferguson), and Prince Edward (who married Di look-alike Sophie Rhys-Jones).

But it's Prince Charles' sons who generate the tabloid buzz these days. Handsome Prince William (b. 1982), a graduate of Scotland's St. Andrews University and an officer in both the Royal Air Force and Royal Navy, serves as the royal family's public face at many charity events, when he's not fulfilling his ongoing military obligations. There's endless speculation about his romantic interests, especially about his long-time, on-again-off-again girlfriend, Kate Middleton (a commoner he met at university). Whomever he marries may eventually become Britain's queen.

Redheaded Prince Harry (b. 1984) made a media splash as a bad boy when he wore a Nazi armband (as an ill-advised joke) to a costume party. Since then, he's proved his mettle as a career soldier. His combat deployment to Iraq was cancelled because of fears his presence would endanger fellow troops, but he served two months in Afghanistan (early 2008). In 2008, he and his regiment did charity work in Africa, and since then he's been training to become a pilot with the Army Air Corps. Harry's love life, like his brother's, is a popular topic for the tabloids.

For more on the monarchy, see www.royal.gov.uk.

the York and Lancaster families fought the Wars of the Roses, so-called because of the symbolic white and red flowers associated with the combatants. Battles, intrigues, kings, nobles, and ladies imprisoned and executed in the Tower—it's a wonder the country survived its rulers.

England was finally united by the "third-party" Tudor family. Henry VIII, a Tudor, was England's Renaissance king. He was handsome, athletic, highly sexed, a poet, a scholar, and a musician. He was also arrogant, cruel, gluttonous, and paranoid. He went through six wives in 40 years, divorcing, imprisoning, or beheading them when they no longer suited his needs.

Henry "divorced" England from the Catholic Church, establishing the Protestant Church of England (the Anglican Church) and setting in motion years of religious squabbles. He also "dissolved" the monasteries (circa 1540), left just the shells of many formerly glorious abbeys dotting the countryside, and pocketed their land and wealth for the Crown.

Henry's daughter, Queen Elizabeth I, who reigned for 45 years, made England a great trading and naval power (defeating the Spanish Armada), and presided over the Elizabethan era of great writers (such as William Shakespeare) and scientists (such as Francis Bacon). But Elizabeth never married, so the English Parliament asked the Protestant ruler to the north, Scotland's King James (Elizabeth's cousin), if he'd like to inherit the English throne. The two nations have been tied together ever since.

The longstanding quarrel between Britain's divine-right kings and Parliament's nobles finally erupted into a civil war (1643). Parliament forces under the Protestant Puritan farmer Oliver Cromwell defeated—and beheaded—James' son, King Charles I. This civil war left its mark on much of what you'll see in Britain. Eventually, Parliament invited Charles' son to take the throne. This "restoration of the monarchy" was accompanied by a great colonial expansion and the rebuilding of London (including Christopher Wren's St. Paul's Cathedral), which had been devastated by the Great Fire of 1666.

Britain grew as a naval superpower, colonizing and trading with all parts of the globe—although some upstart colonies in America "revolted" in 1776 and left the empire. Admiral Horatio Nelson's victory over Napoleon's fleet at the Battle of Trafalgar in 1805 secured her naval superiority ("Britannia rules the waves"), and 10 years later, the Duke of Wellington stomped Napoleon on land at Waterloo. Nelson and Wellington—both buried in London's St. Paul's Cathedral—are memorialized by many arches, columns, and squares that you'll see throughout Britain.

Economically, Britain led the world into the Industrial Age with her mills, factories, coal mines, and trains. By the time of Queen Victoria's reign (1837–1901), Britain was at its zenith of power, with a colonial empire that covered one-fifth of the world.

The 20th century was not kind to Britain. After decades of rebellion, Ireland finally gained its independence—except for the more Protestant north. Two world wars devastated Britain's population, and the Nazi blitzkrieg reduced much of London to rubble. The colonial empire dwindled to almost nothing, and Britain lost its superpower economic status. The war over the Falkland Islands in 1982 showed how little of the British Empire is left—and how determined the British are to hang on to what remains.

Another post-empire hot spot—Northern Ireland, plagued by the "Troubles" between Catholics and Protestants—is cooling off. In the spring of 2007, the unthinkable happened: Leaders of the ultra-nationalist party sat down with those of the ultra-unionist party, and London returned control of Northern Ireland to the popularly elected Northern Ireland Assembly. Perhaps most important of all, after almost 40 years, the British army withdrew most of its forces from Northern Ireland.

The tradition (if not the substance) of greatness continues, presided over by Queen Elizabeth II, her husband, Prince Philip, and their son Prince Charles. With economic problems, the marital turmoil of Charles and the late Princess Diana, and a relentless popular press, the royal family has had a tough time. But the Queen has stayed above it all, and most British people still jump at an opportunity to see royalty. With the 1997 death of Princess Diana and the historic outpouring of grief, it was clear that the concept of royalty was still alive and well as Britain entered the third millennium.

Queen Elizabeth, who turns 84 in 2010, marked her 57th year on the throne in 2009. While many wonder who will succeed her, the case is fairly straightforward: The Queen sees her job as a life-long position, and, legally, Charles (who wants to be king) cannot be skipped over for his son William. Given the longevity in the family (the Queen's mum, born in August of 1900, made it to 101 before she died in 2002), Charles is in for a long wait.

British Politics Today

Politically, Britain is ruled by the House of Commons, with some guidance from the mostly figurehead Queen and the House of Lords. Just as the United States Congress is dominated by Democrats and Republicans, Britain's Parliament is dominated by two parties: Labour and Conservative ("Tories"). (A smaller third party, the Liberal Democrats, often sides with Labour.)

The prime minister is the chief executive. He's not directly elected by voters; rather, he assumes power as the head of the party that wins a majority in Parliamentary elections. Instead of imposing term limits, the Brits allow their prime minister to choose when to leave office. The ruling party also gets to choose when to hold elections, as long as it's within five years of the previous one—so prime ministers carefully schedule elections for times that (they hope) their party will win.

In the 1980s, Conservatives were in charge under Prime Ministers Margaret Thatcher and John Major. As proponents of traditional, Victorian values—community, family, hard work, thrift, and trickle-down economics—they took a Reaganesque approach to Britain's serious social and economic problems.

In 1997, a huge Labour victory brought Tony Blair to the prime ministership. Labour began shoring up a social-service system (health care, education, the minimum wage) undercut by years of Conservative rule. Blair's Labour Party was "New Labour"—akin to Clinton's "New Democrats"—meaning they were fiscally conservative but attentive to the needs of the people. Conservative Party fears of big-spending, bleeding-heart liberalism proved unfounded. The Labour-controlled Parliament was also more open to integration with Europe.

Tony Blair started out as a respected and well-liked PM. But after he followed US President George W. Bush into war with Iraq, his popularity took a nosedive. In May of 2007, Blair announced that he would resign; a few weeks later, his chancellor of the exchequer and longtime colleague, Gordon Brown, was sworn in as Britain's new prime minister.

Looking to the future, London is gearing up to host the 2012 Olympic Games.

Challenges Facing Today's Britain

Great as Britain is, the country has its share of challenges. You'll likely hear people talking about some of the following hot-button topics during your visit: the economy, the war in Afghanistan, terrorism, immigration, and binge-drinking.

Economically, Great Britain's industrial production is about 5 percent of the world's total. The British economy was strong—with inflation, unemployment, and interest rates all low—before the global financial crisis that began in 2008. But, like the US, Britain has suffered from bad loans, falling house prices, and a high unemployment rate—about 7.6 percent in mid-2009, the worst in more than a decade.

British forces ended combat operations in Iraq in April 2009—but troops remain in Afghanistan, and every new casualty re-invigorates public debate about the merits and possible outcomes of this war.

Like the US, Britain has been coping with its own string of terrorist threats and attacks. On the morning of July 7, 2005, London's commuters were rocked by four different bombs that killed dozens across the city. In the summer of 2006, authorities foiled a plot to carry liquid bombs onto a plane (resulting in the liquid ban air travelers are still experiencing today). On June 29, 2007—just two days after Gordon Brown became prime minister—two car bombs were discovered (and defused) near London's Piccadilly Circus, and the next day, a flaming car drove into the baggage-claim level at Glasgow Airport. Most Brits have accepted that they now live with the possibility of terrorism at home—and that life must go on.

Britain has taken aggressive measures to prevent future attacks, such as installing "CCTV" (closed-circuit) surveillance cameras everywhere, in both public and private places. (You'll frequently see signs warning you that you're being filmed.) These cameras have already proved helpful in piecing together the events leading up to an attack, but as Brits trade their privacy for security,

Prime Minister Gordon Brown

Brown, who comes from a humble fishing village in Scotland, was an academic whiz kid who entered the University of Edinburgh at age 16. While he earned a doctorate in history there, politics became his overriding passion—enough to ruin a love affair with a Romanian princess. As he rose through the Labour Party ranks, he gained a reputation as a staid and gruff policy wonk. At first accused by the national press of being shifty-eyed (and therefore untrustworthy), Brown later revealed he was actually blind in his left eye from an old rugby injury.

Brown remained a bachelor well into his forties; his wife, Sarah, (whom he married in 2000) initially preferred to avoid the limelight—which wasn't helping the Browns' popularity. In summer 2009, however, she suddenly came out of hiding, making sure to be photographed at trendy events, and posting daily Twitter updates (in mid-2009, she had 500,000 followers). Of the Browns' three children, one lived only 10 days, and another has been diagnosed with cystic fibrosis—one of the few aspects of Brown's personal life that has garnered him sympathy.

Brown refused to disavow Britain's Iraq involvement, further damaging Labour's popularity. The British media continue to mercilessly lampoon the beleaguered Brown as gloomy, plodding, and boring. As Britain's financial woes persist, it's uncertain how long Brown will hold power. The next general election must be held by June of 2010. Polls suggest that Conservative leader David Cameron has a good chance of taking over 10 Downing Street.

many wonder if they've given up too much.

The terrorist threats have also highlighted issues relating to Britain's large immigrant population (nearly 4 million). Second-generation Muslims—born in Britain, but who strongly identify with other Muslims rather than their British neighbors—were responsible for the July 2005 bombs. Some Brits reacted to the event known as "7/7" as if all the country's Muslims were to blame. At the same time, a handful of radical Islamic clerics began to justify the bombers' violent actions. Unemployment and the economic downturn further stretch the already strained relations between communities within Britain.

The large Muslim population is just one thread in the tapestry of today's Britain. Although nine out of 10 Brits are white, the country has large minority groups, mainly from Britain's former overseas colonies: India, Pakistan, Bangladesh, Africa, the Caribbean, and many other places. But despite the tensions between some groups, for the most part Britain is well-integrated, with minorities represented in most (if not all) walks of life.

Another wave of immigration recently hit Britain. Throughout the British Isles, you'll see lots of Eastern Europeans (mostly Poles, Slovaks, and Lithuanians) working in restaurants, cafés, and B&Bs. These transplants—who started arriving after their home countries joined the EU in 2004—can make a lot more money working here than back home. British small-business owners tell me they find these new arrivals to be polite, responsible, and affordable. And though a few Brits complain that the new arrivals are taking jobs away from the natives, and others are frustrated that their English is often far from perfect, for the most part Britain has gracefully absorbed this new set of immigrants.

Over the past several years, Britain has seen an epidemic of binge-drinking among young people. A 2007 study revealed that one out of every three British men, and one out of every five British women, routinely drinks to excess. It's become commonplace for young adults (typically from their mid-teens to mid-20s) to spend weekend nights drinking at pubs and carousing in the streets. (And they ratchet up the debauchery even more when celebrating a "stag night" or "hen night"—bachelor and bachelorette parties.) While sociologists and politicians scratch their heads about the causes and effects of this phenomenon, tourists are complaining about weekend noise and obnoxious (though generally harmless) young drunks on the streets.

Architecture in Britain

From Stonehenge to Big Ben, travelers are storming castle walls, climbing spiral staircases, and snapping the pictures of 5,000 years of architecture. Let's sort it out.

The oldest ruins—mysterious and prehistoric—date from before Roman times, back to 3000 B.C. The earliest sites, such as Stonehenge and Avebury, were built during the Stone and Bronze ages. The remains from these periods are made of huge stones or mounds of earth, even man-made hills, and were created as celestial calendars and for worship or burial. Britain is crisscrossed with lines of these mysterious sights (ley lines). Iron Age people (600 B.C.–A.D. 50) left desolate stone forts. The Romans thrived in Britain from A.D. 50 to 400, building cities, walls, and roads. Evidence of Roman greatness can be seen in lavish villas with ornate mosaic floors, temples uncovered beneath great English churches, and Roman stones in medieval city walls. Roman roads sliced across the island in straight lines. Today, unusually straight rural roads are very likely laid directly on these ancient roads.

As Rome crumbled in the fifth century, so did Roman Britain. Little architecture survives from Dark Ages England, the Saxon period from 500 to 1000. Architecturally, the light was switched on with the Norman Conquest in 1066. As William earned his title "the Conqueror," his French architects built churches and castles in the European Romanesque style.

English Romanesque is called Norman (1066–1200). Norman churches had round arches, thick walls, and small windows; Durham Cathedral and the Chapel of St. John in the Tower of London are prime examples. You'll see plenty of Norman castles—all built to secure the conquest of these invaders from Normandy. The Tower of London, with its square keep, small windows, and spiral stone stairways, is a typical Norman castle.

Gothic architecture (1200–1600) replaced the heavy Norman style with light, vertical buildings, pointed arches, soaring spires, and bigger windows. English Gothic is divided into three stages. Early English (1200–1300) features tall, simple spires; beautifully carved capitals; and elaborate chapter houses (such as the Wells Cathedral). Decorated Gothic (1300–1400) gets fancier, with more elaborate tracery, bigger windows, and ornately carved pinnacles, as you'll see at Westminster Abbey. Finally, the Perpendicular style (1400–1600, also called "rectilinear") returns to square towers and emphasizes straight, uninterrupted vertical lines from ceiling to floor, with vast windows and exuberant decoration, including fan-vaulted ceilings (King's College Chapel at Cambridge). Through this evolution, the structural ribs (arches meeting at the top of the ceilings) became more and more decorative and fanciful (the fanciest being the star and fan vaulting of the Perpendicular style).

As you tour the great medieval churches of Britain, remember that nearly everything is symbolic. For instance, on the tombs of knights, if the figure has crossed legs, he was a Crusader. If his feet rest on a dog, he died at home; however, if the legs rest on a lion, he died in battle. Local guides and books help us modern pilgrims understand at least a little of what we see.

Wales is particularly rich in English castles, which were needed to subdue the stubborn Welsh. Edward I built a ring of powerful castles in Wales, including Conwy and Caernarfon.

Gothic houses were a simple mix of woven strips of thin wood, rubble, and plaster called wattle and daub. The famous black-and-white Tudor (or half-timbered) look came simply from filling in heavy oak frames with wattle and daub.

The Tudor period (1485–1560) was a time of relative peace (the Wars of the Roses were finally over), prosperity, and renaissance. Henry VIII broke with the Catholic Church and "dissolved" (destroyed) the monasteries, leaving scores of Britain's greatest churches as gutted shells. These hauntingly beautiful abbey ruins (Glastonbury, Tintern, Whitby, Rievaulx, Battle, St. Augustine's in Canterbury, St. Mary's in York, and lots more) surrounded by lush lawns are now pleasant city parks.

A Typical Castle

A castle is a fortified residence for a medieval noble. Castles come in all shapes and sizes. The simplest "motte-and-bailey" castle consists of a stone tower (a keep) on a hill (a motte), surrounded by a wall that enclosed a yard (or bailey). Later castles were much bigger, with more rings of walls, more towers, ingenious booby-traps, and comfy buildings for life during peacetime. Though most castles

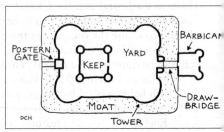

today are ruins, you can mentally reconstruct them if you know the main features. Be aware that you may see several different names for the same thing, depending on the country.

The Keep (or _Donjon_): The heart of the castle complex was a high, strong stone tower that was the lord's home and refuge of last resort. Inside (or nearby) you'd find the Great Hall—the largest room in the castle—serving as throne room, conference center, and dining hall, hosting epic banquets. Upstairs was the solar, the lord's sunlit living room.

The Yard (or Bailey or Ward): Safe within the castle walls was an open courtyard dotted with small half-timbered buildings. In peacetime, knights held jousting tournaments in the yard. During war, when peasants retreated inside the walls for safety, the yard became a mini-village. There was a well and cistern (for crucial water); a kitchen and well-stocked pantry; the chapel; an armory, kennel, and stables; humble cottages for peasants and plusher lodgings for knights; and the garderobe—an outhouse protruding from the wall that emptied into a cesspit.

The Wall: Though the main wall surrounded the inner yard and keep, a castle might also have a series of concentric walls offering more lines of defense and enclosing more yards (e.g., the outer yard or the lower bailey).

Walls were made of ashlar (stone blocks) and stretched like a "curtain wall" between corner towers. The base of the wall might angle out to make it more difficult for invaders to scale the walls. Narrow slits in the walls, called loopholes, allowed soldiers to shoot arrows at the enemy while they remained mostly protected.

Towers: Towers on the castle corners helped shore up the walls and served as lookouts. Inside, they housed chapels, living quarters, or the dungeon. Towers could be square or round (e.g., a drum tower), with either crenellated tops or conical roofs. A turret is a small lookout tower projecting up from the top of the wall, and a bartizan juts out from a corner.

Moat: A ditch circled the wall, often filled with water—but not with crocodiles (despite what you may have seen in cartoons).

Wall Walk (or Allure) and Parapet: Atop the wall was a pathway where guards could patrol and where soldiers stood to fire at the enemy. The soldiers were protected by the parapet, or outer railing of the wall walk. The parapet was studded with stone blocks in a gap-tooth pattern called crenellation. A soldier could hide behind the blocks and shoot through the gaps in between.

Hoardings and Machicolation: Wooden huts called hoardings were built onto the upper parts of the stone walls. They served as watch towers, living quarters, and fighting platforms. A machicolation was a stone ledge jutting out from the wall, fitted with holes in the bottom. If the enemy was scaling the walls, soldiers could drop rocks or boiling oil down through the holes and onto the enemy below.

Gatehouse or Barbican: The castle's main entrance had a variety of ways to control entry. A barbican—a fortified, second gatehouse—might stand outside the castle walls to protect the main gate. In case of attack, a drawbridge could be raised, using counterweights or a chain-and-winch. A heavy iron grill called a portcullis could be lowered across the entrance. If the enemy made it into the gatehouse, soldiers could pour boiling water on them through "murder holes" in the ceiling.

Castles also had a smaller, low-profile postern gate around the side. In peacetime, peasants used this unfortified entrance; in wartime, it became the "sally-port" to launch surprise attacks, or to serve as an escape route.

The Besiegers: Before the era of gunpowder, an attacker's main weapon against a big castle was patience—the siege. Armies surrounded the castle, blocked off all supplies, and waited for the enemy to surrender.

They could also attack by undermining ("sapping") the walls, scaling the walls with ladders, or knocking down the gates with a battering ram—a large log suspended with ropes and swung against the door. A siege tower (or belfry) was a wooden tower on wheels that could be rolled to the castle walls and used like a giant fortified ladder. Catapults such as the mighty trebuchet could hurl a one-ton boulder over the walls.

What We Don't See: Because most castles are old and ruined, we don't see the half-timbered cottages and wooden structures that once fleshed out the stone castles. Look for square holes in ruined walls that once held the beams supporting the wooden floors. We don't see the whitewashed walls, the frescoes, the tapestries used for insulation, shields with coats-of-arms, or the colorful banners that once flew atop towers. We don't see the knights on horseback, troubadours in tights, ladies in cone-shaped hats, earthy peasants, friars in brown robes, or angry soldiers atop the walls, hurling curses at the enemy.

Although few churches were built during the Tudor period, this was a time of house and mansion construction. Heating a home was becoming popular and affordable, and Tudor buildings featured small square windows and many chimneys. In towns, where land was scarce, many Tudor houses grew up and out, getting wider with each overhanging floor.

The Elizabethan and Jacobean periods (1560–1620) were followed by the English Renaissance style (1620–1720). English architects mixed Gothic and classical styles, then Baroque and classical styles. Although the ornate Baroque never really grabbed Britain, the classical style of the Italian architect Andrea Palladio did. Inigo Jones (1573–1652), Christopher Wren (1632–1723), and those they inspired plastered Britain with enough columns, domes, and symmetry to please a Caesar. The Great Fire of London (1666) cleared the way for an ambitious young Wren to put his mark on London forever with a grand rebuilding scheme, including the great St. Paul's Cathedral and more than 50 other churches.

The celebrants of the Boston Tea Party remember Britain's Georgian period (1720–1840) for its lousy German kings. Georgian architecture was rich and showed off by being very classical. Grand ornamental doorways, fine cast-ironwork on balconies and railings, Chippendale furniture, and white-on-blue Wedgwood ceramics graced rich homes everywhere. John Wood Sr. and Jr. led the way, giving the trendsetting city of Bath its crescents and circles of aristocratic Georgian row houses. "Georgian" is English for "Neoclassical."

The Industrial Revolution shaped the Victorian period (1840–1890) with glass, steel, and iron. Britain had a huge new erector set (so did France's Mr. Eiffel). This was also a Romantic period, reviving the "more Christian" Gothic style. London's Houses of Parliament are Neo-Gothic—just 100 years old but looking 700, except for the telltale modern precision and craftsmanship. Whereas Gothic was stone or concrete, Neo-Gothic was often red brick. These were Britain's glory days, and there was more building in this period than in all previous ages combined.

The architecture of modern times obeys the formula "form follows function"—it worries more about your needs than your eyes. Britain treasures its heritage and takes great pains to build tastefully in historic districts and to preserve its many "listed" buildings. With a vital tourist trade, these quaint reminders of its past—and ours—are becoming a valuable part of the British economy.

Typical Church Architecture

History comes to life when you visit a medieval church. Knowing a few simple terms will enrich your experience. Note that not every church will have every feature, and a "cathedral" isn't a type of church architecture, but rather a governing center for a local bishop.

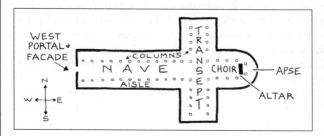

Aisles: The long, generally low-ceilinged arcades that flank the nave.

Altar: The raised area with a ceremonial table (often adorned with candles or a crucifix), where the priest prepares and serves the bread and wine for Communion.

Apse: The space beyond the altar, generally bordered with small chapels.

Choir: A cozy area, often screened off, located within the church nave and near the high altar where services are sung in a more intimate setting.

Cloister: A square-shaped series of hallways surrounding an open-air courtyard, traditionally where monks and nuns got fresh air.

Facade: The outer wall of the church's main (west) entrance, viewable from outside and generally highly decorated.

Groin Vault: An arched ceiling formed where two equal barrel vaults meet at right angles. Less common usage: term for a medieval jock strap.

Narthex: The area (portico or foyer) between the main entry and the nave.

Nave: The long, central section of the church (running west to east, from the entrance to the altar) where the congregation stood through the service.

Transept: The north–south part of the church, which crosses (perpendicularly) the east–west nave. In a traditional Latin cross-shaped floor plan, the transept forms the "arms" of the cross.

West Portal: The main entry to the church (on the west end, opposite the main altar).

British TV

Although it has its share of lowbrow reality programming, much British television is still so good—and so British—that it deserves a mention as a sightseeing treat. After a hard day of castle climbing, watch the telly over tea in the living room of your village B&B.

There are currently five free channels that any television can receive. BBC-1 and BBC-2 are government-regulated and commercial-free. Broadcasting of these two channels (and of the five BBC radio stations) is funded by a mandatory £142-per-year-per-household television and radio license (hmmm, 65 cents per day to escape commercials and public-broadcasting pledge drives). Channels 3, 4, and 5 are privately owned, a little more lowbrow, and have commercials—but those commercials are often clever and sophisticated, providing a fun look at British life. In addition, about 85 percent of households now receive digital cable or satellite television, which offer dozens of specialty channels, similar to those available in North America.

Like the US, Britain is joining the Digital Age, gradually converting its TV signals to digital-only, which requires a digitally equipped set or a converter. By 2013, the old analog signals will be switched off and only digital signals will be broadcast.

Whereas California "accents" fill our airwaves 24 hours a day, homogenizing the way our country speaks, Britain protects and promotes its regional accents by its choice of TV and radio announcers. Ask a local to help you figure out where each person is from.

Commercial-free British TV, though looser than it used to be, is still careful about what it airs and when. But after the 21:00 "watershed" hour, when children are expected to be in bed, some nudity and profanity is allowed, and may cause you to spill your tea.

American programs (such as *Mad Men, Lost, Oprah,* and trash-talk shows) are very popular. The visiting viewer should be sure to tune the TV to a few typical British shows, including a dose of British situation- and political-comedy fun, and the top-notch BBC evening news. British comedies have tickled the American funny bone for years, from sketch comedy *(Monty Python's Flying Circus)* to sitcoms *(Are You Being Served?, Fawlty Towers,* and *Absolutely Fabulous).* A more recent cross-the-pond mega-hit, *The Office,* has made its star Ricky Gervais *the* top name in British comedy today, and has spawned successful adaptations in the US, Germany, France, and French Canada. Quiz shows and reality shows are taken very seriously here *(Who Wants to Be a Millionaire?, American Idol,* and *Dancing with the Stars* are all based on British shows). Jonathan Ross is the David Letterman of Britain for sometimes-edgy late-night talk. For a tear-filled, slice-of-life taste of British soaps dealing in all the controversial issues, watch the popular *Emmerdale, Coronation Street,* or *EastEnders.*

APPENDIX

Contents

Tourist Information

Tourist Information Offices

The **Visit Britain** office in the US is a wealth of knowledge. Check it out: tel. 800-462-2748, www.visitbritain.com, travelinfo @visitbritain.org. Request free maps of London and Britain and any specific information you may want (such as regional information, a garden-tour map, urban cultural activities brochures, and so on). The phone line is mainly intended as a customer service number for their online shop, and isn't staffed (but they do check their messages). For most questions, it's best to enquire by email.

Also try these official tourism board websites: www.visit england.com, www.visitwales.com, and www.visitscotland.com.

In Great Britain, your best first stop in every town is generally the **tourist information office**—abbreviated **TI** in this book. (The **Britain and London Visitors Centre** in London is particularly good—see page 46.) A TI is a great place to get a city map, advice on public transportation (including bus and train schedules), walking-tour information, information on special events, and recommendations for nightlife. For all the help TIs offer, steer clear of their room-finding services (bloated prices, booking fee up to £4, no opinions, and they take a 10 percent cut from your B&B host). Many TIs have information on the entire country or at least the region, so try to pick up maps for destinations you'll be visiting later in your trip. If you're arriving in town after the TI closes, call ahead or pick up a map in a neighboring town.

Communicating

Telephones

Smart travelers use the telephone daily to book or reconfirm rooms, get tourist information, reserve restaurants, confirm tour times, or phone home. This section covers dialing instructions, phone cards, and types of phones.

In sum, the cheapest way to go is to buy an international phone card in Britain and make your calls from hotel-room phones or mobile phones, but not pay phones. The handiest—though pricier—way to make calls is by using a mobile phone (brought from home or purchased in Britain).

How to Dial

Calling from the US to Britain, or vice versa, is simple—once you break the code. The European calling chart in this chapter will walk you through it.

Dialing Domestically Within Britain

Britain, like much of the US, uses an area-code dialing system. If you're dialing within an area code, you just dial the local number to be connected; but if you're calling outside your area code, you have to dial both the area code (which starts with a 0) and the local number.

Area codes are listed in this book and by city on phone-booth walls, and are available from directory assistance (dial 118-500, 64p/min). It's most expensive to call within Britain between 8:00 and 13:00, and cheapest between 17:00 and 8:00. Still, a short call across the country is inexpensive, so don't hesitate to call long distance.

Dialing Internationally

To make an international call, follow these steps:

1. Dial the international access code (00 if you're calling from Britain, 011 from the US or Canada).

2. Dial the country code of the country you're calling (see the European calling chart).

The British Accent

In the olden days, a British person's accent indicated his or her social standing. Eliza Doolittle had the right idea—elocution could make or break you. Wealthier families would send their kids to fancy private schools to learn proper pronunciation. But these days, in a sort of reverse snobbery that has gripped the nation, accents are back. Politicians, newscasters, and movie stars have been favoring deep accents over the Queen's English. While it's hard for American ears to pick out all of the variations, most Brits can determine where a person is from based on their accent...not just the region, but often the village, and even the part of a town.

3. Dial the area code and the local number, keeping in mind that if you're calling Britain, you must drop the initial zero of the area code (the European calling chart lists specifics per country).

Calling from the US to Britain: To call from the US to a recommended London hotel, dial 011 (the US's international access code), 44 (Britain's country code), 20 (London's area code without its initial 0), then 7730-8191 (the hotel's number).

Calling from Britain to the US: To call from London to my office in Edmonds, Washington, I dial 00 (Europe's international access code), 1 (US country code), 425 (Edmonds' area code), and 771-8303.

Note: You might see a + in front of a European number. When dialing the number, replace the + with the international access code of the country you're calling from (00 from Europe, 011 from the US or Canada).

Public Phones

To make calls from public phones, you'll need a lot of coins (Britain doesn't use insertable phone cards, and calls are pricey). Even pre-paid international phone cards, described on page 704, are prohibitively expensive on public phones.

Hotel Room Phones

In-room phones are rare in B&Bs, but if you do have a phone in the room, put it to use for local calls, which are likely cheap (ask for the rates at the front desk first). However, these phones are often a rip-off for long-distance calls, unless you use an international phone card (explained later). Incoming calls are free, making this a cheap way for friends and family to stay in touch (provided they have a good long-distance plan for calls to Europe—and a list of your hotels' phone numbers).

European Calling Chart

Just smile and dial, using this key:
AC = Area Code, LN = Local Number.

European Country	Calling long distance within ...	Calling from the US or Canada to ...	Calling from a European country to ...
Austria	AC + LN	011 + 43 + AC (without the initial zero) + LN	00 + 43 + AC (without the initial zero) + LN
Belgium	LN	011 + 32 + LN (without initial zero)	00 + 32 + LN (without initial zero)
Bosnia-Herzegovina	AC + LN	011 + 387 + AC (without initial zero) + LN	00 + 387 + AC (without initial zero) + LN
Britain	AC + LN	011 + 44 + AC (without initial zero) + LN	00 + 44 + AC (without initial zero) + LN
Croatia	AC + LN	011 + 385 + AC (without initial zero) + LN	00 + 385 + AC (without initial zero) + LN
Czech Republic	LN	011 + 420 + LN	00 + 420 + LN
Denmark	LN	011 + 45 + LN	00 + 45 + LN
Estonia	LN	011 + 372 + LN	00 + 372 + LN
Finland	AC + LN	011 + 358 + AC (without initial zero) + LN	999 + 358 + AC (without initial zero) + LN
France	LN	011 + 33 + LN (without initial zero)	00 + 33 + LN (without initial zero)
Germany	AC + LN	011 + 49 + AC (without initial zero) + LN	00 + 49 + AC (without initial zero) + LN
Gibraltar	LN	011 + 350 + LN	00 + 350 + LN
Greece	LN	011 + 30 + LN	00 + 30 + LN
Hungary	06 + AC + LN	011 + 36 + AC + LN	00 + 36 + AC + LN
Ireland	AC + LN	011 + 353 + AC (without initial zero) + LN	00 + 353 + AC (without initial zero) + LN
Italy	LN	011 + 39 + LN	00 + 39 + LN

European Country	Calling long distance within ...	Calling from the US or Canada to ...	Calling from a European country to ...
Montenegro	AC + LN	011 + 382 + AC (without initial zero) + LN	00 + 382 + AC (without initial zero) + LN
Morocco	LN	011 + 212 + LN (without initial zero)	00 + 212 + LN (without initial zero)
Netherlands	AC + LN	011 + 31 + AC (without initial zero) + LN	00 + 31 + AC (without initial zero) + LN
Norway	LN	011 + 47 + LN	00 + 47 + LN
Poland	LN	011 + 48 + LN (without initial zero)	00 + 48 + LN (without initial zero)
Portugal	LN	011 + 351 + LN	00 + 351 + LN
Slovakia	AC + LN	011 + 421 + AC (without initial zero) + LN	00 + 421 + AC (without initial zero) + LN
Slovenia	AC + LN	011 + 386 + AC (without initial zero) + LN	00 + 386 + AC (without initial zero) + LN
Spain	LN	011 + 34 + LN	00 + 34 + LN
Sweden	AC + LN	011 + 46 + AC (without initial zero) + LN	00 + 46 + AC (without initial zero) + LN
Switzerland	LN	011 + 41 + LN (without initial zero)	00 + 41 + LN (without initial zero)
Turkey	AC (if no initial zero is included, add one) + LN	011 + 90 + AC (without initial zero) + LN	00 + 90 + AC (without initial zero) + LN

APPENDIX

- The instructions above apply whether you're calling a land line or mobile phone.
- The international access codes (the first numbers you dial when making an international call) are 011 if you're calling from the US or Canada, or 00 if you're calling from virtually anywhere in Europe (except Finland, where it's 999).
- To call the US or Canada from Europe, dial 00, then 1 (the country code for the US and Canada), then the area code and number. In short, 00 + 1 + AC + LN = Hi, Mom!

Mobile Phones

For most travelers in Britain, a mobile phone is the best option for making calls (if you need more in-depth information than is provided below, see www.ricksteves.com/phones).

Using Your US Mobile Phone: Your US mobile phone works in Britain if it's GSM-enabled, tri-band or quad-band, and on a calling plan that includes international calls. For example, with a T-Mobile phone, you'll pay $1 per minute to make or receive a call and about $0.35 to send a text message.

You can save money if your phone is electronically "unlocked"—then you can simply buy a **SIM card** (a fingernail-sized chip that stores the phone's information) in Britain. SIM cards, which give you a British phone number, are sold at mobile-phone stores and some newsstand kiosks for £3–10. When you buy the card, you'll also get some prepaid calling time (£15 gives you about 30 minutes). Simply insert the SIM card in your phone (usually in a slot behind the battery), and it'll work like a British mobile phone. When buying a SIM card, always ask about fees for domestic and international calls, roaming charges, and how to check your credit balance and buy more time. To call home, save money by using an international calling card (described below).

Many **smartphones,** such as the iPhone or BlackBerry, work in Britain—but beware of sky-high fees, especially for data down-loading (checking email, browsing the Internet, watching videos, and so on). Ask your provider in advance how to avoid unwittingly "roaming" your way to a huge bill. Some applications allow for cheap or free smartphone calls over a Wi-Fi connection (described later, under "Calling over the Internet").

Using a British Mobile Phone: Local mobile-phone shops all over Britain sell basic phones for around £30–60 (as low as £10 at Carphone Warehouse chain stores). You'll also need to buy a SIM card (explained above) and prepaid credit for making calls. If you remain in the phone's home country, domestic calls are reasonable, and incoming calls are generally free. You'll pay more if you're "roaming" in another country. If your phone is "unlocked," you can swap out its SIM card for a new one when you travel to other countries.

International Phone Cards

These cards are the cheapest way to make international calls from Britain (less than $0.10 a minute to the US; they also work for local calls). There's a catch: British Telecom charges a hefty surcharge for using international calling cards from a pay phone (so instead of 100 minutes for a £5 card, you'll get less than 10 minutes—a miserable deal). But they're still a good deal if you use them when calling from a mobile phone or fixed line (e.g., a hotel-room phone;

ask at the desk if they charge any fees for toll-free calls). The cards are sold all over; look for them at newsstand kiosks and hole-in-the-wall long-distance shops. Ask the clerk which one has the best rates for calls to America. Because cards are occasionally duds, avoid the high denominations. These cards usually work only in the country where they're purchased (unless otherwise noted on the card).

US Calling Cards: These cards, such as the ones offered by AT&T, Verizon, and Sprint, are the worst option. You'll almost always save a lot of money by using a British international calling card instead.

Calling over the Internet

Some things that seem too good to be true...actually are true. If you're traveling with a laptop, you can make calls using **VoIP (Voice over Internet Protocol).** With VoIP, two computers act as the phones, and the Internet-based calls are free (or you can pay a few cents to call from your computer to a telephone). The major providers are Skype (www.skype.com) and Google Talk (www.google.com/talk).

Useful Phone Numbers

Understand the various prefixes—numbers starting with 09 are telephone-sex–type expensive. Numbers that begin with 0800 are toll-free, but numbers with prefixes of 0845, 0870, and 0871 cost around 10p per minute. If you have questions about a prefix, call 100 for free help.

Embassies and Consulates

US Consulate and Embassy: tel. 020/7499-9000, passport info tel. 020/7894-0563, passport services available Mon–Fri 8:30–11:30, plus Mon, Wed, Fri 14:00–16:00 (24 Grosvenor Square, London, Tube: Bond Street, www.usembassy.org.uk)
Canadian High Commission: tel. 020/7258-6600, passport services available Mon–Fri 9:30–13:30 (Trafalgar Square, London, Tube: Charing Cross, www.unitedkingdom.gc.ca)

Emergency Needs
Police and Ambulance: tel. 999

Dialing Assistance
Operator Assistance: tel. 100 (free)
Directory Assistance: tel. 118-500 (64p/min, plus 23p/min connection charge from fixed lines)
International Directory Assistance: tel. 118-505 (£1.99/min, plus 69p connection charge)

Travel Advisories

US Department of State: US tel. 202/647-5225, www.travel.state.gov

Canadian Department of Foreign Affairs: Canadian tel. 800-267-6788, www.dfait-maeci.gc.ca

US Centers for Disease Control and Prevention: US tel. 800-CDC-INFO (800-232-4636), www.cdc.gov/travel

Trains and Buses

Train information for trips within Britain: tel. 0845-748-4950, overseas tel. 011-44-20-7278-5240 (www.nationalrail.co.uk)

Eurostar (Chunnel Info): tel. 0870-518-6186 (www.eurostar.com)

Trains to all points in Europe: tel. 0870-584-8848 (www.raileurope.com)

National Express Buses: tel. 0871-781-8181 (www.nationalexpress.com)

Airports

For online information on the first three airports, check www.baa.co.uk.

Heathrow (flight info): tel. 0870-000-0123

Gatwick (general info): tel. 0870-000-2468 for all airlines, except British Airways—tel. 0870-551-1155 (flights) or 0870-850-9850 (booking)

Stansted (general info): tel. 0870-000-0303

Luton (general info): tel. 01582/405-100 (www.london-luton.com)

London City: tel. 020/7646-0088 (www.londoncityairport.com)

Airlines

Aer Lingus: UK tel. 0870-876-5000, US tel. 800-474-7424 (www.aerlingus.ie)

Air Canada: tel. 0871-220-1111 (www.aircanada.ca)

Alitalia: tel. 0871-424-1424 (www.alitalia.com)

American: tel. 0845-778-9789 (www.aa.com)

bmi: reservations tel. 0870-607-0555, flight info tel. 020/8745-7321 (www.flybmi.com)

British Airways: reservations tel. 0844-493-0787, flight info tel. 0844-493-0777 (www.ba.com)

Brussels Airlines: UK toll tel. 0905-609-5609, 40p/min, US tel. 516/740-5200 (www.brusselsairlines.com)

Continental Airlines: tel. 0845-607-6760 (www.continental.com)

easyJet: tel. 0871-244-2366 (www.easyjet.com)

KLM Royal Dutch/Northwest Airlines: tel. 0870-507-4074 (www.klm.com)

Lufthansa: tel. 0871-945-9747 (www.lufthansa.com)

Ryanair: tel. 0871-246-0000 (www.ryanair.com)

Scandinavian Airlines (SAS): tel. 0871-521-2772 (www.flysas.com)

United Airlines: tel. 0845-844-4777 (www.unitedairlines.co.uk)

US Airways: tel. 0845-600-3300 (www.usair.com)

Heathrow Airport Car-Rental Agencies

Avis: tel. 0844-544-6000 (www.avis.co.uk)

Budget: tel. 0844-544-4600 (www.budget.co.uk)

Enterprise: tel. 020/8897-2100 (www.enterprise.co.uk)

Europcar: tel. 020/8564-3500 (www.europcar.co.uk)

Hertz: tel. 0870-846-0006 (www.hertz.co.uk)

National: tel. 0870-400-4581 (www.nationalcar.co.uk)

The Internet

The Internet can be an invaluable tool for planning your trip (researching and booking hotels, checking bus and train sched-

ules, and so on). It's also useful to get online periodically while you travel—to reconfirm your trip plans, check the weather, catch up on email, blog or post photos from your trip, or call folks back home (explained earlier, under "Calling over the Internet").

Some hotels offer a computer in the lobby with Internet access for guests. Smaller B&Bs may sometimes let you sit at the front desk for a few minutes just to check your email, if you ask politely. If you're traveling with a laptop, see if your hotel has Wi-Fi (wireless Internet access) or a port in your room where you can plug in a cable to get online. Most hotels offer Internet access and/or Wi-Fi for free; others charge a fee.

If your hotel doesn't have access, ask your hotelier to direct you to the nearest place to get online. Most of the towns where I've listed accommodations in this book also have Internet cafés. Many libraries offer free access, but they also tend to have limited opening hours, restrict your online time to 30 minutes, and may require reservations.

Mail

Get stamps at the neighborhood post office, newsstands within fancy hotels, and some mini-marts and card shops. You can arrange for mail delivery to your hotel (allow 10 days for a letter to arrive), but phoning and emailing are so easy that I've dispensed with mail stops altogether.

Transportation

By Car or Train?

Cars are best for three or more traveling together (especially families with small kids), those packing heavy, and those scouring the countryside. Trains and buses are best for solo travelers, blitz tourists, and city-to-city travelers. While a car gives you the ultimate in mobility and freedom, enables you to search for hotels more easily, and carries your bags for you, the train zips you effortlessly from city to city, usually dropping you in the center and near the TI.

Britain has a great train-and-bus system, and travelers who don't want (or can't afford) to drive a rental car can enjoy an excellent tour using public transportation. Britain's 100-mph train system is one of Europe's best. Buses pick you up when the trains let you down.

In Britain, my choice is to connect big cities by train, and to explore rural areas (the Cotswolds, North Wales, the Lake District, and the Highlands) footloose and fancy-free by rental car. The mix works quite efficiently (e.g., London, Bath, Edinburgh, and York by train, with a rental car for the rest). You might consider a BritRail & Drive Pass, which gives you various combinations of rail days and car days to use within two months' time.

Deals on Rails, Wheels, and Wings in Britain

Regular tickets on Britain's great train system (15,000 departures from 2,400 stations daily) are the most expensive per mile in all of Europe. Those who save the most are those who book in advance, leave after rush hour (after 9:30), or ride the bus. Now that Britain has privatized its railways, it can be tricky to track down all your options; a single bus or train route can be operated by several companies. However, one British website covers all train lines (www.nationalrail.co.uk), and another covers all bus and train routes in Britain (www.traveline.org.uk). Another good resource, which has schedules for trains throughout Europe, is German Rail's timetable (http://bahn.hafas.de/bin/query.exe/en).

As with airline tickets, British train tickets can have many different prices for the same journey. A clerk at any station can figure out the cheapest fare for your trip (or call the helpful National Rail folks at tel. 0845-748-4950, 24 hours daily). Savings can be significant. For a London–Edinburgh round-trip (standard class), if you book the day of departure for travel after 9:30, it's £108; the cheapest fare, booked a couple of months in advance as two one-way tickets, is £37.

Though not required on British trains, reservations are free, and a good idea for long journeys or any train travel on Sunday.

Public Transportation Routes in Britain

MAP NOT TO SCALE

London Airports
- **A** Heathrow
- **B** Gatwick
- **C** Luton
- **D** Stansted
- **E** London City

— RAIL
═ EUROSTAR
--- BUS
⋯⋯ FERRY w/ CROSSING TIME (6H)
✈ AIRPORT

Railpasses

Prices listed are for 2009 and are subject to change. For the latest prices, details, and train schedules (and easy online ordering), see my comprehensive *Guide to Eurail Passes* at www.ricksteves.com/rail.

"Standard" is the polite British term for "second" class. "Senior" refers to those age 60 and up. No senior discounts for standard class. "Youth" means under age 26. For each adult or senior BritRail or BritRail England pass you buy, one child (5–15) can travel free with you (ask for the "**Family Pass,**" not available with all passes). Additional kids pay the normal half-adult rate. Kids under 5 travel free.

Note: Overnight journeys begun on the final night of your pass can be completed the day after your pass expires—only BritRail allows this trick. A bunk in a twin sleeper costs $75.

BRITRAIL CONSECUTIVE PASS

	Adult 1st Class	Adult Standard	Senior 1st Class	Youth 1st Class	Youth Standard
3 consec. days	$305	$199	$259	$245	$159
4 consec. days	379	249	319	305	199
8 consec. days	535	359	455	425	285
15 consec. days	799	535	679	639	425
22 consec. days	1015	675	859	809	539
1 month	1195	795	1015	955	635

BRITRAIL FLEXIPASS

	Adult 1st Class	Adult Standard	Senior 1st Class	Youth 1st Class	Youth Standard
3 days in 2 months	$375	$255	$319	$299	$205
4 days in 2 months	465	315	399	375	249
8 days in 2 months	679	459	579	545	365
15 days in 2 months	1025	689	869	819	555

BRITRAIL & DRIVE PASS

Any 4 rail days and 2 car days in 2 months.

	1st Class	Standard Class	Extra Car Day
Mini	$546	$382	$44
Economy	553	389	51
Compact	562	398	60
Compact Auto	592	428	90
Intermed. Auto	605	441	103
Minivan Auto	682	518	180

Prices are per person, two traveling together. Third and fourth persons sharing car buy a regular BritRail pass. To order a Rail & Drive pass, call Rail Europe at 800-438-7245. *Not sold by Europe Through the Back Door.*

Map key:

Approximate point-to-point one-way standard-class fares in US dollars by rail (solid line) and bus (dashed line). First class costs 50 percent more. Add up fares for your itinerary to see whether a railpass will save you money.

BRITRAIL ENGLAND CONSECUTIVE PASS

	Adult 1st Class	Adult Standard	Senior 1st Class	Youth 1st Class	Youth Standard
3 consec. days	$239	$159	$205	$195	$129
4 consec. days	$299	$199	$255	$239	$159
8 consec. days	$429	$285	$365	$345	$229
15 consec. days	$645	$429	$549	$515	$345
22 consec. days	$815	$545	$695	$649	$435
1 month	$959	$639	$815	$765	$515

Covers travel only in England, not Scotland, Wales, or Ireland.

BRITRAIL ENGLAND FLEXIPASS

Type of Pass	Adult 1st Class	Adult Standard	Senior 1st Class	Youth 1st Class	Youth Standard
3 days in 2 months	$305	$205	$259	$245	$165
4 days in 2 months	$379	$255	$319	$305	$205
8 days in 2 months	$549	$369	$465	$439	$295
15 days in 2 months	$819	$549	$699	$655	$439

Covers travel only in England, not Scotland, Wales, or Ireland.

BRITRAIL LONDON PLUS PASS

	Adult 1st Class	Adult Standard
2 out of 8 days	$209	$139
4 out of 8 days	289	225
7 out of 15 days	369	269

Covers much of SE England (see London Plus Coverage Map at www.ricksteves.com/rail). Includes vouchers to cover two trips on the Heathrow, Stansted, or Gatwick Express, separate from your counted travel days, which can be used up to 6 months after validating pass. Many trains are standard class only. The 7 p.m. rule for night trains does not apply. Kids 5–15 half price; under 5 free.

BRITRAIL SCOTTISH FREEDOM PASS

4 out of 8 days	$235
8 out of 15 days	315

Valid in Scotland only, standard class only. Not valid on trains that depart before 9:15am, Mon–Fri. Covers Caledonian MacBrayne and Strathclyde ferry service to Scotland's most popular islands. Discounts on some P&O ferries, some Citylink buses & more. Kids 5–15 half fare; under 5 free.

BRITRAIL PASS PLUS IRELAND

	First Class	Standard Class
5 days in 1 month	$699	$469
10 days in 1 month	1245	839

Covers the entire British Isles (England, Wales, Scotland, Northern Ireland, and the Republic of Ireland). No longer covers ferries. Kids 5-15 pay half fare; under 5 free. No Family Pass, Party Pass, Eurail Discount, nor Off-Peak Special. Consider the cost of separate BritRail and Ireland passes.

Make them at any train station before 18:00 on the day before you travel.

Buying Train Tickets in Advance: The best fares go to those who book their trips well in advance of their journey. (While only a 7-day minimum advance booking is officially required for the cheapest fares, these go fast—especially in summer—so a 6–8 week advance booking is often necessary.) Keep in mind that when booking in advance, return (round-trip) fares are not always cheaper than buying two single (one-way) tickets. Also note that cheap advance tickets often come with the toughest refund restrictions, so be sure to nail down your travel plans before you reserve. To book ahead, you can go to any station, book online at www.nationalrail.co.uk, or call 0845-748-4950 (from the US, call 011-44-20-7278-5240, phone answered 24 hours) to find out the schedule and best fare for your journey; then you'll be referred to the appropriate number to call—depending on the particular rail company—to book your ticket. If you order online, be sure you know what you want; it's tough to reach a person who can change your online reservation. You'll pick up your ticket at the station (unless your order was lost—this service still has some glitches). If you want your ticket mailed to you in the US, you need to allow a couple of weeks and cover the shipping costs. (BritRail passholders, however, cannot use the Web to make reservations.)

Buying Train Tickets en Route: If you'd rather have the flexibility of booking tickets as you go, you can save a few pounds by buying a round-trip ticket, called a "return ticket" (a same-day round-trip, called a "day return," is particularly cheap); buying before 18:00 the day before you depart; traveling after the morning rush hour (this usually means after 9:30 Mon–Fri); and going standard class instead of first class. Preview your options at www.nationalrail.co.uk or www.thetrainline.com.

Senior, Youth, and Family Deals: To get a third off the price of most point-to-point rail tickets, seniors can buy a Senior Railcard (for age 60 and above) and young people can buy a Young Persons Railcard (for ages 16–25, or for full-time students 26 and above with a valid ISIC card). A Family Railcard allows adults to travel cheaper (about 33 percent) while their kids ages 5–15 receive a 60 percent discount for most trips (maximum of 4 adults and 4 kids, www.family-railcard.co.uk). Each card costs £26; see www.railcard.co.uk. These cards are all valid for a year on virtually all trains except special runs such as the Heathrow Express and Eurostar (fill out application at station, brochures on racks in info center, need to show passport). Youths also need to submit a passport-type photo for the Young Persons card.

Railpasses: Consider getting a railpass. The BritRail pass

Sample Train Journey

Here is a typical example of a personalized train schedule printed out by Britain's train stations. At the Llandudno Junction station in North Wales, I told the clerk I wanted to leave after 14:00 for Moreton-in-Marsh in the Cotswolds.

Stations	Arrive	Depart	Class
Llandudno Junction	—	15:27	Standard
Shrewsbury	17:15	17:22	Standard
Wolverhampton	17:58	18:18	Standard
Oxford	19:46	20:21	Standard
Moreton-in-Marsh	20:57	—	

Even though the trip involved three transfers, this schedule allowed me to easily navigate the rails.

Train departures are listed on overhead boards at the station by their final destination (note that your destination could be an intermediate stop on this route and not listed on the overhead). It's helpful to ask at the info desk—or any conductor—for the final destination of your next train so you'll be able to figure out quickly which platform it's departing from. Upon arrival at Wolverhampton, I looked for "Oxford" on the station's overhead train schedule to determine where to catch my train to Moreton-in-Marsh.

Often the conductor on your previous train can even tell you the platform your next train will depart from, but it's wise to confirm.

Lately Britain's train system has experienced a lot of delays, causing more and more travelers to miss their connections. Don't schedule your connections too tightly if you need to be at your destination at a specific time.

comes in "consecutive day" and "flexi" versions, with price breaks for youths, seniors, off-season travelers, and groups of three or more. Most allow one child under 16 to travel free with a paying adult. If you're exploring Britain's backcountry with a BritRail pass, standard class is a good choice since many of the smaller train lines don't even offer first-class cars. BritRail passes cover England as well as Scotland and Wales.

More BritRail options include England-only passes, Scotland-only passes, Britain/Ireland passes, "London Plus" passes (good for travel in most of southeast England but not in London itself), and BritRail & Drive passes (which offer you some rail days and some car-rental days). These BritRail passes, as well as Eurailpasses, get you a discount on the Eurostar train that zips you to continental Europe under the English Channel. These passes are sold outside

of Europe only. For specifics, contact your travel agent or see www
.ricksteves.com/rail.

Buses: Although buses are about a third slower than trains,
they're also a lot cheaper. Round-trip bus tickets usually cost less
than two one-way fares (e.g., London–York one-way costs £26;
round-trip costs £36). And buses go many places that trains don't.
Budget travelers can save a wad with a bus pass. The National
Express sells Brit Xplorer bus passes for unlimited travel on consecutive days (£79/7 days, £139/14 days, £219/28 days, sold over
the counter, non-UK passport required, tel. 0871-781-8181, www
.nationalexpress.com). Check their website to learn about online
Funfare deals; senior/youth/family cards and fares; and discounts
for advance booking.

If you want to take a bus from your last destination to the
nearest airport, you'll find that National Express often offers airport buses. Bus stations are normally at or near train stations (in
London, the bus station is a block southwest of Victoria Station).
The British distinguish between "buses" (for in-city travel with lots
of stops) and "coaches" (long-distance cross-country runs).

A couple of companies offer **backpackers' bus circuits.** These
hop-on, hop-off bus circuits take mostly youth hostellers around
the country super-cheap and easy with the assumption that they'll
be sleeping in the hostels along the way. For instance, **Backpacker
Tours** offers one- to 19-day excursions through England and other
destinations in Great Britain (from about £65/1 day, £90/3 days,
£266/5 days, tel. 0870-745-1046, www.backpackertours.co.uk,
sales@backpackertours.co.uk).

Renting a Car

To rent a car in Britain, you must be at least 23 years old and have
a valid license. An International Driving Permit is recommended,
but not required, if your driver's license has been renewed within
the last year ($15 through your local AAA, plus two passport pho-
tos, www.aaa.com); however, I've frequently rented cars in Britain
and traveled problem-free with just my US license.

Drivers under age 25 may incur a young-driver surcharge,
and some rental companies do not rent to anyone 75 and over. If
you're considered too young or old, look into leasing, which has
less-stringent age restrictions (see "Leasing," later).

Research car rentals before you go. It's cheapest to arrange
most car rentals from the US. Call several companies and look
online to compare rates, or arrange a rental through your hometown travel agent. Two reputable companies among many are
Auto Europe (www.autoeurope.com) and Europe by Car (www
.ebctravel.com). For the best deal, rent by the week with unlimited
mileage (but for long trips, consider leasing). To save money on

gas, ask for a diesel car.

I normally rent the smallest, least-expensive model with a stick-shift. Almost all rentals are manual by default, so if you need an automatic, you must request one in advance; beware that these cars are usually larger models (not as maneuverable on narrow, winding roads). An automatic transmission adds about 50 percent to the car-rental cost over a manual transmission. But weigh this against the fact that in Britain you'll be sitting on the right side of the car, and shifting with your left hand...while driving on the left side of the road. The floor pedals are in the same locations as in the US, and the gears are found in the same basic "H" pattern as at home (i.e., first gear, second, etc.).

Expect to pay about $750 per person (based on 2 people sharing the car) for a small economy car for three weeks with unlimited mileage, including gas, parking, and insurance. Consider leasing (described later) to save money on insurance and taxes. I normally rent a small, inexpensive model like a Ford Fiesta. For a bigger, roomier, more powerful but inexpensive car, move up to a Ford Focus or VW Polo. Minibuses are a great budget way to go for five to nine people.

Compare pick-up costs (downtown can be cheaper than the airport) and explore drop-off options. For a trip covering both Britain and Ireland, you're better off with two separate car rentals. If you pick up the car in a smaller city such as Bath, you'll more likely survive your first day on the English roads. Returning a car at a big-city train station can be tricky; get precise details on the car drop-off location and hours. Note that rental offices usually close from midday Saturday until Monday.

If you drop the car off early or keep it longer, you'll be credited or charged at a fair, prorated price. But keep your receipts in case any questions arise about your billing.

When picking up the car, check it thoroughly and make sure any damage is noted on your rental agreement. Find out how your car's lights, turn signals, wipers, and gas cap function. When you return the car, make sure the agent verifies its condition with you.

Car Insurance Options

When you rent a car, you are liable for a very high deductible, sometimes equal to the entire value of the car. Limit your financial risk in case of an accident by choosing one of these three options: buy Collision Damage Waiver (CDW) coverage from the car-rental company, get coverage through your credit card (free, if your card automatically includes zero-deductible coverage), or buy coverage through Travel Guard.

Although each rental company has its own variation, basic **CDW** costs $15–25 a day (figure roughly 25 percent extra) and reduces your liability, but does not eliminate it. When you pick up the car, you'll be offered the chance to "buy down" the basic deductible to zero (for an additional $10–30/day; this is often called "super CDW").

If you opt for credit-card coverage, there's a catch. You'll technically have to decline all coverage offered by the car-rental company, which means they can place a hold on your card (can be up to the full value of the car). In case of damage, it can be time-consuming to resolve the charges with your credit-card company. Before you decide on this option, quiz your credit-card company about how it works and ask them to explain the worst-case scenario.

Finally, you can buy CDW insurance from Travel Guard ($9/day plus a one-time $3 service fee covers you up to $35,000, $250 deductible, tel. 800-826-4919, www.travelguard.com). It's valid everywhere in Europe except the Republic of Ireland, and some Italian car-rental companies refuse to honor it. Residents of Washington State aren't eligible for this coverage.

For more fine print about car-rental insurance, see www.rick steves.com/cdw.

Leasing

For trips of two and a half weeks or more, leasing (which automatically includes zero-deductible collision and theft insurance) is the best way to go. By technically buying and then selling back the car, you save lots of money on tax and insurance. Leasing provides you a brand-new car with unlimited mileage and a 24-hour emergency assistance program. You can lease for as little as 17 days to as long as six months. Car leases must be arranged from the US. One of many reliable companies offering affordable lease packages is Europe by Car (US tel. 800-223-1516, www.ebctravel.com).

Driving

Bring your driver's license. Seat belts are required, and kids under age 4 must ride in a child-safety seat. An Automobile Association membership for Britain comes with most rentals (www.theaa.com). Understand its towing and emergency road-service benefits.

Driving in Britain is basically wonderful—once you remember to stay on the left and after you've mastered the roundabouts. Every year, however, I get a few notes from traveling readers advising me that, for them, trying to drive in Britain was a nerve-racking and regrettable mistake. If you want to get a little slack on the roads, drop by a gas station or auto shop and buy a green "P" (probationary driver with license) sign to put in your car window (don't get the red "L" sign, which means you're a learner driver without a license and thus prohibited from driving on motorways).

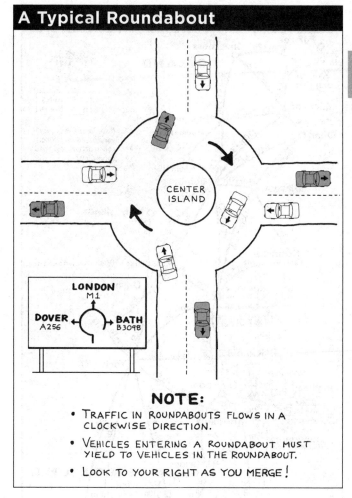

A Typical Roundabout

LONDON
M1

DOVER ← → BATH
A256   B3098

NOTE:

- Traffic in roundabouts flows in a clockwise direction.

- Vehicles entering a roundabout must yield to vehicles in the roundabout.

- Look to your right as you merge!

Many Yankee drivers find the hardest part isn't driving on the left, but steering from the right. Your instinct is to put yourself on the left side of your lane, which means you may spend your first day or two constantly drifting off the road to the left. It can help to remember that the driver always stays close to the center line.

Roundabouts: Don't let roundabouts spook you. After all, you routinely merge into much faster traffic on American highways. Traffic in roundabouts has the right-of-way; entering traffic yields (look to your right as you merge). There are a variety of round-about types; many aren't even "round." You'll probably encounter "double-roundabouts"—figure-eights where you'll slingshot from one roundabout directly into another. Just go with the flow and

APPENDIX

Britain by Car: Mileage and Time

m = miles
h = hours

Note: Your times may vary based on traffic, construction, and road conditions.

Portree
35m 1h
85m • 2h   Inverness
Kyle of Lochalsh   90m • 2.5h   85m • 3h   SCOTLAND
90m • 1.75h
Glencoe   90m • 2.75h
35m • 1h →   Pitlochry
Oban   120m • 3h   60m • 1.5h
125m • 3.25h   70m • 1.5h   St. Andrews
100m • 2.5h   50m • 1h   50m • 1.5h
50m • 1h   Edinburgh
Glasgow   75m • 2h
90m • 2.25h   130m • 3h   Holy Island
135m • 2.5h   100m • 2.5h   125m • 2.75h   80m • 1.75h
Stranraer   145m • 3h   Hadrian's Wall (Housesteads Fort)
65m • 1.5h   50m • 1h   Durham
Keswick (N. Lake Dist.)   85m • 2h
20m • .5h →   120m • 3h   75m • 2h
Windermere (S. Lake Dist.)   90m • 1.75h   Whitby
60m • 1.25h →   35m • 1h
Blackpool   120m • 2.5h
55m   1.25h   York
40m • .75h   60m • 1.25h   Liverpool
Holyhead   Conwy   30m • 1.25h   130m • 3.5h
25m • .5h   30m   75m • 1.5h
15m • .5h   1h   Ruthin   145m • 2.75h   160m • 3h
Caernarfon   30m   60m • 1.5h   220m • 4h
25m • .75h   1h
Snowdonia (Betws-y-Coed)   Iron-bridge Gorge
170m • 4h   70m • 1.5h   ENGLAND
150m • 3.5h   Warwick
WALES   10m • .25h   110m
100m • 2h   Stratford ↓ 2h   Cambridge
65m → 10m • .5h
Cardiff   Bath   Cotswolds (Chipping Campden)   90m • 2h
55m • 1.25h   115m • 2.5h   60m • 1.25h
20m • .75h   60m   Avebury
Wells   30m • 1h   1.5h   85m • 1.75h   London
10m • .25h →   40m • 1h   30m   100m • 2h
Glastonbury   1h   75m • 1.5h
50m • 1.25h   Salisbury (Stonehenge)   Dover

track signs carefully. When approaching an especially complex roundabout, you'll first pass a diagram showing the layout and the various exits. And in many cases, the pavement is painted with which lane you should be in for a particular road or town.

Speed Limits: Speed limits are 30 mph in town, 70 mph on the motorways, and 50 or 60 mph elsewhere. The national sign for 60 mph is a white circle with a black slash. Note that road-surveillance cameras strictly enforce speed limits. Any driver (including foreigners renting cars) photographed speeding will get a nasty bill in the mail. (Cameras—you'll see the foreboding gray boxes—flash on your rear license plate in order not to invade the privacy of anyone sharing the front seat with someone they shouldn't be with.)

Freeways: The shortest distance between any two points is usually the motorway. Road signs can be confusing, too few, and too late. Miss a motorway exit and you can lose 30 minutes. Buy a good map and study it before taking off. Know the cities you'll be lacing together, since road numbers are inconsistent. British road signs are never marked with compass directions (e.g., "A30 West"); instead, you need to know what major town or city you're heading toward ("A30 Penzance"). The driving directions in this book are intended to be used with a good local map. A British road atlas, easily purchased at gas stations in Britain, is money well spent (see "Maps" on page 722).

Fuel: Gas (petrol) costs around $9 per gallon and is self-serve. Diesel rental cars are common; make sure you know what type of gas your car takes before you fill up. Unleaded pumps are usually green.

Driving in Cities: Whenever possible, avoid driving in cities. Be warned that London assesses a congestion charge (see page 52). Most cities have modern ring roads to skirt the congestion. Follow signs to the parking lots outside the city core—most are a five- to ten-minute walk to the center—and avoid what can be an unpleasant network of one-way streets (as in Bath) or roads that are only available to public transportation during the day (as in Oxford).

Driving in Rural Areas: Outside of the big cities and the motorways, British roads tend to be narrow and often lack shoulders. In towns, you may have to cross over the center line just to get around parked cars. Adjust your perceptions of personal space: It's not "my side of the road" or "your side of the road," it's just "the road"—and it's shared as a cooperative adventure. If the road's wide enough, both directions of traffic can pass parked cars simultaneously, but frequently you'll have to take turns—follow the locals' lead and drive defensively. Some narrow country lanes are barely wide enough for one car. Go slowly, and if you encounter an oncoming car, look for the nearest pullout (or "passing place")—the driver who's closest to one is expected to use it, even if they have to back up to reach it. If another car pulls over and blinks its headlights, that means "Go ahead; I'll wait to let you pass." British drivers are quick to offer a friendly wave to thank you for letting them pass (and they appreciate it if you reciprocate). Pull over frequently—to let faster locals pass and to check the map.

Parking: Parking can be confusing. One yellow line marked on the pavement means no parking Monday through Saturday during work hours. Double yellow lines mean no parking at any time. Broken yellow lines mean short stops are OK, but you should always look for explicit signs or ask a passerby. White lines mean you're free to park.

In towns, rather than look for street parking, I generally just pull into the most central and handy pay-and-display parking lot I can find. To "pay and display," feed change into a machine, receive a timed ticket, and display it on the dashboard or stick it to the driver's-side window. Rates are reasonable by US standards, and locals love to share stickers that have time remaining. If you stand by the machine, someone on their way out with time left on their sticker will probably give it to you. Keep a bag of coins in the ashtray or glove box for these machines and for parking meters.

Stock Up: Set your car up for a fun road trip. Establish a cardboard-box munchies pantry. Buy a rack of liter boxes of juice for the trunk, and some Windex and a roll of paper towels (called a "kitchen roll" in Britain) for clearer sightseeing.

Cheap Flights

If you're visiting one or more cities on a longer European trip, consider intra-European airlines. While trains are still the best way to connect places that are close together, a flight can save both time and money on long journeys.

London is the hub for many cheap, no-frills airlines, which affordably connect the city with other destinations in the British Isles and throughout Europe. A visit to www.skyscanner.net sorts the numerous options offered by the many discount airlines, enabling you to see the best schedules for your trip and come up with the best deal. Other good search engines include www .mobissimo.com and www.wegolo.com.

Be aware of the potential drawbacks of flying on the cheap: nonrefundable and nonchangeable tickets, rigid baggage restrictions (and fees if you have more than what's officially allowed), use of airports far outside town, tight schedules that can mean more delays, little in the way of customer assistance if problems arise, and, of course, no frills. To avoid unpleasant surprises, read the small print—especially baggage policies—before you book. If you're traveling with lots of bags, a cheap flight can quickly become a bad deal, due to per-piece baggage fees.

Book in advance. Although you can usually book right up until the flight departs, the cheap seats will often have sold out long before, leaving the most expensive seats for latecomers.

With **bmi,** you can fly relatively inexpensively from London to destinations in the UK and beyond (fares start at £45 one-way to Edinburgh, Dublin, Brussels, or Amsterdam). Call toll tel. 0870-607-0555 or US tel. 800-788-0555 or check www.flybmi.com.

Another low-cost airline, **easyJet** flies from Gatwick, Luton, and Stansted, as well as Liverpool. Prices are based on demand, so the least popular routes make for the cheapest fares, especially if you book early (toll tel. 0905-821-0905, calls 65p/min, www .easyjet.com).

Irish-owned **Ryanair** flies from London (mostly Stansted airport), Liverpool, and Glasgow, to often obscure airports in Dublin, Frankfurt, Stockholm, Oslo, Venice, Turin, and many others. Sample fares: London–Dublin—£50 round-trip (sometimes as low as £30), London–Frankfurt—£45 round-trip (Irish toll tel. 0818-303-030, British toll tel. 0871-246-0000, www.ryanair.com). However, be warned that Ryanair charges additional fees for nearly everything. The company requires a mandatory online-only check-in (£5 charge), from 15 days to four hours before your flight (no airport check-in). When checking in, you must also print out your boarding pass; if you show up without it, there's an additional £40 charge. You can carry on only a small day bag; you'll pay a fee for each checked bag (price depends on number of bags; up to three bags allowed per passenger).

Brussels Airlines (formerly Virgin Express) is a Brussels-based company with good rates and hubs in Bristol, Birmingham, Gatwick, Manchester, and Newcastle (book by phone and pick up ticket at airport an hour before your flight, US tel. 516/740-5200, British toll tel. 0905-609-5609—40p/min, www.brusselsairlines .com).

Resources

Resources from Rick Steves

Rick Steves' Great Britain 2010 is one of more than 30 titles in a series of **books** on European travel, which includes country guide-

books (such as *Rick Steves' England*), city and regional guidebooks (such as *Rick Steves' London*), and my budget-travel skills handbook, *Rick Steves' Europe Through the Back Door.* My phrase books—for French, Italian, German, Spanish, and Portuguese—are practical and budget-oriented. My other books are *Europe 101* (a crash course on art and history, newly expanded and in full color), *Travel as a Political Act* (a travelogue sprinkled with advice for bringing home a global

perspective), *European Christmas* (on traditional and modern-day celebrations), and *Postcards from Europe* (a fun memoir of my travels). For a complete list of my books, see the inside of the last page of this book.

My **TV series**, *Rick Steves' Europe*, covers European destinations in 100 shows, with 10 episodes on Great Britain. My weekly public radio show, *Travel with Rick Steves*, features interviews with travel experts from around the world, including several hours on Great Britain and British culture. All the TV scripts and radio shows (which are easy and free to download to an iPod or other MP3 player) are at www.ricksteves.com.

Take advantage of my free self-guided **audio tours** of the major sights in London. Simply download them from www.ricksteves .com or iTunes (search for "Rick Steves' tours" in the iTunes Store), then transfer them to your iPod or other MP3 player. If your travels take you beyond Britain to France or Italy, download my audio tours of the major sights in Paris, Florence, Rome, and Venice.

Maps

The black-and-white maps in this book, drawn by Dave Hoerlein, are concise and simple. Dave, who is well-traveled in Britain, designed the maps to help you locate recommended places and get to local TIs, where you can pick up more in-depth maps of towns or regions (free or cheap). Better maps are sold at newsstands—

Begin Your Trip at www.ricksteves.com

At our travel website, you'll find a wealth of free information on European destinations, including fresh monthly news and helpful tips from thousands of fellow travelers. You'll also find my latest guidebook updates (www.ricksteves.com/update) and my travel blog.

Our **online Travel Store** offers travel bags and accessories specially designed by Rick Steves to help you travel smarter and lighter. These include my popular carry-on bags (roll-aboard and rucksack versions), money belts, totes, toiletries kits, adapters, other accessories, and a wide selection of guidebooks, planning maps, and DVDs.

Choosing the right **railpass** for your trip—amidst hundreds of options—can drive you nutty. We'll help you choose the best pass for your needs, plus give you a bunch of free extras.

Rick Steves' Europe Through the Back Door travel company offers **tours** with more than two dozen itineraries and about 300 departures reaching the best destinations in this book...and beyond. We offer a 14-day England tour, an 11-day Scotland tour, and a seven-day in-depth London city tour. You'll enjoy great guides, a fun bunch of travel partners (with small groups of around 28), and plenty of room to spread out in a big, comfy bus. You'll find European adventures to fit every vacation length. For all the details, and to get our Tour Catalog and a free Rick Steves Tour Experience DVD (filmed on location during an actual tour), visit www.ricksteves.com or call the Tour Department at 425/608-4217.

before you buy a map, look at it to be sure it has the level of detail you want.

If you'll be lingering in London and want more detail, buy a city map at a London newsstand; the red *Bensons Mapguide* (£3) is excellent. Even the vending-machine maps sold in Tube stations are good. The *Rough Guide* map to London is well-designed (£5, sold at London bookstores). The *Rick Steves' Britain, Ireland & London City Map* has a good map of London ($6, www.ricksteves.com). Many Londoners, along with obsessive-compulsive tourists, rely on the highly detailed *London A–Z* map book (generally £5–7, called "A to Zed" by locals, available at newsstands).

If you're driving, get a road atlas (1 inch equals 3 miles) covering all of Britain. Ordnance Survey, AA, and Bartholomew editions are all available for about £7 at tourist information offices, gas stations, and bookstores. Drivers, hikers, and cyclists may want more in-depth maps for the Cotswolds, the Lake District, and Snowdonia (North Wales).

Other Guidebooks

If you're like most travelers, this book is all you need. But if you're heading beyond my recommended neighborhoods and destinations, $30 for extra maps and books is money well spent. Especially for several people traveling by car, the extra weight and expense are negligible.

The following books are worthwhile, though not updated annually; check the publication date before you buy. *The Lonely Planet* and *Let's Go* guidebooks on London and on Britain are fine budget-travel guides. *Lonely Planet's* guidebooks are more thorough and informative; *Let's Go* books are youth-oriented, with good coverage of nightlife, hostels, and cheap transportation deals. For cultural and sightseeing background, look into Michelin and Cadogan guides to London, England, and Britain. The readable Access guide for London is similarly well-researched. *Secret London* by Andrew Duncan leads the reader on unique walks through a less-touristy London. If you're a literature fan, consider picking up *The Edinburgh Literary Companion* (Lownie).

If you'll be focusing on London or traveling only in England, consider *Rick Steves' London 2010* or *Rick Steves' England 2010*.

Recommended Books and Movies

To get a feel for Great Britain past and present, check out a few of these books and films.

Nonfiction

For a serious historical overview, wade into *A History of Britain*, a three-volume collection by Simon Schama; a companion series is also available on DVD. *A Traveller's History of England* (Daniell), *A Traveller's History of Scotland* (Fisher), and *A History of Wales* (Davies) provide good, succinct summaries of British history.

Other possibilities include the humorous *Notes from a Small Island* (Bryson), *The Matter of Wales* (Morris), and Susan Allen Toth's *My Love Affair with England, England As You Like It,* and *England For All Seasons.*

If you'll be visiting Scotland, consider reading *Crowded with Genius* (Buchan) or *How the Scots Invented the Modern World* (Herman), which explains the influence the Scottish Enlightenment had on the rest of Europe. *The Guynd* is a memoir of a woman who married into a historic Highlands estate.

Fiction

North American readers are already familiar with much British fiction, but here are a few you might have missed.

Classics such as *Mapp & Lucia* (Benson), *The Warden* (Trollope), and *Brideshead Revisited* (Waugh) are always a good place to start. Add to this group anything by Charles Dickens, Jane Austen, the Brontë sisters, Thomas Hardy, and P. G. Wodehouse. *Kidnapped,* by Robert Louis Stevenson, is a fantastic adventure story set in Scotland.

The Pillars of the Earth (Follett), *Sarum* (Rutherfurd), and *Stonehenge* (Cornwell) are all set in and around Salisbury. The heroines of Philippa Gregory's novels (*The Other Boleyn Girl* and *The Queen's Fool,* among others) witness intrigue at the courts of Henry VIII and Elizabeth I, while *Restoration* (Tremain) celebrates the excesses of King Charles II. Sir Thomas More hosts painter Hans Holbein during the Reformation in *Portrait of an Unknown Woman* (Bennett). Sharon Kay Penman brings 13th-century Wales to life in *Here Be Dragons.* And in the romantic, swashbuckling *Outlander* (Gabaldon), the heroine time-travels between the Scotland of 1945 and 1743.

Mystery novels have a long tradition in Britain. *A Morbid Taste for Bones* (Peters) features a Benedictine monk-detective in 12th-century Shropshire. Agatha Christie's Miss Marple was introduced in 1930 in *The Murder at the Vicarage.* And Ian Rankin's troubled Inspector Rebus first gets his man in *Knots and Crosses,* set in modern-day Edinburgh. For a modern mystery, try any of the books in the Inspector Lynley series by Elizabeth George.

Films

Goodbye, Mr. Chips (1939) looks back on a schoolteacher's life in Victorian England. *Mrs. Miniver* (1942), a sentimental WWII picture, won the Academy Award for Best Picture, as did *How Green Was My Valley* (1941), set in a 19th-century Welsh mining village.

If Scotland is on your itinerary, consider viewing the Hitchcock mystery *The 39 Steps* (1935); *I Know Where I'm Going!* (1945), a charming love story filmed on the Island of Mull; the musical *Brigadoon* (1954); and/or the funny, fish-out-of-water flick *Local Hero* (1983).

The Wicker Man (1973), a horror flick, shows a different side of a small Scottish town. *Monty Python and the Holy Grail* (1975) brings the famous comedy troupe's irreverence to Arthurian legend. *Chariots of Fire* (1981) tells the tale of British runners at the 1924 Paris Olympics.

A Room with a View (1985, an adaptation of the E. M. Forster novel) and *The Remains of the Day* (1993) include scenes filmed in rural England. Among the many versions of *Pride and Prejudice,* the 1995 BBC mini-series starring Colin Firth is the winner. The all-star *Gosford Park* (2001) is part comedy, part murder mystery, and part critique of British class stratification in the 1930s. *Hope and Glory* (1987) is a semi-autobiographical story of a boy growing up during WWII's Blitz.

In 1995, Scottish history had a mini-renaissance, with *Braveheart,* winner of the Best Picture Oscar, and *Rob Roy,* which some historians consider the more accurate of the two films. The UK television series *Monarch of the Glen* (2000) features stunning Highland scenery and the eccentric family of a modern-day Laird.

Harry Potter Sights

Harry Potter's story is set in a magical Britain, and all of the places mentioned in the books except London are fictional, but you can visit many real filming locations. Some of the locations are closed to visitors, though, or can be an un-magical disappointment in person. But quicker than you can say "Lumos," let's shine a light on where to get your Harry Potter fix if you're a die-hard fan.

Spoiler Warning: Information in this section will ruin surprises for the three of you who haven't yet read or seen any of the Harry Potter books or movies.

London

In the first film, Harry first realizes his wizard powers when talking with a boa constrictor, filmed at the **London Zoo's Reptile House** in Regent's Park (Tube: Great Portland Street).

London bustles along oblivious to the parallel universe of wizards, hidden in the magical Diagon Alley (filmed, like many of the other fictional settings, on a set at Leavesden Studios, north of London). The goblin-run Gringotts Wizarding Bank, though, was filmed in the real-life marble-floored Exhibition Hall of **Australia House** (Tube: Temple), home of the Australian Embassy.

Harry catches the train to Hogwarts at **King's Cross Station.**

Inside the glass-roofed train station, on a **pedestrian sky bridge** over the tracks, Hagrid gives Harry a train ticket. Harry heads to platform 9¾. You'll find a fun re-creation—complete with a *Platform 9¾* sign and a luggage cart that appears to be disappearing into the wall—on the way to platform 9. (Walk toward the pedestrian bridge and make a left at the arch.)

In film #3, Harry careens through London's lamp-lit streets on a purple three-decker bus that dumps him at The Leaky Cauldron. In this film, the pub's exterior was shot on rough-looking Stoney Street at the southeast edge of **Borough Street Market,** by The Market Porter pub (Tube: London Bridge).

In film #5, the Order of the Phoenix takes to the sky on broomsticks over London, passing by plenty of identifiable land-marks at night. Far beneath them glow the **London Eye, Big Ben,** and **Buckingham Palace.**

In film #6, the **Millennium Bridge** is attacked and collapses into the Thames.

Cinema buffs can visit **Leicester Square** (Tube: Leicester Square), where Daniel Radcliffe and other stars strolled past paparazzi and down red carpets to the Odeon Theater to watch the movies' premieres.

Near Bath

The mysterious side of Hogwarts is often set in the elaborate, fan-vaulted corridors of the **Gloucester Cathedral** cloisters, 50 miles north of Bath. When Harry and Ron set out to save Hermione, they look down a long, dark Gloucester hallway and spot a 20-foot troll at the far end. And it's here that the walls whisper omi-nously to Harry, and letters in blood warn: "Enemies of the heir, beware."

The scene showing Harry being chosen for Gryffindor's Quidditch team was shot in the halls of the 13th-century **Lacock Abbey,** 13 miles east of Bath. Harry attends Professor Snape's class in one of the Abbey's bare, peeling-plaster rooms—appropriate to Snape's temperament. (Mad Max tours include Lacock on its day-trip itinerary; for details, see page 199.)

Oxford

Hogwarts, Harry's prestigious wizarding prep school, is a movie creation, but it's made from a number of locations, many of them real places in Oxford.

Christ Church College—with plenty of Harry-related sights that you can tour—inspired two film sets familiar to Potter fans. In the first film, the kids are ferried to Hogwarts, and then ascend a **stone staircase** that leads into the Great Hall. The high-ceilinged **dining hall** seen throughout the films—tweaked to look much larger on screen—is filled at lunchtime with students at long rows of tables (as it is in the films, minus the weightless candles and flaming braziers).

Later in the first film, Harry sneaks into the restricted book section of Hogwarts Library under a cloak of invisibility. This scene was filmed inside Oxford's **Duke Humfrey's Library.** Hermione reads about the Sorcerer's Stone here, too.

At the end of the first film, Harry awakens from his dark battle into the golden light of the Hogwarts infirmary, filmed in a big-windowed **Divinity School** (downstairs). In film #4, Mad-Eye Moody turns Draco into a ferret on the grounds of **Bodleian Library.**

Durham and Northeast England

In the first film, Harry walks with his white owl, Hedwig, through a snowy cloister courtyard located in **Durham Cathedral** (see page 436). The bird soars up and over the church's twin 13th-century towers.

Harry first learns to fly a broomstick on the green grass of Hogwarts school grounds, filmed inside the walls of **Alnwick Castle,** located 30 miles from Newcastle. In film #2, this is where the Weasleys' flying car crashes into the Whomping Willow.

Scotland

A lot of what you'll see in the exterior shots in the Harry Potter movies—especially scenes of the Hogwarts grounds—was filmed in craggy, cloudy, mysterious Scotland.

The **Hogwarts Express train** that carries Harry, Ron, and Hermione to school each year is filmed along an actual steam-train line. The movies show the train chugging across the real-life **Glenfinnan Viaduct,** where, in film #4, the Dementors stall the train and torture Harry.

Steal Falls, a waterfall at the base of Ben Nevis, is the locale for Harry's battle with a dragon for the Triwizard Tournament in film #4.

Other scenes filmed in the Highlands include a desolate hillside with Hagrid's stone hut in **Glencoe,** which was the main location for outdoor filming in *Azkaban*. Hagrid skips stones across the water at **Loch Eilt,** west of Fort William.

Holidays and Festivals

This list includes many—but not all—major festivals in major cities, plus national holidays observed throughout Great Britain. Some dates have yet to be set. Before planning a trip around a festival, make sure you verify the festival dates by checking the festival's website or contacting the Visit Britain office (listed at the beginning of this chapter). Many sights and banks close down on national holidays—keep it in mind when planning your itinerary.

Many British towns have holiday festivals in late November and early December, with markets, music, and entertainment in the Christmas spirit. Two of these include York's St. Nicholas Fayre (www.yuletideyork.com) and Keswick's Victorian Fayre.

For specifics and a more comprehensive list of festivals, contact the Visit Britain office.

Jan 1	New Year's Day
Jan 2	New Year's Holiday (Scotland)
Feb (one week)	London Fashion Week (www.london fashionweek.co.uk)
Feb 17–22	Jorvik Viking Festival (costumed warriors, battles, www.jorvik-viking-centre.co.uk), York
Feb 27–March 7	Literature Festival (www.bathlitfest.org.uk), Bath
April 2	Good Friday
April 4–5	Easter Sunday and Monday
May 3	Early May Bank Holiday
Mid-May	Jazz Festival, Keswick
May 25–29	Chelsea Flower Show, London (book tickets ahead for this popular event at www.rhs .org.uk/chelsea)
May 28–June 12	International Music Festival (www .bathmusicfest.org.uk), Bath
May 28–June 13	Fringe Festival, Bath (alternative music, dance, and theater; www.bathfringe.co.uk)
May 31	Spring Bank Holiday
Early June	Late Music Festival, York (www.late musicfestival.org.uk)
June 5–6	Beer Festival (music, shows, www .keswickbeerfestival.co.uk), Keswick
June 13	Trooping the Colour, London (military bands and pageantry, Queen's birthday parade)

2010

JANUARY
S	M	T	W	T	F	S
					1	2
3	4	5	6	7	8	9
10	11	12	13	14	15	16
17	18	19	20	21	22	23
24/31	25	26	27	28	29	30

FEBRUARY
S	M	T	W	T	F	S
	1	2	3	4	5	6
7	8	9	10	11	12	13
14	15	16	17	18	19	20
21	22	23	24	25	26	27
28						

MARCH
S	M	T	W	T	F	S
	1	2	3	4	5	6
7	8	9	10	11	12	13
14	15	16	17	18	19	20
21	22	23	24	25	26	27
28	29	30	31			

APRIL
S	M	T	W	T	F	S
				1	2	3
4	5	6	7	8	9	10
11	12	13	14	15	16	17
18	19	20	21	22	23	24
25	26	27	28	29	30	

MAY
S	M	T	W	T	F	S
						1
2	3	4	5	6	7	8
9	10	11	12	13	14	15
16	17	18	19	20	21	22
23/30	24/31	25	26	27	28	29

JUNE
S	M	T	W	T	F	S
		1	2	3	4	5
6	7	8	9	10	11	12
13	14	15	16	17	18	19
20	21	22	23	24	25	26
27	28	29	30			

JULY
S	M	T	W	T	F	S
				1	2	3
4	5	6	7	8	9	10
11	12	13	14	15	16	17
18	19	20	21	22	23	24
25	26	27	28	29	30	31

AUGUST
S	M	T	W	T	F	S
1	2	3	4	5	6	7
8	9	10	11	12	13	14
15	16	17	18	19	20	21
22	23	24	25	26	27	28
29	30	31				

SEPTEMBER
S	M	T	W	T	F	S
			1	2	3	4
5	6	7	8	9	10	11
12	13	14	15	16	17	18
19	20	21	22	23	24	25
26	27	28	29	30		

OCTOBER
S	M	T	W	T	F	S
					1	2
3	4	5	6	7	8	9
10	11	12	13	14	15	16
17	18	19	20	21	22	23
24/31	25	26	27	28	29	30

NOVEMBER
S	M	T	W	T	F	S
	1	2	3	4	5	6
7	8	9	10	11	12	13
14	15	16	17	18	19	20
21	22	23	24	25	26	27
28	29	30				

DECEMBER
S	M	T	W	T	F	S
			1	2	3	4
5	6	7	8	9	10	11
12	13	14	15	16	17	18
19	20	21	22	23	24	25
26	27	28	29	30	31	

June 15–19	Royal Ascot Horse Race (www.ascot.co.uk), Ascot (near Windsor)
June 21–July 4	Wimbledon Tennis Championship, London (www.wimbledon.org)
June 24–27	Royal Highland Show (Scottish county fair, www.royalhighlandshow.org), Edinburgh
July 6–11	International Eisteddfod (folk songs, dances, www.international-eisteddfod.co.uk), Llangollen
July 9–17	Early Music Festival (www.ncem.co.uk/yemf.shtml), York
July 29–Aug 1	Cambridge Folk Festival, Cambridge (buy tickets early at www.cambridge folkfestival.co.uk)
Aug 2	Summer Bank Holiday (Scotland only, not England or Wales)

Aug 6–28	Military Tattoo (massing of bands, www.edinburgh-tattoo.co.uk), Edinburgh
Aug 6–30	Fringe Festival (offbeat theater and comedy, www.edfringe.com), Edinburgh
Aug 13–Sept 5	Edinburgh International Festival (music, dance, shows, www.eif.co.uk)
Aug 29–Nov 7	Illuminations (waterfront light festival), Blackpool
Aug 29–30	Notting Hill Carnival, London (costumes, Caribbean music)
Aug 30	Summer Bank Holiday (England and Wales only, not Scotland)
Sept (one week)	London Fashion Week (www.londonfashionweek.co.uk)
Late Sept	York Festival of Food and Drink (www.yorkfoodfestival.com)
Late Sept	Jane Austen Festival (www.janeausten.co.uk/festival), Bath
Nov 5	Bonfire Night, or Guy Fawkes Night (fireworks, bonfires, effigy-burning of 1605 traitor Guy Fawkes), Britain
Nov 30	St. Andrew's Day, Scotland
Dec 24–26	Christmas holidays
Dec 31–Jan 2	Hogmanay (music, street theater, carnival, www.hogmanay.net), Scotland

Conversions and Climate

Numbers and Stumblers

- In Europe, dates appear as day/month/year, so Christmas is 25/12/10.
- What Americans call the second floor of a building is the first floor in Britain.
- On escalators and moving sidewalks, Brits keep the left "lane" open for passing. Keep to the right.
- When pointing, use your whole hand, palm down.
- When counting with fingers, start with your thumb. If you hold up your first finger to request one item, you'll probably get two.
- To avoid the British version of giving someone "the finger," don't hold up the first two fingers of your hand with your palm facing you. (It looks like a reversed victory sign.)
- And please...don't call your waist pack a "fanny pack."

Metric Conversions (approximate)

Britain uses the metric system for everything but driving measurements. Weight and volume are typically calculated in metric: A kilogram is 2.2 pounds, and a liter is about a quart. The weight of a person is measured by "stone" (one stone equals 14 pounds). Temperatures are generally given in both Celsius and Fahrenheit.

On the road, Britain uses miles and posts speed limits in miles per hour.

1 foot = 0.3 meter	1 square yard = 0.8 square meter
1 yard = 0.9 meter	1 square mile = 2.6 square kilometers
1 mile = 1.6 kilometers	1 ounce = 28 grams
1 centimeter = 0.4 inch	1 quart = 0.95 liter
1 meter = 39.4 inches	1 kilogram = 2.2 pounds
1 kilometer = 0.62 mile	32°F = 0°C

Weights and Measures

1 British pint = 1.2 US pints
1 imperial gallon = 1.2 US gallons, or about 4.5 liters
1 stone = 14 pounds (a 168-pound person weighs 12 stone)

Clothing Sizes

When shopping for clothing, use these US-to-Britain comparisons as general guidelines (but note that no conversion is perfect).
- Women's dresses and blouses: Add 4 (US women's size 10 = UK size 14)
- Men's suits and jackets: US and UK use the same sizing
- Men's shirts: US and UK use the same sizing
- Women's shoes: Subtract 2½ (US size 8 = UK size 5½)
- Men's shoes: Subtract about ½ (US size 9 = UK size 8½)

Climate

First line, average daily high temperature; second line, average daily low; third line, days without rain. For more detailed weather statistics for destinations in this book (as well as the rest of the world), check www.worldclimate.com.

	J	F	M	A	M	J	J	A	S	O	N	D
LONDON												
	43°	44°	50°	56°	62°	69°	71°	71°	65°	58°	50°	45°
	36°	36°	38°	42°	47°	53°	56°	56°	52°	46°	42°	38°
	16	15	20	18	19	19	19	20	17	18	15	16
CARDIFF (SOUTH WALES)												
	45°	45°	50°	56°	61°	68°	69°	69°	64°	58°	51°	46°
	35°	35°	38°	41°	46°	51°	54°	55°	51°	46°	41°	37°
	13	14	18	17	18	17	17	16	14	15	13	13

	J	F	M	A	M	J	J	A	S	O	N	D

YORK

	43°	44°	49°	55°	61°	67°	70°	69°	64°	57°	49°	45°
	33°	34°	36°	40°	44°	50°	54°	53°	50°	44°	39°	36°
	14	13	18	17	18	16	16	17	16	16	13	14

EDINBURGH

	42°	43°	46°	51°	56°	62°	65°	64°	60°	54°	48°	44°
	34°	34°	36°	39°	43°	49°	52°	52°	49°	44°	39°	36°
	14	13	16	16	17	15	14	15	14	14	13	13

Temperature Conversion:
Fahrenheit and Celsius

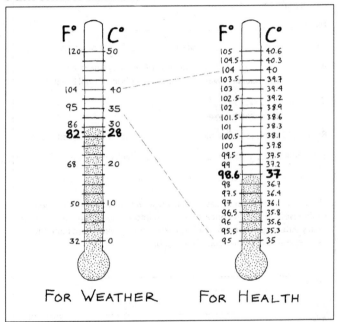

Britain uses both Celsius and Fahrenheit to take its temperature. For a rough conversion from Celsius to Fahrenheit, double the number and add 30. For weather, remember that 28°C is 82°F—perfect. For health, 37°C is just right.

APPENDIX

Hotel Reservation

To: _____   _____
          hotel   *email or fax*

From: _____   _____
          name   *email or fax*

Today's date: _____ /_____ /_____
                  day   *month*   *year*

Dear Hotel _____,
Please make this reservation for me:

Name: _____

Total # of people: _____   # of rooms: _____   # of nights: _____

Arriving: ____ /____ /____   My time of arrival (24-hr clock): _____
             day *month* *year*   (I will telephone if I will be late)

Departing: ____ /____ /____
               day *month* *year*

Room(s): Single____ Double ____ Twin ____ Triple ____ Quad____

With: Toilet ____ Shower ____ Bath ____ Sink only ____

Special needs: View____ Quiet____ Cheapest ____ Ground Floor____

Please email or fax confirmation of my reservation, along with the type of room reserved and the price. Please also inform me of your cancellation policy. After I hear from you, I will quickly send my credit-card information as a deposit to hold the room. Thank you.

_____
Name

_____
Address

_____
City   *State*   *Zip Code*   *Country*

Before hoteliers can make your reservation, they want to know the information listed above. You can use this form as the basis for your email, or you can photocopy this page, fill in the information, and send it as a fax (also available online at www.ricksteves.com/reservation).

Essential Packing Checklist

Whether you're traveling for five days or five weeks, here's what you'll need to bring. Remember to pack light to enjoy the sweet freedom of true mobility. Happy travels!

- ❑ 5 shirts
- ❑ 1 sweater or lightweight fleece jacket
- ❑ 2 pairs pants
- ❑ 1 pair shorts
- ❑ 1 swimsuit (women only—men can use shorts)
- ❑ 5 pairs underwear and socks
- ❑ 1 pair shoes
- ❑ 1 rainproof jacket
- ❑ Tie or scarf
- ❑ Money belt
- ❑ Money—your mix of:
  - ❑ Debit card for ATM withdrawals
  - ❑ Credit card
  - ❑ Hard cash in US dollars ($20 bills)
- ❑ Documents (and back-up photocopies)
- ❑ Passport
- ❑ Printout of airline e-ticket
- ❑ Driver's license
- ❑ Student ID and hostel card
- ❑ Railpass/car rental voucher
- ❑ Insurance details
- ❑ Daypack
- ❑ Sealable plastic baggies
- ❑ Camera and related gear
- ❑ Empty water bottle
- ❑ Wristwatch and alarm clock
- ❑ Earplugs
- ❑ First-aid kit
- ❑ Medicine (labeled)
- ❑ Extra glasses/contacts and prescriptions
- ❑ Sunscreen and sunglasses
- ❑ Toiletries kit
- ❑ Soap
- ❑ Laundry soap
- ❑ Clothesline
- ❑ Small towel
- ❑ Sewing kit
- ❑ Travel information
- ❑ Necessary map(s)
- ❑ Address list (email and mailing addresses)
- ❑ Postcards and photos from home
- ❑ Notepad and pen
- ❑ Journal

If you plan to carry on your luggage, note that all liquids must be in three-ounce or smaller containers and fit within a single quart-size baggie. For details, see www.tsa.gov/travelers.

British–Yankee Vocabulary

For a longer list, plus a dry-witted primer on British culture, see *The Septic's Companion* (Chris Rae).

advert–advertisement

afters–dessert

anticlockwise–counterclockwise

aubergine–eggplant

banger–sausage

bangers and mash–sausage and mashed potatoes

Bank Holiday–legal holiday

bap–small roll

bespoke–custom-made

billion–a thousand of our billions (a million million)

biro–ballpoint pen

biscuit–cookie

black pudding–sausage made from dried blood

bloody–damn

blow off–fart

bobby–policeman ("the Bill" is more common)

Bob's your uncle–there you go, naturally (with a shrug)

boffin–nerd, geek

bollocks–testicles; also used as an exclamation of strong disbelief or disagreement

bolshy–argumentative

bomb–success or failure

bonnet–car hood

boot–car trunk

braces–suspenders

bridle way–path for walkers, bikers, and horse riders

brilliant–cool

brolly–umbrella

bubble and squeak–cabbage and potatoes fried together

bum–butt

candy floss–cotton candy

caravan–trailer

car boot sale–temporary flea market, often for charity

car park–parking lot

casualty–emergency room

cat's eyes–road reflectors

ceilidh (KAY-lee)–informal evening of song and folk fun (Scottish and Irish)

cheap and cheerful–budget but adequate

cheap and nasty–cheap and bad quality

cheers–good-bye or thanks; also a toast

chemist–pharmacist

chicory–endive

chippie–fish-and-chip shop; carpenter

chips–french fries

chock-a-block–jam-packed

chuffed–pleased

cider–alcoholic apple cider

clearway–road where you can't stop

coach–long-distance bus

concession–discounted admission

concs (pronounced "conks")–short for "concession"

cos–romaine lettuce

cotton buds–Q-tips

courgette–zucchini

craic (pronounced "crack")–fun, good conversation (Irish/Scottish and spreading to England)

crisps–potato chips

cuppa–cup of tea

dear–expensive

dicey–iffy, risky

digestives–round graham cookies

dinner–lunch or dinner

diversion–detour

donkey's years–ages, long time

APPENDIX

draughts–checkers
draw–marijuana
dual carriageway–divided highway (four lanes)
dummy–pacifier
elevenses–coffee-and-biscuits break before lunch
elvers–baby eels
face flannel–washcloth
fag–cigarette
fagged–exhausted
faggot–sausage
fancy–to like, to be attracted to (a person)
fanny–vagina
fell–hill or high plain (Lake District)
first floor–second floor
fizzy drink–pop or soda
flutter–a bet
football–soccer
force–waterfall (Lake District)
fortnight–two weeks (shortened from "fourteen nights")
fringe–hair bangs
Frogs–French people
fruit machine–slot machine
full Monty–whole shebang; everything
gallery–balcony
gammon–ham
gangway–aisle
gaol–jail (same pronunciation)
gateau (or gateaux)–cake
gear lever–stick shift
geezer–"dude"
give way–yield
glen–narrow valley (Scotland)
goods wagon–freight truck
green fingers–green thumbs
half eight–8:30 (not 7:30)
heath–open treeless land
hen night–bachelorette party
holiday–vacation
homely–homey or cozy

hoover–vacuum cleaner
ice lolly–Popsicle
interval–intermission
ironmonger–hardware store
ish-more or less
jacket potato–baked potato
jelly–Jell-O
Joe Bloggs–John Q. Public
jumble sale–rummage sale
jumper–sweater
just a tick–just a second
kipper–smoked herring
knackered–exhausted (Cockney: cream crackered)
knickers–ladies' panties
knocking shop–brothel
knock up–wake up or visit (old-fashioned)
ladybird–ladybug
lady fingers–flat, spongy cookie
lady's finger–okra
lager–light, fizzy beer
left luggage–baggage check
lemon squash–lemonade, not fizzy
lemonade–lemon-lime pop, fizzy
let–rent
licenced–restaurant authorized to sell alcohol
lift–elevator
listed–protected historic building
loo–toilet or bathroom
lorry–truck
mac–mackintosh raincoat
mangetout–snow peas
marrow–summer squash
mate–buddy (boy or girl)
mean–stingy
mental–wild, memorable
mews–former stables converted to two-story rowhouses (London)

mobile (MOH-bile)–cell phone

moggie–cat

motorway–freeway

naff–tacky or trashy

nappy–diaper

natter–talk on and on

neep–Scottish for turnip

newsagent–corner store

nought–zero

noughts & crosses–tic-tac-toe

off-licence–liquor store

on offer–for sale

panto, pantomime–fairy-tale play performed at Christmas (silly but fun)

pants–underwear, briefs

pasty (PASS-tee)–crusted savory (usually meat) pie from Cornwall

pavement–sidewalk

pear-shaped–messed up, gone wrong

petrol–gas

pillar box–mailbox

pissed (rude), **paralytic, bev-vied, wellied, popped up, merry, trollied, ratted, rat-arsed, pissed as a newt**–drunk

pitch–playing field

plaster–Band-Aid

publican–pub owner

public school–private "prep" school (e.g., Eton)

pudding–dessert in general

pull, to be on the–on the prowl

punter–customer, especially in gambling

put a sock in it–shut up

queue–line

queue up–line up

quid–pound (money)

randy–horny

rasher–slice of bacon

redundant, made–laid off

Remembrance Day–Veterans' Day

return ticket–round trip

ring up–call (telephone)

roundabout–traffic circle

rubber–eraser

rubbish–bad

sausage roll–sausage wrapped in a flaky pastry

Scotch egg–hard-boiled egg wrapped in sausage meat

self-catering–accommodation with kitchen

Sellotape–Scotch tape

services–freeway rest area

serviette–napkin

setee–couch

shag–intercourse (cruder than in the US)

shandy–lager and 7-Up

silencer–car muffler

single ticket–one-way ticket

skip–Dumpster

sleeping policeman–speed bumps

smalls–underwear

snogging–kissing, making out

sod–mildly offensive insult

sod it, sod off–screw it, screw off

soda–soda water (not pop)

solicitor–lawyer

spanner–wrench

spend a penny–urinate

stag night–bachelor party

starkers–buck naked

starters–appetizers

state school–public school

sticking plaster–Band-Aid

sticky tape–Scotch tape

stone–14 pounds (weight)

stroppy–bad-tempered

subway–underground walkway

suet–fat from animal rendering (sometimes used in cooking)

sultanas–golden raisins
surgical spirit–rubbing alcohol
suspenders–garters
suss out–figure out
swede–rutabaga
ta–thank you
**take the mickey/take the
    piss**–tease
tatty–worn out or tacky
taxi rank–taxi stand
telly–TV
tenement–stone apartment
    house (not necessarily a
    slum)
tenner–£10 bill
theatre–live stage
tick–a check mark
tight as a fish's bum–cheap-
    skate (watertight)
tights–panty hose
tin–can
tip–public dump
tipper lorry–dump truck
top hole–first rate
top up–refill (a drink, mobile-
    phone credit, petrol tank,
    etc.)

torch–flashlight
towel, press-on–panty liner
towpath–path along a river
trainers–sneakers
Tube–subway
twee–quaint, cutesy
twitcher–bird watcher
Underground–subway
verge–grassy edge of road
verger–church official
way out–exit
wee (adj)–small (Scottish)
wee (verb)–urinate
Wellingtons, wellies–rubber
    boots
whacked–exhausted
whinge (rhymes with hinge)–
    whine
wind up–tease, irritate
witter on–gab and gab
yob–hooligan
zebra crossing–crosswalk
zed–the letter Z

INDEX

INDEX

INDEX

INDEX

MAP INDEX

▶ Plan Your Trip

Browse thousands of articles and a wealth of money-saving tips for planning your dream trip. You'll find up-to-date information on Europe's best destinations, packing smart, getting around, finding rooms, staying healthy, avoiding scams and more.

▶ Eurail Passes

Find out, step-by-step, if a rail pass makes sense for your trip—and how to avoid buying more than you need. Get a bunch of free extras!

▶ Graffiti Wall & Travelers' Helpline

Learn, ask, share—our online community of savvy travelers is a great resource for first-time travelers to Europe, as well as seasoned pros.

Rick Steves' Europe Through the Back Door, Inc

Free Audio Tours & Travel Newsletter

Get your nose out of this guide-book and focus on what you'll be seeing with Rick's free audio tours of the greatest sights in Paris, Rome, Florence and Venice.

Subscribe to our free *Travel News* e-newsletter, and get monthly articles from Rick on what's happening in Europe.

▶ Great Gear from Rick's Travel Store

Pack light and right—on a budget—with Rick's custom-designed carry-on bags, roll-aboards, day packs, travel accessories, guidebooks, journals, maps and DVDs of his TV shows.

130 Fourth Avenue North, PO Box 2009 • Edmonds, WA 98020 USA
Phone: (425) 771-8303 • Fax: (425) 771-0833 • www.ricksteves.com

Rick Steves®

TRAVEL SKILLS
Europe Through the Back Door

EUROPE GUIDES
Best of Europe
Eastern Europe
Europe 101
European Christmas
Postcards from Europe

COUNTRY GUIDES
Croatia & Slovenia
England
France
Germany
Great Britain
Ireland
Italy
Portugal
Scandinavia
Spain
Switzerland

CITY & REGIONAL GUIDES
Amsterdam, Bruges & Brussels
Athens & The Peloponnese
Budapest
Florence & Tuscany
Istanbul
London
Paris
Prague & The Czech Republic
Provence & The French Riviera
Rome
Venice
Vienna, Salzburg & Tirol

PHRASE BOOKS & DICTIONARIES
French
French, Italian & German
German
Italian
Portuguese
Spanish

RICK STEVES' EUROPE DVDs
Austria & The Alps
Eastern Europe
England
Europe
France & Benelux
Germany & Scandinavia
Greece, Turkey, Israel & Egypt
Ireland & Scotland
Italy's Cities
Italy's Countryside
Rick Steves' European Christmas
Spain & Portugal
Travel Skills & "The Making Of"

PLANNING MAPS
Britain, Ireland & London
Europe
France & Paris
Germany, Austria & Switzerland
Ireland
Italy
Spain & Portugal

JOURNALS
Rick Steves' Pocket Travel Journal
Rick Steves' Travel Journal

With these apps you can:

▸ Spin the compass icon to switch views between sights, hotels, and restaurant selections—and get details on cost, hours, address, and phone number.

▸ Tap any point on the screen to read Rick's detailed information, including history and suggested viewpoints.

▸ Get a deeper view into Rick's tours with audio and video segments.

Go to iTunes to download the following apps:

Rick Steves' Louvre Tour

Rick Steves' Historic Paris Walk

Rick Steves' Orsay Museum Tour

Rick Steves' Versailles

Rick Steves' Ancient Rome Tour

Rick Steves' St. Peter's Basilica Tour

Once downloaded, these apps are completely self-contained on your iPhone or iPod Touch, so you will not incur pricey roaming charges during use overseas.

Rick Steves books and DVDs are available at bookstores and through online booksellers.
Rick Steves guidebooks are published by Avalon Travel, a member of the Perseus Books Group.
Rick Steves apps are produced by Übermind, a boutique Seattle-based software consultancy firm.

Credits

Researchers
To help update this book, Rick relied on...

Gretchen Strauch

Gretchen lived in St. Andrews, Scotland, for one year, where she studied philosophy and medieval history; her subsequent addictions to Scrumpy Jack and British Kit Kats have kept her coming back ever since. Raised in rural California, she now lives in Seattle and edits the Rick Steves guidebooks.

Lauren Mills

Lauren, a map editor and in-house search engine at Rick Steves, was an ardent Anglophile even before bringing home her British husband as a souvenir. They live in Seattle with their cat Keswick.

Cathy McDonald

Cathy, an editor and researcher for Rick Steves, enjoys England's natural history and how it affects its people. She lives in Seattle, where she has written about the Pacific Northwest for more than 15 years as a freelancer for *The Seattle Times*.

Contributor
Gene Openshaw

Gene is the co-author of seven Rick Steves books. For this book, he wrote material on Europe's art, history, and contemporary culture. When not traveling, Gene enjoys composing music, recovering from his 1973 trip to Europe with Rick, and living everyday life with his daughter.

Images

Location	Photographer
Title Page: Tower Bridge, London	Dominic Bonuccelli
England: Salisbury Cathedral	Cameron Hewitt
London: Houses of Parliament	Rick Steves
Greenwich, Windsor, and Cambridge: Windsor's Changing of the Guard	Lauren Mills
Bath: Pulteney Bridge	Lauren Mills
Near Bath: Avebury Stone Circle	David C. Hoerlein
The Cotswolds: Typical Cotswold Scene	Dominic Bonuccelli
Stratford-upon-Avon: Anne Hathaway's Cottage	Rick Steves
Ironbridge Gorge: The Iron Bridge	Lauren Mills
Blackpool and Liverpool: Blackpool	Rick Steves
The Lake District: Derwentwater	Rick Steves
York: York Minster	Rick Steves
Durham and Northeast England: Durham Cathedral	David C. Hoerlein
Wales: Snowdonia	Cameron Hewitt
North Wales: Snowdonia	David C. Hoerlein
Scotland: Neist Point	Cameron Hewitt
Edinburgh: Edinburgh Castle	Rick Steves
St. Andrews: The Old Course	Cameron Hewitt
Glasgow: Cityscape with the Lighthouse	David C. Hoerlein
Oban and the Southern Highlands: Oban	Jennifer Hauseman
Isle of Skye: Kyleakin Harbor	Cameron Hewitt
Inverness and the Northern Highlands: Inverness	Jennifer Hauseman
Between Inverness and Edinburgh: View from Stirling Castle	Cameron Hewitt

Acknowledgements

Thanks to Cameron Hewitt for his original work on several of the Scotland chapters (particularly St. Andrews and the Isle of Skye), to Jennifer Hauseman for the original version of the Glasgow chapter, and to friends listed in this book who put the "Great" in Great Britain.

Rick Steves' Guidebook Series

Country Guides

Rick Steves' Best of Europe
Rick Steves' Croatia & Slovenia
Rick Steves' Eastern Europe
Rick Steves' England
Rick Steves' France
Rick Steves' Germany
Rick Steves' Great Britain
Rick Steves' Ireland
Rick Steves' Italy
Rick Steves' Portugal
Rick Steves' Scandinavia
Rick Steves' Spain
Rick Steves' Switzerland

City and Regional Guides

Rick Steves' Amsterdam, Bruges & Brussels
Rick Steves' Athens & the Peloponnese
Rick Steves' Budapest
Rick Steves' Florence & Tuscany
Rick Steves' Istanbul
Rick Steves' London
Rick Steves' Paris
Rick Steves' Prague & the Czech Republic
Rick Steves' Provence & the French Riviera
Rick Steves' Rome
Rick Steves' Venice
Rick Steves' Vienna, Salzburg & Tirol

Rick Steves' Phrase Books

French
French/Italian/German
German
Italian
Portuguese
Spanish

Other Books

Rick Steves' Europe 101: History and Art for the Traveler
Rick Steves' Europe Through the Back Door
Rick Steves' European Christmas
Rick Steves' Postcards from Europe
Rick Steves' Travel as a Political Act

Avalon Travel
a member of the Perseus Books Group
1700 Fourth Street
Berkeley, CA 94710

Text © 2009 by Rick Steves
Maps © 2009 by Europe Through the Back Door. All rights reserved.

Printed in the USA by Worzalla
First printing November 2009

ISBN 978-1-59880-293-1
ISSN 1090-6843

For the latest on Rick's lectures, guidebooks, tours, public radio show, and public television
series, contact Europe Through the Back Door, Box 2009, Edmonds, WA 98020, 425/771-
8303, fax 425/771-0833, www.ricksteves.com, rick@ricksteves.com.

Europe Through the Back Door Reviewing Editor: Cameron Hewitt
ETBD Editors: Jennifer Madison Davis, Tom Griffin, Cathy McDonald, Cathy Lu,
    Gretchen Strauch, Sarah McCormic
ETBD Managing Editor: Risa Laib
Research Assistance: Gretchen Strauch, Lauren Mills, Cathy McDonald
Avalon Travel Senior Editor and Series Manager: Madhu Prasher
Avalon Travel Project Editor: Kelly Lydick
Copy Editor: Jennifer Malnick
Proofreader: Janet Walden
Indexer: Claire Splan
Production and Layout: McGuire Barber Design
Cover Design: Kimberly Glyder Design
Graphic Content Director: Laura VanDeventer
Maps and Graphics: David C. Hoerlein, Laura VanDeventer, Brice Ticen, Lauren Mills,
    Barb Geisler, Pat O'Connor, Mike Morgenfeld
Front Matter Color Photos: Cameron Hewitt, Sarah Murdoch, Rick Steves, Dominic
    Bonuccelli
Front Cover Photo: Castle Combe, Cotswolds, England © Peter Adams
Additional Photography: Rick Steves, Cameron Hewitt, Gene Openshaw, Bruce
    VanDeventer, Lauren Mills, David C. Hoerlein, Jennifer Hauseman, Jennifer Schutte,
    Ken Hanley, Sarah Murdoch, Darbi Macy, Dominic Bonuccelli

Foldout Color Map ▶

The foldout map on the opposite page includes:
• A map of Great Britain on one side
• A city map of London on the other side